TENTH EDITION

BUSINESS DATA COMMUNICATIONS AND NETWORKING

JERRY FITZGERALD
Jerry FitzGerald & Associates

ALAN DENNIS
Indiana University

WILEY
JOHN WILEY & SONS, INC.

To Kelly and Alec

VICE PRESIDENT AND EXECUTIVE PUBLISHER *Donald Fowley*
ACQUISITIONS EDITOR *Beth Golub*
PRODUCTION SERVICES MANAGER *Dorothy Sinclair*
PRODUCTION EDITOR *Janet Foxman*
EXECUTIVE MARKETING MANAGER *Christopher Ruel*
CREATIVE Director *Harry Nolan*
SENIOR DESIGNER *Kevin Murphy*
PHOTO EDITOR *Sheena Goldstein*
EDITORIAL ASSISTANT *Lyle Curry*
MEDIA EDITOR *Lauren Sapira*
PRODUCTION SERVICES *Sunitha Arun Bhaskar /Pine Tree Composition*
COVER DESIGN *Michael St. Martine*

This book was set in Times Roman by Laserwords Private Limited, Chennai, India, and printed and bound by R.R. Donnelley-Crawfordsville. The cover was printed by R.R. Donnelley-Crawfordsville.
This book is printed on acid-free paper. ♾

ISBN: 978-0470-05575-5

Printed in the United States of America

10 9 8 7 6 5 4 3

ABOUT THE AUTHORS

Professor Alan Dennis is professor of information systems in the Kelley School of Business at Indiana University and holds the John T. Chambers Chair in Internet Systems. The Chambers Chair was established to honor John Chambers, president and chief executive officer of Cisco Systems, the worldwide leader of networking technologies for the Internet.

Prior to joining Indiana University, Professor Dennis spent nine years as a professor at the University of Georgia, where he won the Richard B. Russell Award for Excellence in Undergraduate Teaching. Professor Dennis has a bachelor's degree in computer science from Acadia University in Nova Scotia, Canada, and an MBA from Queen's University in Ontario, Canada. His Ph.D. in management of information systems is from the University of Arizona. Prior to entering the Arizona doctoral program, he spent three years on the faculty of the Queen's School of Business.

Professor Dennis has extensive experience in the development and application of groupware and Internet technologies and developed a Web-based groupware package called Consensus @nyWARE, now owned by SoftBicycle Corporation. He has won seven awards for theoretical and applied research and has published more than 100 business and research articles, including those in *Management Science, MIS Quarterly, Information Systems Research, Academy of Management Journal, Organization Behavior and Human Decision Making, Journal of Applied Psychology, Communications of the ACM,* and *IEEE Transactions of Systems, Man, and Cybernetics.* His first book was *Getting Started with Microcomputers,* published in 1986. Professor Dennis is also an author (along with Professor Barbara Wixom of the University of Virginia and Professor Robby Roth of the University of Northern Iowa) of *Systems Analysis and Design: An Applied Approach,* also available from Wiley. Professor Dennis is the cochair of the Internet Technologies Track of the Hawaii International Conference on System Sciences. He has served as a consultant to BellSouth, Boeing, IBM, Hughes Missile Systems, the U.S. Department of Defense, and the Australian Army.

Dr. Jerry FitzGerald is the principal in Jerry FitzGerald & Associates, a firm he started in 1977. He has extensive experience in risk analysis, computer security, audit and control of computerized systems, data communications, networks, and systems analysis. He has been active in risk-assessment studies, computer security, audit reviews, designing controls into applications during the new system development process, data communication networks, bank wire transfer systems, and electronic data interchange (EDI) systems. He conducts training seminars on risk analysis, control and security, and data communications networks. Dr. FitzGerald has a Ph.D. in business economics and a master's degree in business economics from the Claremont Graduate School, an

MBA from the University of Santa Clara, and a bachelor's degree in industrial engineering from Michigan State University. He is a certified information systems auditor (CISA) and holds a certificate in data processing (CDP). He belongs to the EDP Auditors Association (EDPAA), the Institute of Internal Auditors (IIA), and the Information Systems Security Association (ISSA). Dr. FitzGerald has been a faculty member at several California universities and a consultant at SRI International.

His publications and software include *Business Data Communications: Basic Concepts, Security and Design,* 4th edition, 1993; *Designing Controls into Computerized Systems,* 2nd edition, 1990; RANK-IT: A Risk Assessment Tool for Microcomputers; CONTROL-IT: A Control Spreadsheet Methodology for Microcomputers; *Fundamentals of Systems Analysis: Using Structured Analysis and Design,* 3rd edition, 1987; *Online Auditing Using Microcomputers; Internal Controls for Computerized Systems;* and over 60 articles in various publications.

PREFACE

Over the past few years, many fundamental changes have occurred in data communications and networking that will shape the future for decades to come. Networking applications such as the Internet and World Wide Web have exploded into the business world. High-speed modems providing megabit data rates (millions of bits per second) over regular telephone lines and cable TV circuits are widely available. New local area network (LAN) and backbone technologies providing gigabit (billions of bits per second) speeds are now available. Metropolitan area network (MAN) and wide area network (WAN) technologies providing terabit (trillions of bits per second) to petabit (quadrillions of bits per second) speeds are on the horizon. The integration of voice and data communication is moving rapidly.

Perhaps the most important change has been the recognition of the strategic importance of communications and networking in both the public and private sector. Today, almost all computers are networked. As we look back on the 1990s, we realize that the importance of the computer was surpassed by the importance of the network.

PURPOSE OF THIS BOOK

Our goal is to combine the fundamental concepts of data communications and networking with practical applications. Although technologies and applications change rapidly, the fundamental concepts evolve much more slowly; they provide the foundation from which new technologies and applications can be understood, evaluated, and compared.

This book has two intended audiences. First and foremost, it is a university textbook. Each chapter introduces, describes, and then summarizes fundamental concepts and applications. Management Focus boxes highlight key issues and describe how networks are actually being used today. Technical Focus boxes highlight key technical issues and provide additional detail. Mini case studies at the end of each chapter provide the opportunity to apply these technical and management concepts. Moreover, the text is accompanied by a detailed Instructor's Manual that provides additional background information, teaching tips, and sources of material for student exercises, assignments, and exams. Finally, our Web page will continue to update the book.

Second, this book is intended for the professional who works in data communications and networking. The book has many detailed descriptions of the technical aspects of communications, along with illustrations where appropriate. Moreover, managerial, technical, and sales personnel can use this book to gain a better understanding of fundamental concepts and trade-offs not presented in technical books or product summaries.

WHAT'S NEW IN THIS EDITION

The tenth edition has five major changes from the ninth edition. First, it includes numerous updates to technologies that have evolved and changed since the last edition went to press. The biggest change has been to the chapter on wireless LANs, as this has undergone major changes in just 2 years.

Second, we have added new hands-on activities to each chapter. The activities are designed to reinforce the key concepts in each chapter, as well as to provide an interesting, practical use of network technology. These activities could be used as demonstrations in class, lab exercises, or activities given as homework. In any event, we believe they will help students better understand key concepts.

Third, this edition includes updates to examples, questions, and exercises throughout the book. We believe these items help to improve students' understanding of key topics. We've also revised three crossword puzzles to the book because we've found that students enjoy puzzles, even those that help them learn.

Fourth, the chapter on network security has been reorganized and updated. This edition focuses on the two major aspects of security (business continuity and intrusion prevention) as well as risk analysis. The topics within the two major aspects have been reorganized to make them easier to understand and easier to teach.

Finally, what is just as important as what has been added is what has been removed. As new technologies arrive it is important to reduce complexity and bulk by removing older technologies that are fading from use. This edition has omitted legacy technologies such as ATM in the backbone, and has reduced the coverage of dial-up modems in favor of cable modems and DSL modems.

Online Animations www.wiley.com/college/fitzgerald

For students and instructors, we're offering online animations that help students visualize basic data communications processes. These animations can be used in the classroom or as a study aid for students. To access the animations, go to the Student Resources site.

Lab Exercises www.wiley.com/college/fitzgerald

This edition includes an online lab manual with many hands-on exercises that can be used in a networking lab. These exercises include configuring routers and servers and other additional practical topics. This edition also include a series of OPNET labs; OPNET is a network simulation tool.

Online Supplements for Instructors www.wiley.com/college/fitzgerald

Instructor's supplements include an Instructor's Manual that includes teaching tips, war stories and answers to end of chapter questions, a Test Bank that includes test questions for each chapter, and Lecture Slides in PowerPoint for classroom presentations. All are available on the Instructor's Resources site.

ACKNOWLEDGMENTS

My thanks to the many people who helped in preparing this edition including my friends at Cisco both current and retired—John Chambers, John Morgridge, and David Alexander. I am indebted to the staff at John Wiley & Sons for their support, including Beth Lang Golub, information systems editor; Janet Foxman, production editor; and Chris Ruel, marketing manager.

I would also like to thank the reviewers for their assistance, often under short deadlines:

Bill Hammerschlag, Dallas County Community College
Elizabeth Baker, Virginia Military Institute
Bob Gregory, Bellevue University
Subodha Kumar, University of Washington
Lauren Eder, Rider University
Nolan J. Taylor, Indiana University
Bruce Tis, Simmons University
Sylvia Perez, Nyack College

Alan Dennis
Bloomington, Indiana
www.kelley.indiana.edu/ardennis

BRIEF CONTENTS

CONTENTS

Part One

INTRODUCTION

Courtesy Cisco Systems, Inc.

Network equipment from Cisco Systems, Inc.

CHAPTER 1

INTRODUCTION TO DATA COMMUNICATIONS

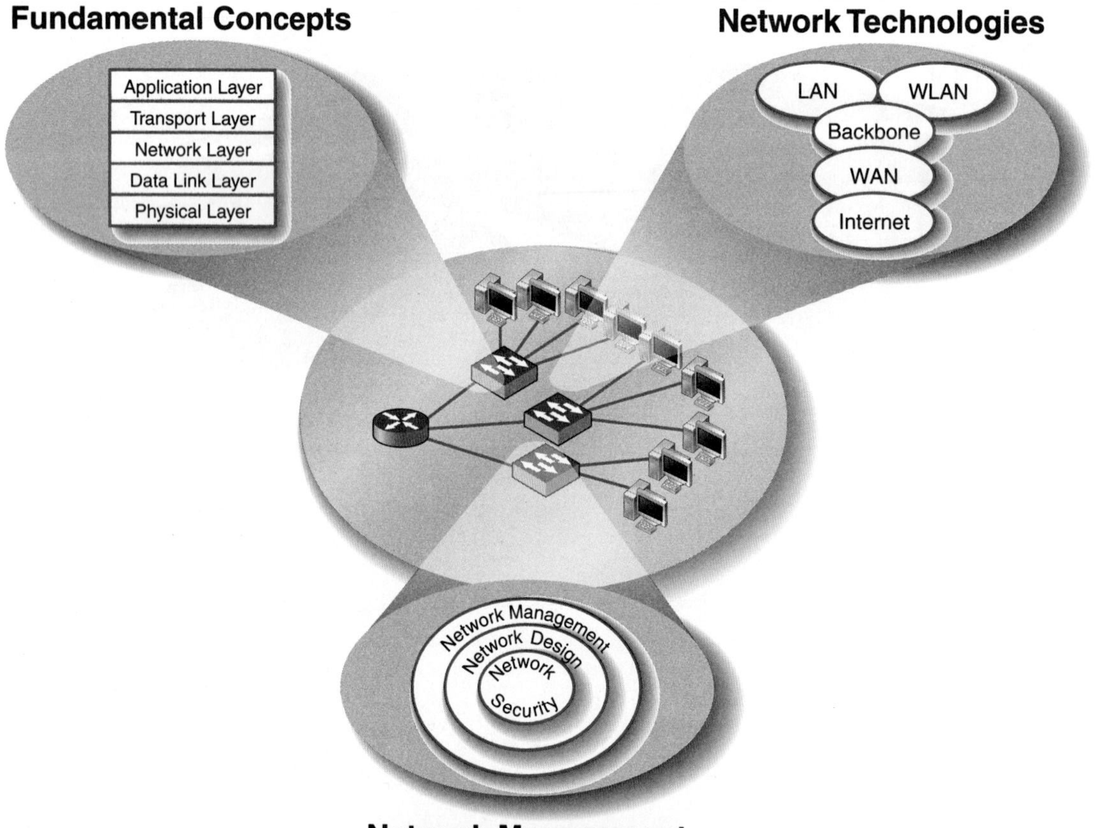

The Three Faces of Networking

THIS CHAPTER introduces the basic concepts of data communications and shows how we have progressed from paper-based systems to modern computer networks. It begins by describing why it is important to study data communications and how the invention of the telephone, the computer, and the Internet has transformed the way we communicate. Next, the basic types and components of a data communication network are discussed. The importance of a network model based on layers and the importance of network standards are examined. The chapter concludes with an overview of three key trends in the future of networking.

OBJECTIVES ▼

- Be aware of the history of communications, information systems, and the Internet
- Be aware of the applications of data communication networks
- Be familiar with the major components of and types of networks
- Understand the role of network layers
- Be familiar with the role of network standards
- Be aware of three key trends in communications and networking

CHAPTER OUTLINE ▼

INTRODUCTION
- A Brief History of Communications in North America
- A Brief History of Information Systems
- A Brief History of the Internet

DATA COMMUNICATIONS NETWORKS
- Components of a Network
- Types of Networks

NETWORK MODELS
- Open Systems Interconnection Reference Model
- Internet Model
- Message Transmission Using Layers

NETWORK STANDARDS
- The Importance of Standards
- The Standards-Making Process
- Common Standards

FUTURE TRENDS
- Pervasive Networking
- The Integration of Voice, Video, and Data
- New Information Services

IMPLICATIONS FOR MANAGEMENT

SUMMARY

INTRODUCTION

What Internet connection should you use? Cable modem or DSL (formally called Digital Subscriber line)? Cable modems are supposedly six times faster than DSL, providing data speeds of 10 mbps to DSL's 1–5 mbps. As we write this, one cable company is using a tortoise to represent DSL in advertisements. So which is faster? We'll give you a hint. Which won the race in the fable, the tortoise or the hare? By the time you finish this book, you'll understand which is faster and why, as well as why choosing the right company as your **Internet service provider (ISP)** is probably more important than choosing the right technology.

Over the past few years, it has become clear that the world has changed forever. We are now in the Information Age—the second Industrial Revolution, according to John Chambers, CEO (chief executive officer) of Cisco Systems, Inc., one of the world's leading networking technology companies. The first Industrial Revolution revolutionized the way people worked by introducing machines and new organizational forms. New companies and industries emerged and old ones died off.

The second Industrial Revolution is revolutionizing the way people work through networking and data communications. The value of a high-speed data communication network is that it brings people together in a way never before possible. In the 1800s, it took several weeks for a message to reach North America by ship from England. By the 1900s, it could be transmitted within the hour. Today, it can be transmitted in seconds. Collapsing the *information lag* to Internet speeds means that people can communicate and access information anywhere in the world regardless of their physical location. In fact, today's problem is that we cannot handle the quantities of information we receive.

Data communications and networking is a truly global area of study, both because the technology enables global communication and because new technologies and applications often emerge from a variety of countries and spread rapidly around the world. The World Wide Web, for example, was born in a Swiss research lab, was nurtured through its first years primarily by European universities, and exploded into mainstream popular culture because of a development at an American research lab.

One of the problems in studying a global phenomenon lies in explaining the different political and regulatory issues that have evolved and currently exist in different parts of the world. Rather than attempt to explain the different paths taken by different countries, we have chosen simplicity instead. Historically, the majority of readers of previous editions of this book have come from North America. Therefore, although we retain a global focus on technology and its business implications, we focus exclusively on North America in describing the political and regulatory issues surrounding communications and networking. We do, however, take care to discuss technological or business issues where fundamental differences exist between North America and the rest of the world (e.g., ISDN [integrated services digital network]) (see Chapter 9).

One of the challenges in studying data communications and networking is that there are many perspectives that can be used. We begin by examining the fundamental concepts of data communications and networking. These concepts explain how data is moved from one computer to another over a network, and represent the fundamental "theory" of how networks operate. The second perspective is from the viewpoint of the technologies in use today—how these theories are put into practice in specific products. From this perspective, we examine how these different technologies work, and when to use which type of technology. The third perspective examines the management of networking technologies, including security, network design, and managing the network on a day-to-day and long-term basis.

In our experience, many people would rather skip over the fundamental concepts, and jump immediately into the network technologies. After all, an understanding of today's technologies is perhaps the most practical aspect of this book. However, network technologies change, and an understanding of the fundamental concepts enables you to better understand new technologies, even though you have not studied them directly.

A Brief History of Communications in North America

Today we take data communications for granted, but it was pioneers like Samuel Morse, Alexander Graham Bell, and Thomas Edison who developed the basic electrical and electronic systems that ultimately evolved into voice and data communication networks.

In 1837, Samuel Morse exhibited a working telegraph system; today we might consider it the first electronic data communication system. In 1841, a Scot named Alexander Bain used electromagnets to synchronize school clocks. Two years later, he patented a printing telegraph—the predecessor of today's fax machines. In 1874, Alexander Graham Bell developed the concept for the telephone at his father's home in Brantford, Ontario, Canada, but it would take him and his assistant, Tom Watson, another two years of work in Boston to develop the first telephone capable of transmitting understandable

MANAGEMENT FOCUS 1.1 CAREER OPPORTUNITIES

It's a great time to be in information technology even after the technology bust. The technology-fueled new economy has dramatically increased the demand for skilled information technology (IT) professionals. The U.S. Bureau of Labor estimates that the number of IT-related jobs will increase by 60 percent between now and 2015. IT employers have responded: Salaries have risen rapidly. Annual starting salaries for our undergraduates at Indiana University range from $50,000 to $65,000. Although all areas of IT have shown rapid growth, the fastest salary growth has been for those with skills in Internet development, networking, and telecommunications. People with a few years of experience in these areas can make $65,000 to $80,000—not counting bonuses.

The demand for networking expertise is growing for two reasons. First, Internet and communication deregulation has significantly changed how businesses operate and has spawned thousands of small start-up companies. Second, a host of new hardware and software innovations have significantly changed the way networking is done.

These trends and the shortage of qualified network experts have also led to the rise in certification. Most large vendors of network technologies, such as Microsoft Corporation and Cisco Systems, Inc., provide certification processes (usually a series of courses and formal exams) so that individuals can document their knowledge. Certified network professionals often earn $10,000 to $15,000 more than similarly skilled uncertified professionals—provided they continue to learn and maintain their certification as new technologies emerge.

conversation in 1876. Later that year, Bell made the first long-distance call (about ten miles) from Paris, Ontario, to his father in Brantford.

When the telephone arrived, it was greeted by both skepticism and adoration, but within five years, it was clear to all that the world had changed. To meet the demand, Bell started a company in the United States, and his father started a company in Canada. In 1879, the first private manual telephone switchboard (private branch exchange, or PBX) was installed. By 1880, the first pay telephone was in use. The telephone became a way of life, because anyone could call from public telephones. The certificate of incorporation for the **American Telephone and Telegraph Company (AT&T)** was registered in 1885. By 1889, AT&T had a recognized logo in the shape of the Liberty Bell with the words Long-Distance Telephone written on it.

In 1892, the Canadian government began regulating telephone rates. By 1910, the Interstate Commerce Commission (ICC) had the authority to regulate interstate telephone businesses in the United States. In 1934, this was transferred to the **Federal Communications Commission (FCC).**

The first transcontinental telephone service and the first transatlantic voice connections were both established in 1915. The telephone system grew so rapidly that by the early 1920s, there were serious concerns that even with the introduction of dial telephones (that eliminated the need for operators to make simple calls) there would not be enough trained operators to work the manual switchboards. Experts predicted that by 1980, every single woman in North America would have to work as a telephone operator if growth in telephone usage continued at the current rate. (At the time, all telephone operators were women.)

The first commercial microwave link for telephone transmission was established in Canada in 1948. In 1951, the first direct long-distance dialing without an operator began. The first international satellite telephone call was sent over the *Telstar I* satellite in 1962. By 1965, there was widespread use of commercial international telephone service via satellite. Fax services were introduced in 1962. Touch-tone telephones were first marketed in 1963. Picturefone service, which allows users to see as well as talk with one another, began operating in 1969. The first commercial packet-switched network for computer data was introduced in 1976.

Until 1968, Bell Telephone/AT&T controlled the U.S. telephone system. No telephones or computer equipment other than those made by Bell Telephone could be connected to the phone system and only AT&T could provide telephone services. In 1968, after a series of lawsuits, the *Carterfone* court decision allowed non-Bell equipment to be connected to the Bell System network. This important milestone permitted independent telephone and modern manufacturers to connect their equipment to U.S. telephone networks for the first time.

Another key decision in 1970 permitted MCI to provide limited long-distance service in the United States in competition with AT&T. Throughout the 1970s, there were many arguments and court cases over the monopolistic position that AT&T held over U.S. communication services. On January 1, 1984, AT&T was divided in two parts under a consent decree devised by a federal judge. The first part, AT&T, provided long-distance telephone services in competition with other **interexchange carriers (IXCs)** such as MCI and Sprint. The second part, a series of seven **regional Bell operating companies**

(RBOCs) or **local exchange carriers (LECs),** provided local telephone services to homes and businesses. AT&T was prohibited from providing local telephone services, and the RBOCs were prohibited from providing long-distance services. Intense competition began in the long-distance market as MCI, Sprint, and a host of other companies began to offer services and dramatically cut prices under the watchful eye of the FCC. Competition was prohibited in the local telephone market, so the RBOCs remained a regulated **monopoly** under the control of a multitude of state laws. The Canadian long-distance market was opened to competition in 1992.

During 1983 and 1984, traditional radio telephone calls were supplanted by the newer cellular telephone networks. In the 1990s, cellular telephones became commonplace and shrank to pocket size. Demand grew so much that in some cities (e.g., New York and Atlanta), it became difficult to get a dial tone at certain times of the day.

In February 1996, the U.S. Congress enacted the Telecommunications Competition and Deregulation Act of 1996. The act replaced all current laws, FCC regulations, and the 1984 consent decree and subsequent court rulings under which AT&T was broken up. It also overruled all existing state laws and prohibited states from introducing new laws. Practically overnight, the local telephone industry in the United States went from a highly regulated and legally restricted monopoly to multiple companies engaged in open competition.

Local and long-distance service in the United States is open for competition. The **common carriers** (RBOCs, IXCs, cable TV companies, and other LECs) are permitted to build their own local telephone facilities and offer services to customers. To increase competition, the RBOCs must sell their telephone services to their competitors at wholesale prices, who can then resell them to consumers at retail prices. Most analysts expected the big IXCs (e.g., AT&T) to quickly charge into the local telephone market, but they were slow to move. Meanwhile, the RBOCs have been aggressively fighting court battles to keep competitors out of their local telephone markets and merging with each other and with the IXCs.

Virtually all RBOCs, LECs, and IXCs have aggressively entered the Internet market. Today, there are thousands of ISPs who provide dial-in and broadband access to the Internet to millions of small business and home users. Most of these are small companies that lease telecommunications circuits from the RBOCs, LECs, and IXCs and use them to provide Internet access to their customers. As the RBOCs, LECs, and IXCs move into the Internet market and provide the same services directly to consumers, the smaller ISPs are facing heavy competition.

International competition should also be heightened by an international agreement signed in 1997 by 68 countries to deregulate (or at least lessen regulation in) their telecommunications markets. The countries agreed to permit foreign firms to compete in their internal telephone markets. Major U.S. firms (e.g., AT&T, BellSouth Corporation) now offer telephone service in many of the industrialized and emerging countries in North America, South America, Europe, and Asia. Likewise, overseas telecommunications giants (e.g., British Telecom) are beginning to enter the U.S. market. This should increase competition in the United States, but the greatest effect is likely to be felt in emerging countries. For example, it costs almost 30 times more to use a telephone in India than it does in the United States.

A Brief History of Information Systems

The natural evolution of information systems in business, government, and home use has forced the widespread use of data communication networks to interconnect various computer systems. However, data communications has not always been considered important.

In the 1950s, computer systems used batch processing, and users carried their punched cards to the computer for processing. By the 1960s, data communication across telephone lines became more common. Users could type their own batches of data for processing using online terminals. Data communications involved the transmission of messages from these terminals to a large central mainframe computer and back to the user.

During the 1970s, online real-time systems were developed that moved the users from batch processing to single transaction-oriented processing. Database management systems replaced the older file systems, and integrated systems were developed in which the entry of an online transaction in one business system (e.g., order entry) might automatically trigger transactions in other business systems (e.g., accounting, purchasing). Computers entered the mainstream of business, and data communications networks became a necessity.

The 1980s witnessed the microcomputer revolution. At first, microcomputers were isolated from the major information systems applications, serving the needs of individual users (e.g., spreadsheets). As more people began to rely on microcomputers for essential applications, the need for networks to exchange data among microcomputers and between microcomputers and central mainframe computers became clear. By the early 1990s, more than 60 percent of all microcomputers in American corporations were networked—connected to other computers.

Today, the microcomputer has evolved from a small, low-power computer into a very powerful, easy-to-use system with a large amount of low-cost software. Today's microcomputers have more raw computing power than a mainframe of the 1990s. Perhaps more surprisingly, corporations today have far more total computing power sitting on desktops in the form of microcomputers than they have in their large central mainframe computers.

Today, the most important aspect of computers is *networking*. The Internet is everywhere, and virtually all computers are networked. Most corporations are rapidly building distributed systems in which information system applications are divided among a network of computers. This form of computing, called client-server computing, will dramatically change the way information systems professionals and users interact with computers. The office of the future that interconnects microcomputers, mainframe computers, fax machines, copiers, teleconferencing equipment, and other equipment will put tremendous demands on data communications networks.

These networks already have had a dramatic impact on the way business is conducted. Networking played a key role—among many other factors—in the growth of Wal-Mart Stores, Inc., into one of the largest forces in the North American retail industry. That process has transformed the retailing industry. Wal-Mart has dozens of mainframes and thousands of network file servers, microcomputers, handheld inventory computers, and networked cash registers. (As an aside, it is interesting to note that every single microcomputer built by IBM in the United States during the third quarter of 1997 was purchased by Wal-Mart.) At the other end of the spectrum, the lack of a sophisticated data communications network was one of the key factors in the bankruptcy of Macy's in the 1990s.

In retail sales, a network is critical for managing inventory. Macy's had a traditional 1970s inventory system. At the start of the season, buyers would order products in large lots to get volume discounts. Some products would be very popular and sell out quickly. When the sales clerks did a weekly inventory and noticed the shortage, they would order more. If the items were not available in the warehouse (and very popular products were often not available), it would take six to eight weeks to restock them. Customers would buy from other stores, and Macy's would lose the sales. Other products, also bought in large quantities, would be unpopular and have to be sold at deep discounts.

In contrast, Wal-Mart negotiates volume discounts with suppliers on the basis of total purchases but does not specify particular products. Buyers place initial orders in small quantities. Each time a product is sold, the sale is recorded. Every day or two, the complete list of purchases is transferred over the network (often via a satellite) to the head office, a distribution center, or the supplier. Replacements for the products sold are shipped almost immediately and typically arrive within days. The result is that Wal-Mart seldom has a major problem with overstocking an unwanted product or running out of a popular product (unless, of course, the supplier is unable to produce it fast enough).

A Brief History of the Internet

The **Internet** is one of the most important developments in the history of both information systems and communication systems because it is both an information system and a communication system. The Internet was started by the U.S. Department of Defense in 1969 as a network of four computers called ARPANET. Its goal was to link a set of computers operated by several universities doing military research. The original network grew as more computers and more computer **networks** were linked to it. By 1974, there were 62 computers attached. In 1983, the Internet split into two parts, one dedicated solely to military installations (called Milnet) and one dedicated to university research centers (called the Internet) that had just under 1,000 host computers or servers.

In 1985, the Canadian government completed its leg of BITNET to link all Canadian universities from coast to coast and provided connections into the American Internet. (BITNET is a competing network to the Internet developed by the City University of New York and Yale University that uses a different approach.) In 1986, the National Science Foundation in the United States created NSFNET to connect leading U.S. universities. By the end of 1987, there were 10,000 servers on the Internet and 1,000 on BITNET.

Performance began to slow down due to increased network traffic, so in 1987, the National Science Foundation decided to improve performance by building a new high-speed backbone network for NSFNET. It leased high-speed circuits from several IXCs and in 1988 connected 13 regional Internet networks containing 170 LANs (local area networks) and 56,000 servers. The National Research Council of Canada followed in 1989 and replaced BITNET with a high-speed network called **CA*net** that used the same communication language as the Internet. By the end of 1989, there were almost 200,000 servers on the combined U.S. and Canadian Internet.

MANAGEMENT FOCUS 1.2 NETWORKS IN THE FIRST GULF WAR

The lack of a good network can cost more than money. During Operation Desert Shield/Desert Storm, the U.S. Army, Navy, and Air Force lacked one integrated logistics communications network. Each service had its own series of networks, making communication and cooperation difficult. But communication among the systems was essential. Each day a navy aircraft would fly into Saudi Arabia to exchange diskettes full of logistics information with the army—an expensive form of "wireless" networking.

This lack of an integrated network also created problems transmitting information from the United States into the Persian Gulf. More than 60 percent of the containers of supplies arrived without documentation. They had to be unloaded for someone to see what was in them and then reloaded for shipment to combat units.

The logistics information systems and communication networks experienced such problems that some Air Force units were unable to quickly order and receive critical spare parts needed to keep planes flying. Officers telephoned the U.S.-based suppliers of these parts and instructed them to send the parts via FedEx.

Fortunately, the war did not start until the United States and its allies were prepared. Had Iraq attacked, things might have turned out differently.

Similar initiatives were undertaken by most other countries around the world, so that by the early 1990s, most of the individual country networks were linked together into one worldwide network of networks. Each of these individual country networks was distinct (each had its own name, access rules, and fee structures), but all networks used the same standards as the U.S. Internet network so they could easily exchange messages with one another. Gradually, the distinctions among the networks in each of the countries began to disappear, and the U.S. name, the Internet, began to be used to mean the entire worldwide network of networks connected to the U.S. Internet. By the end of 1992, there were more than 1 million servers on the Internet.

Originally, commercial traffic was forbidden on the Internet (and on the other individual country networks), because the key portions of these networks were funded by the various national governments and research organizations. In the early 1990s, commercial networks began connecting into NSFNET, CA*net, and the other government-run networks in each country. New commercial online services began offering access to anyone willing to pay, and a connection into the worldwide Internet became an important marketing issue. The growth in the commercial portion of the Internet was so rapid that it quickly overshadowed university and research use. In 1994, with more than 4 million servers on the Internet (most of which were commercial), the U.S. and Canadian governments stopped funding their few remaining circuits and turned them over to commercial firms. Most other national governments soon followed. The Internet had become commercial.

The Internet has continued to grow at a dramatic pace. No one knows exactly how large the Internet is, but estimates suggest there are more than 600 million servers on the Internet, which is still growing rapidly (see www.isc.org). In the mid-1990s, most Internet users were young (under 35 years old) and male, but as the Internet matures, its typical user becomes closer to the underlying average in the population as a whole (i.e., older and more evenly split between men and women). In fact, the fastest growing segment of Internet users is retirees.

DATA COMMUNICATIONS NETWORKS

Data communications is the movement of computer information from one point to another by means of electrical or optical transmission systems. Such systems are often called *data communications networks.* This is in contrast to the broader term *telecommunications,* which includes the transmission of voice and video (images and graphics) as well as data and usually implies longer distances. In general, data communications networks collect data from microcomputers and other devices and transmit that data to a central server that is a more powerful microcomputer, minicomputer, or mainframe, or they perform the reverse process, or some combination of the two. Data communications networks facilitate more efficient use of computers and improve the day-to-day control of a business by providing faster information flow. They also provide message transfer services to allow computer users to talk to one another via electronic mail, chat, and video streaming.

TECHNICAL FOCUS 1.1 INTERNET DOMAIN NAMES

Internet address names are strictly controlled; otherwise, someone could add a computer to the Internet that had the same address as another computer. Each address name has two parts, the computer name and its domain. The general format of an Internet address is therefore computer.domain. Some computer names have several parts separated by periods, so some addresses have the format computer.computer.computer.domain. For example, the main university Web server at Indiana University (IU) is called www.indiana.edu, whereas the Web server for the Kelley School of Business at IU is www.kelley.indiana.edu.

Since the Internet began in the United States, the American address board was the first to assign domain names to indicate types of organization. Some common U.S. domain names are

EDU	for an educational institution, usually a university
COM	for a commercial business
GOV	for a government department or agency
MIL	for a military unit
ORG	for a nonprofit organization

As networks in other countries were connected to the Internet, they were assigned their own domain names. Some international domain names are

CA	for Canada
AU	for Australia
UK	for the United Kingdom
DE	for Germany

New top-level domains that focus on specific types of businesses continue to be introduced, such as

AERO	for aerospace companies
MUSEUM	for museums
NAME	for individuals
PRO	for professionals, such as accountants and lawyers
BIZ	for businesses

Many international domains structure their addresses in much the same way as the United States does. For example, Australia uses *EDU* to indicate academic institutions, so an address such as xyz.edu.au would indicate an Australian university.

For a full list of domain names, see www.iana.org/root/db.

Components of a Network

There are three basic hardware components for a data communications network: a server or host computer (e.g., microcomputer, mainframe), a client (e.g., microcomputer, terminal), and a circuit (e.g., cable, modem) over which messages flow. Both the server and client also need special-purpose network software that enables them to communicate.

The **server** (or **host computer**) stores data or software that can be accessed by the clients. In client-server computing, several servers may work together over the network with a client computer to support the business application.

The **client** is the input-output hardware device at the user's end of a communication circuit. It typically provides users with access to the network and the data and software on the server.

The **circuit** is the pathway through which the messages travel. It is typically a copper wire, although fiber-optic cable and wireless transmission are becoming common. There are many devices in the circuit that perform special functions such as switches and routers.

Strictly speaking, a network does not need a server. Some networks are designed to connect a set of similar computers that share their data and software with each other. Such networks are called **peer-to-peer networks** because the computers function as equals, rather than relying on a central server or host computer to store the needed data and software.

Figure 1.1 shows a small network that has four microcomputers (clients) connected by a **hub** and **cables** (circuit). In this network, messages move through the hub to and from the computers. All computers share the same circuit and must take turns sending messages. The **router** is a special device that connects two or more networks. The router enables computers on this network to communicate with computers on other networks (e.g., the Internet).

The network in Figure 1.1 has three servers. Although one server can perform many functions, networks are often designed so that a separate computer is used to provide different services. The **file server** stores data and software that can be used by computers on the network. The **print server,** which is connected to a printer, manages all printing requests from the clients on the network. The **Web server** stores documents and graphics that can be accessed from any Web browser, such as Internet Explorer. The Web server can respond to requests from computers on this network or any computer on the Internet. Servers are usually microcomputers (often more powerful than the other microcomputers on the network) but may be minicomputers or mainframes.

Types of Networks

There are many different ways to categorize networks. One of the most common ways is to look at the geographic scope of the network. Figure 1.2 illustrates four types of networks: local area networks (LANs), backbone networks (BNs), metropolitan area networks (MANs), and wide area networks (WANs). The distinctions among these are becoming blurry. Some network technologies now used in LANs were originally developed for WANs, whereas some LAN technologies have influenced the development of MAN products. Any rigid classification of technologies is certain to have exceptions.

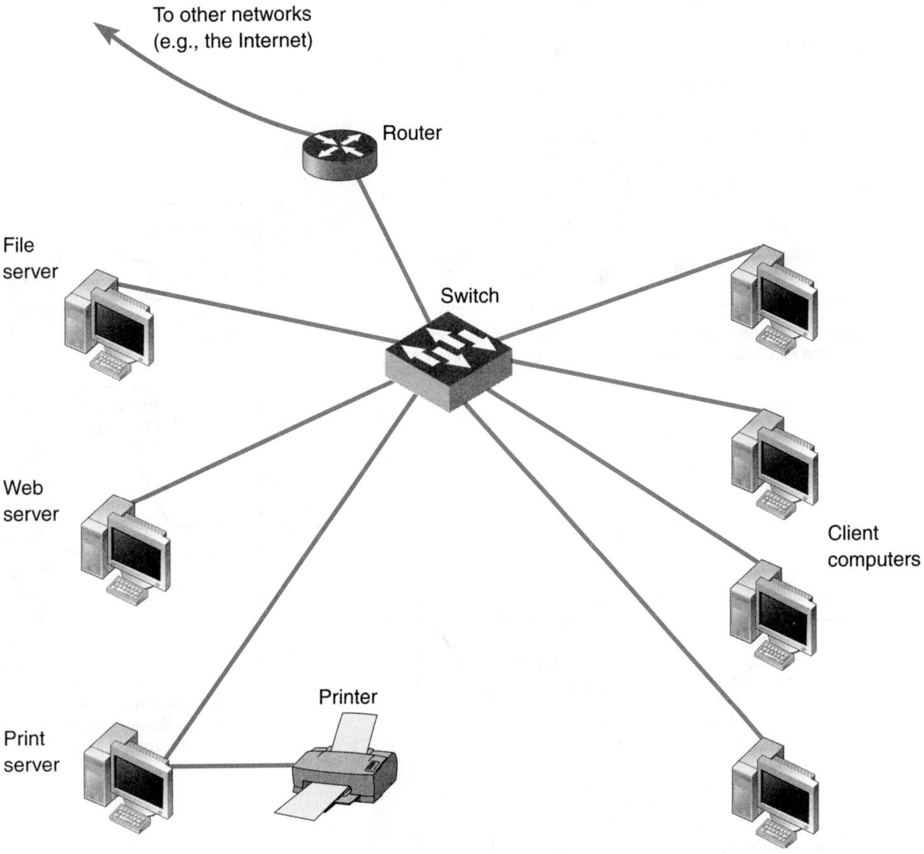

FIGURE 1.1 Example of a local area network (LAN)

A **local area network (LAN)** is a group of microcomputers located in the same general area. A LAN covers a clearly defined small area, such as one floor or work area, a single building, or a group of buildings. LANs often use shared circuits, where all computers must take turns using the same circuit. The upper left diagram in Figure 1.2 shows a small LAN located in the records building at the former McClellan Air Force Base in Sacramento. LANs support high-speed data transmission compared with standard telephone circuits, commonly operating 100 million bits per second (100 Mbps). LANs are discussed in detail in Chapter 6 and wireless LANs in Chapter 7.

Most LANs are connected to a **backbone network (BN),** a larger, central network connecting several LANs, other BNs, MANs, and WANs. BNs typically span from hundreds of feet to several miles and provide very high speed data transmission, commonly 100 to 1,000 Mbps. The second diagram in Figure 1.2 shows a BN that connects the LANs located in several buildings at McClellan Air Force Base. BNs are discussed in detail in Chapter 8.

A **metropolitan area network (MAN)** connects LANs and BNs located in different areas to each other and to WANs. MANs typically span between three and 30 miles. The

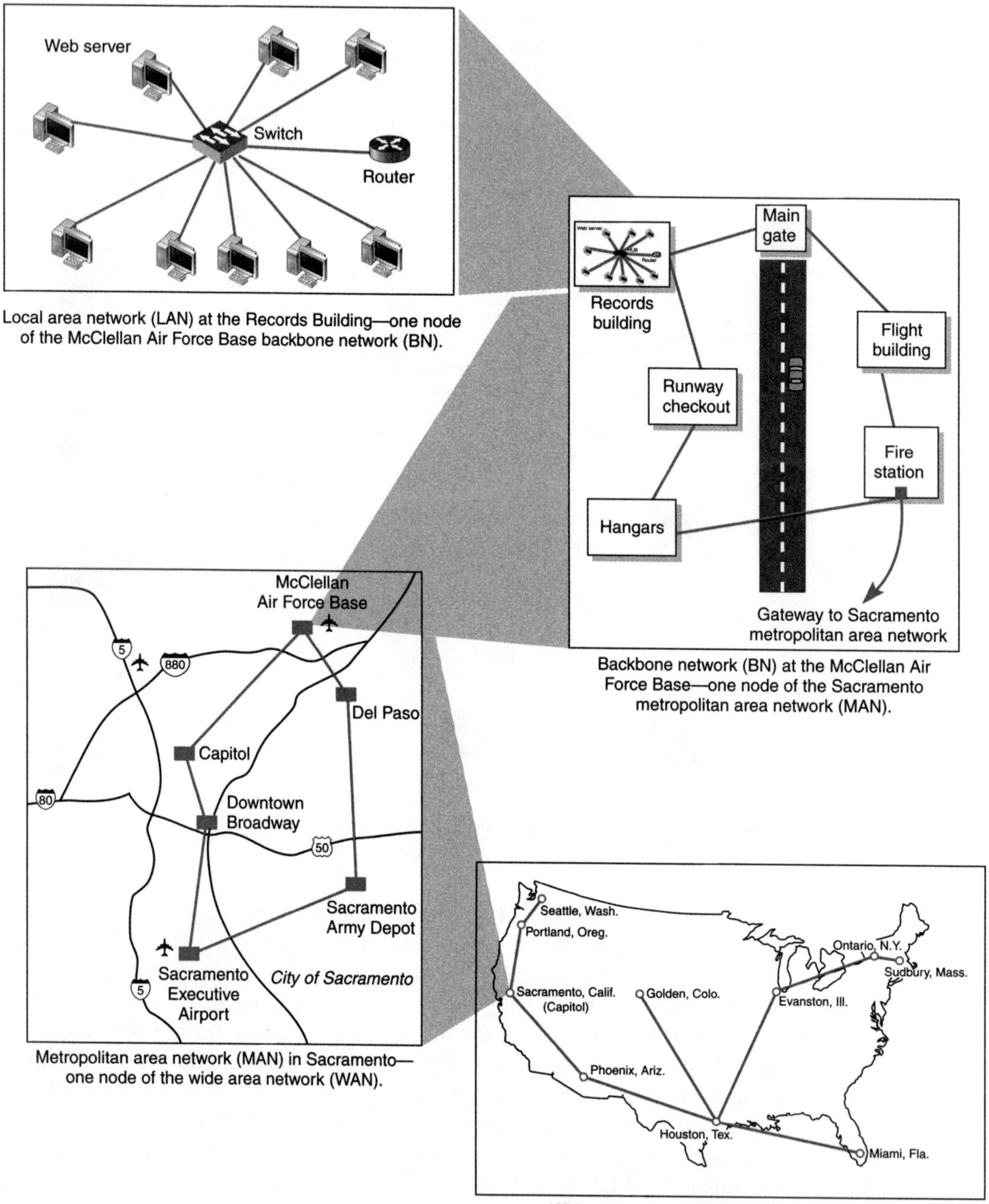

Local area network (LAN) at the Records Building—one node of the McClellan Air Force Base backbone network (BN).

Backbone network (BN) at the McClellan Air Force Base—one node of the Sacramento metropolitan area network (MAN).

Metropolitan area network (MAN) in Sacramento—one node of the wide area network (WAN).

Wide area network (WAN) showing Sacramento connected to nine other cities throughout the U.S.

FIGURE 1.2 The hierarchical relationship of a local area network (LAN) to a backbone network (BN) to a metropolitan area network (MAN) to a wide area network (WAN)

third diagram in Figure 1.2 shows a MAN connecting the BNs at several military and government complexes in Sacramento. Some organizations develop their own MANs using technologies similar to those of BNs. These networks provide moderately fast transmission rates but can prove costly to install and operate over long distances. Unless an organization has a continuing need to transfer large amounts of data, this type of MAN is usually too expensive. More commonly, organizations use public data networks provided by common carriers (e.g., the telephone company) as their MANs. With these MANs, data transmission rates typically range from 64,000 **bits per second** (64 Kbps) to 100 Mbps, although newer technologies provide data rates of 10 *billion bits per second* (10 **gigabits per second,** 10 Gbps). MANs are discussed in detail in Chapter 9.

Wide area networks (WANs) connect BNs and MANs (see Figure 1.2). Most organizations do not build their own WANs by laying cable, building microwave towers, or sending up satellites (unless they have unusually heavy data transmission needs or highly specialized requirements, such as those of the Department of Defense). Instead, most organizations lease circuits from IXCs (e.g., AT&T, MCI, Sprint) and use those to transmit their data. WAN circuits provided by IXCs come in all types and sizes but typically span hundreds or thousands of miles and provide data transmission rates from 64 Kbps to 10 Gbps. WANs are also discussed in detail in Chapter 9.

Two other common terms are **intranets** and **extranets.** An intranet is a LAN that uses the same technologies as the Internet (e.g., Web servers, Java, HTML [Hypertext Markup Language]) but is open to only those inside the organization. For example, although some pages on a Web server may be open to the public and accessible by anyone on the Internet, some pages may be on an intranet and therefore hidden from those who connect to the Web server from the Internet at large. Sometimes an intranet is provided by a completely separate Web server hidden from the Internet. The intranet for the Information Systems Department at Indiana University, for example, provides information on faculty expense budgets, class scheduling for future semesters (e.g., room, instructor), and discussion forums.

An extranet is similar to an intranet in that it, too, uses the same technologies as the Internet but instead is provided to invited users outside the organization who access it over the Internet. It can provide access to information services, inventories, and other internal organizational databases that are provided only to customers, suppliers, or those who have paid for access. Typically, users are given passwords to gain access, but more sophisticated technologies such as smart cards or special software may also be required. Many universities provide extranets for Web-based courses so that only those students enrolled in the course can access course materials and discussions.

NETWORK MODELS

There are many ways to describe and analyze data communications networks. All networks provide the same basic functions to transfer a message from sender to receiver, but each network can use different network hardware and software to provide these functions. All of these hardware and software products have to work together to successfully transfer a message.

One way to accomplish this is to break the entire set of communications functions into a series of **layers,** each of which can be defined separately. In this way, vendors can develop software and hardware to provide the functions of each layer separately. The software or hardware can work in any manner and can be easily updated and improved, as long as the interface between that layer and the ones around it remain unchanged. Each piece of hardware and software can then work together in the overall network.

There are many different ways in which the network layers can be designed. The two most important network models are the Open Systems Interconnection Reference (OSI) model and the Internet model.

Open Systems Interconnection Reference Model

The **Open Systems Interconnection Reference model** (usually called the **OSI model** for short) helped change the face of network computing. Before the OSI model, most commercial networks used by businesses were built using nonstandardized technologies developed by one vendor (remember that the Internet was in use at the time but was not widespread and certainly was not commercial). During the late 1970s, the International Organization for Standardization (ISO) created the Open System Interconnection Subcommittee, whose task was to develop a framework of standards for computer-to-computer communications. In 1984, this effort produced the OSI model.

The OSI model is the most talked about and most referred to network model. If you choose a career in networking, questions about the OSI model will be on the network certification exams offered by Microsoft, Cisco, and other vendors of network hardware and software. However, you will probably never use a network based on the OSI model. Simply put, the OSI model never caught on commercially in North America, although some European networks use it, and some network components developed for use in the United States arguably use parts of it. Most networks today use the Internet model, which is discussed in the next section. However, because there are many similarities between the OSI model and the Internet model, and because most people in networking are expected to know the OSI model, we discuss it here. The OSI model has seven layers (see Figure 1.3).

Layer 1: Physical Layer

The *physical layer* is concerned primarily with transmitting data bits (zeros or ones) over a communication circuit. This layer defines the rules by which ones and zeros are transmitted, such as voltages of electricity, number of bits sent per second, and the physical format of the cables and connectors used.

Layer 2: Data Link Layer

The *data link layer* manages the physical transmission circuit in layer 1 and transforms it into a circuit that is free of transmission errors as far as layers above are concerned. Because layer 1 accepts and transmits only a raw stream of bits without understanding their meaning or structure, the data link layer must create and recognize message boundaries; that is, it must mark where a message starts and where it ends. Another major task of layer 2 is to solve the problems caused by damaged, lost, or duplicate messages so the succeeding layers are shielded from transmission errors. Thus, layer 2 performs error detection and correction. It also decides when a device can transmit so that two computers do not try to transmit at the same time.

<table>
<tr><th>OSI Model</th><th>Internet Model</th><th>Groups of Layers</th><th>Examples</th></tr>
<tr><td>7. Application Layer</td><td rowspan="3">5. Application Layer</td><td rowspan="3">Application Layer</td><td rowspan="3">Internet Explorer and Web pages</td></tr>
<tr><td>6. Presentation Layer</td></tr>
<tr><td>5. Session Layer</td></tr>
<tr><td>4. Transport Layer</td><td>4. Transport Layer</td><td rowspan="2">Internetwork Layer</td><td rowspan="2">TCP/IP Software</td></tr>
<tr><td>3. Network Layer</td><td>3. Network Layer</td></tr>
<tr><td>2. Data Link Layer</td><td>2. Data Link Layer</td><td rowspan="2">Hardware Layer</td><td rowspan="2">Ethernet port, Ethernet cables, and Ethernet software drivers</td></tr>
<tr><td>1. Physical Layer</td><td>1. Physical Layer</td></tr>
</table>

FIGURE 1.3 Network models. OSI = Open Systems Interconnection Reference

Layer 3: Network Layer The *network layer* performs routing. It determines the next computer the message should be sent to so it can follow the best route through the network and finds the full address for that computer if needed.

Layer 4: Transport Layer The *transport layer* deals with end-to-end issues, such as procedures for entering and departing from the network. It establishes, maintains, and terminates logical connections for the transfer of data between the original sender and the final destination of the message. It is responsible for breaking a large data transmission into smaller packets (if needed), ensuring that all the packets have been received, eliminating duplicate packets, and performing flow control to ensure that no computer is overwhelmed by the number of messages it receives. Although error control is performed by the data link layer, the transport layer can also perform error checking.

Layer 5: Session Layer The *session layer* is responsible for managing and structuring all sessions. Session initiation must arrange for all the desired and required services between session participants, such as logging onto circuit equipment, transferring files, using various terminal types, and performing security checks. Session termination provides an orderly way to end the session, as well as a means to abort a session prematurely. It may have some redundancy built in to recover from a broken transport (layer 4) connection in case of failure. The session layer also handles session accounting so the correct party receives the bill.

Layer 6: Presentation Layer The *presentation layer* formats the data for presentation to the user. Its job is to accommodate different interfaces on different terminals or computers so the application program need not worry about them. It is concerned with displaying, formatting, and editing user inputs and outputs. For example, layer 6 might perform data compression, translation between different data formats, and screen formatting. Any function (except those in layers 1 through 5) that is requested sufficiently often to warrant finding a general solution is placed in the presentation layer, although some of these functions can be performed by separate hardware and software (e.g., encryption).

Layer 7: Application Layer The *application layer* is the end user's access to the network. The primary purpose is to provide a set of utilities for application programs. Each user program determines the set of messages and any action it might take on receipt of a message. Other network-specific applications at this layer include network monitoring and network management.

Internet Model

Although the OSI model is the most talked about network model, the one that dominates current hardware and software is a more simple five-layer **Internet model.** Unlike the OSI model that was developed by formal committees, the Internet model evolved from the work of thousands of people who developed pieces of the Internet. The OSI model is a formal standard that is documented in one standard, but the Internet model has never been formally defined; it has to be interpreted from a number of standards.[1] The two models have very much in common (see Figure 1.3); simply put, the Internet model collapses the top three OSI layers into one layer. Because it is clear that the Internet has won the "war," we use the five-layer Internet model for the rest of this book.

Layer 1: The Physical Layer The **physical layer** in the Internet model, as in the OSI model, is the physical connection between the sender and receiver. Its role is to transfer a series of electrical, radio, or light signals through the circuit. The physical layer includes all the *hardware* devices (e.g., computers, modems, and hubs) and physical *media* (e.g., cables and satellites). The physical layer specifies the type of connection and the electrical signals, radio waves, or light pulses that pass through it. Chapter 3 discusses the physical layer in detail.

Layer 2: The Data Link Layer The **data link layer** is responsible for moving a message from one computer to the next computer in the network path from the sender to the receiver. The data link layer in the Internet model performs the same three functions as the data link layer in the OSI model. First, it controls the physical layer by deciding when to transmit messages over the media. Second, it formats the messages by indicating where they start and end. Third, it detects and corrects any errors that have occurred during transmission. Chapter 4 discusses the data link layer in detail.

Layer 3: The Network Layer The **network layer** in the Internet model performs the same functions as the network layer in the OSI model. First, it performs routing, in that it selects the next computer to which the message should be sent. Second, it can find the address of that computer if it doesn't already know it. Chapter 5 discusses the network layer in detail.

[1]Over the years, our view of the Internet layers has evolved, as has the Internet itself. It's now clear that most of the Internet community thinks about networks using a five-layer view, so we'll use it as well. As of this writing, however, Microsoft uses a four-layer view of the Internet for its certification exams.

Layer 4: The Transport Layer The **transport layer** in the Internet model is very similar to the transport layer in the OSI model. It performs two functions. First, it is responsible for linking the application layer software to the network and establishing end-to-end connections between the sender and receiver when such connections are needed. Second, it is responsible for breaking long messages into several smaller messages to make them easier to transmit. The transport layer can also detect lost messages and request that they be resent. Chapter 5 discusses the transport layer in detail.

Layer 5: Application Layer The **application layer** is the application software used by the network user and includes much of what the OSI model contains in the application, presentation, and session layers. It is the user's access to the network. By using the application software, the user defines what messages are sent over the network. Because it is the layer that most people understand best and because starting at the top sometimes helps people understand better, the next chapter, Chapter 2, begins with the application layer. It discusses the architecture of network applications and several types of network application software and the types of messages they generate.

Groups of Layers The layers in the Internet are often so closely coupled that decisions in one layer impose certain requirements on other layers. The data link layer and the physical layer are closely tied together because the data link layer controls the physical layer in terms of when the physical layer can transmit. Because these two layers are so closely tied together, decisions about the data link layer often drive the decisions about the physical layer. For this reason, some people group the physical and data link layers together and call them the **hardware layers.** Likewise, the transport and network layers are so closely coupled that sometimes these layers are called the **internetwork layer.** See Figure 1.3. When you design a network, you often think about the network design in terms of three groups of layers: the hardware layers (physical and data link), the internetwork layers (network and transport), and the application layer.

Message Transmission Using Layers

Each computer in the network has software that operates at each of the layers and performs the functions required by those layers (the physical layer is hardware not software). Each layer in the network uses a formal language, or **protocol,** that is simply a set of rules that define what the layer will do and that provides a clearly defined set of messages that software at the layer needs to understand. For example, the protocol used for Web applications is HTTP (Hypertext Transfer Protocol, which is described in more detail in Chapter 2). In general, all messages sent in a network pass through all layers. All layers except the Physical layer add a **Protocol Data Unit (PDU)** to the message as it passes through them. The PDU contains information that is needed to transmit the message through the network. Some experts use the word "Packet" to mean a PDU. Figure 1.4 shows how a message requesting a Web page would be sent on the Internet.

Application Layer First, the user creates a message at the application layer using a Web browser by clicking on a link (e.g., get the home page at www.somebody.com). The browser translates the user's message (the click on the Web link) into HTTP. The

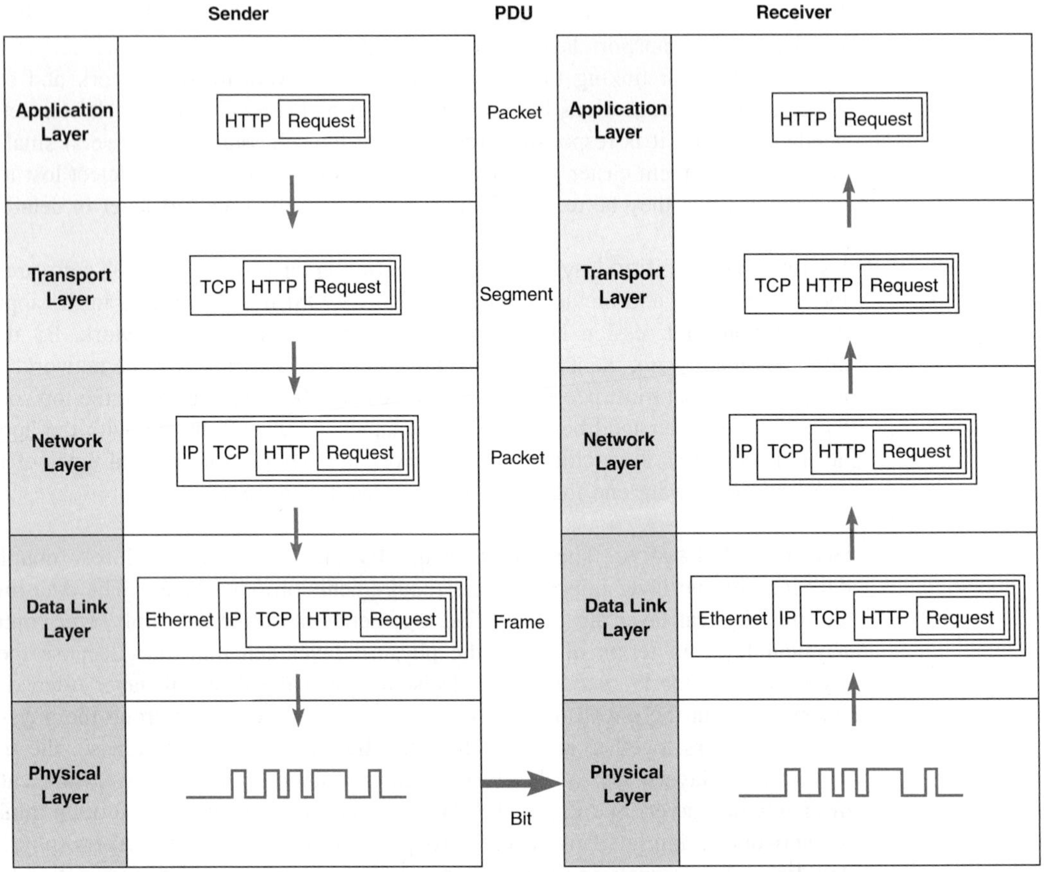

FIGURE 1.4 Message transmission using layers. IP = Internet Protocol; HTTP/Hypertext Transfer Protocol; TCP = Transmission Control Protocol

rules of HTTP define a specific PDU—called an HTTP packet—that all Web browsers must use when they request a Web page. For now, you can think of the HTTP packet as an envelope into which the user's message (*get the Web page*) is placed. In the same way that an envelope placed in the mail needs certain information written in certain places (e.g., return address, destination address), so too does the HTTP packet. The Web browser fills in the necessary information in the HTTP packet, drops the user's request inside the packet, then passes the HTTP packet (containing the Web page request) to the transport layer.

Transport Layer The transport layer on the Internet uses a protocol called TCP (Transmission Control Protocol), and it, too, has its own rules and its own PDUs. TCP is responsible for breaking large files into smaller packets and for opening a connection to the server for the transfer of a large set of packets. The transport layer places the HTTP packet inside a TCP PDU (which is called a TCP segment), fills in the information needed by the TCP segment, and passes the TCP segment (which contains the HTTP packet, which, in turn, contains the message) to the network layer.

Network Layer The network layer on the Internet uses a protocol called IP (Internet Protocol), which has its rules and PDUs. IP selects the next stop on the message's route through the network. It places the TCP segment inside an IP PDU which is called an IP packet, and passes the IP packet, which contains the TCP segment, which, in turn, contains the HTTP packet, which, in turn, contains the message, to the data link layer.

Data Link Layer If you are connecting to the Internet using a LAN, your data link layer may use a protocol called Ethernet, which also has its own rules and PDUs. The data link layer formats the message with start and stop markers, adds error checking information, places the IP packet inside an Ethernet PDU, which is called an Ethernet frame, and instructs the physical hardware to transmit the Ethernet frame, which contains the IP packet, which contains the TCP segment, which contains the HTTP packet, which contains the message.

Physical Layer The physical layer in this case is network cable connecting your computer to the rest of the network. The computer will take the Ethernet frame (complete with the IP packet, the TCP segment, the HTTP packet, and the message) and sends it as a series of electrical pulses through your cable to the server.

When the server gets the message, this process is performed in reverse. The physical hardware translates the electrical pulses into computer data and passes the message to the data link layer. The data link layer uses the start and stop markers in the Ethernet frame to identify the message. The data link layer checks for errors and, if it discovers one, requests that the message be resent. If a message is received without error, the data link layer will strip off the Ethernet frame and pass the IP packet (which contains the TCP segment, the HTTP packet, and the message) to the network layer. The network layer checks the IP address and, if it is destined for this computer, strips off the IP packet and passes the TCP segment, which contains the HTTP packet and the message to the transport layer. The transport layer processes the message, strips off the TCP segment, and passes the HTTP packet to the application layer for processing. The application layer (i.e., the Web server) reads the HTTP packet and the message it contains (the request for the Web page) and processes it by generating an HTTP packet containing the Web page you requested. Then the process starts again as the page is sent back to you.

There are three important points in this example. First, there are many different software packages and many different PDUs that operate at different layers to successfully transfer a message. Networking is in some ways similar to the Russian *Matryoshka,* nested dolls that fit neatly inside each other. This is called encapsulation, because the PDU at a higher level is placed inside the PDU at a lower level so that the lower level PDU encapsulates the higher level one. The major advantage of using different software and protocols is that it is easy to develop new software, because all one has to do is write software for one level at a time. The developers of Web applications, for example, do not need to write software to perform error checking or routing, because those are performed by the data link and network layers. Developers can simply assume those functions are performed and just focus on the application layer. Likewise, it is simple to change the software at any level (or add new application protocols), as long as the interface between that layer and the ones around it remains unchanged.

Second, it is important to note that for communication to be successful, each layer in one computer must be able to communicate with its matching layer in the other computer. For example, the physical layer connecting the client and server must use the same type of electrical signals to enable each to understand the other (or there must be a device to translate between them). Ensuring that the software used at the different layers is the same is accomplished by using *standards.* A standard defines a set of rules, called *protocols,* that explain exactly how hardware and software that conform to the standard are required to operate. Any hardware and software that conform to a standard can communicate with any other hardware and software that conform to the same standard. Without standards, it would be virtually impossible for computers to communicate.

Third, the major disadvantage of using a layered network model is that it is somewhat inefficient. Because there are several layers, each with its own software and PDUs, sending a message involves many software programs (one for each protocol) and many PDUs. The PDUs add to the total amount of data that must be sent (thus increasing the time it takes to transmit), and the different software packages increase the processing power needed in computers. Because the protocols are used at different layers and are stacked on top of one another (take another look at Figure 1.4), the set of software used to understand the different protocols is often called a **protocol stack.**

NETWORK STANDARDS

The Importance of Standards

Standards are necessary in almost every business and public service entity. For example, before 1904, fire hose couplings in the United States were not standard, which meant a fire department in one community could not help in another community. The transmission of electric current was not standardized until the end of the nineteenth century, so customers had to choose between Thomas Edison's direct current (DC) and George Westinghouse's alternating current (AC).

The primary reason for standards is to ensure that hardware and software produced by different vendors can work together. Without networking standards, it would be difficult—if not impossible—to develop networks that easily share information. Standards also mean that customers are not locked into one vendor. They can buy hardware and software from any vendor whose equipment meets the standard. In this way, standards help to promote more competition and hold down prices.

The use of standards makes it much easier to develop software and hardware that link different networks because software and hardware can be developed one layer at a time.

The Standards-Making Process

There are two types of standards: *formal* and *de facto.* A formal standard is developed by an official industry or government body. For example, there are formal standards for applications such as Web browsers (e.g., HTTP, HTML), for network layer software (e.g., IP), data link layer software (e.g., Ethernet IEEE 802.3), and for physical hardware (e.g., V.90 modems). Formal standards typically take several years to develop, during which time technology changes, making them less useful.

De facto standards are those that emerge in the marketplace and are supported by several vendors but have no official standing. For example, Microsoft Windows is a product of one company and has not been formally recognized by any standards organization, yet it is a de facto standard. In the communications industry, de facto standards often become formal standards once they have been widely accepted.

The formal *standardization process* has three stages: specification, identification of choices, and acceptance. The *specification* stage consists of developing a nomenclature and identifying the problems to be addressed. In the *identification of choices* stage, those working on the standard identify the various solutions and choose the optimum solution from among the alternatives. *Acceptance,* which is the most difficult stage, consists of defining the solution and getting recognized industry leaders to agree on a single, uniform solution. As with many other organizational processes that have the potential to influence the sales of hardware and software, standards-making processes are not immune to corporate politics and the influence of national governments.

International Organization for Standardization One of the most important standards-making bodies is the *International Organization for Standardization (ISO),*[2] which makes technical recommendations about data communication interfaces (see www.iso.org). ISO is based in Geneva, Switzerland. The membership is composed of the national standards organizations of each ISO member country.

International Telecommunications Union—Telecommunications Group The **Telecommunications Group (ITU-T)** is the technical standards-setting organization of the United Nations International Telecommunications Union, which is also based in Geneva (see www.itu.int). ITU is composed of representatives from about 200 member countries. Membership was originally focused on just the public telephone companies in each country, but a major reorganization in 1993 changed this, and ITU now seeks members among public- and private-sector organizations who operate computer or communications networks (e.g., RBOCs) or build software and equipment for them (e.g., AT&T).

American National Standards Institute The **American National Standards Institute (ANSI)** is the coordinating organization for the U.S. national system of standards for both technology and nontechnology (see www.ansi.org). ANSI has about 1,000 members from both public and private organizations in the United States. ANSI is a standardization organization, not a standards-making body, in that it accepts standards developed by other organizations and publishes them as American standards. Its role is to coordinate the development of voluntary national standards and to interact with ISO to develop national standards that comply with ISO's international recommendations. ANSI is a voting participant in the ISO.

[2] You're probably wondering why the abbreviation is *ISO,* not *IOS.* Well, *ISO* is a word (not an acronym) derived from the Greek *isos,* meaning "equal." The idea is that with standards, all are equal.

MANAGEMENT FOCUS 1.3 HOW NETWORK PROTOCOLS BECOME STANDARDS

There are many standards organizations around the world, but perhaps the best known is the **Internet Engineering Task Force (IETF).** IETF sets the standards that govern how much of the Internet operates.

The IETF, like all standards organizations, tries to seek consensus among those involved before issuing a standard. Usually, a standard begins as a protocol (i.e., a language or set of rules for operating) developed by a vendor (e.g., HTML [Hypertext Markup Language]). When a protocol is proposed for standardization, the IETF forms a working group of technical experts to study it. The working group examines the protocol to identify potential problems and possible extensions and improvements, then issues a report to the IETF.

If the report is favorable, the IETF issues a **request for comment (RFC)** that describes the proposed standard and solicits comments from the entire world. Most large software companies likely to be affected by the proposed standard prepare detailed responses. Many "regular" Internet users also send their comments to the IETF.

The IETF reviews the comments and possibly issues a new and improved RFC, which again is posted for more comments. Once no additional changes have been identified, it becomes a proposed standard.

Usually, several vendors adopt the proposed standard and develop products based on it. Once at least two vendors have developed hardware or software based on it and it has proven successful in operation, the proposed standard is changed to a draft standard. This is usually the final specification, although some protocols have been elevated to Internet standards, which usually signifies mature standards not likely to change.

The process does not focus solely on technical issues; almost 90 percent of the IETF's participants work for manufacturers and vendors, so market forces and politics often complicate matters. One former IETF chairperson who worked for a hardware manufacturer has been accused of trying to delay the standards process until his company had a product ready, although he and other IETF members deny this. Likewise, former IETF directors have complained that members try to standardize every product their firms produce, leading to a proliferation of standards, only a few of which are truly useful.

SOURCE: "How Networking Protocols Become Standards," *PC Week,* March 17, 1997; "Growing Pains," *Network World,* April 14, 1997.

Institute of Electrical and Electronics Engineers The **Institute of Electrical and Electronics Engineers (IEEE)** is a professional society in the United States whose Standards Association (IEEE-SA) develops standards (see www.standards.ieee.org). The IEEE-SA is probably most known for its standards for LANs. Other countries have similar groups; for example, the British counterpart of IEEE is the Institution of Electrical Engineers (IEE).

Internet Engineering Task Force The IETF sets the standards that govern how much of the Internet will operate (see www.ietf.org). The IETF is unique in that it doesn't really have official memberships. Quite literally anyone is welcome to join its mailing lists, attend its meetings, and comment on developing standards. The role of the IETF and other Internet organizations is discussed in more detail in Chapter 9; also, see the box entitled "How Network Protocols Become Standards."

MANAGEMENT FOCUS 1.4 KEEPING UP WITH TECHNOLOGY

The data communications and networking arena changes rapidly. Significant new technologies are introduced and new concepts are developed almost every year. It is therefore important for network managers to keep up with these changes.

There are at least three useful ways to keep up with change. First and foremost for users of this book is the Web site for this book, which contains updates to the book, additional sections, teaching materials, and links to useful Web sites.

Second, there are literally hundreds of thousands of Web sites with data communications and networking information. Search engines can help you find them. A good initial starting point is the telecom glossary at www.atis.org. Two other useful sites are networkcomputing.com and zdnet.com.

Third, there are many useful magazines that discuss computer technology in general and networking technology in particular, including *Network Computing, Data Communications, Info World, Info Week,* and *CIO Magazine.*

Common Standards

There are many different standards used in networking today. Each standard usually covers one layer in a network. Figure 1.5 outlines some of the most commonly used standards. At this point, these models are probably just a maze of strange names and acronyms to you, but by the end of the book, you will have a good understanding of each of these. Figure 1.5 provides a brief road map for some of the important communication technologies we discuss in this book.

For now, there is one important message you should understand from Figure 1.5: For a network to operate, many different standards must be used simultaneously. The sender of a message must use one standard at the application layer, another one at the transport layer, another one at the network layer, another one at the data link layer, and

Layer	Common Standards
5. Application layer	HTTP, HTML (Web) MPEG, H.323 (audio/video) SMTP, IMAP, POP (e-mail)
4. Transport layer	TCP (Internet and LANs) SPX (Novell LANs)
3. Network layer	IP (Internet and LANs) IPX (Novell LANs)
2. Data link layer	Ethernet (LAN) Frame relay (WAN) T1 (MAN and WAN)
1. Physical layer	RS-232C cable (LAN) Category 5 cable (LAN) V.92 (56 Kbps modem)

FIGURE 1.5 Some common data communications standards. HTML = Hypertext Markup Language; HTTP = Hypertext Transfer Protocol; IMAP = Internet Message Access Protocol; IP = Internet Protocol; IPX = internetwork package exchange; LAN = local area network; MPEG = Motion Picture Experts Group; POP = Post Office Protocol; SPX = sequenced packet exchange; TCP = Transmission Control Protocol

another one at the physical layer. Each layer and each standard is different, but all must work together to send and receive messages.

Either the sender and receiver of a message must use the same standards or, more likely, there are devices between the two that translate from one standard into another. Because different networks often use software and hardware designed for different standards, there is often a lot of translation between different standards.

FUTURE TRENDS

By the year 2010, data communications will have grown faster and become more important than computer processing itself. Both go hand in hand, but we have moved from the computer era to the communication era. There are three major trends driving the future of communications and networking. All are interrelated, so it is difficult to consider one without the others.

Pervasive Networking

Pervasive networking means that communication networks will one day be everywhere; virtually any device will be able to communicate with any other device in the world. This is true in many ways today, but what is important is the staggering rate at which we will eventually be able to transmit data. Figure 1.6 illustrates the dramatic changes over the years in the amount of data we can transfer. For example, in 1980, the capacity of a traditional telephone-based network (i.e., one that would allow you to dial up another computer from your home) was about 300 bits per second (bps). In relative terms, you could picture this as a pipe that would enable you to transfer one speck of dust every second. By the 1990s, we were routinely transmitting data at 9,600 bps, or about a grain of sand every second. By 2000, we were able to transmit either a pea (modem at 56 **Kbps**) or a ping-pong ball (DSL [digital subscriber line] at 1.5 **Mbps**) every second over that same telephone line. In the very near future, we will have the ability to transmit 40 Mbps using fixed point-to-point radio technologies—or in relative terms, about one basketball per second.

Between 1980 and 2005, LAN and backbone technologies increased capacity from about 128 Kbps (a sugar cube per second) to 100 Mbps (a beach ball; see Figure 1.6). Today, backbones can provide 10 **Gbps,** or the relative equivalent of a one-car garage per second.

The changes in WAN and Internet circuits has been even more dramatic (see Figure 1.6). From a typical size of 56 Kbps in 1980 to the 622 Mbps of a high-speed circuit in 2000, most experts now predict a high-speed WAN or Internet circuit will be able to carry 25 **Tbps** (25 terabits, or 25 trillion bits per second) in a few years—the relative equivalent of a skyscraper 50 stories tall and 50 stories wide. Our sources at IBM Research suggest that this may be conservative; they predict a capacity of 1 **Pbps** (1 petabit, or 1 quadrillion bits per second [1 million billion]), which is the equivalent of a skyscraper 300 stories tall and 300 stories wide in Figure 1.6. To put this in perspective in a different way, in 2006, the total size of the Internet was estimated to be 2000 petabits

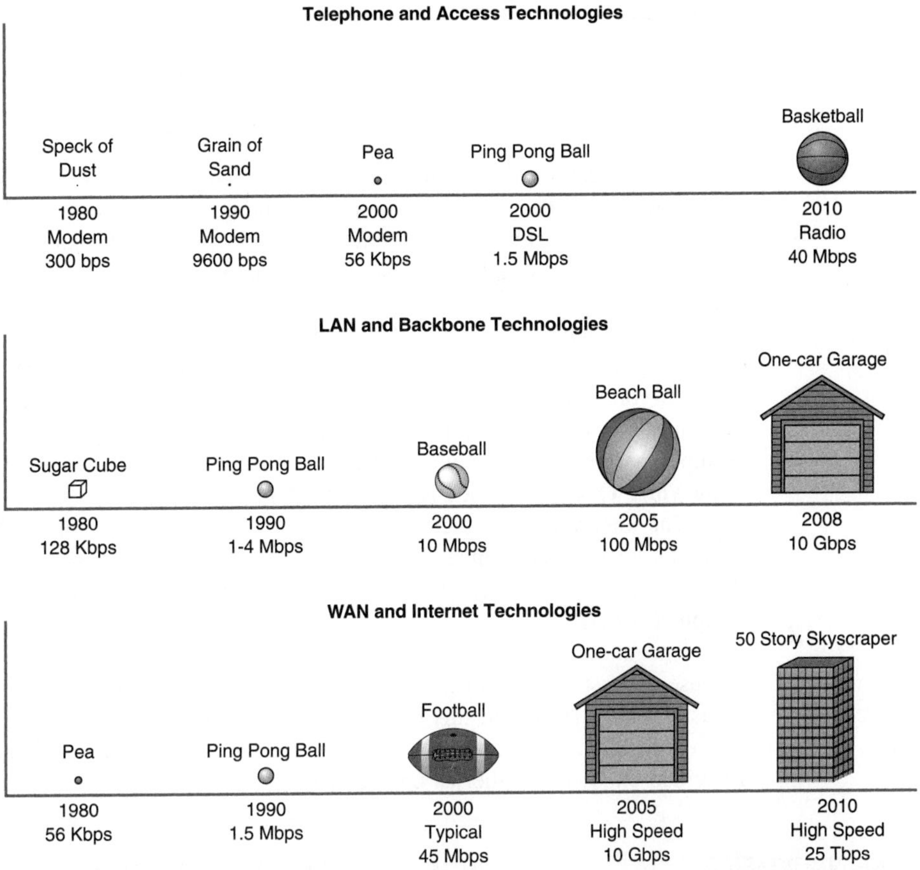

FIGURE 1.6 Relative capacities of telephone, local area network (LAN), backbone network (BN), wide area network (WAN), and Internet circuits. DSL = Digital Subscriber Line

(i.e., adding together every file on every computer in the world that was connected to the Internet). In other words, just *one* 1-Pbps circuit could download the entire contents of today's Internet in about 30 minutes. Of course, no computer in the world today could store that much information—or even just 1 minute's worth of the data transfer.

The term **broadband communication** has often been used to refer to these new highspeed communication circuits. *Broadband* is a technical term that refers to a specific type of data transmission that is used by one of these circuits (e.g., DSL). However, its true technical meaning has become overwhelmed by its use in the popular press to refer to high-speed circuits in general. Therefore, we too will use it to refer to circuits with data speeds of 1 Mbps or higher.

The initial costs of the technologies used for these very high speed circuits will be high, but competition will gradually drive down the cost. The challenge for businesses will be how to use them. When we have the capacity to transmit virtually all the data anywhere we want over a high-speed, low-cost circuit, how will we change the way businesses operate? Economists have long talked about the globalization of world economies. Data communications has made it a reality.

The Integration of Voice, Video, and Data

A second key trend is the integration of voice, video, and data communication, sometimes called **convergence.** In the past, the telecommunications systems used to transmit video signals (e.g., cable TV), voice signals (e.g., telephone calls), and data (e.g., computer data, e-mail) were completely separate. One network was used for data, one for voice, and one for cable TV.

This is rapidly changing. The integration of voice and data is largely complete in WANs. The IXCs, such as AT&T, provide telecommunication services that support data and voice transmission over the same circuits, even intermixing voice and data on the same physical cable. Vonage (www.vonage.com) and Skype (www.skype.com), for example, permit you to use your network connection to make and receive telephone calls using **Voice Over Internet Protocol (VOIP).**

The integration of voice and data has been much slower in LANs and local telephone services. Some companies have successfully integrated both on the same network, but some still lay two separate cable networks into offices, one for voice and one for computer access.

The integration of video into computer networks has been much slower, partly because of past legal restrictions and partly because of the immense communications needs of video. However, this integration is now moving quickly, owing to inexpensive video technologies. Many IXCs are now offering a "triple play" of phone, Internet, and TV video bundled together as one service.

MANAGEMENT FOCUS 1.5 CONVERGENCE IN MARYLAND

The Columbia Association employs 450 full-time and 1,500 part-time employees to operate the recreational facilities for the city of Columbia, Maryland. When Nagaraj Reddi took over as IT director, the Association had a 20-year-old central mainframe, no data networks connecting its facilities, and an outdated legacy telephone network. There was no data sharing; city residents had to call each facility separately to register for activities and provide their full contact information each time. There were long wait times and frequent busy signals.

Reddi wanted a converged network that would combine voice and data to minimize operating costs and improve service to his customers. The Association installed a converged network switch at each facility, which supports computer networks and new digital IP-based phones. The switch also can use traditional analog phones, whose signals it converts into the digital IP-based protocols needed for computer networks. A single digital IP network connects each facility into the Association's WAN, so that voice and data traffic can easy move among the facilities or to and from the Internet.

By using converged services, the Association has improved customer service and also has reduced the cost to install and operate separate voice and data networks.

SOURCE: Cisco Customer Success Story: Columbia Association, www.cisco.com, 2007.

New Information Services

A third key trend is the provision of new information services on these rapidly expanding networks. In the same way that the construction of the American interstate highway system spawned new businesses, so will the construction of worldwide integrated communications networks. The Web has changed the nature of computing so that now, anyone with a computer can be a publisher. You can find information on virtually anything on the Web. The problem becomes one of assessing the accuracy and value of information. In the future, we can expect information services to appear that help ensure the quality of the information they contain. Never before in the history of the human race has so much knowledge and information been available to ordinary citizens. The challenge we face as individuals and organizations is assimilating this information and using it effectively.

Today, many companies are beginning to use **application service providers (ASPs)** rather than developing their own computer systems. An ASP develops a specific system (e.g., an airline reservation system, a payroll system), and companies purchase the service, without ever installing the system on their own computers. They simply use the service, the same way you might use a Web hosting service to publish your own Web pages rather than attempting to purchase and operate your own Web server. Some experts are predicting that by 2010, ASPs will have evolved into **information utilities.** An

MANAGEMENT FOCUS 1.6 INTERNET VIDEO AT REUTERS

For more than 150 years, London-based Reuters has been providing news and financial information to businesses, financial institutions, and the public. As Reuters was preparing for major organizational changes, including the arrival of a new CEO, Tom Glocer, Reuters decided the company needed to communicate directly to employees in a manner that would be timely, consistent, and direct. And they wanted to foster a sense of community within the organization.

Reuters selected a video solution that would reach all 19,000 employees around the world simultaneously, and have the flexibility to add and disseminate content quickly. The heart of the system is housed in London, where video clips are compiled, encoded, and distributed. Employees have a Daily Briefing home page, which presents the day's crucial world news, and a regularly changing 5- to 7-minute high-quality video briefing. Most videos convey essential management information and present engaging and straightforward question-and-answer sessions between Steve Clarke and various executives.

"On the first day, a large number of employees could see Tom Glocer and hear about where he sees the company going and what he wants to do," says Duncan Miller, head of global planning and technology. "Since then, it's provided Glocer and other executives with an effective tool that allows them to communicate to every person in the company in a succinct and controlled manner."

Reuters expected system payback within a year, primarily in the form of savings from reduced management travel and reduced VHS video production, which had previously cost Reuters $215,000 per production. Management also appreciates the personalized nature of the communication, and the ability to get information out within 12 hours to all areas, which makes a huge difference in creating a consistent corporate message.

SOURCE: "Reuters Relies on Internet-Based Video for Optimal Communication," www.cisco.com, 2004.

information utility is a company that provides a wide range of standardized information services, the same way that electric utilities today provide electricity or telephone utilities provide telephone service. Companies would simply purchase most of their information services (e.g., e-mail, Web, accounting, payroll, logistics) from these information utilities rather than attempting to develop their systems and operate their own servers.

IMPLICATIONS FOR MANAGEMENT

At the end of each chapter, we provide key implications for management that arise from the topics discussed in the chapter. The implications we draw focus on improving the management of networks and information systems, as well as implications for the management of the organization as a whole.

There are three key implications for management from this chapter. First, networks and the Internet change almost everything. The ability to quickly and easily move information from distant locations and to enable individuals inside and outside the firm to access information and products from around the world changes the way organizations operate, the way businesses buy and sell products, and the way we as individuals work,

FIGURE 1.7 One server farm with more than 1000 servers
Source: Thomas Koehler/Photothek.net/Digital Railroad, Inc.

live, play, and learn. Companies and individuals that embrace change and actively seek to apply networks and the Internet to better improve what they do, will thrive; companies and individuals that do not, will gradually find themselves falling behind.

Second, today's networking environment is driven by standards. The use of standard technology means an organization can easily mix and match equipment from different vendors. The use of standard technology also means that it is easier to migrate from older technology to a newer technology, because most vendors designed their products to work with many different standards. The use of a few standard technologies rather than a wide range of vendor-specific proprietary technologies also lowers the cost of networking because network managers have fewer technologies they need to learn about and support. If your company is not using a narrow set of industry-standard networking technologies (whether those are de facto standards such as Windows, open standards such as Linux, or formal standards such as 802.11n wireless LANs), then it is probably spending too much money on its networks.

Third, as the demand for network services and network capacity increases, so too will the need for storage and server space. Finding efficient ways to store all the information we generate will open new market opportunities. Today, Google has almost half a million Web servers (see Figure 1.7).

SUMMARY

Introduction The information society, where information and intelligence are the key drivers of personal, business, and national success, has arrived. Data communications is the principal enabler of the rapid information exchange and will become more important than the use of computers themselves in the future. Successful users of data communications, such as Wal-Mart, can gain significant competitive advantage in the marketplace.

Network Definitions A local area network (LAN) is a group of microcomputers or terminals located in the same general area. A backbone network (BN) is a large central network that connects almost everything on a single company site. A metropolitan area network (MAN) encompasses a city or county area. A wide area network (WAN) spans city, state, or national boundaries.

Network Model Communication networks are often broken into a series of layers, each of which can be defined separately, to enable vendors to develop software and hardware that can work together in the overall network. In this book, we use a five-layer model. The application layer is the application software used by the network user. The transport layer takes the message generated by the application layer and, if necessary, breaks it into several smaller messages. The network layer addresses the message and determines its route through the network. The data link layer formats the message to indicate where it starts and ends, decides when to transmit it over the physical media, and detects and corrects any errors that occur in transmission. The physical layer is the physical connection between the sender and receiver, including the hardware devices (e.g., computers, terminals, and modems) and physical media (e.g., cables and satellites). Each layer, except the physical layer, adds a protocol data unit (PDU) to the message.

Standards Standards ensure that hardware and software produced by different vendors can work together. A formal standard is developed by an official industry or government body. De facto standards are those that emerge in the marketplace and are supported by several vendors but have no official standing. Many different standards and standards-making organizations exist.

Future Trends Pervasive networking will change how and where we work and with whom we do business. As the capacity of networks increases dramatically, new ways of doing business will emerge. The integration of voice, video, and data onto the same networks will greatly simplify networks and enable anyone to access any media at any point. The rise in these pervasive, integrated networks will mean a significant increase in the availability of information and new information services such as application service providers (ASPs) and information utilities.

KEY TERMS

American National Standards Institute (ANSI)
application layer
application service provider (ASP)
AT&T
backbone network (BN)
bps
broadband communication
cable
CA*net
circuit
client
common carrier
convergence
data link layer
extranet
Federal Communications Commission (FCC)
file server
Gbps
hardware layer
host computer
hub
information utility
Institute of Electrical and Electronics Engineers (IEEE)
Interexchange carrier (IXC)
International Telecommunications Union—Telecommunications Group (ITU-T)
Internet
Internet Engineering Task Force (IETF)
Internet model
Internet service provider (ISP)
intranet
internetwork layer
Kbps
layers
local area network (LAN)
local exchange carrier (LEC)
Mbps
metropolitan area network (MAN)
monopoly
network
network layer
Open Systems Interconnection Reference model (OSI model)
Pbps
peer-to-peer network
pervasive networking
physical layer
print server
protocol
Protocol Data Unit (PDU)
protocol stack
regional Bell operating company (RBOC)
Request for Comment (RFC)
router
server
standards
Tbps
transport layer
Voice Over Internet Protocol (VOIP)
Web server
wide area network (WAN)

QUESTIONS

1. How can data communications networks affect businesses?
2. Discuss three important applications of data communications networks in business and personal use.
3. Define *information lag* and discuss its importance.
4. Describe the progression of communications systems from the 1800s to the present.
5. Describe the progression of information systems from the 1950s to the present.
6. Describe the progression of the Internet from the 1960s to the present.
7. How do local area networks (LANs) differ from metropolitan area networks (MANs), wide area networks (WANs), and backbone networks (BNs)?
8. What is a circuit?
9. What is a client?
10. What is a host or server?
11. Why are network layers important?
12. Describe the seven layers in the OSI network model and what they do.
13. Describe the five layers in the Internet network model and what they do.
14. Explain how a message is transmitted from one computer to another using layers.
15. Describe the three stages of standardization.
16. How are Internet standards developed?

17. Describe two important data communications standards-making bodies. How do they differ?
18. What is the purpose of a data communications standard?
19. What are three of the largest interexchange carriers (IXCs) in North America?
20. Name two regional Bell operating companies (RBOCs). Which one(s) provide services in your area?
21. Discuss three trends in communications and networking.
22. Why has the Internet model replaced the Open Systems Interconnection Reference (OSI) model?
23. In the 1980s when we wrote the first edition of this book, there were many, many more protocols in common use at the data link, network, and transport layers than there are today. Why do you think the number of commonly used protocols at these layers has declined? Do you think this trend will continue? What are the implications for those who design and operate networks?
24. The number of standardized protocols in use at the application layer has significantly increased since the 1980s. Why? Do you think this trend will continue? What are the implications for those who design and operate networks?

EXERCISES

1-1. Investigate the long-distance carriers (interexchange carriers [IXCs]) and local exchange carriers (LECs) in your area. What services do they provide and what pricing plans do they have for residential users?

1-2. Discuss the issue of communications monopolies and open competition with an economics instructor and relate his or her comments to your data communication class.

1-3. Find a college or university offering a specialized degree in telecommunications or data communications and describe the program.

1-4. Describe a recent data communication development you have read about in a newspaper or magazine and how it may affect businesses.

1-5. Investigate the networks in your school or organization. Describe the important local area networks (LANs) and backbone networks (BNs) in use (but do not describe the specific clients, servers, or devices on them).

1-6. Use the Web to search the Internet Engineering Task (IETF) Web site (www.ietf.org). Describe one standard that is in the request for comment (RFC) stage.

1-7. Discuss how the revolution/evolution of communications and networking is likely to affect how you will work and live in the future.

1-8. Investigate the providers of VOIP phone service using the Internet (e.g., Vonage.com). What services do they provide and what pricing plans do they have for residential users?

MINI-CASES

I. Big E. Bank

Nancy Smith is the director of network infrastructure for Big E. Bank (BEB). BEB has just purchased Ohio Bank (OB), a small regional bank that has 30 branches spread over Ohio. OB has a WAN connecting five cities, in which it has branches, to OB's main headquarters in Columbus. It has a series of MANs in those cities, which in turn connect to the LANs in each of the branches. The OB network is adequate but uses very different data link, network, and transport protocols than those used by BEB's network. Smith's task is to connect OB's network with BEB's network. She has several alternatives. Alternative A is to leave the two networks separate but install a few devices in OB's headquarters to translate between the set of protocols used in the BEB network and those in the OB network so that messages can flow between the two networks. Alternative B is to replace all the WAN, MAN, and LAN network components in OB's entire network so that OB uses the same protocols as BEB and the two can freely communicate. Alternative C is to replace the devices in OB's WAN (and possibly the MANs) so that each city (or each branch, if the MANs are replaced as well) can communicate with the BEB network but leave the LANs in individual branches unchanged. In this case, the device connecting the MAN (or the branch) will translate between the OB protocols and the BEB protocols. Your job is to develop a short list of pros and cons for each alternative and make a recommendation.

II. Global Consultants

John Adams is the chief information officer (CIO) of Global Consultants (GC), a very large consulting firm with offices in more than 100 countries around the the world. GC is about to purchase a set of several Internetbased financial software packages that will be installed in all of their offices. There are no standards at the application layer for financial software but several software companies that sell financial software (call them group A) use one de facto standard to enable their software to work with one another's software. However, another group of financial software companies (call them group B) use a different de facto standard. Although both groups have software packages that GC could use, GC would really prefer to buy one package from group A for one type of financial analysis and one package from group B for a different type of financial analysis. The problem, of course, is that then the two packages cannot communicate and GC's staff would end up having to type the same data into both packages. The alternative is to buy two packages from the same group—so that data could be easily shared—but that would mean having to settle for second best for one of the packages. Although there have been some reports in the press about the two groups of companies working together to develop one common standard that will enable software to work together, there is no firm agreement yet. What advice would you give Adams?

III. Atlas Advertising

Atlas Advertising is a regional advertising agency with offices in Boston, New York, Providence, Washington D.C., and Philadelphia. 1. Describe the types of networks you think they would have (e.g., LANs, BNs, MANs, WANs) and where they are likely to be located. 2. What types of standard protocols and technologies do you think they are using at each layer (e.g., see Figure 1.5)?

IV. Consolidated Supplies

Consolidated Supplies is a medium-sized distributor of restaurant supplies that operates in Canada and several northern U.S. states. They have 12 large warehouses spread across both countries to service their many customers. Products arrive from the manufacturers and are stored in the warehouses until they are picked and put on a truck for delivery to their customers. The networking equipment in their warehouses is old and is starting to give them problems; these problems are expected to increase as the equipment gets older. The vice president of operations, Pat McDonald, would like to replace the existing LANs and add some new wireless LAN technology into all the warehouses, but he is concerned that now may not be the right time to replace the equipment. He has read several technology forecasts that suggest there will be dramatic improvements in networking speeds over the next few years, especially in wireless technologies. He has asked you for advice about upgrading the equipment. Should Consolidated Supplies replace all the networking equipment in all the warehouses now, should it wait until newer networking technologies are available, or should it upgrade some of the warehouses this year, some next year, and some the year after, so that some warehouses will benefit from the expected future improvements in networking technologies?

V. Asia Importers

Caisy Wong is the owner of a small catalog company that imports a variety of clothes and houseware from several Asian countries and sells them to its customers over the Web and by telephone through a traditional catalog. She has read about the convergence of voice and data and is wondering about changing her current traditional, separate, and rather expensive telephone and data services into one service offered by a new company that will supply both telephone and data over her Internet connection. What are the potential benefits and challenges that Asia Importers should consider in making the decision about whether or not to move to one integrated service?

VI. Mega Investments

Mega Investments is a financial services company catering to wealthy individuals. They help these individuals invest their fortunes in stocks, bonds, companies, gold mines, and other investments. Mega Investments has offices in New York, Philadelphia, Toronto, Montreal, and Miami. They recently completed a network upgrade and have standardized all their networks on Ethernet at the data link and physical layers in their LAN, frame relay at the data link and physical layers in their WAN, and TCP/IP at the transport and network layers for all networks. They have recently purchased a similar firm called Caribbean Investments with offices in the Bahamas, Cayman Islands, and St. Martin. Caribbean Investments has an older network that uses token ring at the data link and physical layers in their LAN, and IPX/SPX at the transport and network layers; they have no WAN connections between offices (all data transfer is done by mailing CDs). The older networks still work, but they are starting to show their age; two network cards recently broke and had to be replaced. Mega Investments wants to link the three new offices into their main network and is also considering upgrading those offices to Ethernet and TCP/IP. Outline the pros and cons of upgrading the networks.

CASE STUDY

NEXT-DAY AIR SERVICE

See the Web site.

HANDS-ON ACTIVITY

Convergence at Home

We talked about the convergence of voice, video, and data in this chapter. The objective of this Activity is for you to experience this convergence.

1. Yahoo Instant Messenger is one of the many tools that permit the convergence of voice, video, and text data over the Internet. Use your browser to connect to messenger.yahoo.com and sign-up for Yahoo Instant Messenger; then download and install it—or use the IM tool of your choice. Buy an inexpensive Webcam with a built-in microphone.
2. Get your parents to do the same.
3. Every weekend, talk to your parents using IM text, voice, and video (see Figure 1.8). It's free, so there's no phone bill to worry about, and the video will make everyone feel closer. If you want to feel even closer, connect to them and just leave the voice and video on while you do your homework; no need to talk, just spend time together online.

FIGURE 1.8 Voice, video, and data in Yahoo Instant Messenger

PART TWO

FUNDAMENTAL CONCEPTS

Courtesy Cisco Systems, Inc.

Network switches from Cisco Systems, Inc.

CHAPTER 2
APPLICATION LAYER

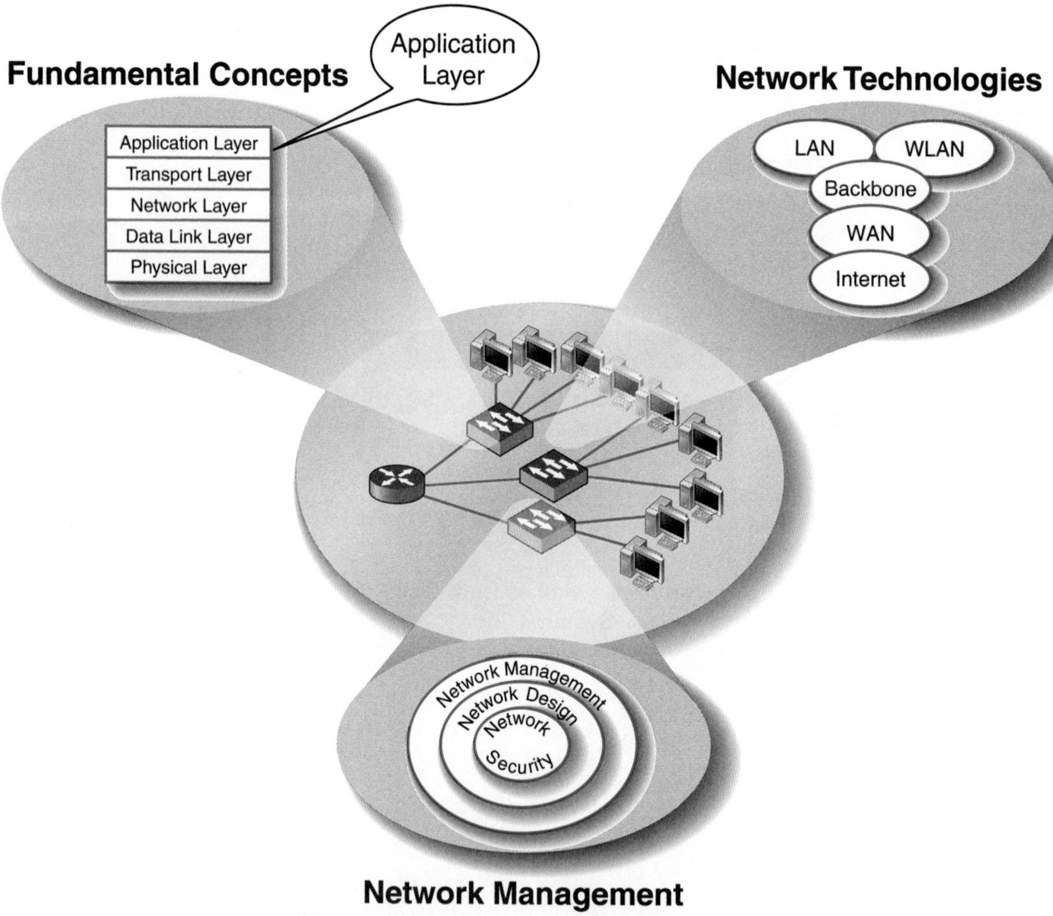

The Three Faces of Networking

THE APPLICATION layer (also called layer 5) is the software that enables the user to perform useful work. The software at the application layer is the reason for having the network because it is this software that provides the business value. This chapter examines the three fundamental types of application architectures used at the application layer (host-based, client-based, client-server). It then looks at the Internet and the primary software application packages it enables: the Web, e-mail, Telnet, FTP, and Instant Messaging.

OBJECTIVES ▼

- Understand host-based, client-based, and client–server application architectures
- Understand how the Web works
- Understand how e-mail works
- Be aware of how FTP, Telnet, and instant messaging works

CHAPTER OUTLINE ▼

INTRODUCTION

Network applications are the software packages that run in the application layer. You should be quite familiar with many types of network software, because it is these application packages that you use when you use the network. In many respects, the only reason for having a network is to enable these applications.

In this chapter, we first discuss three basic architectures for network applications and how each of those architectures affects the design of networks. Because you probably have a good understanding of applications such as the Web and word processing, we will use those as examples of different application architectures. We then examine several common applications used on the **Internet** (e.g., Web, e-mail) and use those to explain how application software interacts with the networks. By the end of this chapter, you should have a much better understanding of the application layer in the network model and what exactly we meant when we used the term protocol data unit in Chapter 1.

APPLICATION ARCHITECTURES

In Chapter 1, we discussed how the three basic components of a network (client computer, server computer, and circuit) worked together. In this section, we will get a bit more specific about how the client computer and the server computer can work together to provide application software to the users. An **application architecture** is the way in which the functions of the application layer software are spread among the clients and servers in the network.

The work done by any application program can be divided into four general functions. The first is **data storage.** Most application programs require data to be stored and retrieved, whether it is a small file such as a memo produced by a word processor or a large database such as an organization's accounting records. The second function is **data access logic,** the processing required to access data, which often means database queries in SQL (structured query language). The third function is the **application logic** (sometimes called business logic), which also can be simple or complex, depending on the application. The fourth function is the **presentation logic,** the presentation of information to the user and the acceptance of the user's commands. These four functions, data storage, data access logic, application logic, and presentation logic, are the basic building blocks of any application.

There are many ways in which these four functions can be allocated between the client computers and the servers in a network. There are four fundamental application architectures in use today. In **host-based architectures,** the server (or host computer) performs virtually all of the work. In **client-based architectures,** the client computers perform most of the work. In **client-server architectures,** the work is shared between the servers and clients. In **peer-to-peer architectures,** computers are both clients and servers and thus share the work. The client-server architecture is the dominant application architecture.

TECHNICAL FOCUS 2.1 CLIENTS AND SERVERS

There are many different types of clients and servers that can be part of a network, and the distinctions between them have become a bit more complex over time. Generally speaking, there are four types of computers that are commonly used as servers:

- A **mainframe** is a very large general-purpose computer (usually costing millions of dollars) that is capable of performing *very* many simultaneous functions, supporting *very* many simultaneous users, and storing *huge* amounts of data.
- A **microcomputer** is the type of computer you use. Microcomputers used as servers can range from a small microcomputer, similar to a desktop one you might use, to one costing $20,000 or more.
- A **cluster** is a group of computers (often microcomputers) linked together so that they act as one computer. Requests arrive at the cluster (e.g., Web requests) and are distributed among the computers so that no one computer is overloaded. Each computer is separate, so that if one fails, the cluster simply bypasses it. Clusters are more complex than single servers because work must be quickly coordinated and shared among the individual computers. Clusters are very scalable because one can always add one more computer to the cluster.
- A **virtual server** is one computer (often a microcomputer) that acts as several servers. Using special software, several operating systems are installed on the same physical computer so that one physical computer appears as several different servers to the network. These virtual servers can perform the same or separate functions (e.g., a printer server, Web server, file server). This improves efficiency (when each server is not fully used, there is no need to buy separate physical computers) and may improve effectiveness (if one virtual server crashes, it does not crash the other servers on the same computer).

There are five commonly used types of clients:

- A *microcomputer* is the most common type of client today. This includes desktop and portable computers, as well as Tablet PCs that enable the user to write with a pen-like stylus instead of typing on a keyboard.
- A **terminal** is a device with a monitor and keyboard but no central processing unit (CPU). **Dumb terminals,** so named because they do not participate in the processing of the data they display, have the bare minimum required to operate as input and output devices (a TV screen and a keyboard). In most cases when a character is typed on a dumb terminal, it transmits the character through the circuit to the server for processing. Every keystroke is processed by the server, even simple activities such as the up arrow.
- A **network computer** is designed primarily to communicate using Internet-based standards (e.g., HTTP, Java) but has no hard disk. It has only limited functionality.
- A **transaction terminal** is designed to support specific business transactions, such as the automated teller machines (ATM) used by banks. Other examples of transaction terminals are point-of-sale terminals in a supermarket.
- A handheld computer, Personal Digital Assistant (PDA), or mobile phone can also be used as a network client.

Host-Based Architectures

The very first data communications networks developed in the 1960s were host-based, with the server (usually a large mainframe computer) performing all four functions. The clients (usually terminals) enabled users to send and receive messages to and from the host computer. The clients merely captured keystrokes, sent them to the server for processing, and accepted instructions from the server on what to display (Figure 2.1).

This very simple architecture often works very well. Application software is developed and stored on the one server along with all data. If you've ever used a terminal (or a microcomputer with Telnet software), you've used a host-based application. There is one point of control, because all messages flow through the one central server. In theory, there are economies of scale, because all computer resources are centralized (but more on cost later).

There are two fundamental problems with host-based networks. First, the server must process all messages. As the demands for more and more network applications grow, many servers become overloaded and unable to quickly process all the users' demands. Prioritizing users' access becomes difficult. Response time becomes slower, and network managers are required to spend increasingly more money to upgrade the server. Unfortunately, upgrades to the mainframes that usually are the servers in this architecture are "lumpy." That is, upgrades come in large increments and are expensive (e.g., $500,000); it is difficult to upgrade "a little."

Client-Based Architectures

In the late 1980s, there was an explosion in the use of microcomputers and microcomputer-based LANs. Today, more than 90 percent of most organizations' total computer processing power now resides on microcomputer-based LANs, not in centralized mainframe computers. Part of this expansion was fueled by a number of low-cost, highly popular applications such as word processors, spreadsheets, and presentation graphics programs. It was also fueled in part by managers' frustrations with application software on host mainframe computers. Most mainframe software is not as easy to use as microcomputer software, is far more expensive, and can take years to develop. In the late 1980s, many large organizations had application development backlogs of two to three years; that is, getting any new mainframe application program written would take years. New York City, for example, had a six-year backlog. In contrast, managers could buy microcomputer packages or develop microcomputer-based applications in a few months.

With client-based architectures, the clients are microcomputers on a LAN, and the server is usually another microcomputer on the same network. The application software

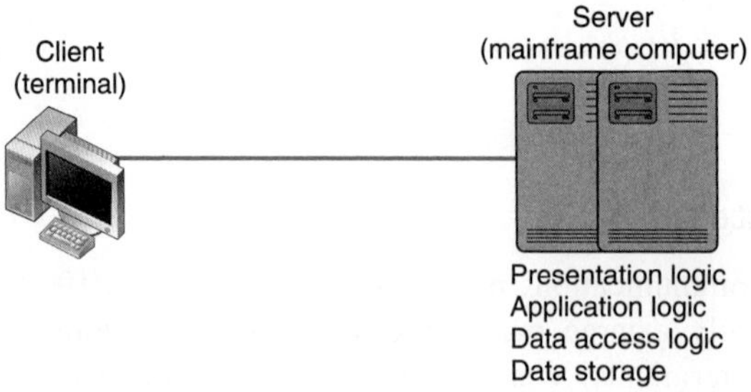

FIGURE 2.1 Host-based architecture

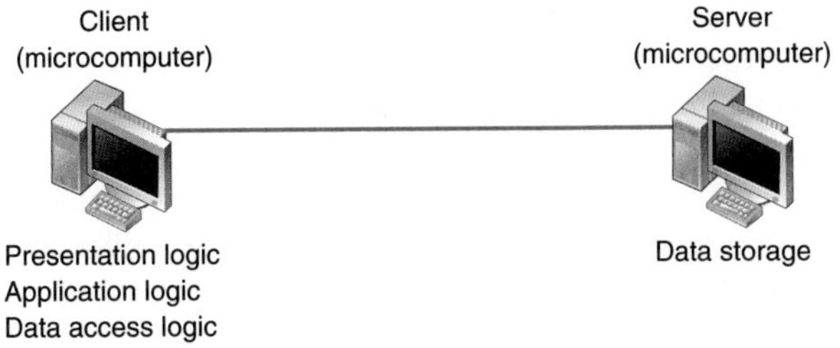

FIGURE 2.2 Client-based architecture

on the client computers is responsible for the presentation logic, the application logic, and the data access logic; the server simply stores the data (Figure 2.2).

This simple architecture often works very well. If you've ever used a word processor and stored your document file on a server (or written a program in Visual Basic or C that runs on your computer but stores data on a server), you've used a client-based architecture.

The fundamental problem in client-based networks is that all data on the server must travel to the client for processing. For example, suppose the user wishes to display a list of all employees with company life insurance. All the data in the database (or all the indices) must travel from the server where the database is stored over the network circuit to the client, which then examines each record to see if it matches the data requested by the user. This can overload the network circuits because far more data is transmitted from the server to the client than the client actually needs.

Client-Server Architectures

Most organizations today are moving to client-server architectures. Client-server architectures attempt to balance the processing between the client and the server by having both do some of the logic. In these networks, the client is responsible for the presentation logic, whereas the server is responsible for the data access logic and data storage. The application logic may either reside on the client, reside on the server, or be split between both.

Figure 2.3 shows the simplest case, with the presentation logic and application logic on the client and the data access logic and data storage on the server. In this case, the client software accepts user requests and performs the application logic that produces database requests that are transmitted to the server. The server software accepts the database requests, performs the data access logic, and transmits the results to the client. The client software accepts the results and presents them to the user. When you used

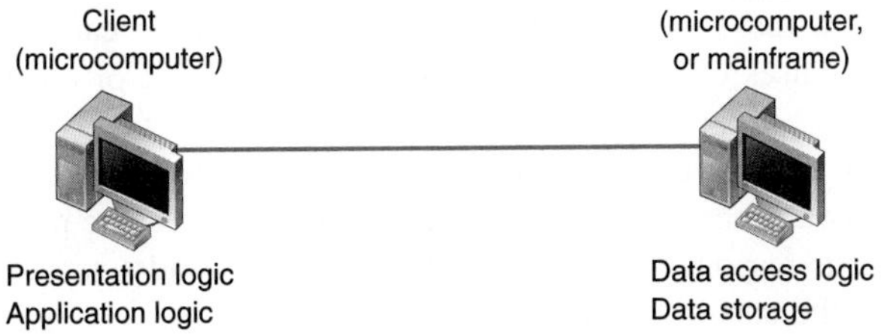

FIGURE 2.3 Two-tier client-server architecture

a Web browser to get pages from a Web server, you used a client-server architecture. Likewise, if you've ever written a program that uses SQL to talk to a database on a server, you've used a client-server architecture.

For example, if the user requests a list of all employees with company life insurance, the client would accept the request, format it so that it could be understood by the server, and transmit it to the server. On receiving the request, the server searches the database for all requested records and then transmits only the matching records to the client, which would then present them to the user. The same would be true for database updates; the client accepts the request and sends it to the server. The server processes the update and responds (either accepting the update or explaining why not) to the client, which displays it to the user.

One of the strengths of client-server networks is that they enable software and hardware from different vendors to be used together. But this is also one of their disadvantages, because it can be difficult to get software from different vendors to work together. One solution to this problem is **middleware,** software that sits between the application software on the client and the application software on the server. Middleware does two things. First, it provides a standard way of communicating that can translate between software from different vendors. Many middleware tools began as translation utilities that enabled messages sent from a specific client tool to be translated into a form understood by a specific server tool.

The second function of middleware is to manage the message transfer from clients to servers (and vice versa) so that clients need not know the specific server that contains the application's data. The application software on the client sends all messages to the middleware, which forwards them to the correct server. The application software on the client is therefore protected from any changes in the physical network. If the network layout changes (e.g., a new server is added), only the middleware must be updated.

There are literally dozens of standards for middleware, each of which is supported by different vendors and each of which provides different functions. Two of the most important standards are Distributed Computing Environment (DCE) and Common Object Request Broker Architecture (CORBA). Both of these standards cover virtually all aspects of the client-server architecture but are quite different. Any client or server software that conforms to one of these standards can communicate with any other software that conforms to the same standard. Another important standard is Open Database Connectivity (ODBC), which provides a standard for data access logic.

Two-Tier, Three-Tier, and n-Tier Architectures

There are many ways in which the application logic can be partitioned between the client and the server. The example in Figure 2.3 is one of the most common. In this case, the server is responsible for the data and the client, the application and presentation. This is called a **two-tier architecture,** because it uses only two sets of computers, one set of clients and one set of servers.

A **three-tier architecture** uses three sets of computers, as shown in Figure 2.4. In this case, the software on the client computer is responsible for presentation logic, an application server is responsible for the application logic, and a separate database server is responsible for the data access logic and data storage.

MANAGEMENT FOCUS 2.1 A MONSTER CLIENT-SERVER ARCHITECTURE

Every spring, Monster.com, one of the largest job sites in the United States, with an average of more than 40 million visits per month, experiences a large increase in traffic. Aaron Braham, vice president of operations, attributes the spike to college students who increase their job search activities as they approach graduation.

Monster.com has 1,000 Web servers, e-mail servers, and database servers at its sites in Indianapolis and Maynard, Massachusetts. The main Web site has a set of load-balancing devices that forward Web requests to the different servers depending on how busy they are.

Braham says the major challenge is that 90 percent of the traffic is not simple requests for Web pages but rather search requests (e.g., what network jobs are available in New Mexico), which require more processing and access to the database servers. Monster.com has more than 1 million job postings and more than 20 million résumés on file, spread across its database servers. Several copies of each posting and résumé are kept on several database servers to improve access speed and provide redundancy in case a server crashes, so just keeping the database servers in sync so that they contain correct data is a challenge.

SOURCE: monster.com case study, www.Dell.com, 2004

An ***n*-tier architecture** uses more than three sets of computers. In this case, the client is responsible for presentation logic, a database server is responsible for the data access logic and data storage, and the application logic is spread across two or more different sets of servers. Figure 2.5 shows an example of an *n*-tier architecture of a groupware product called TCB-Works developed at the University of Georgia. TCB Works has four major components. The first is the Web browser on the client computer that a user uses to access the system and enter commands (presentation logic). The second component is a Web server that responds to the user's requests, either by providing HTML pages and graphics (application logic) or by sending the request to the third component, a set of 28 C programs that perform various functions such as adding comments or voting (application logic). The fourth component is a database server that stores all the data (data access logic and data storage). Each of these four components is separate, making it easy to spread the different components on different servers and to partition the application logic on two different servers.

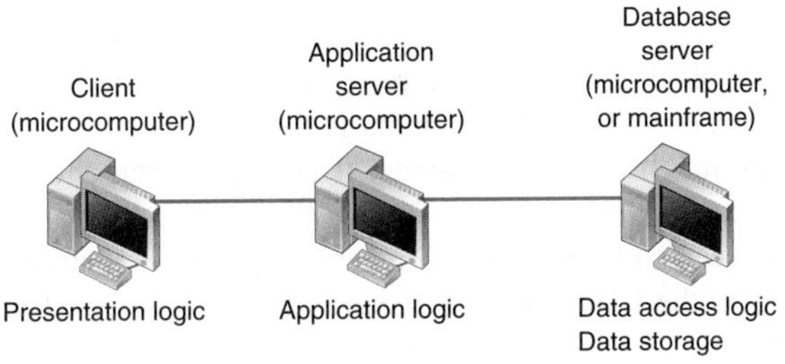

FIGURE 2.4 Three-tier client-server architecture

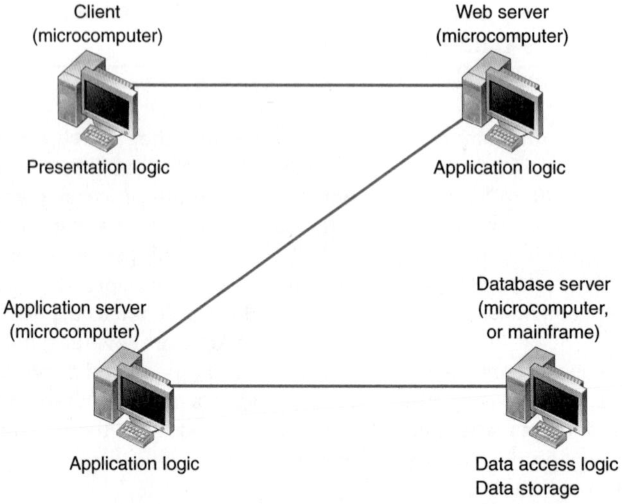

FIGURE 2.5 The *n*-tier client-server architecture

The primary advantage of an *n*-tier client-server architecture compared with a two-tier architecture (or a three-tier compared with a two-tier) is that it separates out the processing that occurs to better balance the load on the different servers; it is more scalable. In Figure 2.5, we have three separate servers, which provides more power than if we had used a two-tier architecture with only one server. If we discover that the application server is too heavily loaded, we can simply replace it with a more powerful server, or even put in two application servers. Conversely, if we discover the database server is underused, we could put data from another application on it.

There are two primary disadvantages to an *n*-tier architecture compared with a two-tier architecture (or a three-tier with a two-tier). First, it puts a greater load on the network. If you compare Figures 2.3, 2.4, and 2.5, you will see that the *n*-tier model requires more communication among the servers; it generates more network traffic so you need a higher capacity network. Second, it is much more difficult to program and test software in *n*-tier architectures than in two-tier architectures because more devices have to communicate to complete a user's transaction.

Thin Clients versus Thick Clients Another way of classifying client-server architectures is by examining how much of the application logic is placed on the client computer. A **thin-client** approach places little or no application logic on the client (e.g., Figure 2.5), whereas a **thick-client** (also called *fat-client*) approach places all or almost all of the application logic on the client (e.g., Figure 2.3). There is no direct relationship between thin and fat client and two-, three- and *n*-tier architectures. For example, Figure 2.6 shows a typical Web architecture: a two-tier architecture with a thin client. One of the biggest forces favoring thin clients is the Web.

Thin clients are much easier to manage. If an application changes, only the server with the application logic needs to be updated. With a thick client, the software on all of the clients would need to be updated. Conceptually, this is a simple task; one simply copies the new files to the hundreds of affected client computers. In practice, it can be a very difficult task.

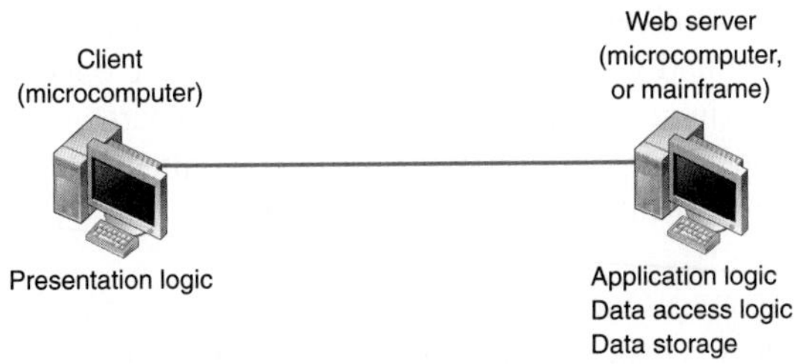

FIGURE 2.6 The typical two-tier thin-client architecture of the Web

Thin-client architectures are the wave of the future. More and more application systems are being written to use a Web browser as the client software, with Java Javascriptor AJAX (containing some of the application logic) downloaded as needed. This application architecture is sometimes called the **distributed computing model.**

Peer-to-Peer Architectures

Peer-to-peer (P2P) architectures are very old, but their modern design became popular in the early 2000s with the rise of P2P file sharing applications (e.g., Napster). With a P2P architecture, all computers act as both a client and a server. Therefore, all computers perform all four functions: presentation logic, application logic, data access logic, and data storage (see Figure 2.7). With a P2P file sharing application, a user uses the presentation, application, and data access logic installed on his or her computer to access the data stored on another computer in the network. With a P2P application sharing network (e.g., grid computing such as seti.org), other users in the network can use others' computers to access application logic as well.

The advantage of P2P networks is that the data can be installed anywhere on the network. They spread the storage throughout the network, even globally, so they can be very resilient to the failure of any one computer. The challenge is finding the data. There must be some central server that enables you to find the data you need, so P2P architectures often are combined with a client-server architecture. Security is a major concern in most P2P networks, so P2P architectures are not commonly used in organizations, except for specialized computing needs (e.g., grid computing).

Choosing Architectures

Each of the preceding architectures has certain costs and benefits, so how do you choose the "right" architecture? In many cases, the architecture is simply a given; the organization

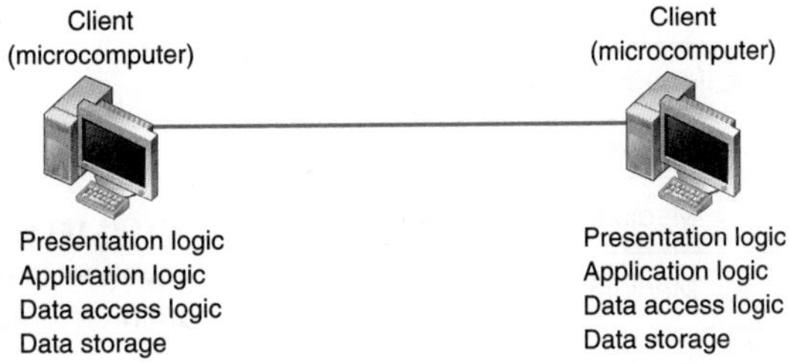

FIGURE 2.7 Peer-to-Peer architecture

has a certain architecture, and one simply has to use it. In other cases, the organization is acquiring new equipment and writing new software and has the opportunity to develop a new architecture, at least in some part of the organization. There are at least three major sets of factors to consider (Figure 2.8). Because P2P architectures are seldom used in organizations, we do not consider them in this section.

Cost of Infrastructure One of the strongest forces driving companies toward client-server architectures is cost of infrastructure (the hardware, software, and networks that will support the application system). Simply put, microcomputers are more than 1,000 times cheaper than mainframes for the same amount of computing power. The microcomputers on our desks today have more processing power, memory, and hard disk space than a mainframe of the early 1990s, and the cost of the microcomputers is a fraction of the cost of the mainframe. Therefore, the cost of client-server architectures is lower than that of **server-based architectures,** which rely on mainframes. Client-server architectures also tend to be cheaper than client-based architectures because they place less of a load on networks and thus require less network capacity.

Cost of Development The cost of developing application systems is an important factor when considering the financial benefits of client-server architectures. Developing application software for client-server architectures can be complex. Developing application software for host-based architectures is usually cheaper. The cost differential may change as companies gain experience with client-server applications, as new client-server products are developed and refined, and as client-server standards mature. However, given the inherent complexity of client-server software and the need to coordinate the interactions of software on different computers, there is likely to remain a cost difference.

Even updating the network with a new version of the software is more complicated. In a host-based network, there is one place in which application software is stored; to update the software, you simply replace it there. With client-server networks, you must update all clients and all servers. For example, suppose you want to add a new server and move some existing applications from the old server to the new one. All application software on all fat clients that send messages to the application on the old server must now be changed to send to the new server. Although this is not conceptually difficult, it can be an administrative nightmare.

Scalability **Scalability** refers to the ability to increase or decrease the capacity of the computing infrastructure in response to changing capacity needs. The most scalable architecture is client-server computing because servers can be added to (or removed from) the architecture when processing needs change. For example, in a four-tier client-server

	Host-Based	Client-Based	Client-Server
Cost of infrastructure	High	Medium	Low
Cost of development	Low	Medium	Medium
Scalability	Low	Medium	High

FIGURE 2.8 Factors involved in choosing architectures

architecture, one might have ten Web servers, four application servers, and three database servers. If the application servers begin to get overloaded, it is simple to add another two or three application servers.

Also, the types of hardware that are used in client-server settings (e.g., minicomputers) typically can be upgraded at a pace that most closely matches the growth of the application. In contrast, host-based architectures rely primarily on mainframe hardware that needs to be scaled up in large, expensive increments, and client-based architectures have ceilings above which the application cannot grow because increases in use and data can result in increased network traffic to the extent that performance is unacceptable.

WORLD WIDE WEB

The Web was first conceived in 1989 by Sir Tim Berners-Lee at the European Particle Physics Laboratory (CERN) in Geneva. His original idea was to develop a database of information on physics research, but he found it difficult to fit the information into a traditional data-base. Instead, he decided to use a *hypertext* network of information. With hypertext, any document can contain a link to any other document.

CERN's first Web browser was created in 1990, but it was 1991 before it was available on the Internet for other organizations to use. By the end of 1992, several browsers had been created for UNIX computers by CERN and several other European and American universities, and there were about 30 Web servers in the entire world. In 1993, Marc Andreessen, a student at the University of Illinois, led a team of students that wrote Mosaic, the first graphical Web browser, as part of a project for the university's National Center for Supercomputing Applications (NCSA). By the end of 1993, the Mosaic browser was available for UNIX, Windows, and Macintosh computers, and there were about 200 Web servers in the world. In 1994, Andreessen and some colleagues left NCSA to form Netscape, and a half a dozen other startup companies introduced commercial Web browsers. Within a year, it had become clear that the Web had changed the face of computing forever. NCSA stopped development of the Mosaic browser in 1996, as **Netscape** and Microsoft began to invest millions to improve their browsers.

How the Web Works

The Web is a good example of a two-tier client-server architecture (Figure 2.9). Each client computer needs an application layer software package called a **Web browser.**

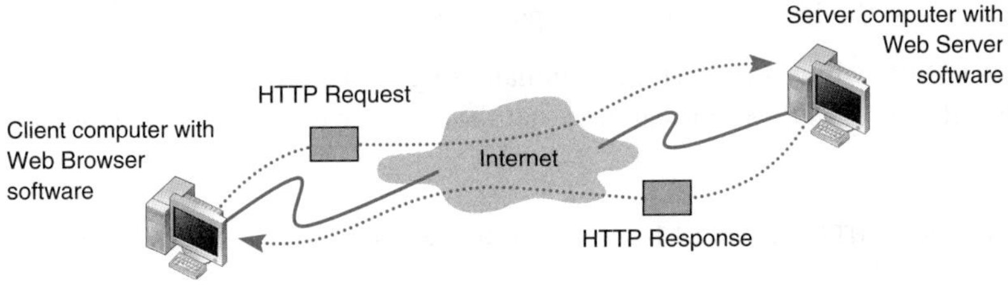

FIGURE 2.9 How the Web works

There are many different browsers, such as Microsoft's Internet Explorer. Each server on the network that will act as a Web server needs an application layer software package called a **Web server.** There are many different Web servers, such as those produced by Microsoft and Apache.

To get a page from the Web, the user must type the Internet **uniform resource locator (URL)** for the page he or she wants (e.g., www.yahoo.com) or click on a link that provides the URL. The URL specifies the Internet address of the Web server and the directory and name of the specific page wanted. If no directory and page are specified, the Web server will provide whatever page has been defined as the site's home page.

For the requests from the Web browser to be understood by the Web server, they must use the same standard **protocol** or language. If there were no standard and each Web browser used a different protocol to request pages, then it would be impossible for a Microsoft Web browser to communicate with an Apache Web server, for example.

The standard protocol for communication between a Web browser and a Web server is **Hypertext Transfer Protocol (HTTP).**[1] To get a page from a Web server, the Web browser issues a special packet called an **HTTP request** that contains the URL and other information about the Web page requested (see Figure 2.9). Once the server receives the HTTP request, it processes it and sends back an **HTTP response,** which will be the requested page or an error message (see Figure 2.9).

This request-response dialogue occurs for every file transferred between the client and the server. For example, suppose the client requests a Web page that has two graphic images. Graphics are stored in separate files from the Web page itself using a different file format than the HTML used for the Web page (in JPEG [Joint Photographic Experts Group] format, for example). In this case, there would be three request-response pairs. First, the browser would issue a request for the Web page, and the server would send the response. Then, the browser would begin displaying the Web page and notice the two graphic files. The browser would then send a request for the first graphic and a request for the second graphic, and the server would reply with two separate HTTP responses, one for each request.

Inside an HTTP Request

The HTTP request and HTTP response are examples of the packets we introduced in Chapter 1 that are produced by the application layer and sent down to the transport, network, data link, and physical layers for transmission through the network. The HTTP response and HTTP request are simple text files that take the information provided by the application (e.g., the URL to get) and format it in a structured way so that the receiver of the message can clearly understand it.

An HTTP request from a Web browser to a Web server has three parts. The first two parts are required; the last is optional. The parts are:

- The **request line,** which starts with a command (e.g., get), provides the Web page and ends with the HTTP version number that the browser understands; the version

[1]The formal specification for HTTP version 1.1 is provided in RFC 2616 on the IETF's Web site. The URL is www.ietf.org/rfc/rfc2616.txt.

number ensures that the Web server does not attempt to use a more advanced or newer version of the HTTP standard that the browser does not understand.

- The **request header,** which contains a variety of optional information such as the Web browser being used (e.g., Internet Explorer) and the date.
- The **request body,** which contains information sent to the server, such as information that the user has typed into a form.

Figure 2.10 shows an example of an HTTP request for a page on our Web server, formatted using version 1.1 of the HTTP standard. This request has only the request line and the request header, because no request body is needed for this request. This request includes the date and time of the request (expressed in Greenwich Mean Time [GMT], the time zone that runs through London) and name of the browser used (Mozilla is the code name for the browser). The "Referrer" field means that the user obtained the URL for this Web page by clicking on a link on another page, which in this case is a list of faculty at Indiana University (i.e., www.indiana.edu/~isdept/faculty.htm). If the referrer field is blank, then it means the user typed the URL him- or herself. You can see inside HTTP headers yourself at www.rexswain.com/httpview.html.

Inside an HTTP Response

The format of an HTTP response from the server to the browser is very similar to the HTTP request. It, too, has three parts, with the first required and the last two optional:

- The **response status,** which contains the HTTP version number the server has used, a status code (e.g., *200* means "okay"; *404* means "not found"), and a reason phrase (a text description of the status code).
- The **response header,** which contains a variety of optional information, such as the Web server being used (e.g., Apache), the date, and the exact URL of the page in the response.
- The **response body,** which is the Web page itself.

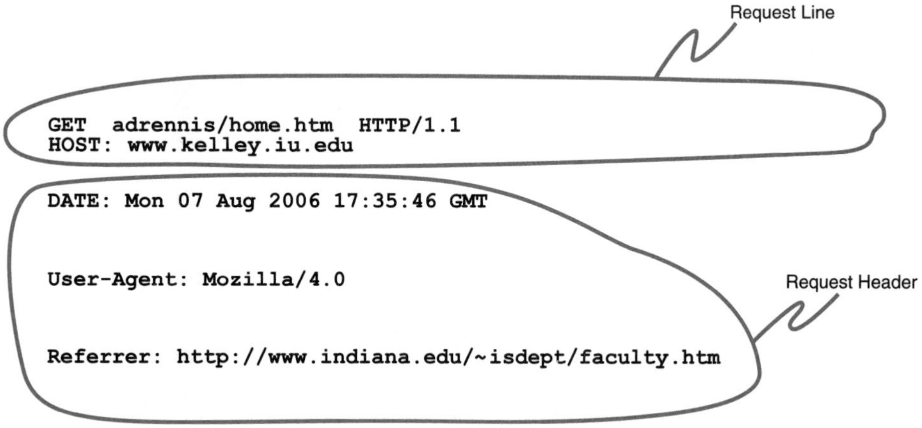

FIGURE 2.10 An example of a request from a Web browser to a Web server using the HTTP (Hypertext Transfer Protocol) standard

Figure 2.11 shows an example of a response from our Web server to the request in Figure 2.10. This example has all three parts. The response status reports "OK," which means the requested URL was found and is included in the response body. The response header provides the date, the type of Web server software used, the actual URL included in the response body, and the type of file. In most cases, the actual URL and the requested URL are the same, but not always. For example, if you request an URL but do not specify a file name (e.g., www.indiana.edu), you will receive whatever file is defined as the home page for that server, so the actual URL will be different from the requested URL.

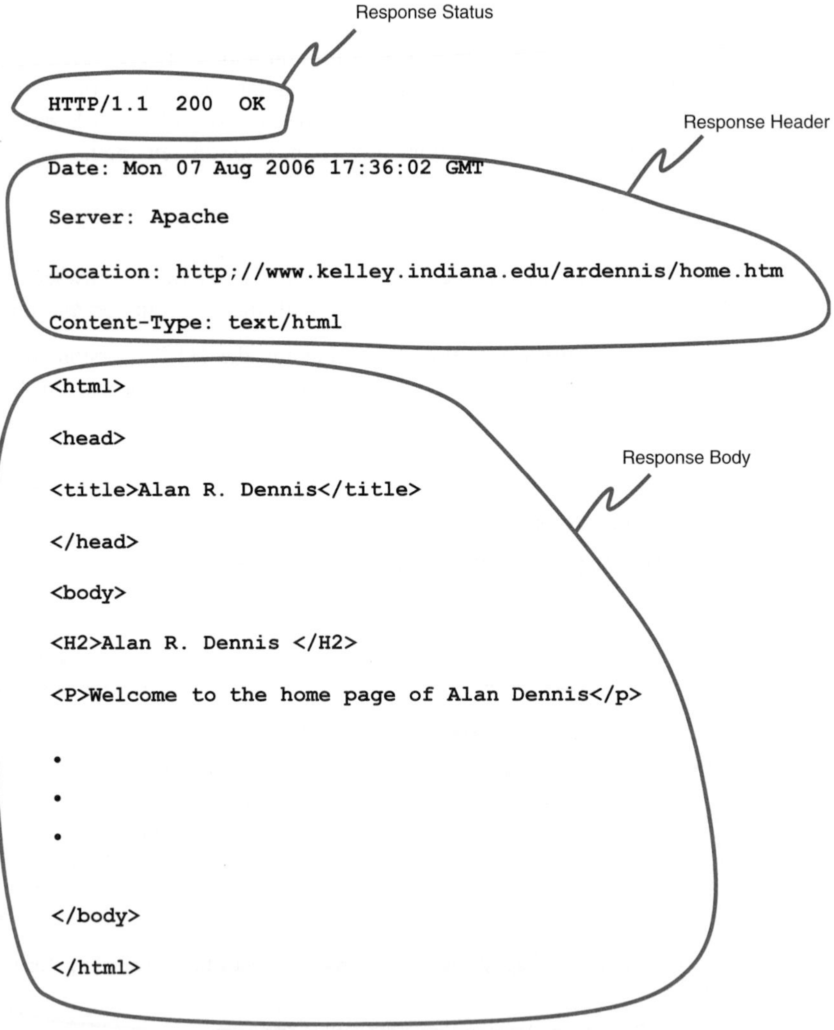

FIGURE 2.11 An example of a response from a Web server to a Web browser using the HTTP standard

MANAGEMENT FOCUS 2.2 FREE SPEECH REIGNS ON THE INTERNET ... OR DOES IT?

In a landmark decision in 1997, the U.S. Supreme Court ruled that the sections of the 1996 Telecommunications Act restricting the publication of indecent material on the Web and the sending of indecent e-mail were unconstitutional. This means that anyone can do anything on the Internet, right?

Well, not really. The court decision affects only Internet servers located in the United States. Each country in the world has different laws that govern what may and may not be placed on servers in their country. For example, British law restricts the publication of pornography, whether on paper or on Internet servers.

Many countries such as Singapore, Saudi Arabia, and China prohibit the publication of certain political information. Because much of this "subversive" information is published outside of their countries, they actively restrict access to servers in other countries.

Other countries are very concerned about their individual cultures. In 1997, a French court convicted Georgia Institute of Technology of violating French language law. Georgia Tech operates a small campus in France that offers summer programs for American students. The information on the campus Web server was primarily in English because classes are conducted in English. This violated the law requiring French to be the predominant language on all Internet servers in France.

The most likely source of problems for North Americans lies in copyright law. Free speech does not give permission to copy from others. It is against the law to copy and republish on the Web any copyrighted material or any material produced by someone else without explicit permission. So don't copy graphics from someone else's Web site or post your favorite cartoon on your Web site, unless you want to face a lawsuit.

The response body in this example shows a Web page in **Hypertext Markup Language (HTML).** The response body can be in any format, such as text, Microsoft Word, Adobe PDF, or a host of other formats, but the most commonly used format is HTML. HTML was developed by CERN at the same time as the first Web browser and has evolved rapidly ever since. HTML is covered by standards produced by the IETF, but Microsoft keeps making new additions to HTML with every release of its browser, so the HTML standard keeps changing.

ELECTRONIC MAIL

Electronic mail (or **e-mail**) was one of the earliest applications on the Internet and is still among the most heavily used today. With e-mail, users create and send messages to one user, several users, or all users on a **distribution list.** Most e-mail software enables users to send text messages and attach files from word processors, spreadsheets, graphics programs, and so on. Many e-mail packages also permit you to filter or organize messages by priority.

Several standards have been developed to ensure compatibility between different e-mail software packages. Any software package that conforms to a certain standard can send messages that are formatted using its rules. Any other package that understands that particular standard can then relay the message to its correct destination; however, if an e-mail package receives a mail message in a different format, it may be unable to process it correctly. Many e-mail packages send using one standard but can understand messages sent in several different standards. The most commonly used standard is SMTP (Simple Mail Transfer Protocol). Other common standards are X.400 and CMC (Common Messaging Calls). In this book, we will discuss only SMTP, but CMC and X.400 both work essentially the same way. SMTP, X.400, and CMC are different from one another (in the same way that English differs from French or Spanish), but several software packages are available that translate between them, so that companies that use one standard (e.g., CMC) can translate messages they receive that use a different standard (e.g., SMTP) into their usual standard as they first enter the company and then treat them as "normal" e-mail messages after that.

How E-mail Works

The **Simple Mail Transfer Protocol (SMTP)** is the most commonly used e-mail standard simply because it is the e-mail standard used on the Internet.[2] E-mail works similarly to how the Web works, but it is a bit more complex. SMTP e-mail is usually implemented as a two-tier thick client-server application, but not always. We first explain how the normal two-tier thick client architecture works and then quickly contrast that with two alternate architectures.

Two-Tier E-mail Architecture

With a two-tier thick client-server architecture, each client computer runs an application layer software package called a **mail user agent,** which is usually more commonly called an e-mail client (Figure 2.11). There are many common e-mail client software packages such as Eudora and Outlook. The user creates the e-mail message using one of these e-mail clients, which formats the message into an SMTP packet that includes information such as the sender's address and the destination address.

The user agent then sends the SMTP packet to a mail server that runs a special application layer software package called a **mail transfer agent,** which is more commonly called mail server software (see Figure 2.12).

This e-mail server reads the SMTP packet to find the destination address and then sends the packet on its way through the network—often over the Internet—from mail server to mail server, until it reaches the mail server specified in the destination address (see Figure 2.12). The mail transfer agent on the destination server then stores the message in the receiver's mailbox on that server. The message sits in the mailbox assigned to the user who is to receive the message until he or she checks for new mail.

The SMTP standard covers message transmission between mail servers (i.e., mail server to mail server) and between the originating e-mail client and its mail server. A different standard is used to communicate between the receiver's e-mail client and his or her mail server. Two commonly used standards for communication between e-mail

[2]The formal specification for SMTP is provided in RFC 822 at: www.ietf.org/rfc/rfc0821.txt

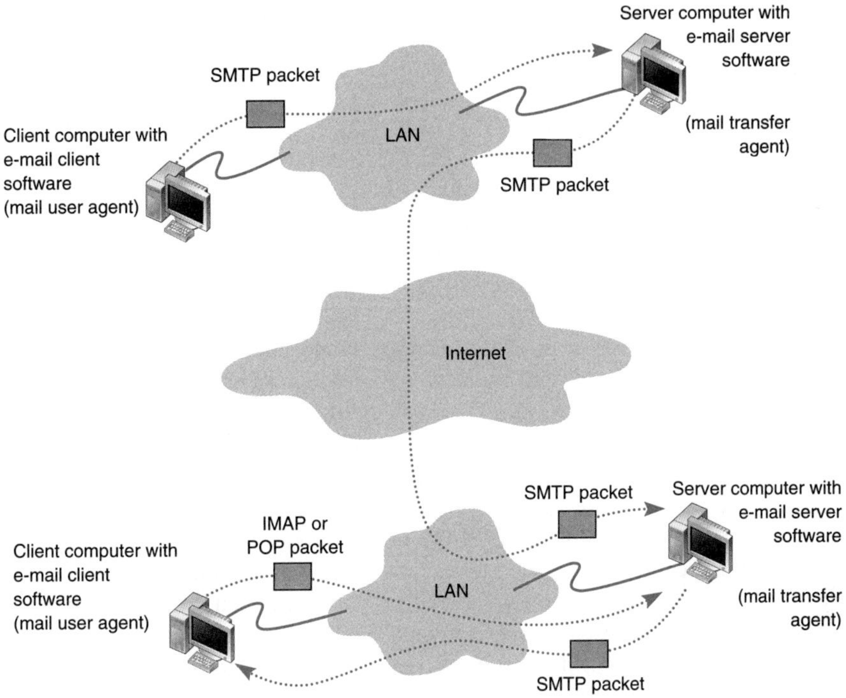

FIGURE 2.12 How SMTP (Simple Mail Transfer Protocol) e-mail works. IMAP = Internet Message Access Protocol; LAN = local area network

client and mail server are **Post Office Protocol (POP)** and **Internet Message Access Protocol (IMAP).** Although there are several important technical differences between POP and IMAP, the most noticeable difference is that before a user can read a mail message with a POP (version 3) e-mail client, the e-mail message must be copied to the client computer's hard disk and deleted from the mail server. With IMAP, e-mail messages can remain stored on the mail server after they are read. IMAP therefore offers considerable benefits to users who read their e-mail from many different computers (e.g., home, office, computer labs) because they no longer need to worry about having old e-mail messages scattered across several client computers; all e-mail is stored on the server until it is deleted.

In our example in Figure 2.12, when the receiver next accesses his or her e-mail, the e-mail client on his or her computer contacts the mail server by sending an IMAP or POP packet that asks for the contents of the user's mailbox. In Figure 2.12, we show this as an IMAP packet, but it could just as easily be a POP packet. When the mail server receives the IMAP or POP request, it sends the original SMTP packet created by the message sender to the client computer, which the user reads with the e-mail client. Therefore, any e-mail client using POP or IMAP must also understand SMTP to create messages and to read messages it receives. Both POP and IMAP provide a host of functions that enable the user to manage his or her e-mail, such as creating mail folders, deleting mail, creating address books, and so on. If the user sends a POP or IMAP request for one of these functions, the mail server will perform the function and send back a POP or IMAP response packet that is much like an HTTP response packet.

Host-Based E-mail Architectures When SMTP was first developed, host-based architectures were the rule, so SMTP was first designed to run on mainframe computers. If you use a text-based version of Linux or UNIX, chances are you are using a host-based architecture for your e-mail.

With this architecture, the client computer in Figure 2.12 would be replaced by a terminal that would send all of the user's keystrokes to the server for processing. The server would then send characters back to the terminal to display. All software would reside on the server. This software would take the user's keystrokes, create the SMTP packet, and then send it on its way to the next mail server.

Likewise, the receiver would use a terminal that would send keystrokes to the server and receive letters back to display. The server itself would be responsible for understanding the user's commands to read a mail message and sending the appropriate characters to the user's terminal so he or she could read the e-mail message. If you had been wondering why the SMTP standard does not include the delivery of the message to the receiver's client computer, you should now understand. Because no software existed on the receiver's terminal, the SMTP standard did not include any specification about how the receiver's mail server software should display messages. Communication between the mail server and the receiver's terminal was left to the e-mail software package running on the server. Because each package and each terminal was different, no standards were developed to cover communication between the terminal and the server.

Three-Tier Thin Client-Server Architecture The three-tier thin client-server e-mail architecture uses a Web server and Web browser to provide access to your e-mail. With this architecture, you do not need an e-mail client on your client computer. Instead, you use your Web browser. This type of e-mail is sometimes called Web-based e-mail and is provided by a variety of companies such as Hotmail and Yahoo.

You use your browser to connect to a page on a Web server that lets you write the e-mail message by filling in a form. When you click the send button, your Web browser sends the form information to the Web server inside an HTTP request (Figure 2.13). The Web server runs a program (written in C or Perl, for example) that takes the information from the HTTP request and builds an SMTP packet that contains the e-mail message. Although not important to our example, it also sends an HTTP response back to the client. The Web server then sends the SMTP packet to the mail server, which processes the SMTP packet as though it came from a client computer. The SMTP packet flows through the network in the same manner as before. When it arrives at the destination mail server, it is placed in the receiver's mailbox.

When the receiver wants to check his or her mail, he or she uses a Web browser to send an HTTP request to a Web server (see Figure 2.13). A program on the Web server (in C or Perl, for example) processes the request and sends the appropriate IMAP (or POP) request to the mail server. The mail server responds with an IMAP (or POP) packet, which a program on the Web server converts into an HTTP response and sends to the client. The client then displays the e-mail message in the Web browser.

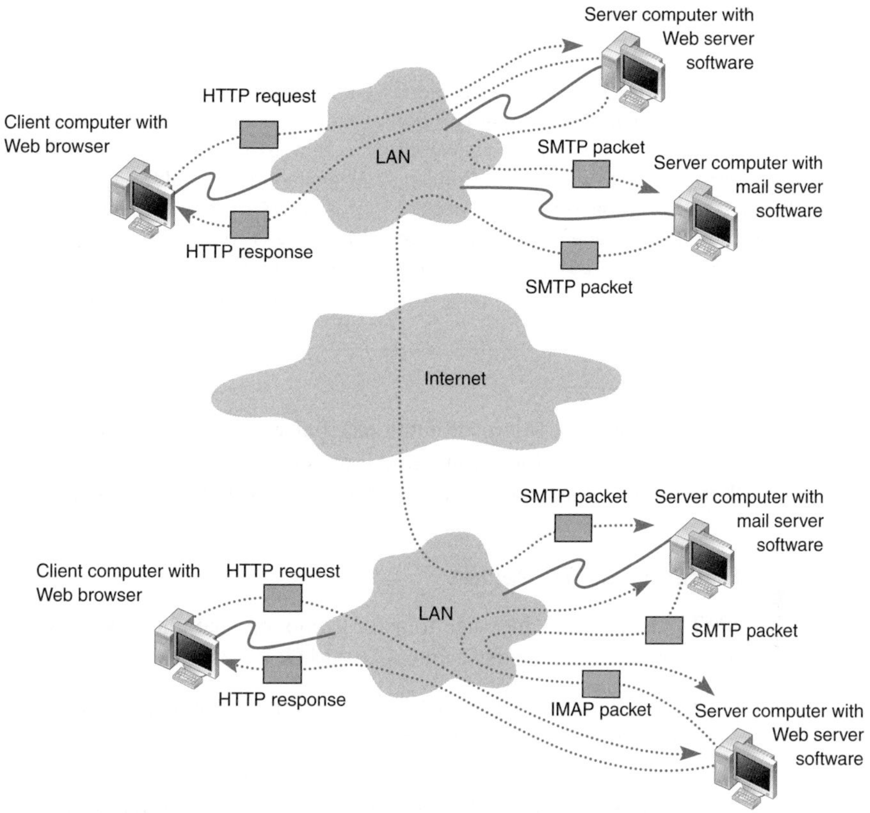

FIGURE 2.13 Inside the Web. HTTP = Hypertext Transfer Protocol; IMAP = Internet Message Access Protocol; LAN = local area network; SMTP = Simple Mail Transfer Protocol

A simple comparison of Figures 2.12 and 2.13 will quickly show that the three-tier approach using a Web browser is much more complicated than the normal two-tier approach. So why do it? Well, it is simpler to have just a Web browser on the client computer rather than to require the user to install a special e-mail client on his or her computer and then set up the special e-mail client to connect to the correct mail server using either POP or IMAP. It is simpler for the user to just type the URL of the Web server providing the mail services into his or her browser and begin using mail. This also means that users can check their e-mail from a public computer anywhere on the Internet.

It is also important to note that the sender and receiver do not have to use the same architecture for their e-mail. The sender could use a two-tier client-server architecture, and the receiver, a host-based or three-tier client-server architecture. Because all communication is standardized using SMTP between the different mail servers, how the users interact with their mail servers is unimportant. Each organization can use a different approach.

In fact, there is nothing to prevent one organization from using all three architectures simultaneously. At Indiana University, we usually access our e-mail through an

TECHNICAL FOCUS 2.2 SMTP Transmission

SMTP (Simple Mail Transfer Protocol) is an older protocol, and transmission using it is rather complicated. If we were going to design it again, we would likely find a simpler transmission method. Conceptually, we think of an SMTP packet as one packet. However, SMTP mail transfer agents transmit each element within the SMTP packet as a separate packet and wait for the receiver to respond with an "OK" before sending the next element.

For example, in Figure 2.14, the sending mail transfer agent would send the *from* address and wait for an OK from the receiver. Then it would send the *to* address and wait for an OK. Then it would send the date, and so on, with the last item being the entire message sent as one element.

e-mail client (e.g., Microsoft Outlook), but we also access it over the Web because many of us travel internationally and find it easier to borrow a Web browser with Internet access than to borrow an e-mail client and set it up to use the Indiana University mail server.

Inside an SMTP Packet

SMTP defines how message transfer agents operate and how they format messages sent to other message transfer agents. An SMTP packet has two parts:

- The **header,** which lists source and destination e-mail addresses (possibly in text form [e.g., "Pat Smith"]) as well as the address itself (e.g., psmith@somewhere.com), date, subject, and so on.
- The **body,** which is the word *DATA,* followed by the message itself.

Figure 2.14 shows a simple e-mail message formatted using SMTP. The header of an SMTP message has a series of fields that provide specific information, such as the sender's e-mail address, the receiver's address, date, and so on. The information in quotes on the *from* and *to* lines is ignored by SMTP; only the information in the angle brackets is used in e-mail addresses. The *message ID* field is used to provide a

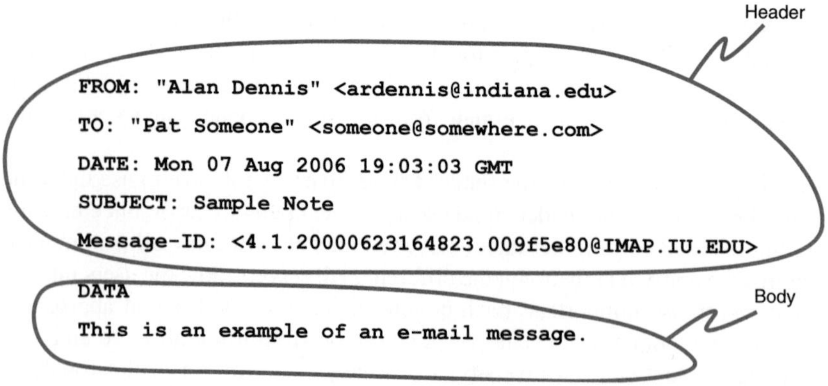

FIGURE 2.14 An example of an e-mail message using the SMTP (Simple Mail Transfer Protocol) standard

unique identification code so that the message can be tracked. The message body contains the actual text of the message itself.

Listserv Discussion Groups

A list server (or **Listserv**) group is simply a mailing list of users who have joined together to discuss some topic. Listserv groups are formed around just about every topic imaginable, including cooking, skydiving, politics, education, and British comedy. Some are short lived, whereas others continue indefinitely. Some permit any member to post messages; others permit only certain members to post messages. Most businesses have Listservs organized around job functions, so that it is easy to reach everyone in a particular department.

There are two parts to every Listserv. The first part, the *Listserv processor,* processes commands such as requests to subscribe, unsubscribe, or to provide more information about the Listserv. The second part is the *Listserv mailer.* Any message sent to the Listserv mailer is resent to everyone on the mailing list. To use a Listserv, you need to know the addresses of both the processor and the mailer.

To subscribe to a Listserv, you send an e-mail message to the Listserv processor, which adds your name to the list (see "Listserv Commands" for the message format). It is important that you send this message to the processor, not the mailer; otherwise, your subscription message will be sent to everyone on the mailing list, which might be embarrassing.

For example, suppose you want to join a Listserv on widgets that has a processor address of listerv @abc.com, and the mailer address is widget-1 @abc.com. To subscribe, you send an e-mail message to listerv @abc.com containing the text: *subscribe widget-1 your name.* To send a message to everyone on this Listserv, you would e-mail your message to widget-1 @abc.com.

Attachments in Multipurpose Internet Mail Extension

As the name suggests, SMTP is a simple standard that permits only the transfer of text messages. It was developed in the early days of computing, when no one had even thought about using e-mail to transfer nontext files such as graphics or word processing documents. Several standards for nontext files have been developed that can operate together with SMTP, such as **Multipurpose Internet Mail Extension (MIME),** uuencode, and binhex.

Each of the standards is different, but all work in the same general way. The MIME software, which exists as part of the e-mail client, takes the nontext file such as a Power-Point graphic file, and translates each byte in the file into a special code that looks like regular text. This encoded section of "text" is then labeled with a series of special fields understood by SMTP as identifying a MIME-encoded attachment and specifying information about the attachment (e.g., name of file, type of file). When the receiver's e-mail client receives the SMTP message with the MIME attachment, it recognizes the MIME "text" and uses its MIME software (that is part of the e-mail client) to translate the file from MIME "text" back into its original format.

TECHNICAL FOCUS 2.3 LISTSERV COMMANDS

There are many different commands that can be sent to the Listserv processor to perform a variety of functions. These commands are included as lines of text in the e-mail message sent to the processor. Each command must be placed on a separate line. Some useful commands include

- SUBSCRIBE: listserv-mailer-name your-name: Subscribes you to a mailing list (e.g., *subscribe maps-1 robin jones*)
- UNSUBSCRIBE: listserv-mailer-name your-name: Unsubscribes you from the mailing list (e.g., *unsubscribe maps-1 robin jones*)
- HELP: Requests the Listserv to e-mail you a list of its commands
- LIST: Requests the Listserv to e-mail you a list of all Listserv groups that are available on this Listserv processor
- LIST DETAILED: Requests the Listserv to e-mail you a detailed description of all Listserv groups that are available on this Listserv processor and are public

OTHER APPLICATIONS

There are literally thousands of applications that run on the Internet and on other networks. Most application software that we develop today, whether for sale or for private internal use, runs on a network. We could spend years talking about different network applications and still cover only a small number.

Fortunately, most network application software works in much the same way as the Web or e-mail. In this section, we will briefly discuss only four commonly used applications: File Transfer Protocol (FTP), Telnet, instant messaging (IM), and Video conferencing.

File Transfer Protocol

File Transfer Protocol (FTP), is an old application that enables you to send and receive files over the Internet. FTP works in a similar manner as HTTP. FTP requires an application layer program on the client computer and a FTP server application program on a server. There are many software packages that use the FTP standard, such as WS-FTP. The user uses his or her client to send FTP requests to the FTP server. The FTP server processes these requests and sends back FTP packets containing the requested file.[3]

Most FTP sites require users to have permission before they can connect and gain access to the files. Access is granted by providing an account name with a password. For example, a network manager or Web-master would write a Web page using software on his or her client computer and then use FTP to send it to a specific account on the Web server.

[3]The formal specification for FTP is provided in RFC 2640 on the IETF's Web site: www.ietf.org/rfc/rfc2640.txt.

A Day in the Life: Network Manager

It was a typical day for a network manager. It began with the setup and troubleshooting for a videoconference. Videoconferencing is fairly routine activity but this one was a little different; we were trying to videoconference with a different company who used different standards than we did. We attempted to use our usual web-based videoconferencing but could not connect. We fell back to ISDN-based videoconferencing over telephone lines, which required bringing in our videoconferencing services group. It took two hours but we finally had the technology working.

The next activity was building a Windows database server. This involved installing software, adding a server into our ADS domain, and setting up the user accounts. Once the server was on the network, it was critical to install all the security patches for both the operating system and database server. We receive so many security attacks that it is our policy to install all security patches on the same day that new software or servers are placed on the network or the patches are released.

After lunch, the next two hours was spent in a boring policy meeting. These meetings are a necessary evil to ensure that the network is well-managed. It is critical that users understand what the network can and can't be used for, and our ability to respond to users' demands. Managing users' expectations about support and use rules helps ensure high user satisfaction.

The rest of the day was spent refining the tool we use to track network utilization. We have a simple intrusion detection system to detect hackers, but we wanted to provide more detailed information on network errors and network utilization to better assist us in network planning.

With thanks to Jared Beard

Telnet

Telnet enables users to log in to servers (or other clients). Telnet requires an application layer program on the client computer and an application layer program on the server or host computer. There are many programs that conform to the Telnet standard, such as EWAN. Once Telnet makes the connection from the client to the server, you must use the account name and password of an authorized user to login.

Because Telnet was designed in the very early days of the Internet, it assumes your client is a dumb terminal. Therefore, when you use Telnet, you are using a host-based architecture. All keystrokes you type in the Telnet client are transferred one by one to the server for processing. The server processes those commands—including simple keystrokes such as up arrow or down arrow—and transfers the results back to the client computer, which displays the letters and moves the cursor as directed by the server.[4]

Telnet can be useful because it enables you to access your server or host computer without sitting at its keyboard. Most network managers use Telnet to work on servers, rather than physically sitting in front of them and using their keyboards. Telnet also poses a great security threat, because it means that anyone on the Internet can attempt to log in to your account and use it as he or she wishes. Two commonly used security precautions are to prohibit remote logins via Telnet unless a user specifically asks for his or her account to be authorized for it and to permit remote logins only from a specific set of

[4]The formal specification for Telnet is provided in RFC 854 and RFC 2355 on the IETF's Web site. The URLs are www.ietf.org/rfc/rfc0854.txt and www.ietf.org/rfc/rfc2355.txt, respectively.

MANAGEMENT FOCUS 2.3 TAGGING PEOPLE

Joseph Krull has a chip on his shoulder—well, in his shoulder to be specific. Krull is one of a small but growing number of people who have a Radio Frequency Identification (RFID) chip implanted in their bodies.

RFID technology has been used to identify pets, so that lost pets can be easily reunited with their owners. Now, the technology is being used for humans.

Krull has a blown left pupil from a skiing accident. If he were injured in an accident and unable to communicate, an emergency room doctor might misinterpret his blown pupil as a sign of a major head injury and begin drilling holes to relieve pressure. Now doctors can use the RFID chip to identify Krull and quickly locate his complete medical records on the Internet.

Critics say such RFID chips pose huge privacy risks because they enable any firms using RFID to track users such as Krull. Retailers, for example, can track when he enters and leaves their stores.

Krull doesn't care. He believes the advantages of having his complete medical records available to any doctor greatly outweighs the privacy concerns.

SOURCE: "RFID IS really getting under people's skin," *NetworkWorld,* April 4, 2005, p. 1.

Internet addresses. For example, the Web server for this book will accept Telnet logins only from computers located in the same building. Chapter 11 discusses network security.

Instant Messaging

One of the fastest growing Internet applications is **instant messaging (IM).** With IM, you can exchange real-time typed messages or chat with your friends. Some IM software also enables you to verbally talk with your friends in the same way as you might use the telephone or to use cameras to exchange real-time video in the same way you might use a videoconferencing system. Several types of IM currently exist, including ICQ and AOL Instant Messenger.

IM works in much the same way as the Web. The client computer needs an IM client software package, which communicates with an IM server software package that runs on a server. When the user connects to the Internet, the IM client software package sends an IM request packet to the IM server informing it that the user is now online. The IM client software package continues to communicate with the IM server to monitor what other users have connected to the IM server. When one of your friends connects to the IM server, the IM server sends an IM packet to your client computer so that you now know that your friend is connected to the Internet. The server also sends a packet to your friend's client computer so that he or she knows that you are on the Internet.

With the click of a button, you can both begin chatting. When you type text, your IM client creates an IM packet that is sent to the IM server (Figure 2.15). The server then retransmits the packet to your friend. Several people may be part of the same chat session, in which case the server sends a copy of the packet to all of the client computers. IM also provides a way for different servers to communicate with one another, and for the client computers to communicate directly with each other. IM will also do Voice and Video.

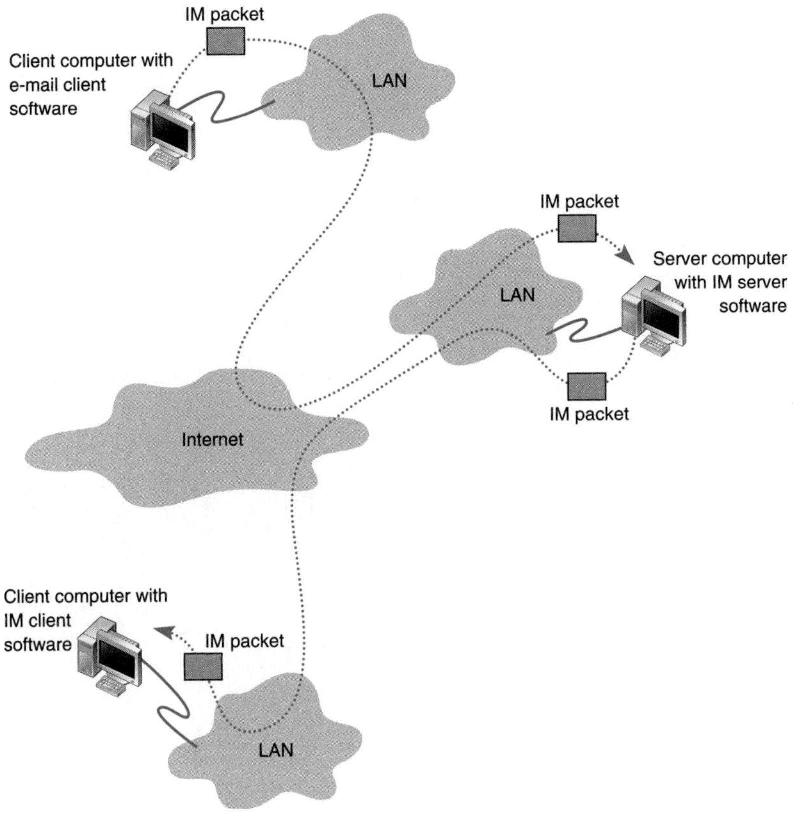

FIGURE 2.15 How instant messaging (IM) works. LAN = local area network

Videoconferencing

Videoconferencing provides real-time transmission of video and audio signals to enable people in two or more locations to have a meeting. In some cases, videoconferences are held in special-purpose meeting rooms with one or more cameras and several video display monitors to capture and display the video signals (Figure 2.16). Special audio microphones and speakers are used to capture and play audio signals. The audio and video signals are combined into one signal that is transmitted though a MAN or WAN to people at the other location. Most of this type of videoconferencing involves two teams in two separate meeting rooms, but some systems can support conferences of up to eight separate meeting rooms. Some advanced systems provide telepresence, which is of such high quality that you feel you are face-to-face with the other participants.

The fastest growing form of videoconferencing is **desktop videoconferencing.** Small cameras installed on top of each computer permit meetings to take place from individual offices (Figure 2.17). Special application software (e.g., Yahoo IM, Net Meeting) is installed on the client computer and transmits the images across a network to application software on a videoconferencing server. The server then sends the signals to the other client computers that want to participate in the videoconference. In some cases, the clients can communicate with one another without using the server. The cost of

FIGURE 2.16 A Cisco telepresence system
Source: Cisco Systems Inc. (from their telepresence brochure):
http://cisco.com/en/US/prod/collateral/ps7060/ps8329/ps8330/ps7073/prod_brochure0900aecd8054c7bd.pdf

desktop videoconferencing ranges from less than $20 per computer for inexpensive systems to more than $1,000 for high-quality systems. Some systems have integrated conferencing software with desktop videoconferencing, enabling participants to communicate verbally and, by using applications such as white boards, to attend the same meeting while they are sitting at the computers in their offices.

The transmission of video requires a lot of network capacity. Most videoconferencing uses data compression to reduce the amount of data transmitted. Surprisingly, the most common complaint is not the quality of the video image but the quality of the voice transmissions. Special care needs to be taken in the design and placement of microphones and speakers to ensure quality sound and minimal feedback.

Most videoconferencing systems were originally developed by vendors using different formats, so many products were incompatible. The best solution was to ensure that all hardware and software used within an organization was supplied by the same vendor and to hope that any other organizations with whom you wanted to communicate used the same equipment. Today, three standards are in common use: **H.320, H.323,** and **MPEG-2** (also called ISO 13818-2). Each of these standards was developed by different organizations and is supported by different products. They are not compatible, although some application software packages understand more than one standard. H.320 is designed for room-to-room videoconferencing over high-speed telephone lines. H.323

FIGURE 2.17 Virtual Margaret
Source: Courtesy Cisco Systems, Inc

is a family of standards designed for desktop videoconferencing and just simple audio conferencing over the Internet. MPEG-2 is designed for faster connections, such as a LAN or specially designed, privately operated WAN.

Webcasting is a special type of one-directional videoconferencing in which content is sent from the server to the user. The developer creates content that is downloaded as needed by the users and played by a plug-in to a Web browser. At present, there are no standards for Webcast technologies, but the products by RealNetworks.com are the de facto standards.

IMPLICATIONS FOR MANAGEMENT

The first implication for management from this chapter is that the primary purpose of a network is to provide a worry-free environment in which applications can run. The network itself does not change the way an organization operates; it is the applications that the network enables that have the potential to change organizations. If the network does not easily enable a wide variety of applications, this can severely limit the ability of the organization to compete in its environment.

The second implication is that over the past few years there has been a dramatic increase in the number and type of applications that run across networks. In the early 1990s, networks primarily delivered e-mail and organization-specific application traffic (e.g. accounting transactions, database inquiries, inventory data). Today's traffic contains large amounts of e-mail, Web packets, videoconferencing, telephone calls, instant messaging, music, and organization-specific application traffic. Traffic has been growing much more rapidly than expected and each type of traffic has different implications for the best network design, making the job of the network manager much more complicated. Most organizations have seen their network operating costs grow significantly even though the cost per packet (i.e., the cost divided by the amount of traffic) has dropped significantly over the last ten years.

MANAGEMENT FOCUS 2.4 MEET VIRTUAL MARGARET

Margaret worked for Cisco Systems, Inc., in San Jose, California, for three years as the executive assistant to Martin de Beer, the vice president of the emerging markets group. With the rising cost of living in the San Jose, she decided to move to Dallas, Texas. Margaret didn't want to leave Cisco, and Cisco didn't want to lose her. However, her job as an executive assistant required regular face-to-face interaction with her boss and the other members of the team.

The solution was telepresence. Cisco installed a 65-inch high-definition plasma screen, a camera, microphone, speaker, and lighting array at her desk in San Jose, and at her desk in Dallas. When she arrives at work in Dallas, she connects to her desk in San Jose and begins her day. She is immediately available to all who pass her desk—in either location. Cisco installed a second telepresence unit in the conference room in San Jose, so with a push of a button, Margaret can join any meeting in the conference room.

"In the beginning, there were a lot of people stopping by," she says. "Mouths would drop open when people saw me, as if in disbelief and amazement of what they were seeing. Now, as folks get used to seeing me day in and day out, it is business as usual. One interesting thing that I noted in the beginning was that I felt like I was on camera all the time, and it made me feel a little self-conscious. Now, I don't even remember that I'm on camera. It feels like I'm still in San Jose—for eight hours a day, I'm fully engaged in the business at Cisco's headquarters."

SOURCE: "Meet Virtual Margaret," www.Cisco.com, 2008.

SUMMARY

Application Architectures There are four fundamental application architectures. In host-based networks, the server performs virtually all of the work. In client-based networks, the client computer does most of the work; the server is used only for data storage. In client-server networks, the work is shared between the servers and clients. The client performs all presentation logic, the server handles all data storage and data access logic, and one or both perform the application logic. With peer-to-peer networks, client computers also play the role of a server. Client-server networks can be cheaper to install and often better balance the network loads but are more complex to develop and manage.

World Wide Web One of the fastest growing Internet applications is the Web, which was first developed in 1990. The Web enables the display of rich graphical images, pictures, full-motion video, and sound. The Web is the most common way for businesses to establish a presence on the Internet. The Web has two application software packages, a Web browser on the client and a Web server on the server. Web browsers and servers communicate with one another using a standard called HTTP. Most Web pages are written in HTML, but many also use other formats. The Web contains information on just about every topic under the sun, but finding it and making sure the information is reliable are major problems.

Electronic Mail With e-mail, users create and send messages using an application-layer software package on client computers called user agents. The user agent sends the mail to a server running an application-layer software package called a mail transfer agent, which then forwards the message through a series of mail transfer agents to the mail transfer agent on the receiver's server. E-mail is faster and cheaper than regular mail and can substitute for telephone conversations in some cases. Several standards have been developed to ensure compatibility between different user agents and mail transfer agents such as SMTP, POP, and IMAP.

KEY TERMS

application architecture
application logic
client-server architecture
cluster
data access logic
data storage
desktop videoconferencing
distributed computing model
distribution list
dumb terminal
e-mail
File Transfer Protocol (FTP)
H.320
H.323
host-based architecture
HTTP request
HTTP response
Hypertext Markup Language (HTML)
Hypertext Transfer Protocol (HTTP)
instant messaging (IM)
Internet
Internet Mail Access Protocol (IMAP)
Listserv
mail transfer agent
mail user agent
mainframe
microcomputer
middleware
MPEG-2
Multipurpose Internet Mail Extension (MIME)
Netscape
network computer
n-tier architecture
peer-to-peer architecture
Post Office Protocol (POP)
presentation logic
protocol
request body
request header
request line
response body
response header
response status
scalability
server-based architecture
Simple Mail Transfer Protocol (SMTP)
SMTP head
SMTP body
Telnet
terminal
thick client
thin client
three-tier architecture
transaction terminal
two-tier architecture
uniform resource locator (URL)
videoconferencing
virtual server
World Wide Web
Web browser
Web casting
Web server

QUESTIONS

1. What are the different types of application architectures?
2. Describe the four basic functions of an application software package.
3. What are the advantages and disadvantages of host-based networks versus client-server networks?
4. What is middleware, and what does it do?
5. Suppose your organization was contemplating switching from a host-based architecture to client-server. What problems would you foresee?
6. Which is less expensive: host-based networks or client-server networks? Explain.
7. Compare and contrast two-tier, three-tier, and *n*-tier client-server architectures. What are the technical differences, and what advantages and disadvantages does each offer?
8. How does a thin client differ from a thick client?
9. What is a network computer?
10. What do the following tools enable you to do: the Web, e-mail, FTP, Telnet?
11. For what is HTTP used? What are its major parts?
12. For what is HTML used?
13. Describe how a Web browser and Web server work together to send a Web page to a user.
14. Can a mail sender use a 2-tier architecture to send mail to a receiver using a 3-tier architecture? Explain.
15. Describe how mail user agents and mail transfer agents work together to transfer mail messages.
16. What roles do SMTP, POP, and IMAP play in sending and receiving e-mail on the Internet?
17. What are the major parts of an e-mail message?
18. What is a virtual server?
19. What is FTP, and why is it useful?
20. What is Telnet, and why is it useful?
21. What is a Listserv and how could you use it to get information?
22. Explain how instant messaging works.
23. Compare and contrast the application architecture for videoconferencing and the architecture for e-mail.

24. Which of the common application architectures for e-mail (two-tier client server, Web-based) is "best"? Explain.
25. Some experts argue that thin-client client-server architectures are really host-based architectures in disguise and suffer from the same old problems. Do you agree? Explain.
26. You can use a Web browser to access an FTP server simply by putting *ftp://* in front of the URL (e.g., ftp://xyz.abc.com). If that server has FTP server software installed, then the FTP server will respond instead of the Web server. What is your browser doing differently to access the FTP server? Hint: This question is more difficult than it seems, because we haven't explained how the server knows to pass certain types of packets to the right software (i.e., HTTP requests to the Web server software and SMTP packets to the e-mail software). At this point, don't worry about it. Linking the network to the application layer is the job of the transport layer, which is explained in Chapter 5.
27. Will the Internet become an essential business tool like the telephone or will it go the way of the dinosaurs? Discuss.

EXERCISES

2-1. Investigate the use of the four major architectures by a local organization (e.g., your university). Which architecture(s) does it use most often and what does it see itself doing in the future? Why?

2-2. What are the costs of client-server versus host-based architectures? Search the Web for at least two different studies and be sure to report your sources. What are the likely reasons for the differences between the two?

2-3. Investigate the costs of dumb terminals, network computers, minimally equipped microcomputers, and top-of-the-line microcomputers. Many equipment manufacturers and resellers are on the Web, so it's a good place to start looking.

2-4. What application architecture does your university use for e-mail? Explain.

MINI-CASES

I. Deals-R-Us Brokers (Part 1)

Fred Jones, a distant relative of yours and president of Deals-R-Us Brokers (DRUB), has come to you for advice. DRUB is a small brokerage house that enables its clients to buy and sell stocks over the Internet, as well as place traditional orders by phone or fax. DRUB has just decided to offer a set of stock analysis tools that will help its clients more easily pick winning stocks, or so Fred tells you. Fred's information systems department has presented him with two alternatives for developing the new tools. The first alternative will have a special tool developed in C++ that clients will download onto their computers to run. The tool will communicate with the DRUB server to select data to analyze. The second alternative will have the C++ program running on the server, the client will use his or her browser to interact with the server.

a. Classify the two alternatives in terms of what type of application architecture they use.
b. Outline the pros and cons of the two alternatives and make a recommendation to Fred about which is better.

II. Deals-R-Us Brokers (Part 2)

Fred Jones, a distant relative of yours and president of Deals-R-Us Brokers (DRUB), has come to you for advice. DRUB is a small brokerage house that enables its clients to buy and sell stocks over the Internet, as well as place traditional orders by phone or fax. DRUB has just decided to install a new e-mail package. One vendor is offering an SMTP-based two-tier client-server architecture. The second vendor is offering a Web-based e-mail architecture. Fred doesn't understand either one but thinks the Web-based one should be better because, in his words, "the Web is the future."

a. *Briefly* explain to Fred, in layperson's terms, the differences between the two.
b. Outline the pros and cons of the two alternatives and make a recommendation to Fred about which is better.

III. Accurate Accounting

Diego Lopez is the managing partner of Accurate Accounting, a small accounting firm that operates a dozen offices in California. Accurate Accounting provides audit and consulting services to a growing number of small- and medium-sized firms, many of which are high technology firms. Accurate Accounting staff typically spend many days on-site with clients during their consulting and audit projects, but has increasingly been using e-mail and Instant Messenger (IM) to work with clients. Now, many firms are pushing Accurate Accounting to adopt videoconferencing. Diego is concerned about what videoconferencing software and hardware to install. While Accurate Accounting's e-mail system enables it to exchange e-mail with any client, using IM has proved difficult because Accurate Accounting has had to use one IM software package with some companies and different IM software with others. Diego is concerned that videoconferencing may prove to be as difficult to manage as IM. "Why can't IM work as simply as e-mail?" he asks. "Will my new videoconferencing software and hardware work as simply as e-mail, or will it be IM all over again?" Prepare a response to his questions.

IV. Ling Galleries

Howard Ling is a famous artist with two galleries in Hawaii. Many of his paintings and prints are sold to tourists who visit Hawaii from Hong Kong and Japan. He paints 6–10 new paintings a year, which sell for $50,000 each. The real money comes from the sales of prints; a popular painting will sell 1,000 prints at a retail price of $1,500 each. Some prints sell very quickly, while others do not. As an artist, Howard paints what he wants to paint. As a businessman, Howard also wants to create art that sells well. Howard visits each gallery once a month to talk with clients, but enjoys talking with the gallery staff on a weekly basis to learn what visitors say about his work and to get ideas for future work. Howard has decided to open two new galleries, one in Hong Kong and one in Tokyo. How can the Internet help Howard with the two new galleries?

CASE STUDY

NEXT-DAY AIR SERVICE

See the Web site.

HANDS-ON ACTIVITY

Looking Inside Your HTTP Packets

Figures 2.10 and 2.11 show you inside one HTTP request and one HTTP response that we captured. The objective of this Activity is for you to see inside HTTP packets that you create.

1. Use your browser to connect to www.rexswain.com/httpview.html. You will see the screen in Figure 2.18.
2. In box labeled URL, type any URL you like and click Submit. You will then see something like the screen in Figure 2.19. In the middle of the screen, under the label "Sending Request:" you will see the exact HTTP packet that your browser generated.
3. If you scroll this screen down, you'll see the exact HTTP response packet that the server sent back to you. In Figure 2.20, you'll see the response from the Indiana University Web server. You'll notice that at the time we did this, Indiana University was using the Apache Web server.
4. Try this on several sites around the Web to see what Web server they use. For example, Microsoft uses the Microsoft IIS Web server, while Cisco uses Apache. Some companies set their Web servers not to release this information.

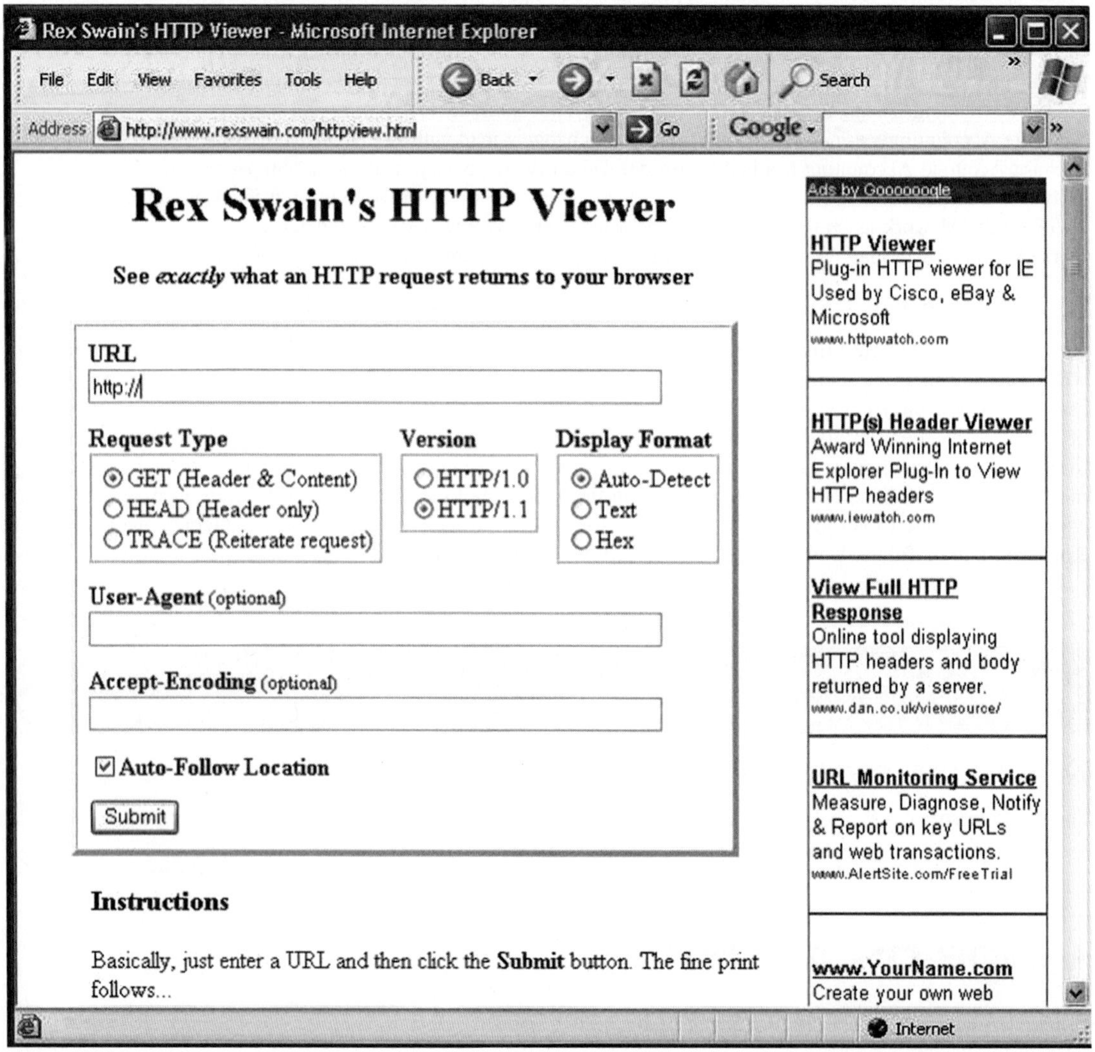

FIGURE 2.18 The HTTP Viewer

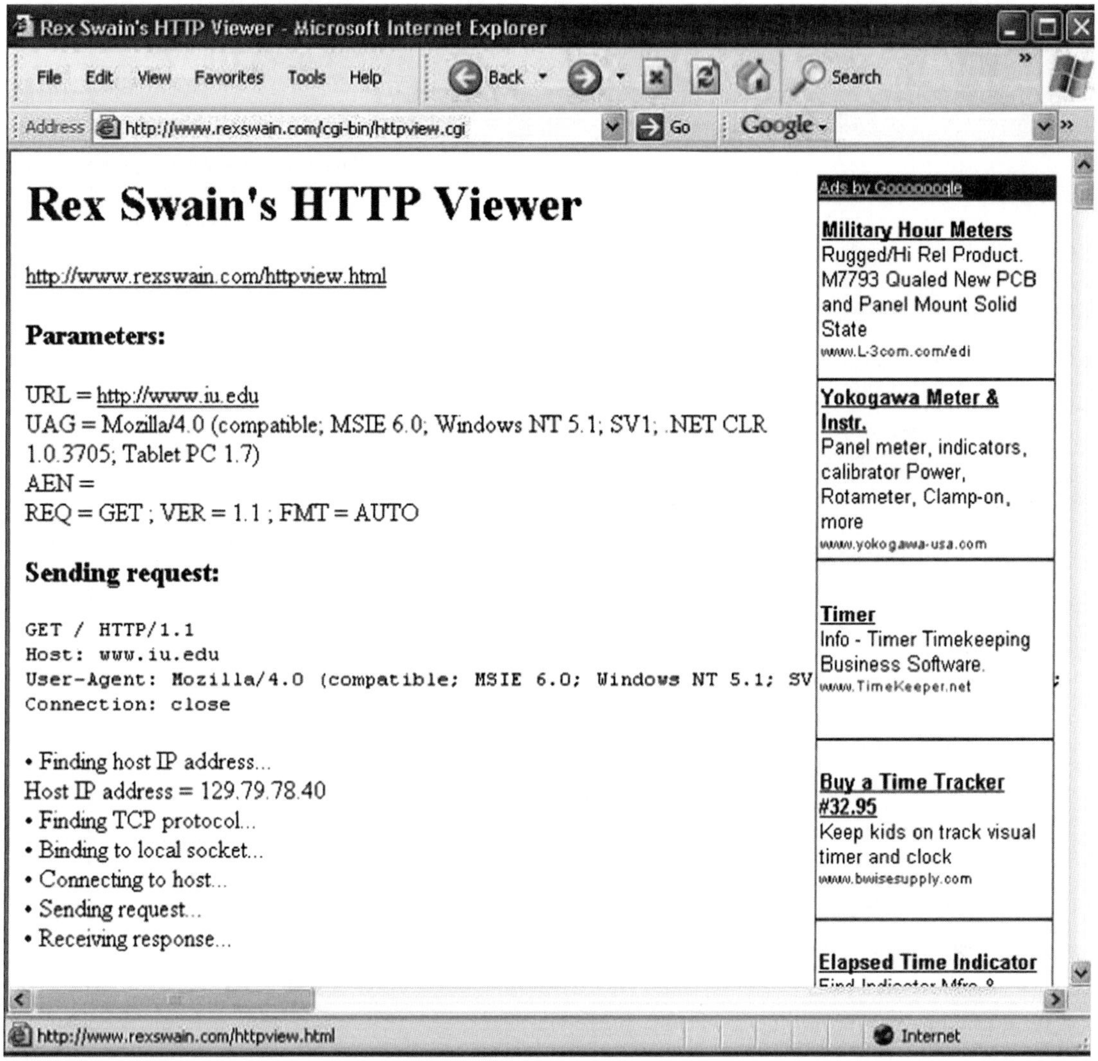

FIGURE 2.19 Looking inside an HTTP request

HANDS-ON ACTIVITY

Tracing Your E-mail

Most e-mail today is spam, unwanted commercial e-mail, or phishing, fake e-mail designed to separate you from your money. Criminals routinely send fake e-mails that try to get you to tell them your login information for your bank or your PayPal account, so they can steal the information, login as you, and steal your money.

It is very easy to fake a return address on an e-mail, so simply looking to make sure that an e-mail has a valid sender is not sufficient to ensure that the e-mail was actually sent by the person or company that claims to have sent it. However, every SMTP e-mail packet contains information in its header about who actually sent the

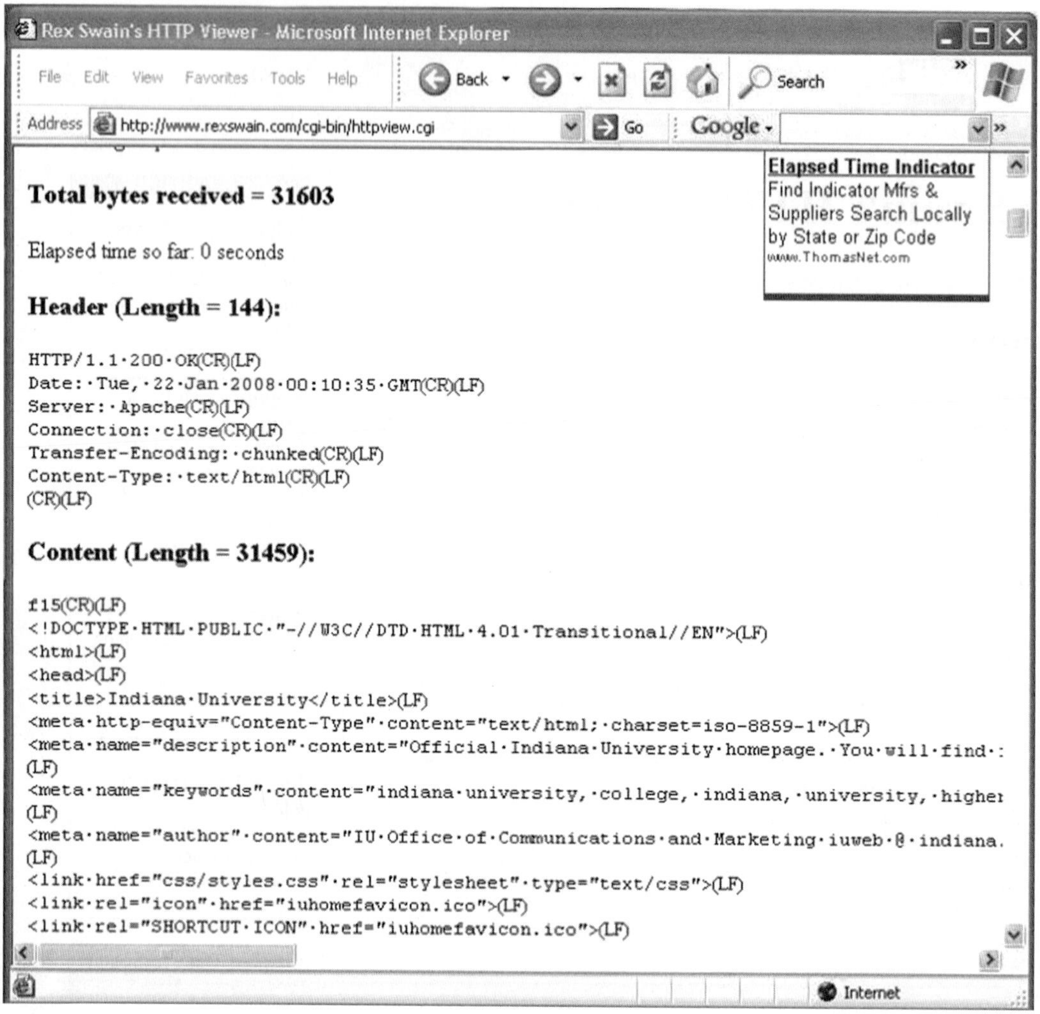

FIGURE 2.20 Looking inside an HTTP response

e-mail. You can read this information yourself, or you can use a tool designed to simplify the process for you. The objective of this Activity is for you to trace an e-mail you have received to see if the sending address on the e-mail is actually the organization that sent it.

There are many tools you can use to trace your e-mail. We like a tool called eMail Tracker Pro, which has a free version that lasts 15 days.

1. Go to www.emailtrackerpro.com and download and install eMail Tracker Pro.
2. Login to your e-mail and find an e-mail message you want to trace. I recently received an e-mail supposedly from Wachovia Bank; the sender's e-mail address was aw-login@wachovia.com.
3. After you open the e-mail, find the option that enables you to view the Internet header or source of the message (in Microsoft Outlook, click the Options tab and look at the bottom of the box that pops up). Figure 2.21 shows the e-mail I received and how to find the SMTP header (which Outlook calls the Internet header). Copy the entire SMTP header to the clipboard.

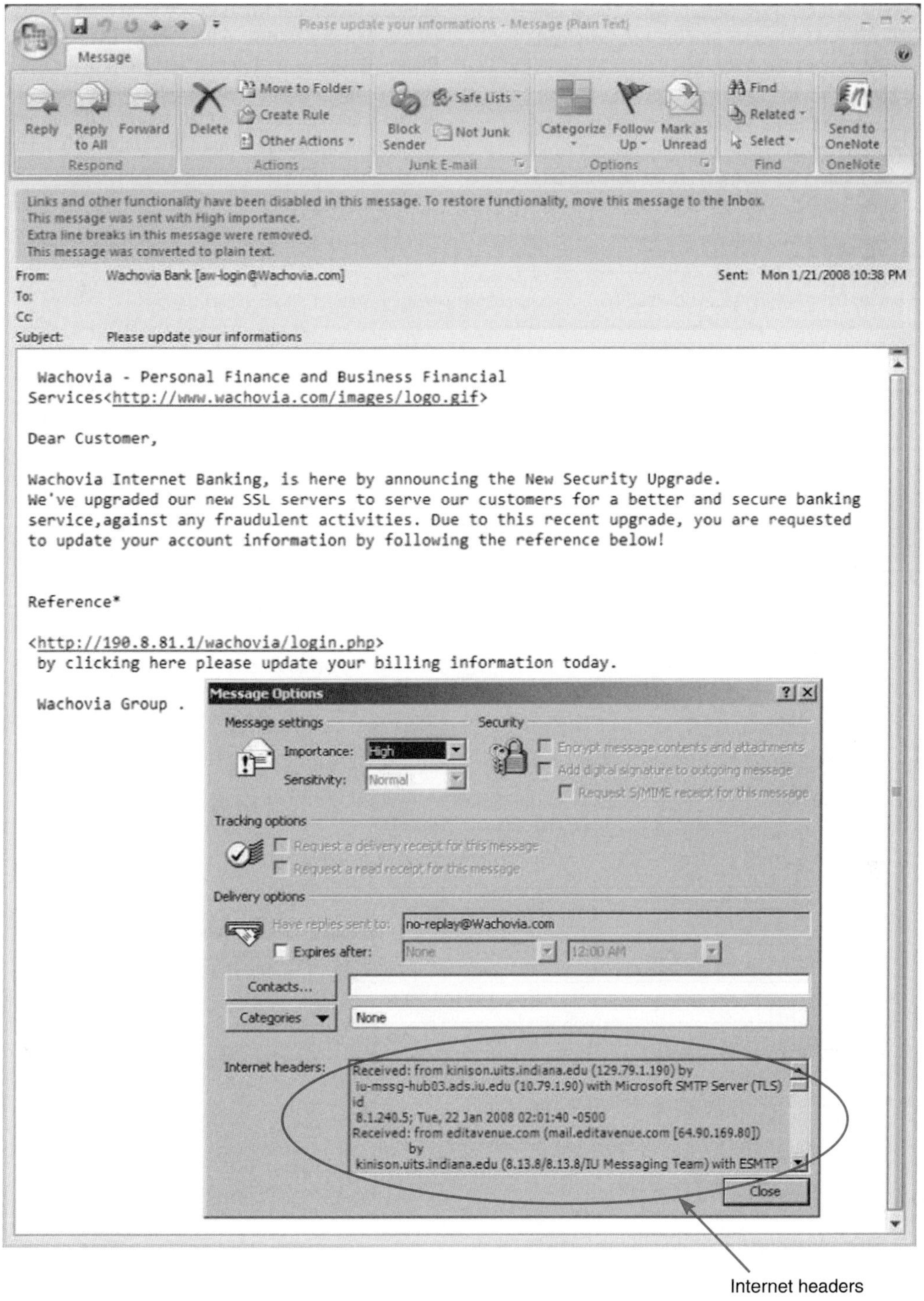

FIGURE 2.21 Viewing the SMTP packet header

4. Start eMail Tracker Pro. Select Trace an email, and paste the SMTP header into the box provided. Click Trace to start the trace.
5. It may take up to 30 seconds to trace the e-mail, so be patient. Figure 2.22 shows the results from the e-mail I received. The e-mail supposedly from Wachovia Bank was actually from a company named Musser and Kouri Law whose primary contact is Musser Ratliff, CPA, which uses SBC in Plano, Texas, as its Internet service provider. We suspect that someone broke into this company's network and used their e-mail server without permission, or fraudulently used this company's name and contact information on its domain registration.

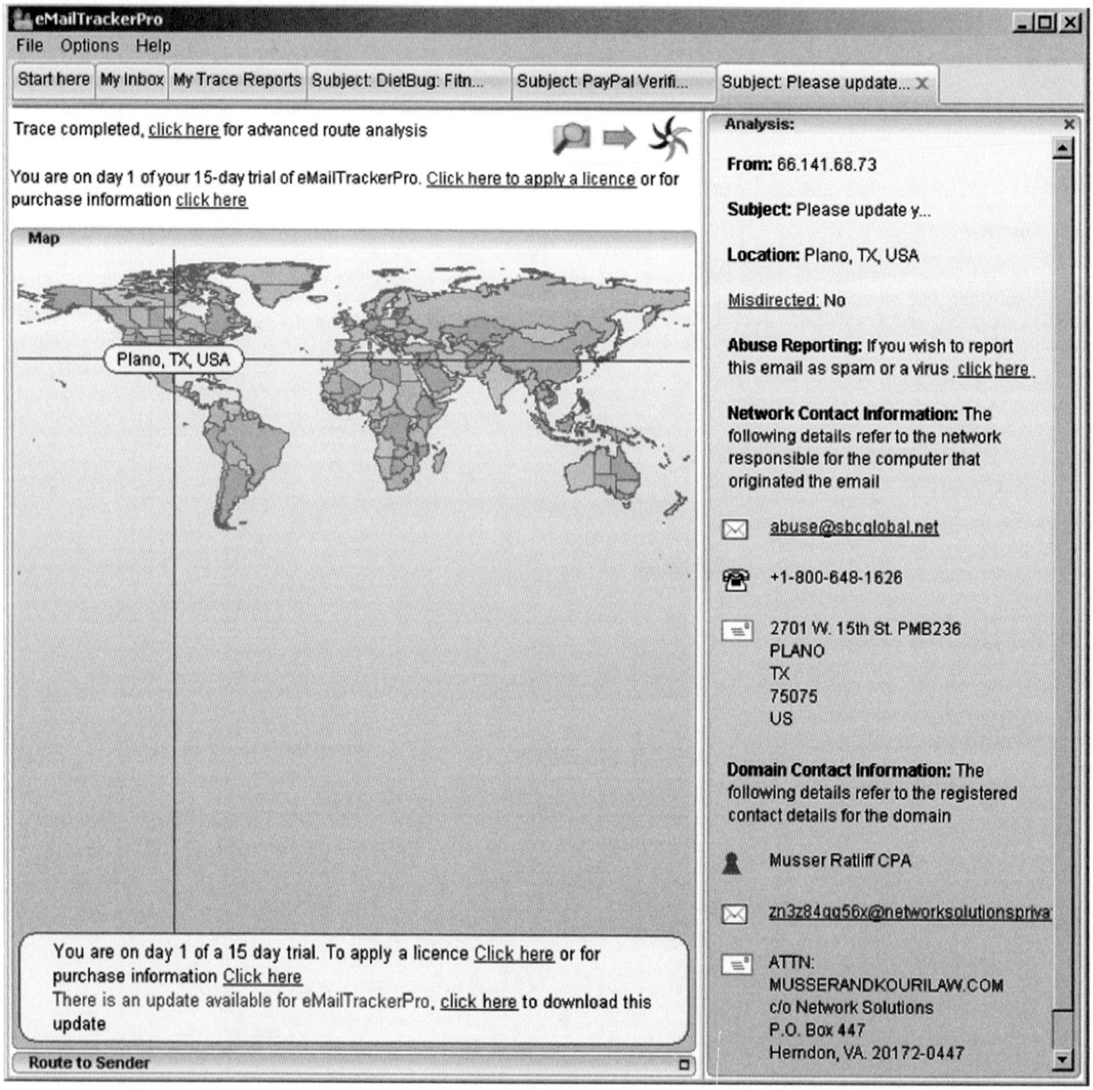

FIGURE 2.22 Viewing the source of the SMTP packet

CHAPTER 3

PHYSICAL LAYER

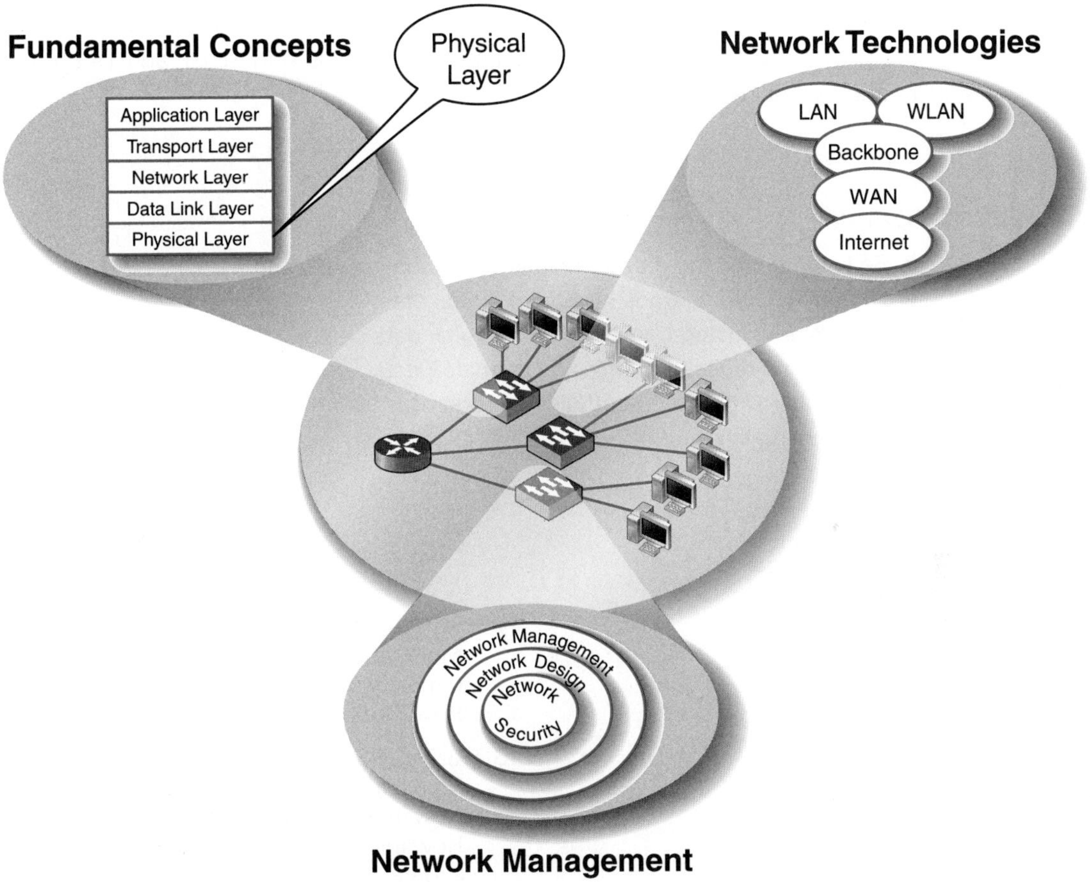

The Three Faces of Networking

THE PHYSICAL layer (also called layer 1) is the physical connection between the computers and/or devices in the network. This chapter examines how the physical layer operates. It describes the most commonly used media for network circuits and explains the basic technical concepts of how data is actually transmitted through the media. Four different types of transmission are described: digital transmission of digital computer data; analog transmission of digital computer data; digital transmission of analog voice data; and combined analog–digital transmission of digital data. You do not need an engineering-level understanding of the topics to be an effective user and manager of data communication applications. It is important, however, that you understand the basic concepts, so this chapter is somewhat technical.

OBJECTIVES ▼

- Be familiar with the different types of network circuits and media
- Understand digital transmission of digital data
- Understand analog transmission of digital data
- Understand digital transmission of analog data
- Be familiar with analog and digital modems
- Be familiar with multiplexing

CHAPTER OUTLINE ▼

INTRODUCTION

This chapter examines how the physical layer operates. The physical layer is the network hardware including servers, clients, and circuits, but in this chapter we focus on the circuits and on how clients and servers transmit data through them. The circuits are usually a combination of both physical media (e.g., cables, wireless transmissions) and special-purpose devices that enable the transmissions to travel through the media. Special-purpose devices such as repeaters are discussed in more detail in Chapter 4, whereas devices such as hubs, switches, and routers are discussed in Chapter 6 and 7.

The word **circuit** has two very different meanings in networking, and sometimes it is hard to understand which meaning is intended. Sometimes, we use the word *circuit* to refer to the **physical circuit**—the actual wire—used to connect two devices. In this case, we are referring to the physical media that carries the message we transmit, such as the twisted-pair wire used to connect a computer to the LAN in an office. In other cases, we are referring to a **logical circuit** used to connect two devices, which refers to the transmission characteristics of the connection, such as when we say a company has a T1 connection into the Internet. In this case, T1 refers not to the physical media (i.e., what type of wire is used) but rather to how fast data can be sent through the connection.[1] Often, each physical circuit is also a logical circuit, but as you will see in the section on multiplexing, sometimes it is possible to have one physical circuit—one wire—carry several separate logical circuits and vice versa: have one logical circuit travel over several physical circuits.

There are two fundamentally different types of data that can flow through the circuit: *digital* and *analog*. Computers produce digital data that are binary, either on or off, 0 or 1. In contrast, telephones produce analog data whose electrical signals are shaped like the sound waves they transfer; they can take on any value in a wide range of possibilities, not just 0 or 1.

Data can be transmitted through a circuit in the same form they are produced. Most computers, for example, transmit their digital data through digital circuits to printers and other attached devices. Likewise, analog voice data can be transmitted through telephone networks in analog form. In general, networks designed primarily to transmit digital computer data tend to use digital transmission, and networks designed primarily to transmit analog voice data tend to use analog transmission (at least for some parts of the transmission).

Data can be converted from one form into the other for transmission over network circuits. For example, digital computer data can be transmitted over an analog telephone circuit by using a modem. A modem at the sender's computer translates the computer's digital data into analog data that can be transmitted through the voice communication circuits, and a second modem at the receiver's end translates the analog transmission back into digital data for use by the receiver's computer.

[1]Don't worry about what a T1 circuit is at this point. All you need to understand is that a T1 circuit is a specific type of circuit with certain characteristics, the same way we might describe gasoline as being unleaded or premium. We discuss T1 circuits in Chapter 9.

Likewise, it is possible to translate analog voice data into digital form for transmission over digital computer circuits using a device called a **codec.** Once again, there are two codecs, one at the sender's end and one at the receiver's end. Why bother to translate voice into digital? The answer is that digital transmission is "better" than analog transmission. Specifically, digital transmission offers five key benefits over analog transmission:

- Digital transmission produces fewer errors than analog transmission. Because the transmitted data is binary (only two distinct values), it is easier to detect and correct errors.
- Digital transmission permits higher maximum transmission rates. Fiber-optic cable, for example, is designed for digital transmission.
- Digital transmission is more efficient. It is possible to send more data through a given circuit using digital rather than analog transmission.
- Digital transmission is more secure because it is easier to encrypt.
- Finally, and most importantly, integrating voice, video, and data on the same circuit is far simpler with digital transmission.

For these reasons, most long-distance telephone circuits built by the telephone companies and other common carriers over the past decades use digital transmission. In the future, most transmissions (voice, data, and video) will be sent digitally.

Regardless of whether digital or analog transmission is used, transmission requires the sender and receiver to agree on two key parameters. First, they have to agree on the *symbols* that will be used: what pattern of electricity, light, or radio wave will be used to represent a 0 and a 1. Once these symbols are set, the sender and receiver have to agree on the **symbol rate:** How many symbols will be sent over the circuit per second? Analog and digital transmission are different, but both require a commonly agreed on set of symbols, and a symbol rate.

In this chapter, we first describe the basic types of circuits and examine the different media used to build circuits. Then we explain how data is actually sent through these media using digital and analog transmission.

CIRCUITS

Circuit Configuration

Circuit configuration is the basic physical layout of the circuit. There are two fundamental circuit configurations: point-to-point and multipoint. In practice, most complex computer networks have many circuits, some of which are point-to-point and some of which are multipoint.

Figure 3.1 illustrates a **point-to-point circuit,** which is so named because it goes from one point to another (e.g., one computer to another computer). These circuits sometimes are called *dedicated circuits* because they are dedicated to the use of these two computers. This type of configuration is used when the computers generate enough data to fill the capacity of the communication circuit. When an organization builds a network

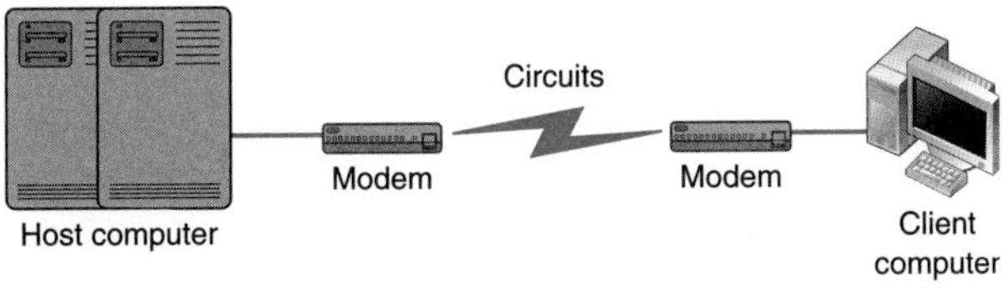

FIGURE 3.1 Point-to-point circuit

using point-to-point circuits, each computer has its own circuit running from itself to the other computers. This can get very expensive, particularly if there is some distance between the computers.

Figure 3.2 shows a **multipoint circuit** (also called a *shared circuit*). In this configuration, many computers are connected on the same circuit. This means that each must share the circuit with the others. The disadvantage is that only one computer can use the circuit at a time. When one computer is sending or receiving data, all others must wait. The advantage of multipoint circuits is that they reduce the amount of cable required and typically use the available communication circuit more efficiently. Imagine the number of circuits that would be required if the network in Figure 3.2 was designed with separate point-to-point circuits. For this reason, multipoint configurations are cheaper than point-to-point circuits. Thus, multipoint circuits typically are used when each computer does not need to continuously use the entire capacity of the circuit or when building point-to-point circuits is too expensive. Wireless circuits are almost always multipoint circuits because multiple computers use the same radio frequencies and must take turns transmitting.

Data Flow

Circuits can be designed to permit data to flow in one direction or in both directions. Actually, there are three ways to transmit: simplex, half-duplex, and full-duplex (Figure 3.3).

Simplex is one-way transmission, such as that with radios and TVs.

Half-duplex is two-way transmission, but you can transmit in only one direction at a time. A half-duplex communication link is similar to a walkie-talkie link; only one

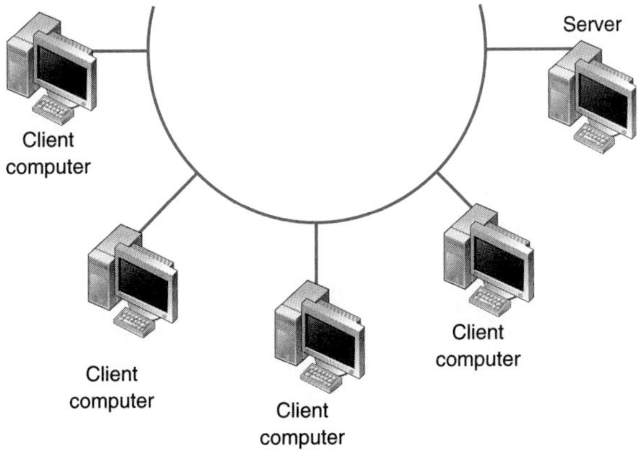

FIGURE 3.2 Multipoint circuit

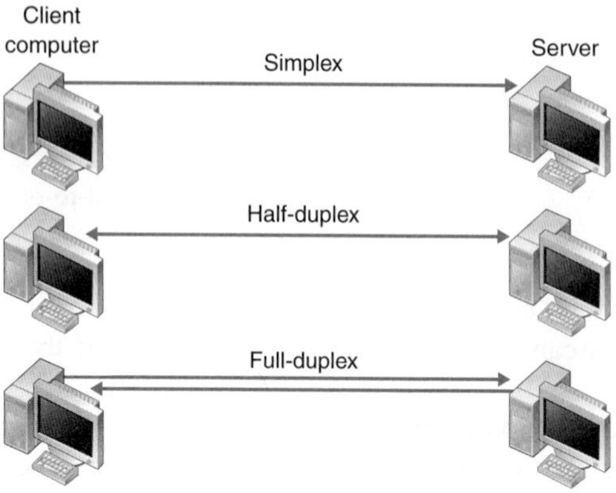

FIGURE 3.3 Simplex, half-duplex, and full-duplex transmissions

computer can transmit at a time. Computers use *control signals* to negotiate which will send and which will receive data. The amount of time half-duplex communication takes to switch between sending and receiving is called **turnaround time** (also called **retrain time** or reclocking time). The turnaround time for a specific circuit can be obtained from its technical specifications (often between 20 and 50 milliseconds). Europeans sometimes use the term *simplex circuit* to mean a half-duplex circuit.

With **full-duplex transmission,** you can transmit in both directions simultaneously, with no turnaround time.

How do you choose which data flow method to use? Obviously, one factor is the application. If data always need to flow only in one direction (e.g., from a remote sensor to a host computer), then simplex is probably the best choice. In most cases, however, data must flow in both directions.

The initial temptation is to presume that a full-duplex channel is best; however, each circuit has only so much capacity to carry data. Creating a full-duplex circuit means that the available capacity in the circuit is divided—half in one direction and half in the other. In some cases, it makes more sense to build a set of simplex circuits in the same way a set of one-way streets can speed traffic. In other cases, a half-duplex circuit may work best. For example, terminals connected to mainframes often transmit data to the host, wait for a reply, transmit more data, and so on, in a turn-taking process; usually, traffic does not need to flow in both directions simultaneously. Such a traffic pattern is ideally suited to half-duplex circuits.

Multiplexing

Multiplexing means to break one high-speed physical communication circuit into several lower-speed logical circuits so that many different devices can simultaneously use it but still "think" that they have their own separate circuits (the multiplexer is "*transparent*"). It is multiplexing (specifically, wavelength division multiplexing [WDM], discussed later in this section) that has enabled the almost unbelievable growth in network capacity discussed in Chapter 1; without WDM, the Internet would have collapsed in the 1990s.

Multiplexing often is done in multiples of 4 (e.g., 8, 16). Figure 3.4 shows a four-level multiplexed circuit. Note that two multiplexers are needed for each circuit:

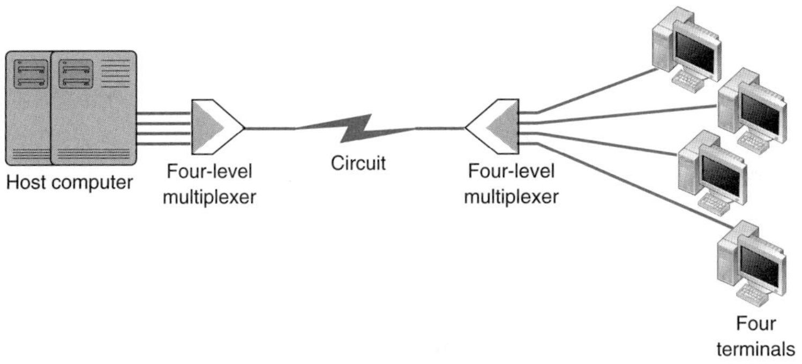

FIGURE 3.4 Multiplexed circuit

one to combine the four original circuits into the one multiplexed circuit and one to separate them back into the four separate circuits.

The primary benefit of multiplexing is to save money by reducing the amount of cable or the number of network circuits that must be installed. For example, if we did not use multiplexers in Figure 3.4, we would need to run four separate circuits from the clients to the server. If the clients were located close to the server, this would be inexpensive. However, if they were located several miles away, the extra costs could be substantial.

There are four types of multiplexing: frequency division multiplexing (FDM), time division multiplexing (TDM), statistical time division multiplexing (STDM), and WDM.

Frequency Division Multiplexing **Frequency division multiplexing (FDM)** can be described as dividing the circuit "horizontally" so that many signals can travel a single communication circuit simultaneously. The circuit is divided into a series of separate channels, each transmitting on a different frequency, much like series of different radio or TV stations. All signals exist in the media at the same time, but because they are on different frequencies, they do not interfere with each other.

Figure 3.5 illustrates the use of FDM to divide one circuit into four **channels.** Each channel is a separate logical circuit, and the devices connected to them are unaware that their circuit is multiplexed. In the same way that radio stations must be assigned separate frequencies to prevent interference, so must the signals in a FDM circuit. The **guardbands** in Figure 3.5 are the unused portions of the circuit that separate these frequencies from each other.

With FDM, the total capacity of the physical circuit is simply divided among the multiplexed circuits. For example, suppose we had a physical circuit with a data rate of 64 Kbps that we wanted to divide into four circuits. We would simply divide the 64 Kbps among the four circuits and assign each circuit 16 Kbps. However, because FDM needs guardbands, we also have to allocate some of the capacity to the guardbands, so we might actually end up with four circuits, each providing 15 Kbps, with the remaining 4 Kbps allocated to the guardbands. There is no requirement that all circuits be the same size, as you will see in a later section. FDM was commonly used in older telephone systems, which is why the bandwidth on older phone systems was only 3,000 Hz, not the 4,000 Hz actually available—1,000 Hz were used as guardbands, with the voice signals traveling between two guardbands on the outside of the channel.

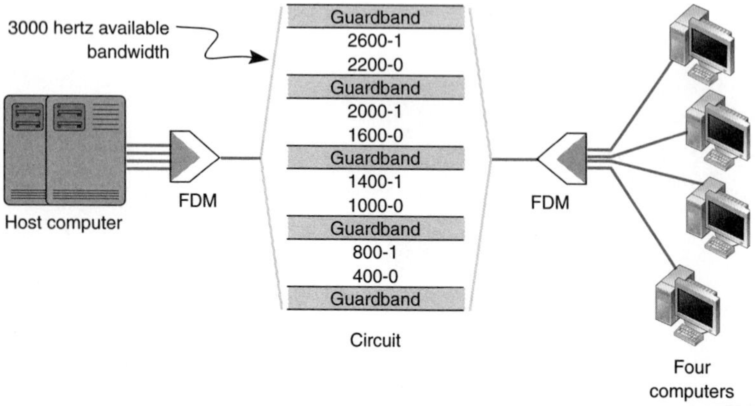

FIGURE 3.5 Frequency division multiplex (FDM) circuit

Time Division Multiplexing **Time division multiplexing (TDM)** shares a communication circuit among two or more terminals by having them take turns, dividing the circuit vertically, so to speak. Figure 3.6 shows the same four terminals connected using TDM. In this case, one character is taken from each computer in turn, transmitted down the circuit, and delivered to the appropriate device at the far end (e.g., one character from computer A, then one from B, one from C, one from D, another from A, another from B, and so on). Time on the circuit is allocated even when data are not being transmitted, so that some capacity is wasted when terminals are idle. TDM generally is more efficient than FDM because it does not need guardbands. Guardbands use "space" on the circuit that otherwise could be used to transmit data. Therefore, if one divides a 64-Kbps circuit into four circuits, the result would be four 16-Kbps circuits.

Statistical Time Division Multiplexing **Statistical time division multiplexing (STDM)** is the exception to the rule that the capacity of the multiplexed circuit must

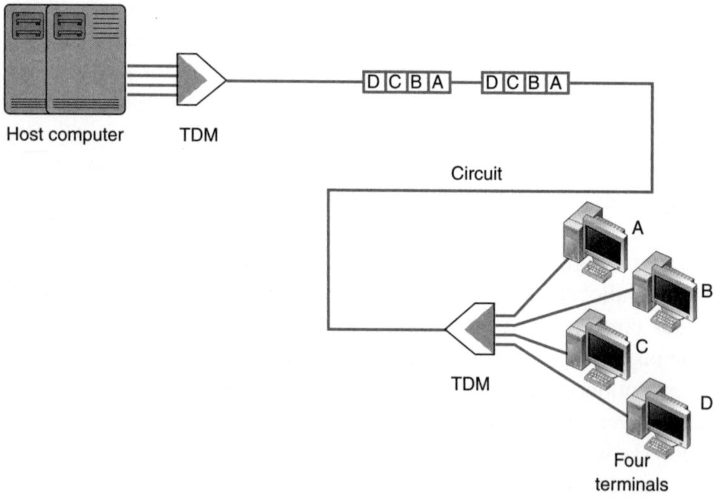

FIGURE 3.6 Time division multiplex (TDM) circuit

equal the sum of the circuits it combines. STDM allows more terminals or computers to be connected to a circuit than does FDM or TDM. If you have four computers connected to a multiplexer and each can transmit at 64 Kbps, then you should have a circuit capable of transmitting 256 Kbps (4 × 64 Kbps). However, not all computers will be transmitting continuously at their maximum transmission speed. Users typically pause to read their screens or spend time typing at lower speeds. Therefore, you do not need to provide a speed of 256 Kbps on this multiplexed circuit. If you assume that only two computers will ever transmit at the same time, 128 Kbps would be enough. STDM is called *statistical* because selection of transmission speed for the multiplexed circuit is based on a statistical analysis of the usage requirements of the circuits to be multiplexed.

The key benefit of STDM is that it provides more efficient use of the circuit and saves money. You can buy a lower-speed, less-expensive circuit than you could using FDM or TDM. STDM introduces two additional complexities. First, STDM can cause time delays. If *all* devices start transmitting or receiving at the same time (or just more than at the statistical assumptions), the multiplexed circuit cannot transmit all the data it receives because it does not have sufficient capacity. Therefore, STDM must have internal memory to store the incoming data that it cannot immediately transmit. When traffic is particularly heavy, you may have a 1- to 30-second delay. The second problem is that because the logical circuits are not permanently assigned to specific devices as they are in FDM and TDM, the data from one device are interspersed with data from other devices. The first message might be from the third computer, the second from the first computer, and so on. Therefore, we need to add some address information to each packet to make sure we can identify the logical circuit to which it belongs. This is not a major problem, but it does increase the complexity of the multiplexer and also slightly decreases efficiency, because now we must "waste" some of the circuit's capacity in transmitting the extra address we have added to each packet.

Wavelength Division Multiplexing

Wavelength division multiplexing (WDM) is a version of FDM used in fiber-optic cables. When fiber-optic cables were first developed, the devices attached to them were designed to use only one color of light generated by a laser or LED. With one commonly used type of fiber cable, the data rate is 622 Mbps (622 million bits per second). At first, the 622-Mbps data rate seemed wonderful. Then the amount of data transferred over the Internet began doubling at fairly regular intervals, and several companies began investigating how we could increase the amount of data sent over existing fiber-optic cables.

The answer, in hindsight, was obvious. Light has different frequencies (i.e., colors), so rather than building devices to transmit using only one color, why not send multiple signals, each in a different frequency, through the same fiber cable? By simply attaching different devices that could transmit in the full spectrum of light rather than just one frequency, the capacity of the existing fiber-optic cables could be dramatically increased, with no change to the physical cables themselves.

WDM works by using lasers to transmit different frequencies of light (i.e., colors) through the same fiber-optic cable. As with FDM, each logical circuit is assigned a different frequency, and the devices attached to the circuit don't "know" they are multiplexed over the same physical circuit.

MANAGEMENT FOCUS 3.1 NASA's Ground Communications Network

NASA's communications network is extensive because its operations are spread out around the world and into space. The main Deep Space Network is controlled out of the Jet Propulsion Laboratory (JPL) in California. JPL is connected to the three main Deep Space Communications Centers (DSCCs) that communicate with NASA spacecraft. The three DSCCs are spread out equidistantly around the world so that one will always be able to communicate with spacecraft no matter where they are in relation to the earth: Canberra, Australia; Madrid, Spain; and Goldstone, California.

Figure 3.7 shows the JPL network. Each DSCC has four large-dish antennas ranging in size from 85 to 230 feet (26 to 70 meters) that communicate with the spacecraft. These send and receive operational data such as telemetry, commands, tracking, and radio signals. Each DSCC also sends and receives administrative data such as e-mail, reports, and Web pages, as well as telephone calls and video.

The three DSCCs and JPL use Ethernet local area networks (LANs) that are connected to multiplexers that integrate the data, voice, and video signals for transmission. Satellite circuits are used between Canberra and JPL and Madrid and JPL. Fiber-optic circuits are used between JPL and Goldstone.

Dense WDM (DWDM) is a variant of WDM that further increases the capacity of WDM by adding TDM to WDM. Today, DWDM permits up to 40 simultaneous circuits, each transmitting up to 10 Gbps, giving a total network capacity in *one* fiber-optic cable of 400 Gbps (i.e., 400 billion bits per second). Remember, this is the same physical cable that until recently produced only 622 Mbps; all we've changed are the devices connected to it.

DWDM is a relatively new technique, so it will continue to improve over the next few years. As we write this, DWDM systems have been announced that provide 128 circuits, each at 10 Gbps (1.28 terabits per second [1.28 Tbps]) in one fiber cable. Experts predict that DWDM transmission speeds should reach 25 Tbps (i.e., 25 trillion bits per second) within a few years (and possibly 1 petabit [Pbps], or 1 million billion bits per second)—all on that same single fiber-optic cable that today typically provides 622 Mbps. Once we reach these speeds, the most time-consuming part of the process is converting from the light used in the fiber cables into the electricity used in the computer devices used to route the messages through the Internet. Therefore, many companies are now developing computer devices that run on light, not electricity.

Inverse Multiplexing

Multiplexing uses one high-speed circuit to transmit a set of several low-speed circuits. It can also be used to do the opposite. **Inverse multiplexing (IMUX)** combines several low-speed circuits to make them appear as one high-speed circuit to the user (Figure 3.8).

One of the most common uses of IMUX is to provide T1 circuits for WANs. T1 circuits provide data transmission rates of 1.544 Mbps by combining 24 slower-speed circuits (64 Kbps). As far as the users are concerned, they have access to one high-speed circuit, even though their data actually travel across a set of slower circuits. T1 and other circuits are discussed in Chapter 9.

Until recently, there were no standards for IMUX. If you wanted to use IMUX, you had to ensure that you bought IMUX circuits from the same vendor so both clients

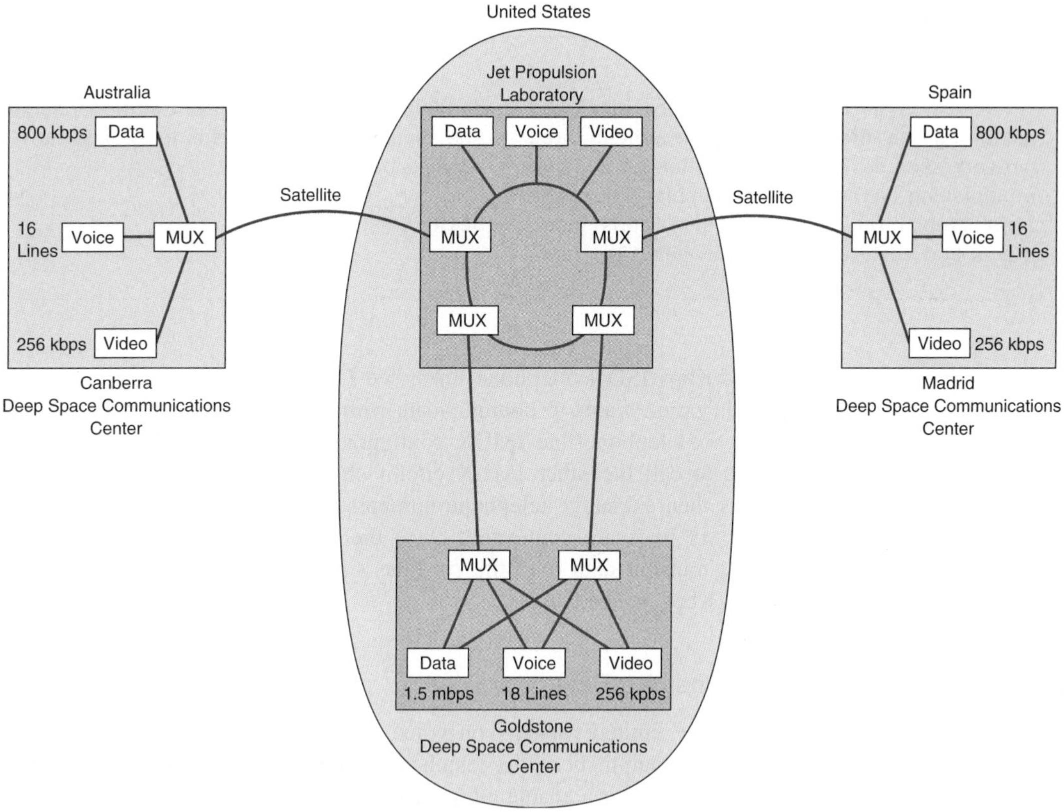

FIGURE 3.7 NASA's Deep Space Communications Centers ground communications network. MUX = multiplexer

or hosts could communicate. Several vendors have recently adopted the **BONDING** standard (**Bandwidth on Demand Interoperability Networking Group**). Any IMUX circuit that conforms to the BONDING standard can communicate with any other IMUX circuit that conforms to the same standard. BONDING splits outgoing messages from one client or host across several low-speed telephone lines and combines incoming messages from several telephone lines into one circuit so that the client or host "thinks" it has a faster circuit.

The most common use for BONDING is for room-to-room videoconferencing. In this case, organizations usually have the telephone company install six telephone lines into their videoconferencing room that are connected to the IMUX. (The telephone lines

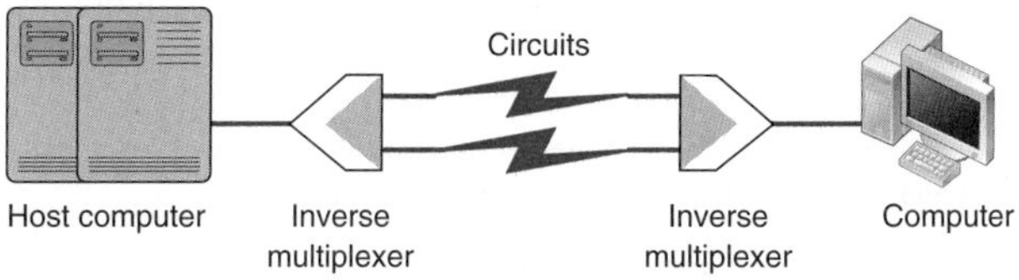

FIGURE 3.8 Inverse multiplexer

MANAGEMENT FOCUS 3.2 GET MORE BANDWIDTH FOR LESS

Upstart network provider Yipes is among the first to offer metropolitan area network services based on wavelength division multiplexing (WDM). It offers circuits that range from 1 Mbps up to 1 Gbps in 1-Mbps increments and costs anywhere between 10 percent and 80 percent of the cost of traditional services. The challenge Yipes faces is to expand its WDM services beyond the MAN.

SOURCE: Yipes.com.

are usually 64-Kbps ISDN telephone lines; see Chapter 9 for a description of ISDN.) When an organization wants to communicate with another videoconferencing room that has a similar six-telephone-line IMUX configuration, the first IMUX circuit uses one telephone line to call the other IMUX circuit on one of its telephone lines. The two IMUX circuits then exchange telephone numbers and call each other on the other five lines until all six lines are connected. Once the connection has been established, the IMUX circuits transmit data over the six lines simultaneously, thus giving a total data rate of 6×64 Kbps $= 384$ Kbps.

How DSL Transmits Data

The reason for the limited capacity on voice telephone circuits lies with the telephone and the switching equipment at the telephone company offices. The actual twisted-pair wire in the local loop is capable of providing much higher data transmission rates. **Digital subscriber line (DSL)** is one approach to changing the way data are transmitted in the local loop to provide higher-speed data transfer. DSL is a family of techniques that combines analog transmission and FDM to provide a set of voice and data circuits. There are many different types of DSL, so many in fact that DSL is sometimes called xDSL, where the *x* is intended to represent one of the many possible flavors. Chapter 10 examines the different types of DSL.

With DSL, a DSL modem (called **customer premises equipment [CPE]**) is installed in the customer's home or office and another DSL modem is installed at the telephone company switch closest to the customer's home or office. The modem is first an FDM device that splits the physical circuit into three logical circuits: a standard voice circuit used for telephone calls, an upstream data circuit from the customer to the telephone switch, and a downstream data circuit from the switch to the customer. TDM is then used within the two data channels to provide a set of one or more individual channels that can be used to carry different data. A combination of amplitude and phase modulation is used in the data circuits to provide the desired data rate (the exact combination depends on which flavor of DSL is used).[2] One version of DSL called G.Lite ASDL provides one voice circuit, a 1.5-Mbps downstream circuit, and a 384-Kbps upstream channel.

[2]DSL is rapidly changing because it is so new. More information can be found from the DSL forum (www.dslforum.org) and the ITU-T (www.itu.int) under standard G.992.

COMMUNICATION MEDIA

The *medium* (or *media,* if there is more than one) is the physical matter or substance that carries the voice or data transmission. Many different types of transmission media are currently in use, such as copper (wire), glass or plastic (fiber-optic cable), or air (radio, infrared, microwave, or satellite). There are two basic types of media. **Guided media** are those in which the message flows through a physical media such as a twisted-pair wire, coaxial cable, or fiber-optic cable; the media "guides" the signal. **Wireless media** are those in which the message is broadcast through the air, such as infrared, microwave, or satellite.

In many cases, the circuits used in WANs are provided by the various common carriers who sell usage of them to the public. We call the circuits sold by the common carriers *communication services.* Chapter 9 describes specific services available in North America. The following sections describe the medium and the basic characteristics of each circuit type, in the event you were establishing your own physical network, whereas Chapter 9 describes how the circuits are packaged and marketed for purchase or lease from a common carrier. If your organization has leased a circuit from a common carrier, you are probably less interested in the media used and more interested in whether the speed, cost, and reliability of the circuit meets your needs.

Guided Media

Twisted-Pair Cable

One of the most commonly used types of guided media is **twisted-pair cable,** insulated pairs of wires that can be packed quite close together (Figure 3.9). The wires usually are twisted to minimize the electromagnetic interference between one pair and any other pair in the bundle. Your house or apartment probably has a set of two twisted-pair wires (i.e., four wires) from it to the telephone company network. One pair is used to connect your telephone; the other pair is a spare that can be used for a second telephone line. The twisted-pair cable used in LANs are usually packaged as four sets of pairs as shown in Figure 3.9, whereas bundles of several thousand

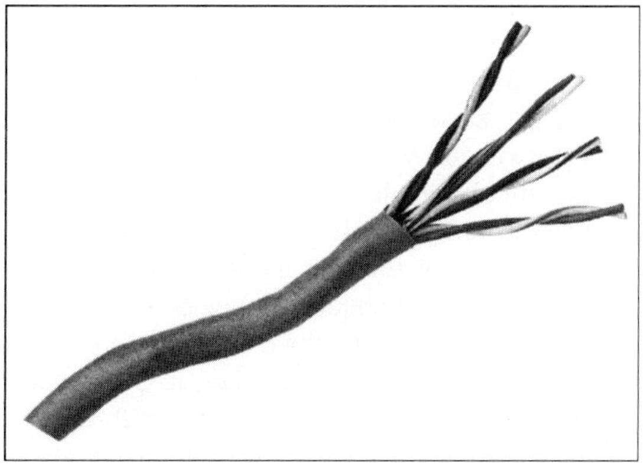

FIGURE 3.9 Category 5e twisted-pair wire
Source: Courtesy South Hills Datacomm

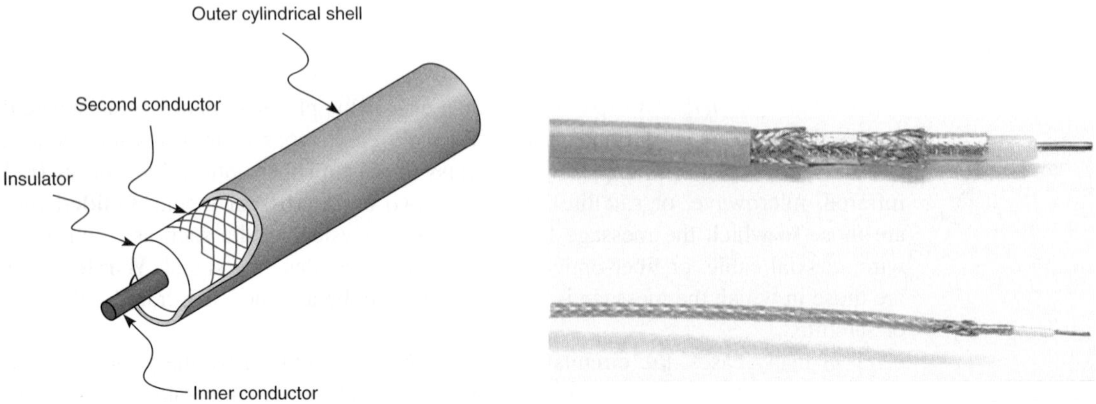

FIGURE 3.10 Coaxial cables. Thinnet and Thicknet Ethernet cables (right) and cross-sectional view (left)

wire pairs are placed under city streets and in large buildings. The specific types of twisted-pair cable used in LANs, such as Cat 5e and Cat 6, are discussed in Chapter 6.

Coaxial Cable **Coaxial cable** is a type of guided media that is quickly disappearing (Figure 3.10). Coaxial cable has a copper core (the inner conductor) with an outer cylindrical shell for insulation. The outer shield, just under the shell, is the second conductor. Because they have additional shielding provided by their multiple layers of material, coaxial cables are less prone to interference and errors than basic low-cost twisted-pair wires. Coaxial cables cost about three times as much as twisted-pair wires but offer few additional benefits other than better shielding. One can also buy specially shielded twisted-pair wire that provides the same level of quality as coaxial cable but at half its cost. For this reason, few companies are installing coaxial cable today, although some still continue to use existing coaxial cable that was installed years ago.

Fiber-Optic Cable Although twisted-pair is the most common type of guided media, **fiber-optic cable** also is becoming widely used. Instead of carrying telecommunication signals in the traditional electrical form, this technology uses high-speed streams of light pulses from lasers or LEDs (light-emitting diodes) that carry information inside hair-thin strands of glass called optical fibers. Figure 3.11 shows a fiber-optic cable and depicts the optical core, the cladding (metal coating), and how light rays travel in optical fibers.

The earliest fiber-optic systems were *multimode,* meaning that the light could reflect inside the cable at many different angles. Multimode cables are plagued by excessive signal weakening (attenuation) and dispersion (spreading of the signal so that different parts of the signal arrive at different times at the destination). For these reasons, early multimode fiber was usually limited to about 500 meters. Graded-index multimode fiber attempts to reduce this problem by changing the refractive properties of the glass fiber so that as the light approaches the outer edge of the fiber, it speeds up, which compensates for the slightly longer distance it must travel compared with light in the center of the fiber. Therefore, the light in the center is more likely to arrive at the same time as the

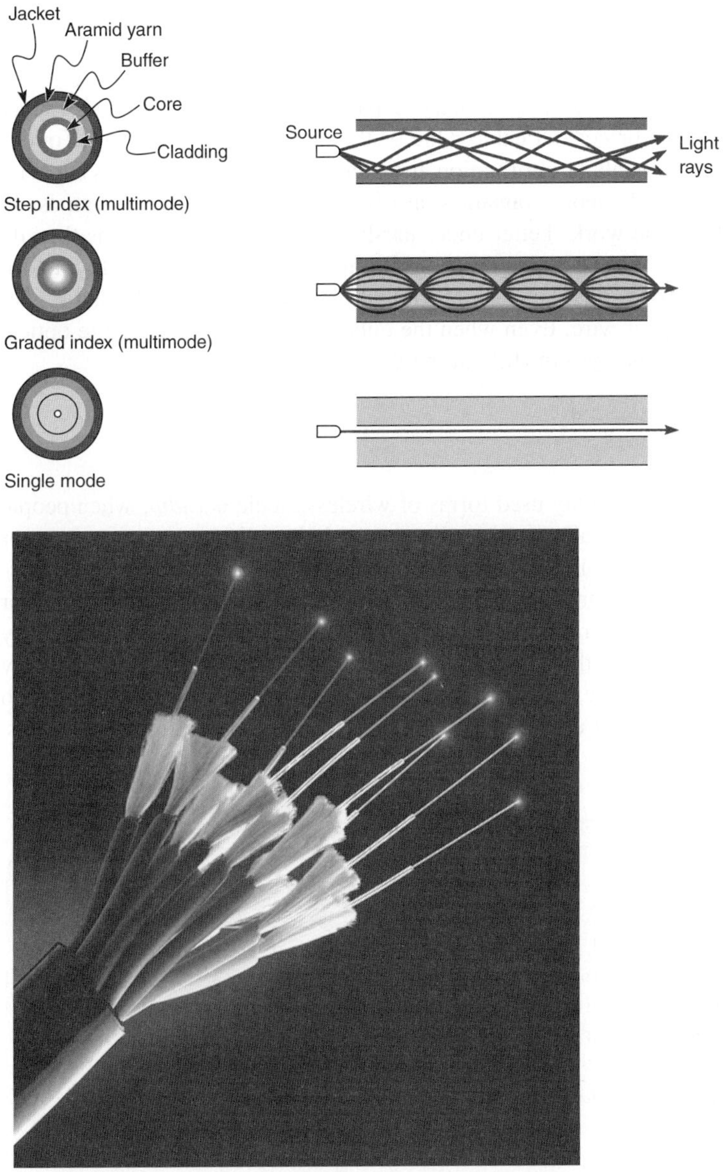

FIGURE 3.11 Fiber-optic cable

Source: Courtesy South Hills Datacomm

light that has traveled at the edges of the fiber. This increases the effective distance to just under 1,000 meters.

Single-mode fiber-optic cables transmit a single direct beam of light through a cable that ensures the light reflects in only one pattern, in part because the core diameter has been reduced from 50 microns to about 5 to 10 microns. This smaller-diameter core allows the fiber to send a more concentrated light beam, resulting in faster data transmission speeds and longer distances, often up to 100 kilometers. However, because the light source must be perfectly aligned with the cable, single-mode products usually use lasers (rather than the LEDs used in multimode systems) and therefore are more expensive.

Fiber-optic technology is a revolutionary departure from the traditional copper wires of twisted-pair cable or coaxial cable. One of the main advantages of fiber optics is that it can carry huge amounts of information at extremely fast data rates. This capacity makes it ideal for the simultaneous transmission of voice, data, and image signals. In most cases, fiber-optic cable works better under harsh environmental conditions than do its metallic counterparts. It is not as fragile or brittle, it is not as heavy or bulky, and it is more resistant to corrosion. Also, in case of fire, an optical fiber can withstand higher temperatures than can copper wire. Even when the outside jacket surrounding the optical fiber has melted, a fiber-optic system still can be used.

Wireless Media

Radio One of the most commonly used forms of wireless media is *radio;* when people used the term *wireless,* they usually mean **radio transmission.** When you connect your laptop into the network wirelessly, you are using radio transmission. Radio data transmission uses the same basic principles as standard radio transmission. Each device or computer on the network has a radio receiver/transmitter that uses a specific frequency range that does not interfere with commercial radio stations. The transmitters are very low power, designed to transmit a signal only a short distance, and are often built into portable computers or handheld devices such as phones and personal digital assistants.

MANAGEMENT FOCUS 3.3 **NETWORKING AUSTRALIA**

The Southern Cross Trans-Pacific Optical Research Testbed (SX TransPORT), will fundamentally change the way that Australian scientists and researchers participate in global research initiatives. The network, built at a cost of almost of $50 million, provides two 10-Gbps (10 billion bits per second) capacity fiber optic circuits.

The fiber optic cables, which run at the bottom of the Pacific Ocean, connect very high-speed Australian networks to very high-speed networks in the United States. One of the 10-Gbps circuits will connect through Hawaii and terminate in the U.S. at Hillsboro, Oregon, where it will interconnect with the Pacific Wave very high speed network. The second 10-Gbps circuit will terminate at San Luis Obispo in California and interconnect into other very high speed networks in the United States.

SX TransPORT is expected to facilitate research in astronomy, an area where Australia is a global leader. Australia is one of the nations likely to host major internationally-funded next-generation radiotelescopes, SKA (Square Kilometer Array) and LOFAR (Low Frequency Array). These telescopes will be able to peer back into the earliest days of the universe, and answer fundamental questions about how the first stars and galaxies came into being. But the scientific and technological benefits from hosting these telescopes, plus the hundreds of millions of dollars of international investment in them, will only come to Australia if overseas researchers can access these telescopes at gigabit speeds.

SOURCE: "Southern Cross Trans-pacific Optical Research Testbed for Australian researchers gets underway," *Lightwave,* 11 December, 2003.

Wireless technologies for LAN environments, such as IEEE 802.11n, are discussed in more detail in Chapter 7.

Infrared **Infrared transmission** uses low-frequency light waves (below the visible spectrum) to carry the data through the air on a direct line-of-sight path between two points. This technology is similar to the technology used in infrared TV remote controls. It is prone to interference, particularly from heavy rain, smoke, and fog that obscure the light transmission. Infrared transmitters are quite small but are seldom used for regular communication among portable or handheld computers because of their line-of-sight transmission requirements. Infrared is not very common, but it is sometimes used to transmit data from building to building.

Microwave **Microwave transmission** is an extremely high-frequency radio communication beam that is transmitted over a direct line-of-sight path between any two points. As its name implies, a microwave signal is an extremely short wavelength, thus the word *micro* wave. Microwave radio transmissions perform the same functions as cables. For example, point A communicates with point B via a through-the-air microwave transmission path, instead of a copper wire cable. Because microwave signals approach the frequency of visible light waves, they exhibit many of the same characteristics as light waves, such as reflection, focusing, or refraction. As with visible light waves, microwave signals can be focused into narrow, powerful beams that can be projected over long distances. Just as a parabolic reflector focuses a searchlight into a beam, a parabolic reflector also focuses a high-frequency microwave into a narrow beam. Towers are used to elevate the radio antennas to account for the earth's curvature and maintain a clear line-of-sight path between the two parabolic reflectors; see Figure 3.12.

MANAGEMENT FOCUS 3.4

MUNICH AIRPORT PROVIDES WIRELESS HOTSPOTS

Munich is Germany's second-largest commercial airport, handling over 23 million passengers per year. It began offering wireless Internet access in its terminal buildings and main concourse in October 2001 and was the first wireless local area network provider to give users a choice of Internet Service Providers (ISP).

Travelers can use their home or work ISP when on the move, greatly simplifying access and billing. ISPs, which will benefit from increased loyalty and revenues, are already planning to use the pioneering multi-service provider concept elsewhere, so ultimately users may be able to travel wherever they want without having to change ISP or pay additional fees.

The hotspots are located throughout the airport. Users simply have to turn on their wireless-equipped computers and they will immediately have access to the network. If they are not existing customers of one of the offered ISPs, they can choose to access the Internet by paying €5.00–€8.00 per hour, depending upon the ISP.

SOURCE: "Munich Airport Uses Cisco Technology to Break New WiFi Ground with the World's First Multiple ISP Hotspot" www.cisco.com, and "Wireless LAN pilot project a success. Up to 3,000 users a month tap in to wireless Internet access," www.munich-airport.de.

FIGURE 3.12 A Microwave tower. The round antennas are microwave antennas and the straight antennas are cell phone antennas
Source: Matej, Pribelsky listock photo

This transmission medium is typically used for long-distance data or voice transmission. It does not require the laying of any cable, because long-distance antennas with microwave repeater stations can be placed approximately 25 to 50 miles apart. A typical long-distance antenna might be ten feet wide, although over shorter distances in the inner cities, the dish antennas can be less than two feet in diameter. The airwaves in larger cities are becoming congested because so many microwave dish antennas have been installed that they interfere with one another.

Satellite **Satellite transmission** is similar to microwave transmission except instead of transmission involving another nearby microwave dish antenna, it involves a satellite many miles up in space. Figure 3.13 depicts a geosynchronous satellite. *Geosynchronous* means that the satellite remains stationary over one point on the earth. One disadvantage of satellite transmission is the *propagation delay* that occurs because the signal has to

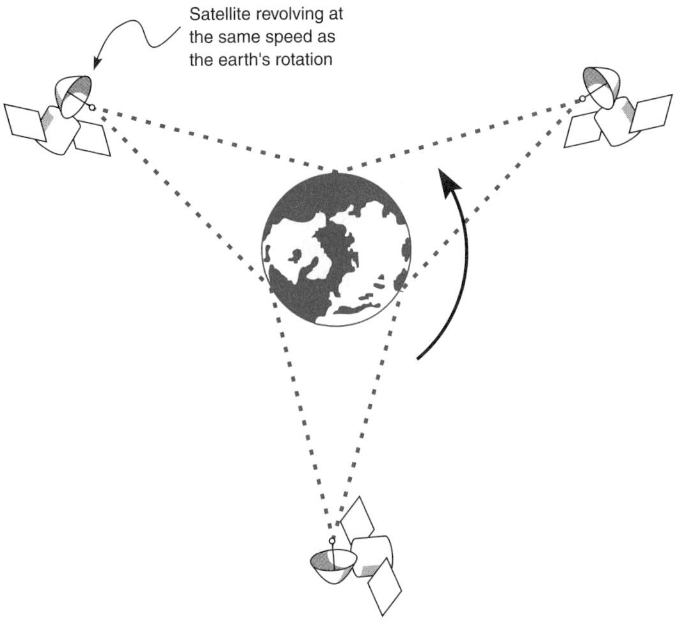

FIGURE 3.13 Satellites in operation

travel out into space and back to earth, a distance of many miles that even at the speed of light can be noticeable. Low earth orbit (LEO) satellites are placed in lower orbits to minimize propogation delay. Satellite transmission is sometimes also affected by *raindrop attenuation* when satellite transmissions are absorbed by heavy rain. It is not a major problem, but engineers need to work around it.

MANAGEMENT FOCUS 3.5 SATELLITE COMMUNICATIONS IMPROVE PERFORMANCE

Boyle Transportation hauls hazardous materials nationwide for both commercial customers and the government, particularly the U.S. Department of Defense. The Department of Defense recently mandated that hazardous materials contractors use mobile communications systems with up-to-the-minute monitoring when hauling the department's hazardous cargoes.

After looking at the alternatives, Boyle realized that it would have to build its own system. Boyle needed a relational database at its operations center that contained information about customers, pickups, deliveries, truck location, and truck operating status. Data is distributed from this database via satellite to an antenna on each truck. Now, at any time, Boyle can notify the designated truck to make a new pickup via the bidirectional satellite link and record the truck's acknowledgment.

Each truck contains a mobile data terminal connected to the satellite network. Each driver uses a keyboard to enter information, which transmits the location of the truck. This satellite data is received by the main offices via a leased line from the satellite earth station.

This system increased productivity by an astounding 80 percent over 2 years; administration costs increased by only 20 percent.

Media Selection

Which media are best? It is hard to say, particularly when manufacturers continue to improve various media products. Several factors are important in selecting media (Figure 3.14).

- The *type of network* is one major consideration. Some media are used only for WANs (microwaves and satellite), whereas others typically are not (twisted-pair, coaxial cable, radio, and infrared), although we should note that some old WAN networks still use twisted-pair cable. Fiber-optic cable is unique in that it can be used for virtually any type of network.
- *Cost* is always a factor in any business decision. Costs are always changing as new technologies are developed and as competition among vendors drives prices down. Among the guided media, twisted-pair wire is generally the cheapest, coaxial cable is somewhat more expensive, and fiber-optic cable is the most expensive. The cost of the wireless media is generally driven more by distance than any other factor. For very short distances (several hundred meters), radio and infrared are the cheapest; for moderate distances (several hundred miles), microwave is cheapest; and for long distances, satellite is cheapest.
- *Transmission distance* is a related factor. Twisted pair wire, coaxial cable, infrared, and radio can transmit data only a short distance before the signal must be regenerated. Twisted-pair wire and radio typically can transmit up to 100 to 300 meters, and coaxial cable and infrared typically between 200 and 500 meters. Fiber optics can transmit up to 75 miles, with new types of fiber-optic cable expected to reach more than 600 miles.

Guided Media						
Media	**Network Type**	**Cost**	**Transmission Distance**	**Security**	**Error Rates**	**Speed**
Twisted Pair	LAN	Low	Short	Good	Low	Low-high
Coaxial Cable	LAN	Moderate	Short	Good	Low	Low-high
Fiber Optics	Any	High	Moderate-long	Very good	Very low	High-very high

Radiated Media						
Media	**Network Type**	**Cost**	**Transmission Distance**	**Security**	**Error Rates**	**Speed**
Radio	LAN	Low	Short	Poor	Moderate	Moderate
Infrared	LAN, BN	Low	Short	Poor	Moderate	Low
Microwave	WAN	Moderate	Long	Poor	Low-moderate	Moderate
Satellite	WAN	Moderate	Long	Poor	Low-moderate	Moderate

FIGURE 3.14 Media summary. BN = backbone network; LAN = local area network; WAN = wide area network

- *Security* is primarily determined by whether the media is guided or wireless. Wireless media (radio, infrared, microwave, and satellite) are the least secure because their signals are easily intercepted. Guided media (twisted pair, coaxial, and fiber optics) are more secure, with fiber optics being the most secure.
- *Error rates* are also important. Wireless media are most susceptible to interference and thus have the highest error rates. Among the guided media, fiber optics provides the lowest error rates, coaxial cable the next best, and twisted-pair cable the worst, although twisted-pair cable is generally better than the wireless media.
- *Transmission speeds* vary greatly among the different media. It is difficult to quote specific speeds for different media because transmission speeds are constantly improving and because they vary within the same type of media, depending on the specific type of cable and the vendor. In general, both twisted-pair cable and coaxial cable can provide data rates of between 1 and 100 Mbps (1 million bits per second), whereas fiber-optic cable ranges between 100 Mbps and 10 Gbps (10 billion bits per second). Radio and infrared generally provide 1 to 50 Mbps, as do microwave and satellite.

DIGITAL TRANSMISSION OF DIGITAL DATA

All computer systems produce binary data. For these data to be understood by both the sender and receiver, both must agree on a standard system for representing the letters, numbers, and symbols that compose messages. The **coding scheme** is the language that computers use to represent data.

Coding

A *character* is a symbol that has a common, constant meaning. A character might be the letter *A* or *B,* or it might be a number such as *1* or *2.* Characters also may be special symbols such as ? or &. Characters in data communications, as in computer systems, are represented by groups of *bits* that are binary zeros (0) and ones (1). The groups of bits representing the set of characters that are the "alphabet" of any given system are called a *coding scheme,* or simply a *code.*

A *byte* is a group of consecutive bits that is treated as a unit or character. One byte normally is composed of 8 bits and usually represents one character; however, in data communications, some codes use 5, 6, 7, 8, or 9 bits to represent a character. For example, representation of the character *A* by a group of 8 bits (say, 01 000 001) is an example of coding.

There are three predominant coding schemes in use today. **United States of America Standard Code for Information Interchange (USASCII,** or, more commonly, **ASCII**) is the most popular code for data communications and is the standard code on most microcomputers. There are two types of ASCII; one is a seven-bit code that has 128 valid character combinations, and the other is an eight-bit code that has 256 combinations. The number of combinations can be determined by taking the number 2 and raising it to the power equal to the number of bits in the code because each bit has two possible values, a 0 or a 1. In this case $2^7 = 128$ characters or $2^8 = 256$ characters.

A second commonly used coding scheme is **ISO 8859,** which is standardized by the International Standards Organization, ISO 8859 is an eight-bit code that includes the ASCII codes plus non-English letters used by many European languages (e.g., letters with acents). If you look closely at Figure 2.20, you will see that HTML often uses ISO 8859.

Unicode is the other commonly used coding scheme. There are many different versions of Unicode. UTF-8 is an eight-bit version which is very similar to ASCII. UTF-16, which uses 16-bits per character (i.e. two bytes, called a "word"), is used by Windows. By using more bits, UTF-16 can represent many more characters beyond the usual English or Latin characters, such as Cyrillic or Chinese.

We can choose any pattern of bits we like to represent any character we like, as long as all computers understand what each bit pattern represents. Figure 3.15 shows the eight-bit binary bit patterns used to represent a few of the characters we use in ASCII.

Transmission Modes

Parallel **Parallel transmission** is the way the internal transfer of binary data takes place inside a computer. If the internal structure of the computer is eight-bit, then all eight bits of the data element are transferred between main memory and the central processing unit simultaneously on eight separate connections. The same is true of computers that use a 32-bit structure; all 32 bits are transferred simultaneously on 32 connections.

Figure 3.16 shows how all eight bits of one character could travel down a parallel communication circuit. The circuit is physically made up of eight separate wires, wrapped in one outer coating. Each physical wire is used to send one bit of the eight-bit character. However, as far as the user is concerned (and the network for that matter),

Character	ASCII
A	01000001
B	01000010
C	01000011
D	01000100
E	01000101
a	01100001
b	01100010
c	01100011
d	01100100
e	01100101
1	00110001
2	00110010
3	00110011
4	00110100
!	00100001
$	00100100

FIGURE 3.15 Binary numbers used to represent different characters using ASCII

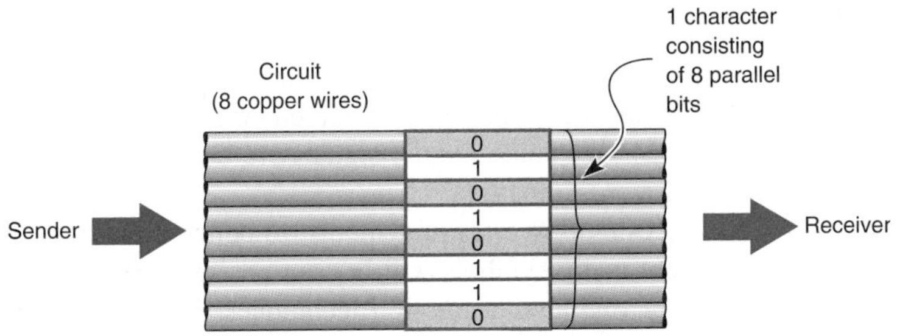

FIGURE 3.16 Parallel transmission of an 8-bit code

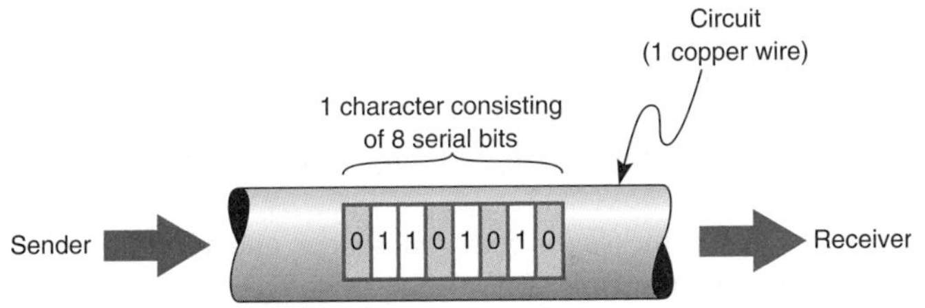

FIGURE 3.17 Serial transmission of an 8-bit code

there is only one circuit; each of the wires inside the cable bundle simply connects to a different part of the plug that connects the computer to the bundle of wire.

Serial **Serial transmission** means that a stream of data is sent over a communication circuit sequentially in a bit-by-bit fashion as shown in Figure 3.17. In this case, there is only one physical wire inside the bundle and all data must be transmitted over that one physical wire. The transmitting device sends one bit, then a second bit, and so on, until all the bits are transmitted. It takes *n* iterations or cycles to transmit *n* bits. Thus, serial transmission is considerably slower than parallel transmission—eight times slower in the case of 8-bit ASCII (because there are 8 bits). Compare Figure 3.17 with Figure 3.16.

TECHNICAL FOCUS 3.1 BASIC ELECTRICITY

There are two general categories of electrical current: direct current and alternating current. *Current* is the movement or flow of electrons, normally from positive (+) to negative (−). The plus (+) or minus (−) measurements are known as **polarity**. *Direct current* (DC) travels in only one direction, whereas *alternating current* (AC) travels first in one direction and then in the other direction.

A copper wire transmitting electricity acts like a hose transferring water. We use three common terms when discussing electricity. *Voltage* is defined as electrical pressure—the amount of electrical force pushing electrons through a circuit. In principle, it is the same as pounds per square inch in a water pipe. *Amperes* (amps) are units of electrical flow, or volume. This measure is analogous to gallons per minute for water. The *watt* is the fundamental unit of electrical power. It is a rate unit, not a quantity. You obtain the wattage by multiplying the volts by the amperes.

Digital Transmission

Digital transmission is the transmission of binary electrical or light pulses in that it only has two possible states, a 1 or a 0. The most commonly encountered voltage levels range from a low of +3/−3 to a high of +24/−24 volts. Digital signals are usually sent over wire of no more than a few thousand feet in length.

All digital transmission techniques require a set of symbols (to define how to send a 1 and a 0), and the symbol rate (how many symbols will be sent per second).

Figure 3.18 shows four types of digital transmission techniques. With **unipolar** signaling, the voltage is always positive or negative (like a DC current). Figure 3.18 illustrates a unipolar technique in which a signal of 0 volts (no current) is used to transmit a zero, and a signal of +5 volts is used to transmit a 1.

An obvious question at this point is this: If 0 volts means a zero, how do you send no data? This is discussed in detail in Chapter 4. For the moment, we will just say that there are ways to indicate when a message starts and stops, and when there are no messages to send, the sender and receiver agree to ignore any electrical signal on the line.

To successfully send and receive a message, both the sender and receiver have to agree on how often the sender can transmit data—that is, on the *symbol rate*. For example, if the symbol rate on a circuit is 64 **Hertz (Hz)** (64,000 symbols per second), then the sender changes the voltage on the circuit once every $^{1}/_{64,000}$ of a

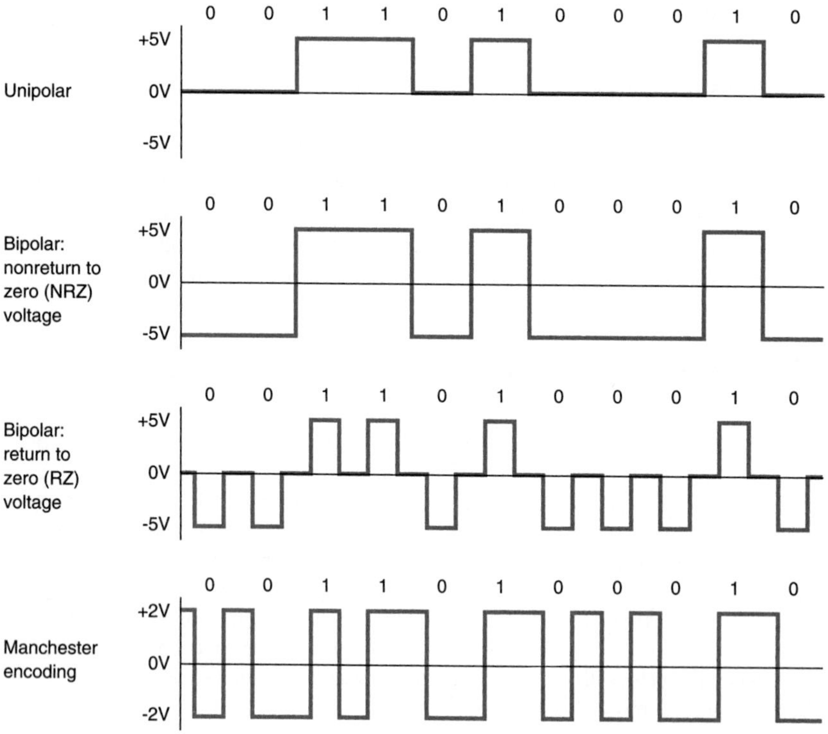

FIGURE 3.18 Unipolar, bipolar, and Manchester signals (digital)

second and the receiver must examine the circuit every $1/_{64,000}$ of a second to read the incoming data.

In **bipolar** signaling, the 1's and 0's vary from a plus voltage to a minus voltage (like an AC current). The first bipolar technique illustrated in Figure 3.18 is called nonreturn to zero (NRZ) because the voltage alternates from +5 volts (a symbol indicating a 1) and −5 volts (a symbol indicating a 0) without ever returning to 0 volts. The second bipolar technique in this figure is called return to zero (RZ) because it always returns to 0 volts after each bit before going to +5 volts (the symbol for a 1) or −5 volts (the symbol for a 0). In Europe, bipolar signaling sometimes is called *double current* signaling because you are moving between a positive and negative voltage potential.

In general, bipolar signaling experiences fewer errors than unipolar signaling because the symbols are more distinct. Noise or interference on the transmission circuit is less likely to cause the bipolar's +5 volts to be misread as a −5 volts than it is to cause the unipolar's 0 volts as a +5 volts. This is because changing the polarity of a current (from positive to negative, or vice versa) is more difficult than changing its magnitude.

How Ethernet Transmits Data

The most common technology used in LANs is Ethernet[3]; if you are working in a computer lab on campus, you are most likely using Ethernet. Ethernet uses digital transmission over either serial or parallel circuits, depending on which version of Ethernet you use. One version of Ethernet that uses serial transmission requires 1/10,000,000 of a second to send one symbol; that is, it transmits 10 million symbols (each of 1 bit) per second. This gives a data rate of 10 Mbps, and if we assume that there are 8 bits in each character, this means that about 1.25 million characters can be transmitted per second in the circuit.

Ethernet uses **Manchester encoding.** Manchester encoding is a special type of bipolar signaling in which the signal is changed from high to low or from low to high in the middle of the signal. A change from high to low is used to represent a 0, whereas the opposite (a change from low to high) is used to represent a 1. See Figure 3.18. Manchester encoding is less susceptible to having errors go undetected, because if there is no transition in midsignal the receiver knows that an error must have occurred.

ANALOG TRANSMISSION OF DIGITAL DATA

Telephone networks were originally built for human speech rather than for data. They were designed to transmit the electrical representation of sound waves, rather than the binary data used by computers. There are many occasions when data need to be transmitted over a voice communications network. Many people working at home still use a modem over their telephone line to connect to the Internet.

[3]If you don't know what Ethernet is, don't worry. We will discuss Ethernet in Chapter 6.

The telephone system (commonly called **POTS** for **plain old telephone service**) enables voice communication between any two telephones within its network. The telephone converts the sound waves produced by the human voice at the sending end into electrical signals for the telephone network. These electrical signals travel through the network until they reach the other telephone and are converted back into sound waves.

Analog transmission occurs when the signal sent over the transmission media continuously varies from one state to another in a wavelike pattern much like the human voice. Modems translate the digital binary data produced by computers into the analog signals required by voice transmission circuits. One modem is used by the transmitter to produce the analog signals and a second by the receiver to translate the analog signals back into digital signals.

The sound waves transmitted through the voice circuit have three important characteristics (see Figure 3.19). The first is the height of the wave, called **amplitude.** Amplitude is measured in decibels (dB). Our ears detect amplitude as the loudness or volume of sound. Every sound wave has two parts, half above the zero amplitude point (i.e., positive) and half below (i.e., negative), and both halves are always the same height.

The second characteristic is the length of the wave, usually expressed as the number of waves per second, or **frequency.** Frequency is expressed in hertz (Hz).[4] Our ears detect frequency as the pitch of the sound. Frequency is the inverse of the length of the sound wave, so that a high frequency means that there are many short waves in a one-second interval, whereas a low frequency means that there are fewer (but longer) waves in 1 second.

The third characteristic is the **phase,** which refers to the direction in which the wave begins. Phase is measured in the number of degrees ($^\circ$). The wave in Figure 3.19 starts up and to the right, which is defined as 0° phase wave. Waves can also start down and to the right (a 180° phase wave), and in virtually any other part of the sound wave.

Modulation

When we transmit data through the telephone lines, we use the shape of the sound waves we transmit (in terms of amplitude, frequency, and phase) to represent different data

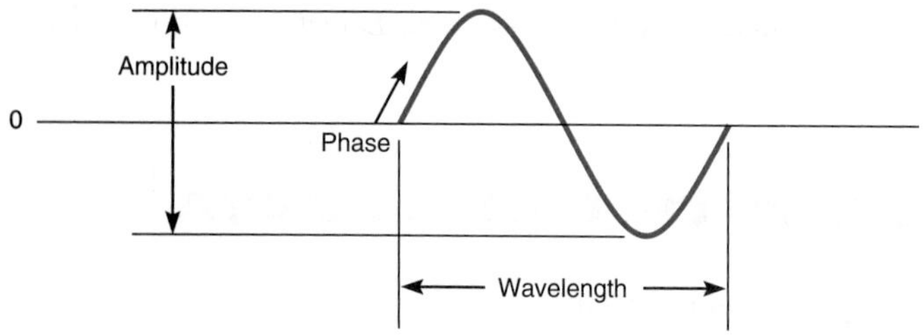

FIGURE 3.19 Sound wave

[4]Hertz is the same as **"cycles per second"**; therefore, 20,000 Hertz is equal to 20,000 cycles per second. One hertz (HZ) is the same as 1 cycle per second. One kilohertz (KHZ) is 1,000 cycles per second (kilocycles); 1 megahertz (MHZ) is 1 million cycles per second (megacycles); and 1 gigahertz (GHZ) is 1 billion cycles per second.

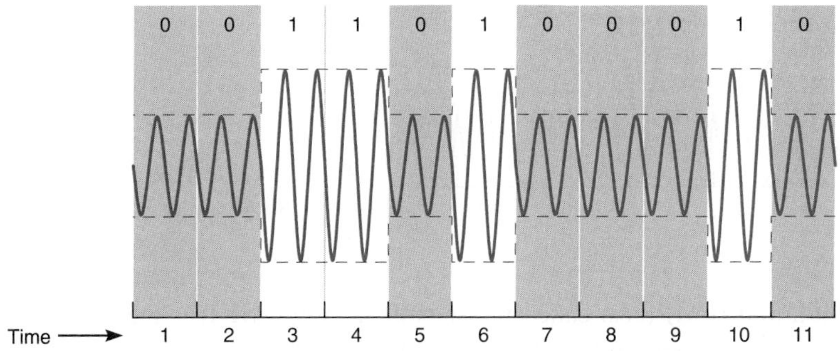

FIGURE 3.20 Amplitude modulation

values. We do this by transmitting a simple sound wave through the circuit (called the **carrier wave**) and then changing its shape in different ways to represent a 1 or a 0. *Modulation* is the technical term used to refer to these "shape changes." There are three fundamental modulation techniques: amplitude modulation, frequency modulation, and phase modulation. Once again, the sender and receiver have to agree on what symbols will be used (what amplitude, frequency, and phase will represent a 1 and a 0) and on the symbol rate (how many symbols will be sent per second).

Basic Modulation With **amplitude modulation (AM)** (also called **amplitude shift keying [ASK]**), the amplitude or height of the wave is changed. One amplitude is the symbol defined to be 0, and another amplitude is the symbol defined to be a 1. In the AM shown in Figure 3.20, the highest amplitude symbol (tallest wave) represents a binary 1 and the lowest amplitude symbol represents a binary 0. In this case, when the sending device wants to transmit a 1, it would send a high-amplitude wave (i.e., a loud signal). AM is more susceptible to noise (more errors) during transmission than is frequency modulation or phase modulation.

Frequency modulation (FM) (also called **frequency shift keying [FSK]**) is a modulation technique whereby each 0 or 1 is represented by a number of waves per second (i.e., a different frequency). In this case, the amplitude does not vary. One frequency (i.e., a certain number of waves per second) is the symbol defined to be a 1, and a different frequency (a different number of waves per second) is the symbol defined to be a 0. In Figure 3.21, the higher-frequency wave symbol (more waves per time period) equals a binary 1, and the lower frequency wave symbol equals a binary 0.

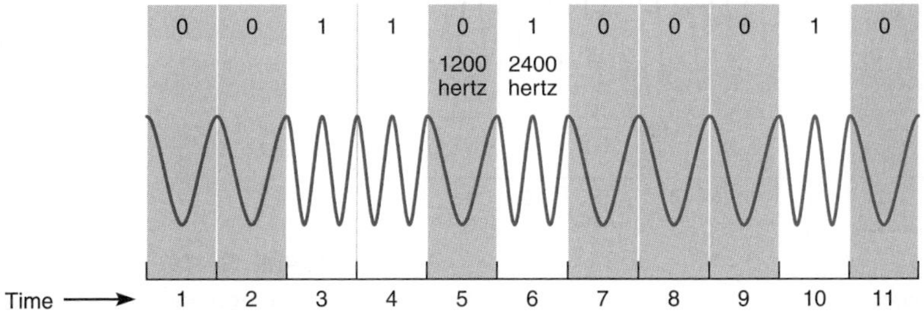

FIGURE 3.21 Frequency modulation

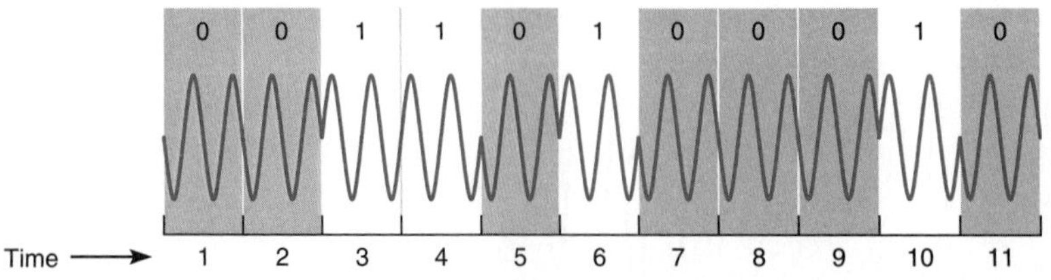

FIGURE 3.22 Phase modulation

Phase modulation (PM) (also called **phase shift keying [PSK]**) is the most difficult to understand. *Phase* refers to the direction in which the wave begins. Until now, the waves we have shown start by moving up and to the right (this is called a 0° phase wave). Waves can also start down and to the right. This is called a phase of 180°. With phase modulation, one phase symbol is defined to be a 0 and the other phase symbol is defined to be a 1. Figure 3.22 shows the case where a phase of 0° symbol is defined to be a binary 0 and a phase of 180° symbol is defined to be a binary 1.

Sending Multiple Bits Simultaneously

Each of the three basic modulation techniques (AM, FM, and PM) can be refined to send more than 1 bit at one time. For example, basic AM sends 1 bit per wave (or *symbol*) by defining two different amplitudes, one for a 1 and one for a 0. It is possible to send 2 bits on one wave or symbol by defining four different amplitudes. Figure 3.23 shows the case where the highest-amplitude wave is defined to be a symbol representing two bits, both 1's. The next highest amplitude is the symbol defined to mean first a 1 and then a 0, and so on.

This technique could be further refined to send 3 bits at the same time by defining 8 different symbols, each with different amplitude levels or 4 bits by defining 16 symbols, each with different amplitude levels, and so on. At some point, however, it becomes very difficult to differentiate between the different amplitudes. The differences are so small that even a small amount of noise could destroy the signal.

This same approach can be used for FM and PM. Two bits could be sent on the same symbol by defining four different frequencies, one for 11, one for 10, and so on, or

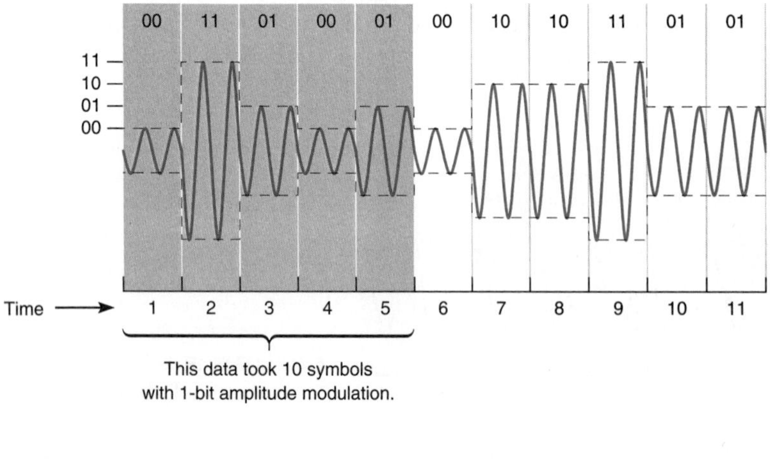

FIGURE 3.23 Two-bit amplitude modulation

by defining four phases (0°, 90°, 180°, and 270°). Three bits could be sent by defining symbols with eight frequencies or eight phases (0°, 45°, 90°, 135°, 180°, 225°, 270°, and 315°). These techniques are also subject to the same limitations as AM; as the number of different frequencies or phases becomes larger, it becomes difficult to differentiate among them.

It is also possible to combine modulation techniques—that is, to use AM, FM, and PM techniques on the same circuit. For example, we could combine AM with four defined amplitudes (capable of sending 2 bits) with FM with four defined frequencies (capable of sending 2 bits) to enable us to send 4 bits on the same symbol.

One popular technique is **quadrature amplitude modulation (QAM).** QAM involves splitting the symbol into eight different phases (3 bits) and two different amplitudes (1 bit), for a total of 16 different possible values. Thus, one symbol in QAM can represent 4 bits. A newer version of QAM called 64-QAM sends 6 bits per symbol and is used in wireless LANs.

Bit Rate versus Baud Rate versus Symbol Rate

The terms **bit rate** (i.e., the number bits per second transmitted) and **baud rate** are used incorrectly much of the time. They often are used interchangeably, but they are not the same. In reality, the network designer or network user is interested in bits per second because it is the bits that are assembled into characters, characters into words and, thus, business information.

A *bit* is a unit of information. A *baud* is a unit of signaling speed used to indicate the number of times per second the signal on the communication circuit changes. Because of the confusion over the term *baud rate* among the general public, ITU-T now recommends the term *baud rate* be replaced by the term *symbol rate.* The bit rate and the symbol rate (or baud rate) are the same only when one bit is sent on each symbol. For example, if we use AM with two amplitudes, we send one bit on one symbol. Here, the bit rate equals the symbol rate. However, if we use QAM, we can send 4 bits on every symbol; the bit rate would be four times the symbol rate. If we used 64-QAM, the bit rate would be six times the symbol rate. Virtually all of today's modems send multiple bits per symbol.

Capacity of a Circuit

The data capacity of a circuit is the fastest rate at which you can send your data over the circuit in terms of the number of bits per second. The **data rate** (or bit rate) is calculated by multiplying the number of bits sent on each symbol by the maximum symbol rate. As we discussed in the previous section, the number of bits per symbol depends on the modulation technique (e.g., QAM sends 4 bits per symbol).

The maximum symbol rate in any circuit depends on the bandwidth available and the signal-to-noise ratio (the strength of the signal compared with the amount of noise in the circuit). The **bandwidth** is the difference between the highest and the lowest frequencies in a band or set of frequencies. The range of human hearing is between 20 Hz and 14,000 Hz, so its bandwidth is 13,880 Hz. The maximum symbol rate for analog transmission is usually the same as the bandwidth as measured in Hertz. If the circuit is very noisy, the maximum symbol rate may fall as low as 50 percent of the bandwidth. If the circuit has very little noise, it is possible to transmit at rates up to the bandwidth.

Digital transmission symbol rates can reach as high as two times the bandwidth for techniques that have only one voltage change per symbol (e.g., NRZ). For digital techniques that have two voltage changes per symbol (e.g., RZ, Manchester), the maximum symbol rate is the same as the bandwidth.

Standard telephone lines provide a bandwidth of 4,000 Hz. Under perfect circumstances, the maximum symbol rate is therefore about 4,000 symbols per second. If we were to use basic AM (1 bit per symbol), the maximum data rate would be 4,000 **bits per second (bps).** If we were to use QAM (4 bits per symbol), the maximum data rate would be 4 bits per symbol × 4,000 symbols per second = 16,000 bps. A circuit with a 10 MHz bandwidth using 64-QAM could provide up to 60 Mbps.

How Modems Transmit Data

The **modem** (an acronym for *mo*dulator/*dem*odulator) takes the digital data from a computer in the form of electrical pulses and converts them into the analog signal that is needed for transmission over an analog voice-grade circuit. There are many different types of modems available today from dial-up modems to cable modems. For data to be transmitted between two computers using modems, both need to use the same type of modem. Fortunately, several standards exist for modems, and any modem that conforms to a standard can communicate with any other modem that conforms to the same standard.

A modem's data transmission rate is the primary factor that determines the throughput rate of data, but it is not the only factor. **Data compression** can increase throughput of data over a communication link by literally compressing the data. **V.44,** the ISO standard for data compression, uses **Lempel-Ziv encoding.** As a message is being transmitted, Lempel-Ziv encoding builds a dictionary of two-, three-, and four-character combinations that occur in the message. Anytime the same character pattern reoccurs in the message, the index to the dictionary entry is transmitted rather than sending the actual data. The reduction provided by V.44 compression depends on the actual data sent but usually averages about 6:1 (i.e., almost six times as much data can be sent per second using V.44 as without it).

DIGITAL TRANSMISSION OF ANALOG DATA

In the same way that digital computer data can be sent over analog telephone networks using analog transmission, analog voice data can be sent over digital networks using digital transmission. This process is somewhat similar to the analog transmission of digital data. A pair of special devices called *codecs* (*co*de/*dec*ode) is used in the same way that a pair of modems is used to translate the data to send across the circuit. One codec is attached to the source of the signal (e.g., a telephone or the local loop at the end office) and translates the incoming analog voice signal into a digital signal for transmission across the digital circuit. A second codec at the receiver's end translates the digital data back into analog data.

Translating from Analog to Digital

Analog voice data must first be translated into a series of binary digits before they can be transmitted over a digital circuit. This is done by sampling the amplitude of the sound wave at regular intervals and translating it into a binary number. Figure 3.24 shows an example where eight different amplitude levels are used (i.e., each amplitude level is represented by three bits). The top diagram shows the original signal, and the bottom diagram, the digitized signal.

A quick glance will show that the digitized signal is only a rough approximation of the original signal. The original signal had a smooth flow, but the digitized signal has

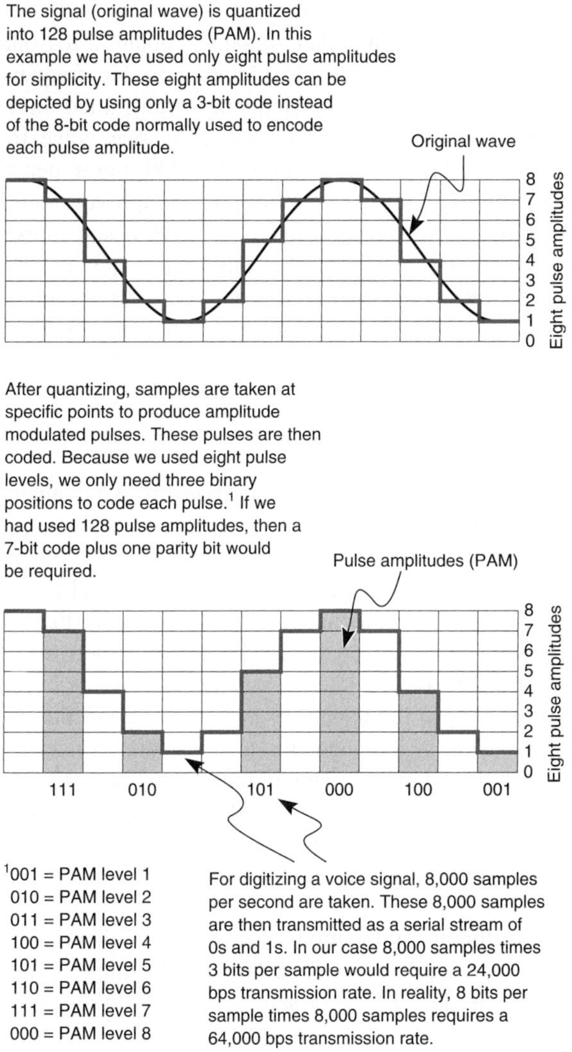

FIGURE 3.24 Pulse amplitude modulation (PAM)

jagged "steps." The difference between the two signals is called **quantizing error.** Voice transmissions using digitized signals that have a great deal of quantizing error sound metallic or machinelike to the ear.

There are two ways to reduce quantizing error and improve the quality of the digitized signal, but neither is without cost. The first method is to increase the number of amplitude levels. This minimizes the difference between the levels (the "height" of the "steps") and results in a smoother signal. In Figure 3.24, we could define 16 amplitude levels instead of eight levels. This would require four bits (rather than the current three bits) to represent the amplitude, thus increasing the amount of data needed to transmit the digitized signal.

No amount of levels or bits will ever result in perfect-quality sound reproduction, but in general, seven bits ($2^7 = 128$ levels) reproduces human speech adequately. Music, on the other hand, typically uses 16 bits ($2^{16} = 65{,}536$ levels).

The second method is to sample more frequently. This will reduce the "length" of each "step," also resulting in a smoother signal. To obtain a reasonable-quality voice signal, one must sample at least twice the highest possible frequency in the analog signal. You will recall that the highest frequency transmitted in telephone circuits is 4,000 Hz. Thus, the methods used to digitize telephone voice transmissions must sample the input voice signal at a minimum of 8,000 times per second. Sampling more frequently than this (called *oversampling*) will improve signal quality. RealNet works.com, which produces Real Audio and other Web-based tools, sets its products to sample at 48,000 times per second to provide higher quality. The iPod and most CDs sample at 44,100 times per second and use 16 bits per sample to produce almost error-free music. MP3 players often sample less frequently and use fewer bits per sample to produce smaller transmissions, but the sound quality may suffer.

How Telephones Transmit Voice Data

When you make a telephone call, the telephone converts your analog voice data into a simple analog signal and sends it down the circuit from your home to the telephone company's network. This process is almost unchanged from the one used by Bell when he invented the telephone in 1876. With the invention of digital transmission, the common carriers (i.e., the telephone companies) began converting their voice networks to use digital transmission. Today, all of the common carrier networks use digital transmission, except in the **local loop** (sometimes called the *last mile*), the wires that run from your home or business to the telephone switch that connects your local loop into the telephone network. This **switch** contains a codec that converts the analog signal from your phone into a digital signal. This digital signal is then sent through the telephone network until it hits the switch for local loop for the person you are calling. This switch uses its codec to convert the digital signal used inside the phone network back into the analog signal needed by that person's local loop and telephone. See Figure 3.25.

There are many different combinations of sampling frequencies and numbers of bits per sample that could be used. For example, one could sample 4,000 times per second using 128 amplitude levels (i.e., 7 bits) or sample at 16,000 times per second using 256 levels (i.e., 8 bits).

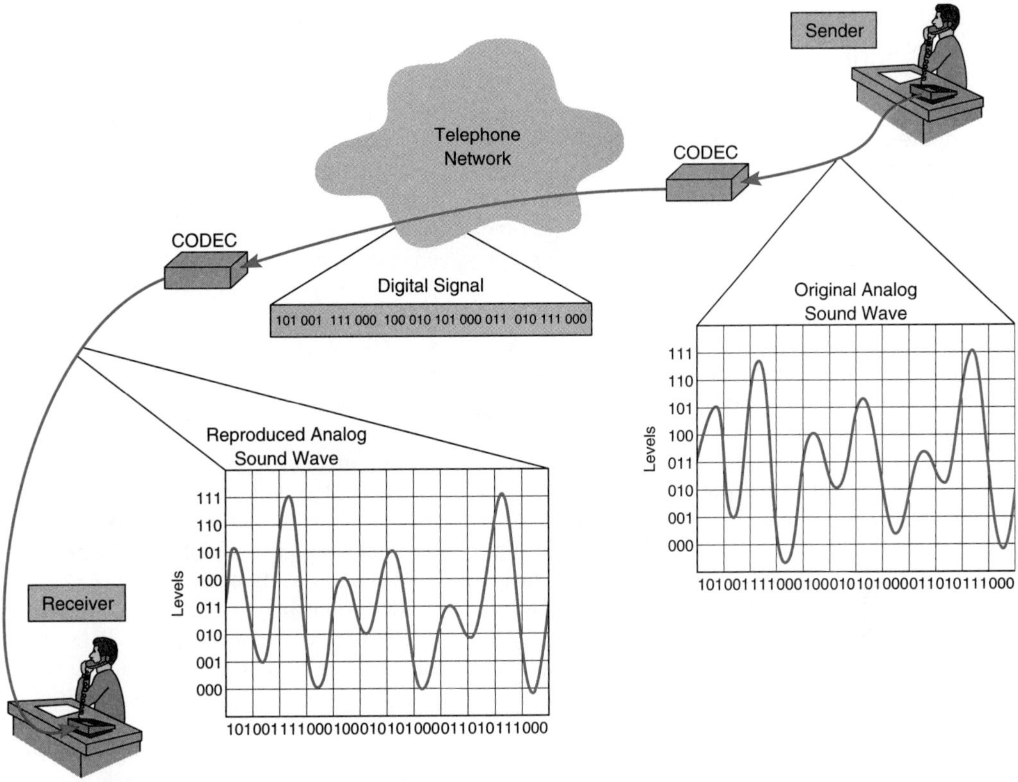

FIGURE 3.25 Pulse amplitude modulation (PAM)

The North American telephone network uses **pulse code modulation (PCM).** With PCM, the input voice signal is sampled 8,000 times per second. Each time the input voice signal is sampled, 8 bits are generated.[5] Therefore, the transmission speed on the digital circuit must be 64,000 bps (8 bits per sample $\times$ 8,000 samples per second) to transmit a voice signal when it is in digital form. Thus, the North American telephone network is built using millions of 64 Kbps digital circuits that connect via codecs to the millions of miles of analog local loop circuits into the users' residences and businesses.

How Instant Messenger Transmits Voice Data

A 64 Kbps digital circuit works very well for transmitting voice data because it provides very good quality. The problem is that it requires a lot of capacity.

Adaptive differential pulse code modulation (**ADPCM**) is the alternative used by IM and many other applications that provide voice services over lower-speed digital circuits. ADPCM works in much the same way as PCM. It samples incoming voice signal 8,000 times per second and calculates the same 8-bit amplitude value as PCM. However, instead of transmitting the 8-bit value, it transmits the *difference* between the 8-bit value

[5]Seven of those bits are used to represent the voice signal, and 1 bit is used for control purposes.

MANAGEMENT FOCUS

3.6 Networking Your Car

Cars are increasingly becoming computers on wheels. About 30% of the cost of a car lies in its electronics—chips, networks, and software. Computers have been used in cars for many years for driving control (e.g., engine management systems, antilock brakes, air bag controls), but as CD players, integrated telephones (e.g., Cadillac's OnStar), and navigation systems become more common, the demands on car networks are quickly increasing. More manufacturers are moving to digital computer controls rather than traditional analog controls for many of the car's basic functions (e.g., BMW's iDrive), making the car network a critical part of car design.

In many ways, a car network is similar to a local area network. There are a set of devices (e.g., throttle control, brakes, fuel injection, CD player, navigation system) connected by a network. Traditionally, each device has used its own proprietary protocol. Today, manufacturers are quickly moving to adopt standards to ensure that all components work together across one common network. One common standard is Media-Oriented Systems Transport (MOST). Any device that conforms to the MOST standard can be plugged into the network and can communicate with the other devices.

The core of the MOST standard is a set of 25 or 40 megabit per second fiber-optic cables that run throughout the car. Fiber-optic cabling was chosen over more traditional coaxial or twisted pair cabling because it provides a high capacity sufficient for most future predicted needs, is not susceptible to interference, and weighs less than coaxial or twisted pair cables. Compared to coaxial or twisted pair cables, fiber-optic cables saves hundreds of feet of cabling and tens of pounds of weight in a typical car. Weight is important in car design, whether it is a high performance luxury sedan or an economical entry level car, because increased weight decreases both performance and gas mileage.

As digital devices such as Bluetooth phones and Wi-Fi wireless computer networks become standard on cars, the push to digital networks will only increase.

SOURCE: "That Network is the MOST," *Roundel,* October 2003, pp. 31-37; "Networks drive the car of the future," *NetworkWorld,* May 23, 2005, pp. 70-74.

in the last time interval and the current 8-bit value (i.e., how the amplitude has *changed* from one time period to another). Because analog voice signals change slowly, these changes can be adequately represented by using only 4 bits. This means that ADPCM can be used on digital circuits that provide only 32 Kbps (4 bits per sample × 8,000 samples per second = 32,000 bps).

Several versions of ADPCM have been developed and standardized by the ITU-T. There are versions designed for 8 Kbps circuits (which send 1 bit 8,000 times per second) and 16 Kbps circuits (which send 2 bits 8,000 times per second), as well as the original 32 Kbps version. However, there is a trade-off here. Although the 32 Kbps version usually provides as good a sound quality as that of a traditional voice telephone circuit, the 8 Kbps and 16 Kbps versions provide poorer sound quality.

Voice over Internet Protocol (VoIP)

Voice over Internet Protocol (VoIP, pronounced voyp) is commonly used to transmit phone conversations over digital networks. VoIP is a relatively new standard that uses digital telephones with built-in codecs to convert analog voice data into digital data

FIGURE 3.26 VoIP phone
Source: Cisco Systems, Inc.

(see Figure 3.26). Because the codec is built into the telephone, the telephone transmits digital data and therefore can be connected directly into a Local Area Network, in much the same manner as a typical computer. Because VoIP phones operate on the same networks as computers, we can reduce the amount of wiring needed; with VoIP, we need to operate and maintain only one network throughout our offices, rather than two separate networks—one for voice and one for data. However, this also means that data networks with VoIP phones must be designed to operate in emergencies (to enable 911 calls) even when the power fails; they must have uninterruptable power supplies (UPS) for all network circuits.

One commonly used VoIP standard is G.722 wideband audio, which is a version of ADPCM that operates at 64 Kbps. It samples 8,000 times per second and produces eight bits per sample.

Because VoIP phones are digital, they can also contain additional capabilities. For example, high-end VoIP phones often contain computer chips to enable them to download and install small software applications so that they can function in many ways like computers.

IMPLICATIONS FOR MANAGEMENT

In the past, networks used to be designed so that the physical cables transported data in the same form in which the data was created: analog voice data generated by telephones used to be carried by analog transmission cables and digital computer data used to be carried by digital transmission cables. Today, it is simple to separate the different types of data (analog voice or digital computer) from the actual physical cables used to carry the data. In most cases, the cheapest and highest-quality media are digital, which means that most data today are transmitted in digital form. Thus the convergence of voice and video and data at the physical layers is being driven primarily by business reasons: digital is better.

The change in physical layers also has implications for organizational structure. Voice data used to be managed separately from computer data because they use different types of networks. As the physical networks converge, so too do the organizational units responsible for managing the data. Today, more organizations are placing the management of voice telecommunications into their information systems organizations.

This also has implications for the telecommunications industry. Over the past five years, the historical separation between manufacturers of networking equipment used in organizations and manufacturers of networking equipment used by the telephone companies has crumbled. There have been some big winners and losers in the stock market from the consolidation of these markets.

SUMMARY

Circuits Networks can be configured so that there is a separate circuit from each client to the host (called a point-to-point configuration) or so that several clients share the same circuit (a multipoint configuration). Data can flow through the circuit in one direction only (simplex), in both directions simultaneously (full duplex), or by taking turns so that data sometimes flow in one direction and then in the other (half duplex). A multiplexer is a device that combines several simultaneous low-speed circuits on one higher-speed circuit so that each low-speed circuit believes it has a separate circuit. In general, the transmission capacity of the high-speed circuit must equal or exceed the sum of the low-speed circuits.

Communication Media Media are either guided, in that they travel through a physical cable (e.g., twisted-pair wires, coaxial cable, or fiber-optic cable), or wireless, in that they are broadcast through the air (e.g., radio, infrared, microwave, or satellite). Among the guided media, fiber-optic cable can transmit data the fastest with the fewest errors and offers greater security but costs the most; twisted-pair wire is the cheapest and most commonly used. The choice of wireless media depends more on distance than on any other factor; infrared and radio are the cheapest for short distances, microwave is cheapest for moderate distances, and satellite is cheapest for long distances.

Digital Transmission of Digital Data Digital transmission (also called baseband transmission) is done by sending a series of electrical (or light) pulse through the media. Digital transmission is preferred to analog transmission because it produces fewer errors; is more efficient; permits higher maximum transmission rates; is more secure; and simplifies the integration of voice, video, and data on the same circuit. With unipolar digital transmission, the voltage changes between 0 volts to represent a binary 0 and some positive value (e.g., +15 volts) to represent a binary 1. With bipolar digital transmission, the voltage changes polarity (i.e., positive or negative) to represent a 1 or a 0. Bipolar is less susceptible to errors. Ethernet uses Manchester encoding, which is a version of unipolar transmission.

Analog Transmission of Digital Data Modems are used to translate the digital data produced by computers into the analog signals for transmission in today's voice communication circuits. Both the sender and receiver need to have a modem. Data is transmitted by changing (or modulating) a carrier sound wave's amplitude (height), frequency (length), or phase (shape) to indicate a binary 1 or 0. For example, in amplitude modulation, one amplitude is defined to be a 1 and another amplitude is defined to be a 0. It is possible to send more than 1 bit on every symbol (or wave). For example, with amplitude modulation, you could send 2 bits on each wave by defining four amplitude levels. The capacity or maximum data rate that a circuit can transmit is determined by multiplying the symbol rate (symbols per second) by the number of bits per symbol. Generally (but not always), the symbol rate is the same as the bandwidth, so bandwidth is often used as a measure of capacity. V.44 is a data compression standard that can be combined with any of the foregoing types of modems to reduce the amount of data in the transmitted signal by a factor of up to six. Thus, a V.92 modem using V.44 could provide an effective data rate of $56{,}000 \times 6 =$ 336, 000 bps.

Digital Transmission of Analog Data Because digital transmission is better, analog voice data is sometimes converted to digital transmission. Pulse code modulation (PCM) is the most commonly used technique. PCM samples the amplitude of the incoming voice signal 8,000 times per second and uses 8 bits to represent the signal. PCM produces a reasonable approximation of the human voice, but more sophisticated techniques are needed to adequately reproduce more complex sounds such as music.

KEY TERMS

adaptive differential pulse code modulation (ADPCM)
American Standard Code for Information Interchange (ASCII)
amplitude
amplitude modulation (AM)
amplitude shift keying (ASK)
analog transmission
bandwidth
baud rate
bipolar
bit rate
bits per second (bps)
Bandwidth on Demand Interoperability Networking Group (BONDING)
carrier wave
channel
circuit
circuit configuration
coaxial cable
codec
coding scheme
customer premises equipment (CPE)
cycles per second
data compression
data rate
digital subscriber line (DSL)
digital transmission
fiber-optic cable
frequency
frequency division multiplexing (FDM)
frequency modulation (FM)
frequency shift keying (FSK)
full-duplex transmission
guardband
guided media
half-duplex transmission
Hertz (Hz)
infrared transmission
inverse multiplexing (IMUX)
ISO 8859
Lempel-Ziv encoding
local loop
logical circuit
Manchester encoding
Microwave transmission
modem
multipoint circuit
multiplexing
parallel transmission
phase
phase modulation (PM)
phase shift keying (PSK)
physical circuit
plain old telephone service (POTS)
point-to-point circuit
polarity
pulse code modulation (PCM)
quadrature amplitude modulation (QAM)
quantizing error
radio transmission
retrain time
satellite transmission
serial transmission
simplex
statistical time division multiplexing (STDM)
switch
symbol rate
time division multiplexing (TDM)
turnaround time
twisted-pair cable
unicode
unipolar
Voice over Internet Protocol (VoIP)
wavelength division multiplexing (WDM)
wireless media
V.44

QUESTIONS

1. How does a multipoint circuit differ from a point-to-point circuit?
2. Describe the three types of data flows.
3. Describe three types of guided media.
4. Describe four types of wireless media.
5. How does analog data differ from digital data?
6. Clearly explain the differences among analog data, analog transmission, digital data, and digital transmission.
7. Explain why most telephone company circuits are now digital.
8. What is coding?

9. Briefly describe three important coding schemes.
10. How is data transmitted in parallel?
11. What feature distinguishes serial mode from parallel mode?
12. How does bipolar signaling differ from unipolar signaling? Why is Manchester encoding more popular than either?
13. What are three important characteristics of a sound wave?
14. What is bandwidth? What is the bandwidth in a traditional North American telephone circuit?
15. Describe how data could be transmitted using amplitude modulation.
16. Describe how data could be transmitted using frequency modulation.
17. Describe how data could be transmitted using phase modulation.
18. Describe how data could be transmitted using a combination of modulation techniques.
19. Is the bit rate the same as the symbol rate? Explain.
20. What is a modem?
21. What is quadrature amplitude modulation (QAM).
22. What is 64-QAM?
23. What factors affect transmission speed?
24. What is oversampling?
25. Why is data compression so useful?
26. What data compression standard uses Lempel-Ziv encoding? Describe how it works.
27. Explain how pulse code modulation (PCM) works.
28. What is quantizing error?
29. What is the term used to describe the placing of two or more signals on a single circuit?
30. What is the purpose of multiplexing?
31. How does DSL (digital subscriber line) work?
32. Of the different types of multiplexing, what distinguishes
    a. frequency division multiplexing (FDM)?
    b. time division multiplexing (TDM)?
    c. statistical time division multiplexing (STDM)?
    d. wavelength division multiplexing (WDM)?
33. What is the function of inverse multiplexing (IMUX)?
34. If you were buying a multiplexer, why would you choose either TDM or FDM? Why?
35. Some experts argue that modems may soon become obsolete. Do you agree? Why or why not?
36. What is the maximum capacity of an analog circuit with a bandwidth of 4,000 Hz using QAM?
37. What is the maximum data rate of an analog circuit with a 10 MHz bandwidth using 64-QAM and V.44?
38. What is the capacity of a digital circuit with a symbol rate of 10 MHz using Manchester encoding?
39. What is the symbol rate of a digital circuit providing 100 Mbps if it uses bipolar NRz signaling?
40. What is VoIP?

EXERCISES

3-1. Investigate the costs of dumb terminals, network computers, minimally equipped microcomputers, and top-of-the-line microcomputers. Many equipment manufacturers and resellers are on the Web, so it's a good place to start looking.

3-2. Investigate the different types of cabling used in your organization and where they are used (e.g., LAN, backbone network).

3-3. Three terminals (T_1, T_2, T_3) are to be connected to three computers (C_1, C_2, C_3) so that T_1 is connected to C_1, T_2 to C_2, and T_3 to C_3. All are in different cities. T_1 and C_1 are 1,500 miles apart, as are T_2 and C_2, and T_3 and C_3. The points T_1, T_2, and T_3 are 25 miles apart, and the points C_1, C_2, and C_3 also are 25 miles apart. If telephone lines cost $1 per mile, what is the line cost for three?

3-4. A few Internet service providers in some areas now have BONDING IMUXs and offer their use to businesses wanting faster Internet access. Search the Web or call your local ISPs to see if they offer this service and if so, how much it costs.

3-5. Draw how the bit pattern 01101100 would be sent using
a. Single-bit AM
b. Single-bit FM
c. Single-bit PM
d. Two-bit AM (i.e., four amplitude levels)
e. Two-bit FM (i.e., four frequencies)
f. Two-bit PM (i.e., four different phases)
g. Single-bit AM combined with single-bit FM
h. Single-bit AM combined with single-bit PM
i. Two-bit AM combined with two-bit PM

3-6. If you had to download a 20-page paper of 400K (bytes) from your professor, approximately how long would it take to transfer it over the following circuits? Assume that control characters add an extra 10 percent to the message.
a. Dial-up modem at 33.6 Kbps
b. Cable modem at 384 Kbps
c. Cable modem at 1.5 Mbps
d. If the modem includes V.44 data compression with a 6:1 data compression ratio, what is the data rate in bits per second you would actually see in choice c above?

MINI-CASES

I. Eureka! (Part 1)

Eureka! is a telephone- and Internet-based concierge service that specializes in obtaining things that are hard to find (e.g., Super Bowl tickets, first-edition books from the 1500s, Fabergé eggs). It currently employs 60 staff members who collectively provide 24-hour coverage (over three shifts). They answer the phones and respond to requests entered on the Eureka! Web site. Much of their work is spent on the phone and on computers searching on the Internet. The company has just leased a new office building and is about to wire it. What media would you suggest the company install in its office and why?

II. Eureka! (Part 2)

Eureka! is a telephone and Internet-based concierge service that specializes in obtaining things that are hard to find (e.g., Super Bowl tickets, first-edition books from the 1500s, Fabergé eggs). It currently employs 60 staff members who work 24 hours per day (over three shifts). Staff answer the phone and respond to requests entered on the Eureka! Web site. Much of their work is spent on the phone and on computers searching on the Internet. What type of connections should Eureka! consider from its offices to the outside world, in terms of phone and Internet? Outline the pros and cons of each alternative below and make a recommendation. The company has four alternatives:

1. Should it use traditional analog services, with standard voice lines, and use modems to dial into its ISP ($40 per month for each voice line plus $20 per month for each Internet access line)?
2. Should the company use standard voice lines but use DSL for its data ($40 per month per line for both services)?
3. Should the company separate its voice and data needs, using standard analog services for voice but finding some advanced digital transmission services for data ($40 per month for each voice line and $300 per month for a circuit with 1.5 Mbps of data)?
4. Should the company search for all digital services for both voice and data ($60 per month for an all-digital circuit that provides two PCM phone lines that can be used for two voice calls, one voice call and one data call at 64 Kbps, or one data call at 128 Kbps)?

III. Amalgamated Stores

Amalgamated Stores is a chain of 50 discount retail clothing stores. Each store has its own computers that are connected over the company's WAN to the central corporate computer via a TDM multiplexer. Each store uses the network primarily to exchange accounting, payroll, and inventory data to and from the corporate head office. The data is gathered into batches of data and transmitted at different times during the day. The network is also used for e-mail, although this is of secondary importance. A sales representative at Discount Networks has approached Amalgamated Stores and suggested that by installing Discount Networks' newest STDM multiplexer, Amalgamated Stores can save money by buying smaller, lower-capacity WAN network circuits for each store without changing the store network. Even though the WAN circuits will be smaller and cheaper, the new STDM multiplexer can still enable all the computers in the store to communicate normally with the central corporate computer. Would you recommend buying the STDM multiplexer? Why or why not? Would you recommend purchasing it if Amalgamated Stores was planning to change its credit card authorization system (used to verify customers' credit cards as they pay for merchandise) to use this network? Why or why not?

IV. Speedy Package

Speedy Package is a same-day package delivery service that operates in Chicago. Each package has a shipping label that is attached to the package and is also electronically scanned and entered into Speedy's data network when the package is picked up and when it is delivered. The electronic labels are transmitted via a device that operates on a cell phone network. 1. Assuming that each label is 1000 bytes long, how long does it take to transmit one label over the cell network, assuming that the cell phone network operates at 14 kbps (14,000 *bits* per second and that there are 8 bits in a byte)? 2. If Speedy were to upgrade to the new, faster digital phone network that transmits data at 114 Kbps (114,000 *bits* per second), how long would it take to transmit a label?

V. Networking Australia

Reread Management Focus 3.3. What other alternatives do you think that Southern Cross considered? Why do you think they did what they did?

VI. Boyle Transportation

Reread Management Focus 3.5. What other alternatives do you think that Boyle Transportation considered? Why do you think they did what they did?

VII. NASA's Ground Network

Reread Management Focus 3.1. What other alternatives do you think that NASA considered? Why do you think they did what they did?

CASE STUDY

NEXT-DAY AIR SERVICE

See the Web site.

HANDS-ON ACTIVITY

Looking Inside Your Cable

One of the most commonly used types of local network cable is Category 5 unshielded twisted pair cable, commonly called "Cat 5." Cat 5 (and an enhanced version called Cat 5e) are used in Ethernet LANs. If you have installed a LAN in your house or apartment, you probably used Cat 5 or Cat 5e.

Figure 3.27 shows a picture of a typical Cat 5 cable. Each end of the cable has a connector called an RJ-45 connector that enables the cable to be plugged into a computer or network device. If you look closely at the connector you will see there are 8 separate "pins." You might think that this would mean the Cat 5 can transmit data in parallel, but it doesn't do this. Cat 5 is used for serial transmission.

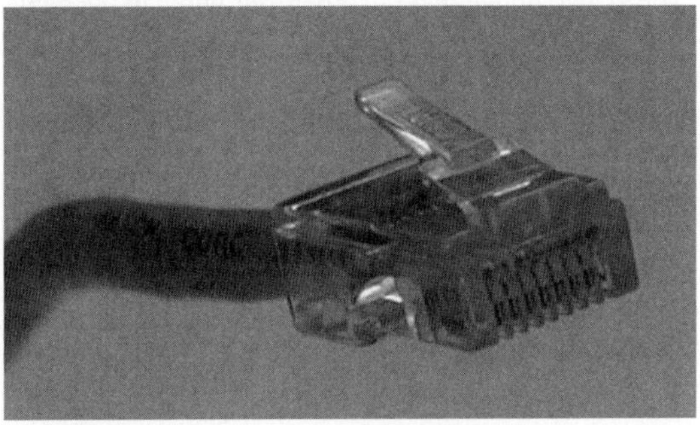

FIGURE 3.27 Cat 5 cable

If you have an old Cat 5 cable (or are willing to spend a few dollars to buy cheap cable), it is simple to take the connector off. Simply take a pair of scissors and cut through the cable a few inches from the connector. Figure 3.28 shows the same Cat 5 cable with the connector cut off. You can see why twisted pair is called twisted pair: a single Cat 5 cable contains four separate sets of twisted pair wires for a total of eight wires.

Unfortunately, this picture is in black and white so it is hard to see the different colors of the eight wires inside the cable. Figure 3.29 lists the different colors of the wires and what they are used for under the EIA/TIA 568B standard (the less common 568A standard uses the pins in different ways). One pair of wires (connected to pins 1 and 2) is used to transmit data from your computer into the network. When your computer transmits, it sends the same data on both wires; pin 1 (transmit+) transmits the data normally and pin 2 (transmit–) transmits the same data with reversed polarity. This way if an error occurs, the hardware will likely detect a different signal on the two cables. For example, if there is a sudden burst of electricity with a positive polarity (or a negative polarity), it will change only one of the transmissions from negative to positive (or vice versa) and leave the other transmission unchanged. Electrical pulses generate a magnetic field that has very bad side effects on the other wires. To minimize this, the two transmit wires are twisted together so that the other wires in the cable receive both a positive and a negative polarity magnetic field from the wires twisted around each other, which cancel each other out.

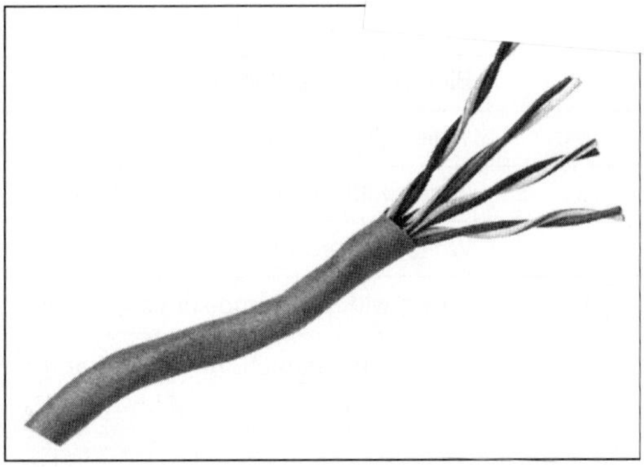

FIGURE 3.28 Inside a Cat 5 cable
Source: Courtesy South Hills Datacomm

Figure 3.29 also shows a separate pair of wires for receiving transmissions from the network (pin 3 (receive+) and pin 6 (receive–)). These wires work exactly the same way as transmit+ and transmit–but are used by the network to send data to your computer. You'll notice that they are also twisted together in one pair of wires, even though they are not side-by-side on the connector.

Figure 3.29 shows the pin functions from the viewpoint of your computer. If you think about it, you'll quickly realize that the pin functions at the network end of the cable are reversed; that is, pin 1 is receive+ because it is the wire that the network uses to receive the transmit+ signal from your computer. Likewise, pin 6 at the network end is the transmit–wire because it is the wire on which your computer receives the reversed data signal.

Pin number	Color (EIA/TIA 568B standard)	Name
1	White with orange stripe	Transmit +
2	Orange with white stripe or solid orange	Transmit –
3	White with green stripe	Receive +
4	Blue with white stripe or solid blue	Not used
5	White with blue stripe	Not used
6	Green with white stripe or solid green	Receive –
7	White with brown stripe or solid brown	Not used
8	Brown with white stripe or solid brown	Not used

FIGURE 3.29 Pin connection for Cat 5 at the computer end

The separate set of wires for transmitting and receiving means that Cat 5 is designed for full-duplex transmission. It can send and receive at the same time because one set of wires is used for sending data and one set for receiving data. However, Cat 5 is not often used this way. Most hardware that uses Cat 5 is designed to operate in a half-duplex mode, even though the cable itself is capable of full duplex.

You'll also notice that the other four wires in the cable are not used. Yes, that's right; they are simply wasted.

HANDS-ON ACTIVITY

Making MP3 Files

MP3 files are good examples of analog to digital conversion. It is simple to take an analog signal—such as your voice—and convert it into a digital file for transmission or playback. In this activity, we will show you how to record your voice and see how different levels of digital quality affect the sound.

First, you need to download a sound editor and MP3 converter. One very good sound editor is Audacity—and it's free. Go to audacity.sourceforge.net and download and install the audacity software. You will also need the plug-in called LAME (an MP3 encoder) which is also free and available at lame.sourceforge.net.

Use Audacity to record music or your voice (you can use a cheap microphone). Audacity records in very high quality, but will produce MP3 files in whatever quality level you choose.

Once you have the file recorded, you can edit the Preferences to change the File Format to use in saving the MP3 file. Audacity/LAME offers a wide range of qualities. Try recording at least three different quality levels. For example, for high quality you could use 320 Kbps, which means the recording uses 320 Kbps of data per second. In other words the number of samples per second times the number of bits per sample produces equals 320 Kbps. For regular quality, you could use 128 Kbps. For low quality, you could use 16 Kbps.

Create each of these files and listen to them to hear the differences in quality produced by the quantizing error. The differences should be most noticeable for music. A recording at 24 Kbps is often adequate for voice, but music will require a better quality encoding.

CHAPTER 4

DATA LINK LAYER

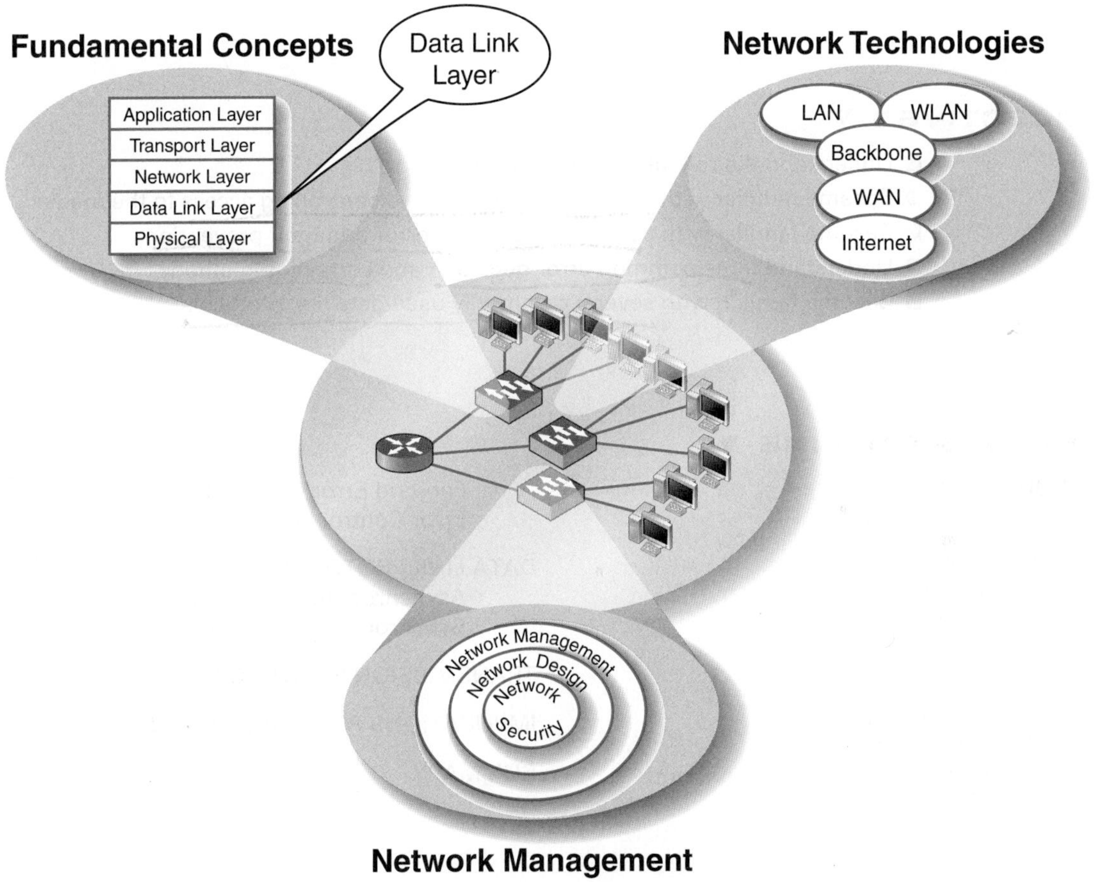

The Three Faces of Networking

THE DATA link layer (also called layer 2) is responsible for moving a message from one computer or network device to the next computer or network device in the overall path from sender or receiver. It controls the way messages are sent on the physical media. Both the sender and receiver have to agree on the rules or *protocols* that govern how they will communicate with each other. A *data link protocol* determines who can transmit at what time, where a message begins and ends, and how a receiver recognizes and corrects a transmission error. In this chapter, we discuss these processes, as well as several important sources of errors.

OBJECTIVES ▼

- Understand the role of the data link layer
- Become familiar with two basic approaches to controlling access to the media
- Become familiar with common sources of error and their prevention
- Understand three common error detection and correction methods
- Become familiar with several commonly used data link protocols

CHAPTER OUTLINE ▼

INTRODUCTION

In Chapter 1, we introduced the concept of layers in data communications. The data link layer sits between the physical layer (hardware such as the circuits, computers, and multiplexers described in Chapter 3) and the network layer (that performs addressing and routing, as described in Chapter 5).

The data link layer is responsible for sending and receiving messages to and from other computers. Its job is to reliably move a message from one computer over one circuit to the next computer where the message needs to go.

The data link layer performs two main functions, and therefore is often divided into two sublayers. The first sublayer (called the **logical link control [LLC] sublayer**) is the data link layer's connection to the network layer above it. At the sending computer, the LLC sublayer software is responsible for communicating with the network layer software (e.g., IP) and for taking the network layer Protocol Data Unit (PDU)—usually an IP packet—and surrounding it with a data link layer PDU—often an Ethernet frame. At the receiving computer, the LLC sublayer software removes the data link layer PDU and passes the message it contains (usually an IP packet) to the network layer software.

The second sublayer (called the **media access control [MAC] sublayer**) controls the physical hardware. The MAC sublayer software at the sending computer controls how and when the physical layer converts bits into the physical symbols that are sent down the circuit. At the receiving computer, the MAC sublayer software takes the data link layer PDU from the LLC sublayer, converts it into a stream of bits, and controls when the physical layer actually transmits the bits over the circuit. At the receiving computer, the MAC sublayer receives a stream of bits from the physical layer and translates it into a coherent PDU, ensures that no errors have occurred in transmission, and passes the data link layer PDU to the LLC sublayer.

Both the sender and receiver have to agree on the rules or *protocols* that govern how their data link layers will communicate with each other. A *data link protocol* performs three functions:

- Controls when computers transmit (*media access control*)
- Detects and corrects transmission errors (*error control*)
- Identifies the start and end of a message by using a PDU (*message delineation*)

MEDIA ACCESS CONTROL

Media access control refers to the need to control when computers transmit. With point-to-point full-duplex configurations, media access control is unnecessary because there are only two computers on the circuit and full duplex permits either computer to transmit at any time.

Media access control becomes important when several computers share the same communication circuit, such as a point-to-point configuration with a half-duplex configuration that requires computers to take turns, or a multipoint configuration in which several computers share the same circuit. Here, it is critical to ensure that no two computers attempt to transmit data at the same time—but if they do, there must be a way to recover from the problem. There are two fundamental approaches to media access control: controlled access and contention.

Controlled Access

Most computer networks managed by a host mainframe computer use controlled access. In this case, the mainframe controls the circuit and determines which clients can access media at what time.

Polling is the process of sending a signal to a client (a computer or terminal) that gives it permission to transmit or asks it to receive. With polling, the clients store all messages that need to be transmitted. Periodically, the server (usually a mainframe computer) *polls* the client to see if it has data to send. If the client has data to send, it does so. If the client has no data to send, it responds negatively, and the server asks another client if it has data to send.

In other words, polling is like a classroom situation in which the instructor calls on the students who raise their hands. The instructor acts like the server. To gain access to the media, students raise their hands and the instructor recognizes them so they can contribute. When they have finished, the instructor again takes charge and allows someone else to comment.

There are several types of polling. With **roll-call polling,** the server works consecutively through a list of clients, first polling client 1, then client 2, and so on, until all are polled. Roll-call polling can be modified to select clients in priority so that some get polled more often than others. For example, one could increase the priority of client 1 by using a polling sequence such as 1, 2, 3, 1, 4, 5, 1, 6, 7, 1, 8, 9.

Typically, roll-call polling involves some waiting because the server has to poll a client and then wait for a response. The response might be an incoming message that was waiting to be sent, a negative response indicating nothing is to be sent, or the full "time-out period" may expire because the client is temporarily out of service (e.g., it is malfunctioning or the user has turned it off). Usually, a timer "times out" the client after waiting several seconds without getting a response. If some sort of fail-safe time-out is not used, the system poll might lock up indefinitely on an out-of-service client.

With **hub polling** (often called **token passing**), one computer starts the poll and passes it to the next computer on the multipoint circuit, which sends its message and passes the poll to the next. That computer then passes the poll to the next, and so on, until it reaches the first computer, which restarts the process again.

Contention

Contention is the opposite of *controlled access.* Computers wait until the circuit is free (i.e., no other computers are transmitting) and then transmit whenever they have data to send. Contention is commonly used in Ethernet LANs.

As an analogy, suppose that you are talking with some friends. Each person tries to get the floor when the previous speaker finishes. Usually, the others yield to the first person who jumps in at the precise moment the previous speaker stops. Sometimes two

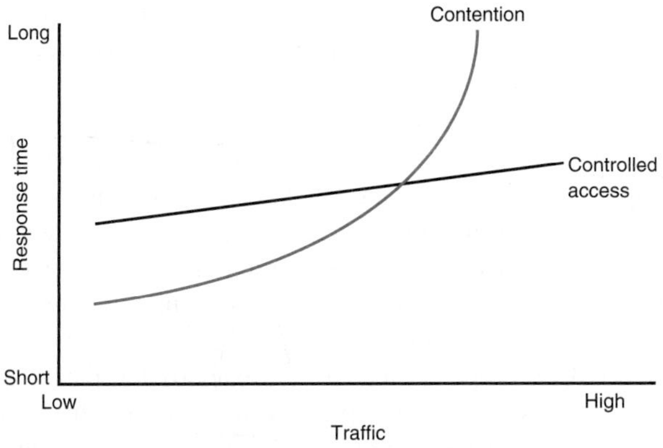

FIGURE 4.1 Relative response times

people attempt to talk at the same time, so there must be some technique to continue the conversation after such a verbal collision occurs.

Relative Performance

Which media access control approach is best: controlled access or contention? There is no simple answer. The key consideration is throughput—which approach will permit the most amount of user data to be transmitted through the network.

In general, contention approaches work better than controlled approaches for small networks that have low usage. In this case, each computer can transmit when necessary, without waiting for permission. Because usage is low, there is little chance of a collision. In contrast, computers in a controlled access environment must wait for permission, so even if no other computer needs to transmit, they must wait for the poll.

The reverse is true for large networks with high usage: controlled access works better. In high-volume networks, many computers want to transmit, and the probability of a collision using contention is high. Collisions are very costly in terms of throughput because they waste circuit capacity during the collision and require both computers to retransmit later. Controlled access prevents collisions and makes more efficient use of the circuit, and although response time does increase, it does so more gradually (Figure 4.1).

The key to selecting the best access control technique is to find the crossover point between controlled and contention. Although there is no one correct answer, because it depends on how many messages the computers in the network transmit, most experts believe that the crossover point is often around 20 computers (lower for busy computers, higher for less-busy computers). For this reason, when we build shared multipoint circuits like those often used in LANs or wireless LANs, we try to put no more than 20 computers on any one shared circuit.

ERROR CONTROL

Before learning the control mechanisms that can be implemented to protect a network from errors, you should realize that there are *human errors* and *network errors*. Human errors, such as a mistake in typing a number, usually are controlled through the application program. Network errors, such as those that occur during transmission, are controlled by the network hardware and software.

There are two categories of network errors: *corrupted data* (data that have been changed) and *lost data.* Networks should be designed to (1) prevent, (2) detect, and (3) correct both corrupted data and lost data. We begin by examining the sources of errors and how to prevent them and then turn to error detection and correction.

Network errors are a fact of life in data communications networks. Depending on the type of circuit, they may occur every few hours, minutes, or seconds because of noise on the lines. No network can eliminate all errors, but most errors can be prevented, detected, and corrected by proper design. IXCs that provide data transmission circuits provide statistical measures specifying typical **error rates** and the pattern of errors that can be expected on the circuits they lease. For example, the error rate might be stated as 1 in 500,000, meaning there is 1 bit in error for every 500,000 bits transmitted.

Normally, errors appear in bursts. In a **burst error,** more than 1 data bit is changed by the error-causing condition. In other words, errors are not uniformly distributed in time. Although an error rate might be stated as 1 in 500,000, errors are more likely to occur as 100 bits every 50,000,000 bits. The fact that errors tend to be clustered in bursts rather than evenly dispersed is both good and bad. If the errors were not clustered, an error rate of 1 bit in 500,000 would make it rare for 2 erroneous bits to occur in the same character. Consequently, simple character-checking schemes would be effective at detecting errors. When errors are #ore or less evenly distrib#ted, it is not di#ficult to gras# the me#ning even when the error #ate is high, as it is in this #entence (1 charac#er in 20). But burst errors are the rule rather than the exception, often obliterating 100 or more bits at a time. This makes it more difficult to recover the meaning, so more reliance must be placed on error detection and correction methods. The positive side is that there are long periods of error-free transmission, meaning that very few messages encounter errors.

Sources of Errors

Line noise and *distortion* can cause data communication errors. The focus in this section is on electrical media such as twisted-pair wire and coaxial cable, because they are more likely to suffer from noise than are optical media such as fiber-optic cable. In this case, noise is undesirable electrical signals (for fiber-optic cable, it is undesirable light). Noise is introduced by equipment or natural disturbances, and it degrades the performance of a communication circuit. Noise manifests itself as extra bits, missing bits, or bits that have been "flipped" (i.e., changed from 1 to 0 or vice versa). Figure 4.2 summarizes the major sources of error and ways to prevent them. The first six sources listed there are the most important; the last three are more common in analog rather than digital circuits.

Line outages are a catastrophic cause of errors and incomplete transmission. Occasionally, a communication circuit fails for a brief period. This type of failure may be caused by faulty telephone end office equipment, storms, loss of the carrier signal, and any other failure that causes a short circuit. The most common cause of line outages are storms that cause damage to circuits or facilities.

White noise or **Gaussian noise** (the familiar background hiss or static on radios and telephones) is caused by the thermal agitation of electrons and therefore is inescapable.

Source of Error	What Causes It	How to Prevent It
Line outages	Storms, accidents	
White noise	Movement of electrons	Increase signal strength
Impulse noise	Sudden increases in electricity (e.g., lightning)	Shield or move the wires
Cross-talk	Multiplexer guardbands too small or wires too close together	Increase the guardbands or move or shield the wires
Echo	Poor connections	Fix the connections or tune equipment
Attenuation	Gradual decrease in signal over distance	Use repeaters or amplifiers
Intermodulation noise	Signals from several circuits combine	Move or shield the wires
Jitter	Analog signals change phase	Tune equipment
Harmonic distortion	Amplifier changes phase	Tune equipment

FIGURE 4.2 Sources of errors and ways to minimize them

Even if the equipment were perfect and the wires were perfectly insulated from any and all external interference, there still would be some white noise. White noise usually is not a problem unless it becomes so strong that it obliterates the transmission. In this case, the strength of the electrical signal is increased so it overpowers the white noise; in technical terms, we increase the signal-to-noise ratio.

Impulse noise (sometimes called *spikes*) is the primary source of errors in data communications. Impulse noise is heard as a click or a crackling noise and can last as long as $^1/_{100}$ of a second. Such a click does not really affect voice communications, but it can obliterate a group of data, causing a burst error. At 1.5 Mbps, 15,000 bits would be changed by a spike of $^1/_{100}$ of a second. Some of the sources of impulse noise are voltage changes in adjacent lines, lightning flashes during thunderstorms, fluorescent lights, and poor connections in circuits.

Cross-talk occurs when one circuit picks up signals in another. You experience cross-talk during telephone calls when you hear other conversations in the background. It occurs between pairs of wires that are carrying separate signals, in multiplexed links carrying many discrete signals, or in microwave links in which one antenna picks up a minute reflection from another antenna. Cross-talk between lines increases with increased communication distance, increased proximity of the two wires, increased signal strength, and higher-frequency signals. Wet or damp weather can also increase cross-talk. Like white noise, cross-talk has such a low signal strength that it normally is not bothersome.

Echoes can cause errors. Echoes are caused by poor connections that cause the signal to reflect back to the transmitting equipment. If the strength of the echo is strong enough to be detected, it causes errors. Echoes, like cross-talk and white noise, have such a low signal strength that they normally are not bothersome. Echoes can also occur in fiber-optic cables when connections between cables are not properly aligned.

Attenuation is the loss of power a signal suffers as it travels from the transmitting computer to the receiving computer. Some power is absorbed by the medium or is lost before it reaches the receiver. As the medium absorbs power, the signal becomes weaker, and the receiving equipment has less and less chance of correctly interpreting the data.

This power loss is a function of the transmission method and circuit medium. High frequencies lose power more rapidly than do low frequencies during transmission, so the received signal can thus be distorted by unequal loss of its component frequencies. Attenuation increases as frequency increases or as the diameter of the wire decreases.

Intermodulation noise is a special type of cross-talk. The signals from two circuits combine to form a new signal that falls into a frequency band reserved for another signal. This type of noise is similar to harmonics in music. On a multiplexed line, many different signals are amplified together, and slight variations in the adjustment of the equipment can cause intermodulation noise. A maladjusted modem may transmit a strong frequency tone when not transmitting data, thus producing this type of noise.

Jitter may affect the accuracy of the data being transmitted because minute variations in amplitude, phase, and frequency always occur. The generation of a pure carrier signal in an analog circuit is impossible. The signal may be impaired by continuous and rapid gain and/or phase changes. This jitter may be random or periodic. Phase jitter during a telephone call causes the voice to fluctuate in volume.

Harmonic distortion usually is caused by an amplifier on a circuit that does not correctly represent its output with what was delivered to it on the input side. *Phase hits* are short-term shifts "out of phase," with the possibility of a shift back into phase.

In general, errors are more likely to occur in wireless, microwove, or satellite transmission than transmission through cables. Therefore, error detection is more important when using radiated media than guided media.

Error Prevention

There are many techniques to prevent errors (or at least reduce them), depending on the situation. *Shielding* (protecting wires by covering them with an insulating coating) is one of the best ways to prevent impulse noise, cross-talk, and intermodulation noise. Many different types of wires and cables are available with different amounts of shielding. In general, the greater the shielding, the more expensive the cable and the more difficult it is to install.

Moving cables away from sources of noise (especially power sources) can also reduce impulse noise, cross-talk, and intermodulation noise. For impulse noise, this means avoiding lights and heavy machinery. Locating communication cables away from power cables is always a good idea. For cross-talk, this means physically separating the cables from other communication cables.

Cross-talk and intermodulation noise is often caused by improper multiplexing. Changing multiplexing techniques (e.g., from FDM to TDM) or changing the frequencies or size of the guardbands in FDM can help.

Many types of noise (e.g., echoes, white noise, jitter, harmonic distortion) can be caused by poorly maintained equipment or poor connections and splices among cables. This is particularly true for echo in fiber-optic cables, which is almost always caused by poor connections. The solution here is obvious: Tune the transmission equipment and redo the connections.

To avoid attenuation, telephone circuits have **repeaters** or **amplifiers** spaced throughout their length. The distance between them depends on the amount of power lost per unit length of the transmission line. An amplifier takes the incoming signal,

MANAGEMENT FOCUS 4.1 FINDING THE SOURCE OF IMPULSE NOISE

Several years ago, the University of Georgia radio station received FCC (Federal Communications Commission) approval to broadcast using a stronger signal. Immediately after the station started broadcasting with the new signal, the campus backbone network (BN) became unusable because of impulse noise. It took two days to link the impulse noise to the radio station, and when the radio station returned to its usual broadcast signal, the problem disappeared.

However, this was only the first step in the problem. The radio station wanted to broadcast at full strength, and there was no good reason for why the stronger broadcast should affect the BN in this way. After two weeks of effort, the problem was discovered. A short section of the BN ran above ground between two buildings. It turned out that the specific brand of outdoor cable we used was particularly tasty to squirrels. They had eaten the outer insulating coating off of the cable, making it act like an antennae to receive the radio signals. The cable was replaced with a steel-coated armored cable so the squirrels could not eat the insulation. Things worked fine when the radio station returned to its stronger signal.

increases its strength, and retransmits it on the next section of the circuit. They are typically used on analog circuits such as the telephone company's voice circuits. The distance between the amplifiers depends on the amount of attenuation, although 1- to 10-mile intervals are common. On analog circuits, it is important to recognize that the noise and distortion are *also* amplified, along with the signal. This means some noise from a previous circuit is regenerated and amplified each time the signal is amplified.

Repeaters are commonly used on digital circuits. A repeater receives the incoming signal, translates it into a digital message, and retransmits the message. Because the message is recreated at each repeater, noise and distortion from the previous circuit are not amplified. This provides a much cleaner signal and results in a lower error rate for digital circuits.

Error Detection

It is possible to develop data transmission methodologies that give very high **error detection** performance. The only way to do error detection is to send extra data with each message. These error detection data are added to each message by the data link layer of the sender on the basis of some mathematical calculations performed on the message (in some cases, error-detection methods are built into the hardware itself). The receiver performs the same mathematical calculations on the message it receives and matches its results against the error-detection data that were transmitted with the message. If the two match, the message is assumed to be correct. If they don't match, an error has occurred.

In general, the larger the amount of error-detection data sent, the greater the ability to detect an error. However, as the amount of error-detection data is increased, the throughput of useful data is reduced, because more of the available capacity is used to transmit these error-detection data and less is used to transmit the actual message itself.

Assume we are using even parity with 8-bit ASCII.
The letter *V* in 8-bit ASCII is encoded as 01101010.
Because there are four 1's (an even number), parity is set to 0.
This would be transmitted as 011010100.

Assume we are using even parity with 8-bit ASCII.
The letter *W* in 8-bit ASCII is encoded as 00011010.
Because there are three 1's (an odd number), parity is set to 1.
This would be transmitted as 000110101.

FIGURE 4.3 Using parity for error detection

Therefore, the **efficiency** of data throughput varies inversely as the desired amount of error detection is increased.

Three well-known *error-detection methods* are parity checking, checksum, and cyclic redundancy checking.

Parity Checking

One of the oldest and simplest error-detection methods is *parity.* With this technique, one additional bit is added to each byte in the message. The value of this additional **parity bit** is based on the number of 1's in each byte transmitted. This parity bit is set to make the total number of 1's in the byte (including the parity bit) either an even number or an odd number. Figure 4.3 gives an example.

A little thought will convince you that any single error (a switch of a 1 to a 0 or vice versa) will be detected by parity, but it cannot determine which bit was in error. You will know an error occurred, but not what the error was. But if *two* bits are switched, the **parity check** will not detect any error. It is easy to see that parity can detect errors only when an odd number of bits have been switched; any even number of errors cancel one another out. Therefore, the probability of detecting an error, given that one has occurred, is only about 50 percent. Many networks today do not use parity because of its low error-detection rate. When parity is used, protocols are described as having **odd parity** or **even parity.**

Checksum

With the **checksum** technique, a checksum (typically one byte) is added to the end of the message. The checksum is calculated by adding the decimal value of each character in the message, dividing the sum by 255, and using the remainder as the checksum. The receiver calculates its own checksum in the same way and compares it with the transmitted checksum. If the two values are equal, the message is presumed to contain no errors. Use of checksum detects close to 95 percent of the errors for multiple-bit burst errors.

Cyclical Redundancy Check

One of the most popular error-checking schemes is **cyclical redundancy check (CRC).** It adds 8, 16, 24, or 32 bits to the message. With CRC, a message is treated as one long binary number, *P*. Before transmission, the data link layer (or hardware device) divides *P* by a fixed binary number, *G,* resulting in a whole number, *Q,* and a remainder, *R/G*. So, $P/G = Q + R/G$. For example, if

$P = 58$ and $G = 8$, then $Q = 7$ and $R = 2$. G is chosen so that the remainder, R, will be either 8 bits, 16 bits, 24 bits, or 32 bits.[1]

The remainder, R, is appended to the message as the error-checking characters before transmission. The receiving hardware divides the received message by the same G, which generates an R. The receiving hardware checks to ascertain whether the received R agrees with the locally generated R. If it does not, the message is assumed to be in error.

CRC performs quite well. The most commonly used CRC codes are CRC-16 (a 16-bit version), CRC-CCITT (another 16-bit version), and CRC-32 (a 32-bit version). The probability of detecting an error is 100 percent for all errors of the same length as the CRC or less. For example, CRC-16 is guaranteed to detect errors if 16 or fewer bits are affected. If the burst error is longer than the CRC, then CRC is not perfect but is close to it. CRC-16 will detect about 99.998 percent of all burst errors longer than 16 bits, whereas CRC-32 will detect about 99.99999998 percent of all burst errors longer than 32 bits.

Error Correction via Retransmission

Once error has been detected, it must be corrected. The simplest, most effective, least expensive, and most commonly used method for error correction is retransmission. With retransmission, a receiver that detects an error simply asks the sender to retransmit the message until it is received without error. This is often called **Automatic Repeat reQuest (ARQ).** There are two types of ARQ: stop-and-wait and continuous.

Stop-and-Wait ARQ

With **stop-and-wait ARQ,** the sender stops and waits for a response from the receiver after each data packet. After receiving a packet, the receiver sends either an **acknowledgment (ACK),** if the packet was received without error, or a **negative acknowledgment (NAK),** if the message contained an error. If it is an NAK, the sender resends the previous message. If it is an ACK, the sender continues with the next message. Stop-and-wait ARQ is by definition a half-duplex transmission technique (Figure 4.4).

Continuous ARQ

With **continuous ARQ,** the sender does not wait for an acknowledgment after sending a message; it immediately sends the next one. Although the messages are being transmitted, the sender examines the stream of returning acknowledgments. If it receives an NAK, the sender retransmits the needed messages. The packets that are retransmitted may be only those containing an error (called **Link Access Protocol for Modems [LAP-M]**) or may be the first packet with an error and all those that followed it (called **Go-Back-N ARQ**). LAP-M is better because it is more efficient.

Continuous ARQ is by definition a full-duplex transmission technique, because both the sender and the receiver are transmitting simultaneously. (The sender is sending messages, and the receiver is sending ACKs and NAKs.) Figure 4.5 illustrates the flow of messages on a communication circuit using continuous ARQ. Continuous ARQ

[1]CRC is actually more complicated than this because it uses polynominal division, not "normal" division as illustrated here. Ross Willams provides an excellent tutorial on CRC at www.ross.net/crc/crcpaper.html.

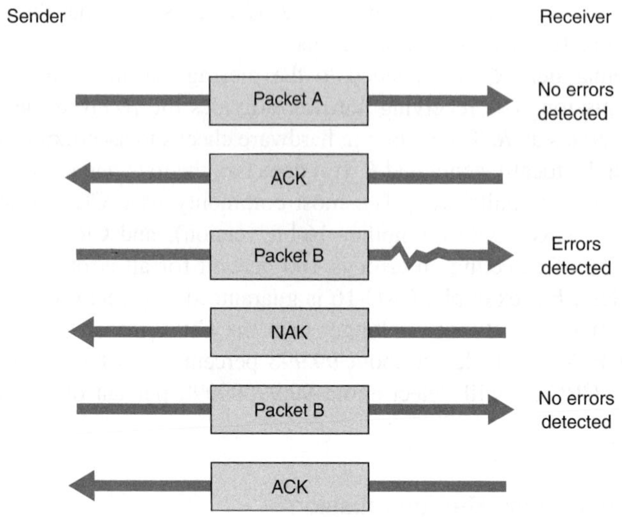

FIGURE 4.4
Stop-and-wait ARQ (Automatic Repeat reQuest). ACK = acknowledgment; NAK = negative acknowledgment

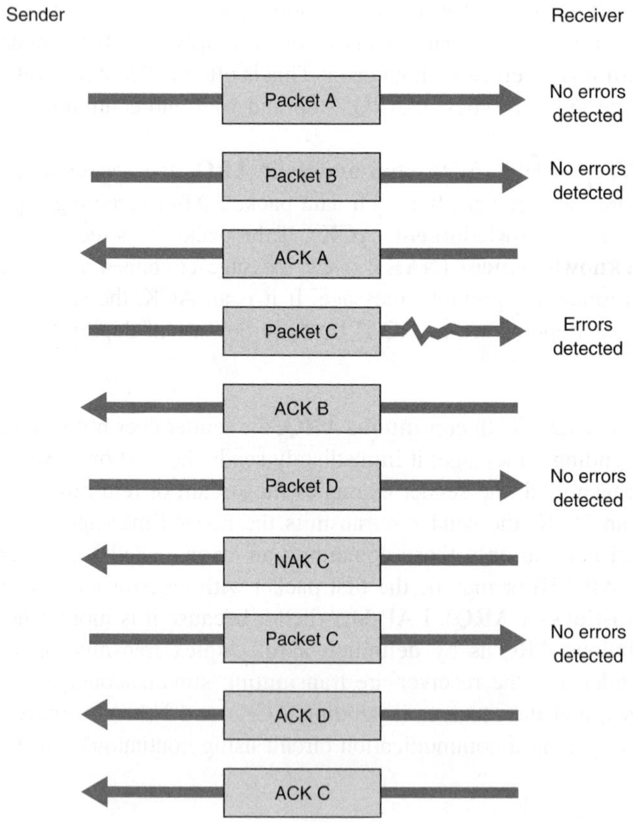

FIGURE 4.5
Continuous ARQ (Automatic Repeat reQuest). ACK = acknowledgment; NAK = negative acknowledgment

is sometimes called **sliding window** because of the visual imagery the early network designers used to think about continuous ARQ. Visualize the sender having a set of messages to send in memory stacked in order from first to last. Now imagine a window that moves through the stack from first to last. As a message is sent, the window expands to cover it, meaning that the sender is waiting for an ACK for the message. As an ACK is received for a message, the window moves forward, dropping the message out of the bottom of the window, indicating that it has been sent and received successfully.

Continuous ARQ is also important in providing **flow control**, which means ensuring that the computer sending the message is not transmitting too quickly for the receiver. For example, if a client computer was sending information too quickly for a server computer to store a file being uploaded, the server might run out of memory to store the file. By using ACKs and NAKs, the receiver can control the rate at which it receives information. With stop-and-wait ARQ, the receiver does not send an ACK until it is ready to receive more packets. In continuous ARQ, the sender and receiver usually agree on the size of the sliding window. Once the sender has transmitted the maximum number of packets permitted in the sliding window, it cannot send any more packets until the receiver sends an ACK.

Forward Error Correction

Forward error correction uses codes containing sufficient redundancy to prevent errors by detecting and correcting them at the receiving end *without* retransmission of the original message. The redundancy, or extra bits required, varies with different schemes. It ranges from a small percentage of extra bits to 100 percent redundancy, with the number of error-detecting bits roughly equaling the number of data bits. One of the characteristics of many error-correcting codes is that there must be a minimum number of error-free bits between bursts of errors.

Forward error correction is commonly used in satellite transmission. A round trip from the earth station to the satellite and back includes a significant delay. Error rates can fluctuate depending on the condition of equipment, sunspots, or the weather. Indeed, some weather conditions make it impossible to transmit without some errors, making forward error correction essential. Compared with satellite equipment costs, the additional cost of forward error correction is insignificant.

Error Control in Practice

In the OSI model (see Chapter 1), error control is defined to be a layer-2 function—it is the responsibility of the data link layer. However, in practice, we have moved away from this. Most network hardware and software available today provide an error control function at the data link layer, but it is turned off. Most network cables are very reliable and errors are far less common than they were in the 1980s.

Therefore, most data link layer software today is configured to detect errors, but *not* correct them. Any time a packet with an error is discovered, it is simply discarded. The exceptions to this tend to be wireless technologies and a few WAN technologies where errors are more common.

The implication from this is that error correction must be performed by software at higher layers. This software must be able to detect lost packets (i.e., those that have

TECHNICAL FOCUS 4.1 How Forward Error Correction Works

To see how error-correcting codes work, consider the example of a forward error checking code in Figure 4.6, called a **Hamming code,** after its inventor, R. W. Hamming. This code is a very simple approach, capable of correcting 1-bit errors. More sophisticated techniques (e.g., Reed–Solomon) are commonly used today, but this will give you a sense of how they work.

The Hamming code associates even parity bits with unique combinations of data bits. With a 4-data-bit code as an example, a character might be represented by the data-bit configuration 1010. Three parity bits, P_1, P_2, and P_4, are added, resulting in a 7-bit code, shown in the upper half of Figure 4.6. Notice that the data bits (D_3, D_5, D_6, D_7) are 1010 and the parity bits (P_1, P_2, P_4) are 101.

As depicted in the upper half of Figure 4.6, parity bit P_1 applies to data bits D_3, D_5, and D_7. Parity bit P_2 applies to data bits D_3, D_6, and D_7. Parity bit P_4 applies to data bits D_5, D_6, and D_7. For the example, in which D_3, D_5, D_6, D_7 = 1010, P_1 must equal 1 because there is only a single 1 among D_3, D_5 and D_7 and parity must be even. Similarly, P_2 must be 0 because D_3 and D_6 are 1's. P_4 is 1 because D_6 is the only 1 among D_5, D_6, and D_7.

Now, assume that during the transmission, data bit D_7 is changed from a 0 to a 1 by line noise. Because this data bit is being checked by P_1, P_2, and P_4, all 3 parity bits now show odd parity instead of the correct even parity. D_7 is the only data bit that is monitored by all 3 parity bits; therefore, when D_7 is in error, all 3 parity bits show an incorrect parity. In this way, the receiving equipment can determine which bit was in error and reverse its state, thus correcting the error without retransmission.

The lower half of the figure is a table that determines the location of the bit in error. A 1 in the table means that the corresponding parity bit indicates a parity error. Conversely, a 0 means the parity check is correct. These 0's and 1's form a binary number that indicates the numeric location of the erroneous bit. In the previous example, P_1, P_2, and P_4 checks all failed, yielding 111, or a decimal 7, the subscript of the erroneous bit.

been discarded) and request the sender to retransmit them. This is commonly done by the transport layer using continuous ARQ as we shall see in the next chapter.

DATA LINK PROTOCOLS

In this section, we outline several commonly used data link layer protocols, which are summarized in Figure 4.7. Here we focus on message delineation, which indicates where a message starts and stops, and the various parts or *fields* within the message. For example, you must clearly indicate which part of a message or packet of data is the error-control portion; otherwise, the receiver cannot use it properly to determine if an error has occurred. The data link layer performs this function by adding a PDU to the packet it receives from the network layer. This PDU is called frame.

Asynchronous Transmission

Asynchronous transmission often is referred to as start-stop transmission because the transmitting computer can transmit a character whenever it is convenient, and the

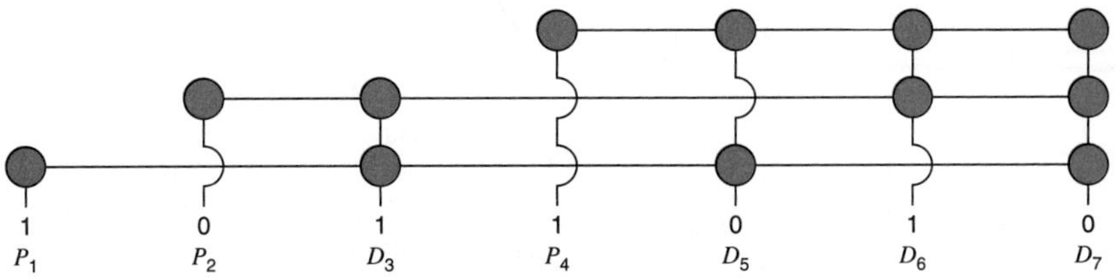

Checking relations between parity bits (P) and data bits (D)

0 = Corresponding parity check is correct 1 = Corresponding parity check fails P_4 P_2 P_1	Determines in which bit the error occured
0 0 0	→ no error
0 0 1	→ P_1
0 1 0	→ P_2
0 1 1	→ D_3
1 0 0	→ P_4
1 0 1	→ D_5
1 1 0	→ D_6
1 1 1	→ D_7

Interpreting parity bit patterns

FIGURE 4.6 Hamming code for forward error correction

Protocol	Size	Error Detection	Retransmission	Media Access
Asynchronous transmission	1	Parity	Continuous ARQ	Full Duplex
Synchronous protocols				
SDLC	*	16-bit CRC	Continuous ARQ	Controlled Access
HDLC	*	16-bit CRC	Continuous ARQ	Controlled Access
Ethernet	*	32-bit CRC	Stop-and-wait ARQ	Contention
PPP	*	16-bit CRC	Continuous ARQ	Full Duplex

*Varies depending on the message length.

ARQ = Automatic Repeat reQuest; CRC = cyclical redundancy check; HDLC = high-level data link control; PPP = Point-to-Point Protocol; SDLC = synchronous data link control.

FIGURE 4.7 Protocol summary

receiving computer will accept that character. It is typically used on point-to-point full-duplex circuits (i.e., circuits that have only two computers on them), so media access control is not a concern. If you use VT100 protocol, or connect to a UNIX or Linux computer using Telnet, chances are you are using asynchronous transmission.

With **asynchronous transmission,** each character is transmitted independently of all other characters. To separate the characters and synchronize transmission, a **start bit** and a **stop bit** are put on the front and back of *each* individual character. For example,

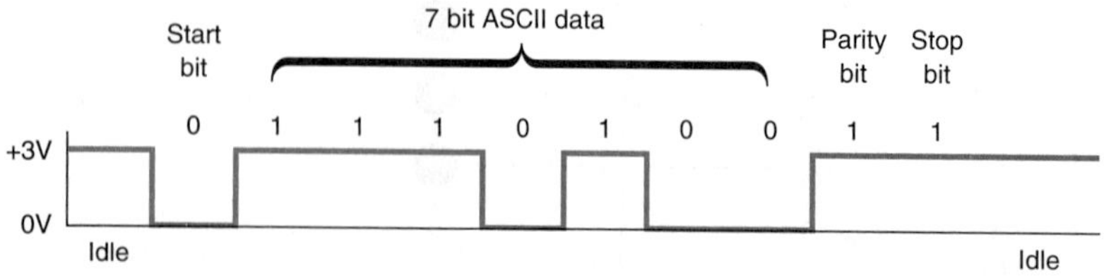

FIGURE 4.8 Asynchronous transmission. ASCII = United States of America Standard Code for Information Interchange

if we are using 7-bit ASCII with even parity, the total transmission is 10 bits for each character (1 start bit, 7 bits for the letter, 1 parity bit, 1 stop bit).

The start bit and stop bit are the opposite of each other. Typically, the start bit is a 0 and the stop bit is a 1. There is no fixed distance between characters because the terminal transmits the character as soon as it is typed, which varies with the speed of the typist. The recognition of the start and stop of each message (called **synchronization**) takes place for each individual character because the start bit is a signal that tells the receiver to start sampling the incoming bits of a character so the data bits can be interpreted into their proper character structure. A stop bit informs the receiver that the character has been received and resets it for recognition of the next start bit.

When the sender is waiting for the user to type the next character, no data is sent; the communication circuit is idle. This idle time really is artificial—some signal always must be sent down the circuit. For example, suppose we are using a unipolar digital signaling technique where +5 volts indicates a 1 and 0 volts indicates a 0 (see Chapter 3). Even if we send 0 volts, we are still sending a signal, a 0 in this case. Asynchronous transmission defines the *idle signal* (the signal that is sent down the circuit when no data are being transmitted) as the same as the stop bit. When the sender finishes transmitting a letter and is waiting for more data to send, it sends a continuous series of stop bits. Figure 4.8 shows an example of asynchronous transmission.

Some older protocols have two stop bits instead of the traditional single stop bit. The use of both a start bit and a stop bit is changing; some protocols have eliminated the stop bit altogether.

Synchronous Transmission

With **synchronous transmission,** all the letters or data in one group of data is transmitted at one time as a block of data. This block of data is called a **frame.** For example, a terminal or microcomputer will save all the keystrokes typed by the user and transmit them only when the user presses a special "transmit" key. In this case, the start and end of the entire frame must be marked, not the start and end of each letter. Synchronous transmission is often used on both point-to-point and multipoint circuits. For multipoint circuits, each packet must include a destination address and a source address, and media access control is important.

The start and end of each frame (synchronization) sometimes is established by adding synchronization characters (SYN) to the start of the frame. Depending on the protocol, there may be anywhere from one to eight SYN characters. After the SYN characters, the transmitting computer sends a long stream of data that may contain thousands of bits. Knowing what code is being used, the receiving computer counts off the

Flag	Address	Control	Message	Frame check sequence	Flag
8 bits	8 bits	8 bits	Variable length	32 bits	8 bits

FIGURE 4.9 SDLC (synchronous data link control) frame layout

appropriate number of bits for the first character, assumes this is the first character, and passes it to the computer. It then counts off the bits for the second character, and so on.

In summary, asynchronous data transmission means each character is transmitted as a totally independent entity with its own start and stop bits to inform the receiving computer that the character is beginning and ending. Synchronous transmission means whole blocks of data are transmitted as frames after the sender and the receiver have been synchronized.

There are many protocols for synchronous transmission. We discuss four commonly used synchronous data link protocols.

Synchronous Data Link Control

Synchronous data link control (SDLC) is a mainframe protocol developed by IBM in 1972 that is still in use today. It uses a controlled-access media access protocol. If you use a 3270 protocol, you're using SDLC.

Figure 4.9 shows a typical SDLC *frame.* Each SDLC frame begins and ends with a special bit pattern (01111110), known as the *flag.* The *address field* identifies the destination. The length of the address field is usually 8 bits but can be set at 16 bits; all computers on the same network must use the same length. The *control field* identifies the kind of frame that is being transmitted, either information or supervisory. An *information frame* is used for the transfer and reception of messages, frame numbering of contiguous frames, and the like. A *supervisory frame* is used to transmit acknowledgments (ACKs and NAKs). The *message field* is of variable length and is the user's message. The *frame check sequence field* is a 32-bit CRC code (some older versions use a 16-bit CRC).

High-Level Data Link Control

High-level data link control (HDLC) is a formal standard developed by the ISO often used in WANs. HDLC is essentially the same as SDLC, except that the address and control fields can be longer. HDLC also has several additional benefits that are beyond the scope of this book, such as a larger sliding window for continuous ARQ. It uses a controlled-access media access protocol. One variant, **Link Access Protocol–Balanced (LAP-B),** uses the same structure as HDLC but is a scaled-down version of HDLC (i.e., provides fewer of those benefits mentioned that are "beyond the scope of this book"). A version of HDLC called Cisco HDLC (cHDLC) includes a network protocol field. cHDLC and HDLC have gradually replaced SDLC.

Ethernet

Ethernet is a very popular LAN protocol, conceived by Bob Metcalfe in 1973 and developed jointly by Digital, Intel, and Xerox in the 1970s. Since then, Ethernet has been further refined and developed into a formal standard called **IEEE 802.3**ac. There are several versions of Ethernet in use today. Ethernet uses a contention media access protocol.

There are several standard versions of Ethernet. Figure 4.10a shows an Ethernet 803.3ac frame. The frame starts with a 7-byte *preamble* which is a repeating pattern of

Preamble	Start of Frame	Destination Address	Source Address	VLAN Tag	Length	DSAP	SSAP	Control	Data	Frame Check Sequence
7 bytes	1 byte	6 bytes	6 bytes	4 bytes	2 bytes	1 byte	1 byte	1-2 bytes	46-1,500 bytes	4 bytes

FIGURE 4.10a Ethernet 802.3ac frame layout

Preamble	Start of Frame	Destination Address	Source Address	Type	Data	Frame Check Sequence	Flag
7 bytes	1 byte	6 bytes	6 bytes	2 bytes	46-1,500 bytes	4 bytes	8 bytes

FIGURE 4.10b Ethernet II frame layout

ones and zeros (10101010). This is followed by a *start of frame delimiter,* which marks the start of the frame. The *destination address* specifies the receiver, whereas the *source address* specifies the sender. The *length* indicates the length in 8-bit bytes of the message portion of the frame. The *VLAN tag* field is an optional four-byte address field used by virtual LANs (VLANs), which are discussed in Chapter 8. The Ethernet frame uses this field only when VLANs are in use; otherwise the field is omitted, and the length field immediately follows the source address field. When the VLAN tag field is in use, the first two bytes are set to the number 24,832 (hexadecimal 81-00), which is obviously an impossible packet length. When Ethernet sees this length, it knows that the VLAN tag field is in use. When the length is some other value, it assumes that VLAN tags are not in use and that the length field immediately follows the source address field. The *DSAP* and *SSAP* are used to pass control information between the sender and receiver. These are often used to indicate the type of network layer protocol the packet contains (e.g., TCP/IP or IPX/SPX, as described in Chapter 5). The *control field* is used to hold the frame sequence numbers and ACKs and NAKs used for error control, as well as to enable the data link layers of communicating computers to exchange other control information. The last 2 bits in the first byte are used to indicate the type of control information being passed and whether the control field is 1 or 2 bytes (e.g., if the last 2 bits of the control field are 11, then the control field is 1 byte in length). In most cases, the control field is 1-byte long. The maximum length of the message is about 1,500 bytes. The frame ends with a CRC-32 *frame check sequence* used for error detection.

Ethernet II is another commonly used version of Ethernet. Like SDLC, it uses a preamble and a flag to mark the start and end of the frame. It has the same source and destination address format as Ethernet 802.3ac. The type field is used to specify an ACK frame or the type of network layer packet the frame contains (e.g., IP). The data and frame check sequence fields are the same as Ethernet 802.3ac.

Newer versions of these two types of Ethernet permits jumbo frames with up to 9,000 bytes of user data in the message field. Some vendors are experimenting with super jumbo frames that can hold up to 64,000 bytes. Neither jumbo nor super jumbo frame sizes have been standardized, but jumbo frames are common for some types of Ethernet such as gigabit Ethernet (see Chapter 6).

Point-to-Point Protocol **Point-to-Point Protocol (PPP)** was developed in the early 1990s and is often used in WANs. It is designed to transfer data over a point-to-point circuit but provides an address so that it can be used on multipoint circuits. Figure 4.11

A Day in the Life: Network Support Technician

When a help call arrives at the help desk, the help desk staff (first-level support) spends up to 10 minutes attempting to solve the problem. If they can't, then the problem is passed to the second-level support, the network support technician.

A typical day in the life of a network support technician starts by working on computers from the day before. Troubleshooting usually begins with a series of diagnostic tests to eliminate hardware problems. The next step, for a laptop, is to remove the hard disk and replace it with a hard disk containing a correct standard image. If the computer passes those tests then the problem is usually software. Then the fun begins.

Once a computer has been fixed it is important to document all the hardware and/or software changes to help track problem computers or problem software. Sometimes a problem is new but relatively straightforward to correct once it has been diagnosed. In this case, the technician will change the standard support process followed by the technicians working at the help desk to catch the problem before it is escalated to the network support technicians. In other cases, a new entry is made into the organization's technical support knowledge base so that if another technician (or user) encounters the problem it is easier for him or her to diagnose and correct the problem. About 10% of the time the network technician is spent documenting solutions to problems.

Network support technicians also are the ones who manage new inventory and set up and configure new computers as they arrive from the manufacturer. They are also the ones responsible for deploying new software and standard desktop images across the network. Many companies also set aside standard times for routine training; in our case, every Friday, several hours is devoted to regular training.

With thanks to Doug Strough

Flag	Address	Control	Protocol	Data	Frame Check Sequence	Flag
1 byte	1 byte	1 byte	2 bytes	Variable Length	2 or 4 bytes	1 byte

FIGURE 4.11 PPP frame layout

shows the basic layout of a PPP frame, which is very similar to an SDLC or HDLC frame. The frame starts with a flag, and has a one-byte address (which is not used on point-to-point circuits). The control field is typically not used. The protocol field indicates what type of data packet the frame contains (e.g., an IP packet). The data field is variable in length and may be up to 1,500 bytes. The frame check sequence is usually a CRC-16, but can be a CRC-32. The frame ends with a flag.

TRANSMISSION EFFICIENCY

One objective of a data communication network is to move the highest possible volume of accurate information through the network. The higher the volume, the greater the resulting network's efficiency and the lower the cost. Network efficiency is affected by characteristics of the circuits such as error rates and maximum transmission speed, as well as by the speed of transmitting and receiving equipment, the error-detection and control methodology, and the protocol used by the data link layer.

Each protocol we discussed uses some bits or bytes to delineate the start and end of each message and to control error. These bits and bytes are necessary for the transmission to occur, but they are not part of the message. They add no value to the user, but they count against the total number of bits that can be transmitted.

Each communication protocol has both information bits and overhead bits. **Information bits** are those used to convey the user's meaning. **Overhead bits** are used for purposes such as error checking and marking the start and end of characters and packets. A parity bit used for error checking is an overhead bit because it is not used to send the user's data; if you did not care about errors, the overhead error checking bit could be omitted and the users could still understand the message.

Transmission efficiency is defined as the total number of information bits (i.e., bits in the message sent by the user) divided by the total bits in transmission (i.e., information bits plus overhead bits). For example, let's calculate the transmission efficiency of asynchronous transmission. Assume we are using 7-bit ASCII. We have 1 bit for parity, plus 1 start bit and 1 stop bit. Therefore, there are 7 bits of information in each letter, but the total bits per letter is 10 (7 + 3). The efficiency of the asynchronous transmission system is 7 bits of information divided by 10 total bits, or 70 percent.

In other words, with asynchronous transmission, only 70 percent of the data rate is available for the user; 30 percent is used by the transmission protocol. If we have a communication circuit using a dial-up modem receiving 56 Kbps, the user sees an effective data rate (or throughput) of 39.2 Kbps. This is very inefficient.

We can improve efficiency by reducing the number of overhead bits in each message or by increasing the number of information bits. For example, if we remove the stop bits from asynchronous transmission, efficiency increases to 7/9, or 77.8 percent. The throughput of a dial-up modem at 56 Kbps would increase 43.6 Kbps, which is not great but is at least a little better.

The same basic formula can be used to calculate the efficiency of synchronous transmission. For example, suppose we are using SDLC. The number of information bits is calculated by determining how many information characters are in the message. If the message portion of the frame contains 100 information characters and we are using an 8-bit code, then there are $100 \times 8 = 800$ bits of information. The total number of bits is the 800 information bits plus the overhead bits that are inserted for delineation and error control. Figure 4.9 shows that SDLC has a beginning flag (8 bits), an address (8 bits), a control field (8 bits), a frame check sequence (assume we use a CRC-32 with 32 bits), and an ending flag (8 bits). This is a total of 64 overhead bits; thus, efficiency is $800/(800 + 64) = 92.6$ percent. If the circuit provides a data rate of 56 Kbps, then the effective data rate available to the user is about 51.9 Kbps.

This example shows that synchronous networks usually are more efficient than asynchronous networks and some protocols are more efficient than others. The longer the message (1,000 characters as opposed to 100), the more efficient the protocol. For example, suppose the message in the SDLC example were 1,000 bytes. The efficiency here would be 99.2 percent, or 8,000/(8000 + 64), giving an effective data rate of about 55.6 Kbps.

The general rule is that the larger the message field, the more efficient the protocol. So why not have 10,000-byte or even 100,000-byte packets to really increase efficiency? The answer is that anytime a frame is received containing an error, the entire frame must be retransmitted. Thus, if an entire file is sent as one large packet (e.g., 100K) and 1 bit is received in error, all 100,000 bytes must be sent again. Clearly, this is a waste of capacity. Furthermore, the probability that a frame contains an error increases with the

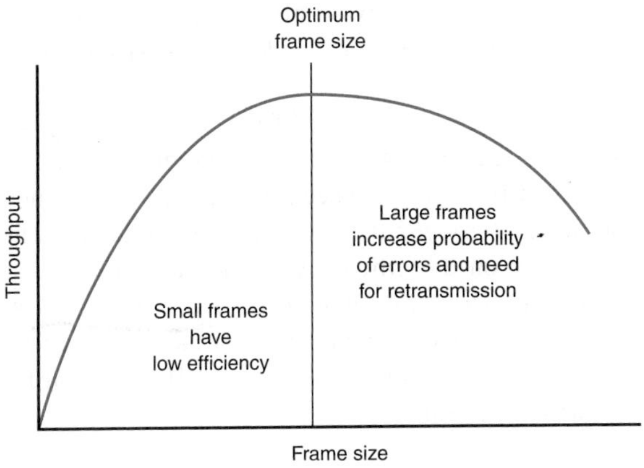

FIGURE 4.12 Frame size effects on throughput

size of the frame; larger frames are more likely to contain errors than are smaller ones, simply due to the laws of probability.

Thus, in designing a protocol, there is a trade-off between large and small frames. Small frames are less efficient but are less likely to contain errors and cost less (in terms of circuit capacity) to retransmit if there is an error (Figure 4.12).

Throughput is the total number of information bits received per second, after taking into account the overhead bits and the need to retransmit frames containing errors. Generally speaking, small frames provide better throughput for circuits with more errors, whereas larger frames provide better throughput in less-error-prone networks. Fortunately, in most real networks, the curve shown in Figure 4.12 is very flat on top, meaning that

MANAGEMENT FOCUS 4.2 SLEUTHING FOR THE RIGHT FRAME SIZE

Optimizing performance in a network, particularly a client–server network, can be difficult because few network managers realize the importance of the frame size. Selecting the right—or the wrong—frame size can have greater effects on performance than anything you might do to the server.

Standard Commercial, a multinational tobacco and agricultural company, noticed a decrease in network performance when they upgraded to a new server. They tested the effects of using frame sizes between 500 bytes to 32,000 bytes. In their tests, a frame size of 512 bytes required a total of 455,000 bytes transmitted over their network to transfer the test messages. In contrast, the 32,000-byte frames were far more efficient, cutting the total data by 44 percent to 257,000 bytes.

However, the problem with 32,000-byte frames was a noticeable response time delay because messages were saved until the 32,000-byte frames were full before transmitting.

The ideal frame size depends on the specific application and the pattern of messages it generates. For Standard Commercial, the ideal frame size appeared to be between 4,000 and 8,000. Unfortunately, not all network software packages enable network managers to fine-tune frame sizes in this way.

SOURCE: "Sleuthing for the Right Packet Size," *InfoWorld*, January 16, 1995.

there is a range of frame sizes that provide almost optimum performance. Frame sizes vary greatly among different networks, but the ideal frame size tends to be between 2,000 and 10,000 bytes.

So why are the standard sizes of Ethernet frames about 1,500 bytes? Because Ethernet was standardized many years ago when errors were more common. Jumbo and super jumbo frame sizes emerged from higher speed, highly error free fiber-optic networks.

Calculating the actual *throughput* of a data communications network is complex because it depends not only on the efficiency of the data link protocol but also on the error rate and number of retransmissions that occur. *Transmission rate of information bits (TRIB)* is a measure of the effective number of information bits that is transmitted over a communication circuit per unit of time. The basic TRIB equation from ANSI is shown in Figure 4.13, along with an example.

FORMULA FOR CALCULATING TRIB

$$\text{TRIB} = \frac{\text{Number of information bits accepted}}{\text{Total time required to get the bits accepted}}$$

$$\text{TRIB} = \frac{K(M - C)\,(1 - P)}{(M/R) + T}$$

where K = information bits per character

M = frame length in characters

R = data transmission rate in characters per second

C = average number of noninformation characters per frame (control characters)

P = probability that a frame will require retransmission because of error

T = time between frames in seconds, such as modem delay/turnaround time on half duplex and propogation delay on satellite transmission. This is the time required to reverse the direction of transmission from send to receive or receive to send on a half-duplex circuit. It can be obtained from the modem specification book and may be referred to as *reclocking time*.

The following TRIB example shows the calculation of throughput assuming a 4,800-bps half-duplex circuit.

$$\text{TRIB} = \frac{7(400 - 10)\,(1 - 0.01)}{(400/600) + 0.025} = 3{,}908 \text{ bits per second}$$

where K = 7 bits per character (information)

M = 400 characters per frame

R = 600 characters per second (derived from 4,800 bps divided by 8 bits/character)

C = 10 control characters per frame

P = 0.01 (10^{-2}) or 1 retransmission per 100 blocks transmitted—1%

T = 25 milliseconds (0.025) turnaround time

If all factors in the calculation remain constant except for the circuit, which is changed to full duplex (no turnaround time delays, T = 0), then the TRIB increases to 4,504 bps.

Look at the equation where the turnaround value (T) is 0.025. If there is a further propagation delay time of 475 milliseconds (0.475), this figure changes to 0.500. For demonstrating how a satellite channel affects TRIB, the total delay time is now 500 milliseconds. Still using the figures above (except for the new 0.500 delay time), we reduce the TRIB for our half-duplex satellite link to 2,317 bps, which is almost half of the full-duplex (no turnaround time) 4,054 bps.

FIGURE 4.13 Calculating TRIB (transmission rate of information bits)

IMPLICATIONS FOR MANAGEMENT

You can think of the data link layer protocol as the fundamental "language" spoken by networks. This protocol must be compatible with the physical cables that are used, but in many cases the physical cables can support a variety of different protocols. Each device on the network speaks a particular data link layer protocol. In the past, there were literally dozens of protocols that were used; each protocol was custom-tailored to specific needs of the devices and application software in use. Where different devices or cables from different parts of the organization were connected, we used a translator to convert from the data link protocol spoken by one device into the protocol spoken by another device.

As the Internet has become more prominent and as it has become more important to move data from one part of an organization to the other, the need to translate among different data link layer protocols has become more and more costly. It is now more important to provide a few widely used protocols for all networks than to custom tailor protocols to the needs of specific devices or applications. Today, businesses are moving rapidly to reduce the number of different protocols spoken by their networking equipment and converge on a few standard protocols that are used widely throughout the network.

We still do use different protocols in different parts of the network where there are important reasons for doing so. For example, local area networks often have different needs than wide area networks, so their data link layer protocols typically are still different, but even here we are seeing a few organizations move to standardize protocols.

This move to standardize data link layer protocols means that networking equipment and networking staff need to understand fewer protocols—their job is becoming simpler, which in turn means that the cost to buy and maintain network equipment and to train networking staff is gradually decreasing (and the side benefit to students is that there are fewer protocols to learn!). The downside, of course, is that some applications may take longer to run over protocols are not perfectly suited to them. As network capacities in the physical layer continue to increase, this has proven to be far less important than the significant cost savings that can be realized from standardization.

SUMMARY

Media Access Control Media access control refers to controlling when computers transmit. There are three basic approaches. With roll-call polling, the server polls client computers to see if they have data to send; computers can transmit only when they have been polled. With hub polling or token passing, the computers themselves manage when they can transmit by passing a token to one other; no computer can transmit unless it has the token. With contention, computers listen and transmit only when no others are transmitting. In general, contention approaches work better for small networks that have low levels of usage, whereas polling approaches work better for networks with high usage.

Sources and Prevention of Error Errors occur in all networks. Errors tend to occur in groups (or bursts) rather than 1 bit at a time. The primary sources of errors are impulse noises (e.g., lightning), cross-talk, echo, and attenuation. Errors can be prevented (or at least reduced) by shielding the cables; moving cables away from sources of noise and power sources; using repeaters (and, to a lesser extent, amplifiers); and improving the quality of the equipment, media, and their connections.

Error Detection and Correction All error-detection schemes attach additional error-detection data, based on a mathematical calculation, to the user's message. The receiver performs the same calculation on incoming messages, and if the results of this calculation do not match the error-detection data on the incoming message, an error has occurred. Parity, checksum, and CRC are the most common error-detection schemes. The most common error-correction technique is simply to ask the sender to retransmit the message until it is received without error. A different approach, forward error correction, includes sufficient information to allow the receiver to correct the error in most cases without asking for a retransmission.

Message Delineation Message delineation means to indicate the start and end of a message. Asynchronous transmission uses start and stop bits on each letter to mark where they begin and end. Synchronous techniques (e.g., SDLC, HDLC, Ethernet, PPP) group blocks of data together into frames that use special characters or bit patterns to mark the start and end of entire messages.

Transmission Efficiency and Throughput Every protocol adds additional bits to the user's message before sending it (e.g., for error detection). These bits are called overhead bits because they add no value to the user; they simply ensure correct data transfer. The efficiency of a transmission protocol is the number of information bits sent by the user divided by the total number of bits transferred (information bits plus overhead bits). Synchronous transmission provides greater efficiency than does asynchronous transmission. In general, protocols with larger frame sizes provide greater efficiency than do those with small frame sizes. The drawback to large frame sizes is that they are more likely to be affected by errors and thus require more retransmission. Small frame sizes are therefore better suited to error-prone circuits, and large frames, to error-free circuits.

KEY TERMS

acknowledgment (ACK)
amplifier
asynchronous transmission
attenuation
Automatic Repeat reQuest (ARQ)
burst error
checksum
contention
continuous ARQ
cross-talk
cyclical redundancy check (CRC)
echo
efficiency
error detection with retransmission
error prevention
error rate
Ethernet (IEEE 802.3)
even parity
flow control
forward error correction
frame
Gaussian noise
Go-Back-N ARQ
Hamming code
harmonic distortion
high level data link control (HDLC)
hub polling
impulse noise
information bits
intermodulation noise
jitter
line noise
line outage
Link Access Protocol-Balanced (LAP-B)
Link Access Protocol for Modems (LAP-M)
logical link control (LLC) sublayer
media access control
media access control (MAC) sublayer
negative acknowledgment (NAK)
odd parity
overhead bits
parity bit
parity check
Point-to-Point Protocol (PPP)
polling
repeater
roll-call polling
sliding window
start bit
stop-and-wait ARQ
stop bit
synchronization
synchronous transmission
throughput
token passing
transmission efficiency
white noise

QUESTIONS

1. What does the data link layer do?
2. What is media access control, and why is it important?
3. Under what conditions is media access control unimportant?
4. Compare and contrast roll-call polling, hub polling (or token passing), and contention.
5. Which is better, controlled access or contention? Explain.
6. Define two fundamental types of errors.
7. Errors normally appear in ______, which is when more than 1 data bit is changed by the error-causing condition.
8. Is there any difference in the error rates of lower-speed lines and higher-speed lines?
9. Briefly define *noise*.
10. Describe four types of noise. Which is likely to pose the greatest problem to network managers?
11. How do amplifiers differ from repeaters?
12. What are three ways of reducing errors and the types of noise they affect?
13. Describe three approaches to *detecting* errors, including how they work, the probability of detecting an error, and any other benefits or limitations.
14. Briefly describe how even parity and odd parity work.
15. Briefly describe how checksum works.
16. How does CRC work?
17. How does forward error correction work? How is it different from other error-correction methods?
18. Under what circumstances is forward error correction desirable?
19. Compare and contrast stop-and-wait ARQ and continuous ARQ.
20. Which is the simplest (least sophisticated) protocol described in this chapter?
21. Describe the frame layouts for SDLC, Ethernet and PPP.
22. What is transmission efficiency?
23. How do information bits differ from overhead bits?
24. Are stop bits necessary in asynchronous transmission? Explain using a diagram.
25. During the 1990s, there was intense competition between two technologies (10-Mbps Ethernet and 16-Mbps token ring) for the LAN market. Ethernet was promoted by a consortium of vendors, whereas token ring was primarily an IBM product, even though it was standardized. Ethernet won, and no one talks about token ring anymore. Token ring used a hub-polling–based approach. Outline a number of reasons why Ethernet might have won. Hint: The reasons were both technical and business.
26. Under what conditions does a data link layer protocol need an address?
27. Are large frame sizes better than small frame sizes? Expain.
28. What media access control technique does your class use?
29. Show how the word "HI" would be sent using asynchronous transmission using even parity (make assumptions about the bit patterns needed). Show how it would be sent using Ethernet.

EXERCISES

4-1. Draw how a series of four separate messages would be *successfully* sent from one computer to another if the first message was transferred without error, the second was initially transmitted with an error, the third was initially lost, and the ACK for the fourth was initially lost.

4-2. How efficient would a 6-bit code be in asynchronous transmission if it had 1 parity bit, 1 start bit, and 2 stop bits? (Some old equipment uses 2 stop bits.)

4-3. What is the transmission rate of information bits if you use ASCII (8 bits plus 1 parity bit), a

1;000-character frame, 56 Kbps modem transmission speed, 20 control characters per frame, an error rate of 1 percent, and a 30-millisecond turnaround time? What is the TRIB if you add a half-second delay to the turnaround time because of satellite delay?

4-4. Search the Web to find a software vendor that sells a package that supports each of the following protocols: SDLC, HDLC, Ethernet, and PPP (i.e., one package that supports SDLC, another [or the same] for HDLC and so on).

4-5. Investigate the network at your organization (or a service offered by an IXC) to find out the average error rates.

4-6. What is the efficiency if a 100-byte file is transmitted using Ethernet? A 10,000-byte file?

4-7. What is the propagation delay on a circuit using a LEO satellite orbiting 500 miles above the earth if the speed of the signal is 186,000 miles per second? If the satellite is 22,000 miles above the earth?

4-8. Suppose you are going to connect the computers in your house or apartment. What media would you use? Why? Would this change if you were building a new house?

MINI-CASES

I. Smith, Smith, Smith, and Smith

Smith, Smith, Smith, and Smith is a regional accounting firm that is putting up a new headquarters building. The building will have a backbone network that connects eight LANs (two on each floor). The company is very concerned with network errors. What advice would you give regarding the design of the building and network cable planning that would help reduce network errors?

II. Worldwide Charity

Worldwide Charity is a charitable organization whose mission is to improve education levels in developing countries. In each country where it is involved, the organization has a small headquarters and usually five to ten offices in outlying towns. Staff members communicate with one another via e-mail on older computers donated to the organization. Because Internet service is not reliable in many of the towns in these countries, the staff members usually phone headquarters and use a very simple Linux e-mail system that uses a server-based network architecture. They also upload and download files. What range of frame sizes is likely to be used?

III. Industrial Products

Industrial Products is a small light-manufacturing firm that produces a variety of control systems for heavy industry. They have a network that connects their office building and warehouse that has functioned well for the last year, but over the past week, users have begun to complain that the network is slow. Clarence Hung, the network manager, did a quick check of the number of orders over the past week and saw no real change, suggesting that there has been no major increase in network traffic. What would you suggest that Clarence do next?

IV. Alpha Corp

Alpha Corp. is trying to decide the size of the connection it needs to the Internet. They estimate that they will send and receive a total of about 1,000 e-mails per hour and that each e-mail message is about 1,500 bytes in size. They also estimate that they will send and receive a total of about 3,000 Web pages per hour and that each page is about 40,000 bytes in size. 1. Without considering transmission efficiency, how large an Internet connection would you recommend in terms of bits per second (assuming that each byte is eight bits in length)? 2. Assuming they use a synchronous data link layer protocol with an efficiency of about 90 percent, how large an Internet connection would you recommend? 3. Suppose Alpha wants to be sure that its Internet connection will provide sufficient capacity the next two years, how large an Internet connection would you recommend?

CASE STUDY

NEXT-DAY AIR SERVICE

See the Web site.

HANDS-ON ACTIVITY

Capturing Packets on Your Network

In this chapter, we discussed several data link layer protocols, such as SDLC and Ethernet. The objective of this Activity is for you to see the data link layer frames in action on your network.

Wireshark is one of the many tools that permit users to examine the frames in their network. It is called a packet sniffer because it enables you to see inside the frames and packets that your computer sends, as well as the frames and packets sent by other users on your LAN. In other words, you can eavesdrop on the other users on your LAN to see what Web sites they visit and even the e-mail they send. We don't recommend using it for this reason, but it is important that you understand that someone else could be using Ethereal to sniff your packets to see and record what you are doing on the Internet.

1. Use your browser to connect to www.wireshark.org and download and install the Wireshark software.
2. When you start Wireshark you will see a screen like that in Figure 4.14, minus the two smaller windows on top.
   a. Click Capture
   b. Click Interfaces
   c. Click the Capture button beside your Wireshark connection (wireless LAN or traditional LAN).
3. Wireshark will capture all packets moving through your LAN. To make sure you have something to see, open your Web browser and visit one or two Web sites. After you have captured packets for 30–60 seconds, return to Wireshark and click Stop.
4. Figure 4.15 shows the packets captured on my home network. The top window in Wireshark displays the complete list of packets in chronological order. Each packet is numbered; I've scrolled the window, so the first packet shown is packet 11. Wireshark lists the time, the source IP address, the destination IP address, the protocol, and some additional information about each packet. The IP addresses will be explained in more detail in the next chapter.

For the moment, look at packet number 16, the second HTTP packet from the top. I've clicked on this packet, so the middle window shows the inside of the packet. The first line in this second window says the frame (or packet if you prefer) is 1091 bytes long. It contains an Ethernet II packet, an Internet Protocol (IP) packet, a Transmission Control Protocol (TCP) Packet, and a Hypertext Transfer Protocol (HTTP) packet. Remember in Chapter 1 that Figure 1.4 described how each packet was placed inside another packet

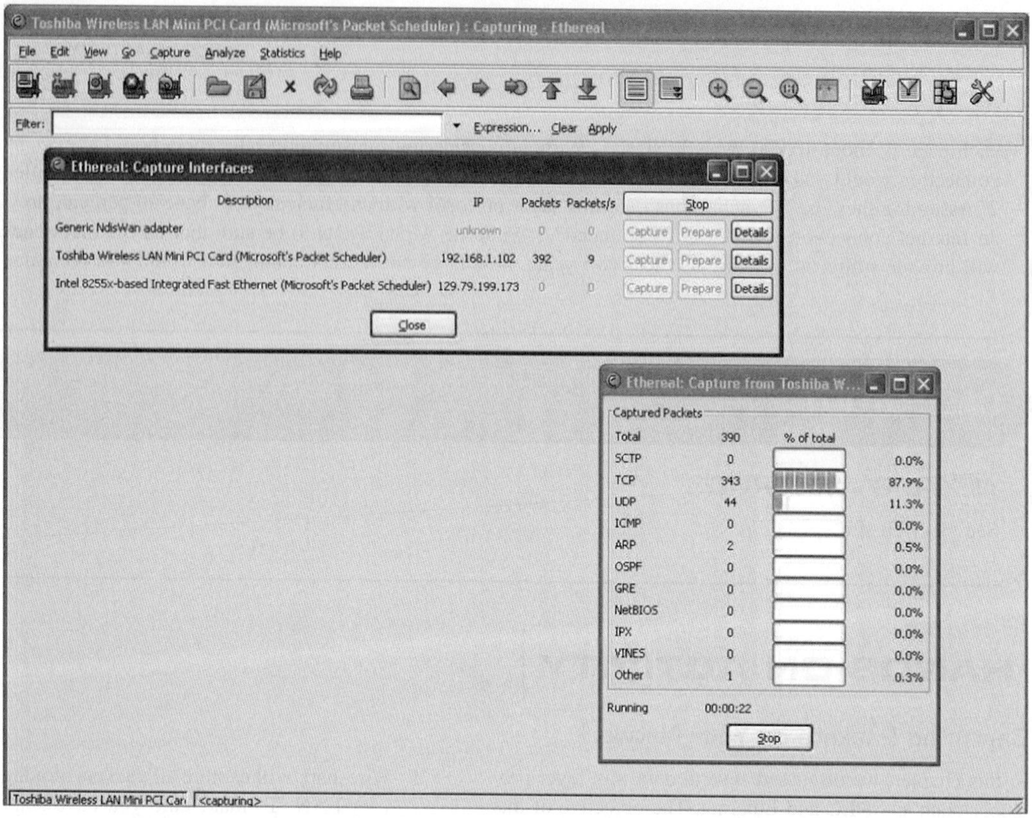

FIGURE 4.14 Capturing packets with Wireshark

as the message moved through the layers and was transmitted.

Click on the plus sign (+) in front of the HTTP packet to expand it. Wireshark shows the contents of the HTTP packet. By reading the data inside the HTTP packet, you can see that this packet was an HTTP request to my.yahoo.com that contained a cookie. If you look closely, you'll see that the sending computer was a Tablet PC—that's some of the optional information my Web browser (Internet Explorer) included in the HTTP header.

The bottom window in Figure 4.15 shows the exact bytes that were captured. The section highlighted in grey shows the HTTP packet. The numbers on the left show the data in hexadecimal format while the data on the right show the text version. The data before the highlighted section is the TCP packet.

From Chapter 2, you know that the client sends an HTTP request packet to request a Web page, and the Web server sends back an HTTP response packet. Packet number 25 in the top window in Figure 4.15 is the HTTP response sent back to my computer by the Yahoo server. You can see that the destination IP address in my HTTP request is the source IP address of this HTTP packet.

5. Figure 4.15 also shows what happens when you click the plus sign (+) in front of the Ethernet II packet to expand it. You can see that this Ethernet packet has a destination address and source address (e.g., 00:02:2d:85:cb:e0).

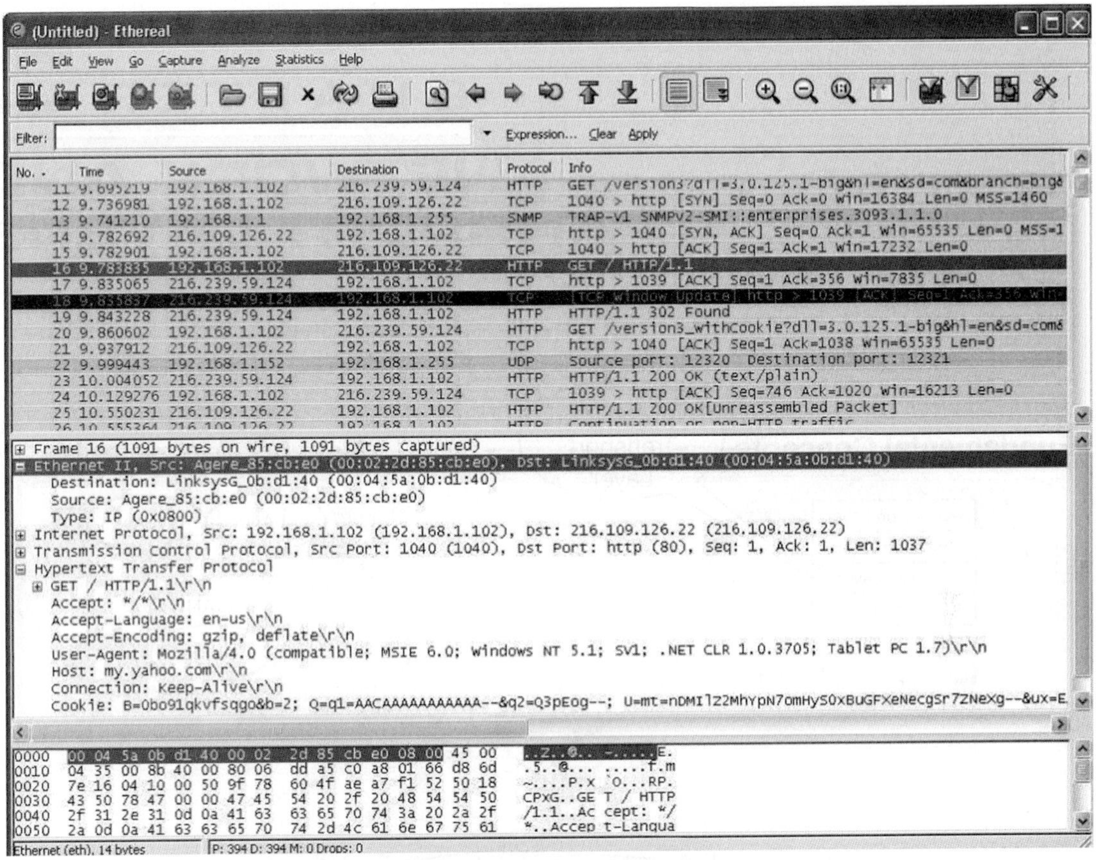

FIGURE 4.15 Analyzing packets with Wireshark

CHAPTER 5

NETWORK AND TRANSPORT LAYERS

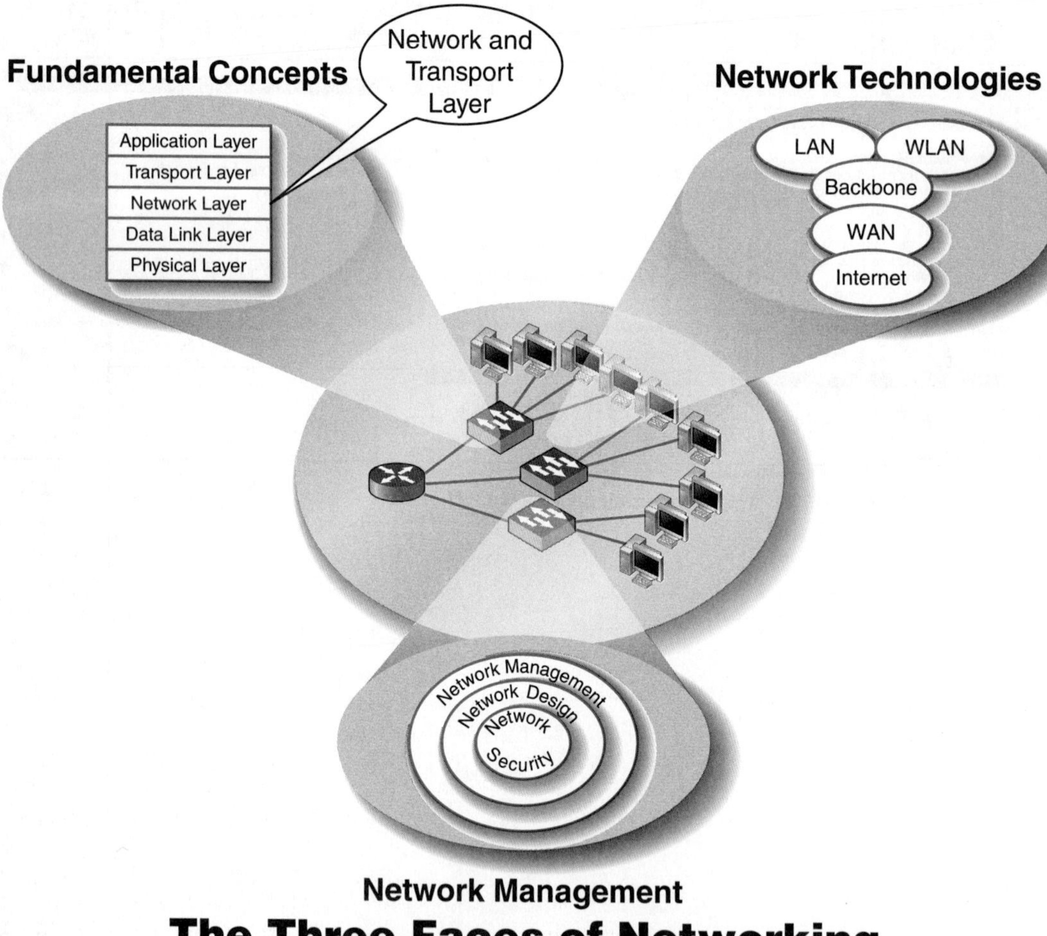

The Three Faces of Networking

THE NETWORK layer and transport layer are responsible for moving messages from end to end in a network. They are so closely tied together that they are usually discussed together. The transport layer (layer 4) performs three functions: linking the application layer to the network, segmenting (breaking long messages into smaller packets for transmission), and session management (establishing an end-to-end connection between the sender and receiver). The network layer (layer 3) performs two functions: routing (determining the next computer to which the message should be sent to reach the final destination) and **addressing** (finding the address of that next computer). There are several standard transport and network layer protocols that specify how packets are to be organized, in the same way that there are standards for data link layer packets. However, only one protocol is in widespread use today: TCP/IP, the protocol used on the Internet. This chapter takes a detailed look at how TCP/IP works.

OBJECTIVES ▼

- Be aware of the TCP/IP protocols
- Be familiar with linking to the application layer, segmenting, and session management
- Be familiar with addressing
- Be familiar with routing
- Understand how TCP/IP works

CHAPTER OUTLINE ▼

INTRODUCTION

The transport and network layers are so closely tied together that they are almost always discussed together. For this reason, we discuss them in the same chapter. There are several different protocols that can be used at the transport and network layers, in the same way there are several different data link layer protocols. TCP/IP is the most commonly used set of protocols and is well on its way to eliminating the other protocols. Therefore, this chapter focuses exclusively on TCP/IP.

The transport layer links the application software in the application layer with the network and is responsible for the end-to-end delivery of the message. The transport layer accepts outgoing messages from the application layer (e.g., Web, e-mail, and so on, as described in Chapter 2) and segments them for transmission. Figure 5.1 shows the application layer software producing an SMTP packet that is split into two smaller TCP

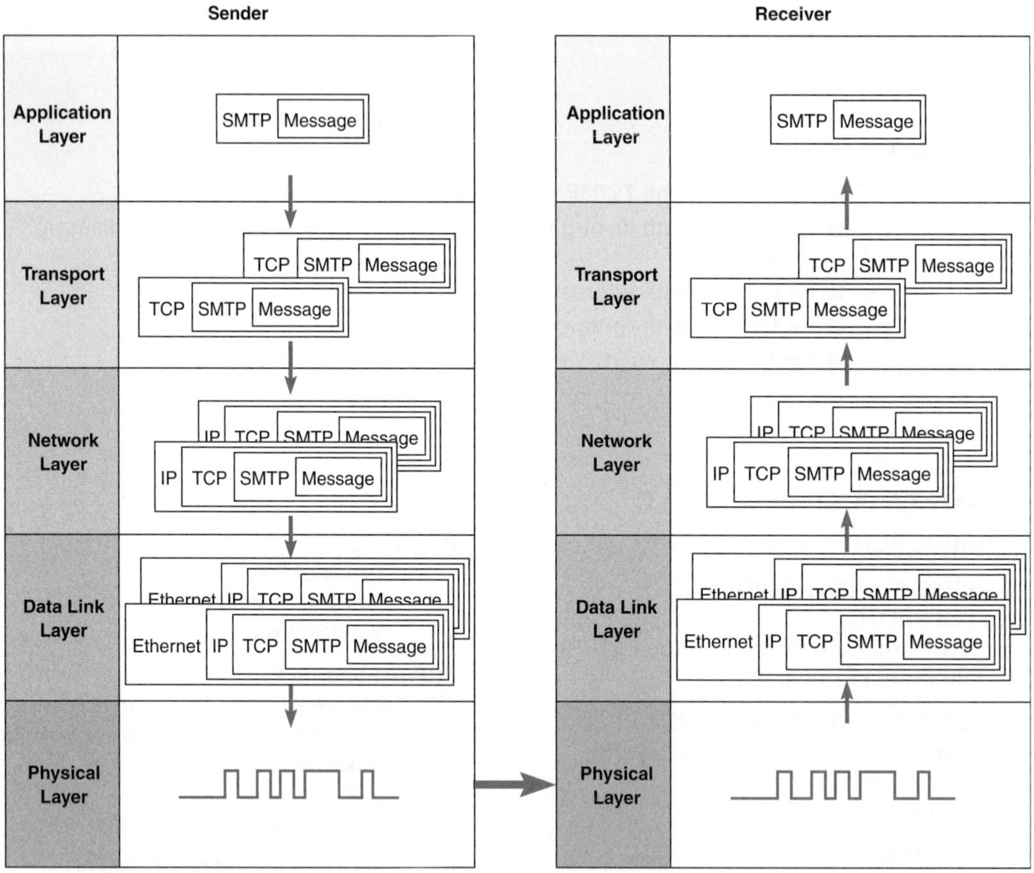

FIGURE 5.1 Message transmission using layers. HTTP = Hypertext Transfer Protocol; IP = Internet Protocol; TCP = Transmission Control Protocol

segments by the transport layer. The Protocol Data Unit (PDU) at the transport layer is called a **segment.** The network layer takes the messages from the transport layer and routes them through the network by selecting the best path from computer to computer through the network (and adds an IP packet). The data link layer adds an Ethernet frame and instructs the physical layer hardware when to transmit. As we saw in Chapter 1, each layer in the network has its own set of protocols that are used to hold the data generated by higher layers, much like a set of *Matryoshka* (nested Russian dolls).

The network and transport layers also accept incoming messages from the data link layer and organize them into coherent messages that are passed to the application layer. For example, as in Figure 5.1 a large e-mail message might require several data link layer frames to transmit. The transport layer at the sender would break the message into several smaller segments and give them to the network layer to route, which in turn gives them to the data link layer to transmit. The network layer at the receiver would receive the individual packets from the data link layer, process them, and pass them to the transport layer, which would reassemble them into the one e-mail message before giving it to the application layer.

In this chapter, we provide a brief look at the transport and network layer protocols, before turning our attention to how TCP/IP works. We first examine the transport layer functions. Addressing and routing are performed by the transport layer and network layers working together, so we will discuss them together rather than separate them according to which part is performed by the transport layer and which by the network layer.

TRANSPORT AND NETWORK LAYER PROTOCOLS

There are many different transport/network layer protocols, but one family of protocols, TCP/IP, dominates. Each transport and network layer protocol performs essentially the same functions, but each is incompatible with the others unless there is a special device to translate between them. Many vendors provide software with *multiprotocol stacks,* which means that the software supports several different transport/network protocols. The software recognizes which protocol an incoming message uses and automatically uses that protocol to process the message. In this chapter, we focus only on TCP/IP. A good overview of protocols, at all layers, is available at: www.protocols.com.

The **Transmission Control Protocol/Internet Protocol (TCP/IP)** was developed for the U.S. Department of Defense's Advanced Research Project Agency network (ARPANET) by Vinton Cerf and Bob Kahn in 1974. TCP/IP is the transport/network layer protocol used on the Internet. It is the world's most popular protocol set, used by almost all BNs, MANs, and WANs. TCP/IP allows reasonably efficient and error-free transmission. Because it performs error checking, it can send large files across sometimes unreliable networks with great assurance that the data will arrive uncorrupted. TCP/IP is compatible with a variety of data link protocols, which is one reason for its popularity.

As the name implies, TCP/IP has two parts. TCP is the transport layer protocol that links the application layer to the network layer. It performs segmenting: breaking the data into smaller PDUs called segments, numbering them, ensuring each segment

Source port	Destination port	Sequence number	ACK number	Header length	Unused	Flags	Flow control	CRC–16	Urgent pointer	Options	User data
16 bits	16 bits	32 bits	32 bits	4 bits	6 bits	6 bits	16 bits	16 bits	16 bits	32 bits	Varies

FIGURE 5.2 Transmission Control Protocol (TCP) segment, ACK = acknowledgment; CRC = cyclical redundancy check

is reliably delivered, and putting them in the proper order at the destination. IP is the network layer protocol and performs addressing and routing. IP software is used at each of the intervening computers through which the message passes; it is IP that routes the message to the final destination. The TCP software needs to be active only at the sender and the receiver, because TCP is involved only when data comes from or goes to the application layer.

Transmission Control Protocol (TCP)

A typical TCP segment has 192-bit header (24 bytes) of control information (Figure 5.2). Among other fields, it contains the source and destination port identifier. The destination port tells the TCP software at the destination to which application layer program the application layer packet should be sent whereas the source port tells the receiver which application layer program the packet is from. The TCP segment also provides a sequence number so that the TCP software at the destination can assemble the segments into the correct order and make sure that no segments have been lost.

The options field is optional, so in many cases it is omitted. In this case, TCP has a length of 20 bytes (160 bits). The header length field is used to tell the receiver how long the TCP packet is, that is, whether the options field is included or not.

TCP/IP has a second type of transport layer protocol called **User Datagram Protocol (UDP).** UDP PDUs are called datagrams. UDP is typically used when the sender needs to send a single small packet to the receiver (e.g., for a DNS request, which we discuss later in this chapter). When there is only one small packet to be sent, the transport layer doesn't need to worry about segmenting the outgoing messages or reassembling them upon receipt, so transmission can be faster. A UDP datagram has only four fields (eight bytes of overhead) plus the application layer packet: source port, destination port, length, and a CRC-16. Unlike TCP, UDP does not check for lost messages, so occasionally a UDP datagram is lost, and the message must be resent.

Internet Protocol (IP)

IP is the network layer protocol. Network layer PDUs are called packets. Two forms of IP are currently in use. The older form is IP version 4 (IPv4), which also has a 192-bit header (24 bytes) (Figure 5.3). This header contains source and destination addresses, packet length, and packet number.

IPv4 is being replaced by IPv6, which has a 320-bit header (40 bytes) (Figure 5.4). The primary reason for the increase in the packet size is an increase in the address size from 32 bits to 128 bits. IPv6's simpler packet structure makes it easier to perform routing and supports a variety of new approaches to addressing and routing.

Version number	Header length	Type of service	Total length	Identifiers	Flags	Packet offset	Hop limit	Protocol	CRC 16	Source address	Destination address	Options	User data
4 bits	4 bits	8 bits	16 bits	16 bits	3 bits	13 bits	8 bits	8 bits	16 bits	32 bits	32 bits	32 bits	Varies

FIGURE 5.3 Internet Protocol (IP) packet (version 4). CRC = cyclical redundancy check

IPv6 was developed because we were running out of IP addresses on the Internet. IPv4 has a four-byte address field, which means there is a theoretical maximum of about 4.2 billion addresses. However, about 500 million of these addresses are reserved and cannot be used, and the way addresses were assigned in the early days of the Internet means that a small number of companies received several million addresses, even when they didn't need all of them. With the increased growth in Internet users, and the explosion in mobile Internet devices, current estimates project that we will run out of IPv4 addresses somewhere between 2012 and 2017.

IPv6 uses a 16-byte long address which provides a theoretical maximum of 3.4×10^{38} addresses—more than enough for the foreseeable future. IPv4 uses decimal to express addresses (e.g., 128.192.55.72), but IPv6 uses hexadecimal (base 16) like Ethernet to express addresses, which makes it slightly more confusing to use. Addresses are eight sets of two byte numbers (e.g., 2001:0890:0600:00d1:0000:0000:abcd:f010), but because this can be long to write, there is a IPv6 "compressed notation" which eliminates the leading zeros within each block and blocks that are all zeros. So the IPv6 address above could also be written as 2001:890:600:d1: :abcd:f010.

Adoption of IPv6 has been slow. Most organizations have not felt the need to change because IPv6 provides few benefits other than the larger address space and requires their staff to learn a whole new protocol. In most cases, the shortage of addresses on the Internet doesn't affect organizations that already have Internet addresses, so there is little incentive to convert to IPv6. Most organizations that implement IPv6 also run IPv4, and IPv6 is not backward-compatible with IPv4, which means that all network devices must be changed to understand both IPV4 and IPv6. The cost of this conversion, along with the few benefits it provides to organizations which do convert, has led a number of commentators to refer to this as the IPv6 "mess." In order to encourage the move to IPv6, the U.S. government required all of its agencies to convert to IPv6 on their WANs and backbone networks by June 2008, but the change was not completed on time.

The size of the message field depends on the data link layer protocol used. TCP/IP is commonly combined with Ethernet. Ethernet has a maximum packet size of 1,492 bytes, so the maximum size of a TCP message field if IPv4 is used is 1,492—24 (the size of the TCP header)—24 (the size of the IPv4 header) = 1, 444.

Version number	Priority	Flow name	Total length	Next header	Hop limit	Source address	Destination address	User data
4 bits	4 bits	24 bits	16 bits	8 bits	8 bits	128 bits	128 bits	Varies

FIGURE 5.4 Internet Protocol (IP) packet (version 6)

MANAGEMENT FOCUS 5.1 **MOVING TO TCP/IP**

Merita Bank in Finland is the Finnish part of the Nordea, the largest financial services group in the Nordic and Baltic region. Merita runs over 3 million transactions on its IBM mainframe computer during a normal banking day, with approximately 190 transactions per second during the peak hour.

Prior to the conversion, Merita's IBM mainframe computer used the Systems Network Architecture (SNA) protocol while its network supporting its many branches used TCP/IP. The inbound data from the branches would arrive at the mainframe network and have to be converted from TCP/IP to SNA before being sent to the mainframe. Likewise, outbound traffic from the mainframe would have to be converted from SNA to TCP/IP before being sent to the branches. Although the network worked, it was not efficient and during periods of high traffic could experience considerable delays.

To eliminate the slow and complex conversion between the TCP/IP-based branch office network and the SNA-based mainframe network, Merita replaced the mainframe's SNA protocol with TCP/IP. Now the network runs significantly faster, and there is one end-to-end protocol. All this, with just changing the network hardware and software on the mainframe and throwing away some old equipment; there were no changes to the branch network or to the application software.

SOURCE: "Merita Bank uses IMS Connect to simplify network connections and increase efficiency," www.ibm.com, 2004.

TRANSPORT LAYER FUNCTIONS

The transport layer links the application software in the application layer with the network and is responsible for segmenting large messages into smaller ones for transmission and for managing the session (the end-to-end delivery of the message). One of the first issues facing the application layer is to find the numeric network address of the destination computer. Different protocols use different methods to find this address. Depending on the protocol—and which expert you ask—finding the destination address can be classified as a transport layer function, a network layer function, a data link layer function, or an application layer function with help from the operating system. In all honesty, understanding how the process works is more important than memorizing how it is classified. The next section discusses addressing at the network layer and transport layer. In this section, we focus on the three unique functions performed by the transport layer: linking the application layer to the network, and segmenting.

Linking to the Application Layer

Most computers have many application layer software packages running at the same time. Users often have Web browsers, e-mail programs, and word processors in use at the same time on their client computers. Likewise, many servers act as Web servers, mail servers, FTP servers, and so on. When the transport layer receives an incoming message, the transport layer must decide to which application program it should be delivered. It makes no sense to send a Web page request to e-mail server software.

With TCP/IP, each application layer software package has a unique **port address.** Any message sent to a computer must tell TCP (the transport layer software) the application layer port address that is to receive the message. Therefore, when an application layer program generates an outgoing message, it tells the TCP software its own port address (i.e., the **source port address**) and the port address at the destination computer (i.e., the **destination port address**). These two port addresses are placed in the first two fields in the TCP segment (see Figure 5.2).

Port addresses can be any 16-bit (2-byte) number. So how does a client computer sending a Web request to a Web server know what port address to use for the Web server? Simple. On the Internet, all port addresses for popular services such as the Web, e-mail, and FTP have been standardized. Anyone using a Web server should set up the Web server with a port address of 80. Web browsers, therefore, automatically generate a port address of 80 for any Web page you click on. FTP servers use port 21, Telnet 23, SMTP 25, and so on. Network managers are free to use whatever port addresses they want, but if they use a nonstandard port number, then the application layer software on the client must specify the correct port number.[1]

Figure 5.5 shows a user running three applications on the client (Internet Explorer, Outlook, and RealPlayer), each of which has been assigned a different port number (1027, 1028, and 7070, respectively). Each of these can simultaneously send and receive data to and from different servers and different applications on the same server. In this case, we see a message sent by Internet Explorer on the client (port 1027) to the Web server software on the xyz.com server (port 80). We also see a message sent by the mail server software on port 25 to the e-mail client on port 1028. At the same time, the RealPlayer software on the client is sending a request to the music server software (port 554) at 123.com.

Segmenting

Some messages or blocks of application data are small enough that they can be transmitted in one frame at the data link layer. However, in other cases, the application data in one "message" is too large and must be broken into several frames (e.g., Web pages, graphic images). As far as the application layer is concerned, the message should be transmitted and received as one large block of data. However, the data link layer can transmit only messages of certain lengths. It is therefore up to the sender's transport layer to break the data into several smaller segments that can be sent by the data link layer across the circuit. At the other end, the receiver's transport layer must receive all these separate segments and recombine them into one large message.

Segmenting means to take one outgoing message from the application layer and break it into a set of smaller segments for transmission through the network. It also means to take the incoming set of smaller segments from the network layer and reassemble them into one message for the application layer. Depending on what the application layer

[1] One way to make a Web server private would be to use a different port number (e.g., 8080). Any Web browser wanting to access this Web server would then have to explicitly include the port number in the URL (e.g., http://www.abc.com:8080).

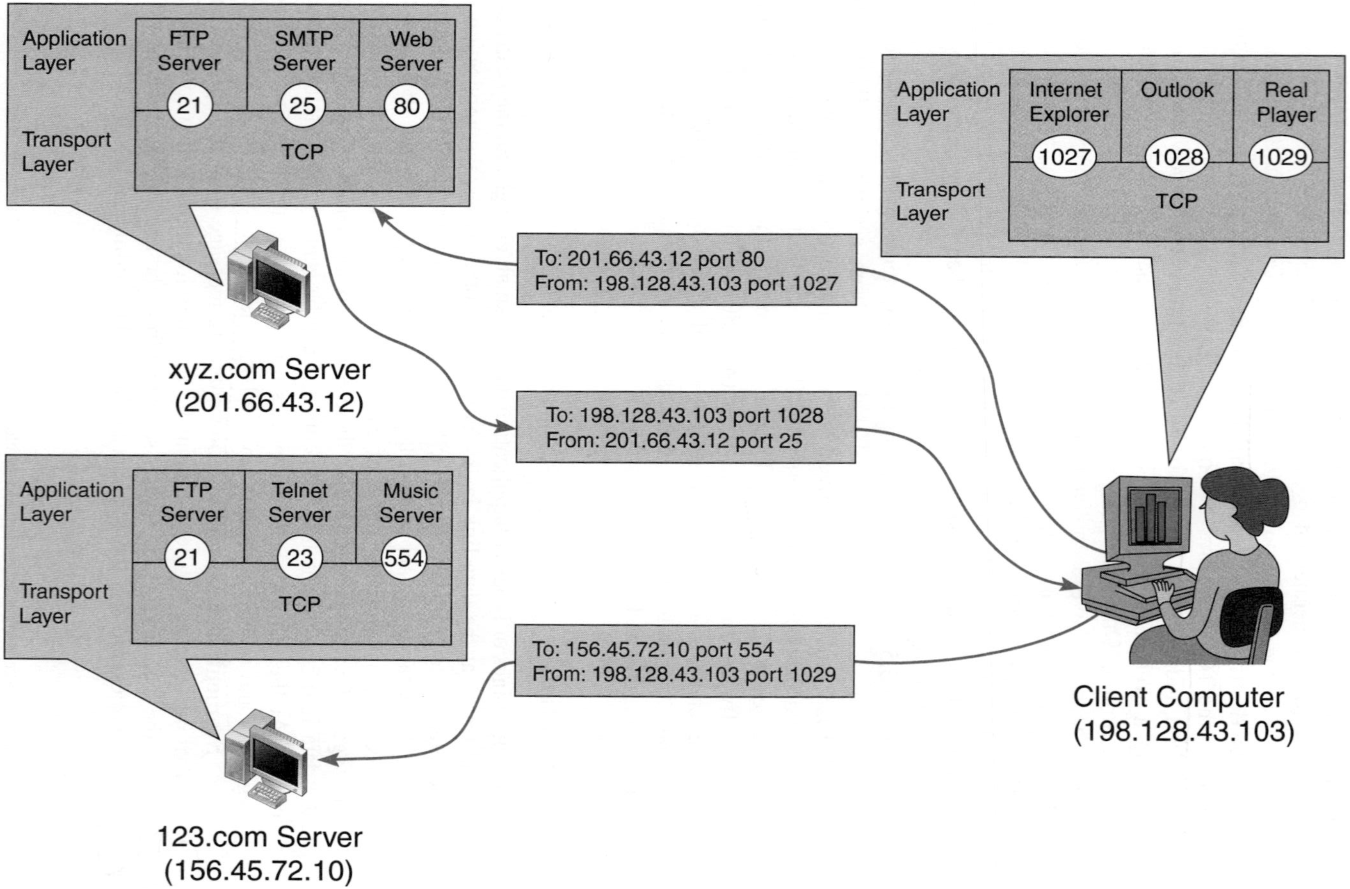

FIGURE 5.5 Linking to application layer services

software chooses, the incoming packets can either be delivered one at a time or held until all packets have arrived and the message is complete. Web browsers, for example, usually request delivery of packets as they arrive, which is why your screen gradually builds a piece at a time. Most e-mail software, on the other hand, usually requests that messages be delivered only after all packets have arrived and TCP has organized them into one intact message, which is why you usually don't see e-mail messages building screen by screen.

The TCP is also responsible for ensuring that the receiver has actually received all segments that have been sent. TCP therefore uses continuous ARQ (see Chapter 4).

One of the challenges at the transport layer is deciding how big to make the segments. Remember, we discussed packet sizes in Chapter 4. When transport layer software is set up, it is told what size segments it should use to make best use of its own data link layer protocols (or it chooses the default size of 536). However, it has no idea what size is best for the destination. Therefore, the transport layer at the sender negotiates with the transport layer at the receiver to settle on the best segment sizes to use. This negotiation is done by establishing a TCP connection between the sender and receiver.

Session Management

A **session** can be thought of as a conversation between two computers. When the sending computer wants to send a message to the receiver, it usually starts by establishing a session with that computer. The sender transmits the segments in sequence until the conversation is done, and then the sender ends the session. This approach to session management is called *connection-oriented* messaging.

Sometimes, the sender only wants to send one short information message or a request. In this case, the sender may choose not to start a session, but just send the one quick message and move on. This approach is called *connectionless messaging*.

Connection-Oriented Messaging

Connection-oriented messaging sets up a *TCP connection* (also called a session) between the sender and receiver. The transport layer software sends a special segment (called a SYN) to the receiver, requesting that a session be established. The receiver either accepts or rejects the session, and together they settle on the segment sizes the session will use.

Once the connection is established, the segments flow between the sender and receiver. TCP uses the continuous ARQ (sliding window) technique described in Chapter 4 to make sure that all segments arrive and to provide flow control.

When the transmission is complete, the sender sends a special segment (called a FIN) to close the session. Once the sender and receiver agree, the session is closed and all record of it is deleted.

Connectionless Messaging

Connectionless messaging means each packet is treated separately and makes its own way through the network. Unlike connection-oriented routing, no connection is established. The sender simply sends the packets as separate, unrelated entities, and it is possible that different packets will take different routes through the network, depending on the type of routing used and the amount of traffic. Because packets following different routes may travel at different speeds, they may arrive out of sequence at their destination. The sender's network layer, therefore, puts a sequence number on each packet, in addition to information about the message stream to which the packet belongs. The network layer must reassemble them in the correct order before passing the message to the application layer.

TCP/IP can operate either as connection-oriented or connectionless. When connection-oriented is desired, TCP is used. When connectionless is desired, the TCP segment is replaced with a User Datagram Protocol (UDP) packet. The UDP packet is much smaller than the TCP packet (only eight bytes).

Connectionless is most commonly used when the application data or message can fit into one single message. One might expect, for example, that because HTTP requests are often very short, they might use UDP connectionless rather than TCP connection-oriented messaging. However, HTTP always uses TCP. All of the application layer software we have discussed so far uses TCP (HTTP, SMTP, FTP, Telnet). UDP is most commonly used for control messages such as addressing (DHCP [Dynamic Host Configuration Protocol], discussed later in this chapter), routing control messages (RIP [Routing Information Protocol], discussed later in this chapter), and network management (SNMP [Simple Network Management Protocol], discussed in Chapter 13).

Quality of Service **Quality of Service (QoS)** routing is a special type of connection-oriented messaging in which different connections are assigned different priorities. For example, videoconferencing requires fast delivery of packets to ensure that the images and voices appear smooth and continuous; they are very time dependent because delays in routing seriously affect the quality of the service provided. E-mail packets, on the other hand, have no such requirements. Although everyone would like to receive e-mail as fast as possible, a 10-second delay in transmitting an e-mail message does not have the same consequences as a 10-second delay in a videoconferencing packet.

With QoS routing, different *classes of service* are defined, each with different priorities. For example, a packet of videoconferencing images would likely get higher priority than would an SMTP packet with an e-mail message and thus be routed first. When the transport layer software attempts to establish a connection (i.e., a session), it specifies the class of service that connection requires. Each path through the network is designed to support a different number and mix of service classes. When a connection is established, the network ensures that no connections are established that exceed the maximum number of that class on a given circuit.

QoS routing is common in certain types of networks (e.g., ATM, as discussed in Chapter 9). The Internet provides several QoS protocols that can work in a TCP/IP environment. **Resource Reservation Protocol (RSVP)** and **Real-Time Streaming Protocol (RTSP)** both permit application layer software to request connections that have certain minimum data transfer capabilities. As one might expect, RTSP is geared toward audio/video streaming applications while RSVP is more general purpose.

RSVP and RTSP are used to create a connection (or session) and request a certain minimum guaranteed data rate. Once the connection has been established, they use *Real-Time Transport Protocol (RTP)* to send packets across the connection. RTP contains information about the sending application, a packet sequence number, and a time stamp so that the data in the RTP packet can be synchronized with other RTP packets by the application layer software if needed.

With a name like Real-Time *Transport* Protocol, one would expect RTP to replace TCP and UDP at the transport layer. It does not. Instead, RTP is combined with UDP. (If you read the previous paragraph carefully, you noticed that RTP does not provide source and destination port addresses.) This means that each real-time packet is first created using RTP and then surrounded by a UDP datagram, before being handed to the IP software at the network layer.

ADDRESSING

Before you can send a message, you must know the destination address. It is extremely important to understand that each computer has several addresses, each used by a different layer. One address is used by the data link layer, another by the network layer, and still another by the application layer.

When users work with application software, they typically use the application layer address. For example, in Chapter 2, we discussed application software that used Internet addresses (e.g., www.indiana.edu). This is an **application layer address** (or a *server name*). When a user types an Internet address into a Web browser, the request is passed to the network layer as part of an application layer packet formatted using the HTTP protocol (Figure 5.6) (see Chapter 2).

The network layer software, in turn, uses a **network layer address.** The network layer protocol used on the Internet is IP, so this Web address (www.indiana.edu) is translated into an IP address that is 4 bytes long when using IPv4 (e.g., 129.79.127.4) (Figure 5.6). This process is similar to using a phone book to go from someone's name to his or her phone number.[2]

The network layer then determines the best route through the network to the final destination. On the basis of this routing, the network layer identifies the **data link layer address** of the next computer to which the message should be sent. If the data link layer is running Ethernet, then the network layer IP address would be translated into an Ethernet address. Chapter 3 shows that Ethernet addresses are six bytes in length,

Address	Example Software	Example Address
Application layer	Web browser	www.kelley.indiana.edu
Network layer	Internet Protocol	129.79.127.4
Data link layer	Ethernet	00-0C-00-F5-03-5A

FIGURE 5.6 Types of addresses

Hex

[2]If you ever want to find out the IP address of any computer, simply enter the command *ping,* followed by the application layer name of the computer at the command prompt (e.g., ping www.indiana.edu).

so a possible address might be 00-0F-00-81-14-00 (Ethernet addresses are usually expressed in hexadecimal) (Figure 5.6).

Assigning Addresses

In general, the data link layer address is permanently encoded in each network card, which is why the data link layer address is also commonly called the physical address or the MAC address. This address is part of the hardware (e.g., Ethernet card) and can never be changed. Hardware manufacturers have an agreement that assigns each manufacturer a unique set of permitted addresses, so even if you buy hardware from different companies, they will never have the same address. Whenever you install a network card into a computer, it immediately has its own data link layer address that uniquely identifies it from every other computer in the world.

Network layer addresses are generally assigned by software. Every network layer software package usually has a configuration file that specifies the network layer address for that computer. Network managers can assign any network layer addresses they want. It is important to ensure that every computer on the same network has a unique network layer address so every network has a standards group that defines what network layer addresses can be used by each organization.

Application layer addresses (or server names) are also assigned by a software configuration file. Virtually all servers have an application layer address, but most client computers do not. This is because it is important for users to easily access servers and the information they contain, but there is usually little need for someone to access someone else's client computer. As with network layer addresses, network managers can assign any application layer address they want, but a network standards group must approve application layer addresses to ensure that no two computers have the same application layer address. Network layer addresses and application layer addresses go hand in hand, so the same standards group usually assigns both (e.g., www.indiana.edu at the application layer means 129.79.78.4 at the network layer). It is possible to have several application layer addresses for the same computer. For example, one of the Web servers in the Kelley School of Business at Indiana University is called both www.kelley.indiana.edu and www.kelley.iu.edu.

Internet Addresses

No one is permitted to operate a computer on the Internet unless they use approved addresses. **ICANN (Internet Corporation for Assigned Names and Numbers)** is responsible for managing the assignment of network layer addresses (i.e., IP addresses) and application layer addresses (e.g., www.indiana.edu). ICANN sets the rules by which new *domain names* (e.g., com, .org, .ca, .uk) are created and IP address numbers are assigned to users. ICANN also directly manages a set of Internet domains (e.g., .com, .org, .net) and authorizes private companies to become domain name registrars for those domains. Once authorized, a registrar can approve requests for application layer addresses and assign IP numbers for those requests. This means that individuals and organizations wishing to register an Internet name can use any authorized registrar for the domain they choose, and different registrars are permitted to charge different fees for their registration services. Many registrars are authorized to issue names and addresses in the ICANN managed domains, as well as domains in other countries (e.g., .ca, .uk, .au).

Several application layer addresses and network layer addresses can be assigned at the same time. IP addresses are often assigned in groups, so that one organization receives a set of numerically similar addresses for use on its computers. For example, Indiana University has been assigned the set of application layer addresses that end in indiana.edu and iu.edu and the set of IP addresses in the 129.79.x.x range (i.e., all IP addresses that start with the numbers 129.79).

In the old days of the Internet, addresses used to be assigned by class. A class A address was one for which the organization received a fixed first byte and could allocate the remaining three bytes. For example, Hewlett-Packard (HP) was assigned the 15.x.x.x address range which has about 16 million addresses. A class B address has the first two bytes fixed, and the organization can assign the remaining two bytes. Indiana University has a class B address, which provides about 65,000 addresses. A class C address has the first three bytes fixed with the organization able to assign the last byte, which provides about 250 addresses.

People still talk about **Internet address classes,** but addresses are no longer assigned in this way and most network vendors are no longer using the terminology. The newer terminology is **classless addressing** in which a slash is used to indicate the address range (it's also called slash notation). For example 128.192.1.0/24 means the first 24 bits (three bytes) are fixed, and the organization can allocate the last byte (eight bits).

One of the problems with the current address system is that the Internet is quickly running out of addresses. Although the four-byte address of IPv4 provides more than 4 billion possible addresses, the fact that they are assigned in sets significantly limits the number of usable addresses. For example, the address range owned by Indiana University includes about 65,000 addresses, but we will probably not use all of them.

The IP address shortage was one of the reasons behind the development of IPv6, discussed previously. Once IPv6 is in wide use, the current Internet address system will be replaced by a totally new system based on 16-byte addresses. Most experts expect that all the current four-byte addresses will simply be assigned an arbitrary 12-byte prefix (e.g., all zeros) so that the holders of the current addresses can continue to use them.

Subnets

Each organization must assign the IP addresses it has received to specific computers on its networks. In general, IP addresses are assigned so that all computers on the same LAN have similar addresses. For example, suppose an organization has just received a set of addresses starting with 128.192.x.x. It is customary to assign all the computers in the same LAN numbers that start with the same first three digits, so the business school LAN might be assigned 128.192.56.x, which means all the computers in that LAN would have IP numbers starting with those numbers (e.g., 128.192.56.4, 128.192.56.5, and so on) (Figure 5.7). The computer science LAN might be assigned 128.192.55.x, and likewise, all the other LANs at the university and the BN that connects them would have a different set of numbers. Each of these LANs is called a TCP/IP **subnet** because computers in the LAN are logically grouped together by IP number.

Routers connect two or more subnets so they have a separate address on each subnet. The routers in Figure 5.7, for example, have two addresses each because they connect two subnets and must have one address in each subnet.

Although it is customary to use the first three bytes of the IP address to indicate different subnets, it is not required. Any portion of the IP address can be designated as a

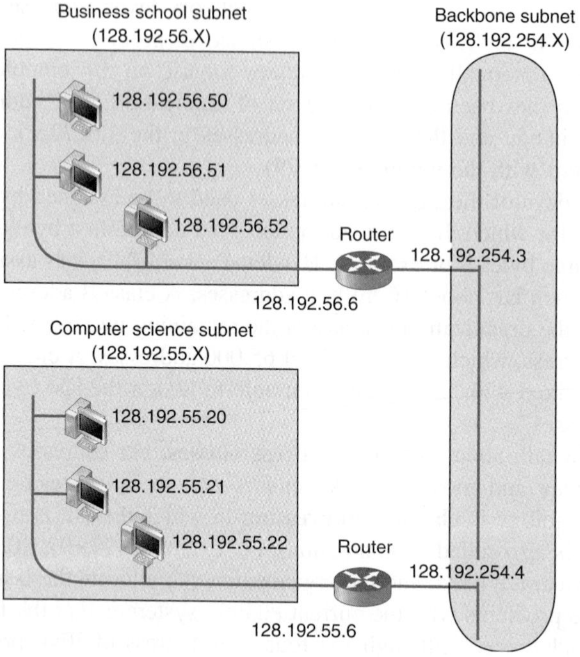

FIGURE 5.7 Address subnets

subnet by using a **subnet mask.** Every computer in a TCP/IP network is given a subnet mask to enable it to determine which computers are on the same subnet (i.e., LAN) that it is on and which computers are outside of its subnet. Knowing whether a computer is on your subnet is very important for message routing, as we shall see later in this chapter.

For example, a network could be configured so that the first two bytes indicated a subnet (e.g., 128.184.x.x), so all computers would be given a subnet mask giving the first two bytes as the subnet indicator. This would mean that a computer with an IP address of 128.184.22.33 would be on the same subnet as 128.184.78.90.

IP addresses are binary numbers, so partial bytes can also be used as subnets. For example, we could create a subnet that has IP addresses between 128.184.55.1 and 128.184.55.127, and another subnet with addresses between 128.184.55.128 and 128.184.55.254.

Dynamic Addressing To this point, we have said that every computer knows its network layer address from a configuration file that is installed when the computer is first attached to the network. However, this leads to a major network management problem. Any time a computer is moved or its network is assigned a new address, the software on each individual computer must be updated. This is not difficult, but it is very time consuming because someone must go from office to office editing files on each individual computer.

The easiest way around this is **dynamic addressing.** With this approach, a server is designated to supply a network layer address to a computer each time the computer connects to the network. This is commonly done for client computers but usually not done for servers.

The most common standard for dynamic addressing is **Dynamic Host Configuration Protocol (DHCP).** DHCP does not provide a network layer address in a configuration file. Instead, there is a special software package installed on the client that instructs it to contact a DHCP server to obtain an address. In this case, when the computer is turned on and connects to the network, it first issues a broadcast DHCP message that is directed to any DHCP server that can "hear" the message. This message asks the server to assign the requesting computer a unique network layer address. The server runs a corresponding DHCP software package that responds to these requests and sends a message back to the client giving it its network layer address (and its subnet mask).

The DHCP server can be configured to assign the same network layer address to the computer (on the basis of its data link layer address) each time it requests an address, or it can *lease* the address to the computer by picking the "next available" network layer address from a list of authorized addresses. Addresses can be leased for as long as the computer is connected to the network or for a specified time limit (e.g., 2 hours). When the lease expires, the client computer must contact the DHCP server to get a new address. Address leasing is commonly used by ISPs for dial-up users. ISPs have many more authorized users than they have authorized network layer addresses because not all users can log in at the same time. When a user logs in, his or her computer is assigned a temporary TCP/IP address that is reassigned to the next user when the first user hangs up.

Dynamic addressing greatly simplifies network management in non-dial-up networks, too. With dynamic addressing, address changes need to be made only to the

TECHNICAL FOCUS 5.1 SUBNET MASKS

Subnet masks tell computers what part of an Internet Protocol (IP) address is to be used to determine whether a destination is on the same subnet or on a different subnet. A subnet mask is a four-byte binary number that has the same format as an IP address. A 1 in the subnet mask indicates that that position is used to indicate the subnet. A 0 indicates that it is not.

A subnet mask of 255.255.255.0 means that the first three bytes indicate the subnet; all computers with the same first three bytes in their IP addresses are on the same subnet. This is because 255 expressed in binary is 11111111.

In contrast, a subnet mask of 255.255.0.0 indicates that the first two bytes refer to the same subnet.

Things get more complicated when we use partial-byte subnet masks. For example, suppose the subnet mask was 255.255.255.128. In binary numbers, this is expressed as:

11111111.11111111.11111111.10000000

This means that the first three bytes plus the first bit in the fourth byte indicate the subnet address.

Likewise, a subnet mask of 255.255.254.0 would indicate the first two bytes plus the first seven bits of third byte indicate the subnet address, because in binary numbers, this is:

11111111.11111111.11111110.00000000

The bits that are ones are called network bits because they indicate which part of an address is the network or subnet part, while the bits that are zeros are called host bits because they indicate which part is unique to a specific computer or host.

DHCP server, not to each individual computer. The next time each computer connects to the network or whenever the address lease expires, the computer automatically gets the new address.

Address Resolution

To send a message, the sender must be able to translate the application layer address (or server name) of the destination into a network layer address and in turn translate that into a data link layer address. This process is called **address resolution.** There are many different approaches to address resolution that range from completely decentralized (each computer is responsible for knowing all addresses) to completely centralized (there is one computer that knows all addresses). TCP/IP uses two different approaches, one for resolving application layer addresses into IP addresses and a different one for resolving IP addresses into data link layer addresses.

Server Name Resolution

Server name resolution is the translation of application layer addresses into network layer addresses (e.g., translating an Internet address such as www.yahoo.com into an IP address such as 204.71.200.74). This is done using the **Domain Name Service (DNS).** Throughout the Internet a series of computers called **name servers** provides DNS services. These name servers have address databases that store thousands of Internet addresses and their corresponding IP addresses. These name servers are, in effect, the "directory assistance" computers for the Internet. Anytime a computer does not know the IP number for a computer, it sends a message to the name server requesting the IP number. There are about a dozen high-level name servers that provide IP addresses for most of the Internet, with thousands of others that provide IP addresses for specific domains.

Whenever you register an Internet application layer address, you must inform the registrar of the IP address of the name server that will provide DNS information for all addresses in that name range. For example, because Indiana University owns the. indiana.edu name, it can create any name it wants that ends in that suffix (e.g., www.indiana.edu, www.kelley.indiana.edu, abc.indiana.edu). When it registers its name, it must also provide the IP address of the DNS server that it will use to provide the IP addresses for all the computers within this domain name range (i.e., everything ending in. indiana.edu). Every organization that has many servers also has its own DNS server, but smaller organizations that have only one or two servers often use a DNS server provided by their ISP. DNS servers are maintained by network managers, who update their address information as the network changes. DNS servers can also exchange information about new and changed addresses among themselves, a process called replication.

When a computer needs to translate an application layer address into an IP address, it sends a special DNS request packet to its DNS server.[3] This packet asks the DNS server to send to the requesting computer the IP address that matches the Internet application layer address provided. If the DNS server has a matching name in its database, it sends

[3]DNS requests and responses are usually short, so they use UDP as their transport layer protocol. That is, the DNS request is passed to the transport layer, which surrounds them in a UDP datagram before handing it to the network layer.

back a special DNS response packet with the correct IP address. If that DNS server does not have that Internet address in its database, it will issue the same request to another DNS server elsewhere on the Internet.[4]

For example, if someone at the University of Toronto asked for a Web page on our server (www.kelley.indiana.edu) at Indiana University, the software on the Toronto client computer would issue a DNS request to the University of Toronto DNS server (Figure 5.8). This DNS server probably would not know the IP address of our server,

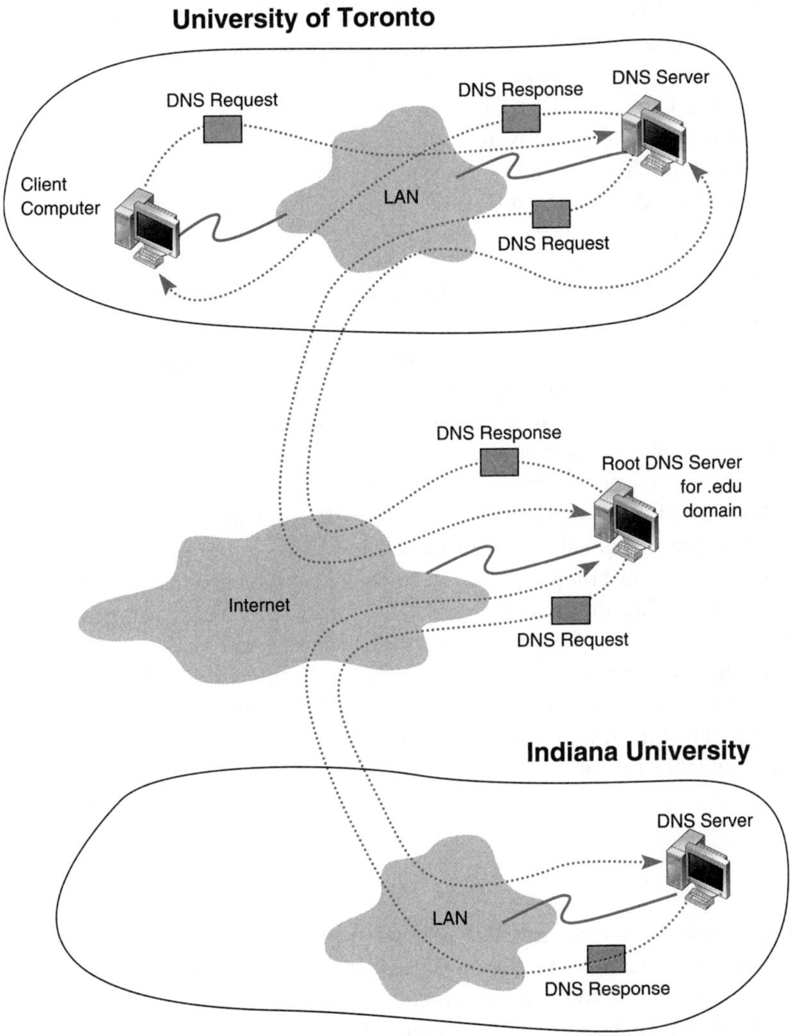

FIGURE 5.8 How the DNS system works

[4]This is called recursive DNS resolution. DNS servers can also use iterative DNS resolution, whereby the client is told that the DNS server does not know the desired address but is given the IP address of another DNS server that can be used to find the address. The client then issues a new DNS request to that DNS server.

so it would forward the request to the DNS root server that it knows stores addresses for the .edu domain. The .edu root server probably would not know our server's IP address either, but it would know that the DNS server on our campus could supply the address. So it would forward the request to the Indiana University DNS server, which would reply to the .edu server with a DNS response containing the requested IP address. The .edu server in turn would send that response to the DNS server at the University of Toronto, which in turn would send it to the computer that requested the address.

This is why it sometimes takes a longer to access certain sites. Most DNS servers know only the names and IP addresses for the computers in their part of the network. Some store frequently used addresses (e.g., www.yahoo.com). If you try to access a computer that is far away, it may take a while before your computer receives a response from a DNS server that knows the IP address.

Once your application layer software receives an IP address, it is stored on your computer in a DNS cache. This way, if you ever need to access the same computer again, your computer does not need to contact a DNS server. The DNS cache is routinely deleted whenever you turn off your computer.

Data Link Layer Address Resolution

To actually send a message, the network layer software must know the data link layer address of the receiving computer. The final destination may be far away (e.g., sending from Toronto to Indiana). In this case, the network layer would *route* the message by selecting a path through the network that would ultimately lead to the destination. (Routing is discussed in the next section.) The first step on this route would be to send the message to its router.

To send a message to another computer in its subnet, a computer must know the correct data link layer address. In this case, the TCP/IP software sends a **broadcast message** to all computers in its subnet. A broadcast message, as the name suggests, is received and processed by all computers in the same LAN (which is usually designed to match the IP subnet). The message is a specially formatted request using **Address Resolution Protocol (ARP)** that says, "Whoever is IP address xxx.xxx.xxx.xxx, please send me your data link layer address." The software in the computer with that IP address then sends an ARP response with its data link layer address. The sender transmits its message using that data link layer address. The sender also stores the data link layer address in its address table for future use.[5]

ROUTING

In many networks, there are various possible routes a message can take to get from one computer to another. For example, in Figure 5.9, a message sent from computer A to computer F could travel first to computer B then to computer C to get to computer F, or it could go to computer D first and then to computer E to get to computer F.

[5]It would be reasonable at this point to guess that because ARP requests and responses are small, they use UDP in the same way that DNS requests and responses do. But they don't. Instead, ARP packets replace both TCP/UDP and IP and are placed directly into the data link layer frame with no transport or network layer PDUs.

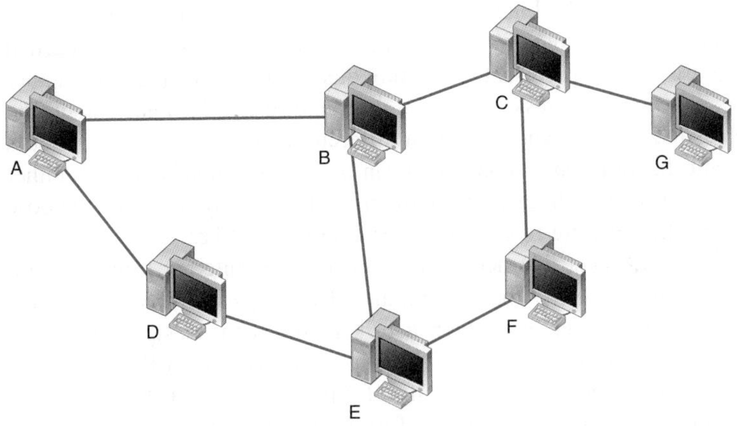

FIGURE 5.9 A typical network

Routing is the process of determining the route or path through the network that a message will travel from the sending computer to the receiving computer. Every computer that performs routing has a **routing table** developed by the network manager that specifies how messages will travel through the network. In its simplest form, the routing table is a two-column table. The first column lists every computer in the network, and the second column lists the computer to which the sending computer should send messages if they are destined for the computer in the first column. Figure 5.10 shows a routing table that might be used by computer B in Figure 5.9.[6]

Obviously, the Internet is more complicated than the simple network in Figure 5.9; it has millions of computers attached. How can we possibly route messages on the Internet? It turns out that most parts of the Internet are connected only to a few other parts of the Internet. That is, any one part of the Internet, such as your university, probably has only two or three connections into the Internet. When messages arrive at the computer that connects your university to the Internet, that computer must choose over which circuit to send the message. Imagine, for example, that computer B in Figure 5.9 is the computer that connects your university to the Internet and that the other computers

Destination	Route
A	A
C	C
D	A
E	E
F	E
G	C

FIGURE 5.10 Routing table

[6]If you ever want to find out the route through the Internet from your computer to any other computer on the Internet, simply enter the command *tracert* followed by the application layer name of the computer at the command line (e.g., tracert www.indiana.edu).

in this figure are different parts of the Internet. Some parts of the Internet are best reached by one circuit (e.g., the part represented by computer A), whereas others are best reached via the other circuit (e.g., the part represented by computer E). In this case, the computer is told that messages sent to IP addresses in a certain range (e.g., 128.x.x.x) should go on one circuit, whereas messages to addresses in a different range (e.g., 12.x.x.x) should go on a different circuit. In some cases, computers can be reached equally well on either circuit (e.g., computer D), in which case the network manager may arbitrarily choose one circuit or configure the software to choose either circuit as it likes.

Imagine yourself as a packet that needs to travel over the Internet from the University of Texas to the University of Alberta (e.g., an HTTP request). As you leave the University of Texas on the Internet, you reach a fork in the path. A sign says *Texas this way—all other destinations straight ahead* (Figure 5.11). Although this sign does not explicitly tell you how to get to the University of Alberta, it is clear that you must continue on straight ahead. As you reach the next fork in the path, there is another sign. Once again, your destination is not listed, but nonetheless, the direction you need to take is clear. The next sign includes your destination (Canada) in a range of destinations, so you turn down that path. The next sign again contains your destination (Alberta) in a range of destinations, so you take that path. At last, you see a sign to your destination. This is one way in which the Internet works.

Because routing is an important function, we often use special-purpose devices called **routers** to build and maintain the routing tables and perform routing. We will explain more about routers in Chapter 8.

Types of Routing

There are three fundamental approaches to routing: centralized routing, static routing, and dynamic routing. As you will see in the TCP/IP Example section later in this chapter, the Internet uses all three approaches.

Centralized Routing

With **centralized routing,** all routing decisions are made by one central computer or router. Centralized routing is commonly used in host-based networks (see Chapter 2), and in this case, routing decisions are rather simple. All computers are connected to the central computer, so any message that needs to be routed is simply sent to the central computer, which in turn retransmits the message on the appropriate circuit to the destination.

Static Routing

Static routing is decentralized, which means that all computers or routers in the network make their own routing decisions following a formal routing protocol. In MANs and WANs, the routing table for each computer is developed by its individual network manager (although network managers often share information). In LANs or backbones, the routing tables used by all computers on the network are usually developed by one individual or a committee. Most decentralized routing protocols are self-adjusting, meaning that they can automatically adapt to changes in the network configuration (e.g., adding and deleting computers and circuits).

With static routing, routing decisions are made in a fixed manner by individual computers or routers. The routing table is developed by the network manager, and it

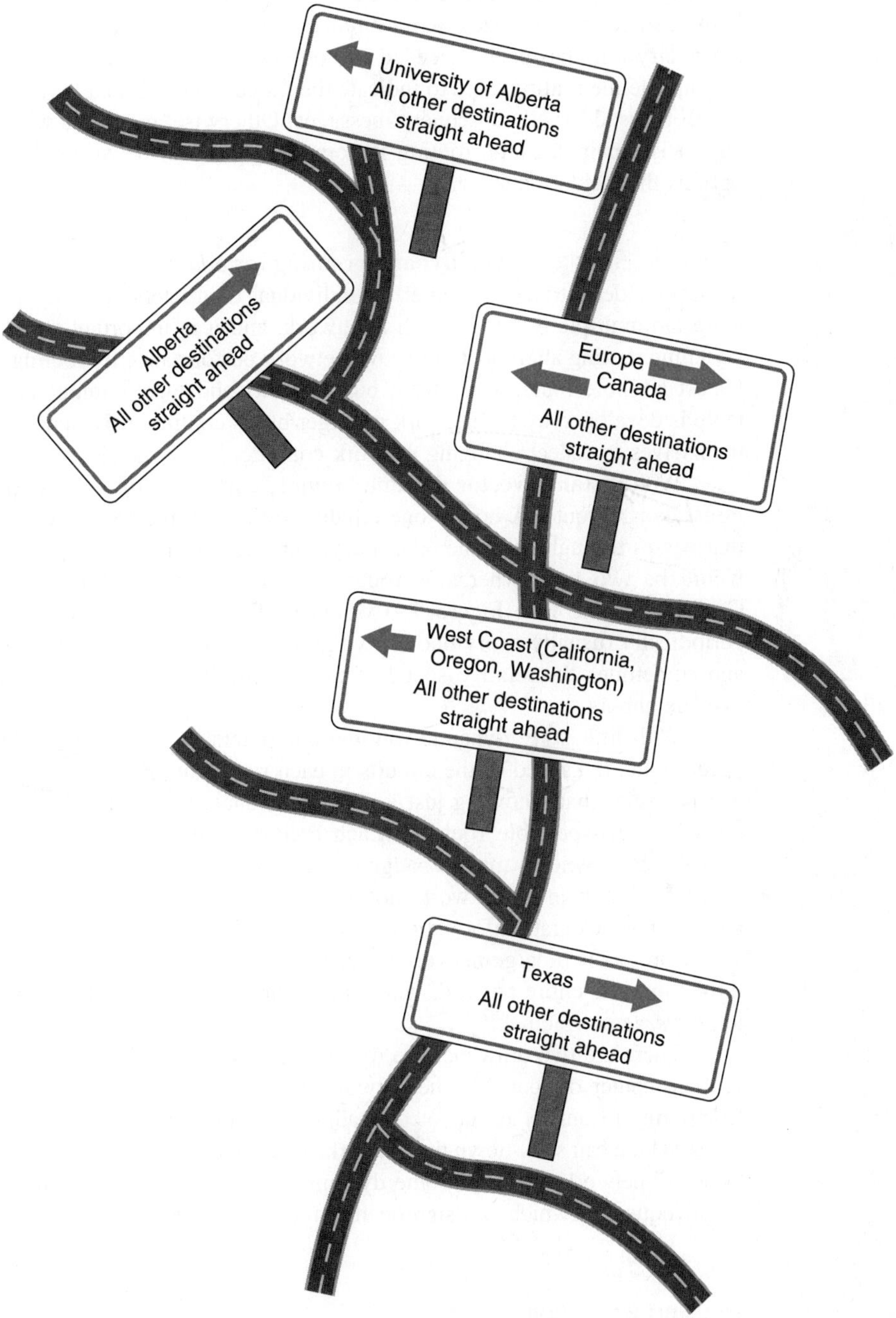

FIGURE 5.11 Internet routing

changes only when computers are added to or removed from the network. For example, if the computer recognizes that a circuit is broken or unusable (e.g., after the data link layer retry limit has been exceeded without receiving an acknowledgment), the computer will update the routing table to indicate the failed circuit. If an alternate route is available, it will be used for all subsequent messages. Otherwise, messages will be stored until the circuit is repaired. Static routing is commonly used in networks that have few routing options that seldom change.

Dynamic Routing

With **dynamic routing** (or *adaptive routing*), routing decisions are made in a decentralized manner by individual computers. This approach is used when there are multiple routes through a network, and it is important to select the best route. Dynamic routing attempts to improve network performance by routing messages over the fastest possible route, away from busy circuits and busy computers. An initial routing table is developed by the network manager but is continuously updated by the computers themselves to reflect changing network conditions.

With **distance vector** dynamic *routing,* computers or routers count the number of **hops** along a route. A hop is one circuit, so that a route from one computer to another that passes through only one other computer (e.g., from A to C through B in Figure 5.9) would be two hops whereas a route that passes through three computers (e.g., A to C via D, E, and F in Figure 5.9) would be four hops. With this approach, computers periodically (usually every one to two minutes) exchange information on the hop count and sometimes the relative speed of the circuits in route and how busy they are with their neighbors.

With **link state** dynamic routing, computers or routers track the number of hops in the route, the speed of the circuits in each route, and how busy each route is. In other words, rather than knowing just a route's distance, link state routing tries to determine how fast each possible route is. Each computer or router periodically (usually every 30 seconds or when a major change occurs) exchanges this information with other computers or routers in the network (not just their neighbors) so that each computer or router has the most accurate information possible. Link state protocols are preferred to distance vector protocols in large networks because they spread more reliable routing information throughout the entire network when major changes occur in the network. They are said to *converge* more quickly.

There are two drawbacks to dynamic routing. First, it requires more processing by each computer or router in the network than does centralized routing or static routing. Computing resources are devoted to adjusting routing tables rather than to sending messages, which can slow down the network. Second, the transmission of routing information "wastes" network capacity. Some dynamic routing protocols transmit status information very frequently, which can significantly reduce performance.

Routing Protocols

A routing protocol is a protocol that is used to exchange information among computers to enable them to build and maintain their routing tables. You can think of a routing protocol as the language that is used to build the signs in Figure 5.11. When new paths are added or paths are broken and cannot be used, messages are sent among computers using the routing protocol.

It can be useful to know all possible routes to a given destination. However, as a network gets quite large, knowing all possible routes becomes impractical; there are simply too many possible routes. Even at some modest number of computers, dynamic routing protocols become impractical because of the amount of network traffic they generate. For this reason, networks are often subdivided into autonomous systems of networks.

An **autonomous system** is simply a network operated by one organization, such as IBM or Indiana University, or an organization that runs one part of the Internet. Remember that we said the Internet was simply a network of networks. Each part of the Internet is run by a separate organization such as AT&T, MCI, and so on. Each part of the Internet or each large organizational network connected to the Internet can be a separate autonomous system.

The computers within each autonomous system know about the other computers in that system and usually exchange routing information because the number of computers is kept manageable. If an autonomous systems grows too large, it can be split into smaller parts. The routing protocols used inside an autonomous system are called **interior routing protocols.**

Protocols used between autonomous systems are called **exterior routing protocols.** Although interior routing protocols are usually designed to provide detailed routing information about all or most computers inside the autonomous systems, exterior protocols are designed to be more careful in the information they provide. Usually, exterior protocols provide information about only the preferred or the best routes rather than all possible routes.

There are many different protocols that are used to exchange routing information. Five are commonly used on the Internet: Border Gateway Protocol (BGP), Internet Control Message Protocol (ICMP), Routing Information Protocol (RIP), Intermediate System to Intermediate System (IS-IS) Open Shortest Path First (OSPF), and Enhanced Interior Gateway Routing Protocol (EIGRP).

Border Gateway Protocol (BGP) is a dynamic distance vector exterior routing protocol used on the Internet to exchange routing information between autonomous systems—that is, large sections of the Internet. Although BGP is the preferred routing protocol between Internet sections, it is seldom used inside companies because it is large, complex, and often hard to administer.

Internet Control Message Protocol (ICMP) is the simplest interior routing protocol on the Internet. ICMP is simply an error-reporting protocol that enables computers to report routing errors to message senders. ICMP also has a very limited ability to update routing tables.[7]

Routing Information Protocol (RIP) is a dynamic distance vector interior routing protocol that is commonly used in smaller networks, such as those operated by one organization. The network manager uses RIP to develop the routing table. When new computers are added, RIP simply counts the number of computers in the possible routes

[7] ICMP is the protocol used by the ping command.

to the destination and selects the route with the least number. Computers using RIP send broadcast messages every minute or so (the timing is set by the network manager) announcing their routing status to all other computers. RIP is used by both TCP/IP and IPX/SPX.

Intermediate System to Intermediate System (IS-IS) is a link state interior routing protocol that is commonly used in large networks. IS-IS is an ISO protocol that has been added to many TCP/IP networks.

Open Shortest Path First (OSPF) is a dynamic link state interior routing protocol that is commonly used on the Internet. It uses the number of computers in a route as well as network traffic and error rates to select the best route. OSPF is more efficient than RIP because it normally doesn't use broadcast messages. Instead, it selectively sends status update messages directly to selected computers or routers. OSPF is the preferred interior routing protocol used by TCP/IP.

TECHNICAL FOCUS 5.2 ROUTING ON THE INTERNET

The Internet is a network of autonomous system networks. Each autonomous system operates its own interior routing protocol while using Border Gateway Protocol (BGP) as the exterior routing protocol to exchange information with the other autonomous systems on the Internet. Although there are a number of interior routing protocols, Open Shortest Path First (OSPF) is the preferred protocol, and most organizations that run the autonomous systems forming large parts of the Internet use OSPF.

Figure 5.12 shows how a small part of the Internet might operate. In this example, there are six autonomous systems (e.g., Sprint, AT&T), three of which we have shown in more detail. Each autonomous system has a **border router** that connects it to the adjacent autonomous systems and exchanges route information via BGP. In this example, autonomous system A is connected to autonomous system B, which in turn is connected to autonomous system C. A is also connected to C via a route through systems D and E. If someone in A wants to send a message to someone in C, the message should be routed through B because it is the fastest route. The autonomous systems must share route information via BGP so that the border routers in each system know what routes are preferred. In this case, B would inform A that there is a route through it to C (and a route to E), and D would inform A that it has a route to E, but D would not inform A that there is a route through it to C. The border router in A would then have to decide which route to use to reach E.

Each autonomous system can use a different interior routing protocol. In this example, B is a rather simple network with only a few devices and routes, and it uses RIP, a simpler protocol in which all routers broadcast route information to their neighbors every minute or so. A and C are more complex networks and use OSPF. Most organizations that use OSPF create a special router called a **designated router** to manage the routing information. Every 15 minutes or so, each router sends its routing information to the designated router, which then broadcasts the revised routing table information to all other routers. If no designated router is used, then every router would have to broadcast its routing information to all other routers, which would result in a very large number of messages. In the case of autonomous system C, which has seven routers, this would require 42 separate messages (seven routers each sending to six others). By using a designated router, we now have only 12 separate messages (the six other routers sending to the designated router, and the designated router sending the complete set of revised information back to the other six).

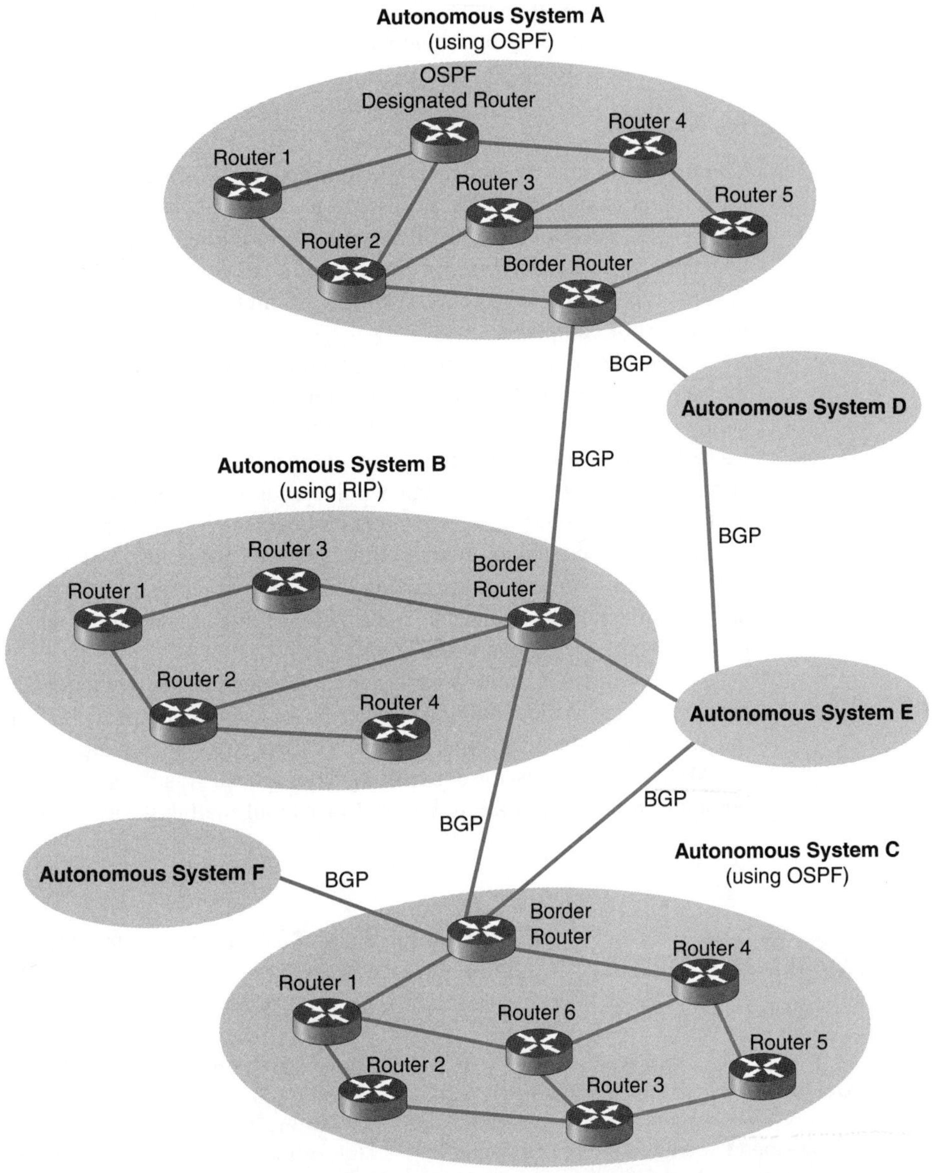

FIGURE 5.12 Routing on the Internet with Border Gateway Protocol (BGP), Open Shortest Path First (OSPF), and Routing Information Protocol (RIP)

Enhanced Interior Gateway Routing Protocol (EIGRP) is a dynamic link state interior routing protocol developed by Cisco and is commonly used inside organizations. As you might expect, EIGRP is an improved version of **Interior Gateway Routing Protocol (IGRP).** EIGRP records information about a route's transmission capacity, delay, reliability, and load. EIGRP is unique in that computer or routers store their own routing table as well as the routing tables for all of their neighbors so they have a more accurate understanding of the network.

Multicasting

The most common type of message in a network is the transmission between two computers. One computer sends a message to another computer (e.g., a client requesting a Web page). This is called a **unicast message.** Earlier in the chapter, we introduced the concept of a *broadcast message* that is sent to all computers on a specific LAN or subnet. A third type of message called a **multicast message** is used to send the same message to a group of computers.

Consider a videoconferencing situation in which four people want to participate in the same conference. Each computer could send the same voice and video data from its camera to the computers of each of the other three participants using unicasts. In this case, each computer would send three identical messages, each addressed to the three different computers. This would work but would require a lot of network capacity. Alternately, each computer could send one broadcast message. This would reduce network traffic (because each computer would send only one message), but every computer on the network would process it, distracting them from other tasks. Broadcast messages usually are transmitted only within the same LAN or subnet, so this would not work if one of the computers were outside the subnet.

The solution is multicast messaging. Computers wishing to participate in a multicast send a message to the sending computer or some other computer performing routing along the way using a special type of packet called **Internet Group Management Protocol (IGMP).** Each multicast group is assigned a special IP address to identify the group. Any computer performing routing knows to route all multicast messages with this IP address

MANAGEMENT FOCUS 5.2

CAPTAIN D'S GETS COOKING WITH MULTICAST

Captain D's has more than 500 company owned and franchised fast food restaurants across North America. Each restaurant has a small low-speed satellite link that can send and receive data at speeds similar to broadband Internet access (384 Kbps to 1.2 Mbps).

Captain D's used to send its monthly software updates to each of its restaurants one at a time, which meant transferring each file 500 times, once to each restaurant. You don't have to be a network wizard to realize that this is slow and redundant.

Captain D's now uses multicasting to send monthly software updates to all its restaurants at once. What once took hours is now accomplished in minutes.

Multicasting also enables Captain D's to send large human resource file updates each week to all restaurants and to transmit computer-based training videos to all restaurants each quarter. The training videos range in size from 500–1000 megabytes, so without multicasting it would be impossible to use the satellite network to transmit the videos.

SOURCE: "Captain D's Gets Cooking with Multicast from XcelleNet," www.xcellenet.com, 2004.

onto the subnet that contains the requesting computer. The routing computer sets the data link layer address on multicast messages to a matching multicast data link layer address. Each requesting computer must inform its data link layer software to process incoming messages with this multicast data link layer address. When the multicast session ends (e.g., the videoconference is over), the client computer sends another IGMP message to the organizing computer or the computer performing routing to remove it from the multicast group.

TCP/IP EXAMPLE

This chapter has discussed the functions of the transport and network layers: linking to the application layer, segmenting, session management, addressing, and routing. In this section, we tie all of these concepts together to take a closer look at how these functions actually work using TCP/IP.

When a computer is installed on a TCP/IP network (or dials into a TCP/IP network), it must be given four pieces of network layer addressing and routing information before it can operate. This information can be provided by a configuration file, or via a DHCP server. The information is

1. Its IP address
2. A subnet mask, so it can determine what addresses are part of its subnet
3. The IP address of a DNS server, so it can translate application layer addresses into IP addresses
4. The IP address of an IP **gateway** (commonly called a router) leading outside of its subnet, so it can route messages addressed to computers outside of its subnet (this presumes the computer is using static routing and there is only one connection from it to the outside world through which all messages must flow; if it used dynamic routing, some routing software would be needed instead)

These four pieces of information are the minimum required. A server would also need to know its application layer address.

In this section, we use the simple network shown in Figure 5.13 to illustrate how TCP/IP works. This figure shows an organization that has four LANs connected by a BN. The BN also has a connection to the Internet. Each building is configured as a separate subnet. For example, Building A has the 128.192.98.x subnet, whereas Building B has the 128.192.95.x subnet. The BN is its own subnet: 128.192.254.x. Each building is connected to the BN via a router that has two IP addresses and two data link layer addresses, one for the connection into the building and one for the connection onto the BN. The organization has several Web servers spread throughout the four buildings. The DNS server and the router onto the Internet are located directly on the BN itself. For simplicity, we will assume that all networks use Ethernet as the data link layer and will only focus on Web requests at the application layer.

In the sections below, we describe how messages are sent through the network. For the sake of simplicity, we will initially ignore the need to establish and close TCP

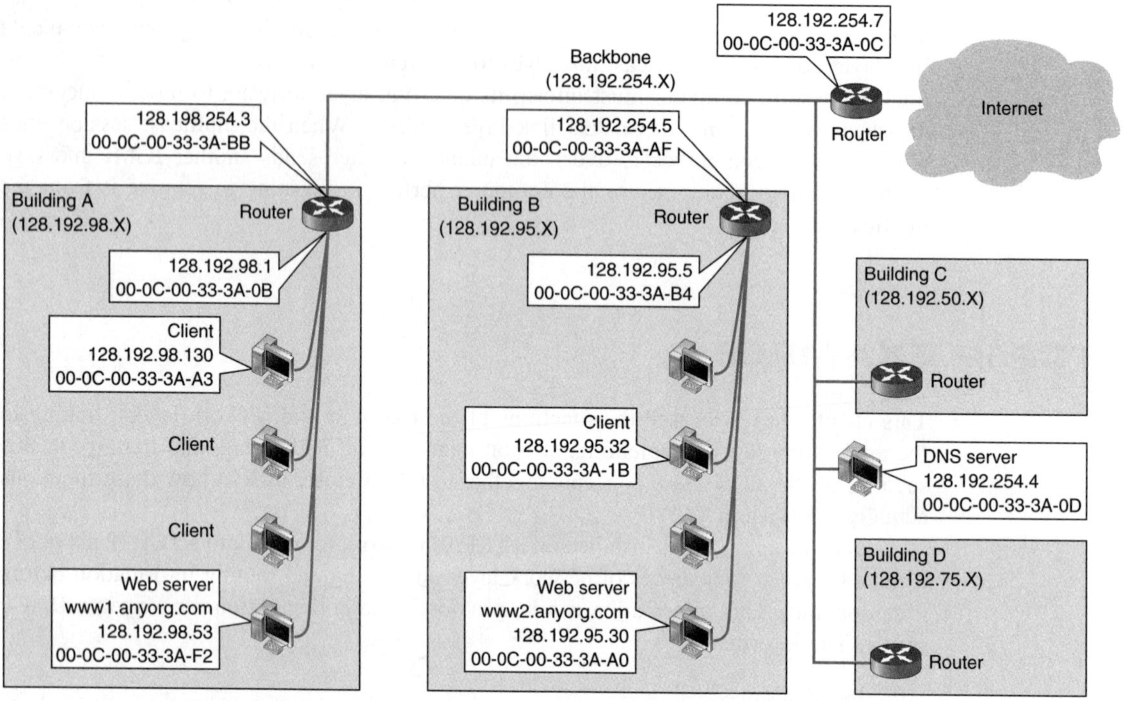

FIGURE 5.13 Example Transmission Control Protocol/Internet Protocol (TCP/IP) network

TECHNICAL FOCUS 5.3 FINDING YOUR COMPUTER'S TCP/IP SETTINGS

If your computer can access the Internet, it must use TCP/IP. In Windows, you can find out your TCP/IP settings by looking at their *properties.* Click on the ***Start*** button and then select ***Control Panel*** and then select ***Network Connections.*** Double click on your ***Local Area Connection*** and then click the ***Support*** tab.

This will show you your computer's IP address, subnet mask, and gateway, and whether the IP address is assigned by a DHCP server. Figure 5.14 shows this information for one of our computers.

If you would like more information, you can click on the ***Details*** button. This second window shows the same information, plus the computer's Ethernet address (called the physical address), as well as information about the DHCP lease and the DNS servers available.

Try this on your computer. If you have your own home network with your own router, there is a chance that your computer has an IP address very similar to ours or someone else's in your class—or the same address, in fact. How can two computers have the same IP address? Well, they can't. This is a security technique called *network address translation* in which one set of "private" IP addresses is used inside a network and a different set of "public" IP addresses is used by the router when it sends the messages onto the Internet. Network address translation is described in detail in Chapter 11.

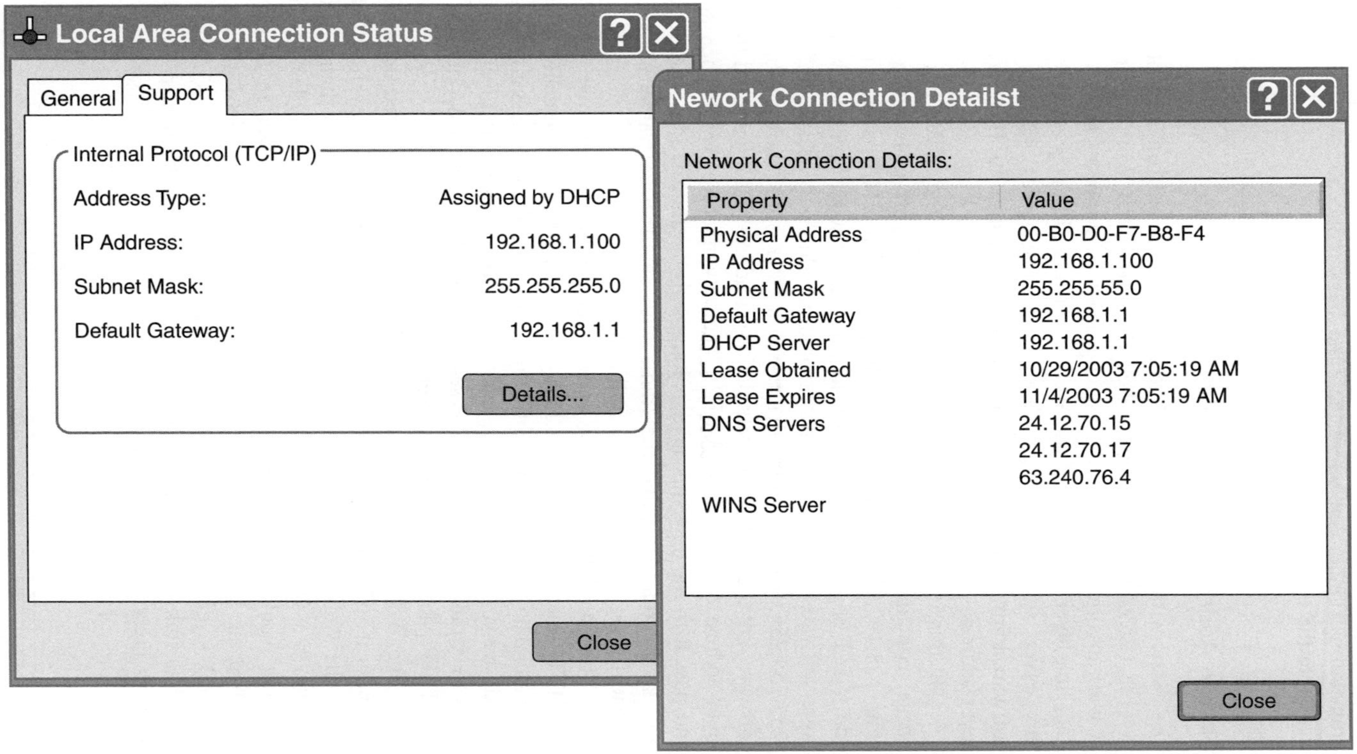

FIGURE 5.14 TCP/IP configuration information

connections. Once you understand the basic concepts, we will then add these in to complete the example.

Known Addresses, Same Subnet

Let's start with the simplest case. Suppose that a user on a client computer in Building A (128.192.98.130) requests a Web page from the Web server in the same building (www1.anyorg.com). We will assume that this computer knows the network layer and data link layer addresses of the Web server (e.g., it has previously requested pages from this server, so the addresses are in its address tables). Because the application layer software knows the IP address of the server, it uses its IP address, not its application layer address.

In this case, the application layer software (i.e., Web browser) passes an HTTP packet containing the user request to the transport layer software requesting a page from 128.192.98.53. The transport layer software (TCP) would take the HTTP packet, add a TCP segment, and then hand it to the network layer software (IP). The network layer software will compare the destination address (128.192.98.53) to the subnet mask (255.255.255.0) and discover that this computer is on its own subnet. The network layer software will then search its data link layer address table and find the matching data link layer address (00-0C-00-33-3A-F2). The network layer would then attach an IP packet and pass it to the data link layer, along with the destination Ethernet address. The data link layer would surround the frame with an Ethernet frame and transmit it over the physical layer to the Web server (Figure 5.15).

The data link layer on the Web server would perform error checking before passing the HTTP packet with the TCP segment and IP packet attached to its network layer software. The network layer software (IP) would then process the IP packet, see that it was destined to this computer, and pass it to the transport layer software (TCP). This software would process the TCP segment, see that there was only one packet, and pass the HTTP packet to the Web server software.

The Web server software would find the page requested, attach an HTTP packet, and pass it to its transport layer software. The transport layer software (TCP) would break the Web page into several smaller segment, each less than 1,500 bytes in length, and attach a TCP segment (with a number to indicate the order) to each. Each smaller segment would then go to the network layer software, get an IP packet attached that specified the IP address of the requesting client (128.192.98.130), and be given to the data link layer with the client's Ethernet address (00-0C-00-33-3A-A3) for transmission. The data link layer on the server would transmit the frames in the order in which the network layer passed them to it.

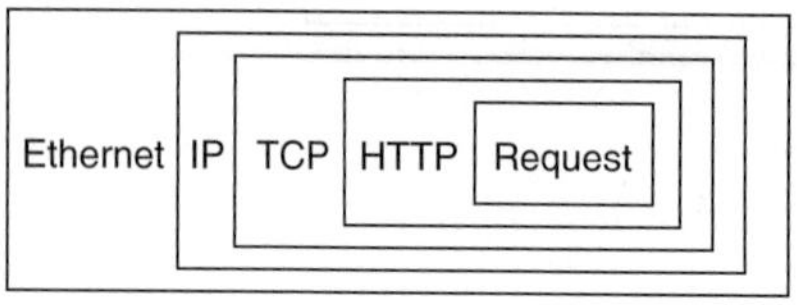

FIGURE 5.15 Packet nesting. HTTP = Hypertext Transfer Protocol; IP = Internet Protocol; TCP = Transmission Control Protocol

The client's data link layer software would receive the frames, perform error checking, and pass the IP packets inside them to the network layer. The network layer software (IP) would check to see that the packets were destined for this computer and pass the TCP segments they contained to the transport layer software. The transport layer software (TCP) would assemble the separate segments, in order, back into one Web page, and pass the HTTP packet in turn to the Web browser to display on the screen.

Known Addresses, Different Subnet

Suppose this time that the same client computer wanted to get a Web page from a Web server located somewhere in Building B (www2.anyorg.com). Again, assume that all addresses are known and are in the address tables of all computers. In this case, the application layer software would pass an HTTP packet to the transport layer software (TCP) with the Internet address of the destination www2.anyorg.com: 128.192.95.30. The transport layer software (TCP) would make sure that the request fit in one segment and hand it to the network layer. The network layer software (IP) would then check the subnet mask and would recognize that the Web server is located outside of its subnet. Any messages going outside the subnet must be sent to the router (128.192.98.1), whose job it is to process the message and send the message on its way into the outside network. The network layer software would check its address table and find the Ethernet address for the router. It would therefore set the data link layer address to the router's Ethernet address on this subnet (00-0C-00-33-3A-0B) and pass the IP packet to the data link layer for transmission. The data link layer would add the Ethernet frame and pass it to the physical layer for transmission.

The router would receive the message and its data link layer would perform error checking and send an acknowledgement before passing the packet to the network layer software (IP). The network layer software would read the IP address to determine the final destination. The router would recognize that this address (128.192.95.30) needed to be sent to the 128.192.95.x subnet. It knows the router for this subnet is 128.192.254.5. It would pass the packet back to its data link layer, giving the Ethernet address of the router (00-0C-00-33-3A-AF).

This router would receive the message (do error checking, etc.) and read the IP address to determine the final destination. The router would recognize that this address (128.192.95.30) was inside its 128.192.95.x subnet and would search its data link layer address table for this computer. It would then pass the packet to the data link layer along with the Ethernet address (00-0C-00-33-3A-A0) for transmission.

The www2.anyorg.com web server would receive the message and process it. This would result in a series of TCP/IP packets addressed to the requesting client (128.192.98.130). These would make their way through the network in reverse order. The Web server would recognize that this IP address is outside its subnet and would send the message to the 128.192.95.5 router using its Ethernet address (00-0C-00-33-3A-B4). This router would then send the message to the router for the 128.192.98.x subnet (128.192.254.3) using its Ethernet address (00-0C-00-33-3A-BB). This router would in turn send the message back to the client (128.192.98.130) using its Ethernet address (00-0C-00-33-3A-A3).

This process would work in the same way for Web servers located outside the organization on the Internet. In this case, the message would go from the client to the 128.192.98.x router, which would send it to the Internet router (128.192.254.7), which would send it to its Internet connection. The message would be routed through the Internet, from router to router until it reached its destination. Then the process would work in reverse to return the requested page.

Unknown Addresses

Let's return to the simplest case (requesting a Web page from a Web server on the same subnet), only this time we will assume that the client computer does not know the network layer or data link layer address of the Web server. For simplicity, we will assume that the client knows the data link layer address of its subnet router, but after you read through this example, you will realize that obtaining the data link layer address of the subnet router is straightforward. (It is done the same way as the client obtains the data link layer address of the Web server.)

Suppose the client computer in Building A (128.192.98.130) wants to retrieve a Web page from the www1.anyorg.com Web server but does not know its addresses. The Web browser realizes that it does not know the IP address after searching its IP address table and not finding a matching entry. Therefore, it issues a DNS request to the name server (128.192.254.4). The DNS request is passed to the transport layer (TCP), which attaches a UDP datagram and hands the message to the network layer.

Using its subnet mask, the network layer (IP) will recognize that the DNS server is outside of its subnet. It will attach an IP packet and set the data link layer address to its router's address.

The router will process the message and recognize that the 128.192.254.4 IP address is on the BN. It will transmit the packet using the DNS server's Ethernet address.

The name server will process the DNS request and send the matching IP address back to the client via the 128.198.98.x subnet router.

The IP address for the desired computer makes its way back to the application layer software, which stores it in its IP table. It then issues the HTTP request using the IP address for the Web server (128.192.98.53) and passes it to the transport layer, which in turn passes it to the network layer. The network layer uses its subnet mask and recognizes that this computer is on its subnet. However, it does not know the Web server's Ethernet address. Therefore, it broadcasts an ARP request to all computers on its subnet, requesting that the computer whose IP address is 128.192.98.53 to respond with its Ethernet address.

This request is processed by all computers on the subnet, but only the Web server responds with an ARP packet giving its Ethernet address. The network layer software on the client stores this address in its data link layer address table and sends the original Web request to the Web server using its Ethernet address.

This process works the same for a Web server outside the subnet, whether in the same organization or anywhere on the Internet. If the Web server is far away (e.g., Australia), the process will likely involve searching more than one name server, but it is still the same process.

TCP Connections

Whenever a computer transmits data to another computer, it must choose whether to use a connection-oriented service via TCP or a connectionless service via UDP. Most application layer software such as Web browsers (HTTP), e-mail (SMTP), FTP, and Telnet use connection-oriented services. This means that before the first packet is sent, the transport layer first sends a SYN segment to establish a session. Once the session is established, then the data packets begin to flow. Once the data are finished, the session is closed with a FIN segment.

In the examples above, this means that the first packet sent is really a SYN segment, followed by a response from the receiver accepting the connection, and then the packets as described above. There is nothing magical about the SYN and FIN segments, they are addressed and routed in the same manner as any other packets. But they do add to the complexity and length of the example.

A special word is needed about HTTP packets. When HTTP was first developed, Web browsers opened a separate TCP session for each HTTP request. That is, when they requested a page, they would open a session, send the single packet requesting the Web page, and close the session at their end. The Web server would open a session, send as many packets as needed to transmit the requested page, and then close the session. If the page included graphic images, the Web browser would open and close a separate session for each request. This requirement to open and close sessions for each request was time consuming and not really necessary. With the newest version of HTTP, Web browsers open one session when they first issue an HTTP request and leave that session open for all subsequent HTTP requests to the same server.

TCP/IP and Network Layers

In closing this chapter, we want to return to the layers in the network model and take another look at how messages flow through the layers. Figure 5.16 shows how a Web request message from a client computer in Building A would flow through the network layers in the different computers and devices on its way to the server in Building B.

The message starts at the application layer of the sending computer (the client in Building A), shown in the upper left corner of the figure, which generates an HTTP packet. This packet is passed to the transport layer, which surrounds the HTTP packet with a TCP segment. This is then passed to the network layer, which surrounds it with an IP frame that includes the IP address of the final destination (128.192.95.30). This in turn is passed to the data link layer, which surrounds it within an Ethernet frame that also includes the Ethernet address of the next computer to which the message will be sent (00-0C-00-33-3A-0B). Finally, this is passed to the physical layer, which converts it into electrical impulses for transmission through the cable to its next stop—the router that serves as the gateway in Building A.

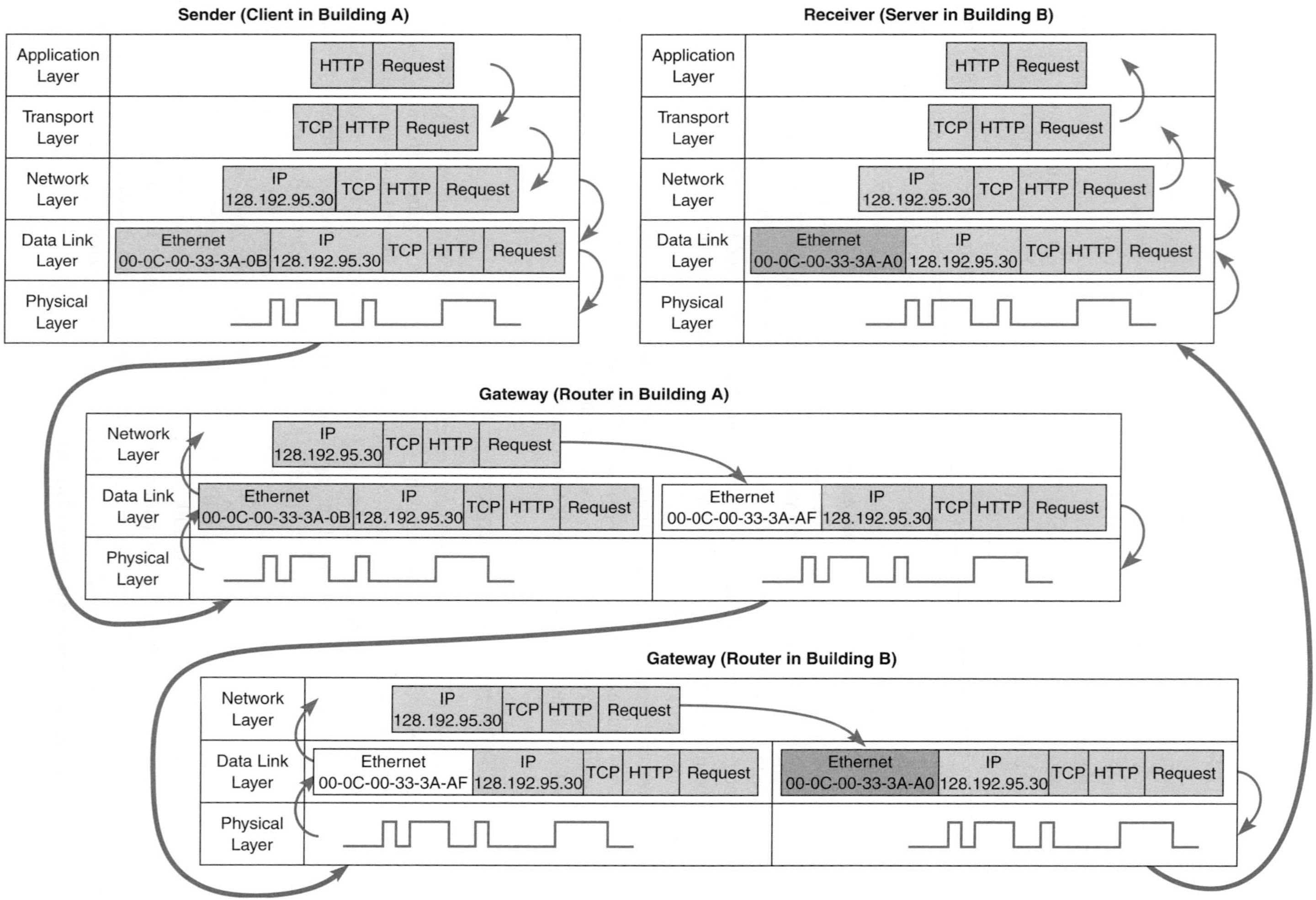

FIGURE 5.16 How messages move through the network layers.
Note: The addresses in this example are destination addresses

When the message arrives at the router in Building A, its physical layer translates it from electrical impulses into digital data and passes the Ethernet frame to the data link layer. The data link layer checks to make sure that the Ethernet frame is addressed to the router, performs error detection, strips off the Ethernet frame, and passes its contents (the IP packet) to the network layer. The routing software running at the network layer looks at the destination IP address, determines the next computer to which the packet should be sent, and passes the outgoing packet down to the data link layer for transmission. The data link layer surrounds the IP packet with a completely new Ethernet frame that contains the destination address of the next computer to which the packet will be sent (00-0C-00-33-3A-AF). In Figure 5.16, this new frame is shown in a different color. This is then passed to the physical layer, which transmits it through the network cable to its next stop—the router that serves as the gateway in Building B.

When the message arrives at the router in Building B, it goes through the same process. The physical layer passes the incoming packet to the data link layer, which checks the destination Ethernet address, performs error detection, strips off the Ethernet frame, and passes the IP packet to the network layer software. The software determines the next destination and passes the IP packet back to the data link layer, which adds a completely new Ethernet frame with the destination address of its next stop (00-0C-00-33-3A-A0)—its final destination.

The physical layer at the server receives the incoming packet and passes it to the data link layer, which checks the Ethernet address, performs error detection, removes the Ethernet frame, and passes the IP packet to the network layer. The network layer examines the final destination IP address on the incoming packet and recognizes that the server is the final destination. It strips off the IP packet and passes the TCP segment to the transport layer, which in turn strips off the TCP segment and passes the HTTP packet to the application layer (the Web server software).

There are two important things to remember from this example. First, at all gateways (i.e., routers) along the way, the packet moves through the physical layer and data

TECHNICAL FOCUS 5.4 PODCASTING

Podcasting is the distribution of audio and video files (e.g., MP3 files) over the Internet. Podcasting uses a relatively old technology (first developed in 2000), but became popular with the introduction of Apple's iPod.

Podcasting requires two things: the content and a channel description file that describes the content. The content is usually MP3 files, audio and/or video. Creating MP3 files is fairly straightforward—see the Hands-On Activity in Chapter 3.

The channel description file describes the overall set of files, called a channel, as well as each individual MP3 file that is available. This file is an XML file that is created according to the **RSS** standard (RSS stands for Rich Site Summary, RDF Site Summary, or Really Simple Syndication, depending upon which version of the standard you read).

Users subscribe to a podcast channel by entering the URL of the channel description RSS file into their favorite aggregation software (e.g., iTunes). The aggregation software regularly reads the RSS file. When it notices that the RSS file contains a new entry for a new MP3 file, the software automatically downloads the new content to the user's iPod.

link layer up to the network layer, but no higher. The routing software operates at the network layer, where it selects the next computer to which the packet should be sent, and passes the packet back down through the data link and physical layers. These three layers are involved at all computers and devices along the way, but the transport and application layers are only involved at the sending computer (to create the application layer packet and the TCP segment) and at the receiving computer (to understand the TCP segment and process the application layer packet). Inside the TCP/IP network itself, messages only reach layer three—no higher.

Second, at each stop along the way, the Ethernet frame is removed and a new one is created. The Ethernet frame lives only long enough to move the message from one computer to the next and then is destroyed. In contrast, the IP packet and the packets above it (TCP and application layer) never change while the message is in transit. They are created and removed only by the original message sender and the final destination.

IMPLICATIONS FOR MANAGEMENT

The implications from this chapter are similar in many ways to the implications from Chapter 4. There used to be several distinct protocols used at the network and transport layers but as the Internet has become an important network, most organizations are moving to the adoption of TCP/IP as the single standard protocol at the transport and network layers. This is having many of the same effects described in Chapter 4: the cost of buying and maintaining networking equipment and the cost of training networking staff is steadily decreasing. However, as we move closer to running out of IP addresses, more organizations will move to IPv6. This will cost a lot, but most organizations will see little business value from the change.

As TCP/IP becomes the dominant transport and network layer protocol for digital data, telephone companies who operate large non-TCP/IP-based networks to carry voice traffic are beginning to wonder whether they too should make the switch to TCP/IP. This has significant financial implications for companies that manufacture large networking equipment used in these networks.

SUMMARY

Transport and Network Layer Protocols TCP/IP are the standard transport and network protocols used today. They perform addressing (finding destination addresses), routing (finding the "best" route through the network), and segmenting (breaking large messages into smaller packets for transmission and reassembling them at the destination).

Transport Layer The transport layer (TCP) uses the source and destination port addresses to link the application layer software to the network. TCP is also responsible for segmeting—breaking large messages into smaller segments for transmission and reassembling them at the receiver's end. When connection-oriented routing is needed, TCP establishes a connection or session from the sender to the receiver. When connectionless routing is needed, TCP is replaced with UDP. Quality of service provides the ability to prioritize packets so that real-time voice packets are transmitted more quickly than simple e-mail messages.

Addressing Computers can have three different addresses: application layer address, network layer address, and data link layer address. Data link layer addresses are usually part of the hardware whereas network layer and application layer addresses are set by software. Network layer and application layer addresses for the Internet are assigned by Internet registrars. Addresses within one organization are usually assigned so that computers in the same LAN or subnet have similar addresses, usually with the same first 3 bytes. Subnet masks are used to indicate whether the first 2 or 3 bytes (or partial bytes) indicate the same subnet. Some networks assign network layer addresses in a configuration file on the client computer whereas others use dynamic addressing in which a DHCP server assigns addresses when a computer first joins the network.

Address Resolution Address resolution is the process of translating an application layer address into a network layer address or translating a network layer address into a data link layer address. On the Internet, network layer resolution is done by sending a special message to a DNS server (also called a name server) that asks for the IP address (e.g., 128.192.98.5) for a given Internet address (e.g., www.kelley.indiana.edu). If a DNS server does not have an entry for the requested Internet address, it will forward the request to another DNS server that it thinks is likely to have the address. That server will either respond or forward the request to another DNS server, and so on, until the address is found or it becomes clear that the address is unknown. Resolving data link layer addresses is done by sending an ARP request in a broadcast message to all computers on the same subnet that asks the computer with the requested IP address to respond with its data link layer address.

Routing Routing is the process of selecting the route or path through the network that a message will travel from the sending computer to the receiving computer. With centralized routing, one computer performs all the routing decisions. With static routing, the routing table is developed by the network manager and remains unchanged until the network manager updates it. With dynamic routing, the goal is to improve network performance by routing messages over the fastest possible route; an initial routing table is developed by the network manager but is continuously updated to reflect changing network conditions, such as message traffic. BGP, RIP, ICMP, EIGRP, and OSPF are examples of dynamic routing protocols.

TCP/IP Example In TCP/IP, it is important to remember that the TCP segments and IP packets are created by the sending computer and never change until the message reaches its final destination. The IP packet contains the original source and ultimate destination address for the packet. The sending computer also creates a data link layer frame (e.g., Ethernet) for each message. This frame contains the data link layer address of the current computer sending the packet and the data link layer address of the next computer in the route through the network. The data link layer frame is removed and replaced with a new frame at each computer at which the message stops as it works its way through the network. Thus, the source and destination data link layer addresses change at each step along the route whereas the IP source and destination addresses never change.

KEY TERMS

address resolution
Address Resolution Protocol (ARP)
addressing
application layer address
autonomous systems
Border Gateway Protocol (BGP)
border router
broadcast message
centralized routing
classless addressing
connectionless messaging
connection-oriented messaging
data link layer address
designated router
destination port address
distance vector routing

Domain Name Service (DNS)
dynamic addressing
Dynamic Host Configuration Protocol (DHCP)
dynamic routing
Enhanced Interior Gateway Routing Protocol (EIGRP)
exterior routing protocol
gateway
hop
Intermediate System to Intermediate System (IS-IS)
Interior Gateway Routing Protocol (IGRP)
interior routing protocol
Internet address classes
Internet Control Message Protocol (ICMP)
Internet Corporation for Assigned Names and Numbers (ICANN)
Internet Group Management Protocol (IGMP)
link state routing
multicast message
name server
network layer address
Open Shortest Path First (OSPF)
port address
Quality of Service (QoS)
Real-Time Streaming Protocol (RTSP)
RSS
Real-Time Transport Protocol (RTP)
Resource Reservation Protocol (RSVP)
router
routing
Routing Information Protocol (RIP)
routing table
segment
segmenting
source port address
static routing
subnet
subnet mask
Transmission Control Protocol/Internet Protocol (TCP/IP)
unicast message
User Datagram Protocol (UDP)

QUESTIONS

1. What does the transport layer do?
2. What does the network layer do?
3. What are the parts of TCP/IP and what do they do? Who is the primary user of TCP/IP?
4. Compare and contrast the three types of addresses used in a network.
5. How is TCP different from UDP?
6. How does TCP establish a session?
7. What is a subnet and why do networks need them?
8. What is a subnet mask?
9. How does dynamic addressing work?
10. What benefits and problems does dynamic addressing provide?
11. What is address resolution?
12. How does TCP/IP perform address resolution from URLs into network layer addresses?
13. How does TCP/IP perform address resolution from IP addresses into data link layer addresses?
14. What is routing?
15. How does decentralized routing differ from centralized routing?
16. What are the differences between connectionless and connection-oriented messaging?
17. What is a session?
18. What is QoS routing and why is it useful?
19. Compare and contrast unicast, broadcast, and multicast messages.
20. Explain how multicasting works.
21. Explain how the client computer in Figure 5.14 (128.192.98.xx) would obtain the data link layer address of its subnet router.
22. Why does HTTP use TCP and DNS use UDP?
23. How does static routing differ from dynamic routing? When would you use static routing? When would you use dynamic routing?
24. What type of routing does a TCP/IP client use? What type of routing does a TCP/IP gateway use? Explain.

25. What is the transmission efficiency of a 10-byte Web request sent using HTTP, TCP/IP, and Ethernet? Assume the HTTP packet has 100 bytes in addition to the 10-byte URL. Hint: Remember from Chapter 4 that *efficiency = user data/total transmission size.*

26. What is the transmission efficiency of a 1,000-byte file sent in response to a Web request HTTP, TCP/IP, and Ethernet? Assume the HTTP packet has 100 bytes in addition to the 1,000-byte file. Hint: Remember from Chapter 4 that *efficiency = user data/total transmission size.*

27. What is the transmission efficiency of a 5,000-byte file sent in response to a Web request HTTP, TCP/IP, and Ethernet? Assume the HTTP packet has 100 bytes in addition to the 5,000-byte file. Assume that the maximum packet size is 1,200 bytes. Hint: Remember from Chapter 4 that *efficiency = user data/total transmission size.*

EXERCISES

5-1. Would you recommend dynamic addressing for your organization? Why?

5-2. Look at your network layer software (either on a LAN or dial-in) and see what options are set—but don't change them! You can do this by using the RUN command to run winipcfg. How do these match the fundamental addressing and routing concepts discussed in this chapter?

5-3. Suppose a client computer (128.192.95.32) in Building B in Figure 5.13 requests a large Web page from the server in Building A (www1.anyorg.com). Assume that the client computer has just been turned on and does not know any addresses other than those in its configuration tables. Assume that all gateways and Web servers know all network layer and data link layer addresses.

a. Explain what messages would be sent and how they would flow through the network to deliver the Web page request to the server.
b. Explain what messages would be sent and how they would flow through the network as the Web server sent the requested page to the client.
c. Describe, but do not explain in detail, what would happen if the Web page contained several graphic images (e.g., GIF [Graphics Interchange Format] or JPEG files).

5-4. Network Solutions provides a service to find who owns domain names and IP addresses. Go to www.networksolutions.com/whois. Find the owner of

a. books.com
b. TV.com
c. 74.128.18.22
d. 129.79.78.188

5-5. What is the subnet portion of the IP address and what is the subnet mask for the following:

a. 12.1.0.0/16
b. 12.1.0.0/24
c. 12.1.0.0/20
d. 12.1.0.0/28

5-6. The puzzle on the next page covers Chapters 2–5.

Across

2. This layer is responsible breaking long messages into smaller packets
4. A class of digital signaling techniques that uses both positive and negative polarity signals
6. The protocol used by the Web
8. The signaling technique used by Ethernet
10. This type of modulation changes the length of the waves
13. Many computers use this protocol to get their IP address
16. A media access control technique good for very busy networks
18. A fast error detection and correction technique
20. This type of routing is best for large busy networks with unpredictable traffic
22. Each separate part of the Internet is called an ________system
24. This application enables you to move files from one computer to another
26. This type of modulation changes the height of the waves
27. Used to identify what part of your address is the subnet
28. In the OSI model, this layer is responsible for error control
30. A media access control technique good for small networks
32. This is used by TCP to connect the application layer
34. Computers use this to find Ethernet addresses
35. This type of routing is best for small networks
36. A one directional circuit
40. A famous network model
41. A good error detection technique
43. This application enables you to use other computers
45. Signals per second
47. A common interior link state routing protocol
49. Computers use this to find IP addresses

Down

1. This layer enables users to access the network
2. Type of multiplexing commonly used on digital circuits
3. This type of logic enables you to enter commands
5. A network in one small area
7. A message that is processed by all computers
9. The signal used to indicate that a message was received without error
11. How many times a circuit signals per second
12. You can read your e-mail with this protocol
14. Most LANs today are set to detect errors but not ________ them
15. The combination of voice, video and data
17. The number of bits per second a circuit can transmit
19. Size of an analog circuit
21. The signal used to indicate that a message was received with an error
23. To transmit several smaller circuits to one larger circuit
25. The network layer protocol used on the Internet
29. A very common source of noise
31. This layer performs routing
33. A transport layer protocol used on the Internet
35. A common email protocol
37. A group responsible for the standardization of common LAN technologies
39. This protocol enables you to send graphic files using e-mail
43. This type of client has a lot of software on it
44. This type of client has little software on it
48. A common interior distance vector routing protocol

MINI-CASES

I. Fred's Donuts

Fred's Donuts is a large regional bakery company that supplies baked goods (e.g., doughnuts, bread, pastries) to cafeterias, grocery stores, and convenience stores in three states. The company has five separate bakeries and office complexes spread over the region and wants to connect the five locations. Unfortunately, the network infrastructure at the five locations has grown up separately and thus there are two different network/transport layer protocols in use (TCP/IP and SPX/IPX). Should the company continue to use the two different protocols or move to one protocol, and if the latter, which one? Explain.

II. Central University

Suppose you are the network manager for Central University, a medium-size university with 13,000 students. The university has 10 separate colleges (e.g., business, arts, journalism), 3 of which are relatively large (300 faculty and staff members, 2,000 students, and 3 buildings) and 7 of which are relatively small (200 faculty and staff, 1,000 students, and 1 building). In addition, there are another 2,000 staff members who work in various administration departments (e.g., library, maintenance, finance) spread over another 10 buildings. There are 4 residence halls that house a total of 2,000 students. Suppose the university has the 128.100.xxx.xxx address range on the Internet. How would you assign the IP addresses to the various subnets? How would you control the process by which IP addresses are assigned to individual computers? You will have to make some assumptions to answer both questions, so be sure to state your assumptions.

III. Connectus

Connectus is a medium-sized Internet Service Provider (ISP) that provides Internet access and data communication services to several dozen companies across the United States and Canada. Most of Connectus' clients have large numbers of traveling sales representatives who use the Connectus network for dial-in access while they are on the road. Connectus also provides fixed data connections for clients' offices. Connectus has dial-in and/or fixed connections centers in about 50 cities and an internal network that connects them. For reliability purposes, all centers are connected with at least two other centers so that if one connection goes down, the center can still communicate with the network. While network volume is fairly predictable for the fixed office location connections, predicting dial-in access volume is more difficult because it depends on how many sales representatives are in which city. Connectus currently uses RIP as its routing protocol, but is considering moving to OSPF. Should it stay with RIP or move to OSPF? Why?

IV. Old Army

Old Army is a large retail store chain operating about 1,000 stores across the United States and Canada. Each store is connected into the Old Army data network, which is used primarily for batch data transmissions. At the end of each day, each store transmits sales, inventory, and payroll information to the corporate head office in Atlanta. The network also supports e-mail traffic, but its use is restricted to department managers and above. Because most traffic is sent to and from the Atlanta headquarters, the network is organized in a hub and spoke design. The Atlanta office is connected to 20 regional data centers, and each regional center is in turn connected to the 30–70 stores in its region. Network volumes have been growing, but at a fairly predictable rate as the number of stores and overall sales volume increases. Old Army currently uses RIP as its routing protocol, but is considering moving to OSPF. Should it stay with RIP or move to OSPF? Why?

V. General Stores

General Stores is a large retail store chain operating about 1,300 stores across the United States and Canada. Each store is connected into the corporate data network. At the end of each day, each store transmits sales and payroll information to the corporate head office in Seattle. Inventory data is transmitted in real time as products are sold to one of a dozen regional distribution centers across North America. The network is also used for credit card validations as customers check out and pay for their purchases. The network supports e-mail traffic, but its use is restricted to department managers and above. The network is designed much like the Internet: one connection from each store goes into a regional network that typically has a series of network connections to other parts of the network. Network volumes have been growing, but at a fairly predictable rate as the number of stores and overall sales volume increases. General Stores is considering implementing a digital telephone service that will allow it to transmit internal telephone calls to other General Stores offices or stores through the data network. Telephone services outside of General Stores will continue to be done normally. General Stores currently uses RIP as its routing protocol, but is considering moving to OSPF. Should it stay with RIP or move to OSPF? Why?

VI. Merita Bank

Reread Management Focus 5.1. What other alternatives do you think that Merita considered? Why do you think they did what they did?

CASE STUDY

NEXT-DAY AIR SERVICE

See the Web site.

HANDS-ON ACTIVITY

Using TCP/IP

In this chapter, we've discussed the basic components of TCP/IP such as IP addresses, subnet masks, DNS requests, and ARP requests. In this activity we'll show you how to explore these items on your computer. Although this activity is designed for Windows computers, most of these commands will also work on Apple computers.

This activity will use the command prompt, so start by clicking START, then RUN, and then type CMD and press enter. You should see the command window, which in Windows is a small window with a black background. Like all other windows you can change its shape by grabbing the corner and stretching it.

IPCONFIG: Reading your computer's settings

In a focus box earlier in the chapter, we showed you how to find your computer's TRCP/IP settings using Windows. You can also do it by using the IPCONFIG command. In the command window, type IPCONFIG/ALL and press enter.

You should see a screen like that shown in Figure 5.17. The middle of the screen will show the TCP/IP information about your computer. You can see the IP address (192.168.1.102 in Figure 5.17), the subnet mask (255.255.255.0), the default gateway, which

```
C:\Documents and Settings\Administrator>ipconfig/all

Windows IP Configuration

        Host Name . . . . . . . . . . . . : ALAN
        Primary Dns Suffix . . . . . . . :
        Node Type . . . . . . . . . . . . : Unknown
        IP Routing Enabled . . . . . . . .: No
        WINS Proxy Enabled . . . . . . . .: No
        DNS Suffix Search List . . . . . .: insightbb.com

Ethernet adapter Local Area Connection:

        Connection-specific DNS Suffix . . .: insightbb.com
        Description . . . . . . . . . . . : Intel(R) PRO/1000 MT Network Connect
ion
        Physical Address . . . . . . . . .: 00-0D-56-D8-8D-96
        Dhcp Enabled . . . . . . . . . . .: Yes
        Autoconfiguration Enabled . . . . : Yes
        IP Address . . . . . . . . . . . .: 192.168.1.102
        Subnet Mask . . . . . . . . . . . : 255.255.255.0
        Default Gateway . . . . . . . . . : 192.168.1.1
        DHCP Server . . . . . . . . . . . : 192.168.1.1
        DNS Servers . . . . . . . . . . . : 63.240.76.4
                                            204.127.198.4
                                            63.240.76.135
        Lease Obtained . . . . . . . . . .: Wednesday, February 20, 2008 8:09:37
 AM
        Lease Expires  . . . . . . . . . .: Tuesday, February 26, 2008 8:09:37 A
M

C:\Documents and Settings\Administrator>
```

FIGURE 5.17 IPCONFIG command

is the IP address of the router leading out of your subnet (192.168.1.1), the DHCP server (192.168.1.1), and the available DNS servers (e.g., 63.240.76.4). Your computer will have similar, but different information. As discussed in Technical Focus 5.3, your computer might be using "private" IP addresses the same as my computer shown in Figure 5.17, so your addresses may be identical to mine. We'll explain how network address translation (NAT) is done in Chapter 11.

PING: Finding other computers

The PING sends a small packet to any computer on the Internet to show you how long it takes the packet to travel from your computer to the target computer and back again. You can ping a computer using its IP address or Web URL. Not all computers respond to ping commands, so not every computer you ping will answer.

Start by pinging your default gateway: just type PING followed by the IP address of your gateway. Figure 5.18 shows that the PING command sends four packets to the target computer and then displays the maximum, minimum, and average transit times. In Figure 5.18, you can see that pinging my gateway is fast: less than one millisecond for the packet to travel from my computer to my router and back again.

Next, ping a well-known Web site in the United States to see the average times taken. Remember that

```
C:\Documents and Settings\Administrator>ping 192.168.1.1

Pinging 192.168.1.1 with 32 bytes of data:

Reply from 192.168.1.1: bytes = 32  time < 1ms  TTL = 64
Reply from 192.168.1.1: bytes = 32  time < 1ms  TTL = 64
Reply from 192.168.1.1: bytes = 32  time < 1ms  TTL = 64
Reply from 192.168.1.1: bytes = 32  time < 1ms  TTL = 64

Ping statistics for 192.168.1.1:
    Packets: Sent = 4, Received = 4, Lost = 0 (0% loss),
Approximate round trip times in milli-seconds:
    Minimum = 0ms, Maximum = 0ms, Average = 0ms
```

```
C:\Documents and Settings\Administrator>ping www.google.com

Pinging www.1.google.com [216.239.37.99] with 32 bytes of data:

Reply from 216.239.37.99: bytes = 32 time = 53ms TTL = 235
Reply from 216.239.37.99: bytes = 32 time = 52ms TTL = 236
Reply from 216.239.37.99: bytes = 32 time = 52ms TTL = 236
Reply from 216.239.37.99: bytes = 32 time = 53ms TTL = 235

Ping statistics for 216.239.37.99:
    Packets: Sent = 4, Received = 4, Lost = 0 (0% loss),
Approximate round trip times in milli-seconds:
    Minimum = 52ms, Maximum = 53ms, Average = 52ms
```

```
C:\Documents and Settings\Administrator>ping www.cityu.edu.hk

Pinging amber.cityu.edu.hk [144.214.5.218] with 32 bytes of data:

Reply from 144.214.5.218: bytes = 32 time = 240ms TTL = 236
Reply from 144.214.5.218: bytes = 32 time = 239ms TTL = 236
Reply from 144.214.5.218: bytes = 32 time = 239ms TTL = 236
Reply from 144.214.5.218: bytes = 32 time = 240ms TTL = 236

Ping statistics for 144.214.5.218:
    Packets: Sent = 4, Received = 4, Lost = 0 (0% loss),
Approximate round trip times in milli-seconds:
    Minimum = 239ms, Maximum = 240ms, Average = 239ms
```

FIGURE 5.18 PING command

not all Web sites will respond to the ping command. In Figure 5.18, you can see that it took an average of 52 milliseconds for a packet to go from my computer to Google and back again. Also note that www.google.com has an IP address of 216.239.37.99.

Now, ping a Web site outside the United States. In Figure 5.18, you can see that it took an average of 239 milliseconds for a packet to go from my computer to the City University of Hong Kong and back again. If you think about it, the Internet is amazingly fast.

```
C:\Documents and Settings\Administrator>arp.-a.

Interface: 192.168.1.102 --- 0x10003
  Internet Address          Physical Address   Type
  192.168.1.1   00-04-5a-0b-d1-40              dynamic
```

```
C:\Documents and Settings\Administrator>ping 192.168.1.152

Pinging 192.168.1.152 with 32 bytes of data:

Reply from 192.168.1.152: bytes = 32 time < 1ms TTL = 64
Reply from 192.168.1.152: bytes = 32 time < 1ms TTL = 64
Reply from 192.168.1.152: bytes = 32 time < 1ms TTL = 64
Reply from 192.168.1.152: bytes = 32 time < 1ms TTL = 64

Ping statistics for 192.168.1.152:
    Packets: Sent = 4, Received = 4, Lost = 0 (0% loss),
Approximate round trip times in milli-seconds:
    Minimum = 0ms, Maximum = 0ms, Average = 0ms
```

```
C:\Documents and Settings\Administrator>arp -a

Interface: 192.168.1.102 --- 0x10003
  Internet Address        Physical Address     Type
  192.168.1.1             00-04-5a-0b-d1-40    dynamic
  192.168.1.152           00-08-e1-00-21-f6    dynamic
```

FIGURE 5.19 ARP command

ARP: Displaying Physical Addresses

Remember that in order to send a message to other computers on the Internet, you must know the physical address (aka data link layer address) of the next computer to send the message to. Most computers on the Internet will be outside your subnet, so almost all messages your computer sends will be sent to your gateway (i.e., the router leaving your subnet). Remember that computers use ARP requests to find physical addresses and store them in their ARP table. To find out what data link layer addresses your computer knows, you can use the ARP command.

At the command prompt, type ARP-A and press enter. This will display the contents of your ARP table. In Figure 5.19, you can see that the ARP table in my computer has only one entry, which means all the messages from my computer since I turned it on have only gone to this one computer—my router. You can also see the physical address of my router: 00-04-5a-0b-d1-40.

If you have another computer on your subnet, ping it and then take a look at your ARP table again. In Figure 5.19, you can see the ping of another computer my subnet (192.168.1.152) and then see the ARP table with this new entry. When I pinged 192.168.1.152, my computer had to find its physical address, so it issued an ARP request and 192.168.1.152 responded with an ARP response, which my computer added into the ARP table before sending the ping.

NSLOOKUP: Finding IP Addresses

Remember that in order to send a message to other computers on the Internet, you must know their IP addresses. Computers use DNS servers to find IP addresses. You can issue a DNS request by using the NSLOOKUP command.

```
C:\Documents and Settings\Administrator>nslookup www.cnn.com
Server: ns1.insightbb.com
Address: 63.240.76.135

Non-authoritative answer:
Name: cnn.com
Addresses: 64.236.16.116, 64.236.24.12, 64.236.24.20, 64.236.24.28
          64.236.29.120, 64.236.16.20, 64.236.16.52, 64.236.16.84
Aliases: www.cnn.com
```

FIGURE 5.20 NSLOOKUP command

Type NSLOOKUP and the URL of a computer on the Internet and press enter. In Figure 5.20, you'll see that www.cnn.com has several IP addresses and is also known as cnn.com

DNS Cache

The IPCONFIG/DISPLAYDNS command can be used to show the contents of the DNS cache. You can experiment with this by displaying the cache, visiting a new Web site with your browser, and then displaying the cache again. Figure 5.21 shows part of the cache on my computer after visiting a number of sites. The DNS cache contains information about all the Web sites I've visited, either directly or indirectly (by having a Web page on one server pull a graphics file off of a different server).

For example, the second entry in this figure is ns1.cisco.com, which has an IP address of 128.107.241.185 (a four-byte long address). The record type is one, which means this is a "host"—that is, a computer on the Internet using IPv4. Because the DNS information might change, all entries have a maximum time to live set by the DNS that provides the information (usually 24 hours); the time to live value is the time in seconds that this entry will remain in the cache until it is removed.

The very last entry in this figure is for ns1.v6.telekom.at. The record type of 28 means that this is a host that uses IPv6, which you can see from the 16-byte long address in the record (2001:890:600:d1: :100).

TRACERT: Finding Routes through the Internet

The TRACERT command will show you the IP addresses of computers in the route from your computer to another computer on the Internet. Many networks have disabled TRACERT for security reasons, so it doesn't always work. Type TRACERT and the URL of a computer on the Internet and press enter. In Figure 5.22, you'll see the route from my computer, through the Insight network, through the AT&T network, through the Level 3 network, and then through the Google network until it reaches the server. TRACERT usually sends three packets, so beside each hop is the total time to reach that hop for each of the three packets. You'll see that it took just over 50 ms for a packet to go from my computer to Google. You'll also see that the times aren't always "right," in that the first packet took 50 ms to reach the bbrl Washington level 3 router (step 9) but only 40 ms to reach the next hop to the car2 Washington Level 3 router (step 10). The time to each hop is measured separately, each with a different packet, so sometimes a packet is delayed longer on one hop or another.

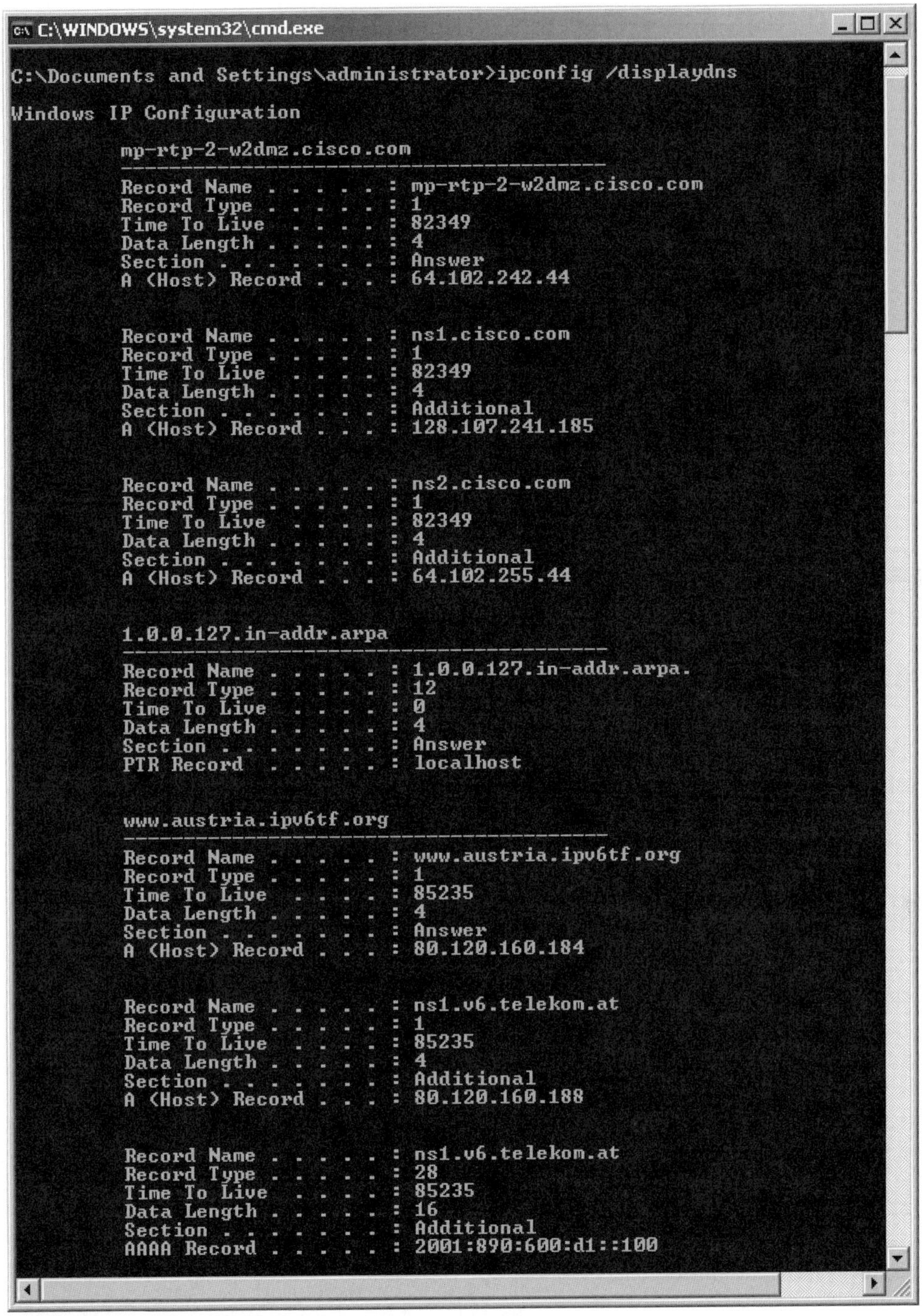

FIGURE 5.21 DNS cache

```
C:\Documents and Settings\Administrator>tracert www.google.com

Tracing route to www.1.google.com [216.239.37.104]
over a maximum of 30 hops:
  1      1 ms     1 ms     1 ms  192.168.1.1
  2      7 ms    10 ms     8 ms  12-220-5-129.client.insightBB.com [12.220.5.129]
  3     11 ms    12 ms    11 ms  12-220-1-78.client.insightBB.com [12.220.1.78]
  4     17 ms    16 ms    16 ms  12-220-0-26.client.insightBB.com [12.220.0.26]
  5     19 ms    18 ms    18 ms  tbr1-p011 901.cgcil.ip.att.net [12.123.4.226]
  6     18 ms    16 ms    16 ms  ggr2-p310.cgcil.ip.att.net [12.123.6.65]
  7     19 ms    18 ms    18 ms  so-9-1.car4.Chicagol.Level3.net [4.68.127.165]
  8     19 ms    18 ms    19 ms  ae-2-52.bbr2.Chicagol.Level3.net [4.68.101.33]
  9     50 ms    39 ms    39 ms  ae-2-0.bbr1.Washington1.Level3.net [4.68.128.201]
 10     40 ms    40 ms    39 ms  ae-12-53.car2.Washington1.Level3.net [4.68.121.83]
 11     53 ms    78 ms    56 ms  unknown.Level3.net [166.90.148.174]
 12     54 ms    52 ms    51 ms  72.14.232.106
 13     55 ms    54 ms    53 ms  216.239.48.96
 14     55 ms    55 ms    54 ms  216.239.48.110
 15     52 ms    51 ms    52 ms  216.239.37.104
Trace complete.
```

FIGURE 5.22 TRACERT command

HANDS-ON ACTIVITY

Watching TCP/IP in Action

This chapter explained how TCP/IP works. The objective of this activity is for you to watch your computer use TCP/IP. The activity in Chapter 4 explained how to download and install Wireshark, a software tool for capturing and analyzing network packets. If you haven't already done so, go to www.wireshark.org and download and install the Wireshark software.

1. Start Wireshark.
2. For this activity, we only want to capture the packets send to and from your computer, so you need to change a Wireshark option.
   a. Click Capture
   b. Click Options
   c. Make sure the check box in front of "Promiscuous mode" is not checked.
3. Select the correct interface in the Interface dropdown (either your Ethernet or wireless interface).
4. Click Start.
5. Start your Web Browser (e.g., Internet Explorer), and watch the packets Wireshark captures.

Figure 5.23 shows the packets I captured that were sent from and to my computer when I used my Web browser to get the home page at www.espn.com. My computer sent and received a combined total of 1,398 packets to load the espn.com home page. That's a lot of packets for one Web page, but it's not unusual.

The top window in Figure 5.23 shows the first 32 packets my computer sent and received in chronological order. The middle window shows the contents of one specific packet that I clicked on in the top window (packet number 6)—but more on that in a moment. My computer has an IP address of 192.168.1.104.

The first two packets in the top window are the ARP request from my computer and the ARP response from my router. My computer did not know the Ethernet address of the router, so before it could send a message, it first had to find the Ethernet address of my router. If you were to click on either of these packets, the middle window below the list of packets would show what that packet contained. If you looked at packet 1 or packet 2, you would see that each has an ARP packet, and an Ethernet frame—no IP packet or TCP segment.

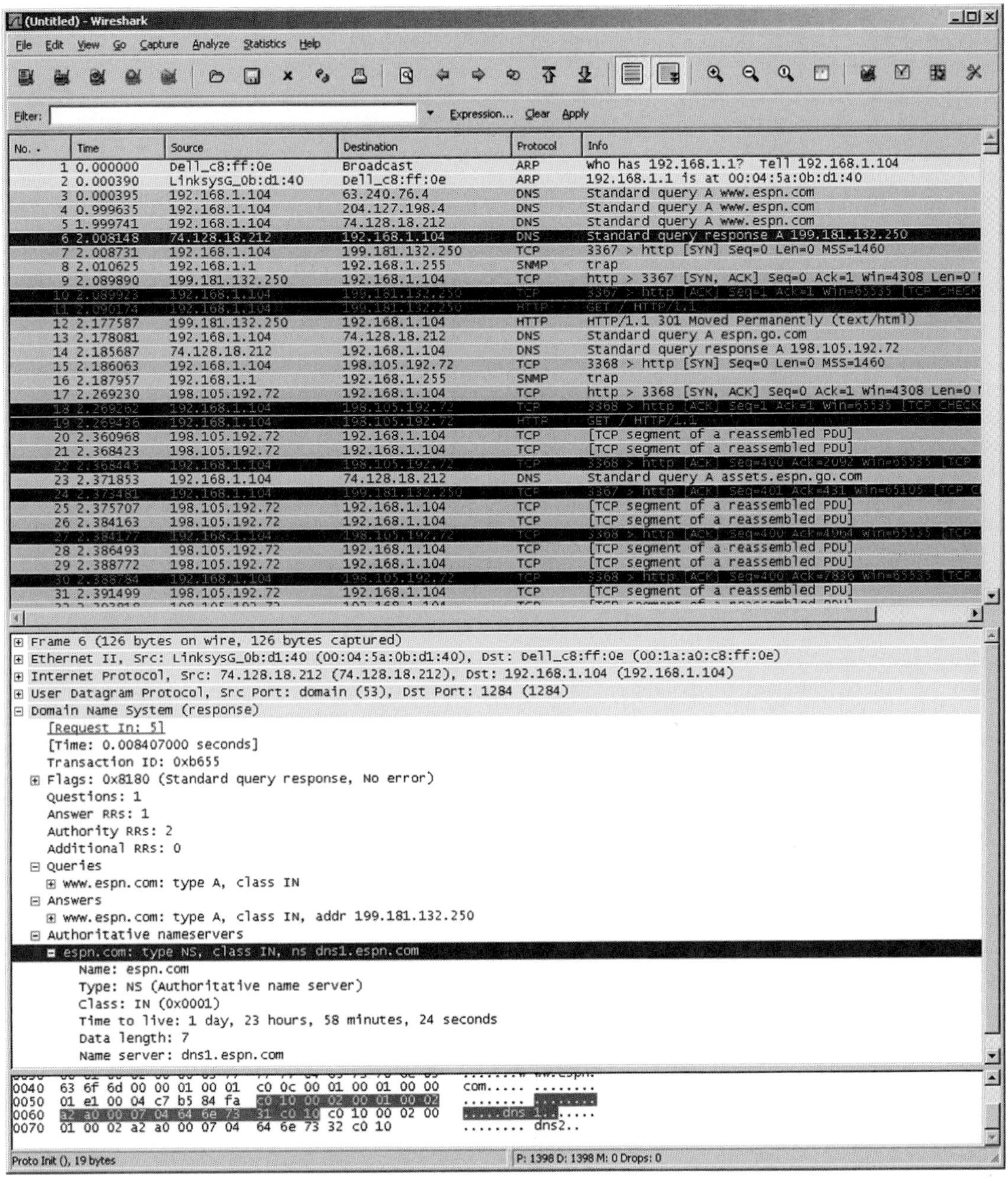

FIGURE 5.23 Wireshark

Packets 3–5 in the top window show the DNS requests sent by my computer. Because I had not visited www.espn.com previously today, my computer did not know the IP address for www.espn.com. My computer has three DNS servers defined in its TCP/IP configuration, so the DNS request for www.espn.com was sent simultaneously to all three. If you were to click on any of these three packets, the middle window would show you that the DNS request packet was placed inside a UDP datagram, inside an IP packet, inside an Ethernet frame.

Packet number 7 is the DNS response packet I received from one of the DNS servers (the one with an IP address of 74.128.18.212). If you were to look up this DNS server's IP address (see Exercise 5-5), you would see that it is owned by Insight Communications, my ISP. The middle window in Figure 5.23 shows the contents of that packet: a DNS response, inside a UDP datagram, inside an IP packet, inside an Ethernet frame. The DNS response packet shows that the DNS server at my ISP received the IP address for www.espn.com from a DNS server called dns1.espn.com.

Once my computer has the IP address for espn.com, it can now send the HTTP request. But first, because HTTP uses connection-oriented messaging, it must open a session at www.espn.com. My computer sends packet 7, which is a TCP SYN segment to open the session, to www.espn.com (whose IP address is 199.181.132.250). The server responds with packet 9, which is a TCP segment acknowledging that the server has accepted my request to open a session and is ready to receive data. My computer then sends packet 10, which is a TCP segment accepting the session from the server.

In the middle of this exchange, you will see packet 8, which was sent by my router (192.168.1.1) to my computer. This is a network management packet (SNMP) which is discussed in Chapter 12.

Next, in packet 11, my computer sends the HTTP request packet to the ESPN server. In packet 12, the server responds with an HTTP response that says the file I requested (the home page on www.espn.com) has been moved to a new URL. If you were to click on packet 12, and look inside the HTTP response packet, you would see that the new URL the server provides is espn.go.com.

My computer then needs to issue a new HTTP request to espn.go.com. However, it doesn't know the IP address of espn.go.com. So it sends packet 13, a DNS request to the DNS server that provided the DNS information to it previously. The DNS server responds with a DNS response containing the needed IP address (packet 14), so my computer is now ready to send the new HTTP packet.

Packets 15–18 are the TCP segments to and from my computer and espn.go.com to create a new session. In packet 19, the computer sends the HTTP request to espn.go.com. In packet 20, espn.go.com (198.105.192.72) responds with an HTTP response containing the first part of the HTML file I requested (the home page for ESPN). If you were to click on packet 20 and open up the TCP segment data that would appear in the middle window, you could read the HTTP response (including the header that shows that ESPN uses Microsoft Web server software).

The HTTP response packet containing the HTML file is large enough that it was spread across many TCP segments. You can see a whole series of TCP segments from the server to my computer (e.g., packets 20, 21, 25, 26, 28, 29, and 31), interspersed by TCP acknowledgments from my computer back to the server.

In packet 23, you will see a new DNS request for assets.espn.go.com. This is because the HTML file includes a graphic file stored on the assets.espn.go.com server. So, before my computer can issue an HTTP request for the file, it must first find the IP address for that server.

You can continue to work through the packet you capture, looking at each in turn to see the pattern of packets that flow between the client and the server, and also looking inside packets to see the protocols used (e.g., UDP versus TCP) and the data they contain.

PART THREE

NETWORK TECHNOLOGIES

Courtesy Cisco Systems, Inc.

A Cisco switch and router

CHAPTER 6

LOCAL AREA NETWORKS

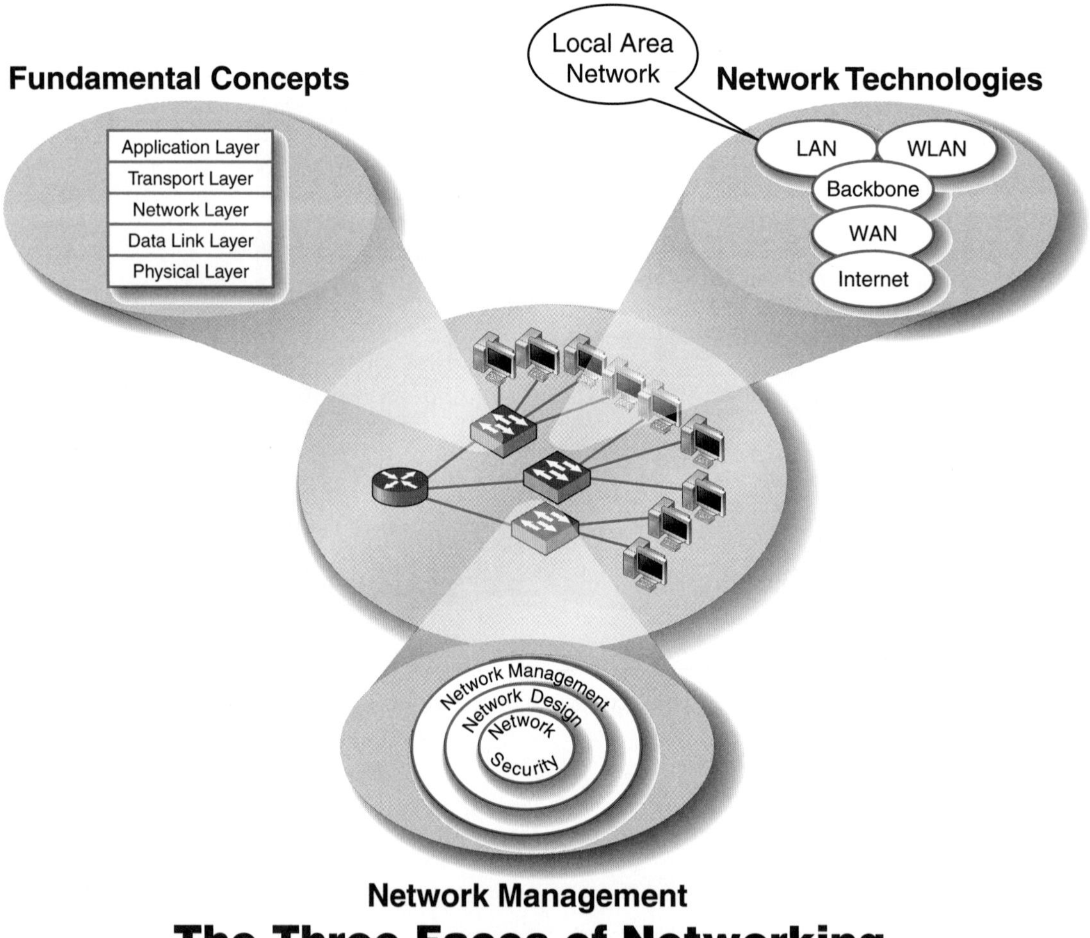

The Three Faces of Networking

THE PRECEDING chapters provided a fundamental understanding of the five basic layers in a typical network. This chapter draws together these concepts to describe a basic LAN. We first summarize the major components of a LAN and then describe the two most commonly used LAN technologies: traditional Ethernet and switched Ethernet. The chapter ends with a discussion of how to design LANs and how to improve LAN performance. In this chapter, we focus only on the basics of LANs; the next chapter describes how LANs and BNs are used together.

OBJECTIVES ▼

- Be aware of the roles of LANs in organizations
- Understand the major components of LANs
- Understand traditional Ethernet LANs
- Understand switched Ethernet LANs
- Understand the best practice recommendations for LAN design
- Be familiar with how to improve LAN performance

CHAPTER OUTLINE ▼

INTRODUCTION

Most large organizations have numerous LANs connected by backbone networks. These LANs also provide access to a variety of servers, mainframe computers, and the Internet. In this chapter, we discuss the fundamental components of a LAN, along with two technologies commonly used in LANs—traditional Ethernet (IEEE 802.3), and switched Ethernet. There used to be many different types of LAN technologies, but gradually the world has changed so that Ethernet dominates. Today, very few organizations consider any LAN technology other than Ethernet. Together, traditional Ethernet and its switched and wireless cousins account for almost all LANs installed today.

Why Use a LAN?

There are two basic reasons for developing a LAN: information sharing and resource sharing. **Information sharing** refers to having users access the same data files, exchange information via e-mail, or use the Internet. For example, a single purchase order database might be maintained so all users can access its contents over the LAN. (Many information-sharing applications were described in Chapter 2.) The main benefit of information sharing is improved decision making, which makes it generally more important than resource sharing.

Resource sharing refers to one computer sharing a hardware device (e.g., printer, an Internet connection) or software package with other computers on the network to save costs. For example, suppose we have 30 computers on a LAN, each of which needs access to a word processing package. One option is to purchase 30 copies of the software and install one on each computer. This would use disk space on each computer and require a significant amount of staff time to perform the installation and maintain the software, particularly if the package were updated regularly.

An alternative is to install the software on the network for all to use. This would eliminate the need to keep a copy on every computer and would free up disk space. It would also simplify software maintenance because any software upgrades would be installed once on the network server; staff members would no longer have to upgrade all computers.

In most cases, not all users would need to access the word processing package simultaneously. Therefore, rather than purchasing a license for each computer in the network, you could instead purchase ten licenses, presuming that only ten users would simultaneously use the software. Of course, the temptation is to purchase only one copy of the software and permit everyone to use it simultaneously. The cost savings would be significant, but this is illegal. Virtually all software licenses require one copy to be purchased for each simultaneous user. Most companies and all government agencies have policies forbidding the violation of software licenses, and many fire employees who knowingly violate them.

One approach to controlling the number of copies of a particular software package is to use **LAN metering software** that prohibits using more copies of a package than there are installed licenses. Many software packages now come in LAN versions that do this automatically, and a number of third-party packages are also available.

Nonetheless, the **Software Publishers Association (SPA)** in Washington, D.C., estimates that about 40 percent of all the software in the world is used illegally—an annual total of more than $40 billion. North America has the lowest rate of **software piracy** (28 percent). Although piracy has been on the decline, it still exceeds 75 percent in many parts of the world, with the exception of western Europe (43 percent), Australia (32 percent), New Zealand (35 percent), and Japan (41 percent). According to SPA, most software sold on eBay is pirated.

The SPA has recently undertaken an aggressive **software audit** program to check the number of illegal software copies on LANs. Whistleblowers receive rewards from SPA, and the violating organizations and employees are brought to court. SPA will work with companies that voluntarily submit to an audit, and it offers an audit kit that scrutinizes networks in search of software sold by SPA members (see www.spa.org).

Dedicated-Server versus Peer-to-Peer LANs

One common way to categorize LANs is by whether they have a dedicated server or whether they operate as a peer-to-peer LAN without a dedicated server. This chapter focuses primarily on dedicated-server LANs because they account for more than 90 percent of all installed LANs, although many of the issues are also common in peer-to-peer networks.

Dedicated Server Networks

As the name suggests, a **dedicated-server LAN** has one or more computers that are permanently assigned as network servers. These servers enable users to share files and often are also used to share printers. A dedicated-server LAN can connect with almost any other network, can handle very large files and databases, and uses sophisticated LAN software. Moreover, high-end dedicated-server LANs can be easily interconnected to form enterprisewide networks or, in some cases, can replace a host mainframe computer. Generally speaking, the dedicated servers are powerful microcomputers or minicomputers. Sometimes servers are organized into a large set of servers on one part of the network called a cluster or **server farm.** Server farms can range from tens to thousands of servers.

In a dedicated-server LAN, the server's usual operating system (e.g., Windows) is replaced by a network operating system (e.g., Linux, Windows Server). Special-purpose network communication software on each client computer is the link between the client computer's operating system and the network operating system on the server. This set of communication software (often called drivers) provides the data link layer and network layer protocols that allow data transmissions to take place. Three software components must work together and in conjunction with the network hardware to enable communications: the network operating system in the dedicated server, the network communication software on the client, and the application software that runs on the server and client computers.

A LAN can have many different types of dedicated servers, such as mail servers, database servers, and Web servers, as discussed in Chapter 2. Other common types are file servers and print servers.

File servers allow many users to share the same set of files on a common, shared disk drive. The hard disk volume can be of any size, limited only by the size of the disk storage itself. Files on the shared disk drive can be made freely available to all network users, shared only among authorized users, or restricted to only one user.

Print servers handle print requests on the LAN. By offloading the management of printing from the main LAN file server or database server, print servers help reduce the load on them and increase network efficiency. Print servers have traditionally been separate computers, but many vendors now sell "black boxes" that perform all the functions of a print server at much less than the cost of a stand-alone computer.

Peer-to-Peer Networks **Peer-to-peer networks** do not require a dedicated server. All computers run network software that enables them to function both as clients and as servers. Authorized users can connect to any computer in the LAN that permits access and use its hard drives and printer as though it were physically attached to their own computers. Peer-to-peer networks often are slower than dedicated server networks because if you access a computer that is also being used by its owner, it slows down both the owner and the network.

In general, peer-to-peer LANs have less capability, support a more limited number of computers, provide less sophisticated software, and can prove more difficult to manage than dedicated-server LANs. However, they are cheaper both in hardware and software. Peer-to-peer LANs are most appropriate for sharing resources in small LANs. We should note that peer-to-peer has become popular for application layer software file sharing on the Internet. This is conceptually similar to peer-to-peer LANs, but quite different in practice.

A Day in the Life: LAN Administrator

Most days start the same way. The LAN administrator arrives early in the morning before most people who use the LAN. The first hour is spent checking for problems. All the network hardware and servers in the server room receive routine diagnostics. All the logs for the previous day are examined to find problems. If problems are found (e.g., a crashed hard disk) the next few hours are spent fixing them. Next, the daily backups are done. This usually takes only a few minutes, but sometimes a problem occurs and it takes an hour.

The next step is to see if there are any other activities that need to be performed to maintain the network. This involves checking e-mail for security alerts (e.g., Windows updates, anti-virus updates). If critical updates are needed, they are done immediately. There are usually e-mails from several users that need to be contacted, either problems with the LAN, or requests for new hardware or software to be installed. These new activities are prioritized into the work queue.

And then the real work begins. Work activities include tasks such as planning for the next roll out of software upgrades. This involves investigating the new software offerings, identifying what hardware platforms are required to run them, and determining which users should receive the upgrades. It also means planning for and installing new servers or network hardware such as firewalls.

Of course, some days can be more exciting than others. When a new virus hits, everyone is involved in cleaning up the compromised computers and installing security patches on the other computers. Sometimes virus attacks can be fun when you see that your security settings work and beat the virus.

With thanks to Steve Bushert

LAN COMPONENTS

There are six components in a traditional LAN (Figure 6.1). The first two are the client computer and the server (but see the earlier section on peer-to-peer networks). Clients and servers have been discussed in Chapter 2, so they are not discussed further here. The other components are network interface cards (NICs), network cables, hubs/switches, and the network operating system.

Network Interface Cards

The **network interface card (NIC)** is used to connect the computer to the network cable and is one part of the physical layer connection among the computers in the network. Most computers come with a NIC built in, but sometimes a separate NIC must be installed; for example, a wireless NIC for a desktop computer (often as a USB device).

Network Cables

Each computer must be physically connected by network cable to the other computers in the network. Just as highways carry all kinds of traffic, the perfect cabling system also should be able to carry all kinds of electronic transmissions within the building. But in practice, it isn't that simple. The selection of a LAN can be influenced greatly by the type of cable that already exists in the building where the LAN is to be installed.

Most LANs are built with **unshielded twisted-pair (UTP) cable, shielded twisted-pair (STP),** or **fiber-optic cable** (although fiber-optic cable is far more commonly used in BNs, which are discussed in the next chapter). Wireless LANs run on infrared or radio frequencies, eliminating the need for cables. (Common cable standards are discussed on the next page. We should add that these cable standards specify the minimum quality cable required; it is possible, for example, to use category 5 UTP wire for a 10Base-T Ethernet.)

Many LANs use a combination of STP and UTP wire. Although initially it appeared that twisted-pair would not be able to meet long-term capacity and distance requirements,

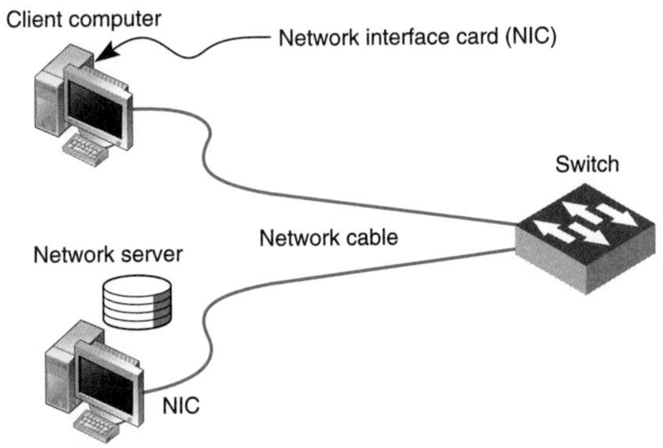

FIGURE 6.1 Local area network components

today UTP is one of the leading LAN cabling technologies. Its low cost makes it very useful. STP is only used in special areas that produce electrical interference, such as factories near heavy machinery or hospitals near MRI scanners.

Fiber-optic cable is even thinner than UTP wire and therefore takes far less space when cabled throughout a building. It also is much lighter, weighing less than 10 pounds per 1,000 feet. Because of its high capacity, fiber-optic cabling is perfect for BNs, although it is beginning to be used in LANs.

Network Hubs and Switches

There are important differences between hubs and switches that we discuss later. For now, we focus on their similar roles. Network **hubs** and **switches** serve two purposes. First, they provide an easy way to connect network cables. A hub or a switch can be thought of as a junction box, permitting new computers to be connected to the network as easily as plugging a power cord into an electrical socket (Figure 6.2). Each connection point where a cable can be plugged in is called a **port.** Each port has a unique number.

TECHNICAL FOCUS 6.1 COMMONLY USED NETWORK CABLE STANDARDS

Name	Type	Maximum Data Rate (Mbps)	Often Used By	Cost[1] ($/foot)
Category 1[2]	UTP	1	Modem	.04
Category 2	UTP	4	Token Ring-4[3]	.35
Category 3	UTP	10	10Base-T Ethernet	.06
Category 4	STP	16	Token Ring-16[3]	.60
Category 5	UTP	100	100Base-T Ethernet	.07
Category 5	STP	100	100Base-T Ethernet	.18
Category 5e[4]	UTP	100	1000Base-T Ethernet	.10
Category 6	UTP	250	1000Base-T Ethernet	.15
Category 7[5]	STP	600	1000Base-T Ethernet	.25
62.5/50	Fiber	1,000	1000Base-F Ethernet	.25

Notes

1. These costs are approximate costs for cable only (no connectors). They often change but will give you a sense of the relative differences in costs among the different options.
2. Category 1 is standard voice-grade twisted-pair wires but it can also be used to support low-speed analog data transmission.
3. Token ring is an old local area network technology seldom used today.
4. Category 5e is an improved version of category 5 that has better insulation and a center plastic pipe inside the cable to keep the individual wires in place and reduce noise from cross-talk, so that it is better suited to 1000Base-T.
5. The standards for category 7 have not been finalized.

FIGURE 6.2 Network hub
Source: Courtesy Cisco Systems, Inc.

Simple hubs and switches are commonly available in 4-, 8-, 16-, and 24-port sizes, meaning that they provide anywhere between 4 and 24 ports into which network cables can be plugged. When no cables are plugged in, the signal bypasses the unused port. When a cable is plugged into a port, the signal travels down the cable as though it were directly connected to the cables attached to the hub. Some switches also enable different types of cables to be connected and perform the necessary conversions (e.g., twisted-pair cable to coaxial cable, coaxial cable to fiber-optic cable).

Second, hubs and switches act as repeaters. Signals can travel only so far in a network cable before they attenuate and can no longer be recognized. (Attenuation was discussed in Chapter 4.) All LAN cables are rated for the maximum distance they can be used (typically 100 meters for **twisted-pair cable**, and 400 meters to several kilometers for fiber-optic cable).

In the early days of LANs, it was common practice to install network cable wherever it was convenient. Little long-term planning was done. Hubs were placed at random

MANAGEMENT FOCUS 6.1

CABLE PROBLEMS AT THE UNIVERSITY OF GEORGIA

Like many organizations, the Terry College of Business at the University of Georgia is headquartered in a building built before the computer age. When local area network cabling was first installed in the early 1980s, no one foresaw the rapid expansion that was to come. Cables and hubs were installed piecemeal to support the needs of the handful of early users.

The network eventually grew far beyond the number of users it was designed to support. The network cabling gradually became a complex, confusing, and inefficient mess. There was no logical pattern for the cables, and there was no network cable plan. Worse still, no one knew where all the cables and hubs were physically located. Before a new user was added, a network technician had to open up a ceiling and crawl around to find a hub. Hopefully, the hub had an unused port to connect the new user, or else the technician would have to find another hub with an empty port.

To complicate matters even more, asbestos was discovered. Now network technicians could not open the ceiling and work on the cable unless asbestos precautions were taken. This meant calling in the university's asbestos team and sealing off nearby offices. Installing a new user to the network (or fixing a network cable problem) now took two days and cost $2,000.

The solution was obvious. The university spent $400,000 to install new category 5 twisted-pair cable to every office and to install a new high-speed fiber-optic backbone network between network segments.

MANAGEMENT FOCUS 6.2 MANAGING NETWORK CABLING

You must consider a number of items when installing cables or when performing cable maintenance. You should:

- Perform a physical inventory of any existing cabling systems and document those findings in the network cable plan.
- Properly maintain the network cable plan. Always update cable documentation immediately on installing or removing a cable or hub. Insist that any cabling contractor provide "as-built" plans that document where the cabling was actually placed, in case of minor differences from the construction plan.
- Establish a long-term plan for the evolution of the current cabling system to whatever cabling system will be in place in the future.
- Obtain a copy of the local city fire codes and follow them. For example, cables used in airways without conduit need to be plenum-certified (i.e., covered with a fire-retardant jacket).
- Conceal all cables as much as possible to protect them from damage and for security reasons.
- Properly number and mark both ends of all cable installations as you install them. If a contractor installs cabling, always make a complete inspection to ensure that all cables are labeled.

intervals to meet the needs of the few users, and cable was laid where it was convenient. The exact placement of the cables and hubs was often not documented, making future expansion more difficult—you had to find the cable and a hub before you could add a new user.

With today's explosion in LAN use, it is critical to plan for the effective installation and use of LAN **cabling.** The cheapest point at which to install network cable is during the construction of the building; adding cable to an existing building can cost significantly more. Indeed, the costs to install cable (i.e., paying those doing the installation and additional construction) are usually substantially more than the cost of the cable itself, making it expensive to reinstall the cable if the cable plan does not meet the organization's needs.

Most buildings under construction today have a separate LAN **cable plan,** as they have plans for telephone cables and electrical cables. The same is true for older buildings in which new LAN cabling is being installed. Most cable plans are similar in style to electrical and telephone plans. Each floor has a telecommunications wiring closet that contains one or more network hubs or switches. Cables are run from each room on the floor to this wiring closet. It is common to install 20 to 50 percent more cables than you actually need, to make future expansion simple. Any reconfiguration or expansion can be done easily by adding a network hub or switch and connecting the unused cables in the wiring closet. This saves the difficulty and expense of installing new cables.

Network Operating Systems

The **network operating system (NOS)** is the software that controls the network. Every NOS provides two sets of software: one that runs on the **network server(s)** and one that runs on the network client(s). The server version of the NOS provides the software that performs the functions associated with the data link, network, and application layers and usually the computer's own operating system. The client version of the NOS provides the software that performs the functions associated with the data link and the network layers and must interact with the application software and the computer's own operating system. Most NOSs provide different versions of their client software that run on different types of computers, so that Windows computers, for example, can function on the same network as Apples. In most cases (e.g., Windows, Linux), the client NOS software is included with the operating system itself.

NOS Server Software The NOS server software enables the file server, print server, or database server to operate. In addition to handling all the required network functions, it acts as the application software by executing the requests sent to it by the clients (e.g., copying a file from its hard disk and transferring it to the client, printing a file on the printer, executing a database request, and sending the result to the client). NOS server software replaces the normal operating system on the server. By replacing the existing operating system, it provides better performance and faster response time because a NOS is optimized for its limited range of operations. Figure 6.3 summarizes several common NOS.

NOS Client Software The NOS software running at the client computers provides the data link layer and network layer. Most operating systems today are designed with

Microsoft Windows Server
One of the most popular NOS is Windows Server, developed by Microsoft Corporation. It provides good file services and adequate print services, as well as an excellent development environment for application services. Windows Server is very similar to the Windows client operating system, so it is straightforward to learn. It works well with Windows client computers, but requires additional software (and effort) to support Apple and Linux clients.

Linux
Linux is an open source operating system first developed by Linus Torvalds at the University of Helsinki. It is the microcomputer version of UNIX, a popular mainframe operating system. Linux provides excellent file, print, and application services. It is more secure than Windows Server, given its origins as a highly secure mainframe operating system and because it is open source. It has a command driven interface (in contrast to Windows' graphical user interface), so it is harder to learn. It works well with Windows, Apple, and Linux client computers.

Apple Mac Operating System
The Apple Mac OS is a version of UNIX, integrated with the Apple graphical user interface to make it easy to use. It provides good file and print services and application development. It is more secure than Windows Server given its origins as a highly secure mainframe operating system. It works well with Apple client computers, but requires additional software (and effort) to support Windows and Linux clients.

FIGURE 6.3 Several common network operating systems

networking in mind. For example, Windows provides built-in software that will enable it to act as a client computer with a Windows Server.

One of the most important functions of a NOS is a *directory service.* Directory services provide information about resources on the network that are available to the users, such as shared printers, shared file servers, and application software. A common example of directory services is Microsoft's **Active Directory Service (ADS).**

ADS works in much the same manner as TCP/IP's DNS service, and in fact ADS servers, called **domain controllers,** can also act as DNS servers. Network resources are typically organized into a hierarchical tree. Each branch on the tree contains a domain, a group of related resources. For example, at a university, one domain might be the resources available within the business school, and another domain might be the resources in the computer science school, while another might be in the medical school. Domains can contain other domains, and in fact the hierarchical tree of domains within one organization can be linked to trees in other organizations to create a *forest* of shared network resources.

Within each domain, there is a server (the domain controller) that is responsible for resolving address information (much like a DNS server resolves address information on the Internet). The domain controller is also responsible for managing authorization information (e.g., who is permitted to use each resource) and making sure that resources are available only to authorized users. Domain controllers in the same tree (or forest) can share information among themselves, so that a domain controller in one part of the tree (or forest) can be configured to permit access to resources to any user that has been approved by another domain controller in a different part of the tree (or forest).

If you login to a Microsoft server or domain controller that provides ADS, you can see all network resources that you are authorized to use. When a client computer wishes to view available resources or access them, it sends a message using an industry standard

TECHNICAL FOCUS 6.2

STORAGE AREA NETWORKS AND NETWORK-ATTACHED STORAGE

New ideas and new terms emerge rapidly in data communications and networking. In recent years, a variant on the local area network (LAN) has emerged. A **storage area network (SAN)** is a LAN devoted solely to data storage. When the amount of data to be stored exceeds the practical limits of servers, the SAN plays a critical role. The SAN has a set of high-speed storage devices and servers that are networked together using a very high speed network (often using a technology called *fiber channel* that runs over a series of multi-gigabit point-to-point fiber-optic circuits). Servers are connected into the normal LAN and to the SAN, which is usually reserved for servers. When data are needed, clients send the request to a server on the LAN, which obtains the information from the devices on the SAN and then returns it to the client.

The devices on the SAN may be a large set of *database servers* or a set of network-attached disk arrays. In other cases, the devices may be **network-attached storage (NAS)** devices. A NAS is not a general-purpose computer like a server that runs a server operating system (e.g., Windows, Linux); it has a small processor and a large amount of disk storage and is designed solely to respond to requests for files and data. NAS can also be attached to LANs where they function as a fast file server.

directory protocol called **lightweight directory services (LDAP)** to the ADS domain controller. The ADS domain controller resolves the textual name in the LDAP request to a network address and—if the user is authorized to access the resource—provides contact information for the resource.

Network Profiles A **network profile** specifies what resources on each server are available on the network for use by other computers and which devices or people are allowed what access to the network. The network profile is normally configured when the network is established and remains in place until someone makes a change. In a LAN, the server hard disk may have various resources that can or cannot be accessed by a specific network user (e.g., data files, printers). Furthermore, a password may be required to grant network access to the resources.

If a device such as a hard disk on one of the network's computers is not included on the network profile, it cannot be used by another computer on the network. For example, if you have a hard disk (C) on your computer and your computer is connected to this LAN but the hard disk is not included on the network profile assignment list, then no other computer can access that hard disk.

In addition to profiling disks and printers, there must be a *user profile* for each person who uses the LAN, to add some security. Each device and each user is assigned various access codes, and only those users who log in with the correct code can use a specific device. Most LANs keep audit files to track who uses which resource. Security is discussed in Chapter 10.

TRADITIONAL ETHERNET (IEEE 802.3)

Almost all LANs installed today use some form of **Ethernet.** Ethernet was originally developed by DEC, Xerox, and Intel but has since become a standard formalized by the IEEE as **IEEE 802.3.**[1] The IEEE 802.3 version of Ethernet is slightly different from the original version but the differences are minor. Likewise, another version of Ethernet has also been developed that differs slightly from the 802.3 standard. In this section, we describe traditional Ethernet which is sometimes called **shared Ethernet.**

Ethernet is a layer 2 protocol, which means it operates at the data link layer. Every Ethernet LAN needs hardware at layer 1, the physical layer, that matches the requirements of the Ethernet software at layer 2. Ethernet is compatible with a variety of layer 3 protocols but is commonly used with TCP/IP.

Topology

Topology is the basic geometric layout of the network—the way in which the computers on the network are interconnected. It is important to distinguish between a logical topology and a physical topology. A **logical topology** is how the network works conceptually,

[1]The formal specification for Ethernet is provided in the 802.3 standard on the IEEE standards Web site. The URL is grouper.ieee.org/groups/802/3.

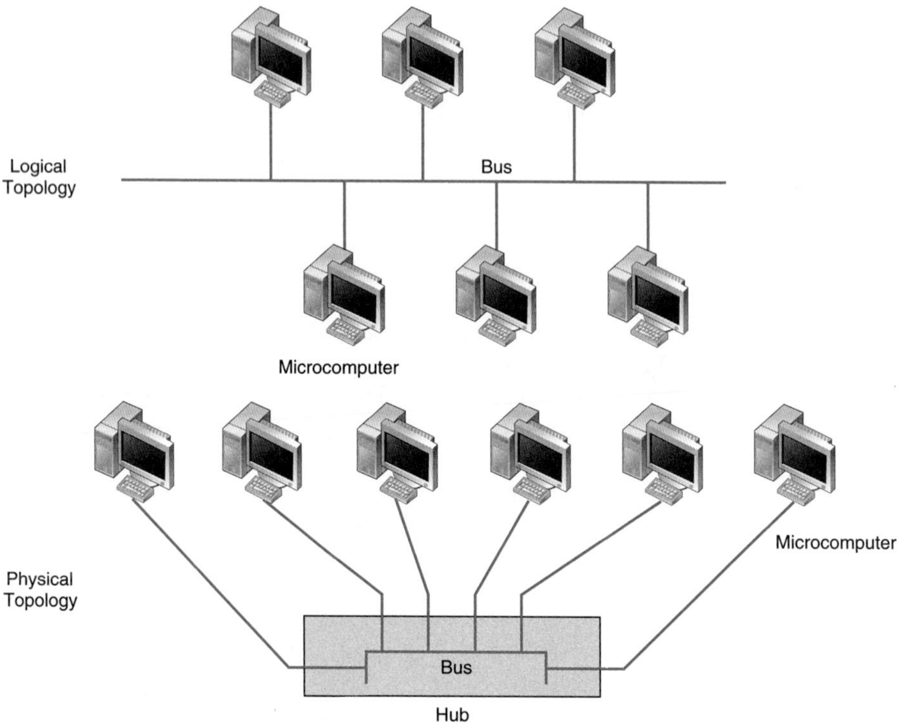

FIGURE 6.4 Ethernet topology

much like a logical data flow diagram (DFD) or logical entity relation diagram (ERD) in systems analysis and design or database design. A **physical topology** is how the network is physically installed, much like a physical DFD or physical ERD.

Ethernet's logical topology is a **bus topology.** All computers are connected to one half-duplex circuit running the length of the network that is called the bus. The top part of Figure 6.4 shows Ethernet's logical topology. All **frames** from any computer flow onto the central cable (or bus) and through it to all computers on the LAN. Every computer on the bus receives *all* frames sent on the bus, even those intended for other computers. Before processing incoming frames, the Ethernet software on each computer checks the data link layer address and processes only those frames addressed to that computer.

The bottom part of Figure 6.4 shows the physical topology of an Ethernet LAN when a hub is used. From the outside, an Ethernet LAN *appears* to be a star topology, because all cables connect to the central hub. Nonetheless, it is logically a bus.

Most Ethernet LANs span sufficient distance to require several hubs. In this case, the hubs are connected via cable in the same manner as any other connection in the network (Figure 6.5).

Media Access Control

When several computers share the same communication circuit, it is important to control their access to the media. If two computers on the same circuit transmit at the same time,

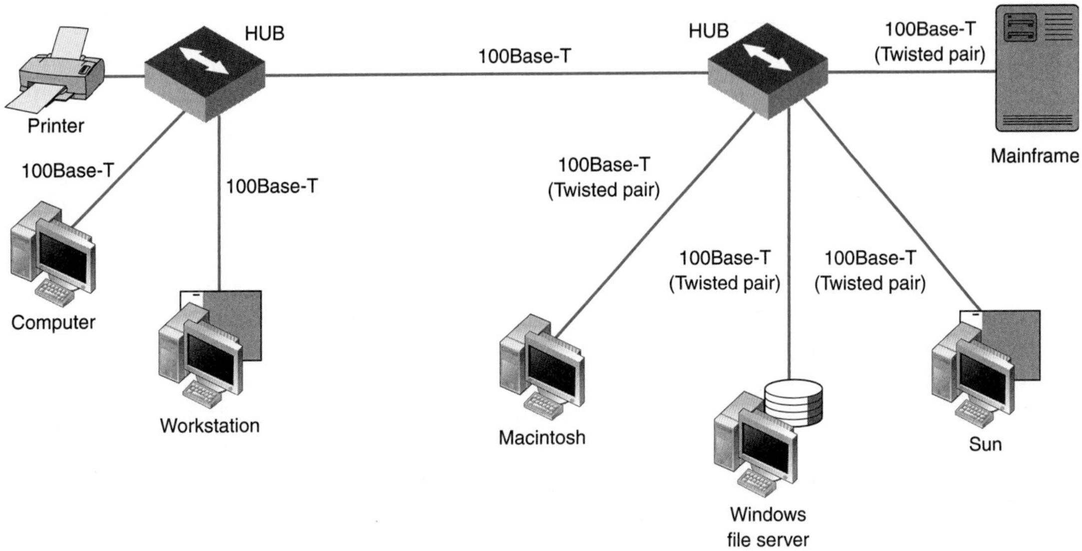

FIGURE 6.5 An example of an Ethernet local area network with two hubs

their transmissions will become garbled. These collisions must be prevented, or if they do occur, there must be a way to recover from them. This is called media access control.

Ethernet uses a contention-based media access control technique called **Carrier Sense Multiple Access with Collision Detection (CSMA/CD).** CSMA/CD, like all contention-based techniques, is very simple in concept: wait until the circuit is free and then transmit. Computers wait until no other devices are transmitting, then transmit their frames. As an analogy, suppose you are talking with a small group of friends (four or five people). As the discussion progresses, each person tries to grab the floor when the previous speaker finishes. Usually, the other members of the group yield to the first person who jumps right after the previous speaker.

Ethernet's CSMA/CD protocol can be termed "ordered chaos." As long as no other computer attempts to transmit at the same time, everything is fine. However, it is possible that two computers located some distance from one another can both listen to the circuit, find it empty, and begin simultaneously. This simultaneous transmission is called a **collision.** The two frames collide and destroy each other.

The solution to this is to listen while transmitting, better known as **collision detection (CD).** If the NIC detects any signal other than its own, it presumes that a collision has occurred and sends a jamming signal. All computers stop transmitting and wait for the circuit to become free before trying to retransmit. The problem is that the computers that caused the collision could attempt to retransmit at the same time. To prevent this, each computer waits a random amount of time after the colliding frame disappears before attempting to retransmit. Chances are both computers will choose a different random amount of time and one will begin to transmit before the other, thus preventing a second collision. However, if another collision occurs, the computers wait a random amount of time before trying again. This does not eliminate collisions completely, but it reduces them to manageable proportions.

Types of Ethernet

Figure 6.6 summarizes the many different types of Ethernet in use today. **10Base-T** runs on very cheap twisted-pair cable up to 100 meters. It was the 10Base-T standard that revolutionized Ethernet and made it the most popular type of LAN in the world. The extremely low cost of 10Base-T made it very inexpensive compared with its foremost competitor, Token Ring. **100Base-T** is the most common form of Ethernet today.

Three other types of Ethernet are common: **1000Base-T** and 1000Base-F (which run at 1 Gbps and are sometimes called **1 GbE**), **10 GbE** (which runs at 10 Gbps), and **40 GbE** (which runs at 40 Gbps). They can use Ethernet's traditional half-duplex approach, but most are configured to use full duplex. Each is also designed to run over fiber-optic cables, but some may also use traditional twisted-pair cables (e.g., Cat 5, Cat 5e). For example, two common versions of 1000Base-F are *1000Base-LX* and *1000Base-SX,* which both use fiber-optic cable, running up to 440 meters and 260 meters, respectively; *1000Base-T,* which runs on four pairs of category 5 twisted-pair cable, but only up to 100 meters[2]; and *1000Base-CX,* which runs up to 24 meters on one category 5 cable. Similar versions of 10 GbE and 40 GbE that use different media are also available.

Some organizations use **10/100 Ethernet,** which is a hybrid that uses either 10Base-T or 100Base-T. 10/100 Ethernet NICs have the ability to run at either 10Base-T or 100Base-T, depending on how they are configured. 10/100 autosense hubs (and switches, as we will discuss shortly) detect the signal transmitted by the client's NIC and will use 10 Mbps or 100 Mbps, depending on which the client uses. 10/100 is useful in the short term as organizations move from 10Base-T to 100base-T or if they are uncertain where they want to use which standard.

Name	Maximum Data Rate	Cables
10Base-T	10 Mbps	UTP cat 3
100Base-T	100 Mbps	UTP cat 5
1000Base-T	1 Gbps	UTP cat 5, UTP cat 5e, UTP cat 6
1000Base-F	1 Gbps	fiber
10 GbE	10 Gbps	UTP cat 5e, UTP cat 6, UTP cat 7, fiber
40 GbE	40 Gbps	fiber

FIGURE 6.6 Types of Ethernet. UTP = unshielded twisted-pair

[2]It would be reasonable to think that 1000Base-T would require 10 category 5 cables because 10 × 100Mps = 1,000 Mbps. However, it is possible to push 100-Mbps cables to faster speeds over shorter distances. Therefore, the category 5 flavor of 1000Base-T uses only 4 pairs of category 5 (i.e., 8 wires) running at 125 Mbps, but over shorter distances than would be normal for 100Base-T. A special form of category 5 cable (called category 5e) has been developed to meet the special needs of 1000Base-T. This same approach is used to run 10 GbE over category 5.

MANAGEMENT FOCUS 6.3 HOSPITAL LEAPS TO 10GBE

The good news was that the LAN at the North Bronx Healthcare Network (NBHN) was predictable; unfortunately that was the bad news, too. With zero network downtime in five years, the old network was "a phenomenally stable environment," says Dan Morreale, CIO. But doctors and nurses using the system also could count on phenomenal delays over its 10 Mbps hubs.

A standard prescription for such a network problem might call for a gigabit Ethernet upgrade. Instead, NBHN skipped a step and upgraded its network to 10 GbE. Morreale says he feared that even 1GbE might be outpaced by the hospital's ballooning LAN capacity needs. In recent years, the hospital added digitized medical-imaging technology, which allows X-rays, MRIs, and other images to be viewed and stored on computers instead of film and videotape. Also, doctors and clinicians commonly dictated notes into their desktop PCs instead of onto dictation minicassettes. That prompted the IT staff to set up servers and storage for the bulky voice note files. Videoconferencing among NBHN staff in separate buildings also was taking off.

In addition to updating its LAN and backbone segments, gigabit Ethernet to the desktop also will be in place to support new medical-imaging systems. "The bandwidth involved with that is not insignificant," Morreale says. For a doctor to view a graphic file, such as an X-ray or cardiology image, involves a 200M-byte file download.

SOURCE: "Bronx Hospital Leaps to 10G," *Network World,* August 8, 2003.

SWITCHED ETHERNET

Switched Ethernet is identical to traditional Ethernet, except that a switch replaces the hub (Figure 6.7). In traditional shared Ethernet, all devices share the same multipoint circuit and must take turns using it. When a frame is sent from one computer to another, it enters the hub, and the hub retransmits it to *all* the computers attached to the hub

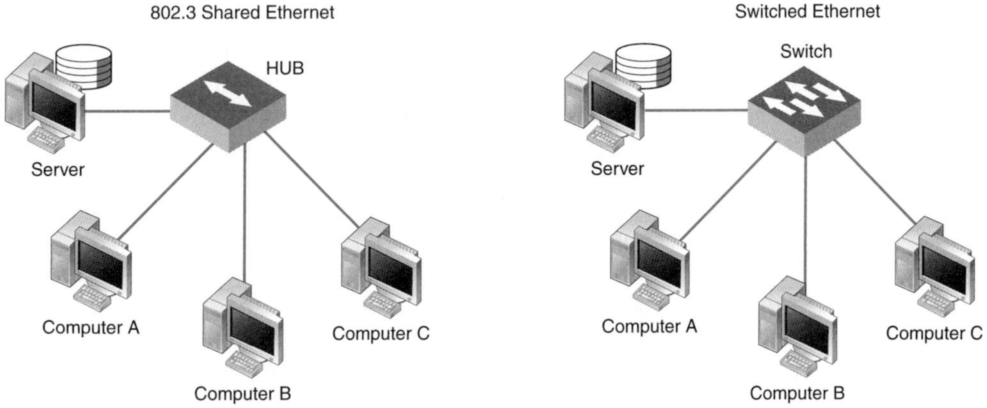

FIGURE 6.7 802.3 Ethernet versus switched Ethernet

(Figure 6.7). Each computer looks at the Ethernet address on incoming frames, and if the address on the packet does not match its address, it discards the packet. This process ensures that no two computers transmit at the same time, because they are always listening and do not transmit when they are receiving a frame, even if the frame is not addressed to them. If the hub did not send the frame to all computers, a computer could begin transmitting at the same time as another computer and never be aware of it.

Topology

With switched Ethernet, the hub is replaced by a *switch* (Figure 6.6). This type of switch is often called a **workgroup switch** because it is designed to support a small set of computers (often 16 to 24) in one LAN. From the outside, the switch looks almost identical to a hub, but inside, it is very different. A switch is an intelligent device with a small computer built-in that is designed to manage a set of separate point-to-point circuits. That means that each circuit connected to a switch is *not* shared with any other devices; only the switch and the attached computer use it. The physical topology looks essentially the same as Ethernet's physical topology: a star. On the inside, the logical topology is a set of separate point-to-point circuits, also a star.

When a switch receives a frame from a computer, it looks at the address on the frame and retransmits the frame only on the circuit connected to that computer, not to all circuits as a hub would. For example, in Figure 6.7, if computer A sends a frame to the switch destined for computer C, the switch retransmits it only on the circuit connected to computer C.

So how does a switch know which circuit is connected to what computer? The switch uses a **forwarding table** that is very similar to the routing tables discussed in Chapter 5. The table lists the Ethernet address of the computer connected to each port on the switch. When the switch receives a frame, it compares the destination address on the frame to the addresses in its forwarding table to find the port number on which it needs to transmit the frame. Because the switch uses the Ethernet address to decide which port to use and because Ethernet is a data link layer or layer-2 protocol, this type of switch is called a **layer-2 switch.** In Chapter 8, we describe other types of switches.

When switches are first turned on, their forwarding tables are empty; they do not know what Ethernet address is attached to what port. Switches *learn* addresses to build the forwarding table. When a switch receives a frame, it reads the frame's data link layer source address and compares this address to its forwarding table. If the address is not in the forwarding table, the switch adds it, along with the port on which the frame was received.

If a switch receives a frame with a destination address that is not in the forwarding table, the switch must still send the frame to the correct destination. In this case, it must retransmit the frame to all ports, except the one on which the frame was received. In this case, the attached computers, being Ethernet and assuming they are attached to a hub, will simply ignore all frames not addressed to them. The one computer for whom the frame is addressed will recognize its address and will process the frame, which includes sending an ACK or a NAK back to the sender. When the switch receives the ACK or NAK, it will add this computer's address and the port number on which the ACK or NAK was received to its forwarding table and then send the ACK or NAK on its way.

So, for the first few minutes until the forwarding table is complete, the switch acts like a hub. But as its forwarding table becomes more complete, it begins to act more and more like a switch. In a busy network, it takes only a few minutes for the switch to learn most addresses and match them to port numbers.

There are three modes in which switches can operate. The first is **cut through switching.** With cut through switching, the switch begins to transmit the incoming packet on the proper outgoing circuit as soon as it has read the destination address in the frame. In other words, the switch begins transmitting before it has received the entire frame. The advantage of this is low **latency** (the time it takes a device from receiving a frame to transmitting it) and results in a very fast network. The disadvantage is that the switch begins transmitting before it has read and processed the frame check sequence at the end of the frame; the frame may contain an error, but the switch will not notice until after almost all of the frame has been transmitted. Cut through switching can only be used when the incoming data circuit has the same data rate as the outgoing circuit.

With the second switching mode, called **store and forward switching,** the switch does not begin transmitting the outgoing frame until it has received the entire incoming frame and has checked to make sure it contains no errors. Only after the switch is sure there are no errors does the switch begin transmitting the frame on the outgoing circuit. If errors are found, the switch simply discards the frame. This mode prevents invalid frame from consuming network capacity, but provides higher latency and thus results in a slower network (unless many frames contain errors). Store and forward switching can be used regardless of whether the incoming data circuit has the same data rate as the outgoing circuit because the entire frame must be stored in the switch before it is forwarded on its way.

The final mode, called **fragment-free switching,** lies between the extremes of cut through and store and forward switching. With fragment-free switching, the first 64 bytes of the frame are read and stored. The switch examines the first 64 bytes (which contain all the header information for the frame) and if all the header data appears correct, the switch presumes that the rest of the frame is error free and begins transmitting. Fragment-free switching is a compromise between cut through and store and forward switching because it has higher latency and better error control than cut through switching, but lower latency and worse error control than store and forward switching. Most switches today use cut through or fragment-free switching.

Media Access Control

Each of the circuits connected to the switch is a separate point-to-point circuit connecting the switch to one computer (or another network device, such as another switch). The switch and the attached computer (or other network device) must share this circuit. Media access control is done in the same manner as traditional Ethernet: each computer (or device) listens before it transmits, and if no one is transmitting, it transmits.

Unlike a hub, in which all attached cables form one shared circuit so that the hub can process only one frame at a time (forcing all attached computers to wait until the one frame is transmitted and it is someone else's turn), a switch is built so that it can simultaneously send or receive frames on *all* the attached circuits. In Figure 6.7, computer A could be sending a frame to the server at the same time as computer B sends one to computer C.

It is possible that two computers may attempt to transmit a frame to the same computer at the same time. For example, both A and B send a frame to C. In this case, the switch chooses which frame to transmit first (usually, the first frame it receives is sent first) and temporarily stores all other frames for that circuit in its internal memory. When the frame is finished and the circuit is again free, the switch then retransmits (or forwards) the temporarily stored frames.

Performance Benefits

Switched Ethernet dramatically improves network performance because each computer has its own dedicated point-to-point circuit, rather than the one common shared multipoint circuit in traditional hub-based Ethernet. Because there are only two devices on each point-to-point circuit (e.g., the switch and a computer), the probability of a collision is lower. Experts believe we can effectively use up to about 95 percent of the switched Ethernet capacity before performance becomes a problem. So each 100Base-T switched circuit effectively has a maximum capacity of about 95 Mbps.

In most LANs, the majority of network traffic is to and from the router that connects the LAN into the backbone network. In most LANs, this circuit is the network bottleneck. Each computer is transmitting at 100 Mbps, but if the circuit to the router is also 100 Mbps, there is often a traffic jam. Many manufacturers now make 100Base-T swiches that provide 100 Mbps circuits to the client computers but a 1 Gbps circuit to the router. Although traffic jams will still occur, the higher speed on the bottleneck circuit will mean they will clear up much more quickly.

THE BEST PRACTICE LAN DESIGN

The past few years have seen major changes in LAN technologies (e.g., gigabit Ethernet, switched Ethernet). As technologies have changed and costs have dropped, so too has our understanding of the best practice design for LANs.

Most organizations today install switched 100Base-T over category 5e wiring for their LANs. It is relatively low cost and fast. Therefore, many vendors have started calling traditional Ethernet a "legacy technology," which means they will continue to support it but will build no new products. Backbone networks often run faster (as we discuss in later chapters), so many organizations are installing 100Base-T switches that have one 1000Base-F port to connect into the backbone.

The cost of switched 100Base-T has dropped dramatically, so it is even cheap enough for home use. A small SOHO switch (SOHO stands for Small Office, Home Office) costs about $30. However, most SOHO users are installing wireless networking because the cost of installing computer cables is far more expensive than buying a wireless card for a desktop computer, so even switched Ethernet may be seen as a legacy technology for the SOHO market. The next chapter discusses wireless networking.

IMPROVING LAN PERFORMANCE

When LANs had only a few users, performance was usually very good. Today, however, when most computers in an organization are on LANs, performance can be a problem. Performance is usually expressed in terms of throughput (the total amount of user data transmitted in a given time period). In this section, we discuss how to improve throughput. We focus on dedicated-server networks because they are the most commonly used type of LANs, but many of these concepts also apply to peer-to-peer networks.

To improve performance, you must locate the **bottleneck,** the part of the network that is restricting the data flow. Generally speaking, the bottleneck will lie in one of two places. The first is the network server. In this case, the client computers have no difficulty sending requests to the network server, but the server lacks sufficient capacity to process all the requests it receives in a timely manner. The second location is the network circuit, connecting the LAN to the corporate BN. In this case, the server can easily process all the client requests it receives, but the circuit lacks enough capacity to transmit all the requests to the server. It is also possible that the bottleneck could lie in the client computers themselves (e.g., they are receiving data too fast for them to process it), but this is extremely unlikely—unless, of course, you are still using old computers!

The first step in improving performance, therefore, is to identify whether the bottleneck lies in the circuit or the server. To do so, you simply watch the utilization of the server during periods of poor performance. If the server utilization is high (e.g., 60 to 100 percent), then the bottleneck is the server; it cannot process all the requests it receives in a timely manner. If the server utilization is low during periods of poor performance (e.g., 10 to 40 percent), then the problem lies with the network circuit; the circuit cannot transmit requests to the server as quickly as necessary. Things become more difficult if

TECHNICAL FOCUS

6.3 ERROR CONTROL IN ETHERNET

Ethernet provides a strong error control method using stop and wait ARQ with a CRC-32 error detection field (see Chapter 4). However, the normal way of installing Ethernet doesn't use stop and wait ARQ.

In the early days of Ethernet, LAN environments were not very reliable, so error control was important. However, today's LAN environments are very reliable; errors seldom occur. Stop and wait ARQ uses considerable network capacity because every time a frame is transmitted, the sender must stop and wait for the receiver to send an acknowledgment. By eliminating the need to stop and wait and the need to send acknowledgments, Ethernet can significantly improve network performance—almost doubling the number of messages that can be transmitted in the same time period. Ethernet does still add the CRC and does still check it for errors, but any frame with an error is simply discarded.

If Ethernet doesn't provide error control, then higher layers in the network model must. In general, TCP is configured to provide error control by using continuous ARQ (see Chapter 5) to ensure that all frames that have been sent are actually received at the final destination. If a frame with an error is discarded by Ethernet, TCP will recognize that a frame has been lost and ask the sender to retransmit. This moves responsibility for error control to the edges of the network (i.e., the sender and receiver) rather than making every computer along the way responsible for ensuring reliable message delivery.

utilization is in the midrange (e.g., 40 to 60 percent). This suggests that the bottleneck may shift between the server and the circuit depending on the type of request, and it suggests that both should be upgraded to provide the best performance.

Now we will focus attention on ways to improve the server and the circuit to remove bottlenecks. These actions address only the supply side of the equation—that is, increasing the capacity of the LAN as a whole. The other way to reduce performance problems is to attack the demand side: reduce the amount of network use by the clients, which we also discuss. Figure 6.8 provides a performance checklist.

Improving Server Performance

Improving server performance can be approached from two directions simultaneously: software and hardware.

Software The NOS is the primary software-based approach to improving network performance. Some NOSs are faster than others, so replacing the NOS with a faster one will improve performance.

Each NOS provides a number of software settings to fine-tune network performance. Depending on the number, size, and type of messages and requests in your LAN, different settings can have a significant effect on performance. The specific settings differ by NOS but often include things such as the amount of memory used for disk caches, the number of simultaneously open files, and the amount of buffer space.

Hardware One obvious solution if your network server is overloaded is to buy a second server (or more). Each server is then dedicated to supporting one set of application

Performance Checklist

Increase Server Performance

- Software
- Fine-tune the network operating system settings
- Hardware
- Add more servers and spread the network applications across the servers to balance the load
- Upgrade to a faster computer
- Increase the server's memory
- Increase the number and speed of the server's hard disk(s)

Increase Client Capacity

- Upgrade to a faster circuit
- Segment the network

Reduce Network Demand

- Move files from the server to the client computers
- Increase the use of disk caching on client computers
- Change user behavior

FIGURE 6.8
Improving local area network performance

software (e.g., one handles e-mail, another handles the financial database, and another stores customer records). The bottleneck can be broken by carefully identifying the demands each major application software package places on the server and allocating them to different servers.

Sometimes, however, most of the demand on the server is produced by one application that cannot be split across several servers. In this case, the server itself must be upgraded. The first place to start is with the server's CPU. Faster CPUs mean better performance. If you are still using an old computer as a LAN server, this may be the answer; you probably need to upgrade to the latest and greatest. Clock speed also matters: the faster, the better. Most computers today also come with CPU-cache (a very fast memory module directly connected to the CPU). Increasing the cache will increase CPU performance.

A second bottleneck is the amount of memory in the server. Increasing the amount of memory increases the probability that disk caching will work, thus increasing performance.

A third bottleneck is the number and speed of the hard disks in the server. The primary function of the LAN server is to process requests for information on its disks. Slow hard disks give slow network performance. The obvious solution is to buy the fastest disk drive possible. Even more important, however, is the number of hard disks. Each computer hard disk has only one read/write head, meaning that all requests must go through this one device. By using several smaller disks rather than one larger disk (e.g., five 200 gigabyte disks rather than one 1 terabyte disk), you now have more read/write heads, each of which can be used simultaneously, dramatically improving throughput. A special type of disk drive called **RAID (redundant array of inexpensive disks)** builds on this concept and is typically used in applications requiring very fast processing of large volumes of data, such as multimedia. Of course, RAID is more expensive than traditional disk drives, but costs have been shrinking. RAID can also provide fault tolerance, which is discussed in Chapter 11.

Several vendors sell special-purpose network servers that are optimized to provide extremely fast performance. Many of these provide RAID and use **symmetric multiprocessing (SMP)** that enables one server to use up to 16 CPUs. Such servers provide excellent performance but cost more than a standard microcomputer (often $5,000 to $15,000).

Improving Circuit Capacity

Improving the capacity of the circuit means increasing the volume of simultaneous messages the circuit can transmit from network clients to the server(s). One obvious approach is simply to buy a bigger circuit. For example, if you are now using a 100Base-T LAN, upgrading to 1000Base-T LAN will improve capacity.

The other approach is to segment the network. If there is more traffic on a LAN than the network circuit and media access protocol can handle, the solution is to divide the LAN into several smaller segments. Breaking a network into smaller parts is called **network segmentation.** By carefully identifying how much each computer contributes to the demand on the server and carefully spreading those computers to different network segments, one can often break a network bottleneck.

Figure 6.9 presents an example in which each network segment is connected into the same server. Most servers can support as many as 16 separate networks or network segments simply by adding one NIC into the server for each network. As the number of NICs in the server increases, however, the server spends more of its processing capacity monitoring and managing the NICs and has less capacity left to process client requests. Most experts recommend no more than three or four NICs per server. There are two ways to create more network segments: one is to use more servers, each dedicated to one or more segments, and the other is to use a BN to connect different segments. BNs are discussed in the next chapter.

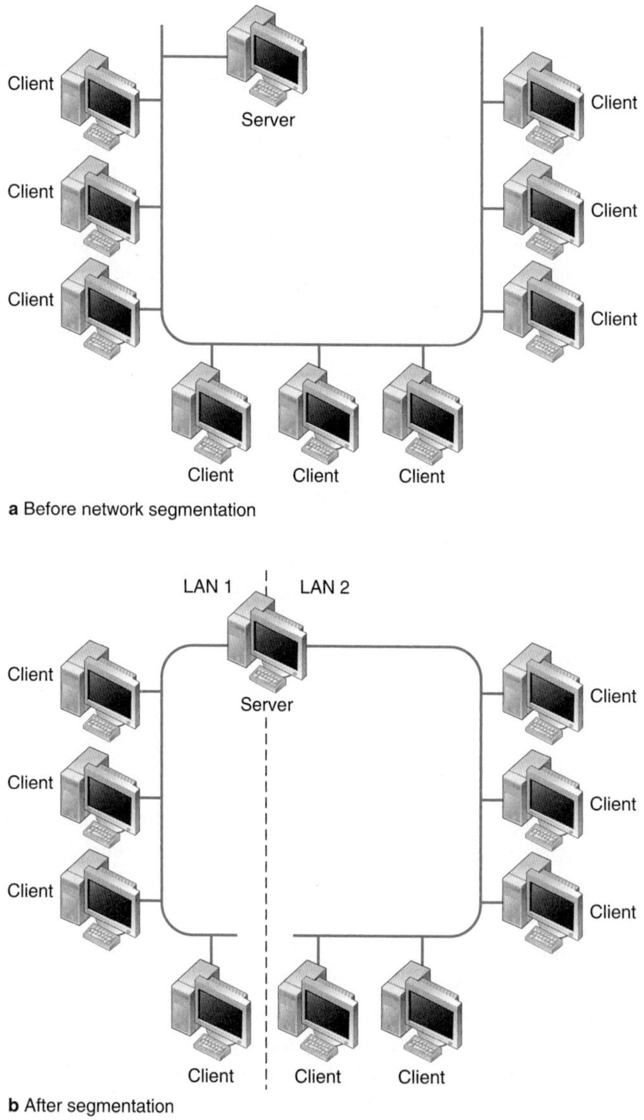

FIGURE 6.9
Network segmentation example

Reducing Network Demand

Upgrading the server hardware and software, choosing a different LAN protocol, or segmenting the LAN are all strategies to increase network capacity. Performance also can be improved by attempting to reduce the demand on the network.

One way to reduce network demand is to move files to client computers. Heavily used software packages that continually access and load modules from the network can place unusually heavy demands on the network. Although user data and messages are often only a few kilobytes in size, today's software packages can be many megabytes in size. Placing even one or two such applications on client computers can greatly improve network performance (although this can create other problems, such as increasing the difficulty in upgrading to new versions of the software).

Another way is to increase the use of disk-caching software on the client machines to reduce the client's need to access disk files stored on the server. For example, most Web browsers store Web pages in their cache so that they can access previously used pages from their hard disks without accessing the network.

Because the demand on most LANs is uneven, network performance can be improved by attempting to move user demands from peak times to off-peak times. For example, early morning and after lunch are often busy times when people check their e-mail. Telling network users about the peak times and encouraging them to change their habits may help; however, in practice, it is often difficult to get users to change. Nonetheless, finding one application that places a large demand on the network and moving it can have a significant impact (e.g., printing several thousand customer records after midnight).

IMPLICATIONS FOR MANAGEMENT

As LANs have standardized on Ethernet, local area networking technology has become a commodity in most organizations. As with most commodities, the cost of LAN equipment (i.e., network interface cards, cabling, hubs, and switches) has dropped significantly. Some vendors are producing high-quality equipment while some new entrants into the market are producing equipment that meets standards but creates opportunities for problems because it lacks the features of more established brands. It becomes difficult for LAN managers to explain to business managers why its important to purchase higher-quality, more expensive equipment when low-cost "standardized" equipment is available.

As costs for LAN equipment drop, LANs are becoming more common in homes, student apartments, and small offices. What once was groundbreaking new technology in the early 1990s has now become a standard consumer product. As LANs become commonplace in homes, apartments, and offices, new software applications will be developed to take advantage of these new capabilities.

Traditional Ethernet is a legacy technology, meaning that manufacturers are no longer creating new products. Most SOHO users are moving quickly to wireless, which means that switched Ethernet is a legacy technology for small SOHO devices; there is little profit to be made in the this market, and many manufacturers will abandon it. We will see a rise in the sales of wireless cards for desktop computers and desktop computers targeted for sale to the SOHO market will come standard with wireless cards in addition to, or instead of, the 100Base-T Ethernet cards we see today. Because 100Base-T Ethernet is the standard for the corporate market, we will see a shift in the design of microcomputers so that there are computers designed for the SOHO market and computers designed for the corporate market.

Decreasing costs for LAN equipment also means that network enabled microprocessor controlled devices that have not normally been thought of as computer technology is becoming less expensive. Therefore, we have seen devices such as copiers turned into network printers and scanners. This trend will increase as electrical appliances such as refrigerators and ovens become network devices. Don't laugh; networked vending machines are already in use.

SUMMARY

Why Use a LAN? The two basic reasons for developing a LAN are information sharing and resource sharing. *Information sharing* refers to business needs that require users to access the same data files, exchange information via e-mail, or search the Internet for information, as discussed in Chapter 2. *Resource sharing* refers to one computer sharing a hardware device (e.g., a printer) or software package with other computers on the network. The main benefit of resource sharing is cost savings whereas the main benefit of information sharing is improved decision making.

Dedicated-Server versus Peer-to-Peer Networks A dedicated-server LAN has one computer that acts as the network server. It can connect with almost any other network, handle very large databases, and use sophisticated LAN software. Moreover, high-end dedicated-server LANs can be interconnected easily to form enterprisewide networks or, in some cases, replace the host mainframe central computer. Common types of dedicated servers include Web servers, application servers, file servers, database servers, print servers, and remote access servers. All computers on a peer-to-peer LAN run special network software that enables them to function both as a client and as a server.

LAN Components The NIC enables the computer to be physically connected to the network cable and provides the physical layer connection among the computers in the network. Most LANs use UTP wires, STP wires, coaxial cable, and/or fiber-optic cable. Network hubs and switches provide an easy way to connect network cables and act as repeaters. Most new buildings built today have a separate LAN cable plan, just as they have plans for telephone cables and for electrical cables. The NOS is the software that performs the functions associated with the data link and the network layers and interacts with the application software and the computer's own operating system. Every NOS provides two sets of software: one that runs on the network server(s) and one that runs on the network client(s). A network profile specifies what resources on each server are available for network use by other computers and which devices or people are allowed what access to the network.

Ethernet (IEEE 802.3) Ethernet, the most commonly used LAN protocol in the world, uses a logical bus topology that has a shared multipoint circuit used by all attached computers and devices although the physical appearance of the network is a star. It uses a contention-based media access technique called CSMA/CD. There are many different types of Ethernet that use different network cabling (e.g., 10Base-T, 100Base-T, 1000Base-T, 10 GbE).

Switched Ethernet With switched Ethernet, a switch replaces the hub, but otherwise, all other components are identical. The switch provides a series of separate point-to-point circuits to the attached devices, so that no device needs to wait for another device before it transmits. When a frame arrives at the switch, the switch reads the Ethernet address and then forwards the frame to the one destination computer. Switched Ethernet has considerably better performance than traditional Ethernet because computers do not have to share circuits with other computers.

Best Practice LAN Design The best practice LAN design today is switched 100Base-T over cat 5e. For SOHO networks, the best LAN choice may be wireless.

Improving LAN Performance Every LAN has a bottleneck, a narrow point in the network that limits the number of messages that can be processed. Generally speaking, the bottleneck will lie in either the network server or the network circuit. Server performance can be improved with a faster NOS that provides better disk caching, by buying more servers and spreading applications among them, or by upgrading the server's CPU, memory, NIC, and the speed and number of its hard disks. Circuit capacity can be improved by using faster technologies (100Base-T rather than 10Base-T) and by segmenting the network into several separate LANs. Overall LAN performance also can be improved by reducing the demand for the LAN by moving files off the LAN, using disk caching on the client computers, and by shifting users' routines.

KEY TERMS

Active Directory Service (ADS)
bottleneck
bus topology
cable plan
cabling
Carrier Sense Multiple Access with Collision Detection (CSMA/CD)
collision
collision detection (CD)
cut through switching
dedicated-server LAN
domain controller
Ethernet
fiber-optic cable
file server
forwarding table
fragment-free switching
frame
hub
IEEE 802.3
information sharing
LAN metering software
latency
layer-2 switch
lightweight directory services (LDAP)
logical topology
network-attached storage (NAS)
network interface card (NIC)
network operating system (NOS)
network profile
network segmentation
network server
peer-to-peer network
physical topology
port
print server
redundant array of inexpensive disks (RAID)
resource sharing
server farm
shared Ethernet
shielded twisted-pair (STP)
software audit
software piracy
Software Publishers Association (SPA)
storage area network (SAN)
store and forward switching
switch
switched Ethernet
symmetric multi-processing (SMP)
topology
twisted-pair cable
unshielded twisted-pair (UTP) cable
workgroup switch
10Base-T
100Base-T
1000Base-T
10/100 Ethernet
1 GbE
10 GbE
40 GbE

QUESTIONS

1. Define *local area network.*
2. What are the distinguishing features of a LAN?
3. What are two reasons for developing LANs?
4. What is the function of LAN metering software?
5. Discuss the legal issue of using single-computer license software on networks.
6. Discuss why it is important for organizations to enforce policies restricting use of employee-owned hardware and software and unauthorized copies of software.
7. In some LANs, most of the computers talk with the server, but others use no server. What are these two approaches called?
8. Describe at least three types of servers.
9. What is a NIC? What is a hub?
10. What media do LANs normally use?
11. What type of cables are commonly used in LANs?
12. Compare and contrast category 5 UTP, category 5e UTP, and category 5 STP.

13. What is a cable plan and why would you want one?
14. What does a NOS do? What are the major software parts of a NOS?
15. What is the most important characteristic of a NOS?
16. What is a network profile?
17. What is Ethernet? How does it work?
18. How does a logical topology differ from a physical topology?
19. Briefly describe how CSMA/CD works.
20. Explain the terms 100Base-T, 100Base-F, 1000Base-T, 10 GbE, and 10/100 Ethernet.
21. How does switched Ethernet differ from traditional Ethernet?
22. How do layer-2 Ethernet switches know where to send the frames they receive? Describe how switches gather and use this knowledge.
23. What are the primary advantages and disadvantages of switched Ethernet?
24. What is a bottleneck and how can you locate one?
25. Describe three ways to improve network performance on the server.
26. Describe three ways to improve network performance on the circuit.
27. Why does network segmentation improve LAN performance?
28. It is said that hooking some computers together with a cable does not make a network. Why?
29. Compare and contrast cut through, store and forward, and fragment-free switching.
30. Is 1 GbE Ethernet really "Ethernet?" Explain.
31. Under what circumstances is switched Ethernet preferred to shared Ethernet? Under what circumstances is shared Ethernet preferred to switched Ethernet?

EXERCISES

6-1. Survey the LANs used in your organization. Are they Ethernet, switched Ethernet, or some other standard? Why?

6-2. Document one LAN (or LAN segment) in detail. What devices are attached, what cabling is used, and what is the topology? What does the cable plan look like?

6-3. You have been hired by a small company to install a simple LAN for their 18 Windows computers. Develop a simple LAN and determine the total cost; that is, select the cables, hubs/switches, and NICs and price them. Assume that the company has no network today and that the office is small enough that you don't need to worry about cable length.

MINI-CASES

I. Designing a New Ethernet

One important issue in designing Ethernet lies in making sure that if a computer transmits a frame, any other computer that attempts to transmit at the same time will be able to hear the incoming frame before it stops transmitting, or else a collision might go unnoticed. For example, assume that we are on earth and send an Ethernet frame over a very long piece of category 5 wire to the moon. If a computer on the moon starts transmitting at the same time as we do on earth and finishes transmitting before our frame arrives at the moon, there will be a collision, but neither computer will detect it; the frame will be garbled, but no one will know why. So, in designing Ethernet, we must make sure that the length of cable in the LAN is shorter than the length of the shortest possible frame that can be sent. Otherwise, a collision could go undetected.

a. Let's assume that the smallest possible message is 64 bytes (including the 33-byte overhead). If we use 10Base-T, how long (in meters) is a 64-byte message? While electricity in the cable travels a bit slower than the speed of light, once you include delays in the electrical equipment in transmitting and receiving the signal, the effective speed is only about 40 million meters per second. (*Hint:* First calculate the number of seconds it would take to transmit the frame then calculate the number of meters the signal would travel in that time, and you have the total length of the frame.)
b. If we use 10 GbE, how long (in meters) is a 64-byte frame?
c. The answer in part b is the maximum distance any single cable could run from a switch to one computer in a switched Ethernet LAN. How would you overcome the problem implied by this?

II. Pat's Petunias

You have been called in as a network consultant by your cousin Pat who operates a successful mail-order flower business. She is moving to a new office and wants to install a network for her telephone operators, who take phone calls and enter orders into the system. The number of operators working varies depending on the time of day and day of the week. On slow shifts, there are usually only 10 operators, whereas at peak times, there are 50. She has bids from different companies to install (1) a shared Ethernet 100Base-T network, or (2) a switched Ethernet 100Base-T network. She wants you to give her some sense of the relative performance of the alternatives so the can compare that with their different costs. What would you recommend?

III. Eureka!

Eureka! is a telephone and Internet-based concierge service that specializes in obtaining things that are hard to find (e.g., Super Bowl tickets, first-edition books from the 1500s, Fabergé eggs). It currently employs staff members who work 24 hours per day (over three shifts), with usually 5 to 7 staff members working at any given time. Staff members answer the phone and respond to requests entered on the Eureka! Web site. Much of their work is spent on the phone and on computers searching on the Internet. They have just leased a new office and are about to wire it. They have bids from different companies to install (a) a shared Ethernet 100Base-T network, (b) a switched Ethernet 100Base-T network, or (c) a 54 mbps wireless network (*Hint:* wireless networks are shared circuit networks). What would you recommend? Why?

IV. Tom's Home Automation

Your cousin Tom runs a small construction company that builds custom houses. He has just started a new specialty service that he is offering to other builders on a subcontracting basis: home automation. He provides a complete service of installing cable in all the rooms in which the homeowner wants data access and installs the necessary networking devices to provide a LAN that will connect all the computers in the house to the Internet. Most homeowners choose to install a DSL or cable modem Internet connection that provides a 1–2 Mbps from the house to the Internet (see Chapter 10). Tom has come to you for advice. What type of cabling (e.g., cat 3, cat 5, cat 5e, cat 6, fiber optic) and what type of networking hardware (e.g., hub or switch) would you recommend? Why?

V. Sally's Shoes

Sally Smith runs a shoe store in the mall that is about 30 feet by 50 feet in size, including a small office and a storage area in the rear. The store has one inventory computer in the storage area and one computer in the office. She is replacing the two cash registers with computers that will act as cash registers but will also be able to communicate with the inventory computer. Sally wants to network the computers with a LAN. What sort of a LAN design would you recommend in terms of cabling and hubs or switches? Draw a picture. Should Sally use peer-to-peer networking or use a dedicated server?

CASE STUDY

NEXT-DAY AIR SERVICE

See the Web site.

HANDS-ON ACTIVITY

Windows Peer-to-Peer Networking

In this chapter, we've discussed two types of LANs: peer-to-peer LANs and dedicated server LANs. This activity will show you how to set up a peer-to-peer LAN for your house or apartment. We first describe file sharing and then discuss printer sharing.

Windows File Sharing

Windows file sharing enables you to select folders on your computer that you can permit others users on your LAN to read and write. There are three steps to create a shared folder.

Step 1. Give your computer an Application Layer Name within a Workgroup

1. Go to Settings → Control Panel → System
2. Click on the Computer Name Tab
3. Click Change
4. Type in a New Computer Name and Workgroup Name. All computers must have the same workgroup name to share files. Each computer within a workgroup must have a unique name.

Step 2. Enable File Sharing

1. Go to Settings → Control Panel → Windows Firewall
2. Click on the Exceptions tab
3. Make sure the box in front of File and Printer Sharing is checked
4. Go to Settings → Control Panel → Network Connections
5. Right click on the LAN connection and click Properties
6. Ensure that the box in front of File and Printer Sharing for Microsoft Networks is checked.

Step 3. Create the Shared Folder

1. Open Windows Explorer
2. Create a new folder
3. Right click the folder name and choose Properties
4. Click on the Sharing tab
5. Avoid the Network Wizard and make sure the boxes in front of Share this Folder and Allow Network Users to change are checked

Once you have created a shared folder, other computers in your workgroup can access it. Move to another computer on your LAN and repeat steps 1 and 2 (and step 3 if you like). Now you can use the shared folder:

1. Double click on My Network Places.
2. Double click on a shared folder
3. Create a file (e.g., using Word) and save it in your shared directory
4. Move the file(s) across computers in your workgroup

If you do this on your home network, anyone with access to your network can access the files in your shared folder. It is much safer to turn off file sharing unless you intentionally want to use it (see Step 2 and make sure the boxes are not checked if you want to prevent file sharing).

Windows Printer Sharing

In the same way you can share folders with other computers in your workgroup you can share printers. To share a printer, do the following on the computer that has the printer connected to it:

1. Go to Settings → Control Panel → Printers and Faxes
2. Right click on a printer and select Properties
3. Click on the Sharing tab
4. Click on Share This Printer

Once you have done this, you can move to other computers on your LAN and install the network on them:

1. Go to Settings → Control Panel → Printers and Faxes
2. Click on Add a Printer
3. In the Welcome to Add a Printer Wizard, click Next
4. Click the Radio Button in front of A Network Printer and click Next
5. Click the Radio Button in front of Browse for a Printer and click Next
6. Select the Network Printer and click Next
7. You can make this printer your default printer or not, and click Next

HANDS-ON ACTIVITY

Tracing Ethernet

TracePlus Ethernet is a network monitoring tool that enables you to see how much network capacity you are using. If you're working from home with a broadband Internet connection, you'll be surprised how little of the Ethernet capacity you're actually using. Your Ethernet connection is probably 100 Mbps (or 54 Mbps if you're

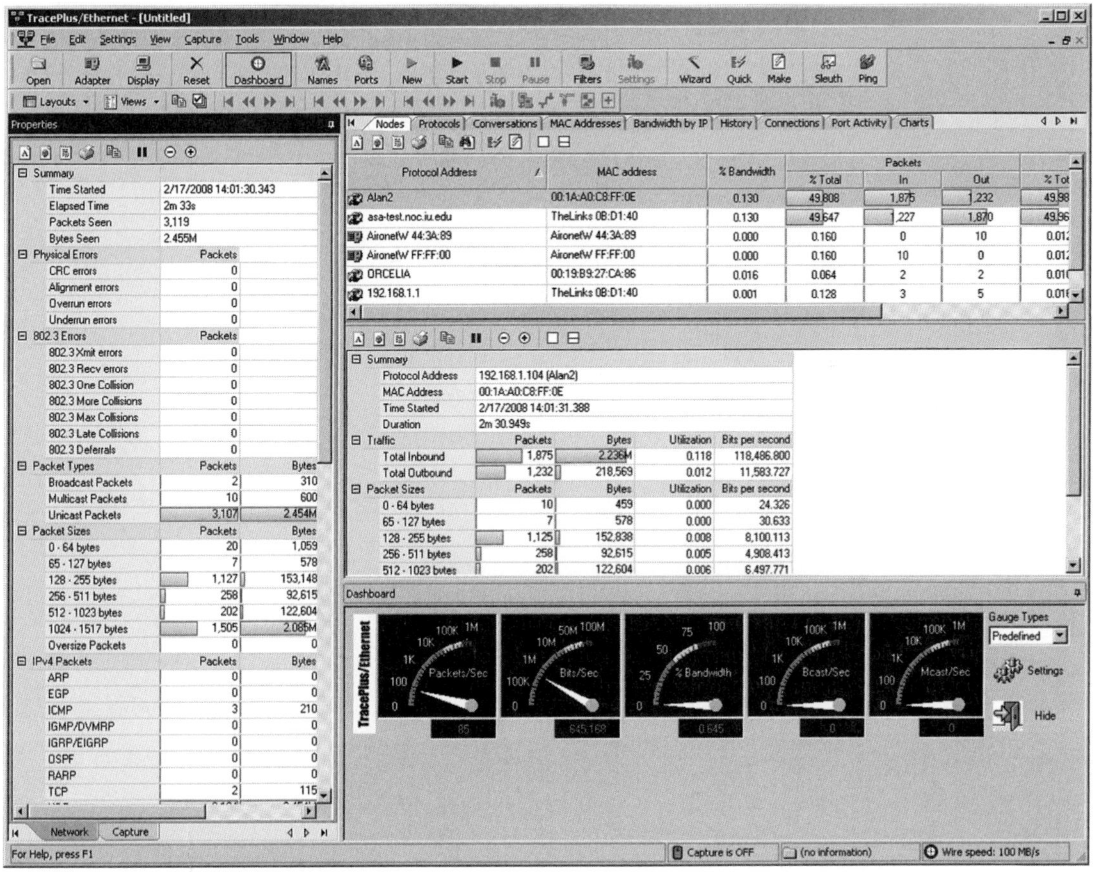

FIGURE 6.10 Trace Plus

using wireless), while your broadband connection is only 1.5 Mbps. The bottleneck is the broadband connection, so you use only 1–2 percent of your Ethernet capacity.

1. Download and install TracePlus. A free trial version of TracePlus is available at Tech Republic (software.techrepublic.com). The URL as we write this is as follows, but it might move, so if this link doesn't work, search on the Tech Republic site: software.techrepublic.com.com/download.aspx?docid=234509.
2. Start TracePlus and monitor your network. Leave it open in one part of your screen as you surf the Internet, check e-mail, or watch a video.

Figure 6.10 shows a sample TracePlus screen while I was surfing the Internet and checking e-mail with Microsoft Outlook. The dashboard at the bottom of the screen shows the real-time usage. You can see that when I took this screen shot, my computer was sending and receiving about 100 packets per second (or if you prefer, 100 frames per second), for a total of just under 1 Mbps of data. This is less than 1 percent of the total Ethernet bandwidth (i.e., network capacity), because I have switched 100Base-T on my computer. The dashboard also shows that I'm sending and receiving almost no broadcast or multicast data.

Immediately above the dashboard is the summary for my computer (192.1681.104 (Alan 2)). In the 2 minutes and 30 seconds of monitoring, my computer received 1,875 inbound packets with a total of 2.236 megabytes of data for a utilization of 0.118 percent. The average bits per second was about 118 Kbps. During the same time, my computer sent slightly fewer outbound packets (1,232), but the average packet was about ten times smaller because the total amount of data sent was only 218,569 bytes. Most packets were in the 128–511 bytes in length, but some were smaller and some were larger.

The Nodes tab in the upper right of the screen shows the nodes on my network that TracePlus can monitor. These include my computer (Alan2), a second computer (Orcelia), my router (192.168.1.1), a wireless access point (Aironet) with two connections (into the LAN and out to the wireless LAN), and the Indiana University VPN server (because I had my VPN connected; Chapter 11 discusses VPNs). You can see that all of these devices have little utilization (under 1 percent), as well as the total number of packets these devices have sent and received. You can click through the other tabs in this area to see the packet distribution.

The panel on the left of the screen shows additional information about the types of packets, errors, and packet sizes.

CHAPTER 7

WIRELESS LOCAL AREA NETWORKS

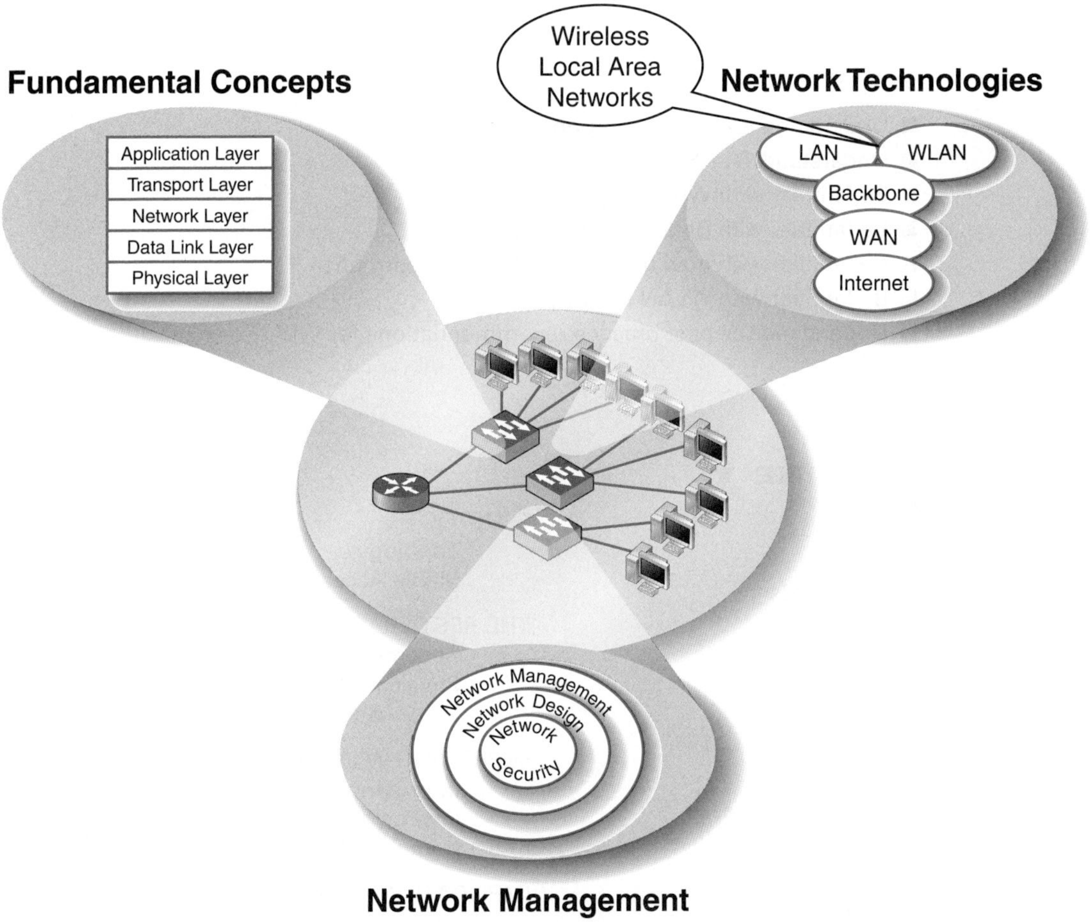

The Three Faces of Networking

ALTHOUGH TRADITIONAL wired Ethernet LANs dominate today's network environment, wireless LANs (WLANs) are common. This chapter describes the basic components of a WLAN and then examines three common wireless technologies: Wi-Fi (IEEE 802.11), WiMAX (IEEE 802.16), and Bluetooth (IEEE 802.15). The chapter ends with a discussion of best practice WLAN design, including security, and how to improve performance.

OBJECTIVES ▼

- Understand the major components of WLANs
- Understand Wi-Fi
- Be familiar with Wi-Max
- Be familiar with Bluetooth WLANs
- Be familiar with how to improve WLAN performance
- Be familiar with WLAN security
- Understand the best practice recommendations for WLAN design

CHAPTER OUTLINE ▼

INTRODUCTION

The use of **Wireless LANs (WLANs)** is growing rapidly. A recent survey of network managers indicated that more than 90 percent of companies are using wireless LANs, usually in addition to traditional wired LANs. Wireless LANs transmit data through the air using radio transmission rather than through twisted-pair cable or fiber-optic cable. This has been one area of networking that has seen the greatest changes in a short amount of time. From a time with no widely accepted standards (2000), we have today gone to an alphabet soup of standards (e.g., 802.11a, 802.11b, 802.11g, 802.11n, 802.15, 802.16d, 802.16e).

WLANs serve the same purpose as LANs: they are used to connect a series of computers in the same small local area to each other and to a backbone network. WLANs are usually not totally wireless in that they are most commonly used to connect a set of wireless computers into a wired network. However, WLANs enable you to use the network in places where it is impractical to put a wired network (either because of cost or access). WLANs can enable staff to pull up a chair and work on the network from a lunchroom, a corridor, or an outdoor patio. WLANs also enable mobile staff to work at different locations in the office building or to move their computers easily from one location to another. WLANs are becoming popular in hospitals, for example, because they enable doctors and nurses to use laptops and tablet PCs to access patient records. WLANs are also popular in airports because they enable business travelers to connect to the Internet from any waiting area.

This chapter examines the basic components of a WLAN and then examines three commonly used WLAN technologies (Wi-Fi, WiMAX, and Bluetooth). The chapter ends with a discussion of best practice recommendations for WLAN design and ways to improve WLAN performance.

As with Ethernet in the previous chapters, the three primary WLAN technologies (Wi-Fi, WiMAX, and Bluetooth) are layer 2 protocols that operate at the data link layer. They too must have physical hardware at layer 1 that meets their requirements and software at layers above them (e.g., TCP/IP) that enables application software to use them.

WLAN COMPONENTS

In the last chapter on LANs, we discussed the three key components of the LAN: the network interface card, the hub/switch, and the cables that connect them. WLANs use the same basic structure. There is a wireless network interface card that is built into a desktop or laptop computer (or can be added later). A wireless access point performs the same functions as a hub or switch. However, instead of cable, there is a set of radio frequencies that are used to transport data (see Figure 7.1). The wireless access point is usually connected via wired Ethernet (often 100Base-T) into a LAN or backbone so the WLAN is connected into the rest of the network.

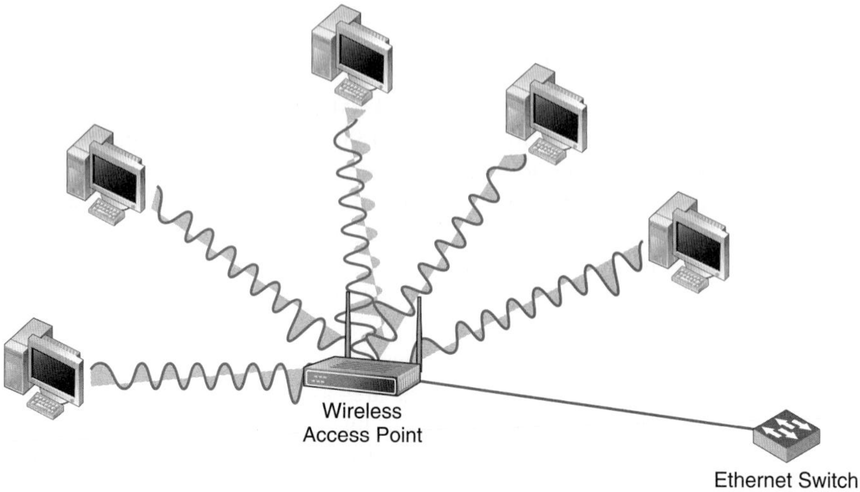

FIGURE 7.1 A wireless access point connected into an Ethernet switch

Network Interface Cards

Each computer has a wireless *network interface card* (*NIC*) that is used to connect the computer into the WLAN. The NIC is a radio transceiver in that it sends and receives radio signals through a short range, usually only about 100 meters or 300 feet. WLAN NICs are available for desktop computers, but laptop computers now come with Wi-Fi NICs built-in.

Access Points

A central wireless **access point (AP)** is a radio transceiver that plays the same role as a hub or switch in wired Ethernet LANs (Figure 7.2). The AP also connects the WLAN into wired LANs, typically using 100Base-T.

The AP in Figure 7.2 has a separate power supply that is plugged into a normal electrical outlet. Some APs use **power over Ethernet (POE)** and need no external power; the power is provided from a POE hub or switch over the unused wires in a category 5/5e cable. POE APs are more expensive, but can be located any where you can run cat 5/5e cable, even if there are no power outlets near by.

The AP acts as a repeater to ensure that all computers within range of the AP can hear the signals of all other computers in the WLAN. All NICs in the WLAN transmit their frames to the AP and then the AP retransmits the frames over the wireless network or over the wired network to their destination. Wireless NICs never communicate with each other directly; they always transmit through the AP. Therefore, if a frame has to be transmitted from one wireless computer to another, it is transmitted twice, once from the sender to the AP and then from the AP to the destination. At first glance this may seem a bit strange because it doubles the number of transmissions in the WLAN. However, very few frames are ever sent from client computer to client computer in a WLAN. Most frames are exchanged between client computers and a server of some kind. For this

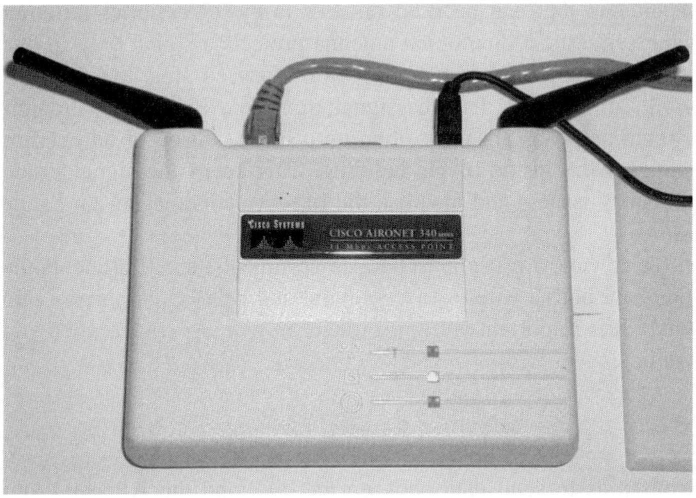

FIGURE 7.2 A wireless access point

reason, servers should never be placed on a WLAN. Even if they are intended to serve clients on a WLAN, they should always be placed on the wired portion of the LAN.

Most WLANs are installed using APs that have **omnidirectional antennas,** which means that the antenna transmits in all directions simultaneously. One common omnidirectional antenna is the dipole antenna shown in Figure 7.3a (nicknamed the "rubber duck" because of its flexibility); see also Figure 7.2. As Figure 7.3a shows, omnidirectional antennas transmit in all directions, both horizontally and vertically. The signal goes in all directions, as well as up and down, although there is often a small dead spot with no signal that is a very small area directly above the antenna.

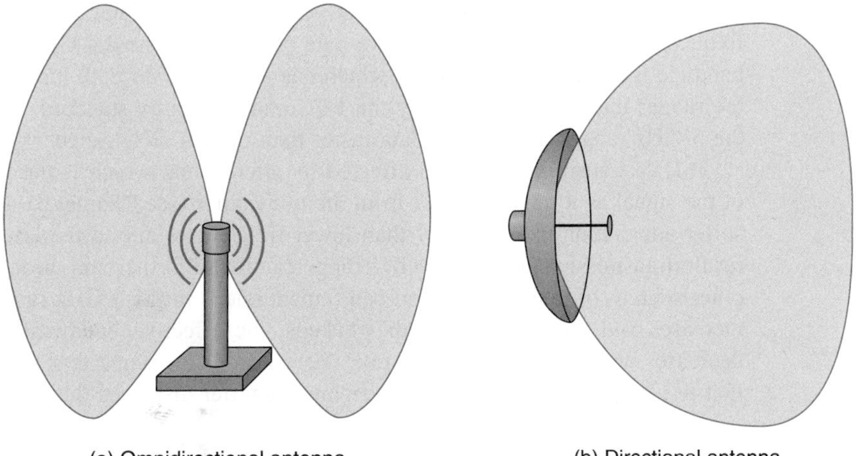

(a) Omnidirectional antenna (b) Directional antenna

FIGURE 7.3 Types of antennas

The other type of antenna that can be used on APs is the **directional antenna** (Figure 7.3b). As the name suggests, a directional antenna projects a signal only in one direction. Because the signal is concentrated in a narrower, focused area, the signal is stronger and therefore will carry farther than the signal from an AP using an omnidirectional antenna. Directional antennas are most often used on the inside of an exterior wall of a building, pointing to the inside of the building. This keeps the signal inside the building (to reduce security issues) and also has the benefit of increasing the range of the AP.

Many wireless routers are sold for use in SOHO environments (small office, home office). The wireless routers are both a wireless access point and a router, and many also contain a 100Base-T switch. It is important not to use the term wireless router when you mean a wireless access point.

Radio Frequencies

WLANs use radio transmissions to send data between the NIC and the AP. All radio transmissions are controlled by the government so that no two radio stations attempt to transmit in the same **frequency range.** In the United States, the Federal Communications Commission (FCC) controls the airwaves. In order to transmit in a certain radio frequency band, you need to get permission.

Most countries (but not all), permit WLANs to operate in two frequency ranges that have been reserved for unlicensed transmissions: the 2.4 GHz range and the 5 GHz range.[1] Japan, for example, uses a slightly different set of frequency ranges. In this book, we will focus on the North American standards. WLANs and other unlicensed transmitters such as cordless phones and baby monitors can use these frequency ranges at will—which means that your WLAN and your cordless phone may interfere with each other. Microwave ovens also use the same frequency range and may cause interference.

The frequency range directly affects the **data rates** that can be transmitted. The larger the frequency range available (called the **bandwidth**), the greater the capacity of the wireless circuit and the faster data can be sent. You can think of the frequency range as the width of a pipe; larger pipes let you move more water per second, and so larger frequency ranges let you move more data per second. The 2.4 GHz range has a smaller bandwidth than the 5 GHz range, which has nothing to do with the technology. It is just the ranges that were allocated by the FCC and chosen by standards groups. As a result, the 5 GHz range can transmit data faster than the 2.4 GHz range.

Data transmission is also affected by attenuation, which is the gradual weakening of the signal as it travels farther from the transmitter (see Chapter 3). Higher frequencies suffer attenuation more quickly than lower frequencies due to the laws of physics. As a result, transmissions in the 2.4 GHz range can travel farther and through more walls and other sources of interference than can transmissions in the 5 GHz range. As interference increases and the signal strength weakens, the effective bandwidth that can be used decreases and capacity and data rate decreases. This means that wireless technologies that use the 5 GHz can transmit over much shorter distances than technologies that use

[1] Some WLAN technologies operate in other frequency ranges.

the 2.4 GHz range. The farther you move from the AP, the worse the data rates as the signal strength weakens.

Most vendors of wireless technologies claim that the range from the AP to computers can be 100–150 meters (300–450 feet). In practice, the range is much shorter as walls absorb the radio waves. The other problem is that as the distance from the AP increases, the maximum speed drops, often very dramatically.

When we design a WLAN it is important to ensure that the APs don't interfere with each other. If all APs transmitted on the same frequency range the transmissions of one AP would interfere with another AP. Therefore, each AP is set to transmit on a different **channel,** very much like the different channels on your TV. Each channel uses a different part of the 2.4 GHz or 5 GHz frequency range so that there is no interference among the different channels. When a computer first starts using the WLAN, its NIC searches all available channels within the appropriate frequency range and then picks the channel that has the strongest signal to use in its communications.

Figure 7.4 shows how a WLAN might be designed using 5 access points, three using omnidirectional antennas and 2 using directional antennas. This configuration uses 3 channels, with each AP configured to use a channel that does not interfere with the APs around it. The distance covered by each AP ranges from 100–500 feet, depending upon interference. Placing the APs and selecting channels to ensure that the entire area is covered and that there is no interference from APs using the same channel is an important design problem. In Figure 7.4, the two APs using channel 1 are at opposite ends of the building, as are the APs using channel 6. The AP using channel 11 is placed in the middle so that its coverage overlaps but does not interfere with the others.

As the user *roams* through a building, the NIC continues to use its original channel until the signal strength starts to drop. When this happens, the NIC again listens to and may attempt to transmit using all of the available channels to find a new channel that has the strongest signal. Some NICs also periodically check for better channels when the channel they are using becomes busy.

One potential problem with WLANs is security. Because anyone within range of a WLAN AP can receive transmissions, eavesdropping is a serious threat. Most WLANs encrypt transmissions so that only authorized computers can decode and read the messages. Security is discussed in detail in Chapter 11 although we briefly discuss WLAN security later in this chapter.

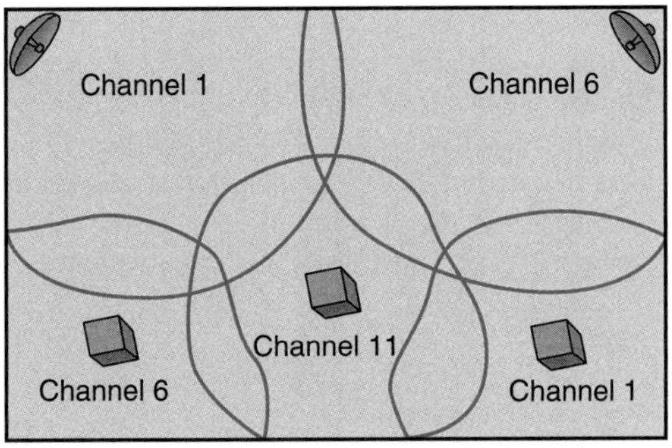

FIGURE 7.4 A WLAN using different channels

WI-FI

Wi-Fi is the commercial name for a set of standards developed by the *IEEE 802.11* standards group. A group of vendors selling 802.11 equipment trademarked the name Wi-Fi to refer to 802.11 because they believe that consumers are more likely to buy equipment with a catchier name than 802.11. Wi-Fi is intended to evoke memories of Hi-Fi, as the original stereo music systems in the 1960s were called.

The 802.11 family of technologies is much like the Ethernet family. The 802.11 standards reuse many of the Ethernet 802.3 components and are designed to connect easily into Ethernet LANs. For these reasons, IEEE 802.11 is often called *wireless Ethernet.* Just as there are several different types of Ethernet (e.g., 10Base-T, 100Base-T, 1000Base-T), there are several different types of 802.11.

Topology

The logical and physical topologies of Wi-Fi are the same as those of shared Ethernet. They are a physical star and a logical bus. There is a central AP to which all computers direct their transmissions (star), but the radio frequencies are shared (bus) so that all computers must take turns transmitting.

Media Access Control

Media access control in Wi-Fi is **Carrier Sense Multiple Access with Collision Avoidance (CSMA/CA),** which is similar to the **contention**-based CSMA/CD approach used

MANAGEMENT FOCUS 7.1 CARNIVAL CRUISE LINES GOES WIRELESS

In 2005, the cruise ship *Carnival Valor* went wireless. "Initially, we had planned to increase the number of workstations in our onboard Internet cafes and to expand Internet access to the staterooms using traditional cat 5 cabling," says Tom McCormick, manager of network engineering for Carnival Cruise Lines. "However, using Cisco wireless technology we are able to provide wireless data access bow-to-stern and, as an added benefit, we were also able to introduce mobile VoIP (Voice over IP wireless telephones) on the same infrastructure." Passengers and crew can access the Internet using any standard laptop or PDA. The ship also provides mobile VoIP phones that can be used anywhere on board.

Designing the network was challenging due to the thick steel bulkheads throughout the ship and the heavy machinery that can often cause radio interference. The network has 217 access points and provides end-to-end voice and data coverage on all decks, including those outdoors. The access points are connected into the traditional wired Ethernet network which connects into a satellite wide area network to provide Internet access. The network also includes special purpose telephone management devices so the VoIP phones can connect into the traditional wired phone network (see Figure 7.5).

SOURCE: G. Knauer, "Voice Goes Wireless," *Packet,* Third Quarter, 2005, pp. 65–69.

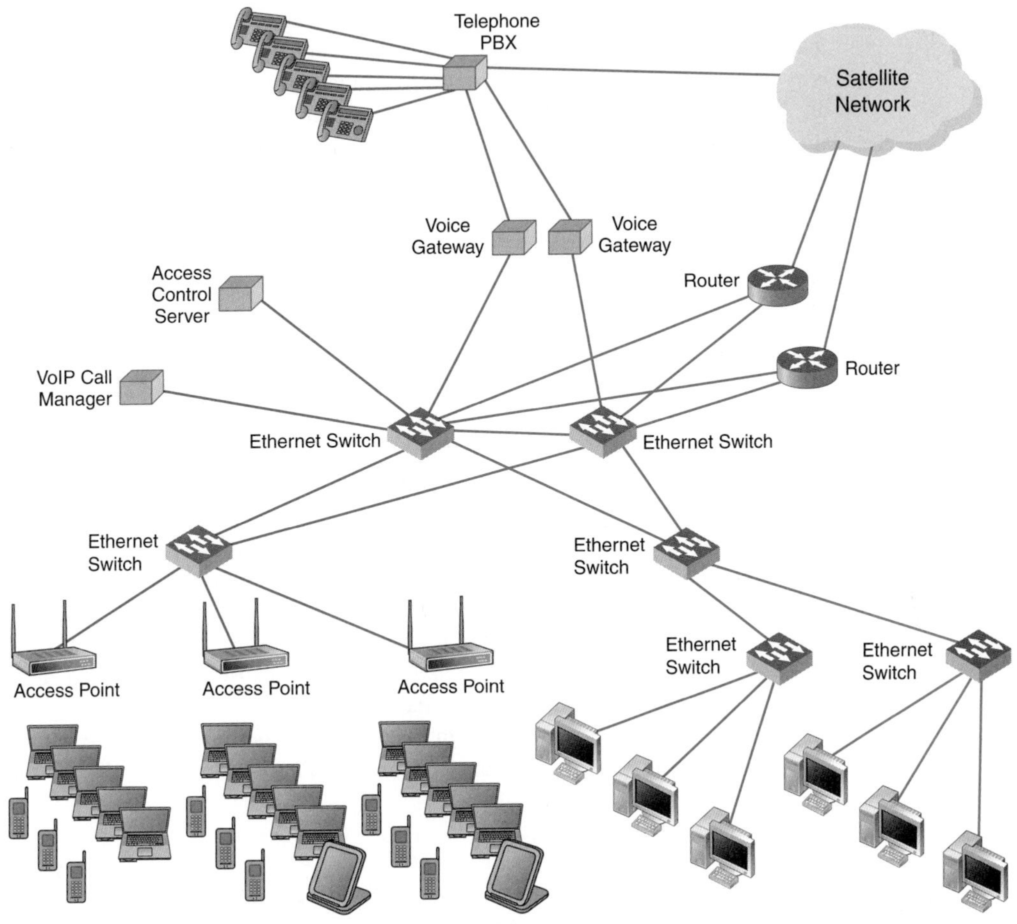

FIGURE 7.5 *Carnival Valor* cruise ship network

by traditional Ethernet. With CSMA/CA, computers listen before they transmit and if no one else is transmitting, they proceed with transmission. Detecting collisions is more difficult in radio transmission than in transmission over wired networks, so Wi-Fi attempts to avoid collisions to a greater extent than traditional Ethernet. CSMA/CA has two media access control approaches.

Distributed Coordination Function The first media access control method is the **distributed coordination function (DCF)** (also called **physical carrier sense method** because it relies on the ability of computers to physically listen before they transmit). With DCF, each frame in CSMA/CA is sent using stop-and-wait ARQ. After the sender transmits one frame, it immediately stops and waits for an ACK from the receiver before attempting to send another frame. When the receiver of a frame detects the end of the frame in a transmission, it waits a fraction of a second to make sure the sender has really stopped transmitting, and then immediately transmits an ACK (or a NAK). The original sender can then send another frame, stop and wait for an ACK, and so on.

While the sender and receiver are exchanging frames and ACKs, other computers may also want to transmit. So when the sender ends its transmission, you might ask why doesn't some other computer begin transmitting before the receiver can transmit an ACK? The answer is that the physical carrier sense method is designed so that the time the receiver waits after the frame transmission ends before sending an ACK is significantly less time than the time a computer must listen to determine that no one else is transmitting before initiating a new transmission. Thus, the time interval between a frame and the matching ACK is so short that no other computer has the opportunity to begin transmitting.

Point Coordination Function The second media access control technique is called the **point coordination function (PCF)** (also called the **virtual carrier sense method**). Not all manufacturers have implemented PCF in their APs. DCF works well in traditional Ethernet because every computer on the shared circuit receives every transmission on the shared circuit. However, in a wireless environment, this is not always true. A computer at the extreme edge of the range limit from the AP on one side may not receive transmissions from a computer on the extreme opposite edge of the AP's range limit. In Figure 7.1, all computers may be within the range of the AP, but may not be within the range of each other. In this case, if one computer transmits, the other computer on the opposite edge may not sense the other transmission and transmit at the same time causing a collision at the AP. This is called the *hidden node problem* because the computers at the opposite edges of the WLAN are hidden from each other.

When the hidden node problem exists, the AP is the only device guaranteed to be able to communicate with all computers on the WLAN. Therefore, the AP must manage

MANAGEMENT FOCUS 7.2 WEST EDMONTON MALL USES WI-FI FOR TOURISM

Being the largest shopping mall in the world (48 city blocks in size) wasn't enough for the West Edmonton Mall, located in Edmonton, Alberta, in western Canada. Every year more than 22 million visitors flock to the mall's 3 hotels, 8 amusement parks, 21 theaters, 110 restaurants, and 800 shops.

Originally planned as a network to serve the 16,500 people who work in the mall, the project quickly grew to gain a competitive edge by enabling visitors to access the Internet. The first phase of the network installed 70 access points in one part of the mall and offered day passes for $11 and month passes for $35.

The response was overwhelming, from both visitors and workers. Visitors can easily surf the Web and e-mail while their children play in the water parks. Many stores have adopted mobile VoIP telephones for their employees.

The network has generated a 120 percent ROI. The next steps to expand the network to the rest of the mall are already in progress. The Mall's owner, Triple Five, is planning to install a similar network in the largest mall in the United States, the Mall of America in Bloomington, Minnesota, which it also owns.

SOURCE: Deborah Mendez-Wilson, "Untethered Utopia," *Network World,* November 21, 2005, pp. 74–76.

the shared circuit using a controlled-access technique, not the contention-based approach of traditional Ethernet. With this approach, any computer wishing to transmit first sends a **request to transmit (RTS)** to the AP, which may or may not be heard by all computers. The RTS requests permission to transmit and to reserve the circuit for the sole use of the requesting computer for a specified time period. If no other computer is transmitting, the AP responds with a **clear to transmit (CTS),** specifying the amount of time for which the circuit is reserved for the requesting computer. All computers hear the CTS and remain silent for the specified time period.

The virtual carrier sense method is optional. It can always be used, never used, or used just for frames exceeding a certain size, as set by the WLAN manager. Controlled-access methods provide poorer performance in low-traffic networks because computers must wait for permission before transmitting rather than just waiting for an unused time period. However, controlled-access techniques work better in high-traffic WLANs because without controlled access there are many collisions. Think of a large class discussion in which the instructor selects who will speak (controlled access) versus one in which any student can shout out a comment at any time.

Types of Wi-Fi

Wi-Fi is one of the fastest changing areas in networking. As we write this textbook, there are three types of Wi-Fi in current use, with a fourth about to be standardized.

802.11a

The IEEE **802.11a** standard provides high speed wireless networking in the 5 GHz range. It is a legacy technology, and no new products are being developed; but some firms still use it. It provides eight channels for indoor use in the United States (plus one channel for outdoor use). The 802.11a standard provides for more or fewer channels in other parts of the world where the radio frequency spectrum regulation is different.[2]

Each channel provides speeds of 54 Mbps under perfect conditions. Because the higher frequency 5 GHz range is used, the distance between the NIC and the AP is 100 meters or 300 feet under perfect conditions; in practice, it is usually less. As interference increases, the data speeds decline, so the farther you are from the AP the lower the data rate you receive. Users at the extreme edge of the range or those facing interference will not be able to communicate at the 54 Mbps. Initial analyses suggest a 54-Mbps data rate is reliable and consistent only up to 50 feet from the AP. Speeds of 20 Mbps are more common, and the speed may even drop to 6 Mbps in the face of interference such as drywall or brick walls.

802.11b

The IEEE **802.11b** standard provides moderate speed wireless networking in the 2.4 GHz range. It is a legacy technology, and no new products are being developed, but some firms still use it. It provides three channels for indoor use in the United States.

[2]The channels are numbers 36, 40, 44, 48, 52, 56, 60, and 64, with 149 being for outdoor use. There are really many more channels as the numbers would suggest, but they overlap with these channels so only these are used in the United States. Other countries use different channels.

The 802.11b standard provides for more or fewer channels in other parts of the world where the radio frequency spectrum regulation is different.[3]

Each channel provides a maximum data rate of 11 Mbps. Only when there is significant interference or the signal begins to weaken because the user is moving far from the WLAN does the data rate change in an attempt to improve signal quality. Thus, for those users close to the center of the WLAN, Mbps is the norm. The range under ideal conditions is 450 feet, although the actual range in practice is closer to 100 feet. The speed may drop to as low as 1 Mbps in the face of interference.

Thus the advantage of 802.11b over 802.11a is that in using the 2.4 GHz frequency range, 802.11b suffers less attenuation and thus the signal has greater range with less decrease in speed as distance from the AP increases. The disadvantage is that 802.11b provides lower speeds than 802.11a.

802.11g The IEEE **802.11g** standard provides high speed wireless networking in the 2.4 GHz range. It will soon be replaced by 802.11n, so it too will be a legacy technology within a year or two. It provides three channels for indoor use in the United States. The 802.11g standards provides for more or fewer channels in other parts of the world whose radio frequency spectrum regulation is different. 802.11g was designed to take the best of both the 802.11a and 802.11b standards and to ultimately replace them.

Each channel provides a maximum data rate of 54 Mbps, with a range under ideal conditions of 300 feet, although the actual range in practice is much less than this. A speed of 20 Mbps is common. The speed may drop to as low as 6 Mbps in the face of interference.

802.11g is designed to be backward compatible with 802.11b, so that 802.11b devices can operate with an 802.11g access point. This will permit the many existing laptop computers that have built-in 802.11b network cards to work with the newer 802.11g access points although they will not be able to operate at the faster speeds provided by 802.11g. Laptops that have built-in 802.11g cards can use the same access points, so both devices can coexist in the WLAN.

However, this backward compatibility comes with a price. 802.11b devices become confused when 802.11g devices operate at high speeds near them, so when an 802.11g access point detects the presence of an 802.11b device, it prohibits 802.11g devices from operating at high speeds.

802.11n The IEEE **802.11n** standard is still under development as we write. Its goal is to provide very high speed wireless networking using both the 2.4 GHz and 5 GHz frequency ranges simultaneously (by using multiple sets of antennas optimized to the different frequencies) to increase the data speeds it can attain. Current drafts of the standard propose speeds of 250 to 300 Mbps, but users are likely to see speeds of 100 Mbps. The range is 450 feet.

[3]In the United States, the channel numbers are 1, 6, and 11. As with 802.11a, there are more channels but they are not used because they overlap, and different channels are used in other countries. When 802.11b was first introduced, a four channel configuration was used (channels 1, 4, 8, and 11). With this approach, the channels overlap to some extent so if you run an AP on channel 1 and another on channel 4, there will some interference between the two APs. Field tests showed that the data rates dropped dramatically due to this interference, so although four channel configurations are possible, the best practice recommendation today is to use a three channel configuration.

As with 802.11g, 802,11n is designed to be backwards compatible with 802.11a, 802.11b, and 802.11g, so that it has the potential to co-exist with, and ultimately replace, all three prior technologies.

Wi-Fi as Public Internet Access

Wi-Fi was initially intended to provide indoor mobile wireless access to organizational LANs and backbones. Many commercial providers now offer Wi-Fi access in public places such as airports and malls, so that users can connect into the Internet and work in public locations. Several towns and commercial providers have also begun to offer outdoor Wi-Fi services as public Internet access.

There are several technical issues in providing large scale public Wi-Fi access, but none are major. The biggest obstacle is political. Some towns have offered these services at no cost or at low cost to residents, which has caused several commercial providers (e.g., Verizon) to complain that the towns are stealing business from them. Several providers have gone to court to stop towns from offering such services. Others have lobbied state governments to introduce laws to prevent towns from offering such services. Fourteen states so far have passed laws prohibiting local governments from offering free or low cost public wireless Internet services. Other states have embraced the idea of low cost public wireless Internet services and have begun encouraging local governments to act.

WIMAX

WiMAX is the commercial name for a set of standards developed by the *IEEE 802.16* standards group. The 802.16 family of technologies is much like the 802.11 family and the Ethernet family. They reuse many of the Ethernet 802.3 components and are designed to connect easily into Ethernet LANs. There are two primary types of WiMAX: fixed and mobile. WiMax is emerging as an Internet access technology in competition with cable modems and DSL as we discuss in Chapter 10.

Topology

The logical and physical topologies of wireless Ethernet are the same as those of 802.11 and shared Ethernet. They are a physical star and a logical bus. There is a central AP to which all computers direct their transmissions (star), but the radio frequencies are shared (bus) so that all computers must take turns transmitting.

Media Access Control

Unlike Ethernet, media access control for WiMAX is controlled access, using a version of the 802.11 point coordination function (PCF).

Types of WiMAX

There are two types of WiMAX.

MANAGEMENT FOCUS 7.3 PUBLIC WI-FI IN TEMPE, ARIZONA

The city of Tempe, home to Arizona State University, has become one of the early leaders in the provision of public Wi-Fi Internet access. Working with several commercial providers, Tempe installed an outdoor Wi-Fi network covering 95 percent of the city's 40 square miles. The neighboring cities of Chandler and Gilbert have also joined the project, meaning that the network eventually will cover 187 square miles. The network is built with 802.11g, meaning that all 802.11g and 802.11b devices can use it.

The network offers access to residents and visitors on an annual, monthly, or daily basis. There is a zone in the merchant district of downtown Tempe that offers free access. Access to City of Tempe and Arizona State University Web sites is also free, regardless of access location.

SOURCE: "City-wide Wi-Fi Project," Tempe City Government, www.tempe.gov/business/wifi; and www.waztempe.com.

802.16d The IEEE **802.16d** standard covers fixed point wireless access, using antennas that are 12–18 inches in size. The goal is to provide wireless connections between one central access point and a set of fixed networks. The most common use of this standard is to connect a set of offices to a central office without using traditional WAN connections (which are discussed in Chapter 9). Under ideal conditions, 802.16d provides 70 Mbps data rates for up to 30 miles. Real world tests of this technology, however, suggest that the maximum effective distance, given the noisy radio frequency ranges it uses, is 5 miles, with effective data rates of 2 Mbps.

A growing use for 802.16d is to connect multiple Wi-Fi public access points to a central switch, so they can connect into the Internet. This eliminates the need to put in wires and enables a quick rollout of new technology.

802.16e The IEEE **802.16e** standard is intended to provide access for mobile users in competition to outdoor Wi-Fi. It provides multiple channels, each with 28 Mbps, although the effective data rate is about 5 Mbps. The effective range is up to 6 miles with a line of sight to the access point or 2.5 miles without a line of sight.

802.16e is a direct competitor to public access Wi-Fi and current cell phone technologies but is incompatible with both. Manufacturers will have to build in separate 802.16e chips and antennas into phones and laptops or users will need to purchase add-on 802.16e NICs.

BLUETOOTH

Bluetooth is the commercial name for the IEEE **802.15** standards, which calls it a **Wireless Personal Area Network (WPAN).** In case you're wondering, Bluetooth's Scandinavian inventor decided to name it after Danish King Harold Bluetooth.

Bluetooth is a strikingly different type of wireless LAN from the others discussed in this chapter. It is not intended as a general-purpose network in competition with

802.11 or 802.16 wireless LANs or 802.3 wired LANs. Its goal is to provide seamless networking of data and/or voice devices in a very small area (up to 10 meters or 30 feet, possibly to increase to about 100 meters or 300 feet with the next generation of technology). Bluetooth can be used to connect many different types of devices, such as keyboards to computers and headsets to mobile phones.

Bluetooth devices are small (about one-third of an inch square) and inexpensive. They are designed to replace short-distance cabling between devices such as keyboards, mice, and a telephone handset and base or to link your PDA to your car so that your door can unlock and automatically open as you approach. Bluetooth provides a basic data rate of 1 Mbps that can be divided into several separate voice and data channels.

Topology

A Bluetooth network is called a **piconet** and consists of no more than eight devices, but can be linked to other piconets to form a larger network. One device is considered the piconet **master,** and all other devices are **slaves.** The master controls the piconet, selecting frequencies and access control used by the master and the slaves. All messages are sent from a slave to the master and from the master to a slave. The slaves do not communicate directly. All devices share the same frequency ranges so the network behaves in the same manner as a shared **bus topology.**

Media Access Control

The master uses a controlled access technique similar to Wi-Fi's PCF approach. Bluetooth uses *frequency-hopping spread-spectrum (FHSS)* in which the 2.4 GHz frequency range is divided into 79 separate channels. Each channel is used in turn to transmit signals. A short burst of data is sent on one frequency and then the sender changes to another frequency channel and broadcasts another burst of data before changing to another channel. There are usually 1,600 channel changes (called *hops*) per second. The master controls which channels will be used, so the master and the slave with which it is communicating are synchronized and both know which frequencies will be used at which point. This approach also minimizes interference because if one frequency channel suffers from interference, it will soon be avoided.

Because Bluetooth operates in the same 2.4-GHz range as Wi-Fi, it has the potential to cause problems for Wi-Fi WLANs. Tests suggest that good management can prevent interference between Bluetooth and Wi-Fi. As long as no Bluetooth piconets are located within 2 meters of a Wi-Fi NIC or AP and as long as only a moderate number of Bluetooth piconets are operating in the same area as a Wi-Fi WLAN, neither the Bluetooth piconets nor the Wi-Fi WLAN appear to suffer any problems.

THE BEST PRACTICE WLAN DESIGN

WiMAX and Bluetooth are not intended to be used for general networking, so we do not include them in our discussions here. Because WLANs are competitors for traditional wired LANs, we also consider the issue of LAN versus WLAN, which is perhaps the more interesting question. We also discuss the physical design of WLANs because the design can be challenging.

Recommendations

Selecting the best wireless technology is usually simple. You pick the newest one, cost permitting. As we write this, 802.11g is the newest standard, but by the time you read it, 802.11n will be available. The initial cost of 802.11n equipment may be expensive, but should drop within six to 12 months.

As new standards are being developed, some manufacturers produce "draft" products. As we write this, there are 802.11n-draft products available (sometimes called "draft-n" products). Because wireless technologies may change as they go through the standards processes, it is never wise to buy a technology based on a "draft" standard. If the 802.11n standard changes as it goes through the last stages of the standards process, 802.11n-draft products will not work with true 802.11n products. Many vendors of draft-n products promise to provide upgrades so that if the standard changes, you will be able to download and install new software in the AP or NIC to make them compatible with the new standard.

Most interesting, perhaps, is the relationship between Wi-Fi and wired Ethernet. The data rates for Wi-Fi are similar to the effective data rates for wired Ethernet networks (see Chapter 6). For most networks, the wired 100Base-T recommended previously still provides the best trade-off between cost and performance. But Wi-Fi networks are a very close competitor for low-traffic environments. In cases where mobility is important or wiring is expensive, Wi-Fi may be the best practice.

Many organizations today are still installing traditional wired networks but are using WLANs as **overlay networks.** They build the usual switched Ethernet networks as the primary LAN, but also install WLANs so that employees can easily move their laptops in and out of the offices and to provide connectivity in places not normally wired such as hallways and lunch rooms.

Physical WLAN Design

We discuss the general principles for network design in Chapter 12, but in this section we discuss some of the issues specific to the design of WLANs. Designing the physical WLAN is more challenging than designing a traditional LAN because the potential for interference means that extra care must be taken in the placement of access points. With the design of LANs there is considerable freedom in the placement of hubs and switches, subject to the maximum limits to the length of network cables. In WLANs, however, the placement of the access points needs to consider both the placement of other access points as well as the sources of interference in the building.

The physical WLAN design begins with a **site survey.** The site survey determines the feasibility of the desired coverage, the potential sources of interference, the current locations of the wired network into which the WLAN will connect, and an estimate of the number of APs required to provide coverage. While the site survey may uncover unexpected sources of interference (e.g., cordless telephones, microwave ovens, industrial equipment), the most common sources of interference are walls. WLANs work very well when there is a clear line of sight between the AP and the wireless computer. The more walls that exist in the environment, the more the wireless signal needs to penetrate the walls and thus the weaker it becomes. The type and thickness of the wall also has an impact; traditional drywall construction provides less interference than does concrete block construction.

An AP with an omnidirectional antenna broadcasts in all directions. Its coverage area is a circle with a certain radius. We can design WLANs using this circle, but because most buildings are square, it is usually easier to design using squares. Figure 7.6 presents the design specifications recommended by Cisco Systems, Inc. for its 802.11g APs. In this figure, R is the radius from the access point in feet, and Z is the length of one side of a square version of the coverage area, also in feet. The table provides the recommended area that an 802.11g AP can cover at a desired data rate. For example, to achieve an 18 Mbps data rate in a standard open office environment, the APs would have to be placed so that users are at most 45 feet from the AP (i.e., R = 45). With a square design template, this would have a square of about 63 feet on every edge (i.e., Z = 63).

If the APs are placed farther apart in this same open office environment, then the data rate would drop. If the APs are placed so that users are 60 feet from the AP (square edge of 85 feet), then the data rate will drop to about 1 Mbps.

Likewise, if the environment is not an open environment, but contains obstacles such as drywall or brick walls, the data rate drops dramatically. For example, in an office with brick walls, using the same 45 foot range to the AP (R = 45) will provide a data rate of only 1 Mbps. Spacing the APs farther apart would result in dead spots with no wireless coverage.

The design specifications for 802.11n will be different than those in Figure 7.6, but as we write this, are not yet available. Since 802.11n is roughly five times faster than 802.11g, it is reasonable to assume that 802.11n would provide about five times faster data rates than those in Figure 7.6.

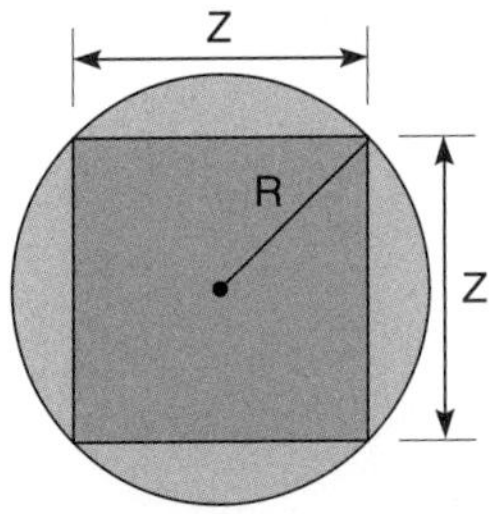

Speed / Building	1 Mbps		5 Mbps		12 Mbps		18 Mbps	
	R	Z	R	Z	R	Z	R	Z
Open office	60	85	55	75	50	70	45	63
Office w/ Drywall	50	70	45	63	42	60	39	55
Office w/ Brick	45	63	42	60	39	55	na	na

Note: R is the radius in feet; Z is the edge of the square in feet

FIGURE 7.6 WLAN design specifications for 802.11g

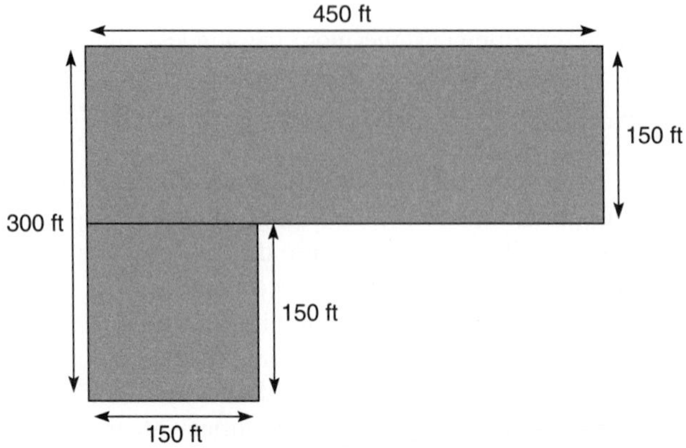

FIGURE 7.7 Sample building drawing

The design process begins with the architectural drawings of the building. Figure 7.7 shows the drawing of a sample building. This building is naturally divided into two parts. The lower left corner presents 150 feet × 150 feet square, while the rest of the building is a 150 ft × 450 feet rectangle. We could, of course, further divide the larger part of the building in smaller sections for design. Let's assume that the large part is an open office environment, while the smaller part is drywalled. If we put two rows of APs in the large area, we could space them so that Z = 75 (two times 75 feet = 150 feet). This would take a total of 12 APs for this area (see Figure 7.8). Figure 7.6 shows that with Z = 75 in an open office environment, the data rate should be about 5 Mbps.

However, if we used this same spacing for the small area with drywall, the 75-feet spacing would not work. Figure 7.6 shows that in an office with drywall, to provide even a 1 Mbps coverage, we need to place the APs with no more than a square spacing (Z) of 70 feet. If we placed the APs using a 75-feet square, there would be dead spots where there was no coverage. Instead, if we place three APs along the 150-feet side, Z = 50, from Figure 7.6 we could expect data rates of 18 Mbps (since the Z value for 18 Mbps is 55, and our WLAN is smaller than this).

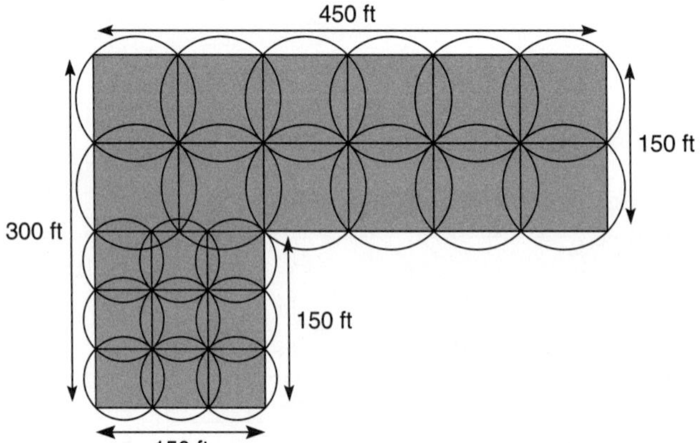

FIGURE 7.8 A Wi-Fi Design

After the initial design is complete, a site survey is done using a temporary AP and a computer or device that can actually measure the strength of the wireless signal. The temporary AP is installed in the area as called for in the initial design, and the computer or device is carried throughout the building measuring the strength of the signal. Actually measuring the strength of the signal in the environment is far more accurate than relying on estimated ranges. The site survey will also locate the placement of power sources and the existing wired network because the AP may require power and in most cases will be connected into the wired network so that the WLAN can communicate with the rest of the network.

The signal strength determines the maximum data rate possible in the WLAN. Under ideal circumstances and if cost is not an issue, many APs will be purchased so that they can be placed close together to provide a strong signal strength that results in a data rate close to the maximum data rate provided by the AP. In general, a 15 percent overlap in coverage between APs at the desired signal strength is sufficient to provide smooth and transparent **roaming** from AP to AP. Each AP is set to transmit on a different wireless channel so that the APs do not interfere with each other. If cost is an issue, fewer APs will be available, and they will need to be placed farther apart to provide a lower signal strength (and slower data rates) at extreme ranges. There may even be some dead spots in less important areas.

Design becomes more difficult in a multistory building because the signals from the APs travel up and down as well as in all horizontal directions. The design must include the usual horizontal mapping but also an added vertical mapping to ensure that APs on different floors do not interfere with one another (Figure 7.9). It becomes even more difficult if your building or set of floors in a large office tower is surrounded by APs of other companies. You have to design your network not to interfere with theirs.

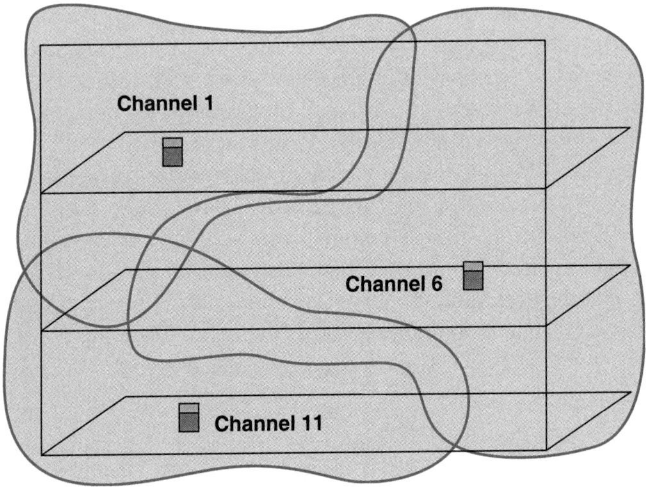

FIGURE 7.9
Multistory WLAN design

WLAN Security

Security is important to all networks and types of technology, but it is especially important for wireless networks. In a traditional wired network such as a LAN, the only way to connect to the network is to enter the offices, find a network connection, and plug into the network. With a WLAN, anyone walking or driving within the range of an AP (even outside the offices) can begin to use the network.

Finding WLANs is quite simple. You just walk or drive around different office buildings with your WLAN-equipped client computer and see if it picks up a signal. There are also many special-purpose software tools available on the Internet that will enable you to learn more about the WLANs you discover, with the intent of helping you to break into them. This type of wireless reconnaissance is often called **wardriving** (see www.wardriving.com). **Warchalking** refers to the practice of writing symbols in chalk on sidewalks and walls to indicate the presence of an unsecured WLAN (see www.warchalking.org).

SSID The most basic security applied to WLANs is to require all client computers wanting to access an AP to include a **Service Set Identifier (SSID)** in all packets. Any packet with the incorrect SSID is not processed by the AP. This provides very basic security but it is easy to break. The SSID is included in all packets in plain text, so any device within range of the AP that has the right software can listen to packets and easily read the SSID they contain. Simply put, using SSID does not provide security.

WEP Another type of wireless security is **Wired Equivalent Privacy (WEP).** With WEP, the AP requires the user to have a *key* in order to communicate with it. All data sent to and from the AP is encrypted so that it can only be understood by computers or devices that have the key.[4] If a computer does not have the correct WEP key, it cannot understand any messages transmitted by the access point and the access point will not accept any data that is not encrypted with the correct key. Encryption is discussed in detail in Chapter 11.

One of the problems with WEP is that the key must be manually typed into the client computer and into the AP. While this is not a major problem in a small WLAN, it does become challenging for large WLANs. Imagine the management time required when a WEP key needs to be changed in an organization with dozens of APs and hundreds of client computers (or hundreds of APs and thousands of computers).

With **Extensible Authentication Protocol (EAP),** the WEP keys are produced dynamically, much like the way in which a DHCP server is used to dynamically produce IP addresses. When an AP using EAP first discovers a new client computer, it requires the user to login before it will communicate with the client computer. The user ID and password supplied by the user are transmitted to a login server, and if the server determines that they are valid the server generates a WEP key that will be used by the AP and client computer to communicate for this session. Once the client logs out or leaves

[4]WEP uses single-key encryption with a 40-bit or 128-bit key length. Only the data payload is encrypted (i.e., the data portion of the LLC PDU in Figure 7.4).

the WLAN, the WEP is discarded and the client must login again and receive a new WEP key.

WEP has a number of serious weaknesses, and most experts agree that a determined hacker can break into a WLAN that uses only WEP security. A good way to think about WEP is that it is like locking your doors when you leave: it won't keep out a professional criminal but it will protect against a casual thief.

MAC Address Filtering With **MAC address filtering,** the AP permits the owner to provide a list of MAC addresses (i.e., layer 2 addresses). The AP only processes frames sent by computers whose MAC address is in the address list; if a computer with a MAC address not in the list sends a frame, the AP ignores it. Unfortunately, this provides no security against a determined hacker. There is software available that will change the MAC address on a wireless NIC, so a determined hacker could use a packet sniffer (e.g., Wireshark) to discover a valid MAC address and then use the software to change his MAC address to one the AP would accept. MAC address filtering is like WEP; it will protect against a casual thief, but not a professional.

WPA **Wi-Fi Protected Access (WPA)** is a newer, more secure type of security. WPA works in ways similar to WEP and EAP: every frame is encrypted using a key, and the key can be fixed in the AP like WEP or can be assigned dynamically as users login like EAP. The difference is that the WPA key is longer than the WEP key and thus is harder to break. More importantly, the key is changed for *every* frame that is transmitted to the client. Each time a frame is transmitted, the key is changed.

802.11i **802.11i** (also called WPA2) is the newest, most secure type of WLAN security. It uses EAP to obtain a master key—in other words, the user logs in to a login server to obtain the master key. Armed with this master key, the user's computer and the AP negotiate a new key that will be used for this session until the users leaves the WLAN. 802.11i uses the Advanced Encryption Standard (AES) discussed in Chapter 11 as its encryption method.

IMPROVING WLAN PERFORMANCE

Improving the performance of WLANs is similar to improving LAN performance. You check the devices in the network (i.e., clients, and APs), the wireless circuits between the computers, and the demand placed on the network.

Improving Device Performance

As we discussed earlier, the presence of one single computer using 802.11b to communicate with an 802.11g AP will reduce the performance of all 802.11g devices using the same WLAN because the AP slows down the 802.11g traffic so it does not confuse the 802.11b device. The same can be said for 802.11g and 802.11n. Therefore, if WLANs with 802.11g (or 802.11n) are widely deployed in your organization and most

MANAGEMENT FOCUS 7.4 MOOCHING WI-FI

If you connect into someone else's Wi-Fi network and start using their Internet connection are you:

a. Guilty of stealing from the owner because you haven't paid them
b. Guilty of stealing from the ISP because you haven't paid them
c. Committing an unethical but not illegal act
d. Really frugal, and not unethical
e. All of the above

According to the St Petersburg, Florida police department, the answer is *a.* They arrested a man named Benjamin Smith for "willfully, knowingly, and without authorization" accessing the network of a homeowner while sitting in a car parked on the street.

According to Verizon and most ISPs, which explicitly prohibit sharing, the answer is *b.* "It's obviously not good for Verizon to have its services given away for free, just as a cable company won't want someone funneling their cable connection next door," said a Verizon spokeswoman.

According to Miss Manners, the answer is *c.* It's not nice to use other people's stuff without asking their permission.

According to Jennifer Granick, executive director of the Center for Internet and Society at Stanford Law School, the answer is *d.* "Such use [i.e., sharing] might be allowed or even encouraged [by the owner]." Unless the owner states you can't enter their network, how do you know you're not invited?

As Lee Tien, a senior staff attorney at the Electronic Frontier Foundation says "Right now, we don't have a way of saying 'Even though my wireless signal is open, I'm saying you can't use it.'" Until we do, the answer is *e.* So, tread carefully. Don't leave your WLAN unsecured or you may be legally inviting others to use it as well as your Internet connection. Likewise, don't intentionally enter someone else's WLAN and use their Internet connection or you might end up like Benjamin Smith—spending the night in jail.

SOURCE: John Cox, "Mooching Wi-Fi," *Network World,* August 8, 2005, pp. 1, 49.

but not all computers use 802.11g, it may be possible to significantly improve performance by replacing the few remaining 802.11b computers with newer 802.11g computers (or 802.11g computers with 802.11n computers.

Not all wireless cards and APs are created equal, despite the move to standardization. Some devices are better designed and thus have a stronger signal at longer ranges. Thus, sometimes performance can be improved by buying high-quality wireless cards and APs from a vendor with a reputation for quality. Some products advertised as "super" or "enhanced" 802.11 products are actually better, but it may be hard for a typical user to tell; the usual network bottleneck in a SOHO network is not the WLAN but the broadband Internet connection.

Improving Circuit Capacity

The simplest way to improve circuit capacity is to upgrade from 802.11a or 802.11b to 802.11g or 802.11n. The faster speeds at greater range should enable computers to quickly see the improved performance.

Reexamining the exact placement of APs is another potential way to improve performance. APs should be placed in an area with the fewest walls between the AP and the devices on the WLAN. This means that most APs will be mounted on ceilings or high up on walls so they can transmit over the top of cubicles and other obstructions. It may be possible to significantly improve performance by placing an AP on a corridor wall rather than in a special-purpose networking closet.

If performance is significantly worse than expected, then it is important to check for sources of interference near the AP and the computers. Bluetooth devices are one source of problems for 802.11b and 802.11g devices. Cordless phones (and baby monitors) also may operate on the same frequency ranges as all three 802.11 standards (2.4 GHz and 5 GHz), so it may be necessary to remove these devices for the WLAN to operate effectively.

Another option is to try different styles of antennas for the AP. Directional antennas focus the radio energy in a smaller range of direction and therefore can produce a stronger signal (with faster throughput) at longer ranges than can omnidirectional antennas. There are also several different styles of both directional and omnidirectional antennas that may better suit different environments.

Reducing Network Demand

One of the most important design rules for improving WLAN performance is never to place a server in a WLAN. All 802.11 WLANs require that all communication is between the individual device and the AP. Therefore, if a server is placed in the WLAN all messages sent from client computers in the WLAN to the server must be sent twice: once from the client to the AP and a second time from the AP to the server. Therefore, performance in the WLAN will be improved if the server is located in the wired portion of the same LAN as the AP (ideally a switched Ethernet LAN) because this will significantly reduce the traffic on the WLAN.

WLANs are most commonly used as overlay networks; they supplement existing wired LANs and are intended to be used primarily by mobile users with laptop computers. It is possible to reduce demand on the WLAN by placing wired LAN jacks in commonly used locations. For example, if there are tables or couches in a lounge that is covered by a WLAN, most mobile users will naturally sit there and use the WLAN. If response times

TECHNICAL FOCUS 7.1 INTERFERENCE AT INDIANA UNIVERSITY

Most of the buildings at Indiana University have both wired and wireless network access. The Kelley School of Business at Indiana University has two major buildings: a modern building built in 2002 and an older building built in 1968. The new building was designed with wireless networks in mind; the old building was not. My office is in the old building.

We have one Wi-Fi access point on our floor which should provide sufficient coverage for the small office tower in which we are located. However, the walls are made of concrete which is hard for wireless signals to penetrate. Figure 7.10 shows the floor plan, the position of the AP, and the data rates that are available at different locations on the floor.

My office is located about 35 feet from the AP (less than 12 meters), which is well within the normal range for high speed access. However, because of the concrete walls, I am unable to receive a signal in most of my office.

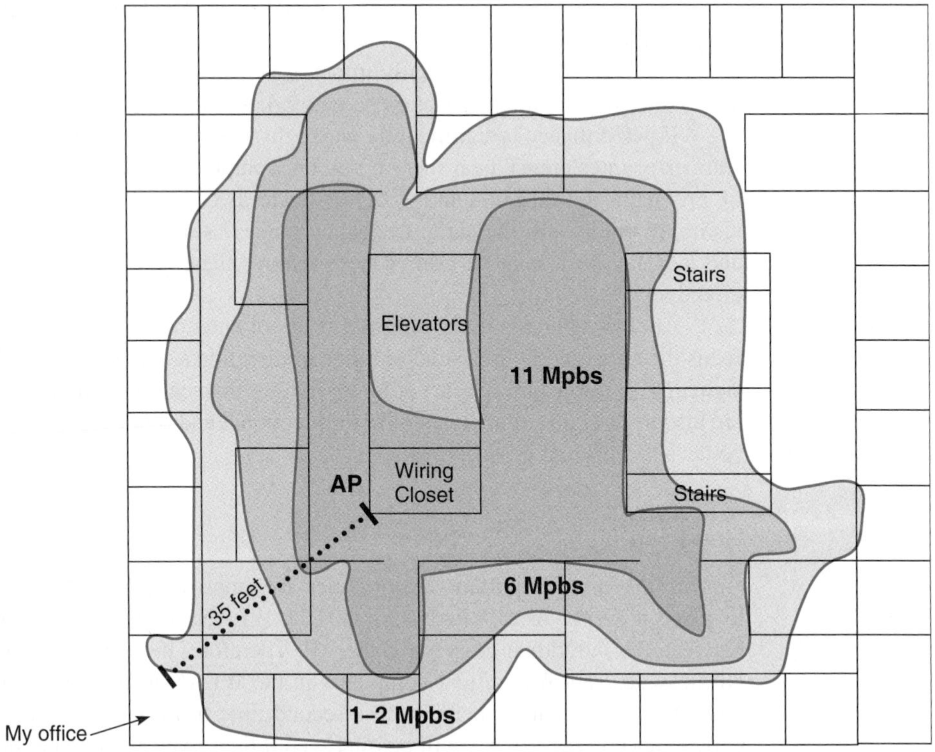

FIGURE 7.10 WLAN coverage on one floor of Indiana University's Kelley School of Business

of the WLAN become a problem, users can plug their laptops into a nearby Ethernet wall jack if offered the opportunity, thus reducing the demand on the WLAN.

IMPLICATIONS FOR MANAGEMENT

As WLANs become commonplace in organizations, accessing organizational networks or the Internet will become routine. Offices, cafeterias, break rooms, and external courtyards will be turned into wireless hotspots. Mobile workers will have access to any data, any time, and any place.

Public access wireless hotspots will become commonplace as people will come to expect the same wireless access in restaurants, malls, and courtyards as they expect in their organizations. WLAN technology will begin to compete with traditional cell phone technology, and providers of cell phones will begin to develop and install new versions of WLAN technologies that have longer ranges.

As WLANs become widely adopted, prices will begin to drop in the same way that the costs of LAN technologies have dropped. Wireless technology will become standard in a multitude of new devices (e.g., handheld computers, shopping carts, door locks) and locations (e.g., city streets, parks, your car). We think the Internet is widespread today; in 5–10 years, it will be truly ubiquitous.

These changes will result in the development of a variety of new Internet applications designed to provide real-time data to consumers in organizations. Entirely new industry segments will be created and businesses will be created and destroyed. This also means that the amount of data flowing through organizational networks and the Internet will continue to grow at its current dizzying pace.

SUMMARY

WLAN Components The NIC is a small radio transmitter/receiver that enables a computer to transmit to and receive from the access point. The access can have a directional or omnidirectional antenna and is usually wired into a traditional wired network. Most WLANs operate in the 2.4 GHZ and 5 GHZ frequency ranges and transmit 100 feet.

Wi-Fi Wi-Fi is the most common type of WLAN. It uses physical star/logical bus topology with both controlled and contention-based media access control. 802.11a provides data rates up to 54 Mbps over short distances, while 802.11b provides data rates up to 11 Mbps over longer distances (up to 500 feet). 802.11g is designed to replace both of these by providing 54 Mbps over longer distances. 802.11n is designed to provide 200 Mbps data rates over these same distances. Both 802.11g and 802.11n are backwards compatible, which means that they can be used with the older standards.

WiMAX WiMAX is designed to provide outdoor 70 Mbps data access over long distances, up to 30 miles, although most real world tests suggest data rates of 5 Mbps up to 6 miles is more common. 802.16d is fixed wireless WiMAX connecting multiple buildings to one center access point, while 801.16e is designed to provide access for mobile users. WiMAX is designed to replace outdoor public access Wi-Fi, but it is unclear which technology will win the battle.

Bluetooth Bluetooth is strikingly different from the other WLANs because its goal is to provide networking of data and/or voice devices in a very small area (up to 10 meters). It is designed to replace short-distance cabling between devices such as keyboards, mice, and a telephone handset. Bluetooth provides a basic data rate of 1 Mbps in the same 2.4-GHz bandwidth as Wi-Fi, but initial tests suggest that there is little interference between Bluetooth and Wi-Fi LANs provided they are not within 2 meters of each other.

Best Practice WLAN Design If mobility is important, Wi-Fi is a viable option to wired LANs. Given the trade-offs in costs and effective data rates, the best LAN for most networks is still the traditional wired LAN discussed in the previous chapter. However, as Wi-Fi becomes more mature, it will provide serious competition.

WLAN Security WLAN security is important because unlike wired LANs, anyone walking or driving by your home or office can connect unnoticed to your WLAN. Two popular approaches to WLAN security, SSID and WEP, provide some security, but neither will stop a determined hacker who knows their weaknesses. Newer security techniques, such as WPA and 802.11i, provide significantly better security.

Improving WLAN Performance WLAN performance can be improved by using name-brand equipment and by ensuring no 802.11b devices operate with an 802.11g AP because just one 802.11b device will slow down the entire WLAN. Performance can also be improved by moving to 802.11g and 802.11n, placing the APs so that fewer walls obstruct their transmission, removing interference (e.g., cordless phones), and switching to more powerful antennas. Network demand can be reduced by ensuring that no servers are placed on the WLAN and by placing additional wired LAN jacks near commonly used locations.

KEY TERMS

access point (AP)
bandwidth
Bluetooth
bus topology
channel
clear to transmit (CTS)
collision
collision avoidance (CSMA/CA)
contention
data rate
directional antenna
distributed coordination function (DCF)
Extensible Authentication Protocol (EAP)
frequency range
MAC address filtering
master
omnidirectional antenna
overlay network
physical carrier sense method
piconet
point coordination function (PCF)
Power over Ethernet (POE)
request to transmit (RTS)
roaming
Service Set Identifier (SSID)
site survey
slave
virtual carrier sense method
warchalking
wardriving
Wi-Fi
Wi-Fi Protected Access (WPA)
WiMAX
Wired Equivalent Privacy (WEP)
Wireless LAN (WLAN)
Wireless Personal Area Network (WPAN)
802.11a
802.11b
802.11g
802.11i
802.11n
802.15
802.16d
802.16e

QUESTIONS

1. Describe the basic components of a wireless network.
2. How do the NIC and AP work together to transmit messages in an 802.11b WLAN?
3. Compare and contrast the two types of antennas.
4. What are two ways in which an omnidirectional antenna differs from a directional antenna?
5. How does Wi-Fi perform media access control?
6. What are the types of Wi-Fi?
7. How does 802.11g differ from 802.11b and 802.11a?
8. What data rates are provided by the different types of Wi-Fi?
9. How does Wi-Fi differ from shared Ethernet in terms of topology, media access control, and error control?
10. How does roaming work?
11. Explain how CSMA/CA DCF works.
12. Explain how CSMA/CA PCF works.
13. How do the effective data rates for Wi-Fi technologies compare to their nominal data rates?
14. Explain the topology and media access control of WiMAX.
15. Compare and contrast the two types of WiMAX.
16. Is WiMAX a competitor to Wi-Fi? Explain.
17. Which type of WiMAX do you think has the greatest future prospects? Why?
18. How does a WPAN differ from a WLAN?
19. Explain the topology and media access control of Bluetooth.
20. What are the best practice recommendations for WLAN design?
21. What is a site survey and why is it important?
22. How do you decide how many APs are needed and where they should be placed for best performance?
23. How much overlap should be provided between APs? Why?

24. Why is security important for WLANs?
25. What are wardriving and warchalking?
26. Explain how SSID works.
27. Explain how WEP works.
28. Explain how EAP works.
29. Explain how 802.11i works.
30. Are today's WLANs secure? Explain.
31. What do you think WLAN security will look like in 3 years?
32. Some people believe Bluetooth is a revolution while others see it as a simple replacement for cables among devices. What do you think? Is Bluetooth a revolution?
33. Given the dramatic changes ahead in WLANs (e.g., IEEE 802.11), would you install a WLAN today? Explain.
34. As IEEE 802.11n becomes widely available, what are the implications for networks of the future? Will 100Base-T still be around or will we eliminate wired offices?
35. Many of the wired and wireless LANs share the same or similar components (e.g., error control). Why?
36. What do you think are the future prospects for Wi-Fi versus WiMAX? Why?
37. What do you think the future is for public access Wi-Fi? Should towns and cities be encouraged to build or be prohibited from building such networks?

EXERCISES

7-1. Survey the WLANs used in your organization. What types of Wi-Fi and/or WiMAX are in use?

7-2. You have been hired by a small company to install a simple WLAN for their 18 Windows computers. Develop a simple WLAN and determine the total costs; that is, select AP and NICs and price them.

7-3. Investigate the current state of wireless security including ideas moving through the IEEE standards process.

7-4. If you live in a large city, explore the downtown area for warchalking. Take pictures and bring them to class.

MINI-CASES

I. General Hospital

General Hospital has five floors, each about 30,000 square feet in size, for a total of about 150,000 square feet. They want to provide a wireless overlay network in addition to their switched 100Base-T. They have a bid for 802.11g access points at a cost of $100 each and a bid for 802.11n access points at a cost of $300 each. They expect to need 200 NICs. 802.11b NICs come built into their laptops and tablets. 802.11n NICs cost about $100 each. What would you recommend? Why?

II. Central University

Central University wants to add a wireless overlay network to one 20,000 square-foot floor in its business school. They have a bid for 802.11g access points at a cost of $100 each and a bid for 802.11n access points at a cost of $300 each. Students will buy their own computers, most of which will come with 802.11n NICs. What would you recommend? Why?

III. South West State University

South West State University installed a series of four Wi-Fi omnidirectional APs spread across the ceiling of the main floor of their library. The main floor has several large, open areas plus two dozen or so small offices spread around the outside walls. The WLAN worked well for one semester, but now more students have laptops with Wi-Fi built in, and performance has deteriorated significantly. What would you recommend that they do? Be sure to support your recommendations.

IV. Household Wireless

Your sister is building a new two-story house (which measures 50 feet long by 30 feet wide) and wants to make sure that it is capable of networking her family's three computers together. She and her husband are both consultants and work out of their home in the evenings and a few days a month (each has a separate office with a computer, plus a laptop from the office that they occasionally use). The kids also have a computer in their playroom. They have several options for networking their home:

a. Wire the two offices and playroom with Ethernet cat 5e cable and put in a 100Base-T switch for $40
b. Install one Wi-Fi access point ($85) and put Wi-Fi cards in the three computers for $50 each (their laptops already have Wi-Fi)
c. Any combination of these options.

What would you recommend? Justify your recommendation.

V. Ubiquitous Offices

Ubiquitous Offices provides temporary office space in cities around the country. They have a standard office layout that is a single floor with outside dimensions of 150 feet wide by 150 feet long. The interior is drywall offices. They have 100Base-T but want to add wireless access as well. How many access points would you buy, and where would you put them? Draw the office and show where the access points would go.

VI. ABC Warehouse

ABC warehouse is a single floor facility with outside dimensions of 100 feet wide by 350 feet long. The interior is open, but there are large metal shelving units throughout the building to hold all the goods in the warehouse. How many access points would you buy, and where would you put them? Draw the warehouse and show where the access points would go.

VII. Metro Motel

Metro Motel is a four-story motel on the outskirts of town. The outside dimensions of the motel are 60 feet wide by 200 feet long, and each story is about 10 feet high. Each floor (except the ground floor) has 20 rooms (drywall construction). There is a central corridor with rooms on both sides. How many access points would you buy, and where would you put them? Draw the motel and show where the access points would go.

CASE STUDY

NEXT-DAY AIR SERVICE

See the Web site.

HANDS-ON ACTIVITY

War-Driving and War-Walking

Wireless LANS are often not secure. It is simple to bring your laptop computer into a public area and listen for wireless networks. This is called War-Driving (if you are in a car) or War-Walking (if you're walking). As long as you do not attempt to use any networks without authorization, War-Driving and War-Walking are quite legal. There are many good software tools available for War-Driving. My favorite is Net Stumbler. It is simple to use, yet powerful.

The first step is to download and install the Net Stumbler software on a laptop computer that has wireless capability. The software is available at www.netstumbler.com. Once you have installed the software, simply walk or drive to a public area and start it up. Figure 7.11 shows an example of the seven networks I discovered in my home town of Bloomington, Indiana when I walked through one building downtown. For each network, Net Stumbler displays the MAC address of the access point (or physical address if you prefer to use that term). It shows the SSID, the channel number the AP is configured to use, the speed of the network, the access point vendor (which can be disabled by the access point owner to increase security), and the type of encryption in use (if any). It also shows the signal strength both by color coding the network (green is good) and by showing the signal-to-noise ratio (SNR) and the strength of the signal and the noise.

In Figure 7.11, you can see a mix of WLANs, both 11 Mbps and 54 Mbps. The channels we usually use for 802.11b and 802.11g are channels 1, 6, and 11. In this figure, you'll see a mix of channels 1 and 6, plus one channel 8 WLAN. 802.11b and 802.11g can be configured to use four channels (1, 4, 8, and 11), although the channels overlap to some extent. So if you run an AP on channel 1 and another on channel 4, there will some interference between the two APs. The best practice recommendation that most companies follow is to use a three-channel configuration. In this building, you can see that most companies are using the three-channel configuration, but one is not; it's using the four-channel configuration.

If you click on an access point in the left panel, Net Stumbler shows you a real time graph of the signal and noise for that network. Figure 7.12 shows how the signal strength changed for one of the networks as I walked through the building. The left edge of the graph shows that the network started with a good signal (the green or light colored area at the top of the bars) was much higher than the noise (the red or dark colored area at the bottom of the bars). As I walked around, the signal became weaker; the signal was barely higher than the noise. As I walked more, the signal dropped so that it was too weak for me to detect it from the noise.

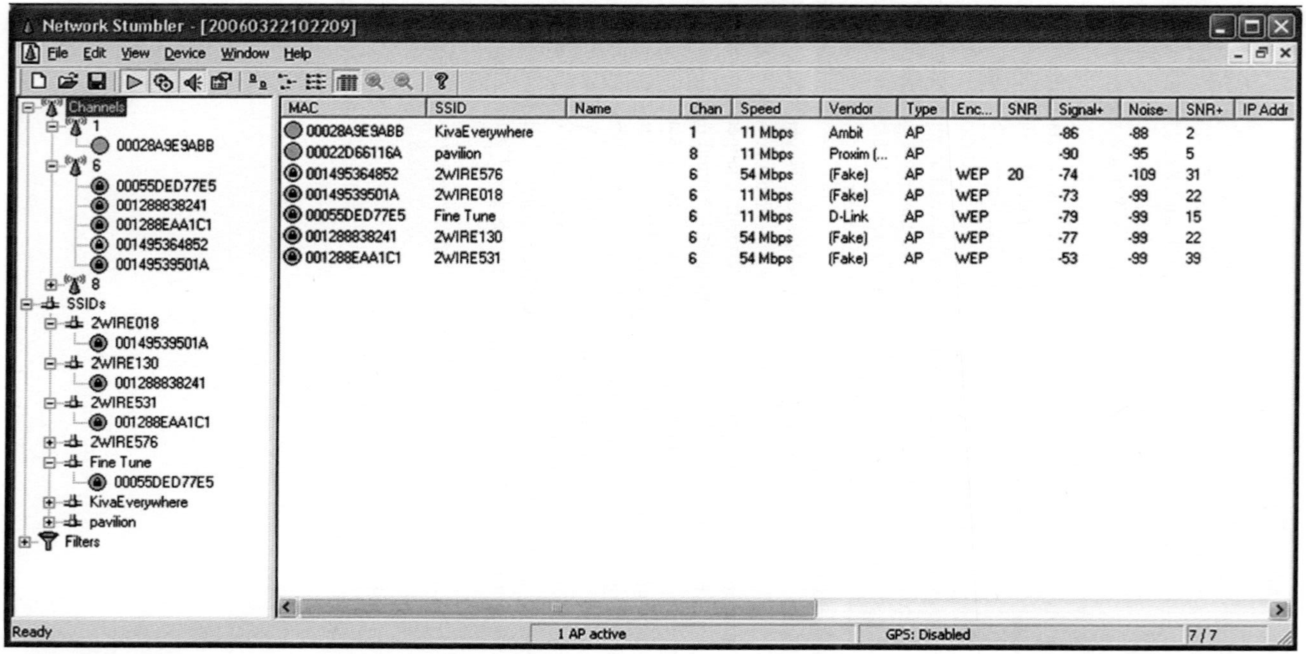

FIGURE 7.11 Networks in one downtown building

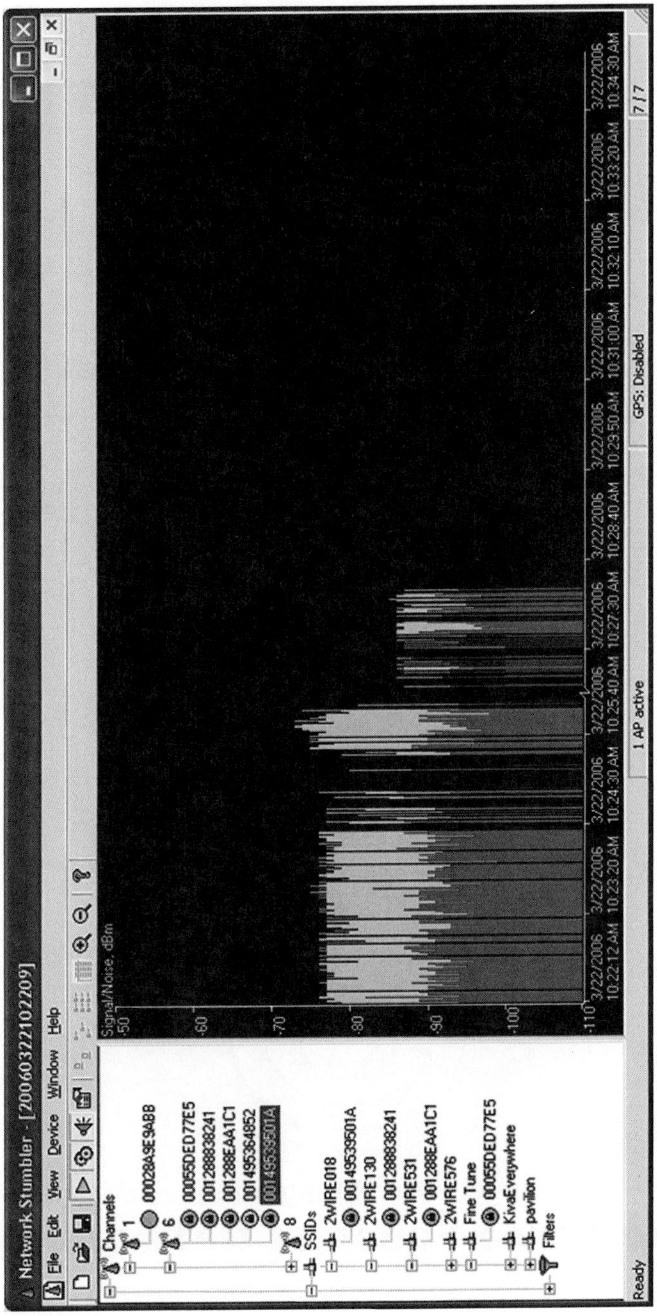

FIGURE 7.12 Changes in signal strength

CHAPTER 8

BACKBONE NETWORKS

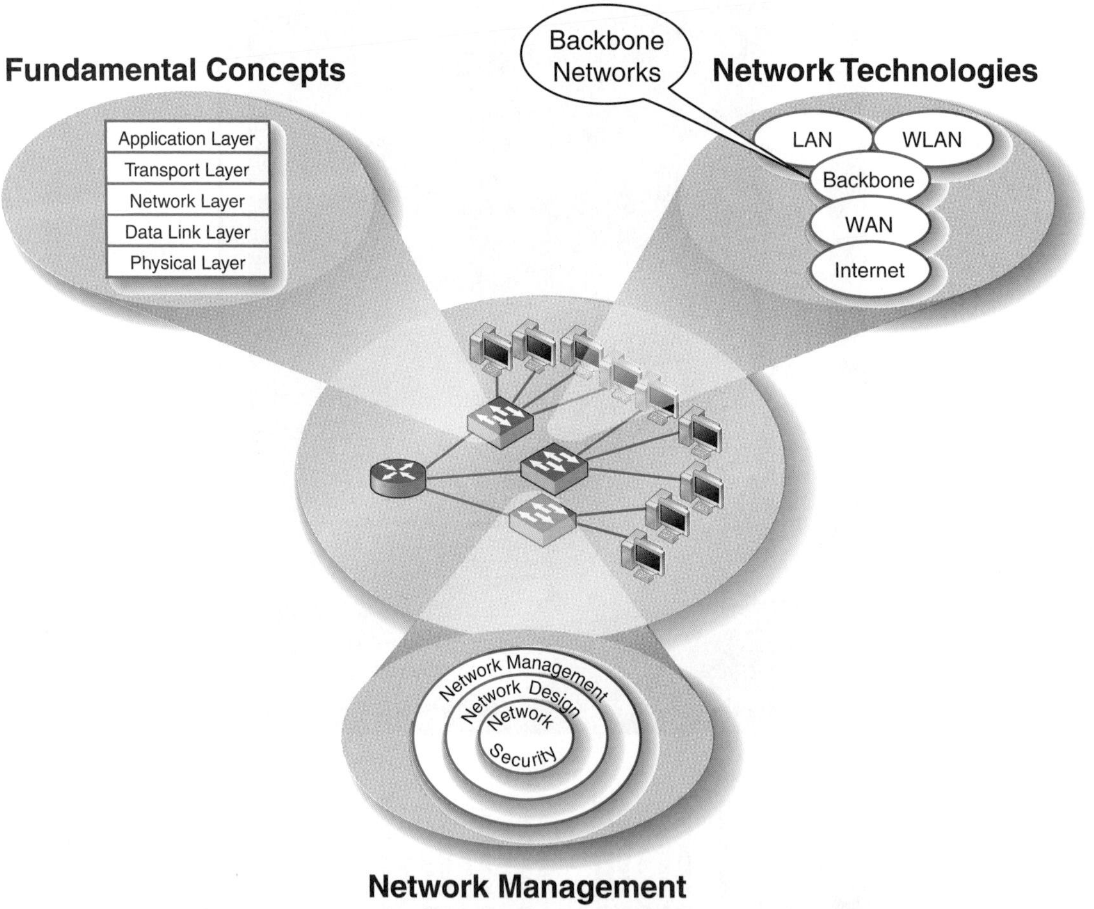

The Three Faces of Networking

THIS CHAPTER examines backbone networks (BNs) that are used to link LANs together and to link BNs to WANs. We begin with the various types of devices used in BNs and discuss several backbone architectures. We then turn to two technologies designed primarily for use in the BN (ATM and gigabit Ethernet). The chapter ends with a discussion of how to improve BN performance and of the future of BNs.

OBJECTIVES ▼

- Understand the internetworking devices used in BNs
- Understand several common backbone architectures
- Be familiar with gigabit Ethernet
- Understand the best practice recommendations for backbone design
- Be aware of ways to improve BN performance

CHAPTER OUTLINE ▼

INTRODUCTION

Most business organizations realize that information must be stored, retrieved, analyzed, acted on, and shared with others at a moment's notice. Without an enterprisewide network or an Internet connection, moving information from one department LAN to another or to customers is difficult.

Interconnecting the organization's diverse networks is critical. A **backbone network (BN)** is a high-speed network that connects many networks. BNs typically use higher-speed circuits to interconnect a series of LANs and provide connections to other

BNs, MANs, WANs, and the Internet. A backbone that connects many BNs spanning several nearby buildings for a single organization is often called a **campus network.** A BN also may be called an **enterprise network** if it connects all networks within a company, regardless of whether it crosses state, national, or international boundaries.

We begin this chapter by describing several commonly used devices in the BN and then showing how those can be used to create different backbone architectures with different performance capabilities. Backbones used to be built with special technologies, but today most BNs use high-speed Ethernet.

BACKBONE NETWORK COMPONENTS

There are two basic components to a BN: the network cable and the hardware devices that connect other networks to the BN. The cable is essentially the same as that used in LANs, except that it is often fiber optic to provide higher data rates. The hardware devices can be computers or special-purpose devices that just transfer messages from one network to another. These include switches, routers, and gateways (Figure 8.1).

Switches

Most *switches* operate at the data link layer. They connect two or more network segments that use the *same* data link and network protocol. They understand only data link layer protocols and addresses. They may connect the *same or different* types of cable. These are the same **layer-2 switches** discussed in Chapter 6 in that they use the data link layer address to forward packets between network segments (Figure 8.2). They learn addresses by reading the source and destination addresses.

Routers

Routers operate at the network layer. Routers connect two or more network segments that use the *same or different* data link protocols but the *same* network protocol. They may connect the *same or different* types of cable. Routers are the "TCP/IP gateways" that we first introduced in Chapter 5. Routers strip off the data link layer packet, process the

Device	Operates At	Packets	Physical Layer	Data Link Layer	Network Layer
Switch	Data link layer	Filtered using data link layer addresses	Same or different	Same	Same
Router	Network layer	Routed using network layer addresses	Same or different	Same or different	Same
Gateway	Network layer	Routed using network layer addresses	Same or different	Same or different	Same or different

FIGURE 8.1 Backbone network devices

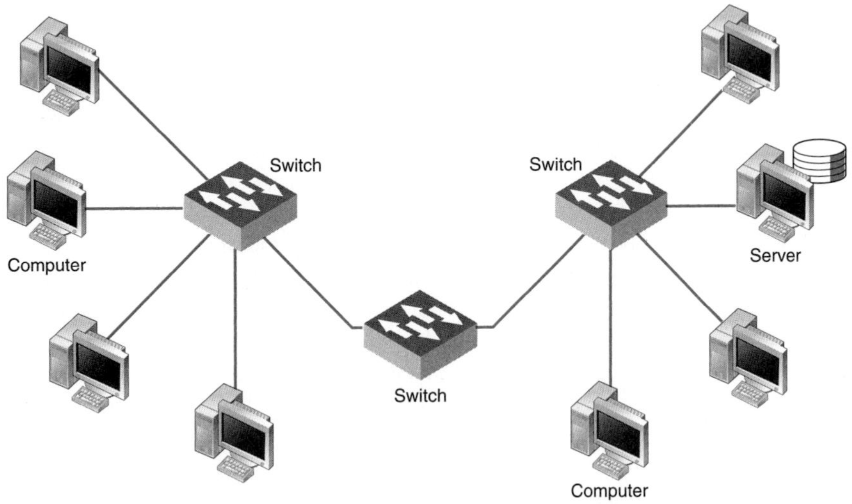

FIGURE 8.2 Use of switches to connect local area network segments

network layer packet, and forward only those messages that need to go to other networks on the basis of their network layer address (Figure 8.3).

Routers may be special purpose devices or special network modules in other devices (e.g., wireless access points for home use often include a built-in router). In general, they perform more processing on each message than switches and therefore operate more slowly.

One major feature of a router is that it can choose the "best" route between networks when there are several possible routes between them. Because a router knows its own

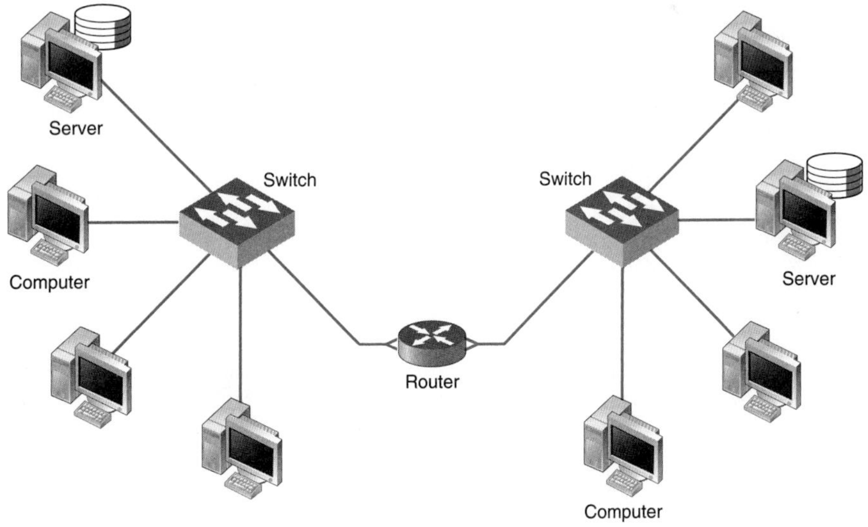

FIGURE 8.3 Use of routers to connect local area networks

location, as well as the packet's final destination, it looks in a routing table to identify the best route or *path.*

One other important difference between a router and a switch is that a router processes only those messages that are specifically addressed to it. Switches process all messages that appear on the network and forward them to the appropriate network on the basis of their data link layer address. Switches simply forward the message unchanged to the other network. In contrast, because routers operate at the network layer, the router's data link layer must first recognize that the incoming message is specifically addressed to the router at the data link layer level before the message is passed to the network layer for processing. The router will then process the message by building an entirely new data link layer packet, then transmit it to the other network.

The router attempts to make no changes to the network layer packet and user data it receives. (As noted previously, it creates a new data link layer packet.) Sometimes, however, changes are needed, such as when the maximum data link layer packet size on one network is different from another, which forces the router to split a message into several smaller messages for transmission.

Gateways

Gateways operate at the network layer and use network layer addresses in processing messages. Gateways are more complex than switches or routers because they are the interface between two or more dissimilar networks. Gateways connect two or more networks that use the *same or different* (usually different) data link and network protocols.

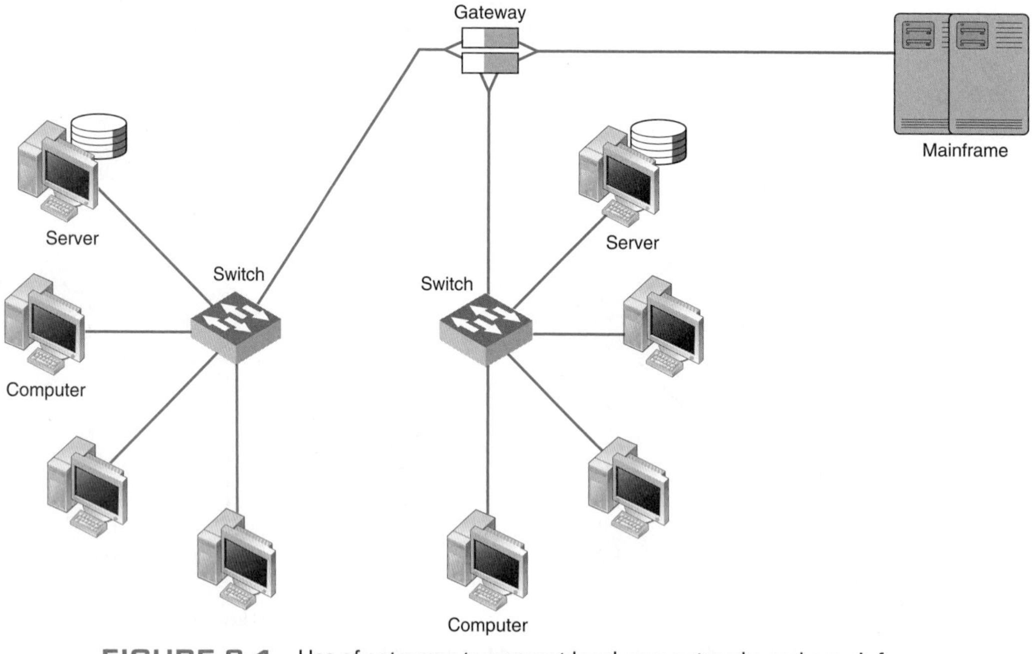

FIGURE 8.4 Use of gateways to connect local area networks and a mainframe

They may connect the *same or different* types of cable. Some gateways operate at the application layer as well. Gateways process only those messages explicitly addressed to them (i.e., using their data link layer address) and route those messages that need to go to other networks (Figure 8.4).

Gateways translate one network layer protocol into another, translate data link layer protocols, and open sessions between application programs, thus overcoming both hardware and software incompatibilities. A gateway may be a stand-alone computer with several NICs and special software or a front-end processor connected to a mainframe computer.

One of the most common uses of gateways is to enable LANs that use TCP/IP and Ethernet to communicate with mainframes that use other protocols. In this case, the gateway converts the microcomputer LAN transmissions into a transmission that looks like it came from a terminal. The gateway provides both the basic system interconnection and the necessary translation between the protocols in both directions. Without this gateway on the LAN, each microcomputer would have to have its own hardware and software in addition to the TCP/IP and Ethernet hardware and software (e.g., software to make the microcomputer act like a terminal). The gateway eliminates the need for

MANAGEMENT FOCUS 8.1 BUILDING A TCP/IP GATEWAY

Transco is the United Kingdom's largest utility company, responsible for gas transfer across a network of 200,000 miles of pipeline and serving the needs of more than 20 million commercial, industrial, and domestic consumers. Transco was formed from the merger of dozens of regional gas boards, and therefore inherited a network composed of a mixture of technologies, many of which were not compatible.

Transco concluded that its new network should be founded on TCP/IP. With many of the Transco sites being in remote outstation locations, the idea also emerged to create a satellite-based WAN carrying IP traffic, thereby removing the high costs and inflexibility of traditional telephone or cable systems.

The outstation locations had a large number of serial-based control and communications devices installed over the years. These were perfectly workable pieces of equipment for which there was no reason to replace. However, the equipment was serial-based with no Ethernet connection and was not compatible with IP.

Therefore, an intermediate communications device was developed to translate the proprietary serial protocol into standard IP-based data. Engineers modified a matchbox-sized Lantronix industrial device server, the Micro IAP, which provides IP and a Web server, thus removing the need for the Transco engineers to write a TCP/IP driver. It simply plugged onto a connector designed as part of the Transco device, providing the unit with TCP/IP connectivity at a stroke.

After the Transco engineers had thoroughly tested the prototype device with the legacy outstations using the proposed protocol, the Micro IAP was added, making the unit Ethernet-enabled and so able to connect into the satellite WAN. Results over the Transco satellite IP system were "outstanding," according to Keith Hand, a Transco telemetry engineer.

SOURCE: "Case Study: Legacy Systems 1: Bringing Ethernet to the Outstations," www.ethernet.industrial-networking.com, 2004.

additional hardware for the microcomputer, and it requires only one connection to the client computer because all data are sent through the LAN.

A Caution

One warning is in order. The terminology used in the marketplace may differ substantially from that in the preceding discussion. Many new types of switches, routers, and gateways are being developed, so that one vendor's "switch" may actually provide the functions of a "router." **Layer-3 switches** function in the same way as layer-2 switches discussed previously, but they switch messages on the basis of their network layer address (usually IP address). These switches provide the best of both switches and routers. They can be used in place of routers but provide the benefits of traditional layer-2 switches: much faster transmission and more simultaneously active ports than routers.

Multiprotocol routers can understand several different network layer protocols. If they receive a message in one protocol, they process it and send it out using the same protocol. Some vendors' multiprotocol routers translate between different network layer protocols (usually TCP/IP and IPX/SPX) so, technically, they are gateways.

BACKBONE NETWORK ARCHITECTURES

The *backbone architecture* refers to the way in which the backbone interconnects the networks attached to it and how it manages the way in which packets from one network move through the backbone to other networks.

While there are an infinite number of ways in which network designers can build backbone networks, there are really only three fundamental architectures that can be combined in different ways. These architectures are routed backbones (routers that move packets on the basis of network layer addresses), switched backbones (switches that move packets based on data link layer addresses), and virtual LANs (switches that move packets through LANs that are built virtually, not using physical location).

These architectures are mixed and matched to build sets of BNs. Before we discuss these architectures, we first must discuss the way in which network designers think about backbone designs and how to combine them; that is, the different layers of backbones that exist in most organizations today.

Backbone Architecture Layers

Network designers often think about three distinct technology layers[1] when they design BNs. The layer closest to the users is the **access layer,** the technology used in the LANs attached to the BN as described in the previous chapter (e.g., 100Base-T, wireless Ethernet) (Figure 8.5). Although the access layer is not part of the BN, the technologies used in the LANs (or access layer) can have major impacts on the design of the backbone.

[1]Try not to confuse the five basic layers in the network model (application layer, transport layer, and so on) with the layers of backbone technology we are describing here. They are different. We would have preferred to use a different word than *layer* to describe these, but unfortunately, that is the term used in the industry.

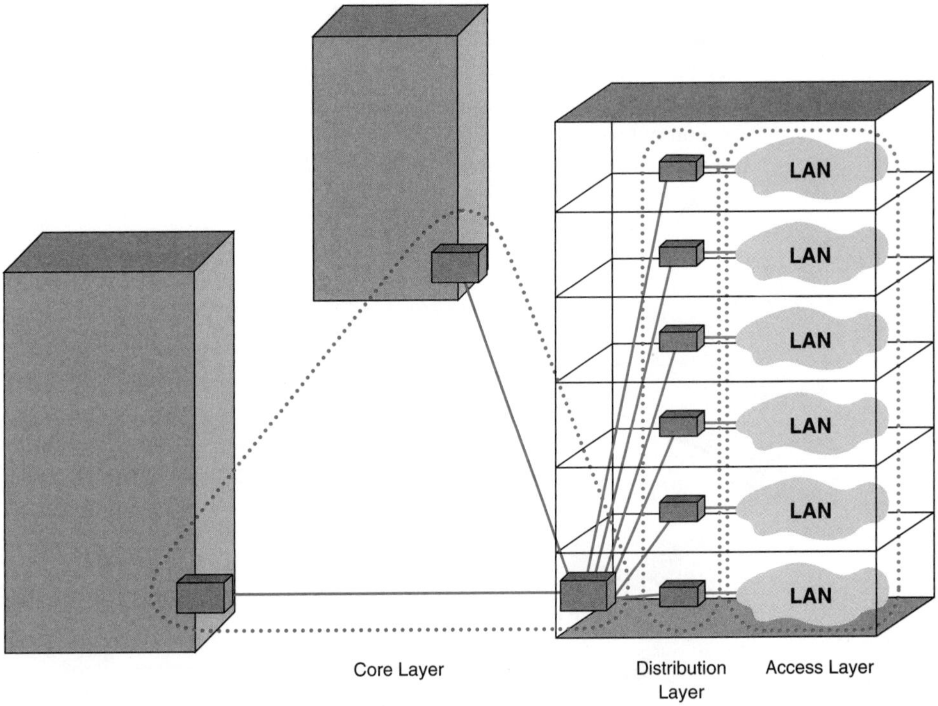

FIGURE 8.5 Backbone network design layers. LAN = local area network

The **distribution layer** is the part of the backbone that connects the LANs together. This is the part of the backbone that contains the "TCP/IP gateways" described in Chapter 5. It usually runs throughout one building.

The **core layer** is the part of the backbone that connects the different BNs together, often from building to building. The core layer is technologies used in the campus network or the enterprise network. Some small organizations are not large enough to have a core layer; their backbone spans only the distribution layer. Other organizations are large enough that they have a core network at several locations that are in turn connected by WANs.

In the sections that follow, we describe the three basic BN architectures and discuss at which layer they are often used. We focus on TCP/IP networks when comparing these architectures. We assume that you are comfortable with the material on TCP/IP in Chapter 5; if you are not, you may want to go back and review the last section of the chapter, entitled TCP/IP Example, before you continue reading.

Switched Backbones

Switched backbones are probably the most common type of BN used in the distribution layer (i.e., within a building); most new building BNs designed today use switched backbones. They also are making their way into the core layer as the campus backbone, but routed backbones still remain common.

Switched backbone networks use a star topology with one switch at its center. Figure 8.6 shows a switched backbone connecting a series of LANs. There is a switch serving each LAN (access layer) which is connected to the backbone switch at the bottom of the figure (distribution layer). This figure implies that the LAN switches are close to the computers in their LANs and farther from the backbone switch. Most organizations now use switched backbones in which all network devices for one part of the building

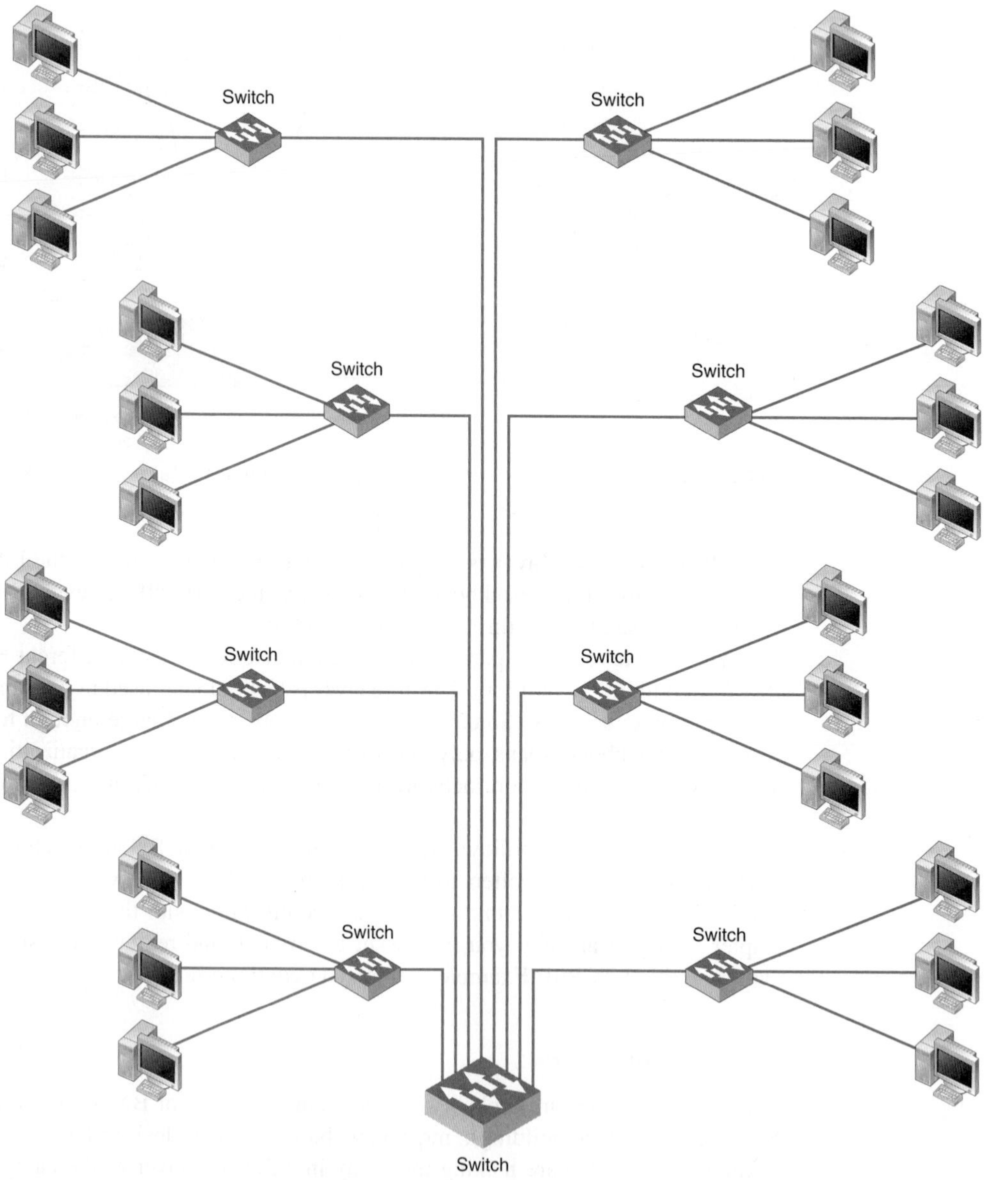

FIGURE 8.6 Switched backbone network design

are physically located in the same room, often in a **rack** of equipment. This form of switched backbone is shown graphically in Figure 8.7. This has the advantage of placing all network equipment in one place for easy maintenance and upgrade, but it does require more cable. In most cases, the cost of the cable itself is only a small part of the overall cost to install the network, so the cost is greatly outweighed by the simplicity of maintenance and the flexibility it provides for future upgrades.

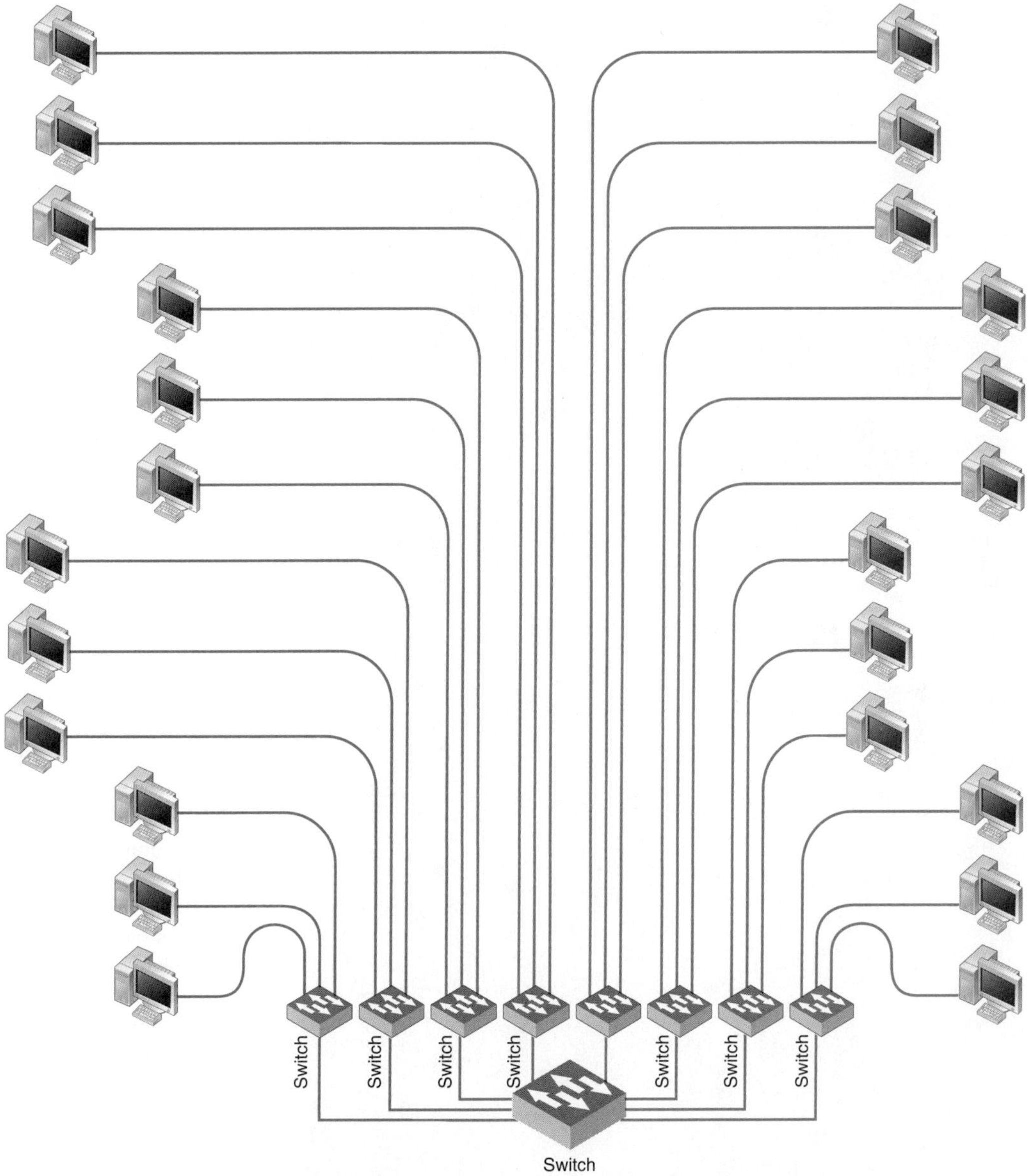

FIGURE 8.7 Rack-mounted switched backbone network design

The room containing the rack of equipment is sometimes called the **main distribution facility (MDF)** or *central distribution facility* (CDF). Figure 8.8 shows a photo of an MDF room at Indiana University. Figure 8.9 shows the equipment diagram of this same room. The cables from all computers and devices in the area served by the MDF (often hundreds of cables) are run into the MDF room. Once in the room, they are connected

FIGURE 8.8 An MDF with rack-mounted equipment. A layer-2 chassis switch with six 100Base-T modules (center of photo) connects to four 24-port 100Base-T switches. The chassis switch is connected to the campus backbone using 1000Base-F over fiber-optic cable. The cables from each room are wired into the rear of the patch panel (shown at the top of the photo), with the ports on the front of the patch panel labeled to show which room is which. Patch cables connect the patch panel ports to the ports on the switches

MANAGEMENT FOCUS 8.2 SWITCHED BACKBONES AT INDIANA UNIVERSITY

At Indiana University we commonly use switched backbones in our buildings. Figure 8.10 shows a typical design. Each floor in the building has a set of switches and access points that serve the LANs on that floor. Each of these LANs and WLANs are connected into a switch for that floor, thus forming a switched backbone on each floor. Typically, we use switched 100Base-T within each floor.

The switch forming the switched backbone on each floor is then connected into another switch in the basement, which provides a switched backbone for the entire building. The building backbone is usually a higher speed network running over fiber-optic cable (e.g., 100Base-F or 1 GbE). This switch, in turn, is connected into a high-speed router that leads to the campus backbone (a routed backbone design).

into the various devices. The devices in the rack are connected among themselves using very short cables called **patch cables.**

With rack-mounted equipment, it becomes simple to move computers from one LAN to another. In the switched backbone design as shown in Figure 8.6, for example,

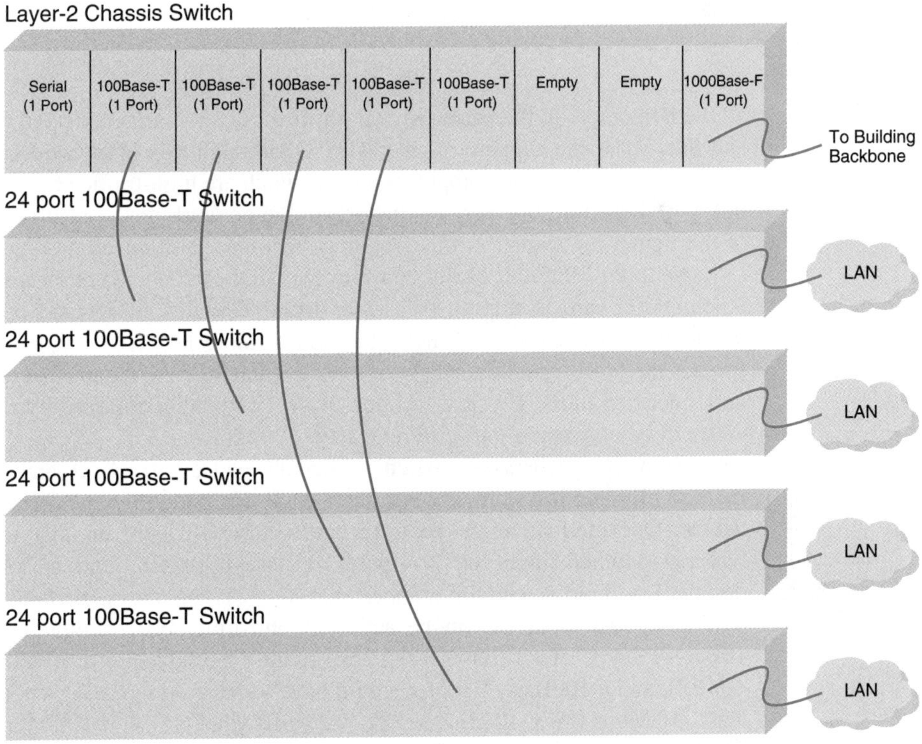

FIGURE 8.9 MDF network diagram

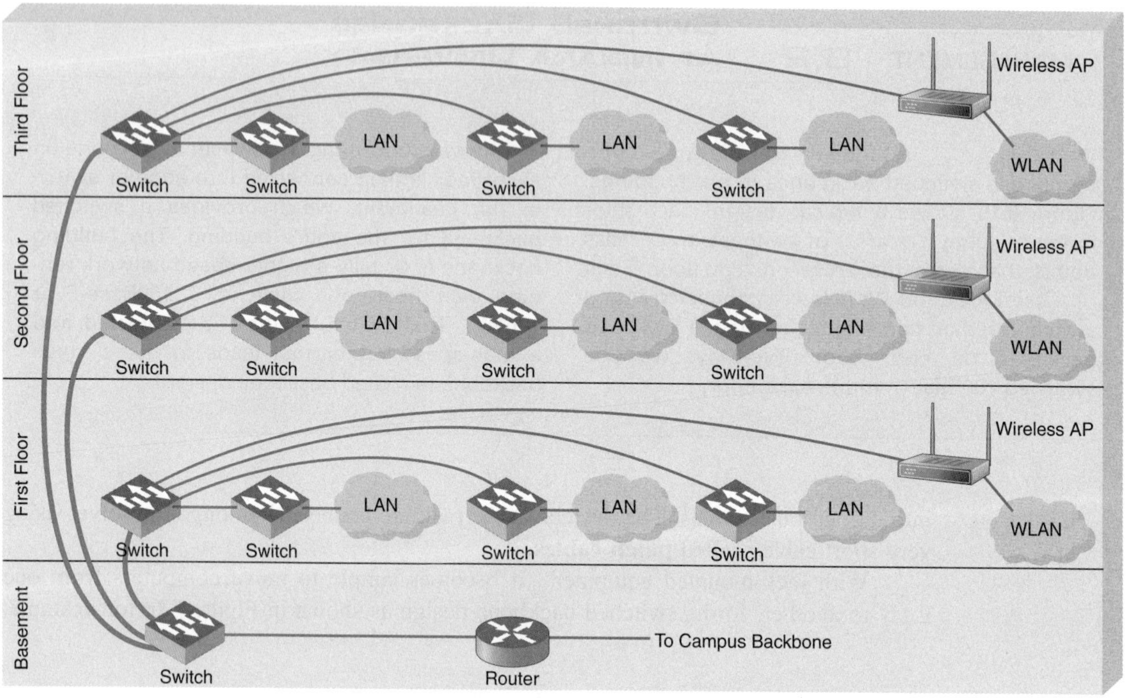

FIGURE 8.10 Switched backbones at Indiana University

all the computers in the same general physical location are connected to the same switch and thus share the capacity of the switch. Although this often works well, it can cause problems if many of the computers on the switch are high-traffic computers. For example, in Figure 8.6, if all the busy computers on the network are located in the upper left area of the figure, the switch in this area may become a bottleneck.

With an MDF, all cables run into the MDF. If one switch becomes overloaded, it is straightforward to unplug the cables from several high-demand computers from the overloaded switch and plug them into one or more less-busy switches. This effectively spreads the traffic around the network more efficiently and means that network capacity is no longer tied to the physical location of the computers; computers in the same physical area can be connected into different network segments.

Sometimes a **chassis switch** is used instead of a rack. A chassis switch enables users to plug **modules** directly into the switch. Each module is a certain type of network device. One module might be a 16-port 100Base-T hub, another might be a router, whereas another might be a 4-port 100Base-T switch, and so on. The switch is designed to hold a certain number of modules and has a certain internal capacity, so that all the modules can be active at one time. For example, a switch with five 10Base-T hubs, two 10Base-T switches (with 8 ports each), a 100Base-T switch (with 4 ports), and a 100Base-T router would have to have an internal switching capacity of at least 710 Mbps ([5 × 10 Mbps] + [2 × 8 × 10 Mbps] + [4 × 100 Mbps] + 100 Mbps = 710 Mbps).

The key advantage of chassis switches is their flexibility. It becomes simple to add new modules with additional ports as the LAN grows and to upgrade the switch to use new technologies. For example, if you want to add gigabit Ethernet, you simply lay the cable and insert the appropriate module into the chassis switch.

Routed Backbones

Routed backbones move packets along the backbone on the basis of their network layer address (i.e., layer-3 address). Routed backbones are sometimes called subnetted backbones or hierarchical backbones and are most commonly used to connect different buildings within the same campus network (i.e., at the core layer).

Figure 8.11 illustrates a routed backbone used at the core layer. A routed backbone is the basic backbone architecture we used to illustrate how TCP/IP worked in Chapter 5. There are a series of LANs (access layer) connected to a switched backbone (distribution layer). Each backbone switch is connected to a router. Each router is connected to a core router (core layer). These routers break the network into separate subnets. The LANs in one building are a separate subnet. Message traffic stays within each subnet unless it specifically needs to leave the subnet to travel elsewhere on the network, in which case the network layer address (e.g., TCP/IP) is used to move the packet. For example, in a switched backbone, a broadcast message (such as an ARP) would be sent to every single computer in the network. A routed backbone ensures that broadcast messages stay in the one network segment (i.e., subnet) where they belong, and are not sent to all computers. This leads to a more efficient network.

Each set of LANs is usually a separate entity, relatively isolated from the rest of the network. There is no requirement that all LANs share the same technologies. Each set of LANs can contain its own server designed to support the users on that LAN, but users can still easily access servers on other LANs over the backbone as needed.

The primary advantage of the routed backbone is that it clearly segments each part of the network connected to the backbone. Each segment (usually a set of LANs or switched backbone) has its own subnet addresses that can be managed by a different network manager. Broadcast messages stay within each subnet and do not move to other parts of the network.

There are two primary disadvantages to routed backbones. First, the routers in the network impose time delays. Routing takes more time than switching, so routed networks can sometimes be slower. Second, routers are more expensive and require more management than switches.

Figure 8.11 shows one core router. Many organizations actually use two core routers to provide better security, as we discuss in Chapter 11.

Virtual LANs

For many years, the design of LANs remained relatively constant. However, in recent years, the introduction of high-speed switches has begun to change the way we think about LANs. Switches offer the opportunity to design radically new types of LANs. Most large organizations today have traditional LANs, but many are considering the

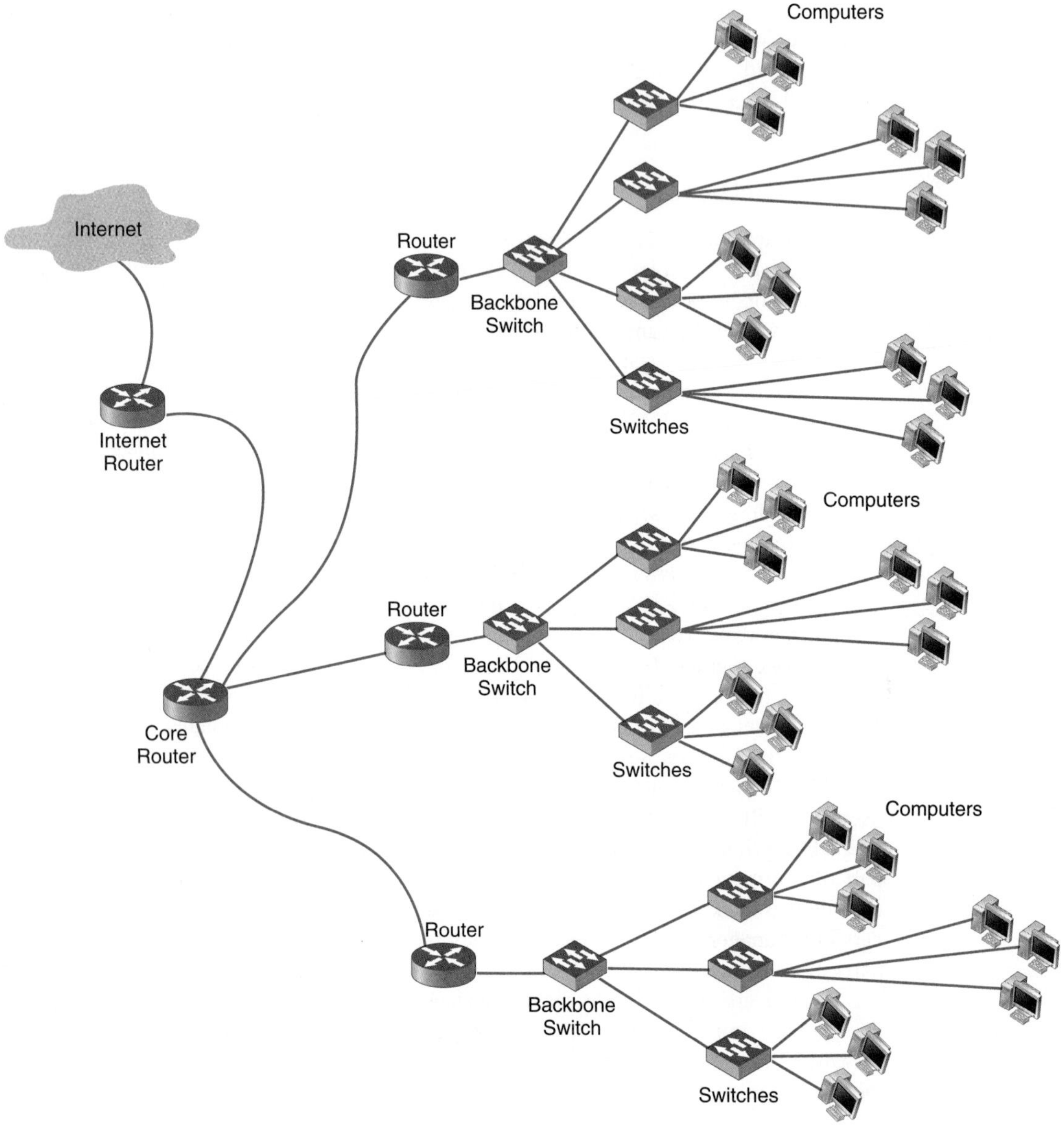

FIGURE 8.11 Routed backbone design

virtual LAN (VLAN), a new type of LAN-BN architecture made possible by intelligent, high-speed switches.

VLANs are networks in which computers are assigned to LAN segments by software rather than by hardware. In the section above, we described how in rack-mounted collapsed BNs a computer could be moved from one hub to another by unplugging its

A Day in the Life: Network Operations Manager

The job of the network operations manager is to ensure that the network operates effectively. The operations manager typically has several network administrators and network managers that report to him or her and is responsible for both day-to-day operations as well as long-term planning for the network. The challenge is to balance daily firefighting with longer term planning; they're always looking for a better way to do things. Network operations managers also meet with users to ensure their needs are met. While network technicians deal primarily with networking technology, a network operations manager deals extensively with both technology and the users.

A typical day starts with administrative work that includes checks on all servers and backup processes to ensure that they are working properly and that there are no security issues. Then it's on to planning. One typical planning item includes planning for the acquisition of new desktop or laptop computers, including meeting with vendors to discuss pricing, testing new hardware and software, and validating new standard configurations for computers. Other planning is done around network upgrades, such as tracking historical data to monitor network usage, projecting future user needs, surveying user requirements, testing new hardware and software, and actually planning the implementation of new network resources.

One recent example of long-term planning was the migration from a Novell file server to Microsoft ADS file services. The first step was problem definition; what were the goals and the alternatives? The key driving force behind the decision to migrate was to make it simpler for the users (e.g., now the users do not need to have different accounts with different passwords) and to make it simpler for the network staff to provide technical support (e.g., now there is one less type of network software to support). The next step was to determine the migration strategy: a Big Bang (i.e., the entire network at once) or a phased implementation (several groups of users at a time). The migration required a technician to access each individual user's computer, so it was impossible to do a Big Bang. The next step was to design a migration procedure and schedule whereby groups of users could be moved at a time (e.g., department by department). A detailed set of procedures and a checklist for network technicians were developed and extensively tested. Then each department was migrated on a one week schedule. One key issue was revising the procedures and checklist to account for unexpected occurrences during the migration to ensure that no data were lost. Another key issue was managing user relationships and dealing with user resistance.

With thanks to Mark Ross

cable and plugging it into a different hub. VLANs provide the same capability via software so that the network manager does not have to unplug and replug physical cables to move computers from one segment to another.

VLANs are often faster and provide greater opportunities to manage the flow of traffic on the LAN and BN than do the traditional LAN and routed BN architecture. However, VLANs are significantly more complex, so they usually are used only for large networks.

The simplest example is a **single-switch VLAN,** which means that the VLAN operates only inside one switch. The computers on the VLAN are connected into the one switch and assigned by software into different VLANs (Figure 8.12). The network manager uses special software to assign the dozens or even hundreds of computers attached to the switch to different VLAN segments. The VLAN segments function in the same way as physical LAN segments or subnets; the computers in the same VLAN act as though they are connected to the same physical switch or hub in a certain subnet. Because VLAN switches can create multiple subnets, they act like layer-3 switches or routers,

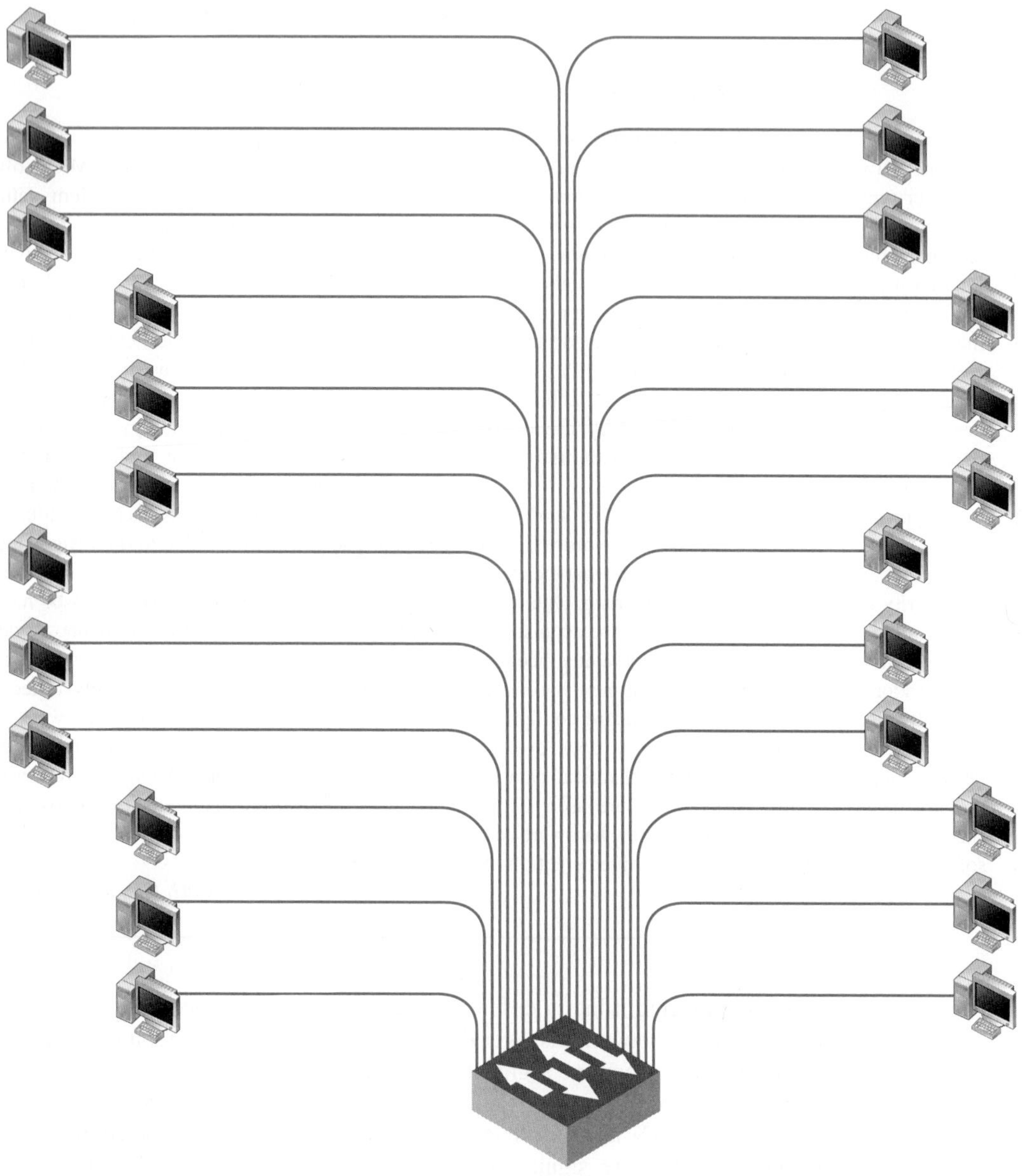

FIGURE 8.12 VLAN-based backbone network design

except the subnets are *inside* the switch, not between switches. Therefore, broadcast messages sent by computers in one VLAN segment are sent only to the computers on the same VLAN.

VLANs can be designed so that they act as though computers are connected via hubs (i.e., several computers share a given capacity and must take turns using it) or via switches (i.e., all computers in the VLAN can transmit simultaneously). Although switched circuits are preferred to the shared circuits of hubs, VLAN switches with the capacity to provide a complete set of switched circuits for hundreds of computers are more expensive than those that permit shared circuits.

We should also note that it is possible to have just one computer in a given VLAN. In this case, that computer has a dedicated connection and does not need to share the network capacity with any other computer. This is commonly done for servers.

Benefits of VLANs

Historically, we have assigned computers to subnets based on geographic location; all computers in one part of a building have placed in the same subnet. With VLANs, we can put computers in different geographic locations in the same subnet. For example, in Figure 8.12 a computer in the lower left could be put on the same subnet as one in the upper right—a separate subnet from all the other computers.

A more common implementation is a **multiswitch VLAN,** in which several switches are used to build the VLANs (Figure 8.13). VLANs are most commonly found in building backbone networks (i.e., access and distribution layers) but are starting to move into core backbones between buildings. In this case, we can now create subnets that span buildings. For example, we could put one of the computers in the upper left of Figure 8.13 in the same subnet as the computers in the lower right, which could be in a completely different building. This enables as to create subnets based on *who* you are,

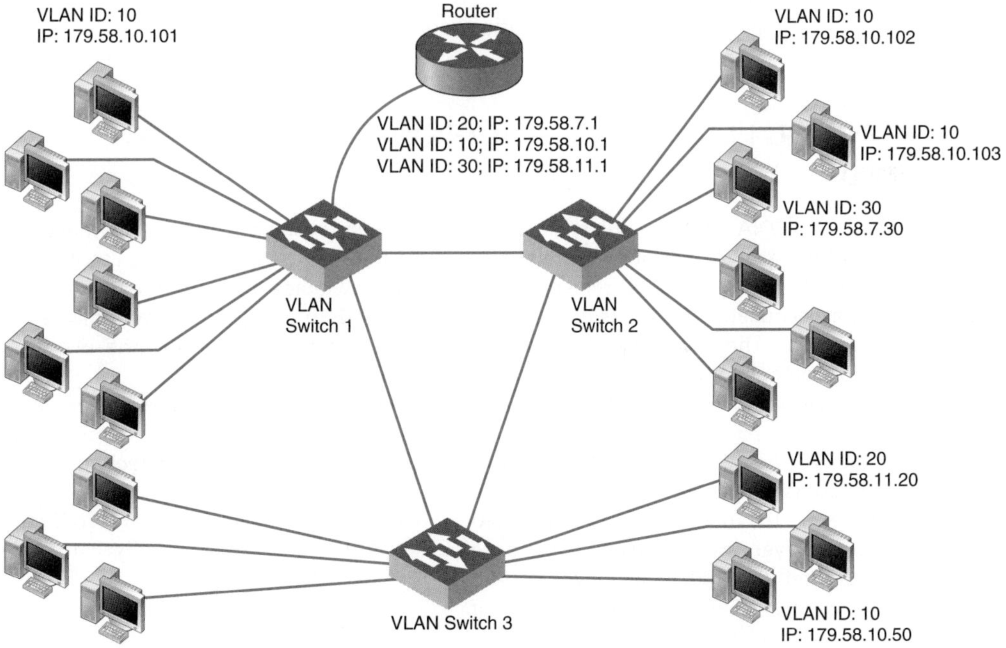

FIGURE 8.13 Multiswitch VLAN-based backbone network design

rather than on *where* you are; we have an accounting subnet and a marketing subnet, not a building A and a building B subnet. We now manage security and network capacity by who you are, not by where your computer is. Because we have several subnets, we need to have a router—but more on that shortly.

VLANs offer two other major advantages compared to the other network architectures. The first lies in their ability to manage the flow of traffic on the LAN and backbone very precisely. VLANs make it much simpler to manage the broadcast traffic that has the potential to reduce performance and to allocate resources to different types of traffic more precisely. The bottom line is that VLANs often provide faster performance than the other backbone architectures.

The second advantage is the ability to prioritize traffic. The VLAN tag information included in the Ethernet packet defines the VLAN to which the packet belongs and also specifies a priority code based on the **IEEE 802.1q** standard (see Chapter 4). As you will recall from Chapter 5, the network and transport layers can use RSVP quality of service (QoS), which enables them to prioritize traffic using different classes of service. RSVP is most effective when combined with QoS capabilities at the data link layer. (Without QoS at the hardware layers, the devices that operate at the hardware layers [e.g., layer-2 switches] would ignore QoS information.) With the Ethernet packet's ability to carry VLAN information that includes priorities, we now have QoS capabilities in the data link layer. This means we can connect VOIP telephones directly into a VLAN switch and configure the switch to reserve sufficient network capacity so that they will always be able to send and receive voice messages.

The biggest drawbacks to VLANs are their cost and management complexity. VLAN switches also are much newer technologies that have only recently been standardized. Such "leading-edge" technologies sometimes introduce other problems that disappear only after the specific products have matured.

MANAGEMENT FOCUS 8.3 VLAN Network at IONA

IONA Technologies, Inc., a 600-person software developer of enterprise middleware, took advantage of its relocation to Waltham, Massachusetts, to redesign its network infrastructure. The new network, designed to support 230 users in one office complex, uses a multiswitch virtual local area network (VLAN) architecture.

IONA has 27 access-layer VLAN switches located close to its users—built into their cubicle walls, to be exact. Up to 24 users are connected to each access-layer switch, using a mixture of 10/100 Ethernet and 1000Base-T over copper cables (e.g., category 5e) (Figure 8.14). Each of the first-level switches are connected via gigabit Ethernet over fiber to a central set of five VLAN switches that form the core of the network. IEEE 802.1q is used to communicate among the access-layer switches and the distribution-layer switches.

Because both the access-layer switches and distribution-layer switches are modular, it is easy for IONA to upgrade when technologies change.

SOURCE: "Middleware Maker Future-Proofs LAN Infrastructure," *Packet*, Cisco Systems, Inc., Second Quarter, 2000.

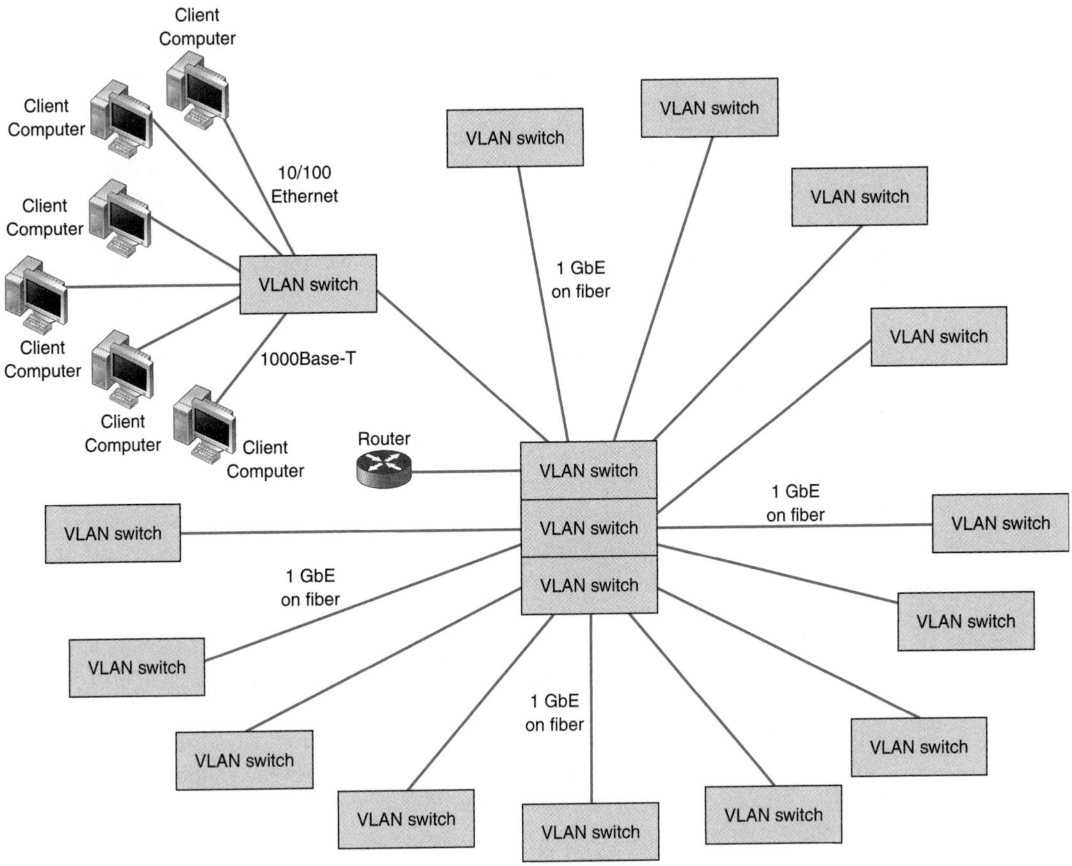

FIGURE 8.14 IONA VLAN (virtual local area network)

How VLANs Work VLANs work somewhat differently than the traditional Ethernet/IP approach described in the previous chapters. Each computer is assigned into a specific VLAN that has a **VLAN ID** number (which ranges from 1 to 1005 or to 4094 depending on whether the extended range standard is used). Each VLAN ID is matched to a traditional IP subnet, so each computer connected to a VLAN switch also receives a traditional IP address assigned by the VLAN switch (the switch acts as a DHCP server; see Chapter 5). Most VLAN switches can support only 255 separate VLANs simultaneously, which means each switch can support up to 255 separate IP subnets, which is far larger than most organizations want in any single device.

Computers are assigned into the VLAN (and the matching IP subnet) based on the physical port on the switch into which they are connected.[2] Don't confuse the physical

[2]One type of VLAN switches used to enable computers to be assigned into VLANs is based on dynamic criteria such as their Ethernet address, but this type of switch has essentially disappeared. The extra cost of dynamic VLAN switches outweighed the benefits they provided and they lost in the marketplace.

port on the switch (which is the jack the cable plugs into) with the TCP port number from Chapter 5; they are different—it's another example of networking using the same word ("port") to mean two different things. The network manager uses software to assign the computers to specific VLANs using their physical port numbers so it is simple to move a computer from one VLAN to another.

When a computer transmits an Ethernet frame, it uses the traditional Ethernet and IP addresses we discussed in previous chapters (e.g., Chapters 4 and 5) to move the frame through the network because it doesn't know that it is attached to a VLAN switch. Recall that as a message moves through the network, the IP address is used to specify the final destination and the Ethernet address is used to move the message from one computer to the next along the route to the final destination. Some devices, such as layer-2 switches, are transparent; the Ethernet frame passes through them unchanged. Other devices, such as routers, remove the Ethernet frame and create a new Ethernet frame to send the message to the next computer. VLANs are transparent—although they do change the frame at times.

Let's use Figure 8.13 to explain how VLAN switches work. We'll assume this network uses the first three bytes to specify the IP subnet. In this example, we have three VLAN switches with three IP subnets (179.58.10.x, 179.58.3.x, and 179.58.11.x) and three VLANs (10, 20, 30). A router is used to enable communication among the different IP subnets.

Suppose a computer connected to switch 2 (IP 179.58.10.102) sends a message to a computer on the same IP subnet that is also connected to switch 2 (IP 179.58.10.103). The sending computer will recognize that the destination computer is in the same IP subnet, create an Ethernet frame with the destination computer's Ethernet address (using ARP if needed to find the Ethernet address), and transmit the frame to VLAN switch 2. When a VLAN switch receives a frame that is destined for another computer in the *same* subnet on the *same* VLAN switch, the switch acts as a traditional layer-2 switch: it forwards the frame unchanged to the correct computer. Remember from Chapter 6 that switches build a forwarding table that lists the Ethernet address of every computer connected to the switch. When a frame arrives at the switch, the switch looks up the Ethernet address in the forwarding table, and if it finds the address, then it forwards the frame to the correct computer. We discuss what happens if the Ethernet address is not in the forwarding table in a moment.

Suppose that a computer wants to send a message to a computer in the same subnet, but that the destination computer is actually on a different VLAN switch. For example in Figure 8.13, suppose this same computer (IP 179.58.10.102) sends a message to a computer on switch 3 (179.58.10.50). The sending computer will act exactly the same because to it, the situation is the same. It doesn't know where the destination computers is; it just knows that the destination is on its own subnet. The sending computer will create an Ethernet frame with the destination computer's Ethernet address (using ARP if needed to find the Ethernet address) and transmit the frame to VLAN switch 2. Switch 2 receives the frame, looks up the destination Ethernet address in its forwarding table, and recognizes that the frame needs to go to switch 3.

VLAN switches use Ethernet 802.1q tagging to move frames from one switch to another. Chapter 4 showed that the layout of an Ethernet frame contains a **VLAN tag** field which VLAN switches use to move frames among switches. When a VLAN switch receives an Ethernet frame that needs to go to a computer on another VLAN switch, it changes the Ethernet frame by inserting the VLAN ID number and a priority code into the VLAN tag field. When a switch is configured, the network administrator defines which VLANs span which switches and also defines **VLAN trunks**—circuits that connect two VLAN switches and enables traffic to flow from one switch to another. As a switch builds its forwarding table, it receives information from other switches and inserts the Ethernet addresses of computers attached to them into its forwarding table along with the correct trunk to use to send frames to them.

In this case, switch 2 receives the frame, and uses the forwarding table to identify that it needs to send the frame over the trunk to switch 3. It changes the frame by inserting the VLAN ID and priority code into the tag field and transmits the frame over the trunk to switch 3. Switch 3 receives the frame, looks the Ethernet address up in its forwarding table, and identifies the specific computer the frame needs to be sent to. The switch removes the VLAN tag information and transmits the revised frame to the destination computer. In this way, neither the sending computer nor the destination computer are aware that the VLAN exists. The VLAN is transparent.

Suppose the same sending computer (179.58.10.102) wants to send a message to a computer on a *different* subnet in the same VLAN (e.g., 179.58.7.30 on the same switch or 179.58.11.20 on switch 3). The sending computer recognizes that the destination is on a different subnet, and therefore creates an Ethernet frame with a destination Ethernet address of its router (179.58.10.1), and sends the frame to switch 2.

At this point, everything works the same as in the previous example. Switch 2 looks up the destination Ethernet address in its forwarding table, and recognizes that the frame needs to go to switch 1 because the router's Ethernet address is listed in the forwarding table as being reachable through switch 1. Switch 2 sets the VLAN tag information and sends the frame over the trunk to switch 1. Switch 1 looks up the destination Ethernet address in its forwarding table, and sees that the router is attached to it. Switch 2 removes the VLAN tag field and sends the frame to the router.

The router is a layer-3 device, so when it receives the message, it strips off the Ethernet frame and reads the IP packet. It looks in its routing table and sees that the destination IP address is within a subnet it controls (either 179.58.7.x or 179.58.11.x depending on which destination computer the packet was sent to). The router creates a new Ethernet frame and sets the destination Ethernet address to the destination computer (using an ARP if needed) and sends the frame to switch 1.

Switch 1 reads the Ethernet address and looks it up in its forwarding table. It discovers the frame needs to go to switch 2 (for 179.58.7.30) or switch 3 (for 179.58.11.20), sets the VLAN tag field, and forwards the frame over the trunk to the correct switch. This switch in turn removes the VLAN tag information and sends the frame to the correct computer.

Up to this point, we've been talking about unicast messages—messages from one computer to another—that are the majority of network traffic. However, what about broadcast messages such as ARPs that are sent to all computers in the same subnet? Each computer on a VLAN switch is assigned into a subnet with a matching VLAN ID. When a computer issues a broadcast message, the switch identifies the VLAN ID of the sending computer and then sends the frame to all other computers that have the same VLAN ID. These computers may be on the same switch, or on different switches. For example, suppose computer 179.58.10.102 issues an ARP to find an Ethernet address (e.g., the router's address). Switch 2 would send the broadcast frame to all attached computers with the same VLAN ID (e.g., 179.58.10.103). Switch 2's trunking information also tells it than VLAN 10 spans switch 1 and switch 3, so it sends the frame to them. They, in turn, use their tables to send it to their attached computers that are in the same VLAN (which includes the router). Note that the router has multiple IP addresses and VLAN IDs because it is connected to several different VLANs and subnets (three, in our example here).

We have also assumed that the VLAN switch has a complete forwarding table—a table that lists all the Ethernet addresses of all the computers in the network. Just like a layer-2 switch, the VLAN switch learns Ethernet addresses as it sends and receives messages. Where the VLAN switch is first turned on, the forwarding table is empty, just like the forwarding table of a layer-2 switch; however, its VLAN ID and trunk tables are complete because these are defined by the network administrator. Suppose the switch has just been turned on and has an empty forwarding table. It receives an Ethernet frame, looks up the destination address in the forwarding table, and does not find where to send it. What happens?

If the VLAN switch were a layer-2 switch, it would send the frame to all ports. However, a VLAN switch can be a bit smarter than this. If you think about how IP works, you will see that an Ethernet frame is *always* sent to a computer in the same IP subnet as the sending computer. Any time a frame needs to move to a different subnet, it goes through a router which sits on both subnets. Think about it for a minute before you continue reading. Therefore, any time the VLAN switch can't find a destination Ethernet address in the forwarding table, it treats the frame as a broadcast frame and sends it to all the computers in the same subnet, which in VLAN terms means all the computers with the same VLAN ID.

This means that a VLAN architecture can improve performance by reducing traffic in the network compared with a switched backbone architecture. Since a switched backbone uses layer-2 switches, all the computers are in the same subnet, and all broadcast traffic goes to all computers. By using a VLAN we can limit where broadcast traffic flows by dividing the network into separate subnets, so that broadcast messages only go to computers in the same subnet.

THE BEST PRACTICE BACKBONE DESIGN

The past few years have seen radical changes in the backbone, both in terms of new technologies (e.g., gigabit Ethernet) and in architectures (e.g., switched backbones, VLANs). Ten years ago, the most common backbone architecture was the routed backbone, connected to a series of shared 10Base-T hubs in the LAN.

Today, the most effective architecture for the distribution layer in terms of cost and performance is a switched backbone (either rack-mounted or using a chassis switch) because it provides the best performance at the least cost. For the core layer, most organizations use a routed backbone. Many large organizations are now implementing VLANs, especially those which have departments spread over multiple buildings, but VLANs add considerable cost and complexity to the network.

MANAGEMENT FOCUS 8.4 MOVING TO GIGABIT ETHERNET

The amount of network traffic at university campuses has exploded over the last few years. This was especially true at the University of Essex. The university was running an FDDI ring as its core backbone that connected to six FDDI distribution layer backbones covering the various administrative and academic departments at the university. This backbone supported approximately 3,800 computers, most of which were located on switched 10Base-T and 10/100 switched LANs, although a few LANs still ran legacy 10Base-2 and shared 10Base-T LANs.

The problem was that the FDDI rings could not be increased from the standard 100 Mbps although traffic had pushed them to the breaking point. So the decision was made to replace the FDDI backbones with gigabit Ethernet.

The new network features a collapsed backbone with a series of 10/100 switches supporting the LANs, each with a fiber-optic gigabit Ethernet connection into a central core router. The new architecture permits the introduction of VLANs, QoS priority queuing, and IGMP multicast filtering, as well as enabling the development of improved security and management facilities.

SOURCE: "Case Study: SMC Networks and the University of Essex," www.ComputerWeekly.com, 2004.

Given the trade-offs in costs, there are several best practice recommendations. First, the best practice architecture is a switched backbone or VLAN for the distribution layer and a routed backbone for the core layer. Second, the best practice recommendation for backbone technology is gigabit Ethernet. Considering the LAN and backbone environments together, the ideal network design is likely to be a mix of layer-2 and layer-3 Ethernet switches. Figure 8.15 shows one likely design. The access layer (i.e., the LANs) uses 100Base-T layer-2 Ethernet switches running on cat 5e or cat 6 twisted-pair cables to provide flexibility for 100Base-T or 1000Base-T. The distribution layer uses layer-2 or layer-3 Ethernet switches that use 100Base-T or more likely 1000Base-T/F (over fiber or cat 6) to connect to the access layer. To provide good reliability, some organizations may provide redundant switches, so if one fails, the backbone continues to operate. The core layer uses layer-3 Ethernet switches running 10 GbE or 40 GbE over fiber.

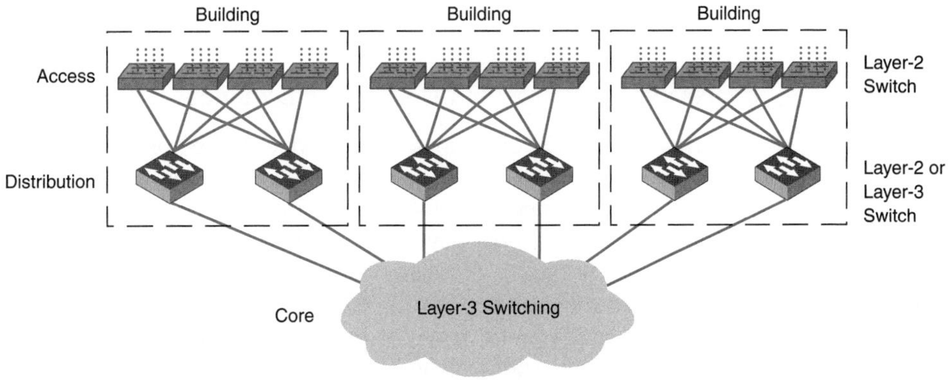

FIGURE 8.15 The best practice network design

TECHNICAL FOCUS 8.1 MULTIPROTOCOL LABEL SWITCHING

Multiprotocol Label Switching (MPLS) is an approach to improving QoS and the movement of packets with different layer-2 protocols through TCP/IP networks.

With MPLS, routers called **Label Switched Routers (LSRs)** are used. The network manager defines a series of **Forwarding Equivalence Classes (FEC)** through the network of LSRs. Each FEC has a reserved data rate and a QoS.

When a packet arrives at the edge of the MPLS network, an edge LSR reads the destination address on the incoming packet. The edge LSR can be configured to use the IP address, the IP address and the source or destination port, or the address in any protocol understood by the LSR. The edge LSR accepts the incoming packet and attaches an MPLS *label* (a packet that contains the FEC address). The edge LSR then forwards the packet to the next LSR as defined in the FEC.

This LSR reads the MPLS label and removes it from the incoming packet, consults its MPLS address table to find the packet's next destination, attaches a new MPLS label with the new FEC address, and forwards the packet to the next LSR in the FEC.

This process continues until the packet reaches the edge LSR closest to its final destination. This edge LSR strips off the MPLS label and forwards the packet outside of the MPLS network in exactly the same format in which it entered the MPLS network.

The advantage of MPLS is that it can easily integrate layer-2 protocols and also provide QoS in an IP environment. It also enables traffic management by enabling the network manager to specify FEC based on both the IP address and the source or destination port.

IMPROVING BACKBONE PERFORMANCE

The method for improving the performance of BNs is similar to that for improving LAN performance. First, find the bottleneck, then solve it (or, more accurately, move the bottleneck somewhere else). You can improve the performance of the network by improving the performance of the computers and other devices in the network, by upgrading the circuits between computers, and by changing the demand placed on the network (Figure 8.16).

Improving Computer and Device Performance

The primary functions of computers and devices in BNs are routing and protocol translations. If the devices and computers are the bottleneck, routing can be improved with faster devices or a faster routing protocol. Static routing is accomplished faster than dynamic routing (see Chapter 5) but obviously can impair circuit performance in high-traffic situations. Dynamic routing is usually used in WANs and MANs because there are many possible routes through the network. BNs often have only a few routes through the network, so dynamic routing may not be too helpful since it will delay processing and increase the network traffic because of the status reports sent through the network. Static routing will often simplify processing and improve performance.

Performance Checklist

Increase Computer and Device Performance
- Change to a more appropriate routing protocol (either static or dynamic)
- Buy devices and software from one vendor
- Increase the devices' memory

Increase Circuit Capacity
- Upgrade to a faster circuit
- Add circuits

Reduce Network Demand
- Change user behavior
- Reduce broadcast messages

FIGURE 8.16 Improving backbone network performance

Most backbone devices are store-and-forward devices. One simple way to improve performance is to ensure that they have sufficient memory. If they don't, the devices will lose packets, requiring them to be retransmitted.

Improving Circuit Capacity

If network circuits are the bottlenecks, there are several options. One is to increase overall circuit capacity (e.g., by going from 100Base-T Ethernet to gigabit Ethernet). Another option is to add additional circuits alongside heavily used ones so that there are several circuits between some devices.

In many cases, the bottleneck on the circuit is only in one place—the circuit to the server. A switched network that provides 100 Mbps to the client computers but a faster circuit to the server (e.g., 1000Base-T) can improve performance at very little cost.

Reducing Network Demand

One way to reduce network demand is to restrict applications that use a lot of network capacity, such as desktop videoconferencing, medical imaging, or multimedia. In practice, it is often difficult to restrict users. Nonetheless, finding one application that places a large demand on the network and moving it can have a significant impact.

Much network demand is caused by broadcast messages, such as those used to find data link layer addresses (see Chapter 5). Some application software packages and NOS modules written for use on LANs also use broadcast messages to send status information to all computers on the LAN. For example, broadcast messages inform users when printers are out of paper, or when the server is running low on disk space. When used in a LAN, such messages place little extra demand on the network because every computer on the LAN gets every message.

This is not the case for routed backbones because messages do not normally flow to all computers, but broadcast messages can consume a fair amount of network capacity in switched backbones. In many cases, broadcast messages have little value outside their individual LAN. Therefore, some switches and routers can be set to filter broadcast messages so that they do not go to other networks. This reduces network traffic and improves performance.

IMPLICATIONS FOR MANAGEMENT

As the technologies used in LANS and WLANs become faster and better, the amount of traffic the backbone network needs to support is increasing at an even faster rate. Coupled with the significant changes in the best practice recommendations for the design of backbone networks, this means that many organizations have had to replace their backbones completely. We would like to think that these have been one-time expenditures, but, as traffic grows, demand placed on the backbone will continue to increase meaning the amount spent on switches and routers for use in the backbone will increase. Designing backbone networks to be easily upgradable is now an important management goal.

As recently as five years ago, ATM was seen as a viable technology for use in backbone networks (ATM is discussed in the next chapter). Today, however, ATM is a legacy backbone technology: no new backbone networks will be installed using it. Therefore, most vendors have stopped the development of ATM technologies intended for use in backbone networks. As vendors stop development of technologies, they more quickly become legacy technologies. The implication is that organizations that still use ATM in their backbone will be faced with a need to invest more funds to replace these outgoing technologies.

On the other hand, as Ethernet moves more extensively into the backbone and pushes out ATM, the costs associated with buying and maintaining backbone devices and training networking staff will continue to decrease, since now there will be one standard technology in use throughout the LAN, WLAN, and backbone. The new focus is on faster and faster versions of Ethernet. While we will spend more on new equipment, performance will increase much more quickly, and the cost to operate the equipment will decrease.

SUMMARY

Network Components There are two basic components to a BN: the network cable and the hardware devices that connect other networks to the backbone. The cable is essentially the same as those used in LANs, except that it is usually fiber optic to provide higher data rates. The hardware devices include routers, gateways, and switches. Switches connect two LAN segments that use the same data link and network protocol and forward only those messages that need to go to other network segments. Routers connect two or more LANs that use the same or different data link protocols but employ the same network protocol. Gateways connect two or more LANs that use the same or different data link and network protocols (usually different). Layer-2 switches are similar to bridges, whereas layer-3 switches are similar to routers.

Backbone Architectures Network designers often think about three distinct technology layers when designing backbones. The access layer is the LAN, the distribution layer connects the LANs together, and the core layer connects the distribution-layer BNs together. The distribution layer is usually a backbone within a building whereas the core layer often connects buildings and is sometimes called the campus network. A routed backbone uses a set of routers or layer-3 switches to connect LANs together and moves messages using layer-3 addresses. A switched backbone uses one device, usually a layer-2 switch, to connect the LANs. A VLAN uses layer-2 or layer-3 switches to build logical or virtual LANs that enable the network manager to assign capacity separate from physical location.

Best Practice Backbone Design The best practice backbone architecture for most organizations is a switched backbone (using a rack or a chassis switch) or VLAN in the distribution layer and a routed backbone in the core layer. The recommended technology is gigabit Ethernet.

Improving Backbone Performance Backbone performance can be improved by choosing the best network layer routing protocols. Upgrading to faster circuits and adding additional circuits on very busy backbones can also improve performance. Finally, one could move servers closer to the end users or reduce broadcast traffic to reduce backbone traffic.

KEY TERMS

access layer
backbone network (BN)
campus network
chassis switch
core layer
distribution layer
enterprise network
forwarding equivalence class (FEC)
gateways
IEEE 802.1q
label switched router (LSR)
layer-2 switch
layer-3 switch
main distribution facility (MDF)
module
multiprotocol label switching (MPLS)
multiprotocol router
multiswitch VLAN
patch cables
rack
routed backbone
router
single-switch VLAN
switched backbone
virtual LAN (VLAN)
VLAN ID
VLAN tag
VLAN trunk

QUESTIONS

1. Compare and contrast switches, routers, and gateways.
2. How does a layer-2 switch differ from a layer-3 switch?
3. How does a router differ from a layer-3 switch?
4. Under what circumstances would you want to use a router?
5. Under what circumstances would you want to use a multiprotocol router?
6. What is an enterprise network?
7. What are the three technology layers important in backbone design?
8. Explain how routed backbones work.
9. Where are routed backbones most commonly used?
10. Explain how switched backbones work.
11. What are the key advantages and disadvantages of routed and switched backbones?
12. Compare and contrast rack-based and chassis-based switched backbones.
13. What is a module and why are modules important?
14. Explain how single-switch VLANs work.
15. Explain how multiswitch VLANs work.
16. What is IEEE 802.1q?
17. What are the advantages and disadvantages of VLANs?
18. How can you improve the performance of a BN?
19. Why are broadcast messages important?
20. What are the preferred architectures used in the technology layers in backbone design?
21. Some experts are predicting that Ethernet will move into the WAN. What do you think?

EXERCISES

8-1. Survey the BNs used in your organization. Do they use Ethernet or some other technology? Why?

8-2. Document one BN in detail. What devices are attached, what cabling is used, and what is the topology? What networks does the backbone connect?

8-3. You have been hired by a small company to install a backbone to connect four 100base-T Ethernet LANs (each using one 24-port hub) and to provide a connection to the Internet. Develop a simple backbone and determine the total cost (i.e., select the backbone technology and price it, select the cabling and price it, select the devices and price them, and so on). Prices are available at www.datacommwarehouse.com, but use any source that is convenient. For simplicity, assume that category 5, category 5e, category 6, and fiber-optic cable have a fixed cost per circuit to buy and install, regardless of distance, of \$50, \$60, \$120, and \$300, respectively.

MINI-CASES

I. Pat's Engineering Works

Pat's Engineering Works is a small company that specializes in complex engineering consulting projects. The projects typically involve one or two engineers who do data intensive analyses for companies. Because so much data are needed, the projects are stored on the company's high-capacity server but moved to the engineers' workstations for analysis. The company is moving into new offices and wants you to design its network. It has a staff of 8 engineers (which is expected to grow to 12 over the next 5 years), plus another 8 management and clerical employees who also need network connections but whose needs are less intense. Design the network. Be sure to include a diagram.

II. Hospitality Hotel

Hospitality Hotel is a luxury hotel whose guests are mostly business travelers. To improve its quality of service, it has decided to install network connections in each of its 600 guest rooms and 12 conference meeting rooms. Last year, the hotel upgraded its own internal networks to switched 100Base-T, but it wants to keep the public network (i.e., the guest and meeting rooms) separate from its private network (i.e., its own computer systems). Your task is to design the public network and decide how to connect the two networks together. Be sure to include a diagram.

III. Transco

Reread Management Focus 8.1. What other alternatives do you think that Transco considered? Why do you think they did what they did?

IV. Central Parking

Reread Management Focus 8.2. What other alternatives do you think that Indiana University considered? Why do you think they did what they did?

V. IONA

Reread Management Focus 8.3. What other alternatives do you think that IONA considered? Why do you think they did what they did?

VI. University of Essex

Reread Management Focus 8.4. What other alternatives do you think that University of Essex considered? Why do you think they did what they did?

VII. Western Trucking

Western Trucking operates a large fleet of trucks that deliver shipments for commercial shippers such as food stores, retailers, and wholesalers. Their main headquarters building and secondary building are shown in Figure 8.17. They currently have a mix of shared 10base-T and switched 10base-T LANs, connected by a series of switches. They want to upgrade to a faster network. Design a new network for them, including the architecture and specific backbone and LAN technologies to be used.

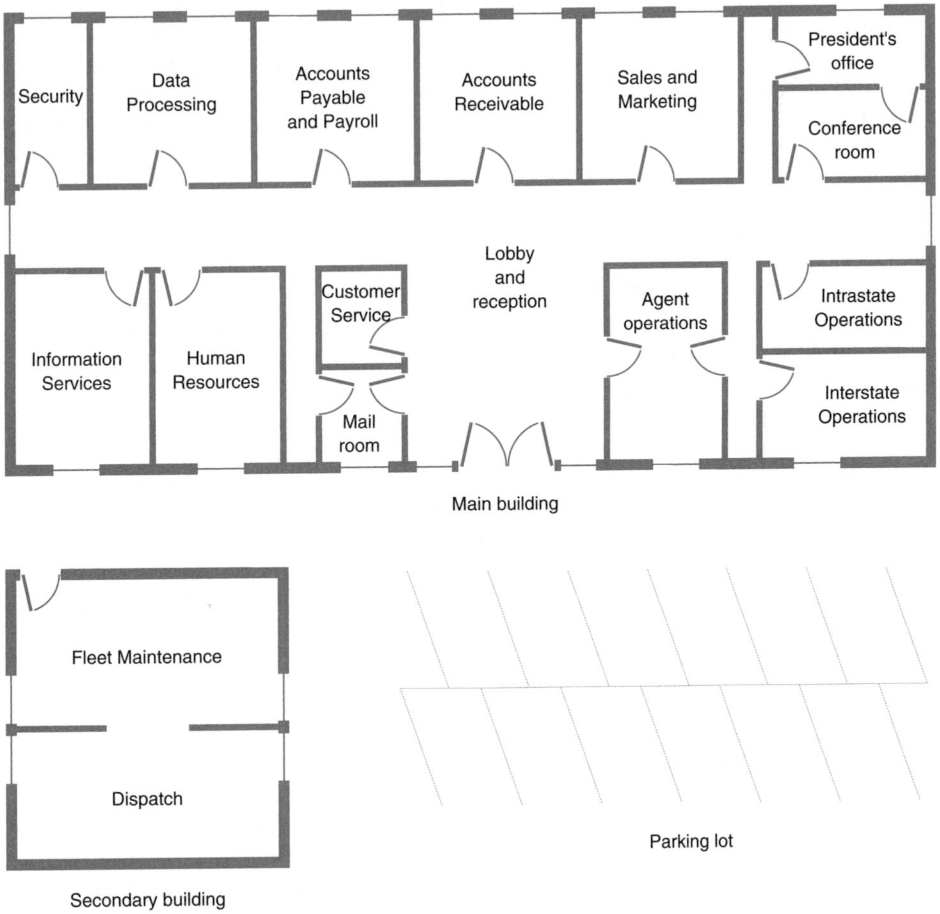

FIGURE 8.17 Facility map of the Western Trucking headquarters

CASE STUDY

NEXT-DAY AIR SERVICE

See the Web site.

HANDS-ON ACTIVITY

Network Mapping

A backbone network connects one or more LANs to each other and usually to the Internet or to another backbone that eventually leads to the Internet. Each of these backbones usually connects many computers.

Network mapping software enables you to generate a map of the computers on all the LANs connected to a backbone. There are many good network mapping packages. Two of my favorites are LANState and LAN Surveyor. LANState is simpler to use but works best for small networks. LAN Surveyor is more complex, but can map large networks.

Both work in the same way. They use the ping command (see Chapter 5) to send IMCP requests to all possible IP addresses in any range you specify. Any computer that responds is added to the map.

Mapping A Small Network

The first step is to download and install LANState. A demo version of the software is available free of charge from 10-Strike Software (www.10-strike.com/lanstate).

You begin by creating a new network map (choose File Create). Then use the Network Map Creation Wizard and choose to Scan an IP-address range. You will be asked to enter an address range. Choose some range, ideally the address range of a small network. I choose to use my home network range (192.168.1.1 through 192.168.1.254). When the scan is complete you will see a list of computers. Click Finish to see a map of these computers.

LANState does not do a good job of drawing a map, but you can rearrange the computers by dragging and dropping them. You can also add lines to make the map look more like a network diagram. Figure 8.18 shows the small network in my house. I have a router (192.168.1.1) that connects a number of computers to the Internet. I also have a wireless access point (192.168.1.100) and a music server (192.168.1.52). When I did this map, three computers were turned on and responded to LANState's pings (192.168.1.102, 192.168.1.103, 192.168.1.111). Computers and devices that are not turned on do not respond to the pings and therefore are not mapped. Since I use dynamic addressing, the addresses of my computers will change every time I turn them on.

You can also left click on any device and choose System Information and General to learn more about that device. Figure 8.18 also shows the information about my son's computer (192.168.1.103). It shows the MAC address (i.e., the Ethernet address), the card manufacturer, and Windows workgroup peer-to-peer network information (i.e., application layer address) for this computer.

Mapping A Large Network

The first step is to download and install LAN Surveyor. A demo version of the software is available free of charge from Solarwinds (www.solarwinds.com/products/lansurveyor). Installing the software and setting it up to run is more complex, so be sure to follow the setup and configuration instructions.

You begin by creating a new network map (choose File New). You will be asked to enter an address range. Choose some range, ideally the address range of a large network. I choose to use part of the Indiana University network (129.79.1.1 through 129.79.1.254). There is no rule preventing you from scanning anyone's network, but many companies (and individuals) feel that scanning their networks is an invasion of privacy, so scan carefully. When the scan is complete, you will see a map of computers.

My scan of this one small part of the Indiana University network found 124 computers. Figure 8.19 shows a partial list of the computers and their IP addresses and host names (i.e., application layer addresses).

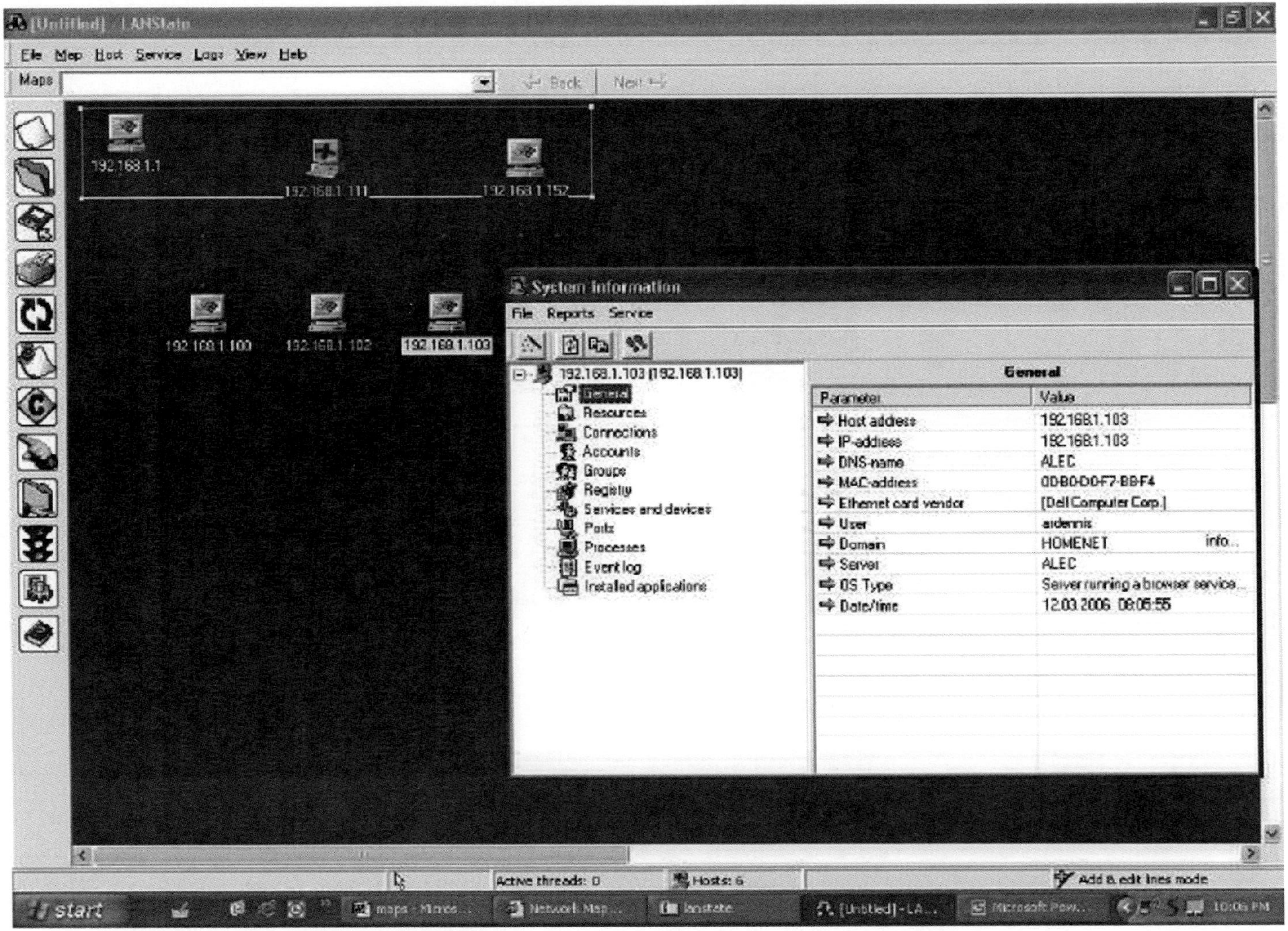

FIGURE 8.18 Network mapping with LANState

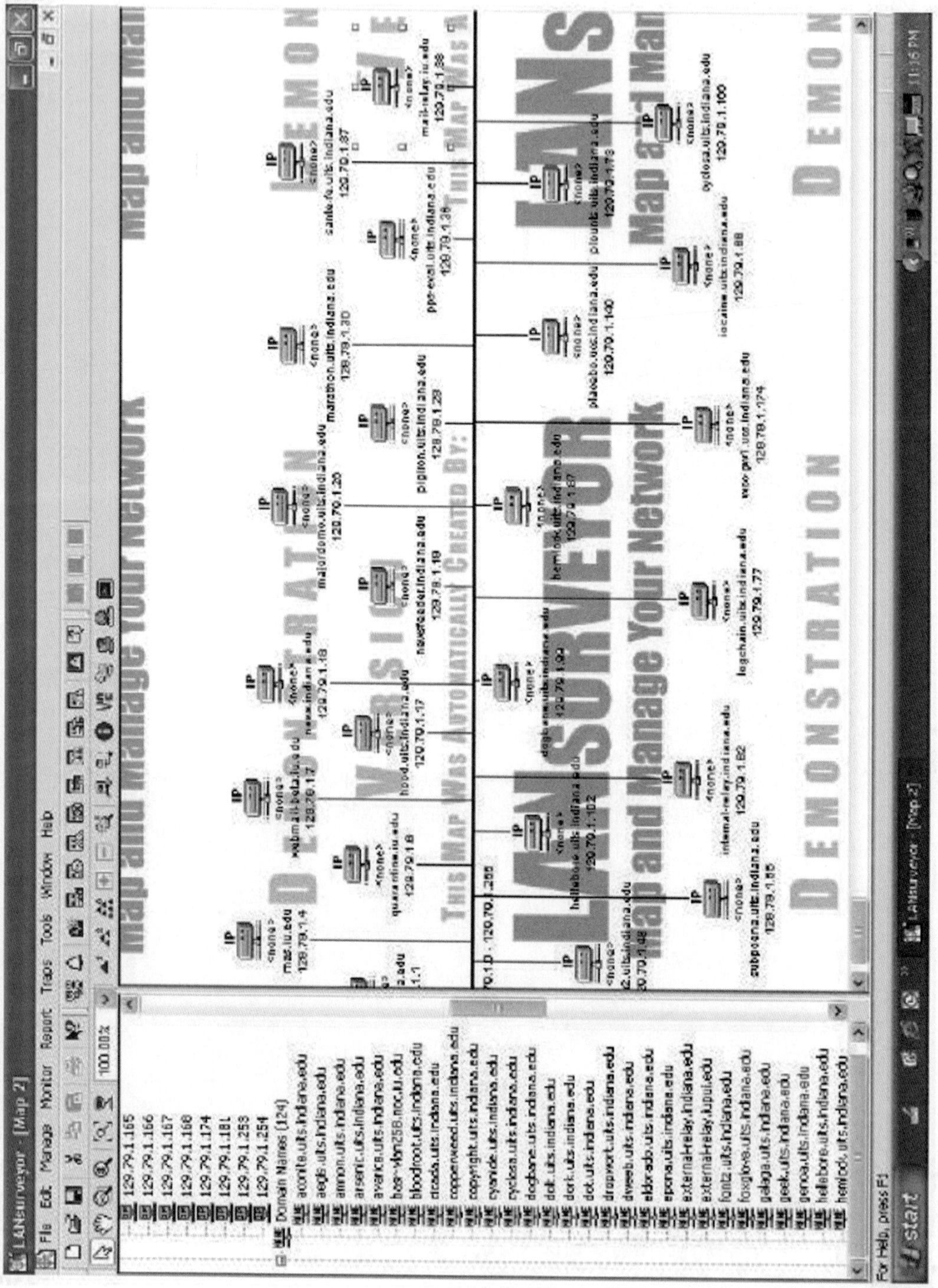

FIGURE 8.19 Network mapping with LAN Surveyor

CHAPTER 9

METROPOLITAN AND WIDE AREA NETWORKS

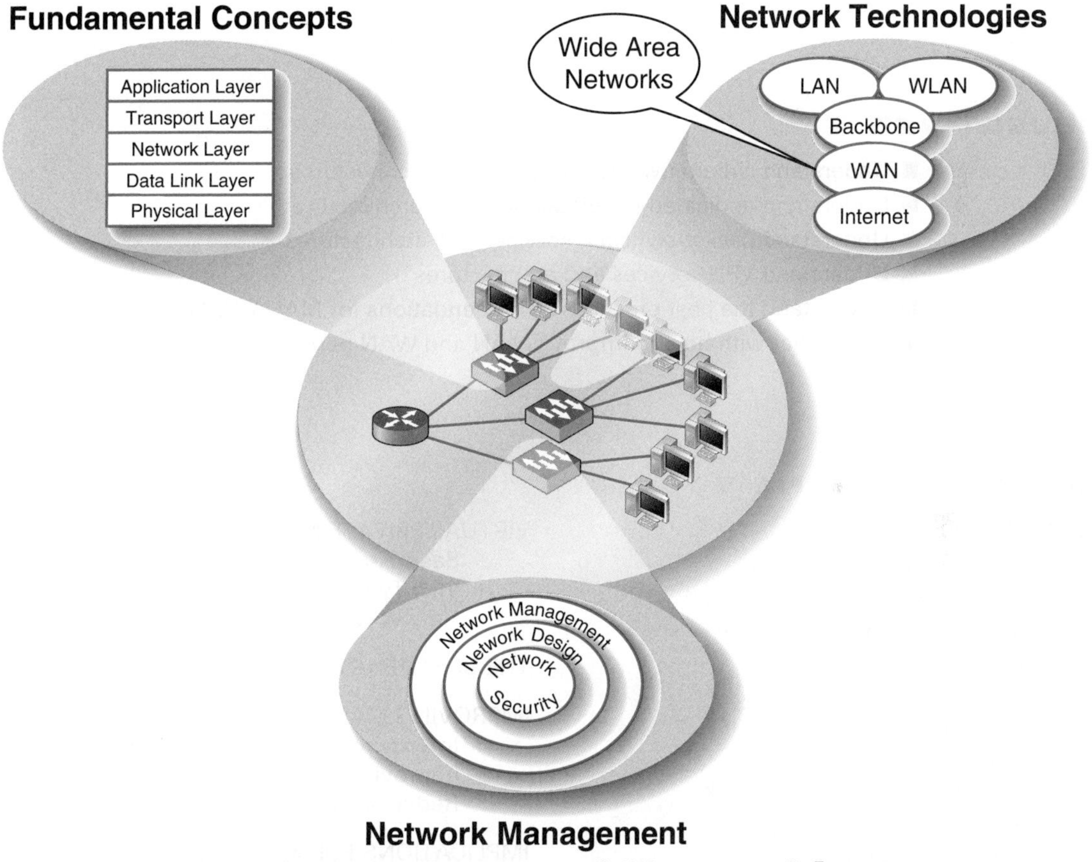

The Three Faces of Networking

MOST ORGANIZATIONS do not build their own metropolitan or long-distance communication circuits, preferring instead to lease them from common carriers or to use the Internet. Therefore, this chapter focuses on the MAN/WAN architectures and telecommunications services offered by common carriers for use in MANs and WANs, not the underlying technology that the carriers use to provide them. We discuss the four principal types of MAN and WAN services that are available: circuit-switched services, dedicated-circuit services, packet-switched services, and virtual private network (VPN) services. We conclude by discussing how to improve MAN and WAN performance and how to select services to build MANs and WANs.

OBJECTIVES ▼

- Understand circuit-switched services and architectures
- Understand dedicated-circuit services and architectures
- Understand packet-switched services and architectures
- Understand VPN services and architectures
- Understand the best practice recommendations for MAN/WAN design
- Be familiar with how to improve MAN and WAN performance

CHAPTER OUTLINE ▼

INTRODUCTION

Metropolitan area networks (MANs) typically span between 3 and 30 miles and connect BNs and LANs. MANs also provide dial-in and dial-out capability to LANs, BNs, and mainframes and access to the Internet. WANs connect BNs and MANs across longer distances, often hundreds or thousands of miles. Figure 1.2 in Chapter 1 shows the roles that LANs, BNs, MANs, and WANs play.

The communication media used in MANs and WANs were described in Chapter 3 (e.g., twisted-pair, wire coaxial cable, fiber optics, microwave, satellite, infrared). Although some organizations build their own MANs and WANs using these media, most do not. Most organizations cannot afford to lay long stretches of cable, build microwave towers, or lease satellites. Instead, most rent or lease circuits from **common carriers,** private companies such as AT&T, Bell Canada, Sprint, BellSouth, and so on that sell or lease communication services and facilities to the public. As a customer, you do not lease physical cables per se; you simply lease circuits that provide certain transmission characteristics. The carrier decides whether it will use twisted-pair, coaxial, fiber optics, or other media for its circuits.

In this chapter, we examine the MAN and WAN architectures and technologies from the viewpoint of a network manager, rather than that of a common carrier. We focus less on internal operations and how the specific technologies work, and more on how these services are offered to network managers and how they can be used to build networks because network managers are less concerned with how the services work and more concerned with how they can use them effectively.

Likewise, we will focus on MAN and WAN services in North America because the majority of our readers are in North America. Although there are many similarities in the way data communications networks and services have evolved in different countries, there also are many differences. Most countries have a federal government agency that regulates data and voice communications. In the United States, the agency is the **Federal Communications Commission (FCC);** in Canada, it is the **Canadian Radio-Television and Telecommunications Commission (CRTC).** Each state or province also has its own **public utilities commission (PUC)** to regulate communications within its borders.

Common carriers are profit oriented, and their primary products are services for voice and data transmissions, both over traditional wired circuits as well as cellular services. Common carriers often supply a broad range of computer-based services, such as the manufacturing and marketing of specialized communication hardware and software. A common carrier that provides local telephone services (e.g., BellSouth) is commonly called a **local exchange carrier (LEC),** whereas one that provides long-distance services (e.g., AT&T) is commonly called an **interexchange carrier (IXC).** As the LECs move into the long-distance market and IXCs move into the local telephone market, this distinction may disappear.

CIRCUIT-SWITCHED NETWORKS

Circuit-switched networks are the oldest and simplest approach to MAN and WAN circuits. These services operate over the **public switched telephone network (PSTN);** that is, the telephone networks operated by the common carriers such as AT&T, BellSouth, and so on. When you telephone someone, you are using the PSTN. The first service we discuss is the dial-up service you use when you call an ISP with a dial-up modem—but first we need to discuss the basic architecture shared by all circuit-switched services.

At this point, you're probably wondering who uses dial-up any more? Most of my students use broadband Internet, which we dicuss in the next chapter. However, statistics show that less than 25 percent of the U.S. and Canadian population has broadband access; believe it or not, most of us still use dial-up—you just won't find many dial-up users on college campuses.

Basic Architecture

Circuit-switched services use a **cloud architecture.** The users lease connection points (e.g., telephone lines) into the common carrier's network, which is called the **cloud**[1] (Figure 9.1). A person (or computer) dials the telephone number of the destination computer and establishes a temporary circuit between the two computers. The computers

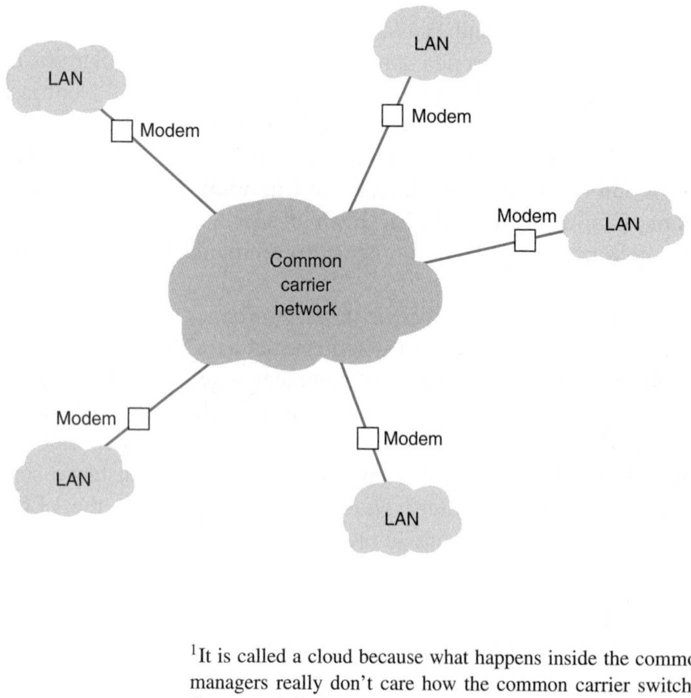

FIGURE 9.1 Dialed circuit services. LAN = local area network

[1] It is called a cloud because what happens inside the common carrier's network is hidden from view. Network managers really don't care how the common carrier switches the circuit inside their network, just as long as the network is fast, accurate, and reliable.

exchange data, and when the task is complete, the circuit is disconnected (e.g., by hanging up the phone).

This architecture is very flexible. Circuits can be established as needed between any computers attached to the cloud at any point. However, data can be transmitted only while a circuit is established, and only to the one location it connects to. If a computer needs to send data to a number of other locations, a series of temporary circuits must be established with and later disconnected from each location, one after another. In general, only a limited number of circuits can be established from or to any one location at a time (e.g., each location has only so many telephone lines).

Cloud-based designs are simpler for the organization because they move the burden of network design and management inside the cloud from the organization to the common carrier. Network managers do not need to worry about the amount of traffic sent between each computer; they just need to specify the amount of traffic entering and leaving each computer and buy the appropriate size and number of connections into the PSTN. However, this comes at a price. Cloud-based designs can be more expensive because users must pay for each connection into the network and pay on the basis of the amount of time each circuit is used. Cloud-based designs are often used when network managers are uncertain of network demand, particularly in a new or rapidly growing network.

There are two basic types of switched-circuit services in use today: POTS and ISDN.

Plain Old Telephone Service

Plain old telephone service (POTS) is the name for the dial-up services you or your parents used at one time. To use POTS, you need to lease a circuit into the network (i.e., a telephone line) and install special equipment (i.e., a modem) to enable your computer to talk to the PSTN. To transfer data to and from another computer on the network, you instruct your modem to dial the other computer's telephone. Once the modem in your computer connects to the modem at the other end, you can transfer data back and forth. When you are done, you hang up and can then call another computer if you wish. Today, POTS is most commonly used to connect to the Internet, but you can also use it to communicate directly with a private non-Internet server.

POTS may use different circuit paths between the two computers each time a number is dialed. Some circuits have more noise and distortion than others, so the quality and maximum data transmission rate can vary. Typical data rates are between 33 kbps and 56 kbps.

Charges for direct dialing are based on the distance between the two telephones (in miles) and the number of minutes the connection is used. Data communications users pay the same rate as voice communications users. In general, most local calls are free, but this depends on the type of local telephone service you have purchased. Long-distance calls are charged at the rate for which you have contracted with your long-distance carrier.

Wide area telephone services (WATSs) are special-rate services that allows calls for both voice communications and data transmission to be purchased in large quantities. For example, you might purchase 100 hours of usage per month for one fixed rate and be charged so many dollars per hour thereafter.

ISDN

The first generation of **integrated services digital network (ISDN)** combines voice, video, and data over the same digital circuit. Because there is a newer version of ISDN, the original version is occasionally called **narrowband ISDN,** but we will just use the term ISDN. ISDN is widely available from a number of common carriers in North America.

To use ISDN, users first need to lease connection points in the PSTN, which are telephone lines just like POTS. Next, they must have special equipment to connect their computers (or networks) into the PSTN. Users need an ISDN **network terminator (NT-1** or **NT-2)** that functions much like a hub, and a NIC (called a **terminal adapter [TA]** or even an "ISDN modem") in all computers attached to the NT-1/NT-2. In most cases, the ISDN service appears identical to the regular dialed telephone service, with the exception that usually (but not always) each device attached to the NT-1/NT-2 needs a unique **service profile identifier (SPID)** to identify it. To connect to another computer using ISDN, you dial that computer's telephone number using the ISDN NIC in much the same way as you would with a modem on a regular telephone line.

ISDN has long been more of a concept than a reliable service in North America. It has been available since the late 1970s, although it has not been widely adopted. Its largest problems are a lack of standards and a lack of interest from common carriers. Acceptance of ISDN has also been slowed because equipment vendors and common carriers have conflicting interpretations of the ISDN standards and because the data rates it offers are low compared with newer services. Skeptics claim that ISDN actually stands for "I still don't know," "I still don't need it" or "It still does nothing." ISDN offers two types of "normal" or narrowband service, plus one higher-speed broadband service.

Basic Rate Interface

Basic rate interface (BRI) (sometimes called basic access service or **2B+D**) provides a communication circuit with two 64-Kbps digital transmission channels (called B channels) and one 16-Kbps control signaling channel (called a D channel). The two B channels handle digitized voice, data, and image transmissions, providing a total of 128 Kbps. The D channel is used for control messages such as acknowledgments, call setup and termination, and other functions such as automatic number identification. Some common carriers sell just one single 64-Kbps channel to those customers needing less capacity than full BRI.

One advantage of BRI is that it can be installed in many existing telephone locations without adding any new cable. If the connection from the customer's telephone to the common carrier's end office is less than 3.5 miles, the ISDN line can use the existing two pairs of twisted-pair wires. The only changes are the end connections at the customer's location and at the carrier's end office. If the connection is longer than 3.5 miles, then new cable will have to be laid.

Primary Rate Interface

Primary rate interface (PRI) (also called primary access service or **23B+D**) is typically offered to commercial customers. It consists of 23 64-Kbps B channels plus 1 64-Kbps D channel. PRI has almost the same capacity as a T1 circuit (1.544 Mbps). In Europe, PRI is defined as 30 B channels plus 1 D channel, making interconnection between America and Europe difficult.

Broadband Integrated Services Digital Network **Broadband ISDN (B-ISDN)** is very different from narrowband ISDN—so different, in fact, that it really is not ISDN. It is a circuit-switched service, but B-ISDN uses ATM to move data from one end point to the other (more on ATM later in this chapter). B-ISDN is backward-compatible with narrowband ISDN, which means it can accept narrowband BRI and PRI transmissions. B-ISDN currently defines three services. The first is a full-duplex channel that operates at 155.52 Mbps; the second provides a full-duplex channel that operates at 622.08 Mbps; and the third is an asymmetrical service with two simplex channels, one from the subscriber at 155.52 Mbps and one from the host to the subscriber at 622.08 Mbps. The first two services are intended for normal bidirectional information exchange. The third (asymmetrical) service is intended to be used for information distribution services such as digital broadcast television.

DEDICATED-CIRCUIT NETWORKS

There are three main problems with POTS and ISDN circuit-switched networks. First, each connection goes through the regular telephone network on a different circuit. These circuits may vary in quality, meaning that although one connection will be fairly clear, the next call may be noisy. Second, the data transmission rates on these circuits are usually low. Generally speaking, transmission rates range from 28.8 Kbps to 56 Kbps for dialed POTS circuits to 128 Kbps to 1.5 Mbps for ISDN circuits. Third, you usually pay per use for circuit-switched services. One alternative is to establish a dedicated-circuit network, in which the user leases circuits from the common carrier for his or her exclusive use 24 hours per day, 7 days per week.

Basic Architecture

With a dedicated-circuit network, you lease circuits from common carriers. All connections are point to point, from one building in one city to another building in the same or a different city. The carrier installs the circuit connections at the two end points of the circuit and makes the connection between them. The circuits still run through the common carrier's cloud, but the network behaves as if you have your own physical circuits running from one point to another (Figure 9.2).

Once again, the user leases the desired circuit from the common carrier (specifying the physical end points of the circuit) and installs the equipment needed to connect computers and devices (e.g., routers or switches) to the circuit. This equipment may include multiplexers or a **channel service unit (CSU)** and/or a **data service unit (DSU);** a CSU/DSU is the WAN equivalent of a NIC in a LAN.

Unlike circuit-switched services that typically use a pay-per-use model, dedicated circuits are billed at a flat fee per month, and the user has unlimited use of the circuit. Once you sign a contract, making changes can be expensive because it means rewiring the buildings and signing a new contract with the carrier. Therefore, dedicated circuits require more care in network design than do switched circuits, both in terms of locations and the amount of capacity you purchase.

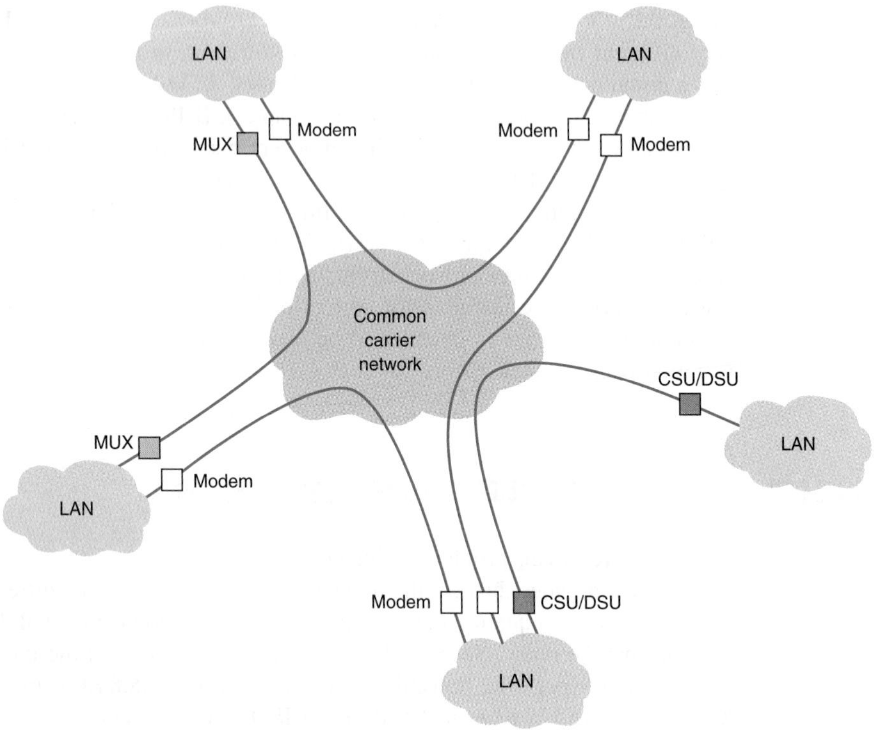

FIGURE 9.2 Dedicated-circuit services. CSU = channel service unit; DSU = data service unit; MUX = multiplexer

There are three basic architectures used in dedicated-circuit networks: ring, star, and mesh. In practice, most networks use a combination of architectures. For example, a **distributed star architecture** has a series of star networks that are connected by a **mesh** or ring architecture.

Ring Architecture A **ring architecture** connects all computers in a closed loop with each computer linked to the next (Figure 9.3). The circuits are full-duplex or half-duplex circuits, meaning that messages flow in both directions around the ring. Computers in the ring may send data in one direction or the other, depending on which direction is the shortest to the destination.

One disadvantage of the ring topology is that messages can take a long time to travel from the sender to the receiver. Messages usually travel through several computers and circuits before they reach their destination, so traffic delays can build up very quickly if one circuit or computer becomes overloaded. A long delay in any one circuit or computer can have significant impacts on the entire network.

In general, the failure of any one circuit or computer in a ring network means that the network can continue to function. Messages are simply routed away from the failed circuit or computer in the opposite direction around the ring. However, if the network is operating close to its capacity, this will dramatically increase transmission times because

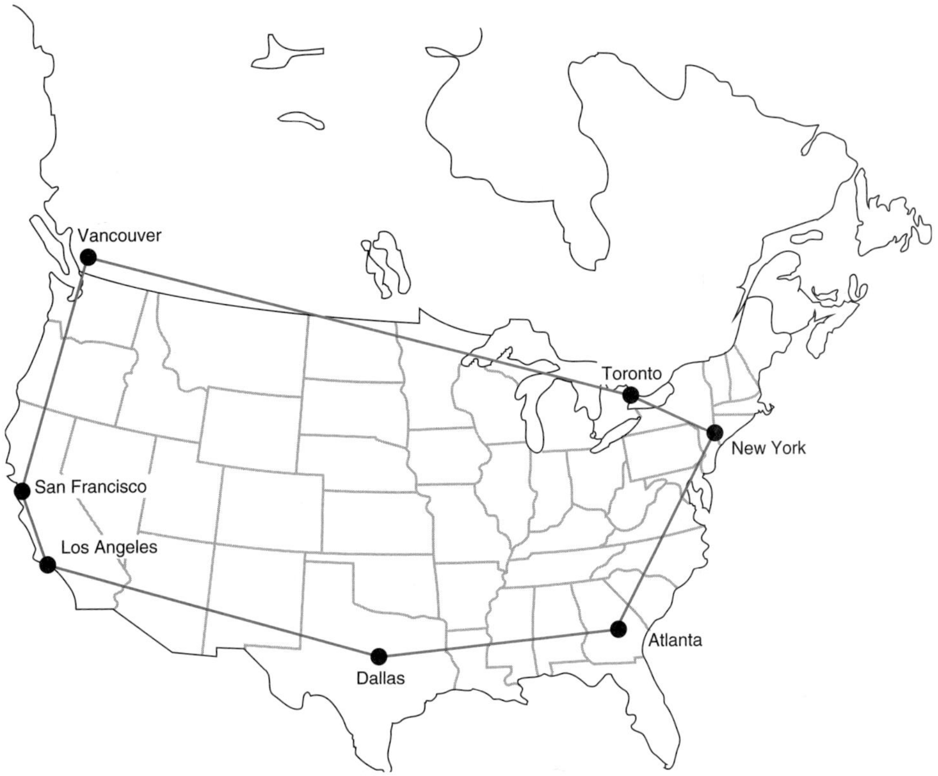

FIGURE 9.3 Ring-based design

the traffic on the remaining part of the network may come close to doubling (because all traffic originally routed in the direction of the failed link will now be routed in the opposite direction through the longest way around the ring).

Star Architecture A **star architecture** connects all computers to one central computer that routes messages to the appropriate computer (Figure 9.4). The star topology is easy to manage because the central computer receives and routes all messages in the network. It can also be faster than the ring network because any message needs to travel through at most two circuits to reach its destination, whereas messages may have to travel through far more circuits in the ring network. However, the star topology is the most susceptible to traffic problems because the central computer must process all messages on the network. The central computer must have sufficient capacity to handle traffic peaks, or it may become overloaded and network performance will suffer.

In general, the failure of any one circuit or computer affects only the one computer on that circuit. However, if the central computer fails, the entire network fails because all traffic must flow through it. It is critical that the central computer be extremely reliable.

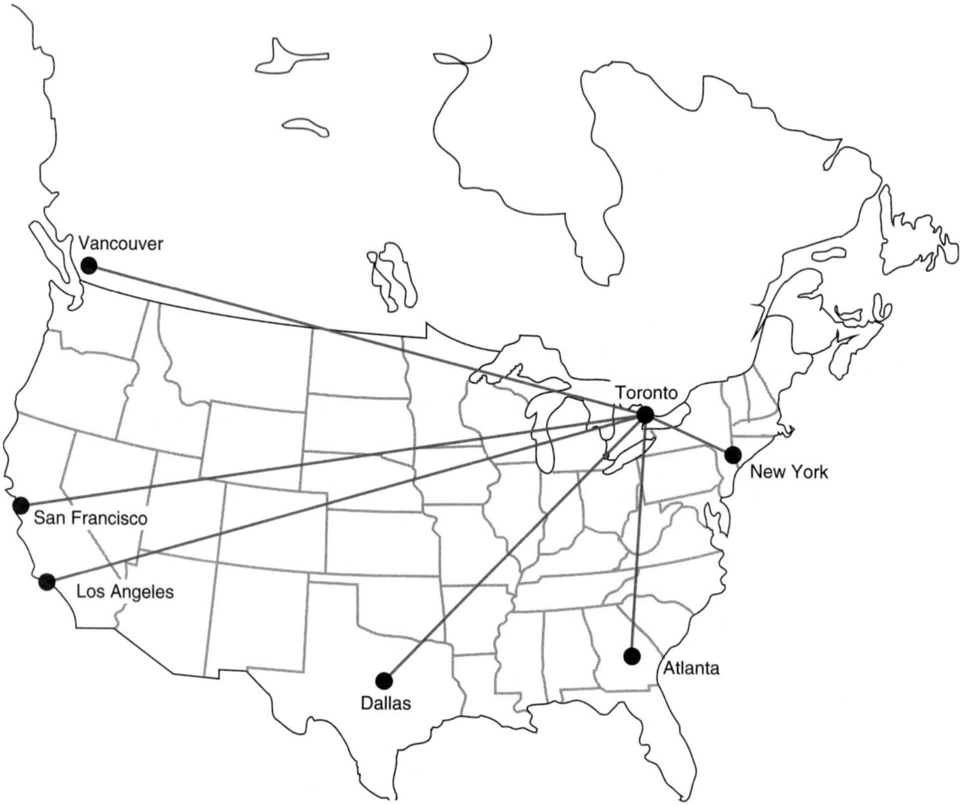

FIGURE 9.4 Star-based design

Mesh Architecture In a **full-mesh architecture,** every computer is connected to every other computer (Figure 9.5a). Full-mesh networks are seldom used because of the extremely high cost. **Partial-mesh architecture** (usually called just **mesh architecture**), in which many, but not all, computers are connected, is far more common (Figure 9.5b). Most WANs use partial-mesh topologies.

The effects of the loss of computers or circuits in a mesh network depend entirely on the circuits available in the network. If there are many possible routes through the network, the loss of one or even several circuits or computers may have few effects beyond the specific computers involved. However, if there are only a few circuits in the network, the loss of even one circuit or computer may seriously impair the network.

In general, mesh networks combine the performance benefits of both ring networks and star networks. Mesh networks usually provide relatively short routes through the network (compared with ring networks) and provide many possible routes through the network to prevent any one circuit or computer from becoming overloaded when there is a lot of traffic (compared with star networks in which all traffic goes through one computer).

The drawback is that mesh networks use decentralized routing so that each computer in the network performs its own routing. This requires more processing by each

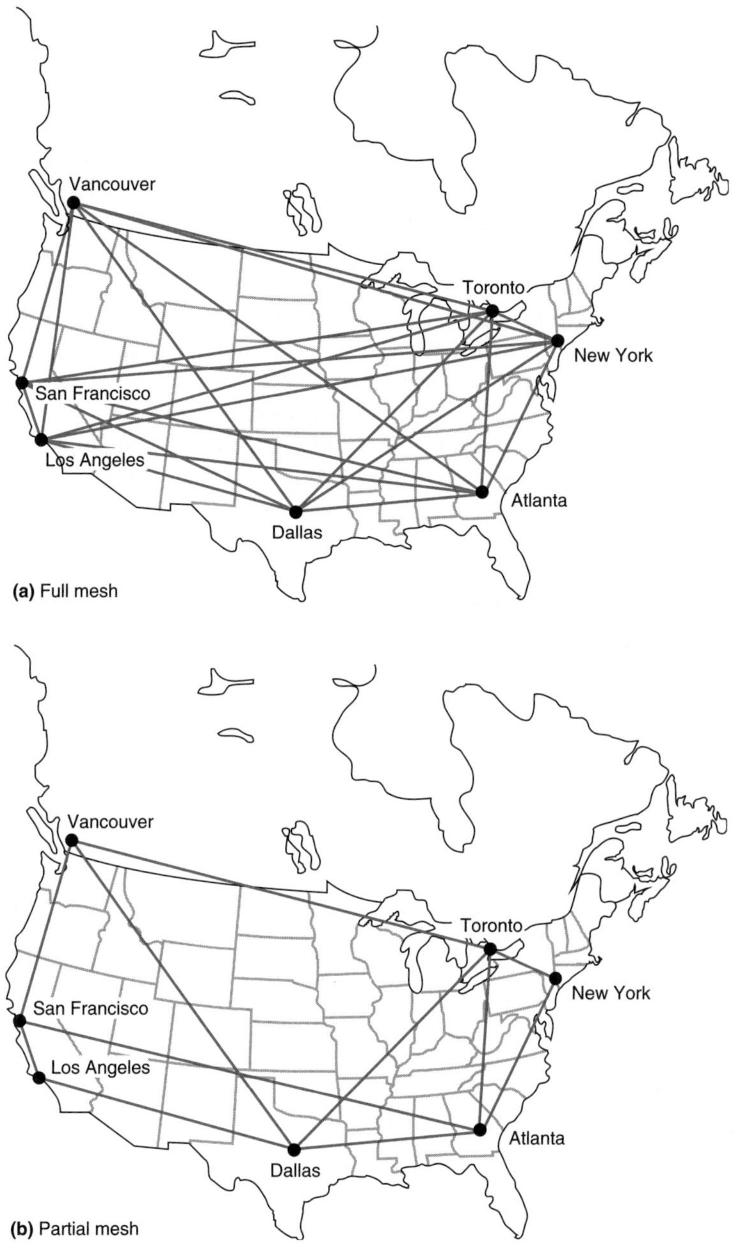

FIGURE 9.5 Mesh design

computer in the network than in star or ring networks. Also, the transmission of network status information (e.g., how busy each computer is) "wastes" network capacity.

There are two types of **dedicated-circuit services** in common use today: T carrier services and synchronous optical network (SONET) services. Both T carrier and SONET have their own data link protocols, which are beyond the focus of this chapter.

T Carrier Services

T carrier circuits are the most commonly used form of dedicated-circuit services in North America today. As with all dedicated-circuit services, you lease a dedicated circuit from one building in one city to another building in the same or different city. Costs are a fixed amount per month, regardless of how much or how little traffic flows through the circuit. There are several types of T carrier circuits (Figure 9.6).

A **T1 circuit** (also called a DS1 circuit) provides a data rate of 1.544 Mbps. T1 circuits can be used to transmit data but often are used to transmit both data and voice. In this case, inverse TDM provides 24 64-Kbps circuits.[2] Digitized voice using PCM requires a 64-Kbps circuit (see Chapter 3), so a T1 circuit enables 24 simultaneous voice channels. Most common carriers make extensive use of PCM internally and transmit most of their voice telephone calls in digital format using PCM, so you will see many digital services offering combinations of the standard PCM 64-Kbps circuit.

A **T2 circuit,** which transmits data at a rate of 6.312 Mbps, is an inverse multiplexed bundle of four T1 circuits. A **T3 circuit** allows transmission at a rate of 44.736 Mbps although most articles refer to this rate as 45 megabits per second. This is equal to the capacity of 28 T1 circuits. T3 circuits are becoming popular as the transmission medium for corporate MANs and WANs because of their higher data rates. At low speed, these T3 circuits can be used as 672 different 64-Kbps channels or voice channels. A **T4 circuit** transmits at 274.176 Mbps, which is equal to the capacity of 178 T1 circuits.

Fractional T1, sometimes called **FT1,** offers portions of a 1.544-Mbps T1 circuit for a fraction of its full cost. Many (but not all) common carriers offer sets of 64 Kbps DS-0 channels as FT1 circuits. The most common FT1 services provide 128 Kbps, 256 Kbps, 384 Kbps, 512 Kbps, and 768 Kbps.

Synchronous Optical Network

The **synchronous optical network (SONET)** is the American standard (ANSI) for high-speed dedicated-circuit services. The ITU-T recently standardized an almost identical service that easily interconnects with SONET under the name **synchronous digital hierarchy (SDH).**

T Carrier Designation	DS Designation	Speed
FT1	DS0	64 Kbps
T1	DS1	1.544 Mbps
T2	DS2	6.312 Mbps
T3	DS3	44.376 Mbps
T4	DS4	274.176 Mbps

FIGURE 9.6 T carrier services

[2]If you multiply 24 circuits by 64 Kbps per circuit, you will get 1.536 Mbps, not 1.544 Mbps. This is because some of the 1.544-Mbps circuit capacity is used by the common carrier for control signals used to frame the data (i.e., mark the start and stop of packets).

SONET Designation	SDH Designation	Speed
OC-1		51.84 Mbps
OC-3	STM-1	155.52 Mbps
OC-12	STM-4	622.08 Mbps
OC-24	STM-8	1.244 Gbps
OC-48	STM-16	2.488 Gbps
OC-192	STM-24	9.953 Gbps
OC-768	STM-256x	39.813 Gbps

FIGURE 9.7 SONET (synchronous optical network) and SDH (synchronous digital hierarchy) services. OC = optical carrier (level)

SONET transmission speeds begin at the OC-1 level (optical carrier level 1) of 51.84 Mbps. Each succeeding rate in the SONET fiber hierarchy is defined as a multiple of OC-1, with SONET data rates defined as high as OC-768, or about 40 Gbps. Figure 9.7 presents the commonly used SONET and SDH services. Each level above OC-1 is created by an inverse multiplexer. Notice that the slowest SONET transmission rate (OC-1) of 51.84 Mbps is slightly faster than the T3 rate of 44.376 Mbps.

PACKET-SWITCHED NETWORKS

Packet-switched networks are quite different from the two types of networks discussed previously. For both circuit-switched and dedicated-circuit networks, a circuit was established between the two communicating computers. This circuit provided a guaranteed data transmission capability that was available for use by only those two computers. For example, if computer A is to transmit data using an ISDN BRI connection to computer B, the connection at both A and B must be available. Once in use for this transmission, it is assigned solely to that transmission. No other transmission is possible

MANAGEMENT FOCUS 9.1 CAREGROUP'S DEDICATED CIRCUIT NETWORK

CareGroup Healthcare System operates six hospitals in the Boston area and uses a metropolitan area network (MAN) and wide area network to connect them together to share clinical data (Figure 9.8). The three major hospitals have relatively high data needs and therefore are connected to one another and the main data center via a MAN that uses a set of SONET OC-1 circuits in a ring architecture.

The other three hospitals, with lower data needs, are connected to the data center via a set of T3 circuits in a star architecture. The data center also has a T3 connection into the Internet to enable its 3,000 or so doctors to access clinical data from their private practice offices or from home.

SOURCE: "Using the Web to Extend Patient Care," *Network World,* May 29, 2000.

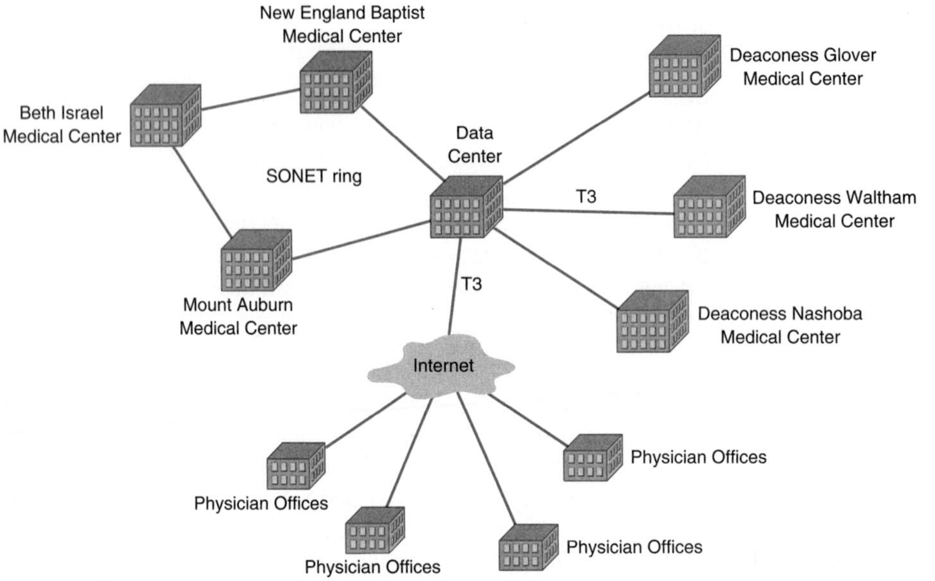

FIGURE 9.8 CareGroup's metropolitan and wide area networks. SONET = synchronous optical network

until the circuit is closed. So, for example, if computer C attempts to reach computer B, it will have to wait until the circuit is closed. In contrast, packet-switched services enable multiple connections to exist simultaneously between computers over the same physical circuit, just like LANs and BNs.

Basic Architecture

With packet-switched services, the user again buys a connection into the common carrier cloud (Figure 9.9). The user pays a fixed fee for the connection into the network (depending on the type and capacity of the service) and is charged for the number of packets transmitted.

The user's connection into the network is a **packet assembly/disassembly device (PAD),** which can be owned and operated by the customer or by the common carrier. The PAD converts the sender's data into the network layer and data link layer packets used by the packet network and sends them through the packet-switched network. At the other end, another PAD reassembles the packets back into the network layer and data link layer protocols expected by the destination and delivers it to the appropriate computer.

One of the key advantages of packet-switched services is that different locations can have different connection speeds into the common carrier cloud. The PAD compensates for differences in transmission speed between sender and receiver; for example, the circuit at the sender might be 1.5 Mbps whereas the receiver only has a 64-Kbps circuit. In contrast, a dial-up circuit or a dedicated circuit must have the same speed at both the sender and receiver.

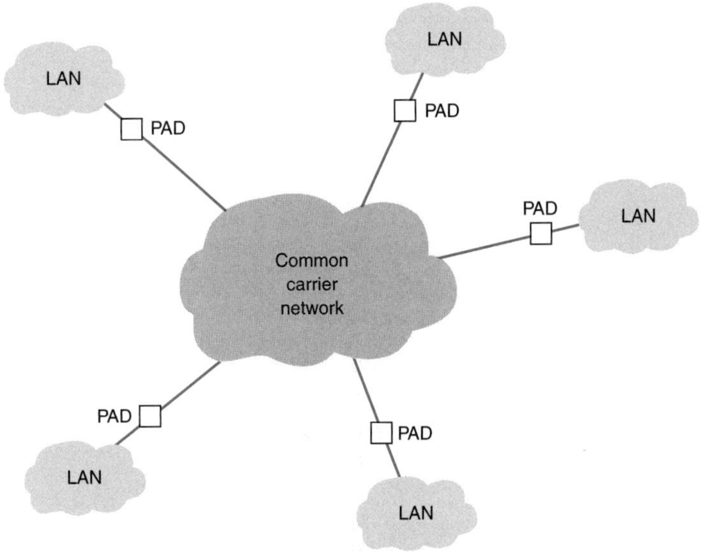

FIGURE 9.9 Packet-switched services. LAN = local area network; PAD = packet assembly/disassembly device

Packet-switched networks enable packets from separate messages with different destinations to be *interleaved* for transmission, unlike switched circuits and dedicated circuits. Packet switching is popular because most data communications consist of short bursts of data with intervening spaces that usually last longer than the actual burst of data. Packet switching takes advantage of this characteristic by interleaving bursts of data from many users to maximize use of the shared communication network. Figure 9.10 shows a packet-switching connection between six different cities. The little boat-shaped figures (shown on the communication circuits) represent individual packets from separate messages.

Although the packets in one data stream may mix with several other data streams during their journey, it is unlikely that packets from two different data streams will travel together during the entire length of their transmission. The two communicating computers do not need to know through which intermediate devices their data are routed because the packet network takes care of it by either of two methods.

The first method, called **datagram,** is a connectionless service. It adds a destination address and sequence number to each packet, in addition to information about the data stream to which the packet belongs. In this case, a route is chosen for each packet as it is accepted into the packet network. Each packet may follow a different route through the network. At the destination address, the sequence number tells the network how to reassemble the packets into a continuous message. The sequence number is necessary because different routes may deliver packets at different speeds, so data packets often arrive out of sequence. Few networks today use datagrams for data transfer.

The second and more common routing method is a connection-oriented approach called a **virtual circuit.** In this case, the packet-switched network establishes what appears to be one end-to-end circuit between the sender and receiver. All packets for that transmission take the same route over the virtual circuit that has been set up for that particular

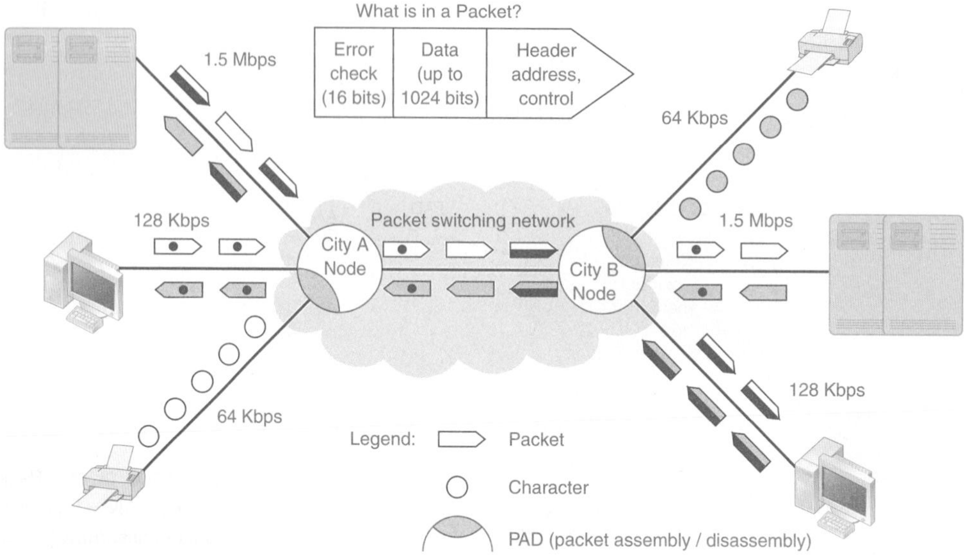

FIGURE 9.10 Packet-switching concepts

transmission. The two computers believe they have a dedicated point-to-point circuit, but in fact, they do not.

Virtual circuits are usually **permanent virtual circuits (PVCs),** which means that they are defined for frequent and consistent use by the network. They do not change unless the network manager changes the network. Some common carriers also permit the use of **switched virtual circuits (SVCs)** although this is not usual. Changing PVCs is done using software, but common carriers usually charge each time a PVC is established or removed. It often takes days or weeks to create or take down PVCs although this is mostly due to poor management by common carriers rather than due to technology issues, so this may change.

Because most network managers build packet-switched networks using PVCs, *most packet-switched networks behave like dedicated-circuit networks.* At first glance, the basic architecture in Figure 9.9 looks very similar to the cloud mesh of switched-circuit services, and in fact, they are very similar because data can move from any computer attached to the cloud to any other on the cloud. However, because virtually all data-intensive networks use PVCs, this means that the network is actually built using virtual circuits that are the software equivalent of the hardware-based dedicated circuits. As a result, packet-switched networks often have star, ring, and mesh topologies similar to those of dedicated-circuit networks. However, because the PVCs are in software, they are much easier to change than the hardware circuits of dedicated-circuit networks.

Most common carriers permit users to specify two different types of data rates that are negotiated per connection and for each PVC as it is established. The **committed information rate (CIR)** is the data rate the PVC must guarantee to transmit. If the network accepts the connection, it guarantees to provide that level of service. Most connections also specify a **maximum allowable rate (MAR),** which is the maximum rate that the network will attempt to provide, over and above the CIR. The circuit will attempt to transmit all packets up to the MAR, but all packets that exceed the CIR are marked as **discard eligible (DE).** If the network becomes overloaded, DE packets are discarded. So although users can transmit more data than the CIR, they do so at a risk of lost packets and the need to retransmit them.

Packet-switched services are often provided by different common carriers than the one from which organizations get their usual telephone and data services. Therefore, organizations often lease a dedicated circuit (e.g., T1) from their offices to the packet-switched network **point of presence (POP).** The POP is the location at which the packet-switched network (or any common carrier network, for that matter) connects into the local telephone exchange.

There are five types of packet-switched services: X.25, ATM, frame relay, switched multimegabit data service, and Ethernet service. Several common carriers (e.g., Sprint) have announced that they intend to stop offering all services except Ethernet and Internet services (see Chapter 10). Other carriers have hinted at the same decision. Over the next few years these technologies may disappear.

X.25

The oldest packet-switched service is **X.25,** a standard developed by ITU-T. X.25 offers datagram, SVC, and PVC services. X.25 uses the LAP-B data link layer protocol and the PLP network-layer protocol. When packets arrive at the PAD, connecting the user's network to the packet-switched network, their data link (e.g., Ethernet) and network layer (e.g., IP) packets are removed and PLP and LAP-B packets are substituted. Packets are moved through the X.25 network in much the same way as in TCP/IP networks, with the LAP-B packet error checked and replaced at each hop in the network. When they arrive at the edge of the X.25 network, new destination protocols (e.g., Ethernet, IP) are created and the message is sent on its way. X.25 is sometimes called a **reliable packet service** because it provides complete error checking and guaranteed delivery on all packets transmitted.

Although common in Europe, X.25 is not widespread in North America. The primary reason is its transmission speed. For many years, the maximum speed into North American X.25 networks was 64 Kbps, but this has increased to 2.048 Mbps, which is the European standard for ISDN. However, for many users, 2.048 Mbps is still not fast enough.

Asynchronous Transfer Mode

Asynchronous transfer mode (ATM), also standardized, is a newer technology than X.25. ATM for BNs was discussed in the previous chapter. ATM for the MAN and WAN is essentially the same.

ATM is similar to X.25 in that it provides packet-switched services, but it has four distinct operating characteristics that differ from X.25. First, ATM performs encapsulation of packets, so packets are delivered unchanged through the network.

Second, ATM provides no error control in the network; error control is the responsibility of the source and destination. (ATM is considered an **unreliable packet service.**)

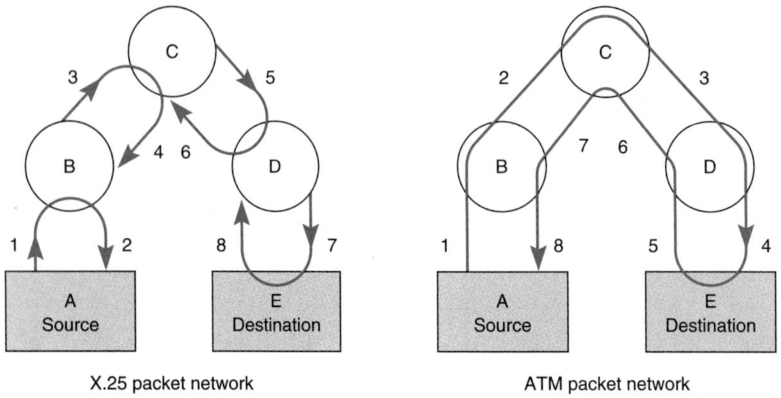

FIGURE 9.11 Asynchronous transfer mode (ATM) compared with X.25 packet switching. With X.25, each node sends an acknowledgment immediately on receiving a packet. With ATM, the final destination sends an acknowledgment, making this technique faster than the X.25 technique

Because the user's data link packet remains intact, it is simple for the devices at the edge of the ATM network to check the error-control information in the packet to ensure that no errors have occurred and to request transmission of damaged or lost packets. Figure 9.11 illustrates the difference in error control between X.25 networks and ATM networks. The left side shows that when an X.25 packet leaves its source A and moves through node B, to node C, to node D, and finally to destination E, each intermediate node acknowledges the packet as it passes. The right side of the figure shows how an ATM packet moves through node B, node C, node D, and on to destination E. When destination E receives the packet correctly, a single acknowledgment is sent back through the nodes to source A, as shown by the numbers *5, 6, 7,* and *8.* Some common carriers have started using the term **fast packet services** instead to refer to these services that do not provide error control—it sounds better for marketing!

Third, ATM provides extensive QoS information that enables the setting of very precise priorities among different types of transmissions: high priority for voice and video, lower priority for e-mail.

Finally, ATM is scalable; it is easy to multiplex basic ATM circuits into much faster ATM circuits. Most common carriers offer ATM circuits that provide the same data transmission rates as SONET: 51.84 Mbps, 466.56 Mbps, 622.08 Mbps, and so on up to 39 Gbps (OC-768). New versions called T1 ATM (1.544 Mbps) and T3 ATM (45 Mbps) are also available.

Frame Relay

Frame relay, just recently standardized, is an even newer packet-switching technology that transmits data faster than X.25 but slower than ATM; it has sometimes been called a poor man's ATM. It is one of the most commonly used WAN services in the world. Like ATM, frame relay performs encapsulation of packets, so packets are delivered unchanged through the network. Like ATM, it is an unreliable packet service because it does not perform error control. Frame relay checks for errors but simply discards packets with errors. It is up to the software at the source and destination to control for lost messages.

Frame relay does not yet provide QoS capabilities, but this is under development. Different common carriers offer frame relay networks with different transmission speeds.

MANAGEMENT FOCUS 9.2 FRAME RELAY IN CALIFORNIA

Ten communities in northern San Diego County, California, work together to provide fire department services to their citizens. The group spans 50 fire stations that needed to quickly and efficiently share voice, video, and computer data.

They implemented a converged frame relay network, using mostly T1 speed circuits (1.5 Mbps) into the frame relay network operated by AT&T. Each fire station has a PAD that connects their station's voice and data network into the AT&T frame relay cloud. The PAD uses MPLS (see Chapter 8) to tag all incoming IP packets with the PVC that leads to the destination address. As the packet leaves the frame relay network, the MPLS information is removed, and an Ethernet frame added for delivery into the destination station's network.

SOURCE: "California Fire Departments Improve Response Time Thanks to Integrated IP Network," ATT.com.

Most offer a range of CIR speeds that include 56 Kbps, 128 Kbps, 256 Kbps, 384 Kbps, 1.5 Mbps, 2 Mbps, and 45 Mbps.

Ethernet Services

Although we have seen rapid increases in capacities and sharp decreases in costs in LAN and BN technologies, changes in MAN and WAN services offered by common carriers

A Day in the Life: Networking and Telecommunications Vice President

A vice president is a person in an executive-level position whose focus is to set the strategic direction for the organization. A vice president has very little to do with the day-to-day operations; much like an Admiral in a Navy fleet, he or she defines the direction, but the individual captains running each ship actually make sure that everything that needs to happen gets done.

The vice president works with the chief information officer (CIO) and other executive leadership of the organization to identify the key organizational goals that have implications for the network. The vice president works with his or her staff to revise the strategic networking plan to ensure that the network is capable of supporting the organization's goals. The key elements of the strategic plan are the networking architectures, key technologies, and vendors. Once the strategy has been set, the vice president's job is to instruct the senior managers to execute the strategy and then let them do their jobs.

In most cases, the changes to the networking strategic plan are relatively minor, but sometimes there are dramatic changes that require a major shift in strategic direction. For example, in recent years, we've seen a major change in the fundamental capabilities of network tools and applications. Our architecture strategy during the 1990s was driven by the fact that network management tools were poor and maintenance costs per server were high; the fundamental architecture strategy was to minimize the number of servers. Today, network management tools are much better, maintenance costs per server are significantly lower, and network traffic has changed both in volume and in the number and complexity of services supported (e.g., Web, e-mail, H.323, IPv6); the strategy today is to provide a greater number of servers, each of which is dedicated to supporting one specific type of traffic.

With thanks to Brian Voss

saw only modest changes in the 1990s. That changed in 2000 with the introduction of several Internet startups (e.g., Yipes) offering **Ethernet services.**

Most organizations today use Ethernet and IP in the LAN and BN environment, yet the MAN/WAN packet network services (X.25, ATM, and frame relay) discussed earlier use different layer-2 protocols. Any LAN or BN traffic, therefore, must be translated or encapsulated into a new protocol and destination addresses generated for the new protocol. This takes time, slowing network throughput. It also adds complexity, meaning that companies must add staff knowledgeable in the different MAN/WAN protocols, software, and hardware these technologies require. This is one reason many common carriers are starting to call these four technologies "legacy technologies," signaling their demise.

Each of the preceding packet services uses the traditional PSTN provided by the common carriers such as AT&T and BellSouth. In contrast, Ethernet services bypass the PSTN; companies offering Ethernet services have laid their own gigabit Ethernet fiber-optic networks in large cities. When an organization signs up for service, the packet network company installs new fiber-optic cables from their citywide MAN backbone into the organization's office complex and connects it to an Ethernet switch. The organization simply plugs its network into its Ethernet switch and begins using the service. All traffic entering the packet network must be Ethernet, using IP or MPLS (see Chapter 8).

Currently, Ethernet services offer CIR speeds of 1 Mbps to 40 Gbps, in 1-Mbps increments at about one quarter the cost of traditional packet-switched networks. Because this is an emerging technology, we should see many changes in the next few years.

VIRTUAL PRIVATE NETWORKS

A **virtual private network (VPN)** provides the equivalent of a private packet-switched network over the public Internet.[3] It involves establishing a series of PVCs that run over the Internet so that the network acts like a set of dedicated circuits over a private packet network.

Basic Architecture

With a VPN, you first lease an Internet connection at whatever access rate and access technology you choose for each location you want to connect. For example, you might lease a T1 circuit from a common carrier that runs from your office to your **Internet service provider (ISP).** You pay the common carrier for the circuit and the ISP for Internet access. Then you connect a **VPN gateway** (a specially designed router or switch) to each Internet access circuit to provide access from your networks to the VPN. The VPN gateways enable you to create PVCs through the Internet that are called *tunnels* (Figure 9.12).

[3]Some common carriers and third-party vendors are now providing VPN services that use their own networks rather than the Internet, but by far the majority of VPN services are Internet-based. In the interest of simplicity, we will focus on Internet-based VPN services.

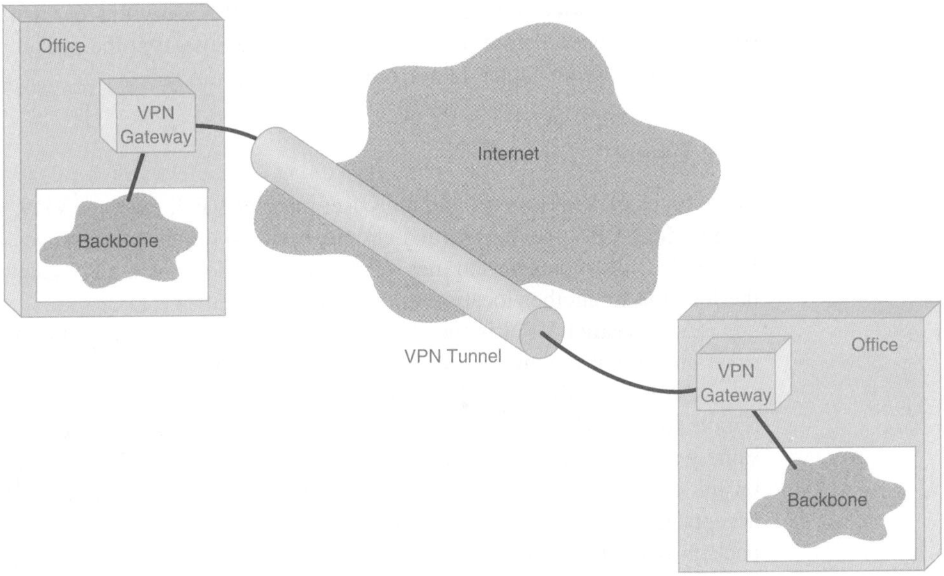

FIGURE 9.12 A virtual private network (VPN). ISP = Internet service provider

The VPN gateway at the sender takes the outgoing packet and encapsulates it with a protocol that is used to move it through the tunnel to the VPN gateway on the other side. The VPN gateway at the receiver strips off the VPN packet and delivers the packet to the destination network. The VPN is transparent to the users; it appears as though a traditional packet-switched network PVC is in use. The VPN is also transparent to the ISP and the Internet as a whole; there is simply a stream of Internet packets moving across the Internet. **VPN software** is commonly used on home computers or laptops to provide the same secure tunnels to people working from offsite.

VPNs operate either at layer 2 or layer 3. A **layer-2 VPN** uses the layer-2 packet (e.g., Ethernet) to select the VPN tunnel and encapsulates the entire packet, starting with the layer-2 packet. Layer-2 tunneling protocol (**L2TP**) is an example of a layer-2 VPN. A **layer-3 VPN** uses the layer-3 packet (e.g., IP) to select the VPN tunnel and encapsulates the entire packet, starting with the layer-3 packet; it discards the incoming layer-2 packet and generates an entirely new layer-2 packet at the destination. **IPSec** is an example of a layer-3 VPN.

The primary advantages of VPNs are low cost and flexibility. Because they use the Internet to carry messages, the major cost is Internet access, which is inexpensive compared with the cost of circuit-switched services, dedicated-circuit services, and packet-switched services from a common carrier. Likewise, anywhere you can establish Internet service, you can quickly put in a VPN.

There are two important disadvantages. First, traffic on the Internet is unpredictable. Sometimes packets travel quickly, but at other times, they take a long while to reach their destination. Although some VPN vendors advertise QoS capabilities, these apply only in the VPN devices themselves; on the Internet, a packet is a packet (at least until Internet 2 becomes more common—see Chapter 10). Second, because the data travels on the Internet, security is always a concern. Most VPN networks encrypt the packet at the source VPN device before it enters the Internet and decrypt the packet at the destination VPN device. (See Chapter 11 for more on encryption.)

VPN Types

Three types of VPNs are in common use: intranet VPN, extranet VPN, and access VPN. An **intranet VPN** provides virtual circuits between organization offices over the Internet. Figure 9.12 illustrates an intranet VPN. Each location has a VPN gateway that connects the location to another location through the Internet.

An **extranet VPN** is the same as an intranet VPN, except that the VPN connects several different organizations, often customers and suppliers, over the Internet.

An **access VPN** enables employees to access an organization's networks from a remote location. Employees have access to the network and all the resources on it in the same way as employees physically located on the network. The user uses VPN software on his or her computer to connect to the VPN device at the office. The VPN gateway accepts the user's log-in, establishes the tunnel, and the software begins forwarding packets over the Internet. An access VPN provides a less expensive connection than having a national toll-free phone number that connects directly into large sets of modems at the organization's office. Compared with a typical ISP-based remote connection, the access VPN is a more secure connection than simply sending packets over the Internet. Figure 9.13 shows an access VPN.

How VPNs Work

When packets move across the Internet, they are much like postcards in the paper mail. Anyone can read what they contain. VPNs provide security by encapsulating (i.e., surrounding) packets in a separate, secure packet that is encrypted. No one can read the encapsulated data without knowing the password that is used to decrypt the packet (we explain how encryption works in Chapter 11). Layer-2 and layer-3 VPNs work very similarly, except that layer-2 VPNs encapsulate the user's data starting with the layer-2 packet (the Ethernet frame) while layer-3 VPNs encapsulate the user's data starting with the layer-3 packet (the IP packet).

Figure 9.13 shows how a layer-3 access VPN using IPSec works. Suppose an employee is working at home with a LAN that uses a router to connect to the Internet via an Internet service provider (ISP) using DSL (we explain how DSL works in the next chapter). When the employee wants to use the VPN, he or she starts the VPN software on his or her computer and uses it to login into the VPN gateway at the office. The VPN software creates a new "interface" on the employee's computer that acts exactly like a separate connection into the Internet. Interfaces are usually hardware connections, but the VPN is a software interface, although the employee's computer doesn't know this—it's just another interface. Computers can have multiple interfaces; a laptop computer often has two interfaces, one for Ethernet and one for wireless Wi-Fi.

The VPN gateway at the office is also as a router and a DCHP server. The VPN gateway assigns an IP address to the VPN interface on the employee's computer that is an IP address in a subnet managed by the VPN gateway. For example, if the VPN

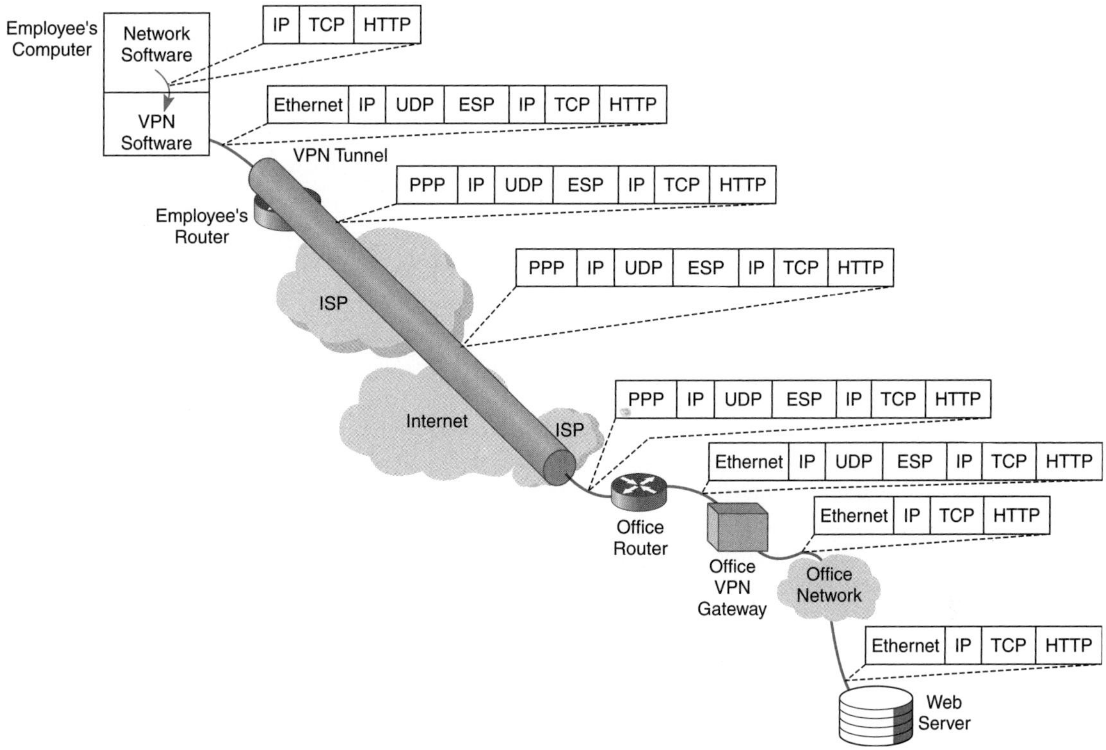

FIGURE 9.13 Using VPN Software

gateway has an IP address of 156.56.198.1 and managed the 156.56.198.x subnet, it would assign an IP address in this subnet domain (e.g., 156.56.198.55).

The employee's computer now thinks it has two connections to the Internet: The traditional interface that has the computer's usual IP address and the VPN interface that has an IP address assigned by the VPN gateway. The VPN software on the employee's computer makes the VPN interface the default interface for all network traffic to and from the Internet, which ensures that all messages leaving the employee's computer flow through the VPN interface to the VPN gateway at the office.

Suppose the employee sends an HTTP request to a Web server at the office (or somewhere else on the Internet). The Web browser software will create an HTTP packet which is passed to the TCP software (which adds a TCP segment), and this in turn is passed to the IP software managing the VPN interface. The IP software creates the IP packet using the source IP address assigned by the VPN gateway. Normally, the IP software would then pass the IP packet to the Ethernet software that manages the Ethernet interface into the employee's LAN, but since the IP packet is being sent out the VPN interface, the IP packet is passed to the VPN software managing the VPN interface. Figure 9.13 shows the message as it leaves the network software and is passed to the VPN for transmission: an HTTP packet, surrounded by a TCP segment, surrounded by an IP packet.

The VPN software receives the IP packet, encrypts it, and encapsulates it (and its contents: the TCP segment and the HTTP packet) with an **Encapsulating Security Payload (ESP)** packet using IPSec encryption. The contents of the ESP packet (the IP packet, the TCP segment and the HTTP packet) are encrypted so that no one except the VPN gateway at the office can read them. You can think of the IPSec packet as an application layer packet whose destination is the office VPN gateway. How do we send an application layer packet over the Internet? Well, we pass it to the TCP software, which is exactly what the VPN software does.

The VPN software passes the ESP packet (and its encrypted contents) to the employee's computer normal Internet interface for transmission. This interface has been sitting around waiting for transmissions, but since the VPN interface is defined as the primary interface to use, it has received no messages to transfer except those from the VPN software.

This interface treats the ESP packet as an application layer packet that needs to be sent to the VPN gateway at the office. It attaches a transport layer packet (a UDP datagram in this case, not a TCP segment). It then passes the ESP packet to the IP software which creates an IP packet with an IP destination address of the VPN gateway at the office and a source IP of the employee's computer's normal Internet interface. It passes this IP packet to the Ethernet software, which adds an Ethernet frame and transmits it to the employee's router.

The employee's router receives the Ethernet frame, strips off the frame, and reads the IP packet. It sees that the packet needs to be sent to the VPN gateway at the office, which means sending the packet to the Employee's ISP over the DSL circuit. Since DSL uses PPP as its layer-2 protocol, it adds a PPP frame and sends the packet over the DSL circuit to the ISP.

The router at the ISP strips off the PPP frame and reads the IP packet, which it uses to route the packet through the Internet. As the packet moves over the Internet, the layer-2 frame changes at each hop, depending on the circuit in use. For example, if the ISP uses a T3 circuit, then the ISP creates an appropriate layer-2 frame to move the packet over the T3 circuit (which usually is a PPP frame).

The packet travels from the Internet to the ISP that connects the office to the Internet and arrives at the office's router. This router will strip off the incoming layer-2 frame (suppose the office uses a T-3 connection with PPP as shown in the figure), read the IP packet, and create an Ethernet frame that will send the packet to the office VPN gateway. The VPN gateway will strip off the Ethernet frame, read the IP packet, strip it off, read the UDP datagram, strip it off, and hand the ESP packet to its VPN software. The VPN gateway's software will decrypt the ESP packet, and deencapsulate the IP packet (and the TCP segment and HTTP packet it contains) from the ESP packet. The VPN gateway now has the IP packet (and the TCP segment and HTTP packet) that was originally created by the software on the employee's computer. The VPN gateway reads this IP packet and creates an Ethernet frame to send it on the next hop to its destination and transmits it into the office network, where it ultimately reaches the Web server. On this last leg of the journey after it leaves the VPN gateway, the packet is not encrypted and can be read like a normal packet on the Internet.

The return path from the Web server back to the employee's computer is very similar. The Web server will process the HTTP request packet and create an HTTP response packet which it sends back to the employee's computer. The source address on the IP packet that the Web server received was the IP address associated with the VPN interface on the employee's computer, so the Web server uses this address as the destination IP address. This packet is therefore routed back to the VPN gateway, because the subnet for this IP address is defined as being in the subnet that the VPN gateway manages. Once again, the return packet is not encrypted on this part of the journey.

When the packet arrives at the VPN gateway, it looks up the VPN IP address in its table and sees the usual IP address of the computer associated with that VPN address. The VPN gateway creates an ESP packet and encrypts the IP packet from the Web server (and the TCP segment and HTTP packet it contains). It then treats the ESP packet as a application layer packet that needs to be sent to the VPN software on the employee's computer; it passes it to its TCP software for a UDP datagram, then to its IP software for an IP packet, and then to its Ethernet software for an Ethernet frame and transmission back through the VPN tunnel.

When the packet eventually reaches the employee's computer, it comes in the normal Internet interface and eventually reaches the TCP software that strips off the UDP datagram. The TCP software sees that the ESP packet inside the UDP datagram is destined for the VPN software (remember that TCP port numbers are used to identify to which application layer software a packet should go). The VPN software removes the ESP packet and passes the IP packet it contains to the IP software, which in turn strips off the IP packet, and passes the TCP segment it contains to the TCP software, which strips off the TCP segments and passes the HTTP packet it contains to the Web browser.

MANAGEMENT FOCUS 9.3 CISCO'S METRO ETHERNET VPN

The Cisco Systems Inc. offices in San Jose, California, used a VPN network over the Internet through four SONET OC-3 links provided by different common carriers (the next chapter discusses the Internet in more detail). Cisco needed more capacity, so when one of the common carriers decided to discontinue its SONET services, Cisco decided to move to metro Ethernet for some of its Internet connection.

Cisco replaced one OC-3 with a 200 Mbps metro Ethernet circuit from AT&T. AT&T installed two parallel 1 Gbps fiber optic circuits from the Cisco office into the AT&T network in San Jose. Only one circuit is in use; the other is a backup in case the first circuit fails.

The circuit connects into the AT&T network through an edge switch whose job is to add MPLS tags to the incoming frames to route them through the AT&T network to their destination. Although the circuit is capable of supporting 1 Gbps of data, this switch limits the circuit capacity to ensure that the circuit does not use more than the 200 Mbps of data that Cisco has contracted for. Cisco's router into the AT&T network is also configured to only enable 200 Mps of data on this circuit. If Cisco needs more capacity, it can change its contract with AT&T and Cisco, and AT&T will change the capacity setting on their switch and router.

The circuit has proven to be very reliable and now provides 200 Mbps at a lower cost than the previous OC-3 circuit. Cisco plans to convert the remaining OC-3 circuits to metro Ethernet in the coming years.

SOURCE: "How Cisco Deployed a High-Speed WAN," Cisco.com.

MANAGEMENT FOCUS 9.4 ENERGY SCIENCES NETWORK

The Energy Sciences Network serves the U.S. Department of Energy and the thousands of corporate and university scientists doing research for it. It is one of the fastest wide area networks in the world because its users, researching high energy physics, human genomics, and climate modeling, routinely move terabyte-sized files across the network.

The current network uses a mixture of very high speed optical Ethernet services as well as high speed ATM, and moderate speed T3 circuits (see Figure 9.14). The Network has always been an early adopter of new technologies, so the San Francisco ring, currently running at 20 Gbps, will upgrade to 100 Gbps Ethernet within the next 2 years as it becomes available. Likewise, the older ATM portions of the network will gradually move to faster Ethernet services.

SOURCE: "ESnet turns to high-speed optical MANs." *NetworkWorld,* May 23, 2005, p. 12.

THE BEST PRACTICE MAN/WAN DESIGN

Developing best practice recommendations for MAN and WAN design is more difficult than for LANs and backbones because the network designer is buying services from different companies rather than buying products. The relatively stable environment enjoyed

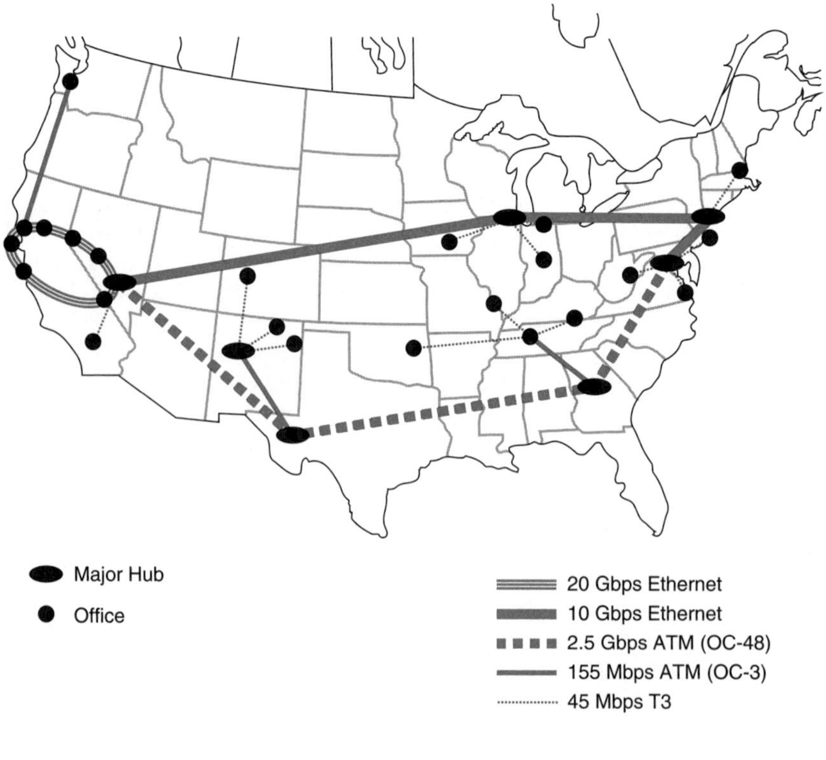

FIGURE 9.14
Energy Sciences Network

by the MAN/WAN common carriers is facing sharp challenges by VPNs at the low end and Ethernet services at the high end. As larger IT and equipment firms begin to enter the VPN and Ethernet services markets, we should see some major changes in the industry and in the available services and costs.

We also need to point out that the technologies in this chapter are primarily used to connect different corporate locations. Technologies primarily used for Internet access (e.g., DSL, cable modem) are discussed in the next chapter.

We use the same two factors as we have previously for LANs and backbones (effective data rates and cost), plus add two additional factors: reliability and network integration. Reliability refers to the ability to predictably send messages as expected. Network integration refers to the ease with which the MAN/WAN service can be used to connect LANs and backbones.

Figure 9.15 summarizes the major services available today for the MAN and WAN, grouped by the type of service. A few patterns should emerge from the table. For small MANs and WANs with low data transmission needs, POTS dial-up services are a reasonable alternative. POTS can be more difficult to integrate with LANs and backbones, so this is a good option only if one is willing to use dial-up connections. Since most of

Type of Service	Nominal Data Rates	Effective Data Rates	Relative Cost	Reliability	Network Integration
Circuit-Switched Services					
POTS	33.6 Kbps to 56 Kbps	33 to 300 Kbps[1]	Low	High	Difficult
ISDN	128 Kbps to 1.5 Mbps	122 Kbps to 1.3 Mbps	Moderate	Moderate	Difficult
B-ISDN	155 Mbps to 622 Mbps	300 Mbps to 1200 Mbps[2]	High	Low	Difficult
Dedicated-Circuit Services					
T Carrier	64 Kbps to 274 Mbps	53 Kbps to 218 Mbps	Moderate	High	Moderate
SONET	50 Mbps to 10 Gbps	48 Mbps to 9.1 Gbps	High	High	Moderate
Packet-Switched Services					
X.25	56 Kbps to 2 Mbps	50 Kbps to 1.5 Mbps	Moderate	High	Difficult
ATM	52 Mbps to 10 Gbps	84 Mbps to 16 Gbps[3]	High	Moderate	Moderate
Frame Relay	56 Kbps to 45 Mbps	56 Kbps to 44 Mbps	Moderate	Moderate	Moderate
Ethernet	1 Mbps to 40 Gbps	900 Kbps to 36 Gbps	Low	High	Simple
VPN Services					
VPN	56 Kbps to 40 Gbps	50 Kbps to 36 Gbps	Very Low	Low	Moderate

Notes:
[1] Assuming data compression and no noise
[2] B-ISDN is full duplex
[3] ATM is full duplex

FIGURE 9.15 MAN/WAN services

this type of network is used for Internet access, we really need to wait until the next chapter before drawing conclusions.

For networks with moderate data transmission needs (64 Kbps–2 Mbps) there are several distinct choices. If cost is more important than reliability, then a VPN is probably a good choice. If you need flexibility in the location of your network connections and you are not completely sure of the volume of traffic you will have between locations, frame relay is probably a good choice. If you have a mature network with predictable demands, then T carrier services is probably a good choice (Figure 9.16).

For high-traffic networks (2 Mbps–45 Mbps), the new Ethernet services are a dominant choice. Some organizations may prefer the more mature—and therefore proven—T3 or frame relay services, depending on whether the greater flexibility of packet services provides value or a dedicated circuit makes more sense.

For very-high-traffic networks (45 Mbps–10 Gbps), Ethernet services again are a dominant choice. And again some organizations may prefer the more mature ATM or SONET services, depending on whether the greater flexibility of packet services provides value or a dedicated circuit makes more sense.

Unless their data needs are stable, network managers often start with more flexible packet-switched services and move to the usually cheaper dedicated-circuit services once their needs have become clear and an investment in dedicated services is safer. Some packet-switched services even permit organizations to establish circuits with a zero-CIR (and rely entirely on the availability of the MAR) so network managers can track their needs and lease only what they need.

Network managers often add a packet network service as an overlay network on top of a network built with dedicated circuits to handle peak data needs; data usually travels over the dedicated-circuit network, but when it becomes overloaded with traffic, the extra traffic is routed to the packet network.

Network Needs	Recommendation
Low Traffic Needs (64 Kbps or less)	POTS if dial-up is acceptable VPN if reliability is less important Frame relay otherwise
Moderate Traffic Needs (64 Kbps to 2 Mbps)	VPN if reliability is less important T1 if network volume is stable and predictable Frame relay otherwise
High Traffic Needs (2 Mbps to 45 Mbps)	Ethernet if available T3 if network volume is stable and predictable Frame relay otherwise
Very High Traffic Needs (45 Mbps to 10 Gbps)	Ethernet if available SONET if network volume is stable and predictable ATM otherwise

FIGURE 9.16
Best practice MAN/WAN recommendations

IMPROVING MAN/WAN PERFORMANCE

Improving the performance of MANs and WANs is handled in the same way as improving LAN performance. You begin by checking the devices in the network, by upgrading the circuits between the computers, and by changing the demand placed on the network (Figure 9.17).

Improving Device Performance

In some cases, the key bottleneck in the network is not the circuits; it is the devices that provide access to the circuits (e.g., routers). One way to improve network performance is to upgrade the devices and computers that connect backbones to the WAN. Most devices are rated for their speed in converting input packets to output packets (called **latency**). Not all devices are created equal; some vendors produce devices with lower latencies than others.

Another strategy is examining the routing protocol, either static or dynamic. Dynamic routing will increase performance in networks that have many possible routes from one computer to another and in which message traffic is "bursty"—that is, in which traffic occurs in spurts, with many messages at one time, and few at others. But dynamic routing imposes an overhead cost by increasing network traffic. In some cases, the traffic and status information sent between computers accounts for more than 50 percent of all WAN message traffic. This is clearly a problem because it drastically reduces the amount of network capacity available for users' messages. Dynamic routing should use no more than 10 to 20 percent of the network's total capacity.

Improving Circuit Capacity

The first step is to analyze the message traffic in the network to find which circuits are approaching capacity. These circuits then can be upgraded to provide more capacity. Less-used circuits can be downgraded to save costs. A more sophisticated analysis

Performance Checklist

Increase Computer and Device Performance
- Upgrade devices
- Change to a more appropriate routing protocol (either static or dynamic)

Increase Circuit Capacity
- Analyze message traffic and upgrade to faster circuits where needed
- Check error rates

Reduce Network Demand
- Change user behavior
- Analyze network needs of all new systems
- Move data closer to users

FIGURE 9.17 Improving performance of metropolitan and local area networks

MANAGEMENT FOCUS 9.5 GIGABIT ETHERNET IN THE NETHERLANDS

SURFnet is the national computer network for education and research in the Netherlands. Demand for network capacity had been rapidly growing as more and more students started using the Internet, so SURFnet began looking for a way to significantly upgrade its WAN that connects more than 50 universities, libraries, and research centers.

SURFnet considered implementing SONET or ATM OC-192, but felt that 10 Gbps Ethernet provided similar data rates, was more familiar to their customers, and was more scaleable. SURFnet has leased fiber from Amsterdam to major regional centers around the Netherlands (Figure 9.18). Each of these regional centers is a POP and in turn provides connections to other universities, libraries, and research centers in its region, often via a 1 Gbps or 100 Mbps Ethernet MAN or WAN. Sometimes SONET, ATM, or E-carrier services (the European equivalent to T carrier services) are used for the regional connections, depending upon the demand.

SOURCE: "Cisco Helps SURFnet Provide 10 Gigabit Ethernet to Higher Education and Research Community," www.cisco.com, 2004.

involves examining *why* circuits are heavily used. For example, in Figure 9.3, the circuit from San Francisco to Vancouver may be heavily used, but much traffic on this circuit may not originate in San Francisco or be destined for Vancouver. It may, for example, be going from Los Angeles to Toronto, suggesting that adding a circuit here would improve performance to a greater extent than upgrading the San Francisco-to-Vancouver circuit.

The capacity may be adequate for most traffic but not for meeting peak demand. One solution may be to add a circuit-switched or packet-switched service that is used only when demand exceeds circuit capacity. The use of a service as a backup for heavy traffic provides the best of both worlds. The lower-cost dedicated circuit is used constantly, and the backup service is used only when necessary to avoid poor response times.

Sometimes a shortage of capacity may be caused by a faulty circuit. As circuits deteriorate, the number of errors increases. As the error rate increases, throughput falls because more messages have to be retransmitted. Before installing new circuits, monitor the existing ones to ensure that they are operating properly or ask the common carrier to do it.

Reducing Network Demand

There are many ways to reduce network demand. One simple step is to require a network impact statement for all new application software developed or purchased by the organization. This focuses attention on the network impacts at an early stage in application development. Another simple approach is to use data compression techniques for all data in the network.

Another sometimes more difficult approach is to shift network usage from peak or high-cost times to lower-demand or lower-cost times. For example, the transmission of detailed sales and inventory reports from a retail store to headquarters could be done

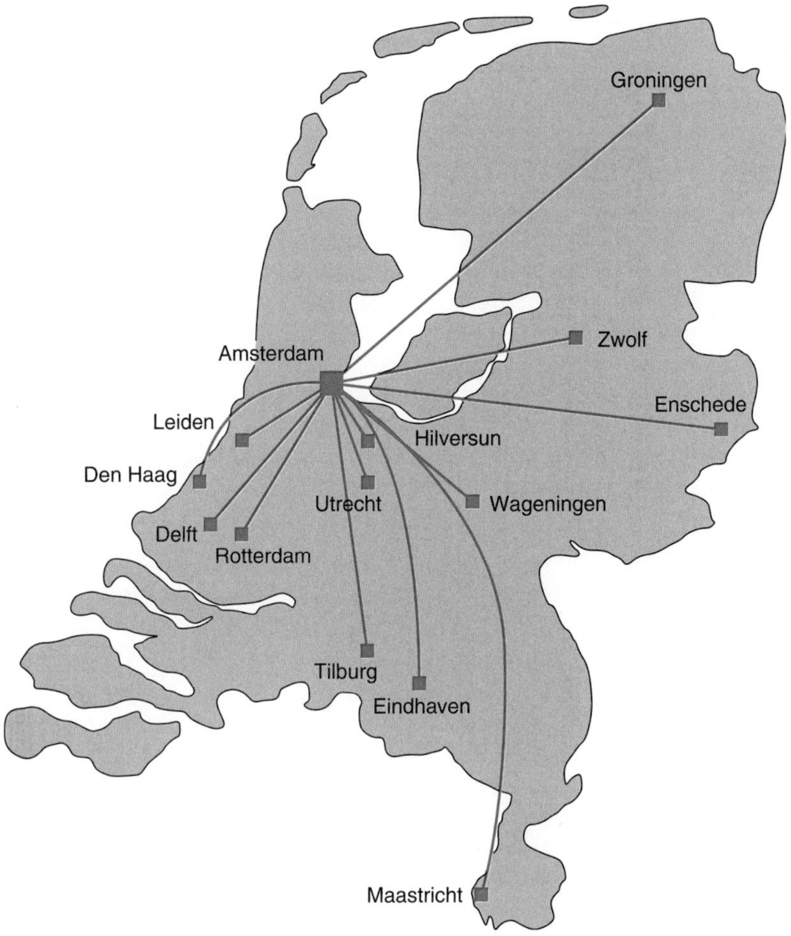

FIGURE 9.18 The SURFnet gigabit Ethernet WAN

after the store closes. This takes advantage of off-peak rate charges and avoids interfering with transmissions requiring higher priority such as customer credit card authorizations.

The network can be redesigned to move data closer to the applications and people who use them. This also will reduce the amount of traffic in the network. Distributed database applications enable databases to be spread across several different computers. For example, instead of storing customer records in one central location, you could store them according to region.

IMPLICATIONS FOR MANAGEMENT

As the amount of digital computer data flowing through MANs and WANs has increased and as those networks have become increasingly digital, the networking and telecommunications vice president role has significantly changed over the past five to ten years.

Traditionally this vice president has been responsible for computer communications; today in most companies, this individual is also responsible for telephone and voice services.

T carrier, SONET, and ATM have traditionally dominated the MAN and WAN market. However, with the growing use of VPNs and Ethernet services, we are beginning to see a major change. In the early 1990s, the costs of MANs and WANs were quite high. As these networks have changed to increasingly digital technologies, and as competition has increased with the introduction of new companies and new technologies (e.g., VPNs, Ethernet services), costs have begun to drop. More firms are now moving to implement software applications that depend upon low-cost MANs and WANs.

The same factors that caused the LAN and BN to standardize on a few technologies (Ethernet, wireless Ethernet) are now acting to shape the future of the MAN and WAN. We believe that within five years, X.25 and ATM, will disappear, replaced by Ethernet and IP services. Within ten years, ISDN, T-carrier, and SONET may also disappear.

These changes have also had significant impacts on the manufacturers of networking equipment designed for MANs and WANs. Market shares and stock prices have shifted dramatically over the last five years in favor of companies with deep experience in backbone technologies (e.g., Ethernet) and Internet technologies (e.g., IP) as those technologies spread into the MAN and WAN market.

SUMMARY

Circuit-Switched Networks Circuit-switched services enable you to define the end points of the WAN without specifying all the interconnecting circuits through carrier's cloud. The user dials the number of the destination computer to establish a temporary circuit, which is disconnected when the data transfer is complete. POTS is traditional dial-up service. BRI ISDN provides a communication circuit with two 64-Kbps digital transmission channels and one 16-Kbps control channel. PRI ISDN consists of 23 64-Kbps data channels and one 64-Kbps control channel. Broadband ISDN, not yet widely available, offers much faster data speeds up to 622 Mbps.

Dedicated-Circuit Networks A dedicated circuit is leased from the common carrier for exclusive use 24 hours per day, 7 days per week. Faster and more noise-free transmissions are possible, but you must carefully plan the circuits you need because changes can be expensive. The three common architectures are ring, star, and mesh. T carrier circuits have a set of digital services ranging from FT1 (64 Kbps) to T1 (1.544 Mbps) to T4 (274 Mbps). A SONET uses fiber optics to provide services ranging from OC-1 (51 Mbps) to OC-12 (622 Mbps).

Packet-Switched Networks Packet switching is a technique in which messages are split into small segments. The user buys a connection into the common carrier cloud and pays a fixed fee for the connection into the network and for the number of packets transmitted. X.25 is an older, traditional service that provides slower service (up to 2 Mbps) but guarantees error-free delivery. ATM does not perform error control, and it offers data rates up to 622 Mbps. Frame relay is a newer packet-switching service with higher data rates (up to 45 Mbps), but it does not perform error control. Ethernet services use Ethernet and IP to transmit packets at speeds between 1 Mbps and 1 Gbps.

VPN Networks A VPN provides a packet service network over the Internet. The sender and receiver have VPN devices that enable them to send data over the Internet in encrypted form through a VPN tunnel. Although VPNs are inexpensive, traffic delays on the Internet can be unpredictable.

The Best Practice MAN/WAN Design For small MANs and WANs with low data transmission needs, POTS dial-up services are a reasonable alternative. For networks with moderate data transmission needs (64 Kbps–2 Mbps), a VPN is a good choice if cost is more important than reliability; otherwise, frame relay or T carrier services are good choices. For high-traffic networks (2 Mbps–45 Mbps), the new Ethernet services are a dominant choice, but some organizations may prefer the more mature—and therefore proven—T3 or frame relay services. For very high-traffic networks (45 Mbps–10 Gbps), Ethernet services are a dominant choice but again some organizations may prefer the more mature ATM or SONET services. Unless their data needs are stable, network managers often start with more flexible packet-switched services and move to the usually cheaper dedicated-circuit services once their needs have become clear and an investment in dedicated services is safer.

Improving MAN/WAN Performance One can improve network performance by improving the speed of the devices themselves and by using a better routing protocol. Analysis of network usage can show what circuits need to be increased or decreased in capacity, what new circuits need to be leased, and when additional switched circuits may be needed to meet peak demand. Reducing network demand may also improve performance. Including a network usage analysis for all new application software, using data compression, shifting usage to off-peak times, establishing priorities for some applications, or redesigning the network to move data closer to those who use it are all ways to reduce network demand.

KEY TERMS

access VPN
asynchronous transfer mode (ATM)
basic rate interface (BRI)
broadband ISDN (B-ISDN)
Canadian Radio-Television and Telecommunications Commission (CRTC)
channel service unit/data service unit (CSU/DSU)
circuit-switched services
cloud
cloud architecture
committed information rate (CIR)
common carrier
datagram
dedicated-circuit services
discard eligible (DE)
distributed star architecture
Ethernet services
Encapsulating Security Payload (ESP)
extranet VPN
fast packet services
Federal Communications Commission (FCC)
fractional T1 (FT1)
frame relay
full-mesh architecture
integrated services digital network (ISDN)
interexchange carrier (IXC)
Internet service provider (ISP)
intranet VPN
IPSec
L2TP
latency
layer-2 VPN
layer-3 VPN
local exchange carrier (LEC)
maximum allowable rate (MAR)
mesh
mesh architecture
narrowband ISDN
network terminator (NT-1, NT-2)
packet assembly/disassembly (PAD)
packet-switched networks
permanent virtual circuit (PVC)
plain old telephone service (POTS)
point of presence (POP)
primary rate interface (PRI)
public switched telephone network (PSTN)
public utilities commission (PUC)
reliable packet services
ring architecture
service profile identifier (SPID)
star architecture
switched virtual circuit (SVC)
synchronous digital hierarchy (SDH)
synchronous optical network (SONET)
T carrier circuit
T1, T2, T3, T4 circuits
terminal adapter (TA)
2B+D
23B+D
unreliable packet services
virtual circuit
virtual private network (VPN)
VPN gateway
VPN software
wide area telephone service (WATS)
X.25

QUESTIONS

1. What are common carriers, local exchange carriers, and interexchange carriers?
2. Who regulates common carriers and how is it done?
3. Explain how a cloud architecture works.
4. What is POTS?
5. How does ISDN work?
6. Compare and contrast BRI, PRI, and B-ISDN.
7. What is a 2B+D?
8. How does broadband ISDN differ from narrowband ISDN?
9. Compare and contrast circuit-switched services, dedicated-circuit services, and packet-switched services.
10. Is a WAN that uses dedicated circuits easier or harder to design than one that uses dialed circuits? Explain.
11. Compare and contrast ring architecture, star architecture, and mesh architecture.
12. What are the most commonly used T carrier services? What data rates do they provide?
13. Distinguish among T1, T2, T3, and T4 circuits.
14. Describe SONET. How does it differ from SDH?
15. How do packet-switching services differ from other WAN services?
16. How is a virtual circuit distinguished from other circuits?
17. Where does packetizing take place?
18. What does a packet contain?
19. How does a reliable packet service differ from an unreliable packet service?
20. How do datagram services differ from virtual circuit services?
21. How does an SVC differ from a PVC?
22. Compare and contrast X.25, frame relay, ATM, and Ethernet services.
23. Which is likely to be the longer-term winner, X.25, frame relay, ATM, or Ethernet services?
24. Explain the differences between CIR and MAR.
25. How do VPN services differ from common carrier services?
26. Explain how VPN services work.
27. Compare the three types of VPN.
28. How can you improve WAN performance?
29. Describe five important factors in selecting WAN services.
30. Are Ethernet services a major change in the future of networking or a technology blip?
31. Are there any MAN/WAN technologies that you would avoid if you were building a network today? Explain.
32. Suppose you joined a company that had a WAN composed of SONET, T carrier services, ATM, and frame relay, each selected to match a specific network need for a certain set of circuits. Would you say this was a well-designed network? Explain.
33. It is said that packet-switched services and dedicated-circuit services are somewhat similar from the perspective of the network designer. Why?

EXERCISES

9-1. Find out the data rates and costs of T carrier and ISDN services in your area.

9-2. Find out the data rates and costs of packet-switched and circuit-switched services in your area.

9-3. Investigate the MAN or WAN of a company in your area. Draw a network map.

9-4. Using Figure 9.13:

a. Suppose the example used a Layer-2 VPN protocol called L2TP. Draw the messages and the packets they would contain.

b. Suppose the web server was an e-mail server. Draw the messages from the e-mail server to the employee's computer. Show what packets would be in the message.

c. Suppose the office connects to its ISP using metro Ethernet. What packets would be in the message from the office router to the ISP?

d. Suppose the employee connects to the ISP using a Layer-2 protocol called XYZ. What packets would be in the message from the employes's router to the ISP?

MINI-CASES

I. Cookies Are Us

Cookies Are Us runs a series of 100 cookie stores across the midwestern United States and central Canada. At the end of each day, the stores express-mail a diskette or two of sales and inventory data to headquarters, which uses the data to ship new inventory and plan marketing campaigns. The company has decided to move to a WAN. What type of a WAN architecture and WAN service would you recommend? Why?

II. MegaCorp

MegaCorp is a large manufacturing firm that operates 5 factories in Dallas, 4 factories in Los Angeles, and 5 factories in Albany, New York. It operates a tightly connected order management system that coordinates orders, raw materials, and inventory across all 14 factories. What type of WAN architecture and WAN service would you recommend? Why?

III. Sunrise Consultancy

Sunrise Consultancy is a medium-sized consulting firm that operates 17 offices around the world (Dallas, Chicago, New York, Atlanta, Miami, Seattle, Los Angeles, San Jose, Toronto, Montreal, London, Paris, Sao Paulo, Singapore, Hong Kong, Sydney, and Bombay). They have been using Internet connections to exchange e-mail and files, but the volume of traffic has increased to the point that they now want to connect the offices via a WAN. Volume is low but expected to grow quickly once they implement a new knowledge management system. What type of a WAN topology and WAN service would you recommend? Why?

IV. CareGroup

Reread Management Focus 9.1. What other alternatives do you think that CareGroup considered? Why do you think they did what they did?

V. Fire Departments

Reread Management Focus 9.2. What other alternatives do you think that the fire departments considered? Why do you think they did what they did?

VI. CISCO Systems Inc.

Reread Management Focus 9.3. What alternatives do you think CISCO systems considered? Why do you think they did what they did?

VII. Energy Sciences Network

Reread Management Focus 9.4. What other alternatives do you think that the Energy Sciences Network considered? Why do you think they did what they did?

VIII. SURFnet

Reread Management Focus 9.5. What other alternatives do you think that SURFnet considered? Why do you think they did what they did?

CASE STUDY

NEXT-DAY AIR SERVICE

See the Web site.

HANDS-ON ACTIVITY

Examining Wide Area Neworks

There are millions of WANs in the world. Some are run by common carriers and are available to the public. Others are private networks run by organizations for their internal use only. Thousands of these networks have been documented on the Web.

Explore the Web to find networks offered by common carriers and compare the types of network circuits they have. Now do the same for public and private organizations to see what they have. Figure 9.19 shows the network map for Quest (www-test.quest.com/largebusiness/enterprisesolutions/downloads/0703-NA_IP_Map2_07.pdf), a large common carrier in the United States. This shows the services offered in each major city, as well as the size of the circuits connecting cities.

Other interesting WAN maps, including dynamic maps, are available from:

Cable and Wireless: www.cw.com/our_network/network_maps

Cogent: www.cogentco.com/htdocs/map.php

Sprint/Nextel: www.sprintworldwide.com/english/maps/

TATA Communications: www.tatacommunications.com/map/gfp.html

HANDS-ON ACTIVITY

Examining VPNs with Wireshark

If you want to see VPNs in action and understand how they protect your data as it moves over the Internet, you can sniff your packets with Wireshark. In order to do this lab, you'll have to have a VPN you can use. This will normally be available from your school.

In this exercise, you'll use Wireshark to sniff the packets with and without the VPN. Before you start, you'll need to download and install Wireshark, a packet sniffer software package, on your computer. See the Hands-On Activity in Chapter 4 for instructions on how to do this.

1. Start the VPN software on your computer.
2. Start a Web browser (e.g., Internet Explorer) and go to a Web site.
3. Start Wireshark and click on the Capture menu item. This will open up a new menu (see the very top of Figure 9.20). Click on Interfaces.
4. This will open a new window that will enable you to select which interface you want to capture packets from. Figure 9.20 shows you the three interfaces I have on my computer. The first interface is a dial-up modem that I never use. The second interface (labeled "Broadcom NetXtreme

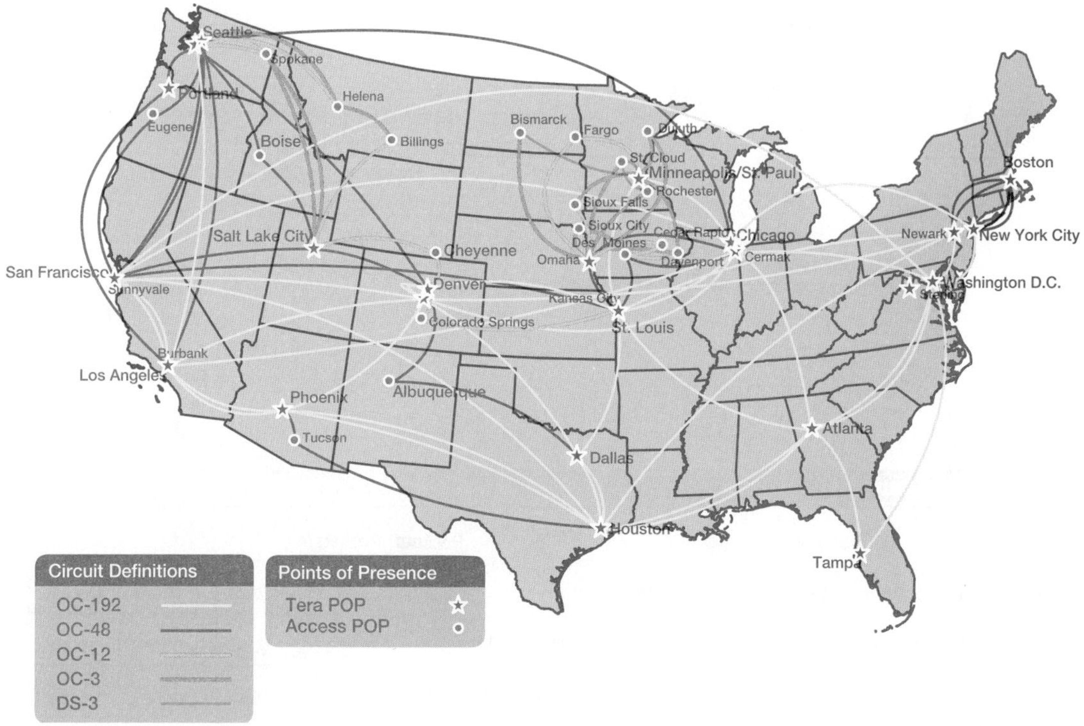

FIGURE 9.19 QUEST'S WAN

Gigabit Ethernet Driver") is my Ethernet local area network. It has the IP address of 192.168.1.104. The third interface (labeled "WN (PPP/SLIP) Interface") is the VPN tunnel; it has an IP address of 156.56.198.144 and only appears when you start the VPN software and login to a VPN gateway. If you do a WhoIs on this IP address (see Chapter 5 for WhoIs), you will see that this IP address is owned by Indiana University. When I logged into my VPN software, it assigned this IP address to the tunnel so that all IP packets that leave my computer over this tunnel will appear to be from a computer on a subnet on the Indiana University campus that is connected to the VPN gateway. Your computer will have different interfaces and IP addresses because your network is different than mine. But, the interfaces should be similar.

5. Start by capturing packets on your regular Ethernet Interface. In my case, this is the second interface. Click on the Start button beside the Ethernet driver (which is 192.168.1.104 on my computer).
6. Go to your Web browser and use it to load a new Web page, which will cause some packets to move through your network.
7. A screen similar to that in Figure 9.21 will appear. After a few seconds, go back to Wireshark and click the Interface menu item and then click Stop.
8. The top window in Figure 9.21 shows the packets that are leaving the computer through the tunnel. Click on a packet to look at it. The middle window in this figure shows what's inside the packet. We see an Ethernet frame, an IP packet, a UDP datagram, and an Encapsulating Security Payload packet (which is the ESP packet). Notice that you cannot see anything inside the ESP packet because its contents are encrypted. All packets in this tunnel will *only* flow to and from my computer (192.168.1.104) and the VPN gateway (156.56.245.15).
9. Now we want to look at the packets that are sent by your computer *into* the VPN tunnel. No one else can see these packets. You can see them only

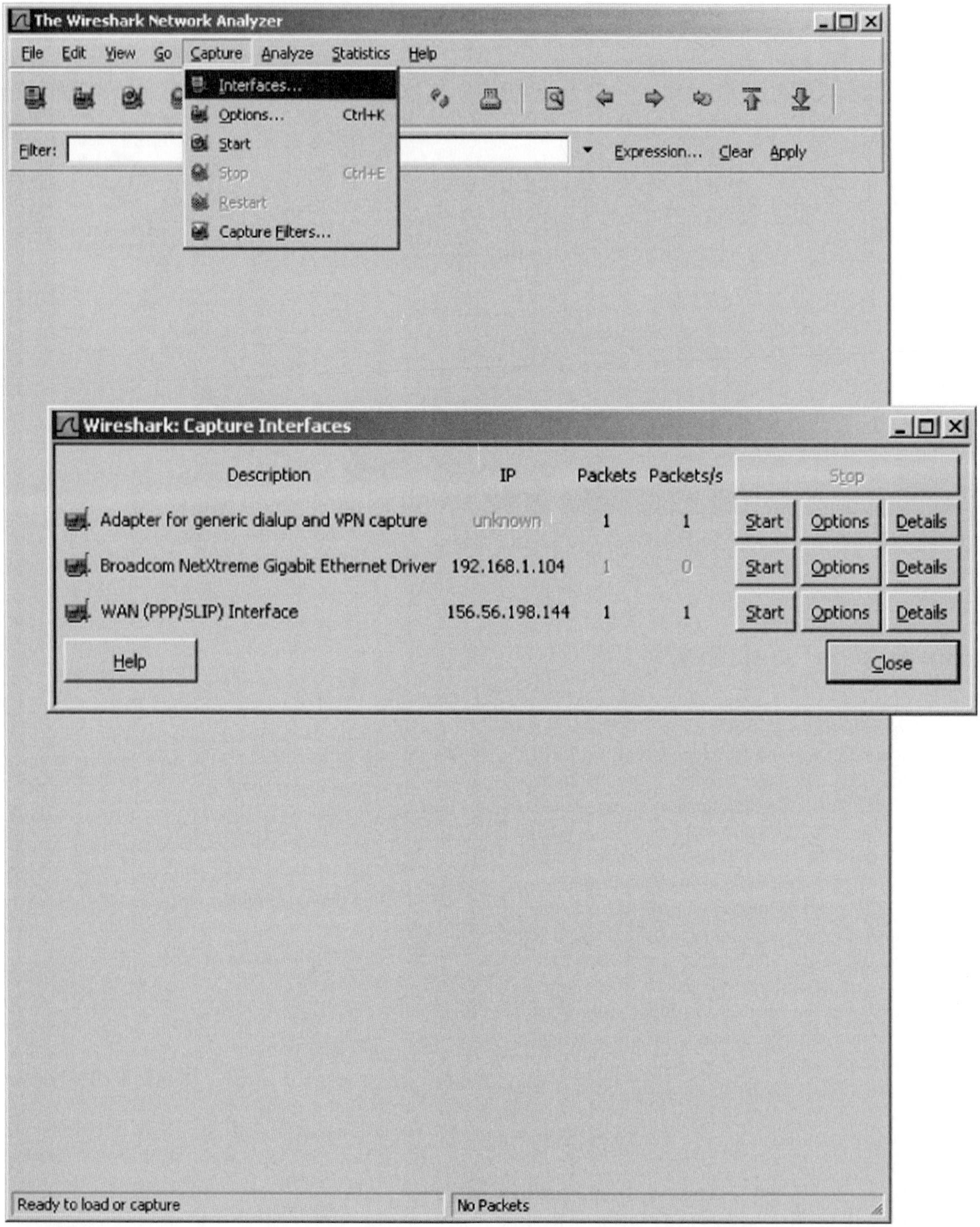

FIGURE 9.20 Starting Wireshark

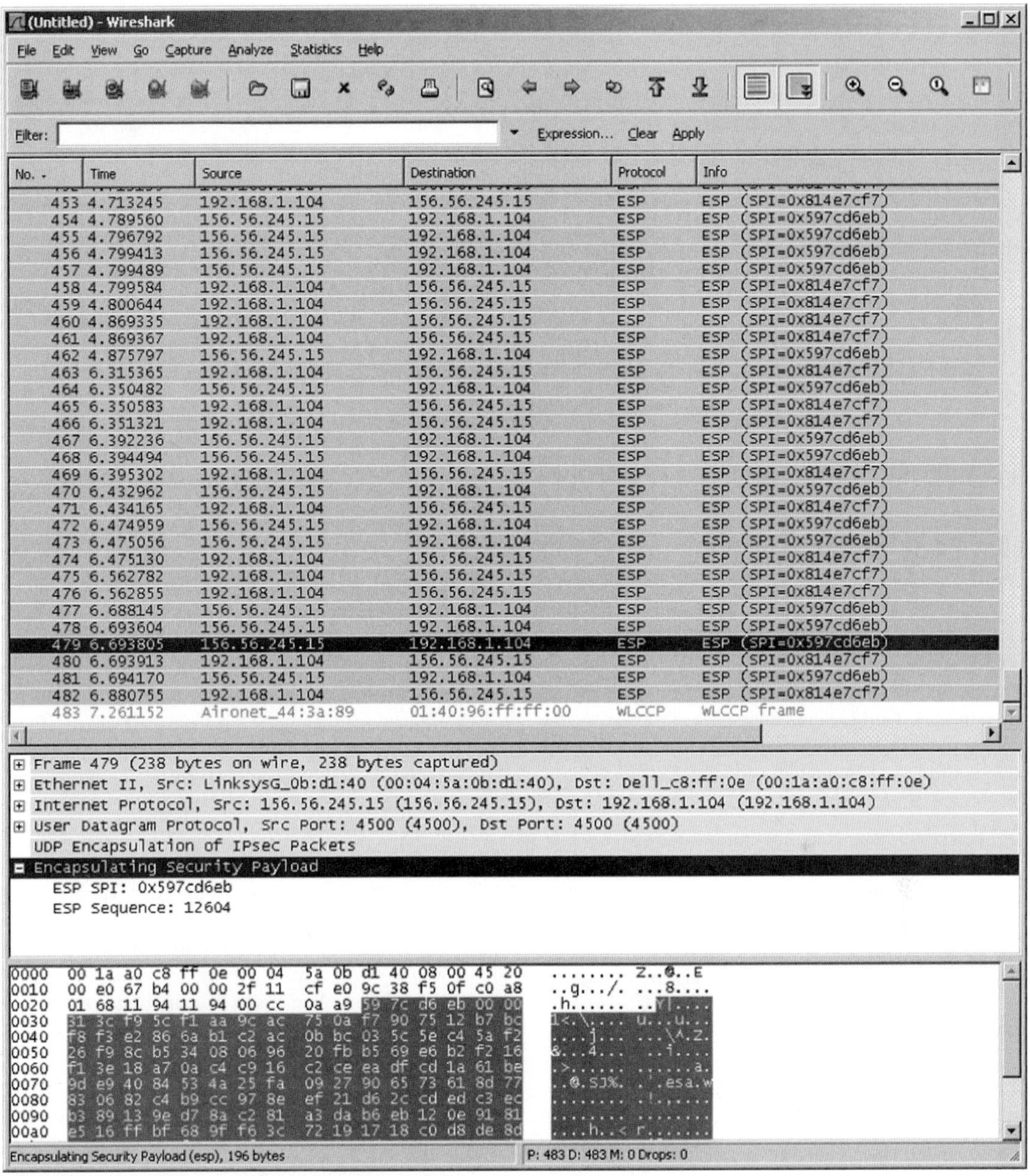

FIGURE 9.21 Viewing encrypted packets

because they are on your computer and you're looking at them as they move from your traditional network software to your VPN software.

10. Click on the Wireshark Capture menu item and click Interfaces.
11. Click on the Start button beside your VPN interface, which in my case in Figure 9.20 is the button in front of 156.56.198.144.
12. Go to your Web browser and use it to load a new Web page, which will cause some packets to move through your network.
13. A screen similar to that in Figure 9.22 will appear. After a few seconds, go back to Wireshark and click the Interface menu item, and then click Stop.
14. The top window in Figure 9.22 shows the packets that are entering the VPN tunnel. Click on an HTTP packet to look at it (you may need to scroll to find one). The middle window in this figure shows what's inside the packet. We see an Ethernet frame, an IP packet, a TCP segment, and an HTTP request (for a page called/enterprise/on www.tatacommunications.com). We can see these because they have not yet entered the VPN software to be encrypted. These are the packets that would normally be sent over the Internet if we have not started the VPN software. Like all normal Internet messages, they can be read by anyone with sniffer software such as Wireshark.

HANDS-ON ACTIVITY

Examining VPNs with Tracert

Tracert is a useful tool for seeing how VPNs affect routing. In order to do this lab, you'll have to have a VPN you can use. This will normally be available from your school.

Tracert is a simple command that comes preinstalled on all Windows and Mac computers. Tracert enables you to see the route that an IP packet takes as it moves over the Internet from one computer to another. Do this activity when you are not on campus.

1. Tracert is command line command, so you first need to start the CMD window. Click Start, then Run, and then type CMD and press enter. This will open the command window, which is usually a small window with a black background. You can change the size and shape of this window, but it is not as flexible as a usual window.
2. We will first trace the route from your computers to two other computers without using the VPN. So make sure your VPN is *not* connected.
3. We'll start by tracing the route from your computer to a computer on the campus of the site you VPN into. In my case, I VPN into my university, which is Indiana University. I can choose to trace the route to any computer on campus. I'll choose our main Web server (www.iu.edu). At the command prompt, type tracert and the URL of a computer on your campus.
4. The top half of Figure 9.23 shows the route from my computer to www.iu.edu. There are 18 hops and it takes about 35 ms. The first hop does not report information because this feature is turned off in the router at my house for security reasons. You can see that my ISP is Comcast (hop 6). If you compare this to the tracert at the end of Chapter 5, you'll notice that my ISP changed (and thus the route into the Internet changed) between the time I wrote Chapter 5 and this chapter; Comcast bought Insight in my town of Bloomington, Indiana.
5. Now trace the route from your computer to another computer on the Internet. The bottom of Figure 9.23 shows the route from my computer to www.google.com. There are 17 hops, and it takes about 35 ms. You'll see that the routes to IU and Google are the same until step 6, and then they diverge.
6. Next we want to see what happens when you have a VPN connection. Start your VPN software and connect into the VPN gateway at your school.
7. Trace the route from your computer to the same computer as in step 3. At the command prompt, type tracert and the URL of a computer on your campus.
8. The top half of Figure 9.24 shows the route from my computer to www.iu.edu. There are two

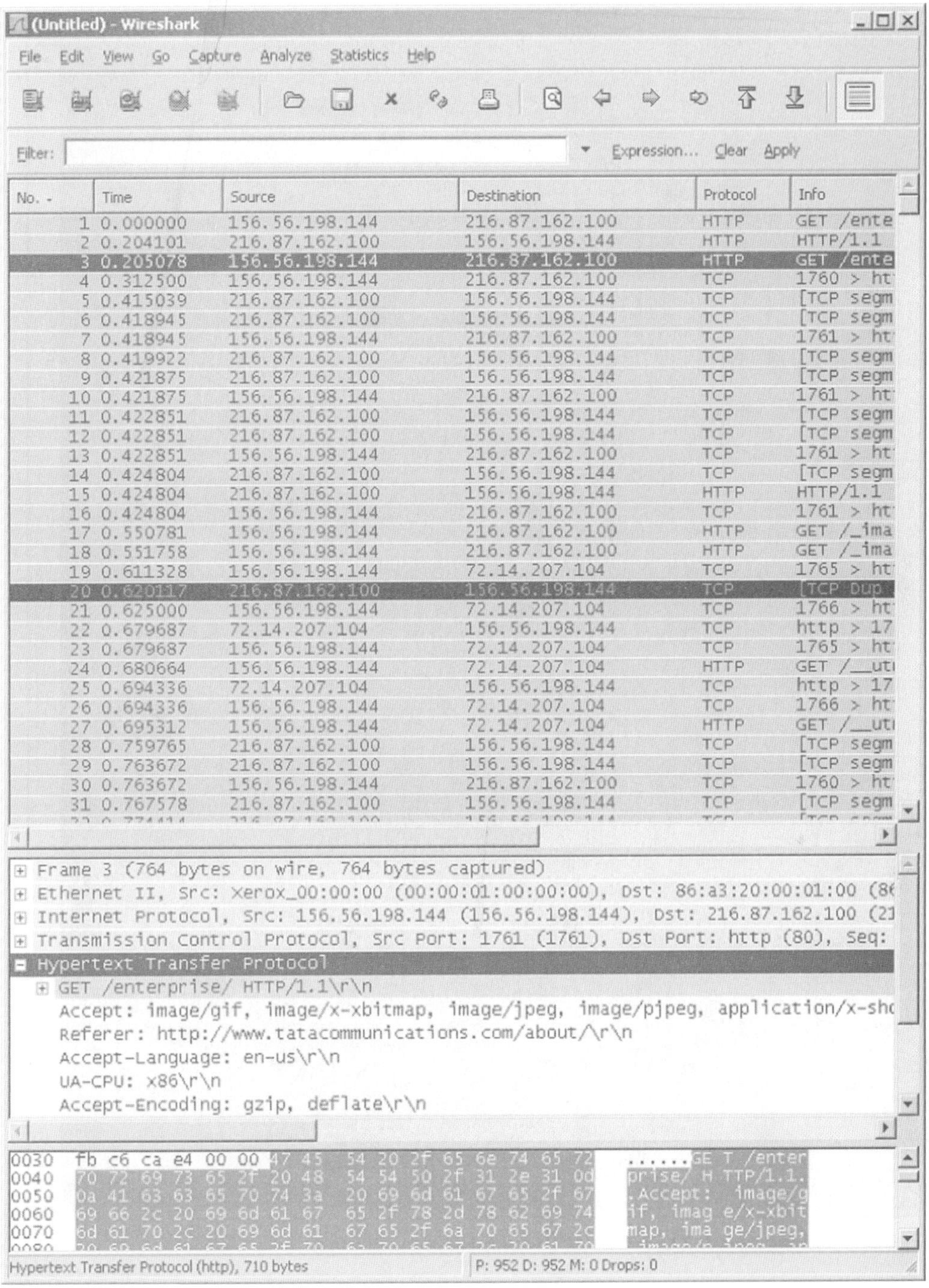

FIGURE 9.22 Packets that enter the VPN tunnel

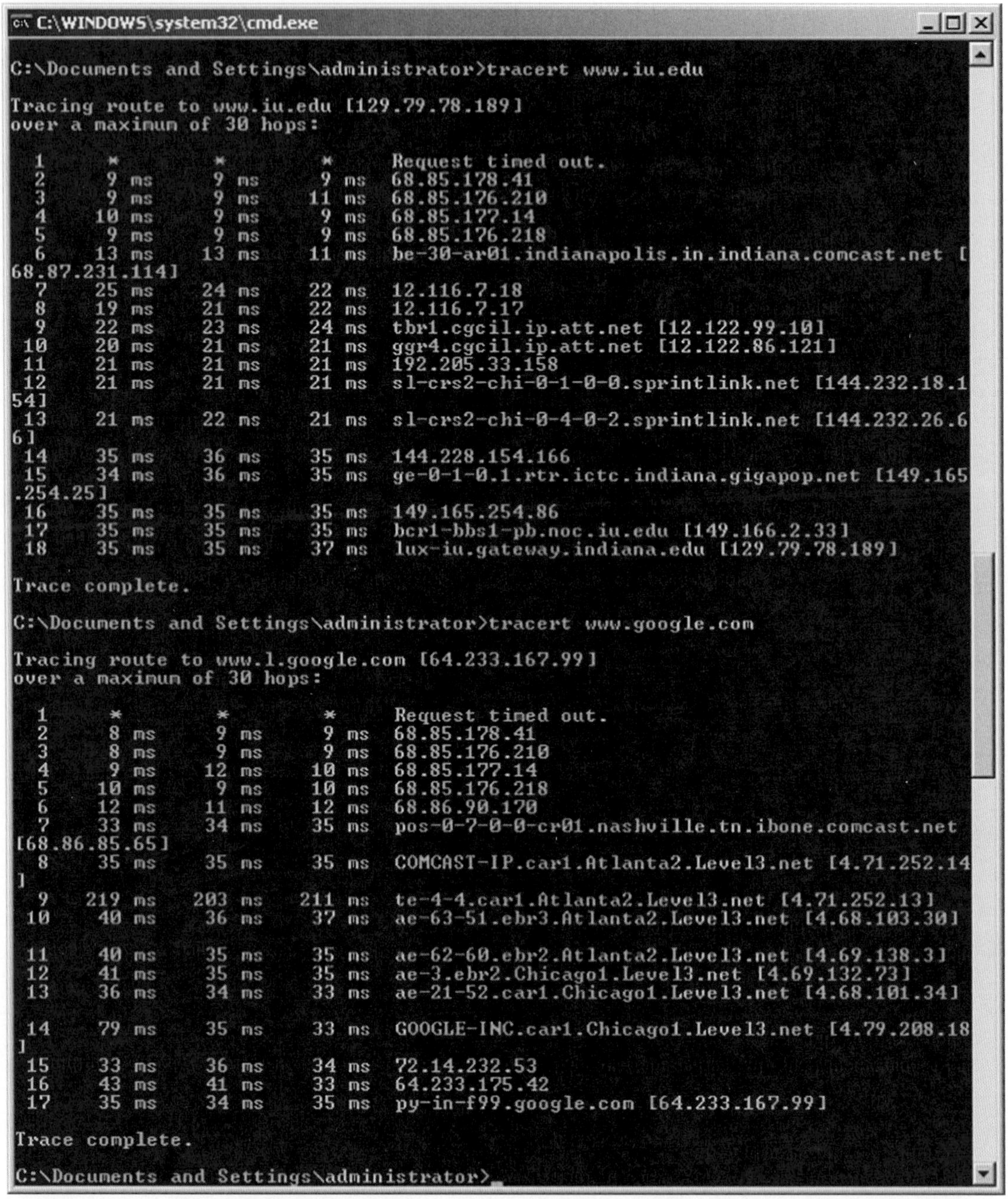

FIGURE 9.23 TraceRt without a VPN

FIGURE 9.24 TraceRt with a VPN

hops and it takes about 35 ms. The VPN is in operation and is transparent to my networking software, which thinks it is on the same subnet as the VPN gateway. Therefore, it thinks there is just one hop from my computer to the subnet's gateway, the VPN gateway. You'll see that the time is still about 35 ms, so the packet is still traveling the same 18 hops to get there; it's just that the tracert packet is encapsulated and doesn't see all the hops through the VPN tunnel.

9. Now do a tracert to the same computer as you did in step 5. The bottom of Figure 9.24 shows the route from my computer to www.google.com. There are nine hops and it takes about 43 ms. Of course, the first hop is really 17 hops and 35 ms; this is again hidden from view. As we explained in the text, when the VPN is connected, all packets go from your computer to the VPN gateway on your campus before being routed to the final destination. You can see from Figure 9.24 that this adds additional hops and time to packets that are not going to your campus, compared to not using the VPN. You can also see that once the packets leave the VPN gateway they are ordinary packets; they are no longer encrypted and protected from view.

The VPN provides security only to and from the VPN gateway on your campus, not beyond it. Therefore, you should use your VPN if you have security concerns to and from campus (e.g., someone sniffing your packets). But if most of your work is going to be off campus, then the VPN increases the time it takes to send and receive packets, and only provides security protection over the last section from your computer to your school's campus. Using the VPN may not be worth the additional response time it imposes on you.

CHAPTER 10

THE INTERNET

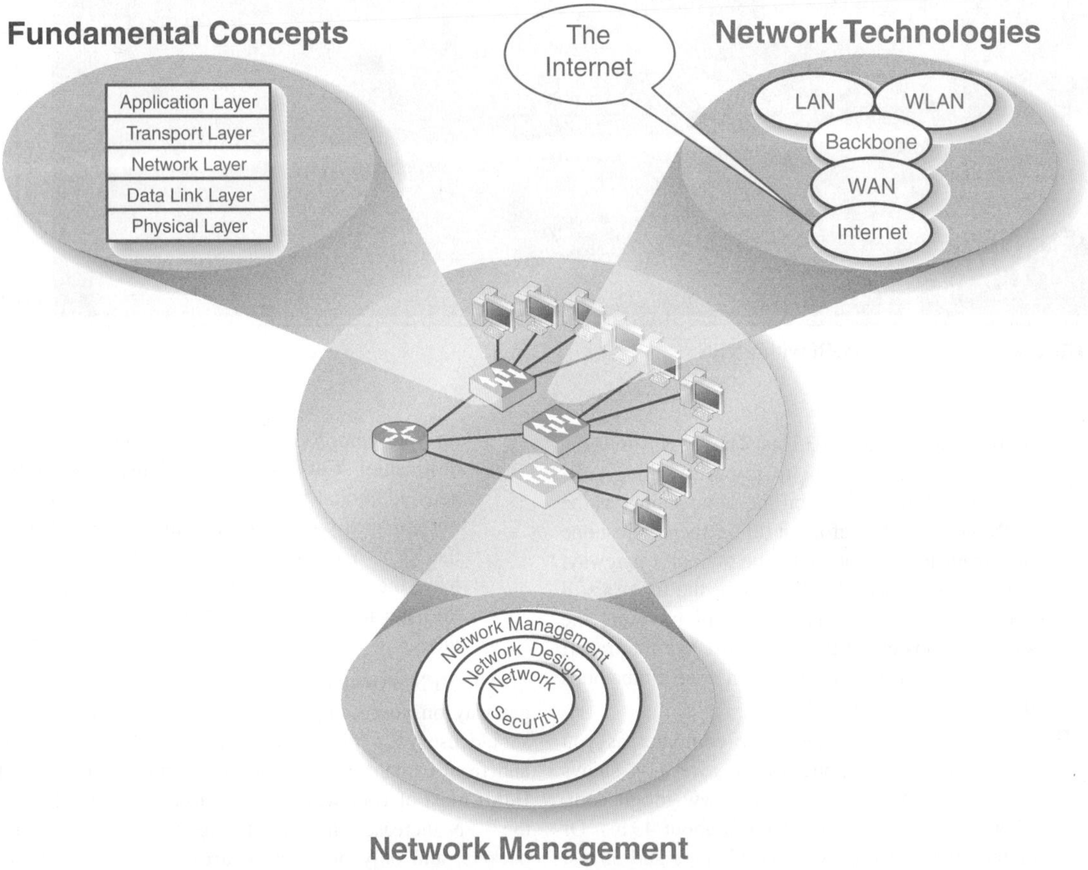

The Three Faces of Networking

THIS CHAPTER examines the Internet in more detail to explain how it works and why it is a network of networks. This chapter also examines Internet access technologies, such as DSL and cable modem, as well as the possible future of the Internet in the form of Internet 2.

OBJECTIVES ▼

- Understand the overall design of the Internet
- Be familiar with DSL, cable modem, and Wireless
- Be familiar with Internet 2

CHAPTER OUTLINE ▼

INTRODUCTION

The Internet is the most used network in the world, but it is also one of the least understood. There is no one network that is *the* Internet. Instead, the Internet is a network of networks—a set of separate and distinct networks operated by various national and state government agencies, nonprofit organizations, and for-profit corporations. The Internet exists only to the extent that these thousands of separate networks agree to use Internet protocols and to exchange data packets among one another.

The Internet is simultaneously a strict, rigidly controlled club in which deviance from the rules is not tolerated and a freewheeling, open marketplace of ideas. All networks that connect to the Internet must rigidly conform to an unyielding set of standards for the transport and network layers; without these standards, data communication would not be possible. At the same time, content and new application protocols are developed freely and without restriction, and quite literally anyone in the world is allowed to comment on proposed changes.

In this chapter, we first explain how the Internet really works and look inside one of the busiest intersections on the Internet, the Chicago network access point, at which about 100 separate Internet networks meet to exchange data. We then turn our attention to how you as an individual can access the Internet and what the Internet may look like in the future.

HOW THE INTERNET WORKS

Basic Architecture

The Internet is hierarchical in structure. At the top are the very large national **Internet service providers (ISPs),** such as AT&T and Sprint, that are responsible for large Internet networks. These **national ISPs,** sometimes called **tier 1 ISPs,** connect together and exchange data at **network access points (NAPs)** (Figure 10.1).

In the early 1990s, when the Internet was still primarily run by the U.S. National Science Foundation (NSF), the NSF established four main NAPs in the United States to connect the major national ISPs. When the NSF stopped funding the Internet, the

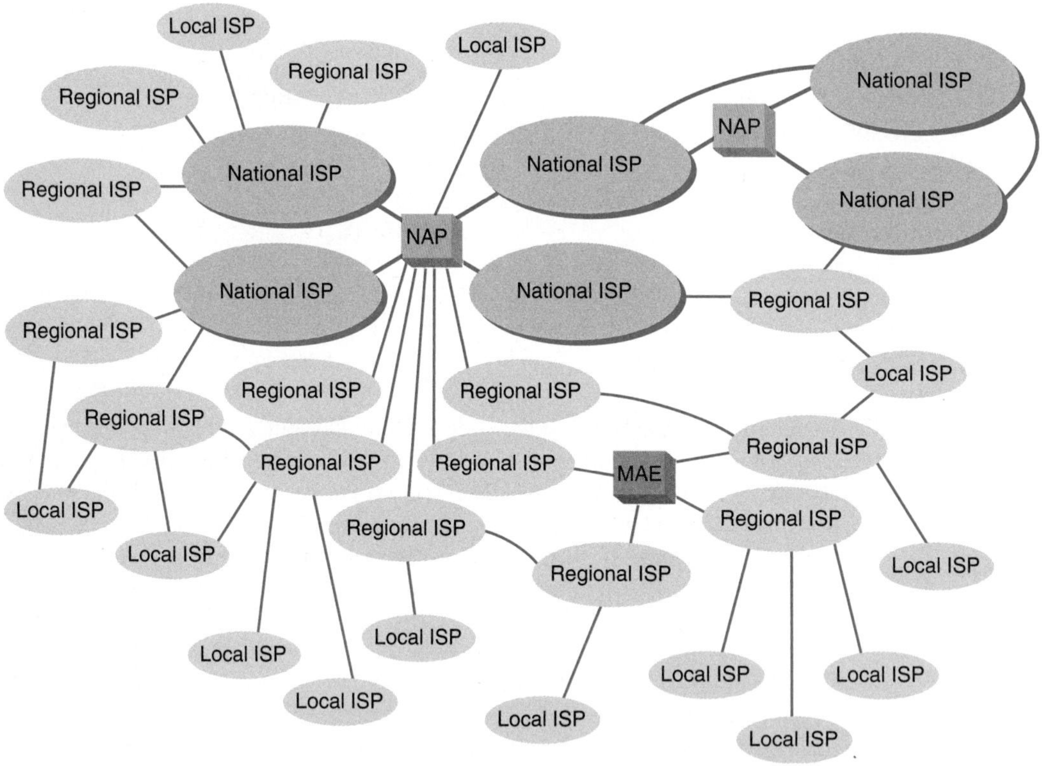

FIGURE 10.1 Basic Internet architecture. ISP = Internet service provider; MAE = metropolitan area exchange; NAP = network access point

companies running these NAPs began charging the national ISPs for connections, so today the NAPs in the United States are all commercial enterprises run by various common carriers such as AT&T and Sprint. As the Internet has grown, so too has the number of NAPs; today there are about a dozen NAPs in the United States with many more spread around the world.

NAPs were originally designed to connect only national ISPs. These national ISPs in turn provide services for their customers and also to **regional ISPs** (sometimes called **tier 2 ISPs**) such as Cogent Communications or France Telcom. These regional ISPs rely on the national ISPs to transmit their messages to national ISPs in other countries. Regional ISPs, in turn, provide services to their customers and to local ISPs (sometimes called **tier 3 ISPs**) who sell Internet access to individuals. As the number of ISPs grew, a new form of NAP called a **metropolitan area exchange (MAE)** emerged. MAEs are smaller versions of NAPs and typically link a set of regional ISPs whose networks come together in major cities (Figure 10.1). Today there are about 50 MAEs in the United States.

Because most NAPs, MAEs, and ISPs now are run by commercial firms, many of the early restrictions on who could connect to whom have been lifted. Indiana University, for example, which might be considered a local ISP because it provides Internet access for about 40,000 individuals, has a direct connection into the Chicago NAP, as do several other universities and large corporations. Regional and local ISPs often will have several connections into other national, regional, and local ISPs to provide backup connections in case one Internet connection fails. In this way, they are not dependent on just one higher-level ISP.

In general, ISPs at the same level do not charge one another for transferring messages they exchange across a NAP or MAE. That is, a national tier 1 ISP does not charge another national tier 1 ISP to transmit its messages. This is called **peering.** Figure 10.1 shows several examples of peering. It is peering that makes the Internet work and has led to the belief that the Internet is free. This is true to some extent, but higher-level ISPs normally charge lower-level ISPs to transmit their data (e.g., a national will charge a regional and a regional will charge a local). And of course, a local ISP will charge individuals like us for access!

In October, 2005, an argument between two national ISPs shut down 45 million Web sites for a week. The two ISPs had a peering agreement but one complained that the other was sending it more traffic than it should so it demanded payment and stopped accepting traffic, leaving large portions of the network isolated from the rest of the Internet. The dispute was resolved, and they began accepting traffic from each other and the rest of the Internet again.

In Figure 10.1, each of the ISPs are **autonomous systems,** as defined in Chapter 5. Each ISP is responsible for running its own interior routing protocols and for exchanging routing information via the BGP exterior routing protocol (see Chapter 5) at NAPs and MAEs and any other connection points between individual ISPs.

Connecting to an ISP

Each of the ISPs is responsible for running its own network that forms part of the Internet. ISPs make money by charging customers to connect to their part of the Internet. Local

ISPs charge individuals for broadband or dial-up access whereas national and regional ISPs (and sometimes local ISPs) charge larger organizations for higher-speed access.

Each ISP has one or more **points of presence (POP).** A POP is simply the place at which the ISP provides services to its customers. To connect into the Internet, a customer must establish a circuit from his or her location into the ISP POP. For individuals, this is often done using a DSL modem, cable modem, or dial-up modem over a traditional telephone line (Figure 10.2). This call connects to the modem pool at the ISP and from there to a **remote-access server (RAS),** which checks the user ID and password to make sure the caller is a valid customer. Once logged in, the user can begin sending TCP/IP packets from his or her computer over the phone to the POP. Figure 10.2 shows a POP using a switched backbone with a layer-2 switch. The POP backbone can take many forms, as we discussed in Chapter 8.

In the next section, we will discuss Internet access technologies such as DSL, cable modem, and Wireless Application Protocol (WAP) in more detail. Customers who need more network capacity simply lease a higher-capacity circuit. Figure 10.2 shows corporate customers with T1, T3, and OC-3 connections into the ISP POP. It is important to note that the customer must pay for both Internet access (paid to the ISP) and for the circuit connecting from their location to the POP (usually paid to the local exchange

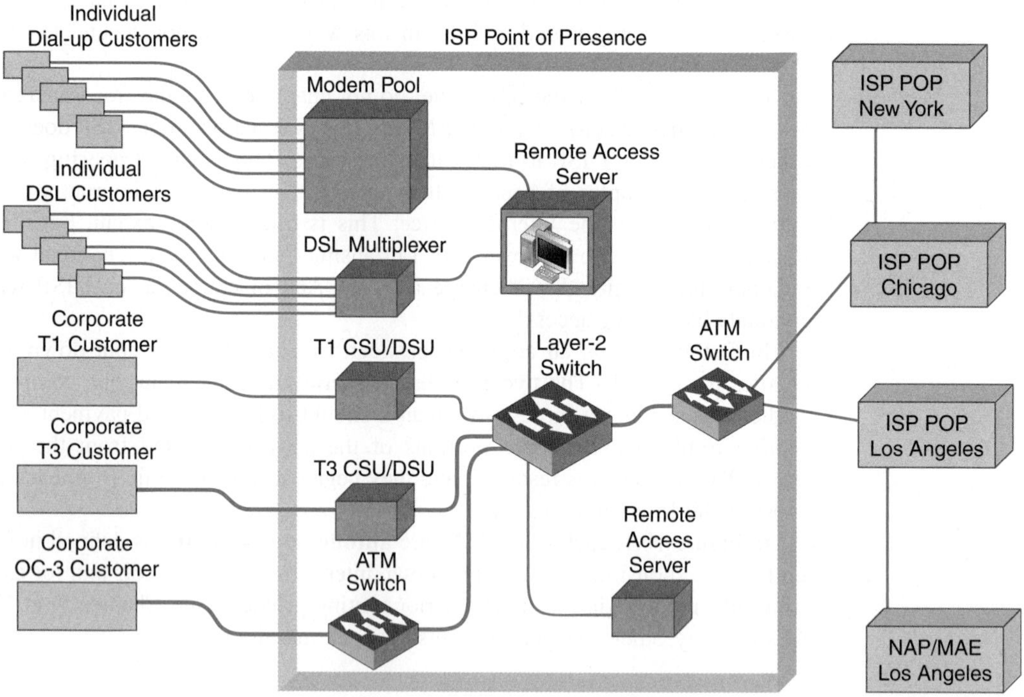

FIGURE 10.2 Inside an Internet service provider (ISP) point of presence (POP). ATM = asynchronous transfer mode; CSU = channel service unit; DSU = data service unit; MAE = metropolitan area exchange; NAP = network access point

MANAGEMENT FOCUS 10.1 INSIDE THE CHICAGO NETWORK ACCESS POINT

The Chicago network access point (NAP) is one of the busiest NAPs in the world. As we write this, it processes an average of about 4 gigabits of data per second.

More than 140 different Internet service providers (ISPs), including national ISPs (e.g., BBN Planet and Sprint), regional ISPs (e.g., Michigan's Merit network), and local ISPs (e.g., Indiana University), as well as ISPs in other countries (e.g., Germany's Tiscali network and the Singapore Advanced Research and Education Network), exchange traffic at the Chicago NAP. At present, most connections are asynchronous transfer mode (ATM) OC-3, or ATM OC-12, and the rest are T3. Pricing starts at about $4,000 per month for T3 and about $4,700 per month for OC-3. (Remember, this is only for Internet access; the ISPs must also lease a T3 or OC-3 circuit from their closest point-of-presence [POP] to the NAP.)

The NAP currently uses a large Cisco ATM switch that connects the more than 140 separate ISP networks (Figure 10.3). The ISP networks exchange IP packets through the NAP. They also exchange routing information through the Border Gateway Protocol (BGP) exterior routing protocol. Normally, the border router at each ISP simply generates BGP packets and sends them to the border routers at the other ISPs connected to the NAP. The Chicago NAP has so many ISPs that this is impossible. Because there are about 140 ISPs, each ISP would send messages to about 140 other ISPs, meaning a total of about 1 million BGP packets moving through the NAP every few minutes.

Instead, the Chicago NAP uses a route server in much the same way large networks based on OSPF (Open Shortest Path First) used designated routers (see "Routing on the Internet" in Chapter 5). The border router in each ISP sends BGP packets just to the NAP route server. The route server consolidates the routing information and then sends BGP packets back to each border router. This results in more efficient processing and only 200 messages every few minutes.

SOURCE: www.aads.net/main.html.

carrier [e.g., BellSouth, AT&T], but sometimes the ISP also can provide circuits). For a T1 connection, for example, a company might pay the local exchange carrier $400 per month to provide the T1 circuit from its offices to the ISP POP and *also* pay the ISP $300 per month to provide the Internet access.

As Figure 10.2 shows, the ISP POP is connected in turn to the other POPs in the ISP's network. Any messages destined for other customers of the same ISP would flow within the ISP's own network. In most cases, the majority of messages entering the POP are sent outside of the ISP's network and thus must flow through the ISP's network to the nearest NAP/MAE, and from there, into some other ISP's network.

This can be less efficient than one might expect. For example, suppose you are connected to the Internet via a local ISP in Minneapolis and request a Web page from another organization in Minneapolis. A short distance, right? Maybe not. If the other organization uses a different local ISP, which in turn uses a different regional ISP, the message may have to travel all the way to the Chicago NAP before it can move between the two separate parts of the Internet.

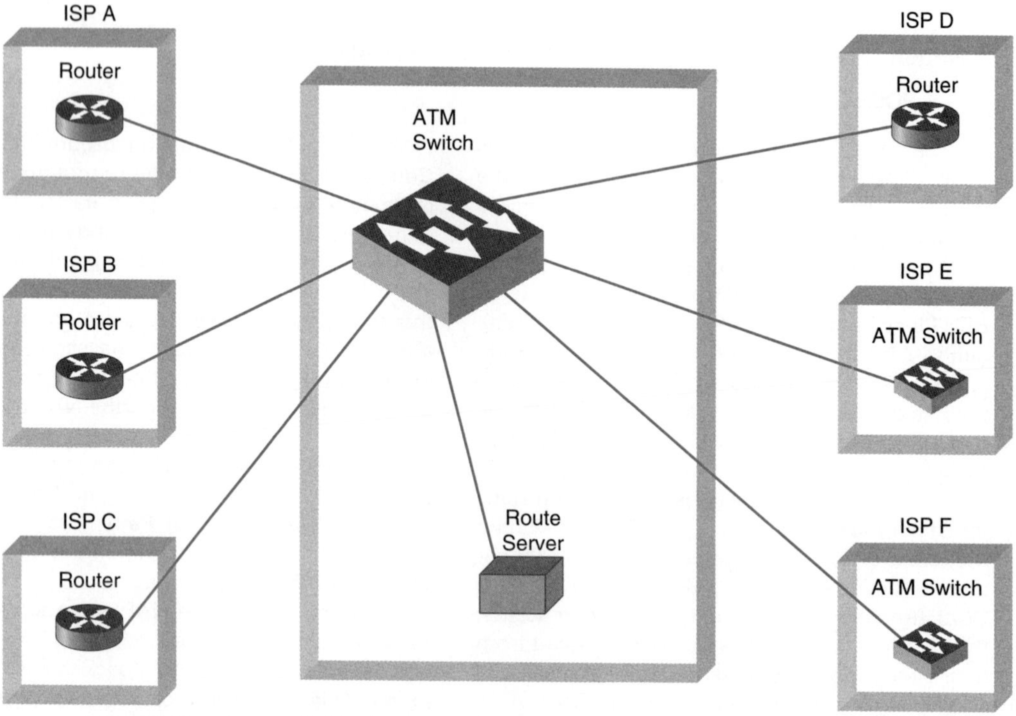

FIGURE 10.3 Inside the Internet's Chicago network access point. ATM = asynchronous transfer mode; ISP = Internet service provider

The Internet Today

Sprint is one of the national ISPs in North America. Figure 10.4 shows Sprint's North American backbone as it existed while we were writing this book; it will have changed by the time you read this. As you can see, Sprint has a number of Internet circuits across the United States and Canada. Many interconnect in Chicago where Sprint connects into the Chicago NAP. Sprint also connects into major NAPs and MAEs in Reston, Virginia; Miami; Los Angeles; San Jose; Palo Alto; Vancouver; Calgary; Toronto; and Montreal. Most of the circuits are SONET OC-12, but a few are OC-48 and OC-192.

Today, the backbone circuits of the major U.S. national ISPs operate at SONET OC-48 and OC-192. Most of the largest national ISPs (e.g., Sprint, Cable & Wireless) plan to convert their principal backbones to OC-192 (10 Gbps). A few are now experimenting with OC-768 (80 Gbps), and several are in the planning stages with OC-3072 (160 Gbps). This is good because the amount of Internet traffic has been growing rapidly. The Internet traffic in the U.S. is expected to reach 80 Tbps (80 trillion bits per second) by 2011.

As traffic increases, ISPs can add more and faster circuits relatively easily, but where these circuits come together at NAPs and MAEs, bottlenecks are becoming more common. Network vendors such as Cisco and Juniper are making larger and larger switches capable of handling these high-capacity circuits, but it is a daunting task. When

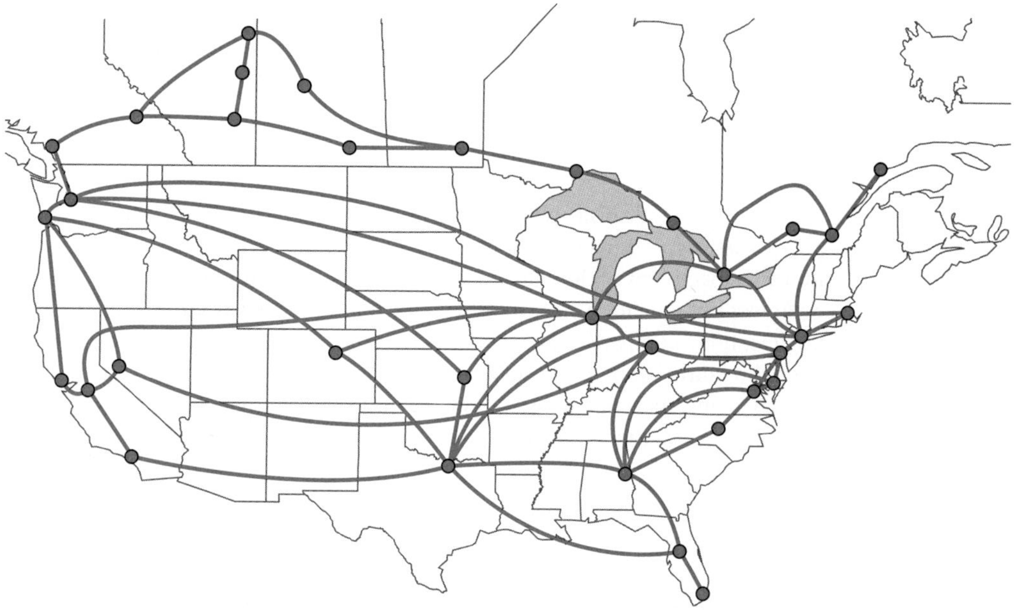

FIGURE 10.4 Sprint's North American Internet backbone

circuit capacities increase by 100 percent, switch manufacturers also must increase their capacities by 100 percent. It is simpler to go from a 622 Mbps circuit to a 10 Gbps circuit than to go from a 20 Gbps switch to a 200 Gbps switch.

The Internet is constantly changing. Up-to-date maps of the major ISPs whose networks make up large portions of the Internet are available at navigators.com/isp.html.

INTERNET ACCESS TECHNOLOGIES

There are many ways in which individuals and organizations can connect to an ISP. Some individuals use 56-Kbps dial-up modems over telephone lines; some use DSL or cable modem. As we discussed in the preceding section, many organizations lease T1 or T3 lines into their ISPs. DSL and cable modem technologies are commonly called **broadband technologies** because they provide higher-speed communications than traditional modems.[1]

It is important to understand that Internet access technologies are used only to connect from one location to an ISP. Unlike the MAN and WAN technologies in the previous chapter, Internet access technologies cannot be used for general-purpose

[1] *Broadband* is a technical term that means "analog transmission" (see Chapter 3). The new broadband technologies often use analog transmission, so they were called broadband. However, the term *broadband* has been corrupted in common usage so that to most people it usually means "high speed."

networking from any point to any point. In this section, we discuss four principal Internet access technologies (DSL, cable modem, fixed wireless, and mobile wireless) and also discuss some future technologies that may become common.

DSL

Digital subscriber line (DSL) is a family of point-to-point technologies designed to provide high-speed data transmission over traditional telephone lines.[2] The reason for the limited capacity on traditional telephone circuits lies with the telephone and the switching equipment at the end offices. The actual cable in the **local loop** from a home or office to the telephone company end office is capable of providing much higher data transmission rates. So conversion from traditional telephone service (POTS) to DSL usually requires just changing the telephone equipment, not rewiring the local loop, which is what has made it so attractive.

Architecture

DSL uses the existing local loop cable but places different equipment on the customer premises (i.e., the home or office) and in the telephone company end office. The equipment that is installed at the customer location is called the **customer premises equipment (CPE).** Figure 10.5 shows one common type of DSL installation. (There are other forms.) The CPE in this case includes a **line splitter** that is used to separate the traditional voice telephone transmission from the data transmissions. The line splitter directs the telephone signals into the normal telephone system so that if the DSL equipment fails, voice communications are unaffected.

The line splitter also directs the data transmissions into a **DSL modem,** which is sometimes also called a DSL router. As you will recall from Chapter 3, this is both a modem and an FDM multiplexer. The DSL modem produces Ethernet 10Base-T packets so it can be connected directly into a computer or to a router and hub and can serve the needs of a small network.

Figure 10.5 also shows the architecture within the local carrier's end office (i.e., the telephone company office closest to the customer premises). The local loops from many customers enter and are connected to the **main distribution facility (MDF).** The MDF works like the CPE line splitter; it splits the voice traffic from the data traffic and directs the voice traffic to the voice telephone network and the data traffic to the **DSL access multiplexer (DSLAM).** The DSLAM demultiplexes the data streams and converts them into ATM data, which are then distributed to the ISPs. Some ISPs are collocated, in that they have their POPs physically in the telephone company end offices. Other ISPs have their POPs located elsewhere.

Types of DSL

DSL services are not available in all locations. In general, DSL services have advanced more quickly in Canada, Europe, Australia, and Asia than in the United States, owing to their newer telephone networks from the end offices to the customer.

[2]DSL is rapidly changing because it is so new. More information can be found from the DSL forum (www.adsl.com, www.dsllife.com) and the ITU-T under standard G.992.

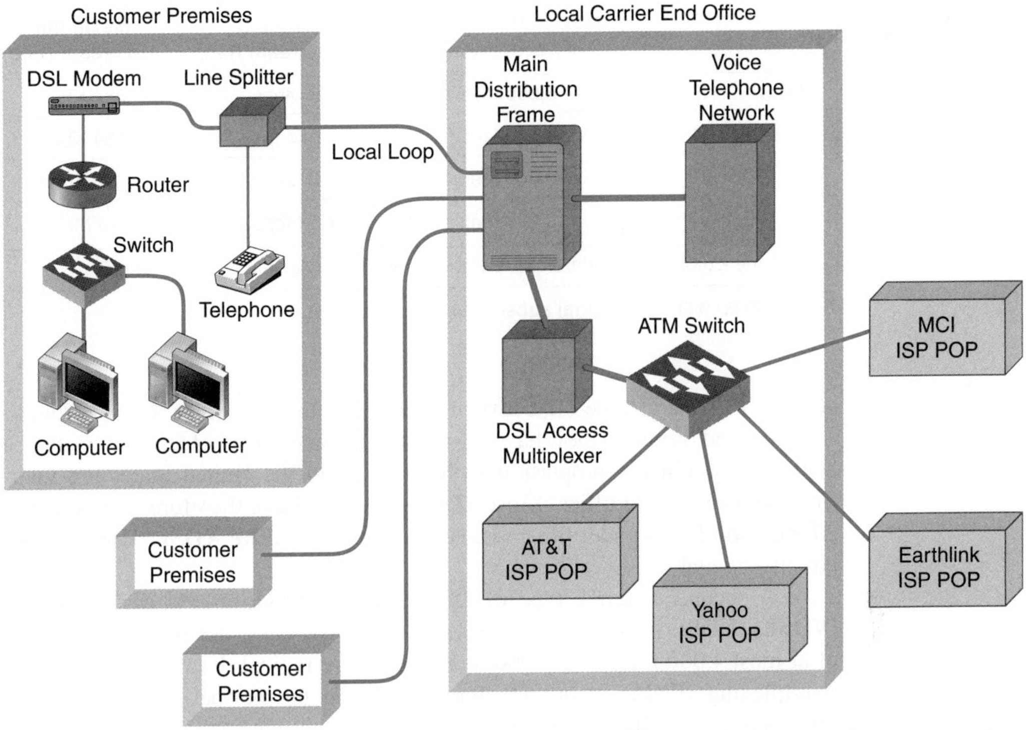

FIGURE 10.5 Digital subscriber line (DSL) architecture. ATM = asynchronous transfer mode; ISP = Internet service provider; POP = point of presence

There are many different types of DSL. The most common type of DSL in use today is **asymmetric DSL (ADSL).** ADSL uses frequency division multiplexing (see Chapter 3) to create three separate channels over the one local loop circuit. One channel is the traditional voice telephone circuit. A second channel is a relatively high-speed simplex data channel downstream from the carrier's end office to the customer. The third channel is a slightly slower duplex data channel primarily used for upstream from the customer to the carrier's end office.[3] ADSL is called asymmetric because its two data channels have different speeds. Each of the two data channels are further multiplexed using time division multiplexing so they can be further subdivided.

The size of the two digital channels depends on the distance from the CPE to the end office. The shorter the distance, the higher the speed, because with a shorter distance, the circuit suffers less attenuation and higher-frequency signals can be used, providing a greater bandwidth for modulation. Figure 10.6 lists the common types of ADSL.

ADSL providers face a challenge in selecting what type of ADSL to offer in a given market. On one hand, customers want the highest speed access possible. However,

[3]Because the second data channel is intended primarily for upstream data communication, many authors imply that this is a simplex channel, but it is actually a set of half-duplex channels.

Type	Maximum Length of Local Loop	Maximum Downstream Rate	Maximum Upstream Rate
ADSL T1 (G.Lite)	18,000 feet	1.5 Mbps	384 Kbps
ADSL E1*	16,000 feet	2.0 Mbps	384 Kbps
ADSL T2	12,000 feet	6 Mbps	640 Kbps
SDSL	18,000 feet	1.5 Mbps	1.5 Mbps
*E1 is the European standard services similar to T1 services in North America.			

FIGURE 10.6 Digital subscriber line data rates

because there is a trade-off between speed and distance, if an ADSL provider chooses a high-speed version, they have just limited the number of customers they can serve because a significant proportion of households in the United States are long distances from the nearest end office. Most ADSL providers have therefore chosen the T1 level of ADSL and offer it under the trademarked name of **G.Lite ADSL.** Higher speed versions are also available.

A second common type of DSL is **very-high-data-rate digital subscriber line (VDSL).** VDSL is asymmetric DSL service designed for use over very short local loops of at most 4,000 feet, with 1,000 feet being more typical. It also uses frequency division multiplexing (FDM) to provide three channels: the normal analog voice channel, an upstream digital channel, and a downstream digital channel. Figure 10.7 lists the types of VDSL we anticipate will become common.

VDSL has several standards that are in use. The exact data speeds and channels are likely to change as manufacturers, telephone companies, and ITU-T gain more experience and as the standards groups attempt to merge competing standards. Several companies are also developing symmetric versions of VDSL in which upstream and downstream channels have the same capacity. We expect major changes to VDSL.

Cable Modems

One alternative to DSL is the **cable modem,** a digital service offered by cable television companies. There are several competing standards, but the **Data over Cable Service Interface Specification (DOCSIS)** standard is the dominant one. DOCSIS is not a formal standard but is the one used by most vendors of **hybrid fiber coax (HFC)** networks

Type	Maximum Length of Local Loop	Maximum Downstream Rate	Maximum Upstream Rate
1/4 OC-1	4,500 feet	13 Mbps	1.6 Mbps
1/2 OC-1	4,000 feet	26 Mbps	2.3 Mbps
OC-1	4,000 feet	52 Mbps	16 Mbps

FIGURE 10.7 Data rates for very-high-data-rate digital subscriber line. OC = optical carrier

(i.e., cable networks that use both fiber-optic and coaxial cable). As with DSL, these technologies are changing rapidly.[4]

Architecture Cable modem architecture is very similar to DSL—with one very important difference. DSL is a point-to-point technology whereas cable modems use *shared* multipoint circuits. With cable modems, each user must compete with other users for the available capacity. Furthermore, because the cable circuit is a multipoint circuit, all messages on the circuit go to all computers on the circuit. If your neighbors were hackers, they could use pocket sniffers such as Ethereal (see Chapter 4) to read all messages that travel over the cable, including yours.

Figure 10.8 shows the most common architecture for cable modems. The cable TV circuit enters the customer premises through a cable splitter that separates the data transmissions from the TV transmissions and sends the TV signals to the TV network and the data signals to the cable modem. The cable modem (both a modem and frequency division multiplexer) translates from the cable data into Ethernet packets,

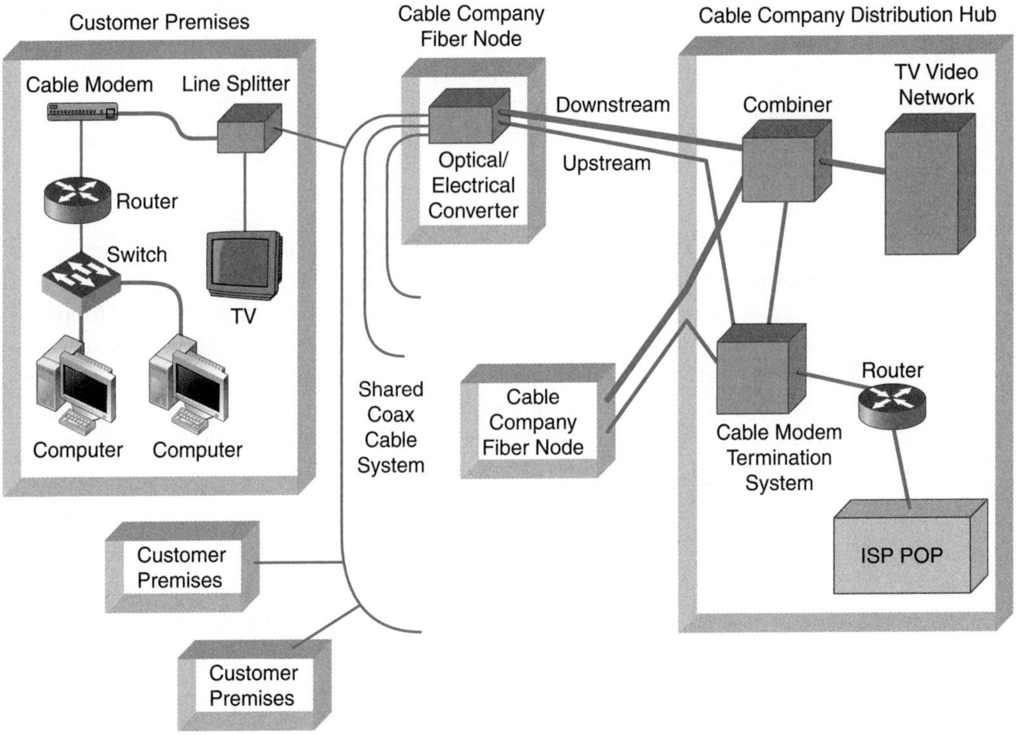

FIGURE 10.8 Cable modem architecture. ISP = Internet service provider; POP = point of presence

[4]More information can be found at www.cablemodem.com and www.cable-modems.org.

which then are directed into a computer to a router and hub for distribution in a small network.

The cable TV cable entering the customer premises is a standard coaxial cable. A typical segment of cable is shared by anywhere from 300 to 1,000 customers, depending on the cable company that installed the cable. These 300 to 1,000 customers share the available data capacity, but of course, not all customers who have cable TV will choose to install cable modems. This coax cable runs to a *fiber node,* which has an **optical-electrical (OE) converter** to convert between the coaxial cable on the customer side and fiber-optic cable on the cable TV company side. Each fiber node serves as many as half a dozen separate coaxial cable runs.

The fiber nodes are in turn connected to the cable company **distribution hub** (sometimes called a headend) through two separate circuits: an upstream circuit and a downstream circuit. The upstream circuit, containing data traffic from the customer, is connected into a **cable modem termination system (CMTS).** The CMTS contains a series of cable modems/multiplexers and converts the data from cable modem protocols into protocols needed for Internet traffic, before passing them to a router connected to an ISP POP. Often, the cable company is an Internet regional ISP, but sometimes it just provides Internet access to a third-party ISP.

The downstream circuit to the customer contains both ordinary video transmissions from the cable TV video network and data transmissions from the Internet. Downstream data traffic enters the distribution hub from the ISP POP and is routed through the CMTS, which produces the cable modem signals. This traffic is then sent to a *combiner,* which combines the Internet data traffic with the ordinary TV video traffic and sends it back to the fiber node for distribution.

Types of Cable Modems The DOCSIS standard provides many types of cable modems. The maximum speed is about 150 Mbps downstream and about 100 Mbps upstream, although most cable TV companies provide at most 27 Mbps downstream and 10 Mbps upstream. Cable modems can be configured to limit capacity, so the most common speeds offered by most cable providers range from 1–10 Mbps downstream and 256 Kbps to 1 Mbps upstream. Of course, this capacity is shared, so an individual user will only see this when no other computers on his or her segment are active.

Fixed Wireless

The most popular types of **fixed wireless** are WiMax (which was discussed in Chapter 7) and **wireless DSL,** which requires a line of sight between the communicating transmitters. For this reason, wireless DSL has limited application because it requires tall buildings or towers to be effective. The most common use today is to provide Internet access to multitenant buildings such as remote office buildings, apartment buildings, and hotels. Transmitters are used to connect the building to the ISP, and DSL is used inside the building to connect to the wireless transceiver (Figure 10.9).

WiMax may become a real competitor to wired Internet services such as cable modem and DSL because several large carriers have formed a new company (Clearwire) to offer 1.5 Mbps WiMax Internet services in major cities throughout the United States.

MANAGEMENT FOCUS 10.2 INTERNET SPEED TEST

The speed of your Internet connection depends upon many things, such as your computer's settings, the connection from your computer to your ISP, and the connections your ISP has into the Internet. There are many Internet sites that enable you to test how fast your Internet connection actually is. Our favorite is speedtest.net.

Fixed wireless comes in both point-to-point and multipoint versions. The point-to-point version is designed to connect only two locations and is often used as backbone between buildings owned by the same organization. The multipoint version is sometimes called point-to-multipoint because there is one central receiver and all other locations communicate only with it. The multipoint version is designed as an alternative to DSL and cable modems and is intended for use by an ISP supporting a small number of customers. Like cable modems, the circuit is a shared circuit, so users must compete for the shared capacity, but most installations are limited to a few dozen users. Data transmission for both versions ranges from 1.5 to 54 Mbps, depending on the vendor.

Other fixed wireless technologies such as *satellite* are also available. Satellite technologies use the satellite for downstream transmissions (from the ISP to the customer) but

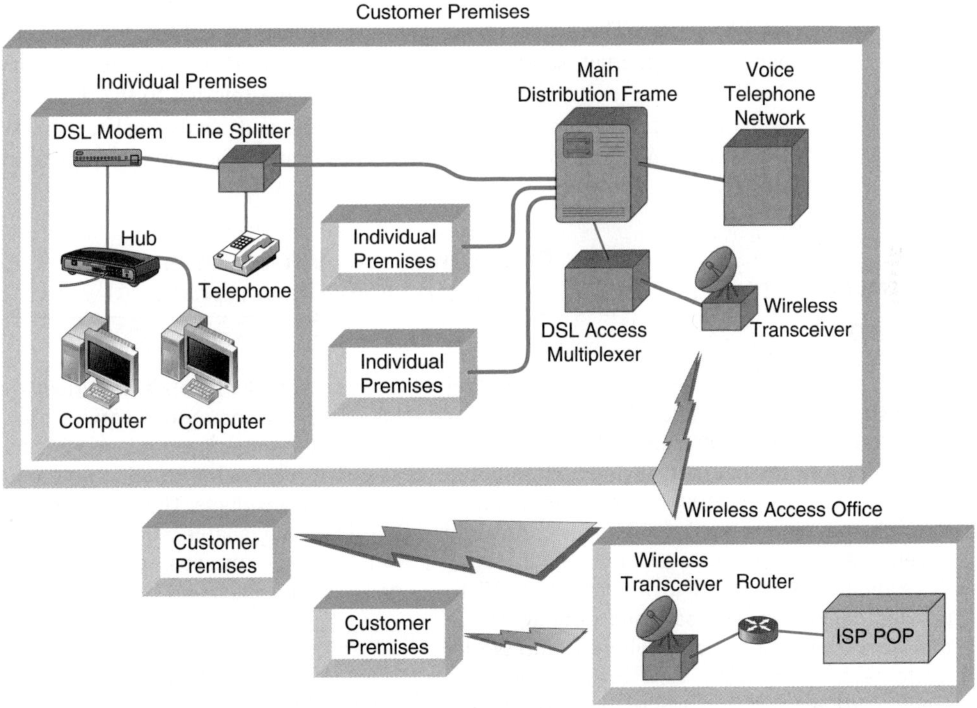

FIGURE 10.9 Fixed wireless architecture. DSL = digital subscriber line; ISP = Internet service provider; POP = point of presence

use traditional dial-up modems for upstream transmissions. Although satellite technology has been available for several years, it has never become really popular.

Mobile Wireless

Mobile wireless technologies enable users to access the Internet from any location where there is mobile wireless service. Widespread mobile wireless Internet access is probably the next major change in networking. Mobile wireless Internet access technologies exist today (e.g., cell phone connections), but most are slow compared with wired access, whether DSL, cable modem, or simply a dial-up modem. The WLAN technologies discussed in Chapter 7 (e.g., 802.11) are primarily intended for use inside one organization although they are also installed in public places such as coffee shops and airports for access to the Internet.

Wireless Application Protocol (WAP) provides a set of application and network protocols called the **Wireless Application Environment (WAE)** to support mobile wireless Internet applications. WAP is designed to enable the use of normal Web applications on computers and devices with small display screens operating over low-speed wireless connections. Figure 10.10 shows the basic WAP architecture.

The WAP client (a mobile phone, palm computer, or laptop computer) runs special WAP software called a WAE user agent. This software generates WAE requests that are similar in many ways to HTTP requests and transmits them wirelessly to a WAP gateway. A transceiver at the WAP gateway passes the requests to a **wireless telephony application (WTA) server.** This server responds to the requests and, if the client has requested a Web page on the Internet, sends a WAE request to a **WAP proxy.** The WAP proxy translates the WAE request into HTTP and sends it over the Internet to the desired Web server.

This Web server responds to the request and sends back to the WAP proxy an HTTP response that contains HTML, JPEG, and other Internet application protocols.

MANAGEMENT FOCUS 10.3

Banking on Wireless Application Protocol

SkandiaBanken, a leading Swedish Internet bank, provides retail banking services to over 350,000 clients. The bank operates entirely via the Internet, having no traditional branches. Customers communicate with the bank through the Web, e-mail, telephones, and now Wireless Application Protocol (WAP) technology.

SkandiaBanken chose to implement WAP to provide customers with safe and easy access to their financial data from anywhere in the world. Customers can securely view their deposit and credit card accounts, execute their credit card payments, make balance inquiries, and pay their bills. Users of the mobile service may also check the foreign exchange, gold, and treasury bill rates, as well as access information on the bank's range of financial products. There is even location-based information available, such as city guides, restaurant reviews, movies, theaters, museums, art galleries, libraries, and other important facilities.

SOURCE: "Financial Institutions Worldwide Use Infinite WAP Server to Offer Mobile Banking," Infinite.com.

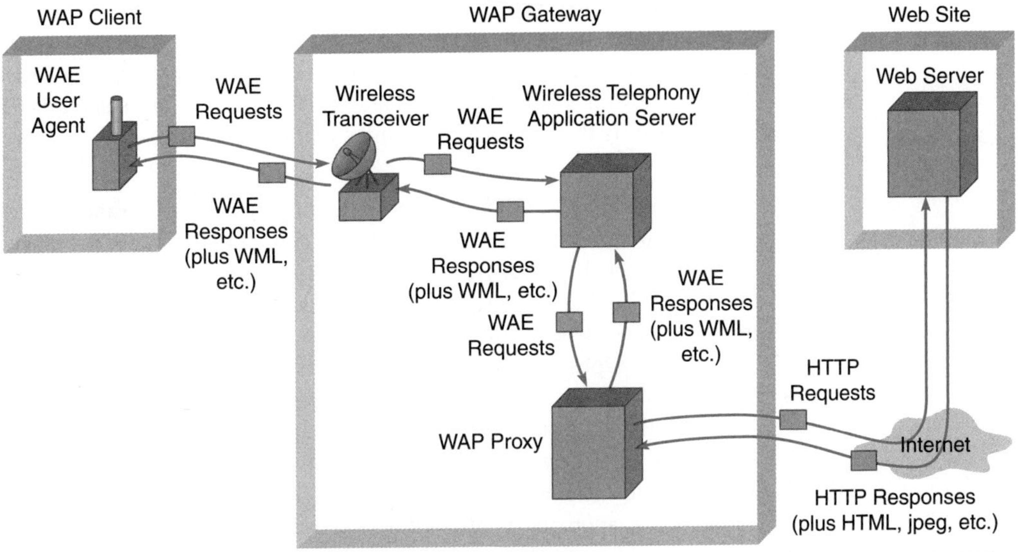

FIGURE 10.10 Mobile wireless architecture for Wireless Application Protocol (WAP) applications. HTML = Hypertext Markup Language; HTTP = Hypertext Transfer Protocol; WAE = Wireless Application Environment; WML = Wireless Markup Language

The WAP proxy in turn translates these into their WAE equivalents and sends them to the WTA server, which sends them to the client.

Future Technologies

Internet access technologies are one of the fastest growth areas in networking, so there are several new technologies that have the potential to become important alternatives to DSL, cable modems, and wireless technologies. In this section, we focus on two up-and-coming technologies: passive optical networking (PON) and Ethernet.

Passive Optical Networking

Passive optical networking (PON), sometimes called **fiber-to-the-home (FTTH),** is exactly what it sounds like: running fiber-optic cable into the home. The traditional set of hundreds of copper telephone lines that run from the telephone company switch office is replaced by one fiber-optic cable that is run past each house or office in the neighborhood. Data is transmitted down the signal fiber cable using wavelength division multiplexing (WDM), providing hundreds or thousands of separate channels. At each subscriber location, a fiber splitter separates the channels belonging to that location and runs them into an optical electrical converter, which then connects to an Ethernet switch.

This approach is called passive optical because the splitters require no electrical current and thus are quicker and easier to install than traditional electrical-based hubs and repeaters. However, because they are passive, the optical signal fades quickly, giving a maximum length of about ten miles.

Each single fiber has a capacity of about 155 Mbps, which must be allocated among the subscribers. This means about 1.5 Mbps if there are 100 subscribers per fiber, or 15 Mbps if there are only ten subscribers. At present, there are no standards for PON and FTTH, but several vendors have joined together to develop standards. The larger problem, of course, is the cost of laying miles and miles of fiber-optic cable.

Ethernet to the Home

Perhaps the most exciting possibility is Ethernet to the home. If we were to start over and design an entirely new network for Internet access from home, we would probably start with Ethernet because of its low cost and popularity in organizational LANs. Using common protocols would make the whole task of networking much simpler for everyone involved.

Pioneered by **Yipes.com,** such an approach is exactly what is being used in several major U.S. cities. With this approach, the common carrier installs a TCP/IP router with 10Base-T or 100Base-T connections into the customer's network and an Ethernet fiber on the other. The IP/Ethernet traffic moves from the router into the carrier's Ethernet MAN and then onto the Internet.

Although this approach is also limited because of the cost of providing Ethernet fiber to the customer, we believe this has great potential. Because conversions between protocols are not required at the customer site, connecting to the network is much simpler than with other Internet access technologies.

INTERNET GOVERNANCE

Because the Internet is a network of networks, no one organization operates the Internet. The closest thing the Internet has to an owner is the **Internet Society (ISOC)** (www.isoc.org). ISOC is an open-membership professional society with more than 175 organizational and 8,000 individual members in over 100 countries, including corporations, government agencies, and foundations that have created the Internet and its technologies. Because membership in ISOC is open, anyone, including students, is welcome to join and vote on key issues facing the Internet.

The ISOC mission is to ensure "the open development, evolution and use of the Internet for the benefit of all people throughout the world."[5] ISOC works in three general areas: public policy, education, and standards. In terms of public policy, ISOC participates in the national and international debates on important issues such as censorship, copyright, privacy, and universal access. ISOC delivers training and education programs targeted at improving the Internet infrastructure in developing nations. The most important ISOC activity lies in the development and maintenance of Internet standards. ISOC works through four interrelated standards bodies: Internet Engineering Task Force (IETF), Internet Engineering Steering Group (IESG), Internet Architecture Board (IAB), and Internet Research Task Force (IRTF).

[5]See www.isoc.org/isoc/mission.

The **Internet Engineering Task Force (IETF)** (www.ietf.org) is a large, open international community of network designers, operators, vendors, and researchers concerned with the evolution of the Internet architecture and the smooth operation of the Internet. IETF works through a series of working groups, which are organized by topic (e.g., routing, transport, security). The **requests for comment (RFCs)** that form the basis for Internet standards are developed by the IETF and its working groups.

Closely related to the IETF is the **Internet Engineering Steering Group (IESG).** The IESG is responsible for technical management of IETF activities and the Internet standards process. It administers the process according to the rules and procedures that have been ratified by the ISOC trustees. The IESG is directly responsible for the actions associated with entry into and movement along the Internet "standards track," including final approval of specifications as Internet standards. Each IETF working group is chaired by a member of the IESG.

Whereas the IETF develops standards and the IESG provides the operational leadership for the IETF working groups, the **Internet Architecture Board (IAB)** provides strategic architectural oversight. The IAB attempts to develop conclusions on strategic issues (e.g., top-level domain names, use of international character sets) that can be passed on as guidance to the IESG or turned into published statements or simply passed directly to the relevant IETF working group. In general, the IAB does not produce polished technical proposals but rather tries to stimulate action by the IESG or

TECHNICAL FOCUS 10.1 Registering an Internet Domain Name

Until the 1990s, there was only a moderate number of computers on the Internet. One organization was responsible for registering domain names (sets of application layer addresses) and assigning IP addresses for each top-level domain (e.g., .COM). Network Solutions, for example, was the sole organization responsible for domain name registrations for the .COM, .NET, and .ORG domains. In October 1998, the **Internet Corporation for Assigned Names and Numbers (ICANN)** was formed to assume responsibility for the IP address space and domain name system management.

In spring 1999, ICANN established the Shared Registration System (SRS) that enabled many organizations to perform domain name registration and address assignment using a shared database. More than 80 organizations are now accredited by ICANN as registrars and are permitted to use the SRS. Each registrar has the right to assign names and addresses in one or more top-level domains. For a list of registrars and the domains they serve, see www.internic.com.

If you want to register a new domain name and obtain an IP address, you can contact any accredited registrar for that top-level domain. One of the oldest privately operated registrars is register.com. Each registrar follows the same basic process for registering a name and assigning an address, but each may charge a different amount for their services. In order to register a name, you must first check to see if it is available (i.e., that no one else has registered it). If the name has already been registered, you can find out who owns it and perhaps attempt to buy it from them.

If the domain name is available, you will need to provide the IP address of the DNS server that will be used to store all IP addresses in the domain. Most large organizations have their own DNS servers, but small companies and individuals often use the DNS of their ISP.

the IETF that will lead to proposals that meet general consensus. The IAB appoints the IETF chairperson and all IESG members, from a list provided by the IETF nominating committee. The IAB also adjudicates appeals when someone complains that the IESG has failed.

The **Internet Research Task Force (IRTF)** operates much like the IETF through small research groups focused on specific issues. Whereas IETF working groups focus on current issues, IRTF research groups work on long-term issues related to Internet protocols, applications, architecture, and technology. The IRTF chairperson is appointed by the IAB.

INTERNET2

The Internet is changing. New applications and access technologies are being developed at lightning pace. But these innovations do not change the fundamental structure of the Internet. It has evolved more slowly because the core technologies (TCP/IP) are harder to change gradually; it is difficult to change one part of the Internet without changing the attached parts.

Many organizations in many different countries are working on dozens of different projects in an attempt to design new technologies for the next version of the Internet.[6] The two primary American projects working on the future Internet got started at about the same time in 1996. The U.S. National Science Foundation provided $100 million to start the **Next Generation Internet (NGI)** program, and 34 universities got together to start what turned into the **University Corporation for Advanced Internet Development (UCAID),** which developed the **Abilene network,** commonly called **Internet2.** In 1997, the Canadian government established the **Advanced Research and Development Network Operations Center (ARDNOC),** which developed **CA*net,** the Canadian project on the future Internet.[7]

Figure 10.11 shows the major high-speed circuits in the Internet2 network and the CA*net network. All the major circuits in these networks are OC-192 (10 Gbps). The two networks peer in Seattle, Chicago, and New York. National Lambda Rail (www.nlr.net) is another major high-speed network that is experimenting with long distance Ethernet (10 GbE) running over fiber-optic circuits.

Each of the networks has a set of access points called **gigapops,** so named because they provide a point of presence at gigabit speeds. Although traditional Internet NAPs provide connections between networks at T1, T3, OC-1, OC-3, and—occasionally—OC-12 speeds, gigapops are designed to provide access at much higher speeds so that different networks can exchange data at much higher rates of speed, usually OC-198 or 10 Gbps. Gigapops also usually provide a wider range of services than traditional NAPs that are primarily just data exchange points.

Besides providing very high-speed Internet connections, these networks are intended to experiment with new protocols that one day may end up on the future Internet.

[6]For a listing of several major international projects, see www.startap.net.

[7]For more information on these projects, see www.internet2.org and www.canarie.ca.

FIGURE 10.11 Selected high-speed Internet 2 backbones

For example, most of these networks run IPv6 as the primary network layer protocol, rather than IPv4. Most are also working on new ways to provide quality of service (QoS) and multicasting. Some, such as Internet2, are also working on developing new applications for a high-speed Internet, such as tele-immersion and videoconferencing.

MANAGEMENT FOCUS 10.4 INSIDE THE PACIFIC/NORTHWEST GIGAPOP

The Pacific/Northwest Gigapop is located in Seattle, Washington, and is run by the University of Washington and University Corporation for Advanced Internet Development (i.e., Internet2). It provides gigabit Ethernet and SONET OC-192 (10 Gbps) connections to several high-speed networks such as Abilene, CA*net, Microsoft, and the Defense Research and Engineering Network, which is funded by the U.S. Department of Defense. It also provides a network access point for these high-speed networks to connect to lower-speed networks of the traditional Internet, such as those run by Sprint, AT&T, Singapore's SingAREN, and Australia's AARNet, as well as a number of universities in the Pacific Northwest.

The basic core of the gigapop is a set of high-speed switches, connected to high-speed routers. High-speed networks, such as Abilene, connect directly into the core devices whereas lower-speed networks connect into the core via a set of routers.

SOURCE: www.pnw-gigapop.net.

IMPLICATIONS FOR MANAGEMENT

Several years ago, there was great concern that the traffic on the Internet would exceed its capacity. The growth of traffic on the Internet was increasing significantly faster than the construction of new Internet circuits; several experts predicted the collapse of the Internet. It did not happen for the simple reason that companies could make money by building new circuits and charging for their use. Today, there are a large number of fiber-optic circuits that have been built but not yet been turned on. Wavelength division multiplexing technologies mean that 10–20 times more data can now be transmitted through the same fiber-optic cable (see Chapter 3). Many countries, companies, and universities are now building the Next Generation Internet using even newer, experimental, very high-speed technologies. The Internet will not soon run out of capacity.

In recent years, there has been a blossoming of new "broadband" technologies for higher speed Internet access. Individuals and organizations can now access the Internet at relatively high speeds—much higher speeds than we would have even considered reasonable 5–10 years ago. This means that it is now simple to move large amounts of data into most homes and businesses in North America. As a result, software applications that use the Internet can provide a much richer multimedia experience than ever before.

In previous chapters, we have described how there has been a significant reduction in a number of different technologies in use in LANs, backbones, MANs, and WANs over the past few years. We are about to enter that stage with regard to Internet access technologies. Today there are many choices; over the next two years a few dominant standards will emerge, and the market will solidify around those standards. Organizations that invest in the technologies that ultimately become less popular will need to invest significant funds to replace those technologies with the dominant standards. The challenge, of course, is to figure out which technology standards will become dominant. Will it be cable modem and DSL, or Ethernet to the home? Only time will tell.

SUMMARY

How the Internet Works The Internet is a set of separate networks, ranging from large national ISPs to midsize regional ISPs to small local ISPs, that connect with one another at NAPs and MAEs. NAPs and MAEs charge the ISPs to connect, but similar-sized ISPs usually do not charge each other to exchange data. Each ISP has a set of points of presence through which it charges its users (individuals, businesses, and smaller ISPs) to connect to the Internet. Users connect to a POP to get access to the Internet. This connection may be via a dial-up modem over a telephone line or via a higher-speed circuit such as DSL, cable modem, or a T1.

DSL DSL enables users to connect to an ISP POP over a standard point-to-point telephone line. The customer installs a DSL modem that connects via Ethernet to his or her computer system. The modem communicates with a DSLAM at the telephone company office, which sends the data to the ISP POP. ADSL is the most common type of DSL and often provides 1.5 Mbps downstream and 384 Kbps upstream. VDSL is a faster version that runs over short distances and has speeds up to 51.8 Mbps.

Cable Modem Cable modems use a shared multipoint circuit that runs through the cable TV cable. They also provide the customer with a modem that connects via Ethernet to his or her computer system. The modem communicates with a CMTS at the cable company office, which sends the data to the ISP POP. The DOCSIS standard is the dominant standard, but there are no standard data rates today. Typical downstream speeds range between 1 Mbps and 10 Mbps, and typical upstream speeds range between 256 Kbps and 1 Mbps.

Wireless Fixed wireless systems provide DSL-like speeds over a single line-of-sight wireless circuit to a multitenant building. Inside the building, DSL is used to provide service to a large number of users over the existing phone lines. Mobile wireless uses cellular telephone technologies to provide access to small hand-held devices using WAP. WAP translates from traditional Internet protocols such as HTTP and HTML into their WAE equivalents for use in the small devices.

Internet Governance The closest the Internet has to an owner is the ISOC, which works on public policy, education, and Internet standards. Standards are developed through four related organizations governed by ISOC. The IETF develops the actual standards through a series of working groups. The IESG manages IETF activities. The IAB sets long-term strategic directions, and the IRTF works on future issues through working groups in much the same way as the IETF.

Internet2 There are many different organizations currently working on the next generation of the Internet, including the Abilene network, vBNS, and CA*net. Although each is working in a slightly different fashion, all join together with one another and parts of the regular Internet at gigapops (gigabit points of presence).

KEY TERMS

Abilene network
Advanced Research and Development Network Operations Center (ARDNOC)
asymmetric DSL (ADSL)
autonomous systems
broadband technologies
cable modem
cable modem termination system (CMTS)
CA*net
customer premises equipment (CPE)
Data over Cable Service Interface Specification (DOCSIS)
digital subscriber line (DSL)
distribution hub
DSL access multiplexer (DSLAM)
DSL modem
fiber-to-the-home (FTTH)
fixed wireless
gigapop
G.Lite ASDL
hybrid fiber coax (HFC)
Internet Architecture Board (IAB)
Internet Corporation for Assigned Names and Numbers (ICANN)
Internet Engineering Steering Group (IESG)

Internet Engineering Task Force (IETF)
Internet Research Task Force (IRTF)
Internet service provider (ISP)
Internet Society (ISOC)
Internet2
line splitter
local ISP
local loop
main distribution facility (MDF)
metropolitan area exchange (MAE)
mobile wireless
national ISP
network access point (NAP)
Next Generation Internet (NGI)
optical-electrical (OE) converter
passive optical networking (PON)
peering
point of presence (POP)
regional ISP
remote-access server (RAS)
request for comment (RFC)
tier 1 ISP
tier 2 ISP
tier 3 ISP
University Corporation for Advanced Internet Development (UCAID)
very-high-data-rate digital subscriber line (VDSL)
WAP proxy
Wireless Application Environment (WAE)
Wireless Application Protocol (WAP)
wireless DSL
wireless telephony application (WTA) server
Yipes.com

QUESTIONS

1. What is the basic structure of the Internet?
2. Explain how the Internet is a network of networks.
3. Compare and contrast an NAP and a MAE.
4. What is a POP?
5. Explain one reason why you might experience long response times in getting a Web page from a server in your own city.
6. What type of circuits are commonly used to build the Internet today? What type of circuits are commonly used to build Internet2?
7. Compare and contrast cable modem and DSL.
8. Explain how DSL works.
9. How does a DSL modem differ from a DSLAM?
10. Explain how ADSL works.
11. Explain how VDSL works.
12. Compare and contrast ADSL and VDSL.
13. Explain how a cable modem works.
14. What is an OE converter? A CMTS?
15. Which is better, cable modem or DSL? Explain.
16. Explain how one type of fixed wireless called wireless DSL works.
17. Compare and contrast mobile wireless and fixed wireless.
18. Explain how WAP works.
19. What are some future technologies that might change how we access the Internet?
20. What is PON, and how does it work?
21. Explain how Ethernet to the home works.
22. What are the principal organizations responsible for Internet governance, and what do they do?
23. How is the IETF related to the IRTF?
24. What are two principal American organizations working on the future of the Internet?
25. What is Internet2?
26. What is a gigapop?
27. There are many different organizations working on their vision of a high-speed Internet. Is this good or bad? Would we be better off just having one organization working on this and coordinating the work?
28. Today, there is no clear winner in the competition for broadband Internet access. What technology or technologies do you think will dominate in two years' time? Why?
29. Some experts believe that in five years, the dial-up modem will have disappeared. What do you think?
30. Many experts predicted that small, local ISPs would disappear as regional and national ISPs began offering local access. This hasn't happened. Why?

EXERCISES

10-1. Describe the current network structure of the Abilene network, the vBNS network, and the CA*net network.

10-2. Provide the service details (e.g., pricing) for at least two high-speed Internet access service providers in your area.

10-3. Some people are wiring their homes for 100Base-T. Suppose a friend who is building a house asks you what—if any—network to put inside the house and what Internet access technology to use. What would you recommend?

10-4. Explore the products available to install wireless Internet access in your home. How much would it cost to install and how much would it cost each month?

10-5. Do the puzzle below.

Across

4. A catchy name for wireless technology
6. You should never put one of these on a WLAN
8. A type of dedicated circuit
9. A commonly used WAN technology
11. Another name for T3
12. WANs often use this type of cable
14. I still don't need it
16. An emerging technologyfor WANs
18. Main distribution facility
20. A common Internet access technology
23. A point where national ISPs connect
25. OC-3 speed in Mbps
26. Your VPN software will log into a VPN ________
28. A commonly used WAN architecture
30. The network design layer most associated with campus backbones
33. Network sniffer software
35. A common WLAN technology
37. T3 speed in Mbps

Down

1. The network design layer most associated with building backbones
2. The maximum data rate that a packet switched network guarantees to provide
3. One of the Inernet 2 networks
5. High speed Internet access technologies are often called this
7. An inexpensive way to provie WAN services over the Internet
8. Switched Ethernet's topology
10. A core backbone is likely to use a ________ design
13. A WAN technology
15. An old packet switched WAN technology
17. This device connects IP subnets
19. A slow speed dedicated circuit
21. A layer-2 device for connecting backbones
22. A good type of wireless security
24. A place where you can connect to a common carrier
27. The network design layer most associated with user computers
29. A backbone deisgn commonly used in buildings
31. The maximum data rate that a packet switched network will permit but doesn't guarantee
32. A common Ethernet speed in Mbps
34. A WAN architecture
36. T1 speed in Mbps v

MINI-CASES

I. Cathy's Collectibles

Your cousin Cathy runs a part-time business out of her apartment. She buys and sells collectibles such as antique prints, baseball cards, and cartoon cells and has recently discovered the Web with its many auction sites. She has begun buying and selling on the Web by bidding on collectibles at lesser-known sites and selling them at a profit at more well-known sites. She downloads and uploads lots of graphics (pictures of the items she's buying and selling). She is getting frustrated with the slow Internet access she has with her 56-Kbps dial-up modem and asks you for advice. DSL is available at a cost of $60 per month for 1.5 Mbps down and 384 Kbps up. Cable modem service is available for a cost of $50 per month for 1.5 Mbps down and 640 Kbps up. Wireless DSL is available in her apartment building for $45 per month for 1.5 Mbps down and 256 Kbps up. Explain the differences in these services and make a recommendation.

II. Surfing Sam

Sam likes to surf the Web for fun, to buy things, and to research for his classes. Suppose the same Internet access technologies are available as in mini-case I above. Explain the differences in these services and make a recommendation.

III. Cookies Are Us

Cookies Are Us runs a series of 100 cookie stores across the midwestern United States and central Canada. At the end of each day, the stores express-mail a diskette or two of sales and inventory data to headquarters, which uses the data to ship new inventory and plan marketing campaigns. They have decided to move data over a WAN or the Internet. What type of a WAN topology and service (see Chapter 9) or Internet connection would you recommend? Why?

IV. Organic Foods

Organic Foods operates organic food stores in Toronto. The store operates like a traditional grocery store but offers only organically grown produce and meat, plus a wide array of health food products. Organic Foods sells memberships, and its 3,000 members receive a discount on all products they buy. There are also special member events and sales promotions each month. Organic Foods wants to open a new Internet site that will enable it to e-mail its members monthly and provide up-to-date information and announcements about new products, sales promotions, and member events on its Web site. it has two options. First, it could develop the software on its own server in its office and connect the office (and the server) to the internet via an ISDN, DSL, T1, or similar connection from its offices to an ISP. Alternately, it could pay the ISP to host the Web site on its servers and just connect the office to the isp for internet service. Costs for several Internet access options are present in mini-case I above. In addition, ISDN service costs $120 per month for BRI and $1,500 per month (plus $1,000 to install) for PRI; T1 service would cost $1,000 to install and $900 per month to operate; frame relay would cost $1,000 to install and $300 per month for 256kps or $500 for 1.5 mbps. web hosting would cost $100–400 per month, depending upon the traffic. which would you recommend and what size of an internet connection would you recommend? justify your choice.

CASE STUDY

NEXT-DAY AIR SERVICE

See the Web site.

HANDS-ON ACTIVITY

Seeing the Internet

The Internet is a network of networks. One way to see this is by using the VisualRoute software. VisualRoute is a commercial package, but provides a demonstration on its Web site. Go to visualroute.visualware.com and register to use their free service. Then enter a URL and watch as the route from your computer to the destination is traced and graphed. Figure 10.12 shows the route from my house in Indiana to the City University of Hong Kong.

Another interesting site is the Internet Traffic Report (www.internettrafficreport.com). This site shows how busy the parts of the Internet are in real time. The main page enables you to see the current status of the major parts of the world, including a "traffic index" that rates performance on a 100 point scale. You can also see the average response time at key Internet NAPs, MAEs, and peering points (at least those that have agreed to be monitored), which is an average of 135 milliseconds as I write this. It also shows the global packet loss rates—the percent of packets discarded due to transmission errors—(an average of 3 percent today).

By clicking on a region of the world you can see the same statistics for routers in that region. If you click on a specific router you can see a graph of its performance over the past 24 hours. Figure 10.13 shows the statistics for one router operated by Sprint.

You can also get traffic reports for Internet 2 netstats .indiana.edu. Figure 10.14 shows the "weathermap" on the Internet 2 Abilene network. Each circuit is color coded (although it's hard to see in this two-color figure). The weathermap shows traffic in both directions because the circuits are full duplex. The circuit from Atlanta to Chicago, for example, is running at 5 percent of capacity, while the circuit from Chicago to Atlanta is running at 10 percent of capacity. You can also click on any circuit to see a graph of traffic over the last 24 hours.

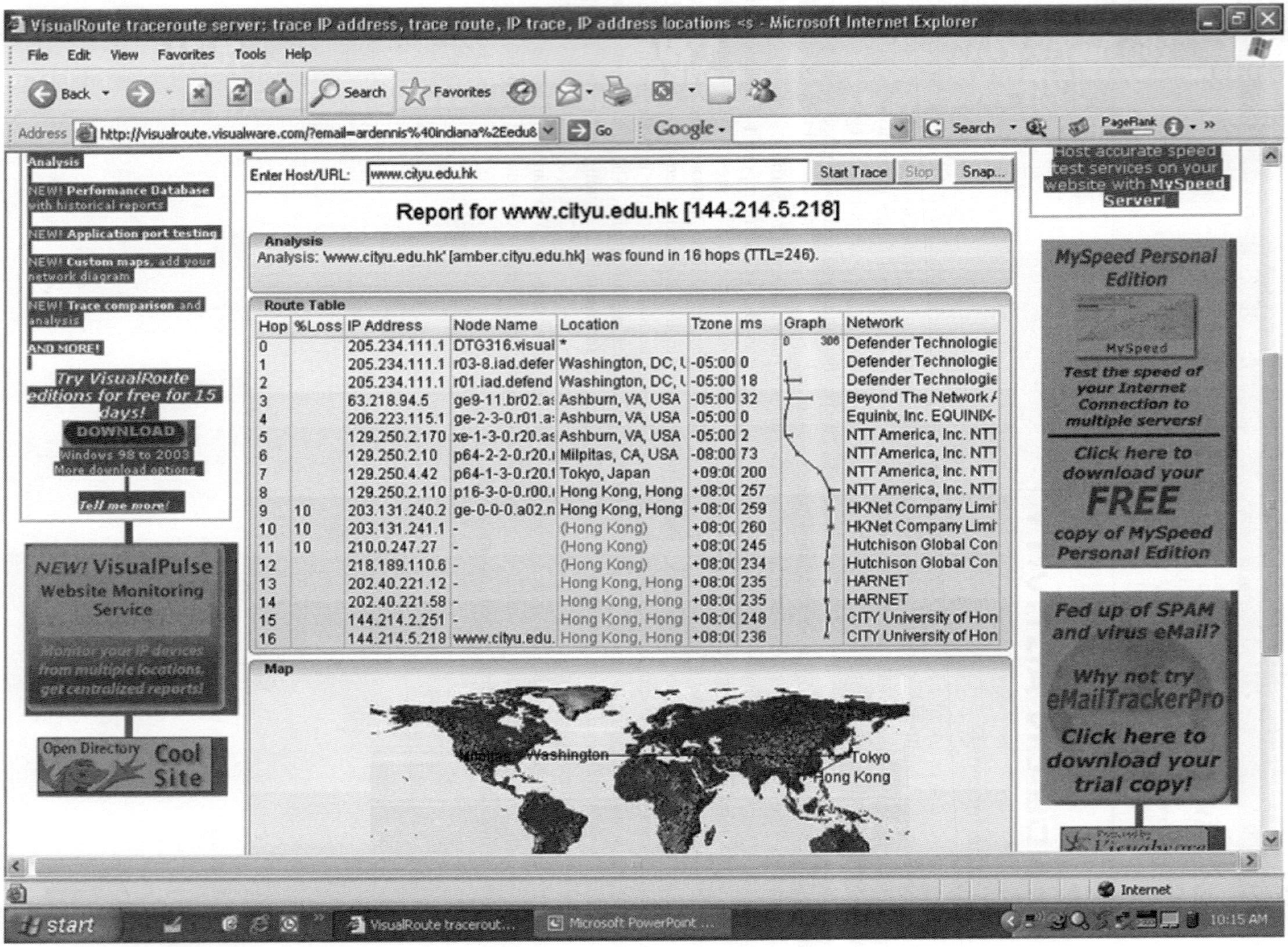

FIGURE 10.12 Visual trace route

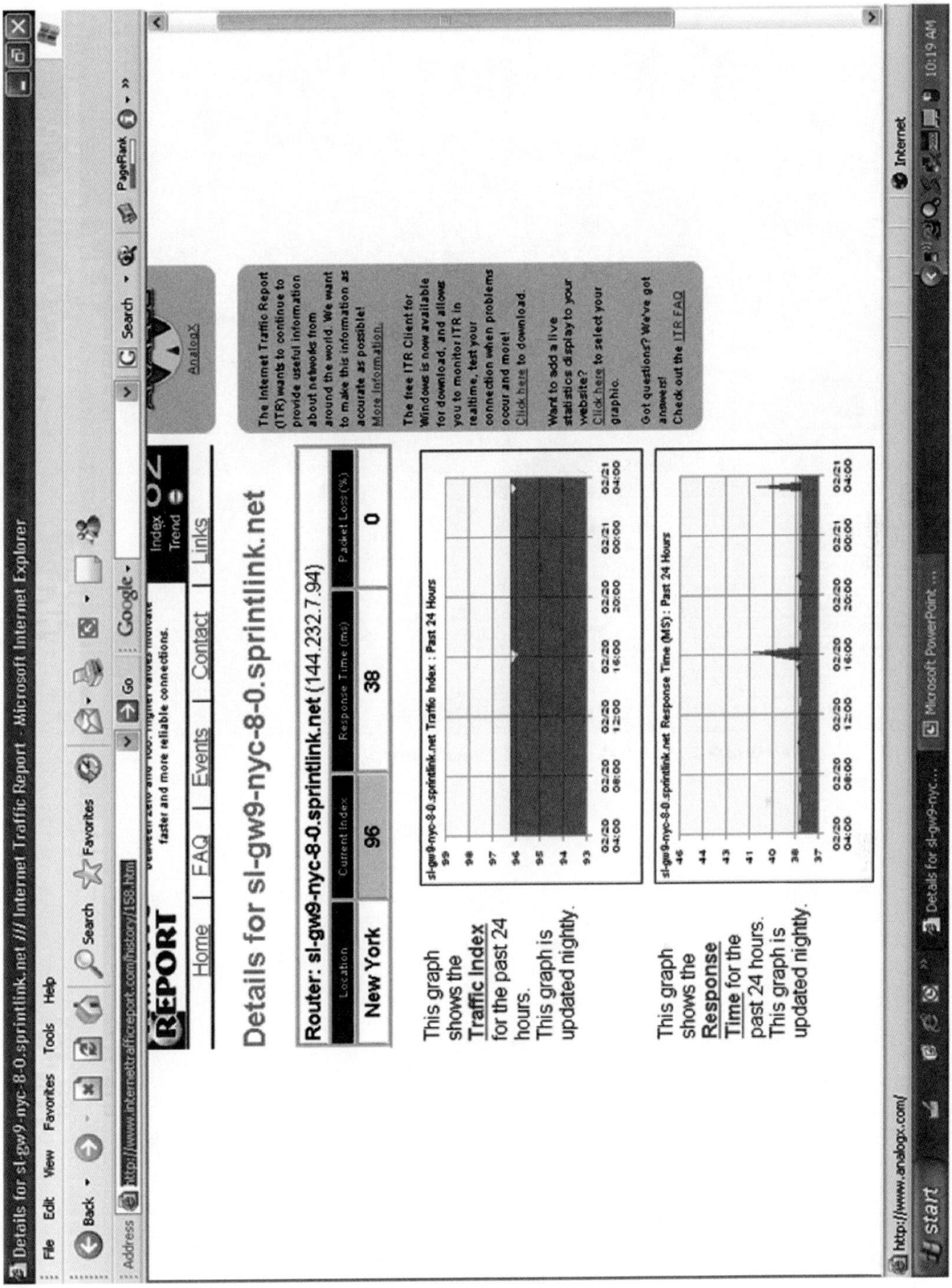

FIGURE 10.13 Internet traffic reports

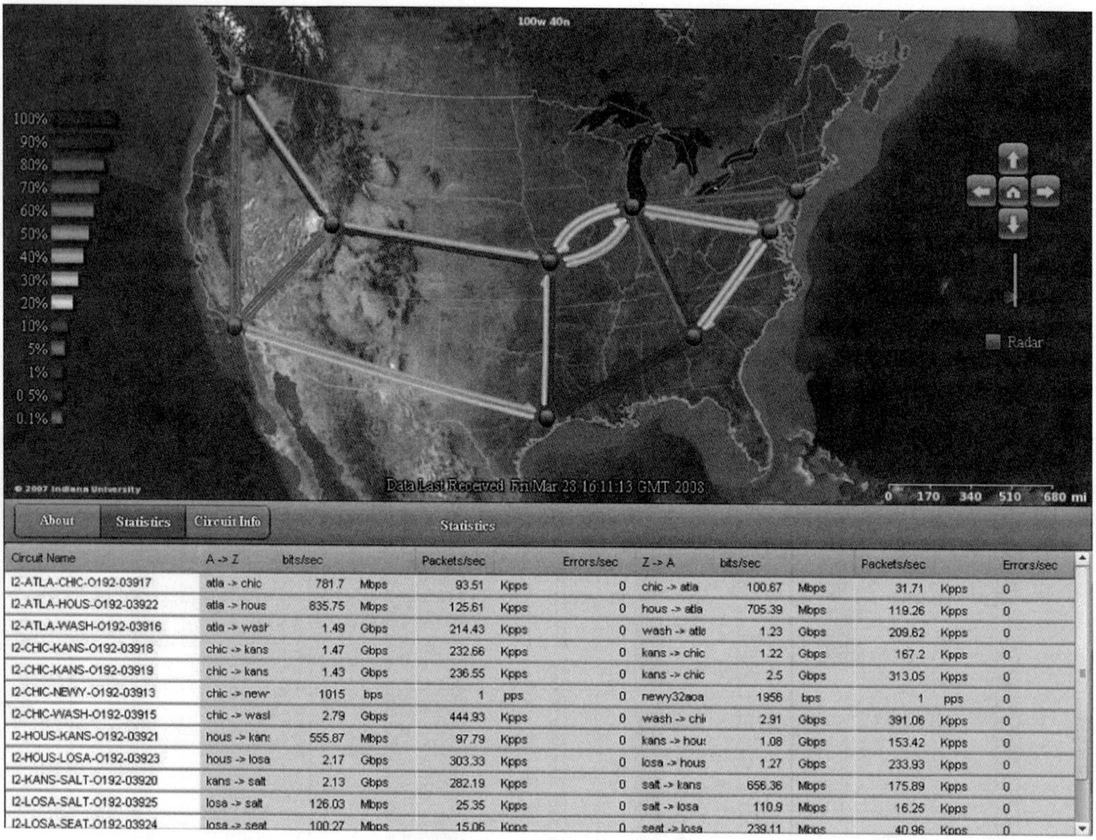

FIGURE 10.14 Internet 2 weathermap

PART FOUR

NETWORK MANAGEMENT

Courtesy Alan Dennis

CHAPTER 11

NETWORK SECURITY[1]

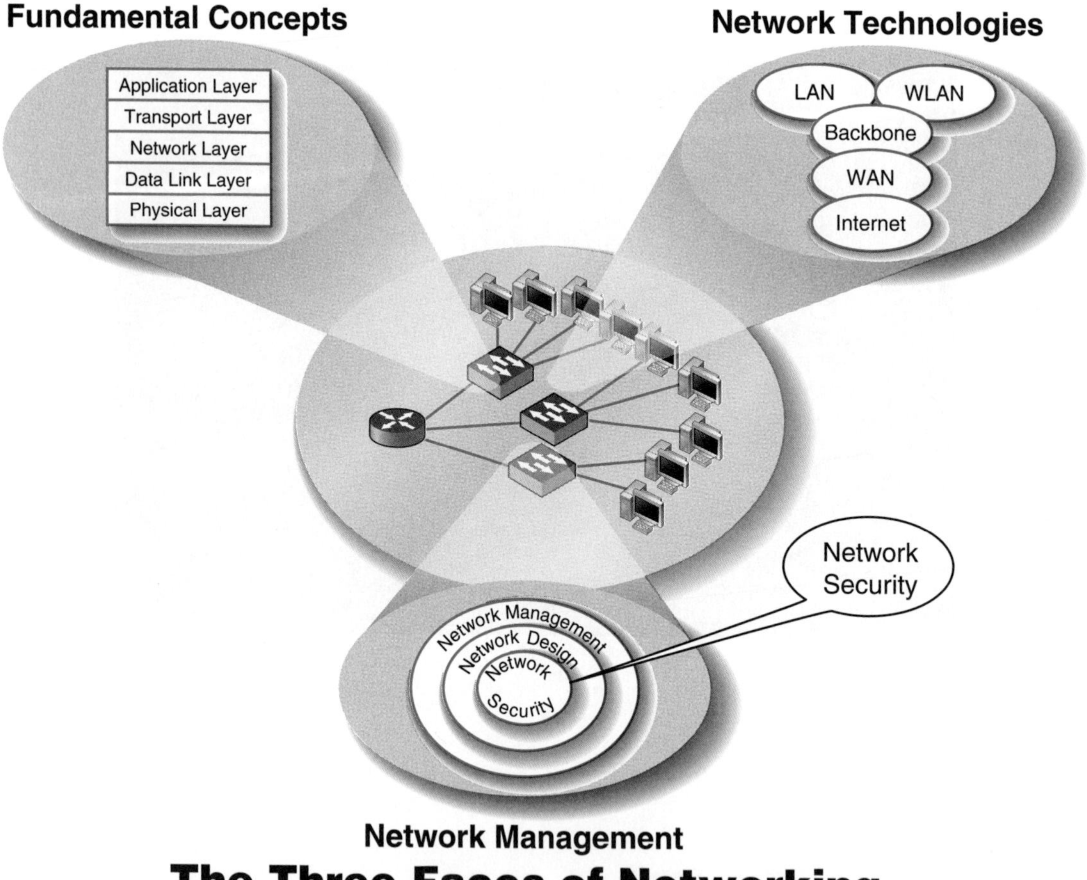

The Three Faces of Networking

[1]This chapter was written by Alan Dennis and Dwight Worker.

THIS CHAPTER describes why networks need security and how to provide it. The first step in any security plan is risk assessment, understanding the key assets that need protection, and assessing the risks to each. There are a variety of steps that can be taken to prevent, detect, and correct security problems due to disruptions, destruction, disaster, and unauthorized access.

OBJECTIVES ▼

- Be familiar with the major threats to network security
- Be familiar with how to conduct a risk assessment
- Understand how to ensure business continuity
- Understand how to prevent intrusion

CHAPTER OUTLINE ▼

INTRODUCTION

Business and government have always been concerned with physical and information security. They have protected physical assets with locks, barriers, guards, and the military since organized societies began. They have also guarded their plans and information with coding systems for at least 3,500 years. What has changed in the last 50 years is the introduction of computers and the Internet.

The rise of the Internet has completely redefined the nature of information security. Now companies face global threats to their networks, and, more importantly, to their data. Viruses and worms have long been a problem, but credit card theft and identity theft, two of the fastest growing crimes, pose immense liability to firms who fail to protect their customers' data. Laws have been slow to catch up, despite the fact that breaking into a computer in the United States—even without causing damage—is now a federal crime punishable by a fine and/or imprisonment. Nonetheless, we have a new kind of transborder cyber crime against which laws may apply but will be very difficult to enforce. The United States and Canada may extradite and allow prosecution of digital criminals operating within their borders, but investigating, enforcing, and prosecuting transnational cyber crime across different borders is much more challenging. And even when someone is caught they face lighter sentences than bank robbers.

Computer security has become increasingly important over the last 5 years with the passage of the Sarbanes-Oxley Act (SOX) and the Health Insurance Portability and Accountability Act (HIPAA). The number of Internet security incidents reported to the **Computer Emergency Response Team (CERT)** has doubled every year up until 2003, when CERT stopped keeping records because there were so many incidents that it was no longer meaningful to keep track.[2] CERT was established by the U.S. Department of Defense at Carnegie Mellon University with a mission to work with the Internet community to respond to computer security problems, raise awareness of computer security issues, and prevent security breaches.

Approximately 70 percent of organizations experienced security breaches in the last 12 months.[3] The median number of security incidents was four, but the top 5 percent of organizations were attacked more than 100 times a year. About 60% reported they suffered a measurable financial loss due to a security problem, with the average loss being about $350,000, which is significantly higher than in previous years. The median loss was much smaller, under $50,000. Experts estimate that worldwide annual losses due to security problems exceed $2 trillion.

Part of the reason for the increase in computer security problems is the increasing availability of sophisticated tools for breaking into networks. Five years ago, someone wanting to break into a network needed to have some expertise. Today, even inexperienced attackers can download tools from a Web site and immediately begin trying to break into networks.

Two other factors are also at work increasing security problems. First, organized crime has recognized the value of computer attacks. Criminal organizations have launched spam campaigns with fraudulent products and claims, created viruses to steal information, and have even engaged in extortion by threatening to disable a small company's network unless it pays them a fee. Computer crime is less risky than traditional crime and also pays a lot better.

[2]CERT maintains a Web site on security at www.cert.org. Another site for security information is www.infosyssec.net.

[3]The statistics in this chapter are based on surveys conducted by CSO magazine (www.csoonline.com) and the Computer Security Institute (www.gocsi.com).

Second, there is considerable evidence that the Chinese military and security services have engaged in a major, ongoing cyberwarfare campaign against military and government targets in the western world.[4] To date these attacks have focused on espionage and disabling military networks. Most large Chinese companies are owned by the Chinese military or security services or by leaders recently departed from these organizations. There is some evidence that China's cyberwarfare campaign has expanded to include industrial espionage against western companies in support of Chinese companies.

As a result, the cost of network security has increased. Firms spent an average of about 5 percent of their total IT budget on network security. The average expenditure was about $1,250 per employee per year—and that's all employees in the organization not per IT employee, so that an organization with 100 employees spends an average of $1.25 million per year on IT security. About 30 percent of organizations had purchased insurance for security risks.

Why Networks Need Security

In recent years, organizations have become increasingly dependent on data communication networks for their daily business communications, database information retrieval, distributed data processing, and the internetworking of LANs. The rise of the Internet with opportunities to connect computers anywhere in the world has significantly increased the potential vulnerability of the organization's assets. Emphasis on network security also has increased as a result of well-publicized security break-ins and as government regulatory agencies have issued security-related pronouncements.

The losses associated with the security failures can be huge. An average annual loss of about $350,000 sounds large enough, but this is just the tip of the iceberg. The potential loss of consumer confidence from a well-publicized security break-in can cost much more in lost business. More important than these, however, are the potential losses from the disruption of application systems that run on computer networks. As organizations have come to depend upon computer systems, computer networks have become "mission-critical." Bank of America, one of the largest banks in the United States, estimates that it would cost the bank $50 million if its computer networks were unavailable for 24 hours. Other large organizations have produced similar estimates.

Protecting customer privacy and the risk of identity theft also drives the need for increased network security. In 1998, the European Union passed strong data privacy laws that fined companies for disclosing information about their customers. In the United States, organizations have begun complying with the data protection requirements of the HIPAA, and a California law providing fines up to $250,000 for each unauthorized disclosure of customer information (e.g., if someone were to steal 100 customer records, the fine could be $25 million).

As you might suspect, the value of the data stored on most organizations' networks and the value provided by the application systems in use far exceeds the cost of the networks themselves. For this reason, the primary goal of network security is to protect organizations' data and application software, not the networks themselves.

[4]John J. Tkacik Jr., "Trojan Dragon: China's Cyber Threat," *Backgrounder,* no. 2106, February 2008, The Heritage Foundation.

Types of Security Threats

For many people, security means preventing intrusion, such as preventing an attacker from breaking into your computer. Security is much more than that, however. There are three primary goals in providing security: confidentiality, integrity, and availability. **Confidentiality** refers to the protection of organizational data from unauthorized disclosure of customer and proprietary data. **Integrity** is the assurance that data have not been altered or destroyed. **Availability** means providing continuous operation of the organization's hardware and software so that staff, customers, and suppliers can be assured of no interruptions in service.

There are many potential threats to confidentiality, integrity, and availability. Figure 11.1 shows some threats to a computer center, the data communication circuits, and the attached computers. In general, security threats can be classified into two broad categories: ensuring business continuity and preventing unauthorized access.

Ensuring **business continuity** refers primarily to ensuring availability, with some aspects of data integrity. There are three main threats to business continuity. *Disruptions* are the loss of or reduction in network service. Disruptions may be minor and temporary. For example, a network switch might fail or a circuit may be cut causing part of the network to cease functioning until the failed component can be replaced. Some users may be affected, but others can continue to use the network. Some disruptions may also be caused by or result in the *destruction* of data. For example, a virus may destroy files, or the "crash" of a hard disk may cause files to be destroyed. Other disruptions may be catastrophic. Natural (or man-made) *disasters* may occur that destroy host computers or large sections of the network. For example, hurricanes, fires, floods, earthquakes, mudslides, tornadoes, or terrorist attacks can destroy large parts of the buildings and networks in their path.

Intrusion refers primarily to confidentiality, but also to integrity, as an intruder may change important data. Intrusion is often viewed as external attackers gaining access to organizational data files and resources from across the Internet. However, almost half of all intrusion incidents involve employees. Intrusion may have only minor effects. A curious intruder may simply explore the system, gaining knowledge that has little value. A more serious intruder may be a competitor bent on industrial espionage who could attempt to gain access to information on products under development, or the details and price of a bid on a large contract, or a thief trying to steal customer credit card numbers or information to carry out identity theft. Worse still, the intruder could change files to commit fraud or theft or could destroy information to injure the organization.

Network Controls

Developing a secure network means developing **controls.** Controls are software, hardware, rules, or procedures that reduce or eliminate the threats to network security. Controls *prevent, detect,* and/or *correct* whatever might happen to the organization because of threats facing its computer-based systems.

Preventive controls mitigate or stop a person from acting or an event from occurring. For example, a password can prevent illegal entry into the system, or a set of second circuits can prevent the network from crashing. Preventative controls also act as

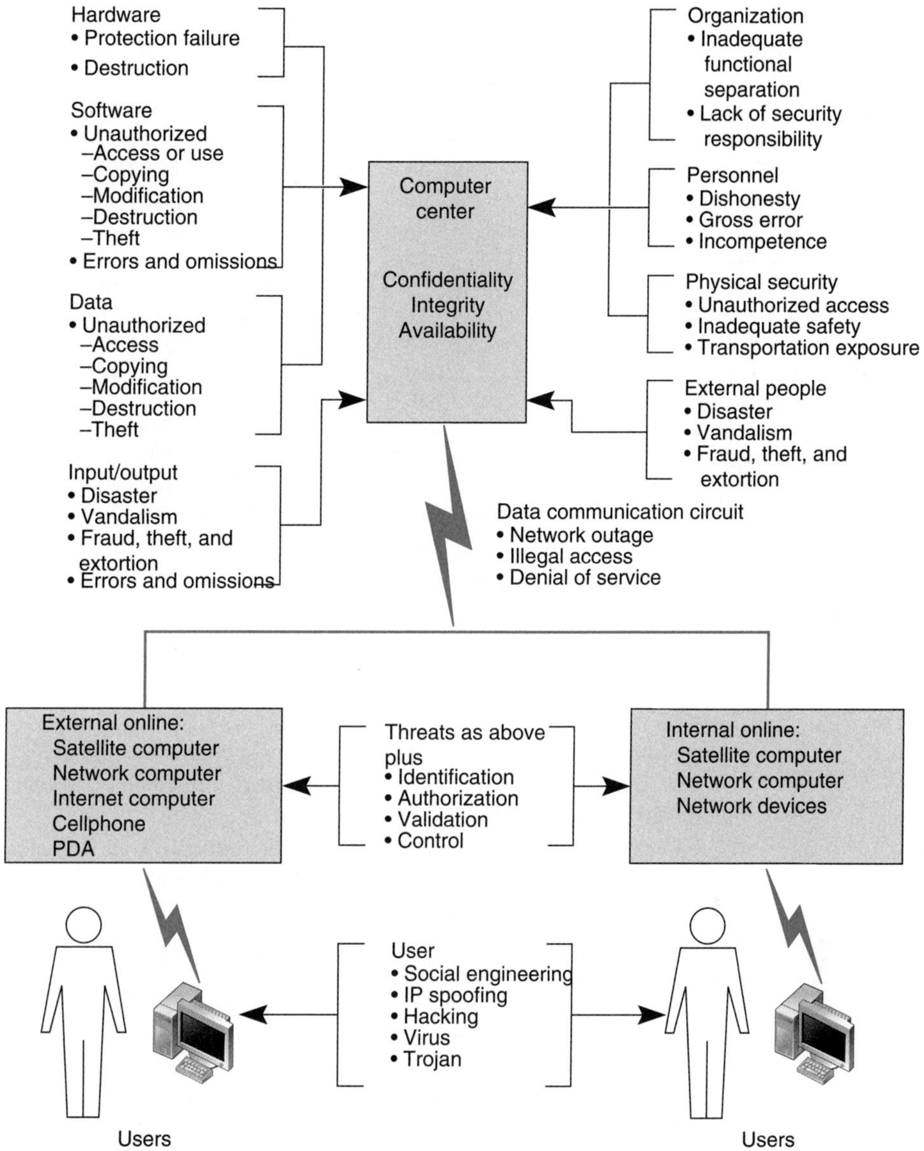

FIGURE 11.1 Some threats to a computer center, data communication circuits, and client computers

a deterrent by discouraging or restraining someone from acting or proceeding because of fear or doubt. For example, a guard or a security lock on a door may deter an attempt to gain illegal entry.

Detective controls reveal or discover unwanted events. For example, software that looks for illegal network entry can detect these problems. They also document an event, a situation, or an intrusion, providing evidence for subsequent action against the individuals

MANAGEMENT FOCUS 11.1 CREDIT CARD DATA THEFT

In May of 2005, hackers broke into a database operated by CardSystems Solutions and stole data on as many as 40 million MasterCard, Visa, and other credit card users. The breach was the largest single data leak in history, affecting one out of every seven credit cards issued in the United States.

The breach was discovered by MasterCard's fraud department, who tracked the stolen data to its source at CardSystems, a third-party processor of credit data. CardSystems processes more than $15 billion in credit card transactions per year, mostly for over 100,000 small- and medium-sized businesses.

The intruder used the Internet to break into a server at a processing center in Tucson, Arizona, that hosted the credit card database. The intruder exploited a known security flaw in the server software.

The theft cost CardSystems millions of dollars and it was acquired by another firm.

A similar theft of 45 million credit cards occured at T.J.Maxx in 2005, but was not discovered until 2007. In this case, the intruder was able to break the encryption used on the stored data. T.J.Maxx says the breach cost $250 million to fix the compromised systems and settle lawsuits.

SOURCE: Robert Lemos, "MasterCard Warns of Massive Credit-Card Breach," *SecurityFocus.com,* 2005-06-17; Paul F. Roberts "Major Card Vendors Stay Mum on Data Breach," *www.eweek.com,* June 20, 2005; "One Year Later: Five Takeaways from the TJX Breach," computer world.com, January 20, 2008.

or organizations involved or enabling corrective action to be taken. For example, the same software that detects the problem must report it immediately so that someone or some automated process can take corrective action.

Corrective controls remedy an unwanted event or an intrusion. Either computer programs or humans verify and check data to correct errors or fix a security breach so it will not recur in the future. They also can recover from network errors or disasters. For example, software can recover and restart the communication circuits automatically when there is a data communication failure.

The remainder of this chapter discusses the various controls that can be used to prevent, detect, and correct threats. We also present a control spreadsheet and risk analysis methodology for identifying the threats and their associated controls. The control spreadsheet provides a network manager with a good view of the current threats and any controls that are in place to mitigate the occurrence of threats.

Nonetheless, it is important to remember that it is not enough just to establish a series of controls; someone or some department must be accountable for the control and security of the network. This includes being responsible for developing controls, monitoring their operation, and determining when they need to be updated or replaced.

Controls must be reviewed periodically to be sure that they are still useful and must be verified and tested. Verifying ensures that the control is present, and testing determines whether the control is working as originally specified.

It is also important to recognize that there may be occasions in which a person must temporarily override a control, for instance when the network or one of its software or hardware subsystems is not operating properly. Such overrides should be tightly controlled, and there should be a formal procedure to document this occurrence should it happen.

RISK ASSESSMENT

One key step in developing a secure network is to conduct a **risk assessment.** This assigns levels of risk to various threats to network security by comparing the nature of the threats to the controls designed to reduce them. It is done by developing a control spreadsheet and then rating the importance of each risk. This section provides a brief summary of the risk assessment process.[5]

Develop a Control Spreadsheet

To be sure that the data communication network and microcomputer workstations have the necessary controls and that these controls offer adequate protection, it is best to build a **control spreadsheet** (Figure 11.2). Threats to the network are listed across the top, organized by business continuity (disruption, destruction, disaster) and intrusion, and the network assets down the side. The center of the spreadsheet incorporates all the controls that *currently* are in the network. This will become the benchmark upon which to base future security reviews.

Threats / Assets (with Priority)	Disruption, Destruction, Disaster					Intrusion		
	Fire	Flood	Power Loss	Circuit Failure	Virus	External Intruder	Internal Intruder	Eaves-drop
(92) Mail server								
(90) Web server								
(90) DNS server								
(50) Computers on sixth floor								
(50) Sixth-floor LAN circuits								
(80) Building A backbone								
(70) Router in building A								
(30) Network software								
(100) Client database								
(100) Financial database								

FIGURE 11.2 Sample control spreadsheet with some assets and threats. DNS = Domain Name Service; LAN = local area network

[5]CERT has developed a detailed risk assessment procedure called OCTAVE^{SM}, which is available at www.cert.org/octave.

TECHNICAL FOCUS 11.1 BASIC CONTROL PRINCIPLES OF A SECURE NETWORK

- The less complex a control, the better.
- A control's cost should be equivalent to the identified risk. It often is not possible to ascertain the expected loss, so this is a subjective judgment in many cases.
- Preventing a security incident is always preferable to detecting and correcting it after it occurs.
- An adequate system of internal controls is one that provides "just enough" security to protect the network, taking into account both the risks and costs of the controls.
- Automated controls (computer-driven) always are more reliable than manual controls that depend on human interaction.
- Controls should apply to everyone, not just a few select individuals.
- When a control has an override mechanism, make sure that it is documented and that the override procedure has its own controls to avoid misuse.
- Institute the various security levels in an organization on the basis of "need to know." If you do not need to know, you do not need to access the network or the data.
- The control documentation should be confidential.
- Names, uses, and locations of network components should not be publicly available.
- Controls must be sufficient to ensure that the network can be audited, which usually means keeping historical transaction records.
- When designing controls, assume that you are operating in a hostile environment.
- Always convey an image of high security by providing education and training.
- Make sure the controls provide the proper separation of duties. This applies especially to those who design and install the controls and those who are responsible for everyday use and monitoring.
- It is desirable to implement entrapment controls in networks to identify attackers who gain illegal access.
- When a control fails, the network should default to a condition in which everyone is denied access. A period of failure is when the network is most vulnerable.
- Controls should still work even when only one part of a network fails. For example, if a backbone network fails, all local area networks connected to it should still be operational, with their own independent controls providing protection.
- Don't forget the LAN. Security and disaster recovery planning has traditionally focused on host mainframe computers and WANs. However, LANs now play an increasingly important role in most organizations but are often overlooked by central site network managers.
- Always assume your opponent is smarter than you.
- Always have insurance as the last resort should all controls fail.

Assets The first step is to identify the assets on the network. An **asset** is something of value and can be either hardware, software, data, or applications. Probably the most important asset on a network is the organization's data. For example, suppose someone destroyed a mainframe worth $10 million. The mainframe could be replaced simply by buying a new one. It would be expensive, but the problem would be solved in a few weeks. Now suppose someone destroyed all the student records at your university so that no one knows what courses anyone had taken or their grades. The cost would far exceed the cost of replacing a $10 million computer. The lawsuits alone would easily exceed $10 million, and the cost of staff to find and reenter paper records would be enormous and certainly would take more than a few weeks. Figure 11.3 summarizes some typical assets.

An important type of asset is the **mission-critical application,** which is an information system that is critical to the survival of the organization. It is an application that cannot be permitted to fail, and if it does fail, the network staff drops everything else to fix it. For example, for an Internet bank that has no brick-and-mortar branches, the Web site is a mission-critical application. If the Web site crashes, the bank cannot conduct business with its customers. Mission-critical applications are usually clearly identified, so their importance is not overlooked.

Once you have a list of assets, they should be evaluated based on their importance. There will rarely be enough time and money to protect all assets completely, so it is important to focus the organization's attention on the most important ones. Prioritizing asset importance is a business decision, not a technology decision, so it is critical that senior business managers be involved in this process.

Threats A **threat** to the data communication network is any potential adverse occurrence that can do harm, interrupt the systems using the network, or cause a monetary loss to the organization. While threats may be listed in generic terms (e.g., theft of data, destruction of data), it is better to be specific and use actual data from the organization being assessed (e.g., theft of customer credit card numbers, destruction of the inventory database).

Once the threats are identified they can be ranked according to their probability of occurrence and the likely cost if the threat occurs. Figure 11.4 summarizes the most common threats and their likelihood of occurring, plus a typical cost estimate, based on several surveys. The actual probability of a threat to your organization and its costs depend upon your business. An Internet bank, for example, is more likely to be a target

Hardware	• Servers, such as mail servers, Web servers, DNS servers, DHCP servers, and LAN file servers • Client computers • Devices such as hubs, switches, and routers
Circuits	• Locally operated circuits such as LANs and backbones • Contracted circuits such as MAN and WAN circuits • Internet access circuits
Network software	• Server operating systems and system settings • Application software such as mail server and Web server software
Client software	• Operating systems and system settings • Application software such as word processors
Organizational data	• Databases with organizational records
Mission-critical applications	• For example, for an Internet bank, its Web site is mission-critical

FIGURE 11.3 Types of assets. DNS = Domain Name Service; DHCP = Dynamic Host Control Protocol; LAN = local area network; MAN = metropolitan area network; WAN = wide area network

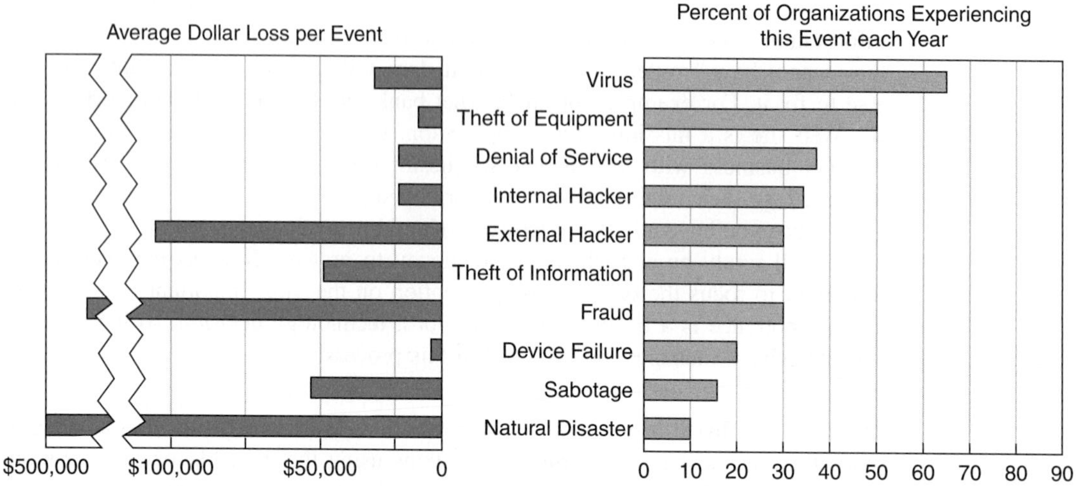

FIGURE 11.4 Likelihood and costs of common risks

of fraud and to suffer a higher cost if it occurs than a restaurant with a simple Web site. Nonetheless, Figure 11.4 provides some general guidance.

From Figure 11.4 you can see that the most likely event is a virus infection, suffered by more than 60 percent of organizations each year. The average cost to clean up a virus that slips through the security system and infects an average number of computers is about $33,000 per virus. Depending upon your background, this was probably not the first security threat that came to mind; most people first think about unknown attackers breaking into a network across the Internet. This does happen, too; unauthorized access by an external hacker is experienced by about 30 percent of all organizations each year, with some experiencing an act of sabotage or vandalism. The average cost to recover after these attacks is $100,000.

Interestingly, companies suffer intrusion by their own employees about as often as by outsiders, although the dollar loss is usually less unless fraud or theft of information is involved. While few organizations experience fraud or theft of information from internal or external attackers, the cost to recover afterward can be very high, both in dollar cost and bad publicity. Several major companies have had their networks broken into and have had proprietary information such as customer credit card numbers stolen. Winning back customers whose credit card information was stolen can be an even greater challenge than fixing the security breach.

You will also see that device failure and computer equipment theft are common problems but usually result in low dollar losses compared to other security violations. Natural disasters (e.g., fire, flood) are also common, and result in high dollar losses.

Denial of service attacks, in which someone external to your organization blocks access to your networks, are also common (35 percent) and somewhat costly ($25,000 per event). Even temporary disruptions in service that cause no data loss can have significant costs. Estimating the cost of denial of service is very organization-specific; the cost of disruptions to a company that does a lot of e-commerce through a Web site is often measured in the millions.

Amazon.com, for example, has revenues of more than $10 million per hour, so if its Web site were unavailable for an hour or even part of an hour it would cost millions of dollars in lost revenue. Companies that do no e-commerce over the Web would have lower costs, but recent surveys suggest losses of $100,000–200,000 per hour are not uncommon for major disruptions of service. Even the disruption of a single LAN has cost implications; surveys suggest that most businesses estimate the cost of lost work at $1,000–5,000 per hour.

There are two "big picture" messages from Figure 11.4. First, the most common threat that has a noticeable cost is viruses. In fact, if we look at the relative probabilities of the different threats, we can see that the threats to business continuity (e.g., virus, theft of equipment, or denial of service) have a greater chance of occurring than intrusion. Nonetheless, given the cost of fraud and theft of information, even a single event can have significant impact.[6]

The second important message is that the threat of intrusion from the outside intruder coming at you over the Internet has increased. For the past 25 years, more organizations reported encountering security breaches caused by employees than by outsiders. This has been true ever since the early 1980s when the FBI first began keeping computer crime statistics and security firms began conducting surveys of computer crime. However, in recent years, the number of external attacks has increased at a much greater rate while the number of internal attacks has stayed relatively constant. Even though some of this may be due to better internal security and better communications with employees to prevent security problems, much of it is simply due to an increase in activity by external attackers and the global reach of the Internet. Today, external attackers pose almost as great a risk as internal employees.

Identify and Document the Controls

Once the specific assets and threats have been identified, you can begin working on the network *controls,* which mitigate or stop a threat, or protect an asset. During this step, you identify the existing controls and list them in the cell for each asset and threat.

Begin by considering the asset and the specific threat, and then describe each control that prevents, detects, or corrects that threat. The description of the control (and its role) is placed in a numerical list, and the control's number is placed in the cell. For example, assume 24 controls have been identified as being in use. Each one is described, named, and numbered consecutively. The numbered list of controls has no ranking attached to it: the first control is number 1 just because it is the first control identified.

Figure 11.5 shows a partially completed spreadsheet. The assets and their priority are listed as rows, with threats as columns. Each cell lists one or more controls that protect one asset against one threat. For example, in the first row, the mail server is currently protected from a fire threat by a Halon fire suppression system, and there is a disaster recovery plan in place. The placement of the mail server above ground level protects against flood, and the disaster recovery plan helps here too.

[6]We should point out, though, that the losses associated with computer fraud are small compared with other sources of fraud.

Threats / Assets (with Priority)	Disruption, Destruction, Disaster					Intrusion		
	Fire	Flood	Power Loss	Circuit Failure	Virus	External Intruder	Internal Intruder	Eavesdrop
(92) Mail server	1, 2	1, 3	4	5, 6	7, 8	9, 10, 11	9, 10	
(90) Web server	1, 2	1, 3	4	5, 6	7, 8	9, 10, 11	9, 10	
(90) DNS server	1, 2	1, 3	4	5, 6	7, 8	9, 10, 11	9, 10	
(50) Computers on sixth floor	1, 2	1, 3			7, 8	10, 11	10	
(50) Sixth-floor LAN circuits	1, 2	1, 3						
(80) Building A backbone	1, 2	1, 3		6				
(70) Router in building A	1, 2	1, 3				9	9	
(30) Network software					7, 8	9, 10, 11	9, 10	
(100) Client database					7, 8	9, 10, 11	9, 10	
(100) Financial database					7, 8	9, 10, 11	9, 10	

Controls

1. Disaster recovery plan
2. Halon fire system in server room; sprinklers in rest of building
3. Not on or below ground level
4. Uninterruptable power supply (UPS) on all major network servers
5. Contract guarantees from interexchange carriers
6. Extra backbone fiber cable laid in different conduits
7. Virus checking software present on the network
8. Extensive user training about viruses and reminders in monthly newsletter
9. Strong password software
10. Extensive user training about password security and reminders in monthly newsletter
11. Application-layer firewall

FIGURE 11.5 Sample control spreadsheet with some assets, threats, and controls. DNS = Domain Name Service; LAN = local area network

Evaluate the Network's Security

The last step in using a control spreadsheet is to evaluate the adequacy of the existing controls and the resulting degree of risk associated with each threat. Based on this assessment, priorities can be established to determine which threats must be addressed immediately. Assessment is done by reviewing each set of controls as it relates to each threat and network component. The objective of this step is to answer the specific question: are the controls adequate to effectively prevent, detect, and correct this specific threat?

The assessment can be done by the network manager, but it is better done by a team of experts chosen for their in-depth knowledge about the network and environment being reviewed. This team, known as the **Delphi team,** is composed of three to nine key people. Key managers should be team members because they deal with both the long-term and day-to-day operational aspects of the network. More important, their participation means the final results can be implemented quickly, without further justification, because they make the final decisions affecting the network.

ENSURING BUSINESS CONTINUITY

Business continuity means that the organization's data and applications will continue to operate even in the face of disruption, destruction, or disaster. A business continuity plan has two major parts: the development of controls that will prevent these events from having a major impact on the organization, and a disaster recovery plan that will enable the organization to recover if a disaster occurs. In this section, we discuss controls designed to prevent, detect, and correct these threats.[7] We focus on the major threats to business continuity: Viruses, theft, denial of service, attacks, device failure, and disasters. Business continuity planning is sometimes overlooked because intrusion is more often the subject of news reports.

Virus Protection

Special attention must be paid to preventing computer **viruses.** Some are harmless and just cause nuisance messages, but others are serious such as destroying data. In most

> **MANAGEMENT FOCUS 11.2 ATTACK OF THE AUDITORS**
>
> Security has become a major issue over the past few years. With the passage of HIPPA and the Sarbanes-Oxley Act, more and more regulations are addressing security. It takes years for most organizations to become compliant, because the rules are vague and there are many ways to meet the requirements.
>
> "If you've implemented commonsense security, you're probably already in compliance from an IT standpoint," says Kim Keanini, Chief Technology Officer of nCricle, a security software firm. "Compliance from an auditing standpoint, however, is something else." Auditors require documentation. It is no longer sufficient to put key network controls in place; now you have to provide documented proof that a control is working, which usually requires event logs of transactions and thwarted attacks.
>
> When it comes to security, Bill Randal, MIS Director of Red Robin Restaurants, can't stress the importance of documentation enough. "It's what the auditors are really looking for," he says. "They're not IT folks, so they're looking for documented processes they can track. At the start of our [security] compliance project, we literally stopped all other projects for other three weeks while we documented every security and auditing process we had in place."
>
> Software vendors are scrambling to ensure than their security software not only performs the functions it is designed to do, but also to improve its ability to provide documentation for auditors.
>
> SOURCE: Oliver Rist, "Attack of the Auditors," *InfoWorld,* March 21, 2005, pp. 34–40.

[7]There are many good business continuity planning sites such as www.disasterrecoveryworld.com.

cases, disruptions or the destruction of data are local and affect only a small number of computers. Such disruptions are usually fairly easy to deal with; the virus is removed and the network continues to operate. Some viruses cause widespread infection, although this has not occurred in recent years.

Most viruses attach themselves to other programs or to special parts on disks. As those files execute or are accessed, the virus spreads. *Macro viruses,* viruses that are contained in documents e-mails, or spreadsheet files, can spread when an infected file is simply opened. Some viruses change their appearances as they spread, making detection more difficult.

A **worm** is special type of virus that spreads itself without human intervention. Many viruses attach themselves to a file and require a person to copy the file, but a worm copies itself from computer to computer. Worms spread when they install themselves on a computer and then send copies of themselves to other computers, sometimes by e-mail, sometimes via security holes in software. (Security holes are described later in this chapter.)

The best way to prevent the spread of viruses is to install **antivirus software** such as that by Symantec. Most organizations automatically install antivirus software on their computers, but many people fail to install them on their home computers. Antivirus software is only as good as its last update, so it is critical that the software be updated regularly. Be sure to set your software to update automatically or do it manualy on a regular basis.

Viruses are often spread by downloading files from the Internet, so do not copy or download files of unknown origin (e.g., music, videos, screen savers), or at least check every file you do download. Always check all files for viruses before using them (even those from friends!). Researchers estimate that ten new viruses are developed every day, so it is important to frequently update the virus information files that are provided by the antivirus software.

Denial-of-Service Protection

With a **denial-of-service attack (DoS),** an attacker attempts to disrupt the network by flooding it with messages so that the network cannot process messages from normal users. The simplest approach is to flood a Web server, mail server, and so on with incoming messages. The server attempts to respond to these, but there are so many messages that it cannot.

One might expect that it would be possible to filter messages from one source IP so that if one user floods the network, the messages from this person can be filtered out before they reach the Web server being targeted. This could work, but most attackers use tools that enable them to put false source IP addresses on the incoming messages so that it is difficult to recognize a message as a real message or a DoS message.

A **distributed denial-of-service attack (DDoS)** is even more disruptive. With a DDoS attack, the attacker breaks into and takes control of many computers on the Internet (often several hundred to several thousand) and plants software on them called a **DDoS agent** (or sometimes a zombie or a bot). The attacker then uses software called a **DDoS handler** (sometimes called a botnet) to control the agents. The handler issues instructions to the computers under the attacker's control, which simultaneously begin sending messages to the target site. In this way, the target is deluged with messages from many different sources, making it harder to identify the DoS messages and greatly increasing the number of messages hitting the target (see Figure 11.6). Some DDos attacks have sent more than one million packets per second at the target.

There are several approaches to preventing DoS and DDoS attacks from affecting the network. The first is to configure the main router that connects your network to the Internet (or the firewall, which will be discussed later in this chapter) to verify that the source address of all incoming messages is in a valid address range for that connection (called **traffic filtering**). For example, if an incoming message has a source address from inside your network, then it is obviously a false address. This ensures that only messages with valid addresses are permitted into the network, although it requires more processing in the router and thus slows incoming traffic.

A second approach is to configure the main router (or firewall) to limit the number of incoming packets that could be DoS/DDoS attack packets that it allows to enter the network, regardless of their source (called **traffic limiting**). Technical Focus box 11.2 describes some of the types of DoS/DDoS attacks and the packets used. Such packets have the same content as legitimate packets that should be permitted into the network. It is a flood of such packets that indicates a DoS/DDoS attack, so by discarding packets over a certain number that arrive each second, one can reduce the impact of the attack.

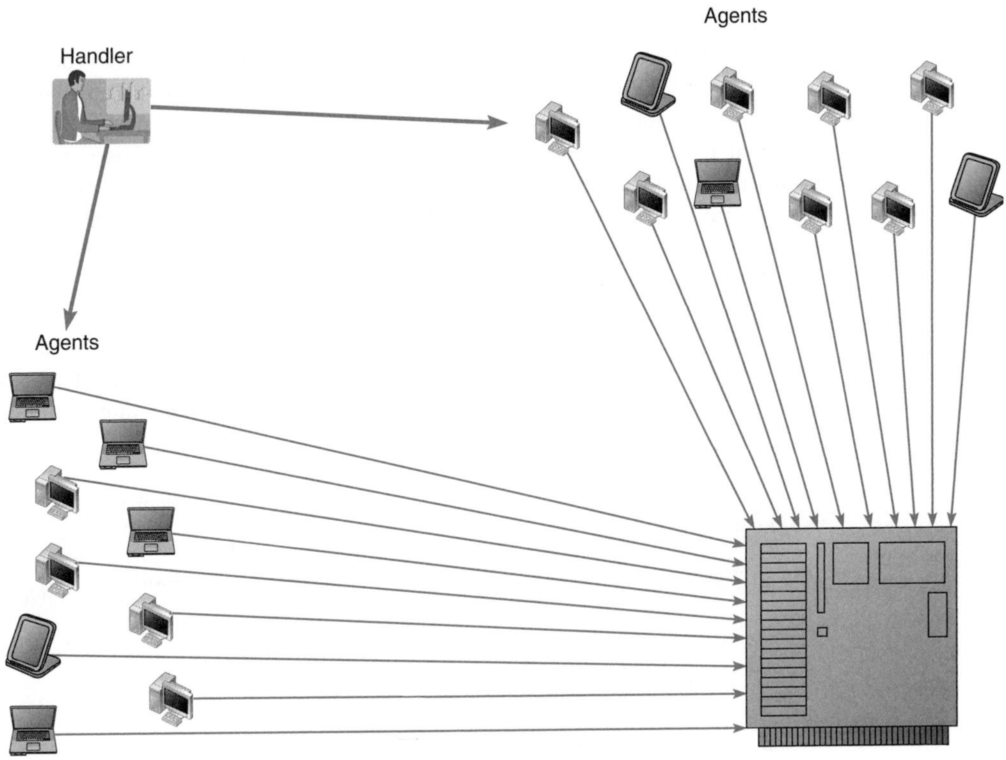

FIGURE 11.6 A distributed denial-of-service attack

MANAGEMENT FOCUS 11.3 A DDoS Attack Takes Down StormPay

StormPay, an e-commerce payment processor, was taken down for several days by a DDoS attack. StormPay is used by many Web hosting companies to process payments. The attack occurred after StormPay froze the account of a controversial service that pays users to view Internet ads. The service was under investigation by the FBI and SEC for running a Ponzi scheme.

The attack was a DNS recursion attack (see Technical Focus 11.2) that sent bogus DNS requests and DNS responses into StormPay's network. About 120,000 computers (zombies) were used in the attack which flooded StormPay's network with 6 gigabits of data per second. After StormPay took action to bring its site back online, the attack switched to the ISPs that host StormPay's sites, which again took StormPay's site offline.

SOURCE: Rich Miller, "Payment Gateway StormPay Battling Sustained DDOS Attack, Netcraft.com, February 10, 2006; Jon Swartz, "Increasing Web Attacks Disrupt Commerce," *USAToday.com,* February 26, 2006.

The disadvantage is that during an attack, some valid packets from regular customers will be discarded so they will be unable to reach your network. Thus the network will continue to operate, but some customer packets (e.g., Web requests, e-mails) will be lost.

A third and more sophisticated approach is to use a special-purpose security device, called a **traffic anomaly detector,** that is installed in front of the main router (or firewall) to perform **traffic analysis.** This device monitors normal traffic patterns and learns what normal traffic looks like. Most DoS/DDoS attacks target a specific server or device so when the anomaly detector recognizes a sudden burst of abnormally high traffic destined for a specific server or device, it quarantines those incoming packets but allows normal traffic to flow through into the network. This results in minimal impact to the network as a whole. The anomaly detector re-routes the quarantined packets to a **traffic anomaly analyzer** (see Figure 11.7). The anomaly analyzer examines the quarantined traffic, attempts to recognize valid source addresses and "normal" traffic, and selects which of the quarantined packets to release into the network. The detector can also inform the router owned by the ISP that is sending the traffic into the organization's network to reroute the suspect traffic to the anomaly analyzer, thus avoiding the main

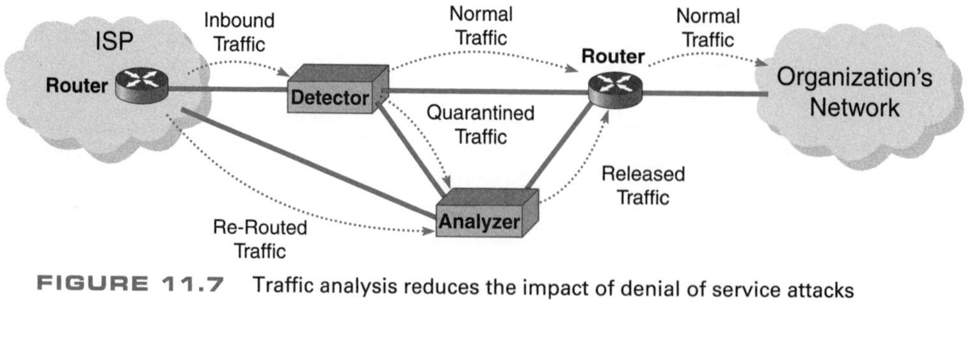

FIGURE 11.7 Traffic analysis reduces the impact of denial of service attacks

TECHNICAL FOCUS 11.2 INSIDE A DOS ATTACK

A DoS attack typically involves the misuse of standard TCP/IP protocols or connection processes so that the target for the DoS attack responds in a way designed to create maximum trouble. Five common types of attacks include:

- **ICMP Attacks:**
  The network is flooded with ICMP echo requests (i.e., pings) that have a broadcast destination address and a faked source address of the intended target. Because it is a broadcast message, every computer on the network responds to the faked source address so that the target is overwhelmed by responses. Because there are often dozens of computers in the same broadcast domain, each message generates dozens of messages at the target.
- **UDP Attacks:**
  This attack is similar to an ICMP attack except that it uses UDP echo requests instead of ICMP echo requests.
- **TCP SYN Floods:**
  The target is swamped with repeated SYN requests to establish a TCP connection, but when the target responds (usually to a faked source address) there is no response. The target continues to allocate TCP control blocks, expects each of the requests to be completed, and gradually runs out of memory.
- **UNIX Process Table Attacks:**
  This is similar to a TCP SYN flood, but instead of TCP SYN packets, the target is swamped by UNIX open connection requests that are never completed. The target allocates open connections and gradually runs out of memory.
- **Finger of Death Attacks:**
  This is similar to the TCP SYN flood, but instead the target is swamped by finger requests that are never disconnected.
- **DNS Recursion Attacks:**
  The attacker sends DNS requests to DNS servers (often within the target's network), but spoofs the from address so the requests appear to come from the target computer which is overwhelmed by DNS responses. DNS responses are larger packets than ICMP, UDP, or SYN responses so the effects can be stronger

SOURCE: "Web Site Security and Denial of Service Protection," www.nwfusion.com.

circuit leading into the organization. This process is never perfect, but is significantly better than the other approaches.

Another possibility under discussion by the Internet community as a whole is to require Internet service providers (ISPs) to verify that all incoming messages they receive from their customers have valid source IP addresses. This would prevent the use of faked IP addresses and enable users to easily filter out DoS messages from a given address. It would make it virtually impossible for a DoS attack to succeed, and much harder for a DDoS attack to succeed. Because small- to medium-sized businesses often have poor security and become the unwilling accomplices in DDoS attacks, many ISPs are beginning to impose security restrictions on them, such as requiring firewalls to prevent unauthorized access (firewalls are discussed later in this chapter).

Theft Protection

One often overlooked security risk is theft. Computers and network equipment are commonplace items that have a good resale value. Several industry sources estimate that over

$1 billion is lost to computer theft each year, with many of the stolen items ending up on Internet auction sites (e.g., eBay).

Physical security is a key component of theft protection. Most organizations require anyone entering their offices to go through some level of physical security. For example, most offices have security guards and require all visitors to be authorized by an organization employee. Universities are one of the few organizations that permit anyone to enter their facilities without verification. Therefore, you'll see most computer equipment and network devices protected by locked doors or security cables so that someone cannot easily steal them.

One of the most common targets for theft is laptop computers. More laptop computers are stolen from employee's homes, cars, and hotel rooms than any other device. Airports are another common place for laptop thefts. It is hard to provide physical security for traveling employees, but most organizations provide regular reminders to their employees to take special care when traveling with laptops. Nonetheless, they are still the most commonly stolen device.

Device Failure Protection

Eventually, every computer network device, cable, or leased circuit will fail. It's just a matter of time. Some computers, devices, cables, and circuits are more reliable than others, but every network manager has to be prepared for a failure.

The best way to prevent a failure from impacting business continuity is to build **redundancy** into the network. For any network component that would have a major impact on business continuity, the network designer provides a second, redundant component. For example, if the Internet connection is important to the organization, the network designer ensures that there are at least two connections into the Internet—each provided by a different common carrier, so that if one common carrier's network goes down, the organization can still reach the Internet via the other common carrier's network. This means, of course, that the organization now requires two routers to connect to the Internet, because there is little use in having two Internet connections if they both run through the same router; if that one router goes down, having a second Internet connection provides no value.

This same design principle applies to the organization's internal networks. If the core backbone is important (and it usually is), then the organization must have two core backbones, each served by different devices. Each distribution backbone that connects to the core backbone (e.g., a building backbone that connects to a campus backbone) must also have two connections (and two routers) into the core backbone.

The next logical step is to ensure that each access layer LAN also has two connections into the distribution backbone. Redundancy can be expensive, so at some point, most organizations decide that not all parts of the network need to be protected. Most organizations build redundancy into their core backbone and their Internet connections, but are very careful in choosing which distribution backbones (i.e., building backbones) and access layer LANs will have redundancy. Only those building backbones and access LANs that are truly important will have redundancy. This is why a risk assessment with a control spreadsheet is important, because it is too expensive to protect the entire network. Most organizations only provide redundancy in mission critical backbones and LANs (e.g., those that lead to servers).

Redundancy also applies to servers. Most organizations use a server farm, rather than a single server, so that if one server fails, the other servers in the server farm continue to operate and there is little impact. Some organizations use **fault-tolerant servers** that contain many redundant components so that if one of its components fails, it will continue to operate.

Redundant arrays of independent disks (RAID) is a storage technology that, as the name suggests, is made of many separate disk drives. When a file is written to a RAID device, it is written across several separate, redundant disks.

There are several types of RAID. RAID 0 uses multiple disk drives and therefore is faster than traditional storage, because the data can be written or read in parallel across several disks, rather than sequentially on the same disk. RAID 1 writes duplicate copies of all data on at least two different disks; this means that if one disk in the RAID array fails, there is no data loss because there is a second copy of the data stored on a different disk. This is sometimes called **disk mirroring,** because the data on one disk is copied (or mirrored) onto another. RAID 2 provides error checking to ensure no errors have occurred during the reading or writing process. RAID 3 provides a better and faster error checking process than RAID 2. RAID 4 provides slightly faster read access than RAID 3 because of the way it allocates the data to different disk drives. RAID 5 provides slightly faster read and write access because of the way it allocates the error checking data to different disk drives. RAID 6 can survive the failure of two drives with no data loss.

Power outages are one of the most common causes of network failures. An **uninterruptable power supply (UPS)** is a device that detects power failures and permits the devices attached to it to operate as long as its battery lasts. UPS for home use are inexpensive and often provide power for up to 15 minutes—long enough for you to save your work and shut down your computer. UPS for large organizations often have batteries that last for an hour and permit mission critical servers, switches, and routers to operate until the organization's backup generator can be activated.

Disaster Protection

A disaster is an event that destroys a large part of the network and computing infrastructure in one part of the organization. Disasters are usually caused by natural forces (e.g., hurricanes, floods, earthquakes, fires), but some can be manmade (e.g., arson, bombs, terrorism).

Avoiding Disaster Ideally, you want to avoid a disaster, which can be difficult. How do you avoid an earthquake? There are, however, some commonsense steps you can take to avoid the full impact of a disaster from affecting your network. The most fundamental is again redundancy; store critical data in at least two very different places, so if a disaster hits one place, your data are still safe.

Other steps depend on the disaster to be avoided. For example to avoid the impact of a flood, key network components and data should never be located near rivers or in the basement of a building. To avoid the impact of a tornado, key network components and data should be located underground. To reduce the impact of fire, a fire suppression

MANAGEMENT FOCUS 11.4 RECOVERING FROM KATRINA

As Hurricane Katrina swept over New Orleans, Ochsner Hospital lost two of its three backup power generators knocking out air conditioning in the 95-degree heat. Fans were brought out to cool patients, but temperatures inside critical computer and networking equipment reached 150 degrees. Kurt Induni, the hospital's network manager, shut down part of the network and the mainframe with its critical patient records system to ensure they survived the storm. The hospital returned to paper-based record keeping, but Induni managed to keep e-mail alive, which became critical when the telephone system failed and a main fiber line was cut. E-mail through the hospital's T-3 line into Baton Rouge became the only reliable means of communication. After the storm, the mainframe was turned back on and the patient records were updated.

While Ochsner Hospital remained open, Kindred Hospital was forced to evacuate patients (under military protection from looters and snipers). The patients' files, all electronic, were simply transferred over the network to other hospitals with no worry about lost records, X-rays, CT scans, and such.

In contrast, the Louisiana court system learned a hard lesson. The court system is administered by each individual parish (i.e., county) and not every parish had a disaster recovery plan or even backups of key documents–many parishes still use old paper files that were destroyed by the storm. "We've got people in jails all over the state right now that have no paperwork and we have no way to offer them any kind of means for adjudication," says Freddie Manit, CIO for the Louisiana Ninth Judicial District Court. No paperwork means no prosecution, even for felons with long records, so many prisoners will simply be released. Sometimes losing data is not the worst thing that can happen.

SOURCE: Phil Hochmuth, "Weathering Katrina," *NetworkWorld,* September 19, 2005, pp. 1, 20; and M. K. McGee, "Storm Shows Benefits, Failures of Technology," *Informationweek,* September 15, 2005, p. 34.

system should be installed in all key data centers. To reduce the impact of terrorist activities, the location of key network components and data should be kept a secret and should be protected by security guards.

Disaster Recovery A critical element in correcting problems from a disaster is the **disaster recovery plan,** which should address various levels of response to a number of possible disasters and should provide for partial or complete recovery of all data, application software, network components, and physical facilities. A complete disaster recovery plan covering all these areas is beyond the scope of this text. Figure 11.8 provides a summary of many key issues. A good example of a disaster recovery plan is MIT's business continuity plan at web.mit.edu/security/www/pubplan.htm. Some firms prefer the term business continuity plan.

The most important elements of the disaster recovery plan are **backup** and **recovery controls** that enable the organization to recover its data and restart its application software should some portion of the network fail. The simplest approach is to make backup copies of all organizational data and software routinely and to store these backup copies off-site. Most organizations make daily backups of all critical information, with less important

Elements of a Disaster Recovery Plan

A good disaster recovery plan should include:

- The name of the decision-making manager who is in charge of the disaster recovery operation. A second manager should be indicated in case the first manager is unavailable.
- Staff assignments and responsibilities during the disaster
- A preestablished list of priorities that states what is to be fixed first
- Location of alternative facilities operated by the company or a professional disaster recovery firm and procedures for switching operations to those facilities using backups of data and software
- Recovery procedures for the data communication facilities (backbone network, metropolitan area network, wide area network, and local area network), servers, and application systems. This includes information on the location of circuits and devices, whom to contact for information, and the support that can be expected from vendors, along with the name and telephone number of the person at each vendor to contact.
- Action to be taken in case of partial damage or threats such as bomb threats, fire, water or electrical damage, sabotage, civil disorders, and vendor failures
- Manual processes to be used until the network is functional
- Prodecures to ensure adequate updating and testing of the disaster recovery plan
- Storage of the data, software, and the disaster recovery plan itself in a safe area where they cannot be destroyed by a catastrophe. This area must be accessible, however, to those who need to use the plan.

FIGURE 11.8 Elements of a disaster recovery plan

information (e.g., e-mail files) backed up weekly. Backups used to be done on tapes that were physically shipped to an off-site location, but more and more, companies are using their WAN connections to transfer data to remote locations (it's faster and cheaper than moving tapes). Backups should always be encrypted (encryption is discussed later in the chapter) to ensure that no unauthorized users can access them.

Continuous data protection (CDP) is another option that firms are using in addition to or instead of regular backups. With CDP, copies of all data and transactions on selected servers are written to CDP servers as the transaction occurs. CDP is more flexible than traditional backups that take snapshots of data at specific times, or disk mirroring, that duplicates the contents of a disk from second to second. CDP enables data to be stored miles from the originating server and time-stamps all transactions to enable organizations to restore data to any specific point in time. For example, suppose a virus brings down a server at 2:45 P.M. The network manager can restore the server to the state it was in at 2:30 P.M. and simply resume operations as though the virus had not hit.

Backups and CDP ensure that important data are safe, but they do not guarantee the data can be used. The disaster recovery plan should include a documented and tested approach to recovery. The recovery plan should have specific goals for different types of disasters. For example, if the main database server was destroyed, how long should it take the organization to have the software and data back in operation by using the backups?

Conversely, if the main data center was completely destroyed, how long should it take? The answers to these questions have very different implications for costs. Having a spare network server or a server with extra capacity that can be used in the event of the loss of the primary server is one thing. Having a spare data center ready to operate within 12 hours (for example) is an entirely different proposition.

While many organizations have a disaster recovery plan, only a few test their plans. A **disaster recovery drill** is much like a fire drill in that it tests the disaster recovery plan and provides staff the opportunity to practice little-used skills to see what works and what doesn't work before a disaster happens and the staff must use the plan for real. Without regular disaster recovery drills, the only time a plan is tested is when it must be used. For example, when an island-wide blackout shut down all power in Bermuda, the backup generator in the British Caymanian Insurance office automatically took over and kept the company operating. However, the key-card security system, which was not on the generator, shut down, locking out all employees and forcing them to spend the day at the beach. No one had thought about the security system and the plan had not been tested.

Organizations are usually much better at backing up important data than are individual users. When did you last backup the data an your computer? What would you do if your computer was stolen or destroyed? There is an inexpensive alternative to CDP for home users. **Online backup** services such as mozy.com enable you to back up the data on your computer to their server on the Internet. You download and install client software that enables you to select what folders to back up. After you back up the data for the first time, which takes a while, the software will run every few hours and automatically back up all changes to the server, so you never have to think about backups again. If you need to recover some or all of your data, you can go to their Web site and download it.

Disaster Recovery Outsourcing

Most large organizations have a two-level disaster recovery plan. When they build networks they build enough capacity and have enough spare equipment to recover from a minor disaster such as loss of a major server or portion of the network (if any such disaster can truly be called minor). This is the first level. Building a network that has sufficient capacity to quickly recover from a major disaster such as the loss of an entire data center is beyond the resources of most firms. Therefore, most large organizations rely on professional disaster recovery firms to provide this second-level support for major disasters.

Many large firms outsource their disaster recovery efforts by hiring **disaster recovery firms** that provide a wide range of services. At the simplest, disaster recovery firms provide secure storage for backups. Full services include a complete networked data center that clients can use when they experience a disaster. Once a company declares a disaster, the disaster recovery firm immediately begins recovery operations using the backups stored on-site and can have the organization's entire data network back in operation on the disaster recovery firm's computer systems within hours. Full services are not cheap, but compared to the potential millions of dollars that can be lost per day from the inability to access critical data and application systems, these systems quickly pay for themselves in time of disaster.

MANAGEMENT FOCUS 11.5 DISASTER RECOVERY HITS HOME

"The building is on fire" were the first words she said as I answered the phone. It was just before noon and one of my students had called me from her office on the top floor of the business school at the University of Georgia. The roofing contractor had just started what would turn out to be the worst fire in the region in more than 20 years although we didn't know it then. I had enough time to gather up the really important things from my office on the ground floor (memorabilia, awards, and pictures from 10 years in academia) when the fire alarm went off. I didn't bother with the computer; all the files were backed up off-site.

Ten hours, 100 firefighters, and 1.5 million gallons of water later, the fire was out. Then our work began. The fire had completely destroyed the top floor of the building, including my 20-computer networking lab. Water had severely damaged the rest of the building, including my office, which, I learned later, had been flooded by almost 2 feet of water at the height of the fire. My computer, and virtually all the computers in the building, were damaged by the water and unusable.

My personal files were unaffected by the loss of the computer in my office; I simply used the backups and continued working—after making new backups and giving them to a friend to store at his house. The Web server I managed had been backed up to another server on the opposite side of campus 2 days before (on its usual weekly backup cycle), so we had lost only 2 days' worth of changes. In less than 24 hours, our Web site was operational; I had our server's files mounted on the university library's Web server and redirected the university's DNS server to route traffic from our old server address to our new temporary home.

Unfortunately, the rest of our network did not fare as well. Our primary Web server had been backed up to tape the night before and while the tapes were stored off-site, the tape drive was not; the tape drive was destroyed and no one else on campus had one that could read our tapes; it took 5 days to get a replacement and reestablish the Web site. Within 30 days we were operating from temporary offices with a new network, and 90 percent of the office computers and their data had been successfully recovered.

Living through a fire changes a person. I'm more careful now about backing up my files, and I move ever so much more quickly when a fire alarm sounds. But I still can't get used to the rust that is slowly growing on my "recovered" computer.

INTRUSION PREVENTION

Intrusion is the second main type of security problem and the one that tends to receive the most attention. No one wants an intruder breaking into their network.

There are four types of intruders who attempt to gain unauthorized access to computer networks. The first are casual intruders who have only a limited knowledge of computer security. They simply cruise along the Internet trying to access any computer they come across. Their unsophisticated techniques are the equivalent of trying doorknobs, and, until recently, only those networks that left their front doors unlocked were at risk. Unfortunately, there are now a variety of hacking tools available on the Internet that enable even novices to launch sophisticated intrusion attempts. Novice attackers that use such tools are sometimes called **script kiddies.**

The second type of intruders are experts in security, but their motivation is the thrill of the hunt. They break into computer networks because they enjoy the challenge and enjoy showing off for friends or embarrassing the network owners. These intruders are called **hackers** and often have a strong philosophy against ownership of data and software. Most cause little damage and make little attempt to profit from their exploits, but those that do can cause major problems. Hackers that cause damage are often called **crackers.**

The third type of intruder is the most dangerous. They are professional hackers who break into corporate or government computers for specific purposes, such as espionage, fraud, or intentional destruction. The U.S. Department of Defense (DoD), which routinely monitors attacks against U.S. military targets, has until recently concluded that most attacks are individuals or small groups of hackers in the first two categories. While some of their attacks have been embarrassing (e.g., defacement of some military and intelligence Web sites), there have been no serious security risks. However, in the late 1990s the DoD noticed a small but growing set of intentional attacks that they classify as exercises, exploratory attacks designed to test the effectiveness of certain software attack weapons. Therefore, they established an **information warfare** program and a new organization responsible for coordinating the defense of military networks under the U.S. Space Command.

The fourth type of intruder is also very dangerous. These are organization employees who have legitimate access to the network, but who gain access to information they are not authorized to use. This information could be used for their own personnel gain, sold to competitors, or fraudulently changed to give the employee extra income. Many security break-ins are caused by this type of intruder.

The key principle in preventing intrusion is to be *proactive.* This means routinely testing your security systems before an intruder does. Many steps can be taken to prevent intrusion and unauthorized access to organizational data and networks, but no network is completely safe. The best rule for high security is to do what the military does: do not keep extremely sensitive data online. Data that need special security are stored in computers isolated from other networks. In the following sections, we discuss the most important security controls for preventing intrusion and for recovering from intrusion when it occurs.

Security Policy

In the same way that a disaster recovery plan is critical to controlling risks due to disruption, destruction, and disaster, a **security policy** is critical to controlling risk due to intrusion. The security policy should clearly define the important assets to be safeguarded and the important controls needed to do that. It should have a section devoted to what employees should and should not do. It should contain a clear plan for routinely training employees—particularly end-users with little computer expertise—on key security rules and a clear plan for routinely testing and improving the security controls in place (Figure 11.9). A good set of examples and templates is available at www.sans.org/resources/policies.

Perimeter Security and Firewalls

Ideally, you want to stop external intruders at the perimeter of your network, so that they cannot reach the servers inside. There are three basic access points into most networks:

Elements of a Security Policy

A good security policy should include:

- The name of the decision-making manager who is in charge of security
- An incident reporting system and a rapid-response team to respond to security breaches in progress
- A risk assessment with priorities as to which assets are most important
- Effective controls placed at all major access points into the network to prevent or deter access by external agents
- Effective controls placed within the network to ensure that internal users cannot exceed their authorized access
- Use of minimum number of controls possible to reduce management time and to provide the least inconvenience to users
- An acceptable use policy that explains to users what they can and cannot do, including guidelines for accessing others' accounts, password security, e-mail rules, and so on
- A procedure for monitoring changes to important network components (e.g., routers, DNS servers)
- A plan to routinely train users regarding security policies and build awareness of security risks
- A plan to routinely test and update all security controls that includes monitoring of popular press and vendor reports of security holes
- An annual audit and review of the security practices

FIGURE 11.9 Elements of a security policy

the Internet, LANS and WLANs, and dial-up access through a modem. Recent surveys suggest that the most common access point for intrusion is the Internet connection (70 percent of organizations experienced an attack from the Internet), followed by LANs and WLANs (30 percent), and dial-up (10 percent). External intruders are most likely to use the Internet connection, while internal intruders are most likely to use the LAN or WLAN. Because the Internet is the most common source of intrusions, the focus of perimeter security is usually on the Internet connection, although physical security and dial-up security are also important.

A **firewall** is commonly used to secure an organization's Internet connection. A firewall is a router or special-purpose device that examines packets flowing into and out of a network and restricts access to the organization's network. The network is designed so that a firewall is placed on every network connection between the organization and the Internet (Figure 11.10). No access is permitted except through the firewall. Some firewalls have the ability to detect and prevent denial-of-service attacks, as well as unauthorized access attempts. Three commonly used types of firewalls are packet-level firewalls, application-level firewalls, and NAT firewalls.

Packet-Level Firewalls

A **packet-level firewall** examines the source and destination address of every network packet that passes through it. It only allows packets into or

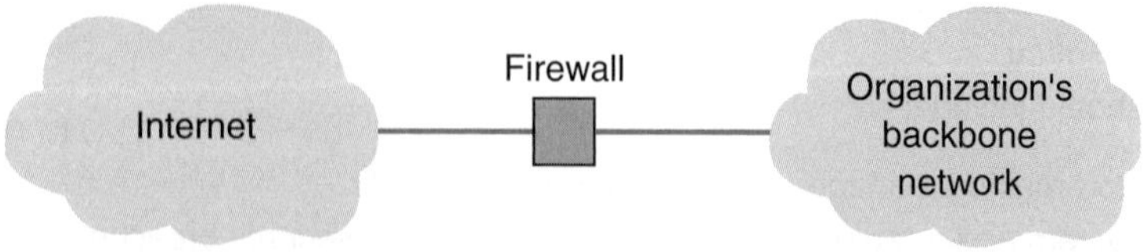

FIGURE 11.10 Using a firewall to protect networks

out of the organization's networks that have acceptable source and destination addresses. In general, the addresses are examined only at the transport layer (TCP port id) and network layer (IP address). Each packet is examined individually, so the firewall has no knowledge of what packets came before. It simply chooses to permit entry or exit based on the contents of the packet itself. This type of firewall is the simplest and least secure because it does not monitor the contents of the packets or why they are being transmitted, and typically does not log the packets for later analysis.

The network manager writes a set of rules (called an **access control list [ACL]**) for the packet level firewall so it knows what packets to permit into the network and what packets to deny entry. Remember that the IP packet contains the source IP address and the destination address and that the TCP segment has the destination port number that identifies the application layer software to which the packet is going. Most application layer software on servers uses standard TCP port numbers. The Web (HTTP) uses port 80 while e-mail (SMTP) uses port 25.

Suppose that the organization had a public Web server with an IP address of 128.192.44.44 and an e-mail server with an address of 128.192.44.45 (see Figure 11.11). The network manager wants to make sure that no one outside of the organization can change the contents of the Web server (e.g., by using telnet or FTP). The ACL could be written to include a rule that permits the Web server to receive HTTP packets from the Internet (but other types of packets would be discarded). For example, the rule would say if the source address is anything, the destination IP address is 128.192.44.44 and the destination TCP port is 80, then permit the packet into the network; see the ACL on the firewall in Figure 11.11. Likewise, we could add a rule to the ACL that would permit SMTP packets to reach the e-mail server: if the source address is anything, the destination is 128.192.44.45 and the destination TCP port is 25, then permit the packet through (see Figure 11.11). The last line in the ACL is usually a rule that says to deny entry to all other packets that have not been specifically permitted (some firewalls come automatically configured to deny all packets other than those explicitly permitted, so this command would not be needed). With this ACL, if an external intruder attempted to use telnet (port 23) to reach the Web server, the firewall would deny entry to the packet and simply discard it.

Although source IP addresses can be used in the ACL, they often are not used. Most hackers have software that can change the source IP address on the packets they send (called **IP spoofing**) so using the source IP address in security rules is not usually worth the effort. Some network managers do routinely include a rule in the ACL that denies entry to all packets coming from the Internet that have a source IP address of a subnet inside the organization, because any such packets must have a spoofed address and therefore obviously are an intrusion attempt.

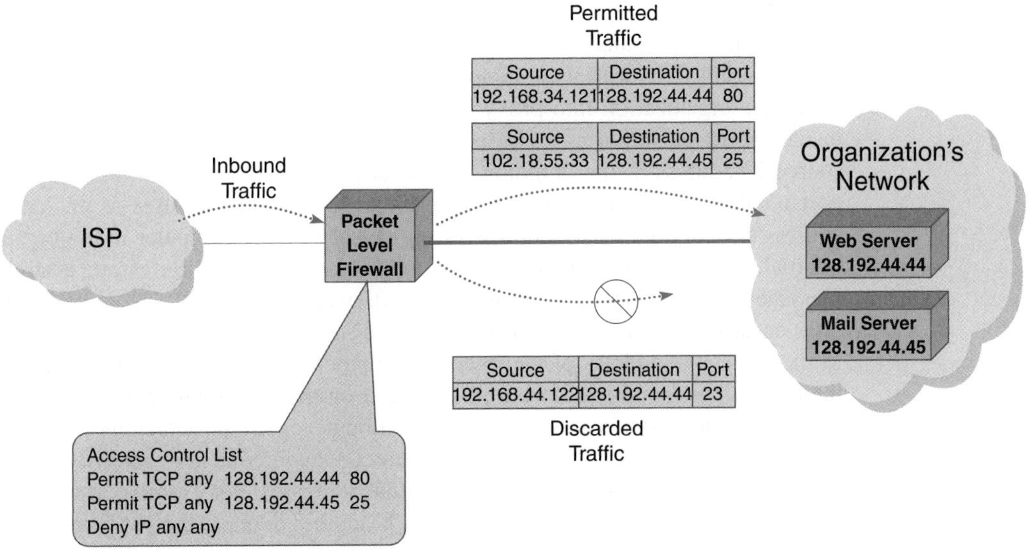

FIGURE 11.11 How packet-level firewalls work

Application-Layer Firewalls An **application-level firewall** is more expensive and more complicated to install and manage than a packet-level firewall, because it examines the contents of the application layer packet and searches for known attacks (see security holes later in this chapter). Application-layer firewalls have rules for each application they can process. For example, most application-layer firewalls can check Web packets (HTTP), e-mail packets (SMTP), and other common protocols. In some cases, special rules must be written by the organization to permit the use of application software it has developed.

Remember from Chapter 5 that TCP uses connection-oriented messaging in which a client first establishes a connection with a server before beginning to exchange data. Application-level firewalls can use *stateful inspection,* which means that they monitor and record the status of each connection and can use this information in making decisions about what packets to discard as security threats.

Many application-level firewalls prohibit external users from uploading executable files. In this way, intruders (or authorized users) cannot modify any software unless they have physical access to the firewall. Some refuse changes to their software unless it is done by the vendor. Others also actively monitor their own software and automatically disable outside connections if they detect any changes.

Network Address Translation Firewalls **Network address translation (NAT)** is the process of converting between one set of public IP addresses that are viewable from the Internet and a second set of private IP addresses that are hidden from people outside of the organization. NAT is transparent, in that no computer knows it is happening. While NAT can be done for several reasons, the most common reason is security. If external intruders on the Internet can't see the private IP addresses inside your organization, they can't attack your computers. Most routers and firewalls today have NAT built into them, even inexpensive routers designed for home use.

The **NAT firewall** uses an address table to translate the private IP addresses used inside the organization into proxy IP addresses used on the Internet. When a computer inside the organization accesses a computer on the Internet, the firewall changes the source IP address in the outgoing IP packet to its own address. It also sets the source port number in the TCP segment to a unique number that it uses as an index into its address table to find the IP address of the actual sending computer in the organization's internal network. When the external computer responds to the request, it addresses the message to the firewall's IP address. The firewall receives the incoming message, and after ensuring the packet should be permitted inside, changes the destination IP address to the private IP address of the internal computer and changes the TCP port number to the correct port number before transmitting it on the internal network.

This way systems outside the organization never see the actual internal IP addresses, and thus they think there is only one computer on the internal network. Most organizations also increase security by using illegal internal addresses. For example, if the organization has been assigned the Internet 128.192.55.X address domain, the NAT firewall would be assigned an address such as 128.192.55.1. Internal computers, however, would *not* be assigned addresses in the 128.192.55.X subnet. Instead, they would be assigned unauthorized Internet addresses such as 10.3.3.55 (addresses in the 10.X.X.X domain are not assigned to organizations but instead are reserved for use by private intranets). Because these internal addresses are never used on the Internet but are always converted by the firewall, this poses no problems for the users. Even if attackers discover the actual internal IP address, it would be impossible for them to reach the internal address from the Internet because the addresses could not be used to reach the organization's computers.[8]

Firewall Architecture Many organizations use layers of NAT, packet-level and application-level firewalls (Figure 11.12). Packet-level firewalls are used as an initial screen from the Internet into a network devoted solely to servers intended to provide public access (e.g., Web servers, public DNS servers). This network is sometimes called the *DMZ* (demilitarized zone) because it contains the organization's servers but does not provide complete security for them. This packet-level firewall will permit Web requests and similar access to the DMZ network servers but will deny FTP access to these servers from the Internet because no one except internal users should have the right to modify the servers. Each major portion of the organization's internal networks has its own NAT firewall to grant (or deny) access based on rules established by that part of the organization.

This figure also shows how a packet sent by a client computer inside one of the internal networks protected by a NAT firewall would flow through the network. The packet created by the client has the client's false source address and the source port

[8]Most routers and firewalls manufactured by Linksys (a manufacturer of networking equipment for home and small office use owned by Cisco) use NAT. Rather than setting the internal address to 10.x.x.x, Linksys sets them to 192.168.1.x, which is another subnet reserved for private intranets. If you have Linksys equipment with a NAT firewall, your internal IP address is likely to be 192.168.1.100.

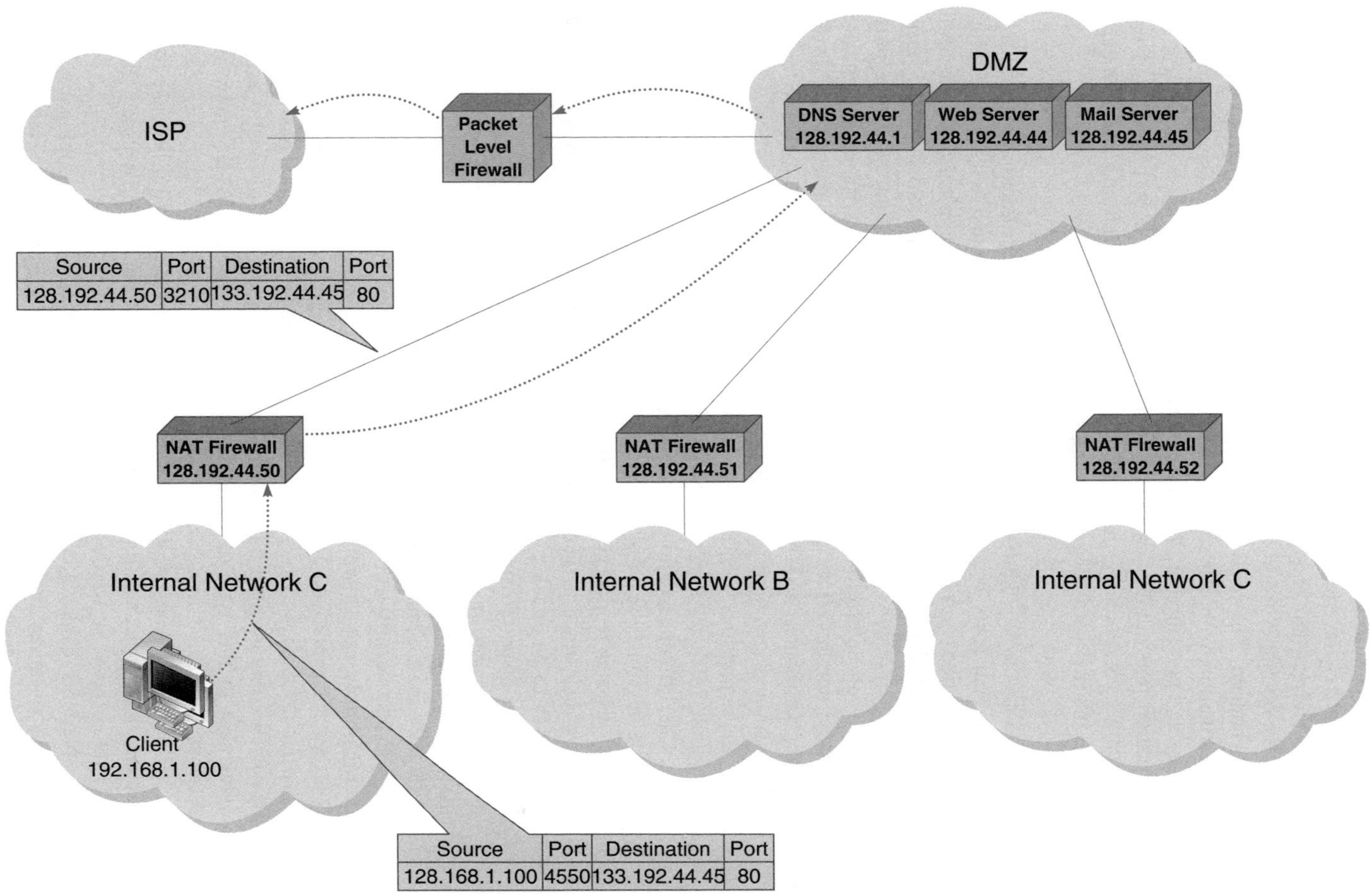

FIGURE 11.12 A typical network design using firewalls

number of the process on the client that generated the packet (an HTTP packet going to a Web server, as you can tell from the destination port address of 80). When the packet reaches the firewall, the firewall changes the source address on the IP packet to its own address and changes the source port number to an index it will use to identify the client computer's address and port number. The destination address and port number are unchanged. The firewall then sends the packet on its way to the destination. When the destination Web server responds to this packet, it will respond using the firewall's address and port number. When the firewall receives the incoming packets it will use the destination port number to identify what IP address and port number to use inside the internal network, change the inbound packet's destination and port number, and send it into the internal network so it reaches the client computer.

Physical Security One important element to prevent unauthorized users from accessing an internal LAN is *physical security:* preventing outsiders from gaining access into the organization's offices, server room, or network equipment facilities. Both main and remote physical facilities should be secured adequately and have the proper controls. Good security requires implementing the proper access controls so that only authorized personnel can enter closed areas where servers and network equipment are located or access the network. The network components themselves also have a level of physical security. Computers can have locks on their power switches or passwords that disable the screen and keyboard.

In the previous section we discussed the importance of locating backups and servers at separate (off-site) locations. Some companies have also argued that by having many servers in different locations you can reduce your risk and improve business continuity. Does having many servers disperse risk, or does it increase the points of vulnerability? A clear disaster recovery plan with an off-site backup and server facility can disperse risk, like distributed server systems. Distributed servers offer many more physical vulnerabilities to an attacker: more machines to guard, upgrade, patch, and defend. Many times these dispersed machines are all part of the same logical domain, which means that breaking into one of them often can give the attacker access to the resources of the others. It is our feeling that a well backed-up, centralized data center can be made inherently more secure than a proliferated base of servers.

Proper security education, background checks, and the implementation of error and fraud controls are also very important. In many cases, the simplest means to gain access is to become employed as a janitor and access the network at night. In some ways this is easier than the previous methods because the intruder only has to insert a listening device or computer into the organization's network to record messages. Three areas are vulnerable to this type of unauthorized access: wireless LANs, network cabling, and network devices.

Wireless LANs are the easiest target for **eavesdropping** because they often reach beyond the physical walls of the organization. Chapter 7 discussed the techniques of WLAN security, so we do not repeat them here.

Network cables are the next easiest target for eavesdropping because they often run long distances and usually are not regularly checked for tampering. The cables owned by the organization and installed within its facility are usually the first choice for eavesdropping. It is 100 times easier to tap a local cable than it is to tap an interexchange

TECHNICAL FOCUS 11.3 DATA SECURITY REQUIRES PHYSICAL SECURITY

The general consensus is that if someone can physically get to your server for some period of time, then all of your information on the computer (except perhaps strongly encrypted data) is available to the attacker.

With a Windows server, the attacker simply boots the computer from the CD drive with a Knoppix version of Linux. (Knoppix is Linux on a CD.) If the computer won't boot from the CD, the attacker simply changes the BIOS to make it boot from the CD. Knoppix finds all the drivers for the specific computer and gives you a Linux desktop that can fully read all of the NTFS or FAT32 files.

But what about Windows password access? Nothing to it. Knoppix completely bypasses it. The attacker can then read, copy, or transmit any of the files on the Windows machine. Similar attacks are also possible on a Linux or Unix server, but they are slightly more difficult.

channel because it is extremely difficult to identify the specific circuits belonging to any one organization in a highly multiplexed switched interexchange circuit operated by a common carrier. Local cables should be secured behind walls and above ceilings, and telephone equipment and switching rooms (wiring closets) should be locked and their doors equipped with alarms. The primary goal is to control physical access by employees or vendors to the connector cables and modems. This includes restricting their access to the wiring closets in which all the communication wires and cables are connected.

Certain types of cable can impair or increase security by making eavesdropping easier or more difficult. Obviously, any wireless network is at extreme risk for eavesdropping because anyone in the area of the transmission can easily install devices to monitor the radio or infrared signals. Conversely, fiber-optic cables are harder to tap, thus increasing security. Some companies offer armored cable that is virtually impossible to cut without special tools. Other cables have built-in alarm systems. The U.S. Air Force, for example, uses pressurized cables that are filled with gas. If the cable is cut, the gas escapes, pressure drops, and an alarm is sounded.

Network devices such as switches and routers should be secured in a locked wiring closet. As discussed in Chapter 6, all messages within a given local area network are actually received by all computers on the LAN although they only process those messages addressed to them. It is rather simple to install a **sniffer program** that records all messages received for later (unauthorized) analysis. A computer with a sniffer program could then be plugged into an unattended switch to eavesdrop on all message traffic. A **secure switch** makes this type of eavesdropping more difficult by requiring a special authorization code to be entered before new computers can be added.

Dial-In Security Dial-in security is important for any organization that permits staff members to access its network via modems. Some dial-up modem controls include changing the modem telephone numbers periodically and keeping telephone numbers confidential. In recent years, **automatic number identification (ANI)** has been used. The network manager can specify several telephone numbers authorized to access each account. When a user successfully logs on to an account, the source of the incoming phone call is identified using ANI and if it is one of the authorized numbers, the login is accepted; otherwise, the host computer or communications server disconnects the call. ANI does not work for users who frequently travel (e.g., sales representatives) because they often call from hotel rooms and have no knowledge of telephone numbers in advance.

Server and Client Protection

Security Holes

Even with physical security and firewalls, the servers and client computers on a network may not be safe because of **security holes.** A security hole is simply a bug that permits unauthorized access. Many commonly used operating systems have major security holes well known to potential intruders. Many security holes have been documented and "patches" are available from vendors to fix them, but network managers may be unaware of all the holes or simply forget to update their systems with new patches regularly.

A complete discussion of security holes is beyond the scope of this book. Many security holes are highly technical; for example, sending a message designed to overflow a memory buffer, thereby placing a short command into a very specific memory area that performs some function. Others are rather simple, but not obvious. For example, the attacker sends a message that lists the server's address as both the sender and the destination, so the server repeatedly sends messages to itself until it crashes.

Once a security hole is discovered, it is quickly circulated through the Internet. The race begins between hackers and security teams; hackers share their discovery with other hackers and security teams share the discovery with other security teams. CERT is the central clearinghouse for major Internet-related security holes, so the CERT team quickly responds to reports of new security problems and posts alerts and advisories on the Web and e-mails them to those who subscribe to its service. The developer of the software with the security hole usually works quickly to fix the security hole and produces a **patch** that corrects the hole. This patch is then shared with customers so they can download and apply it to their systems to prevent hackers from exploiting the hole to break in. Attacks that take advantage of a newly discovered security hole before a patch is developed are called **zero day attacks.** One problem is that many network managers do not routinely respond to such security threats and immediately download and install the patch. Often it takes many months for patches to be distributed to most sites.[9] Do you regularly install all the Windows or Mac updates on your computer?

Other security holes are not really holes but simply policies adopted by computer vendors that open the door for security problems, such as computer systems that come with a variety of preinstalled user accounts. These accounts and their initial passwords are well documented and known to all potential attackers. Network managers sometimes forget to change the passwords on these well-known accounts thus enabling an attacker to slip in.

[9]For an example of one CERT advisory posted about problems with the most common DNS server software used on the Internet, see www.cert.org/advisories/CA-2001-02.html. The history in this advisory shows that it took about eight months for the patch for the previous advisory in this family (issued in November 1999) to be installed on most DNS servers around the world. This site also has histories of more recent advisories.

MANAGEMENT FOCUS 11.6 PATCH AND PRAY

In January 2003, the Slammer worm infected 90 percent of all vulnerable computers on the Internet in just 10 minutes after it was released. Slammer was stopped by ISPs that blocked port 1434, the one Slammer used to propagate itself.

When Slammer subsided, talk focused on patching. Those looking to cast blame cried a familiar refrain: if everyone had just patched their systems, Slammer wouldn't have happened. But that's not true; patching no longer works. Software today is massive (Windows contains over 45 million lines of code) and the rate of sloppy coding (10 to 20 errors per 1,000 lines of code) has led to thousands of vulnerabilities. There are simply too many patches coming too quickly.

Patch writing is usually assigned to entry-level programmers. They fix problems in a race with hackers trying to exploit them. From this patch factory comes a poorly written product that can break as much as it fixes. One patch, for example, worked fine for everyone except the unlucky users who happened to have a certain computer with outdated drivers, which the patch crashed. Sometimes if you just apply patches, you get nailed.

There are two emerging and opposite patch philosophies: either patch more or patch less. Patch-more adherents believe patching isn't the problem, but that manual patching is. Vendors in the patch-more school have created patch management software that automates the process of finding, downloading, and applying patches.

The patch-less school argues that historically only 2 percent of vulnerabilities have resulted in attacks. Therefore, most patches aren't worth applying; they're at best superfluous and, at worst, *add* significant additional risk. Instead, you should improve your security policy (e.g., turn off ports such as 1434 that aren't needed) and pay third parties to determine which patches are really necessary.

SOURCE: "Patch and Pray," www.csoonline.com/read/081303/patch.html, August 2003.

Operating Systems The American government requires certain levels of security in the operating systems and network operating systems it uses for certain applications. The minimum level of security is C2. Most major operating systems (e.g., Windows) provide at least C2. Most widely used systems are striving to meet the requirements of much higher security levels such as B2. Very few systems meet the highest levels of security (A1 and A2).

There has been a long running debate about whether the Windows operating system is less secure than other operating systems such as Linux. Every new attack on Windows systems ignites the debate; Windows detractors repeat "I told you so" while Windows defenders state that this happens mostly because Windows is the obvious system to attack since it is the most commonly used operating system and because of the hostility of the Windows detractors themselves.

There is a critical difference in what applications can do in Windows and in Linux. Linux (and its ancestor Unix) was first written as a multi-user operating system in which different users had different rights. Only some users were system administrators and had the rights to access and make changes to the critical parts of the operating system. All other users were barred from doing so.

In contrast, Windows (and its ancestor DOS) was first written as an operating system for a single personal computer, an environment in which the user was in complete control

TECHNICAL FOCUS

11.4 EXPLOITING A SECURITY HOLE

In order to exploit a security hole, the hacker has to know it's there. So how does a hacker find out? It's simple in the era of automated tools.

First, the hacker has to find the servers on a network. The hacker could start by using network scanning software to systematically probe every IP address on a network to find all the servers on the network. At this point, the hacker has narrowed the potential targets to a few servers.

Second, the hacker needs to learn what services are available on each server. To do this, he or she could use port scanning software to systematically probe every TCP/IP port on a given server. This would reveal which ports are in use and thus what services the server offers. For example, if the server has software that responds to port 80, it is a Web server, while if it responds to port 25, it is a mail server.

Third, the hacker would begin to seek out the exact software and version number of the server software providing each service. For example, suppose the hacker decides to target mail servers. There are a variety of tools that can probe the mail server software, and based on how the server software responds to certain messages, determine which manufacturer and version number of software is being used.

Finally, once the hacker knows which package and version number the server is using, the hacker uses tools designed to exploit the known security holes in the software. For example, some older mail server software packages do not require users to authenticate themselves (e.g., by a userid and password) before accepting SMTP packets for the mail server to forward. In this case, the hacker could create SMTP packets with fake source addresses and use the server to flood the Internet with spam (i.e., junk mail). In another case, a certain version of a well-known e-commerce package enabled users to pass operating system commands to the server simply by including a UNIX pipe symbol (|) and the command to the name of a file name to be uploaded; when the system opened the uploaded file, it also executed the command attached to it.

of the computer and could do anything he or she liked. As a result, Windows applications regularly access and make changes to critical parts of the operating system. There are advantages to this. Windows applications can do many powerful things without the user needing to understand them. These applications can be very rich in features, and more important, they can appear to the user to be very friendly and easy to use. Everything appears to run "out-of-the-box" without modification. Windows has built these features into the core of their systems. Any major rewrite of Windows to prevent this would most likely cause significant incompatibilities with all applications designed to run under previous versions of Windows. To many, this would be a high price to pay for some unseen benefits called "security."

But there is a price for this friendliness. Hostile applications can easily take over the computer and literally do whatever they want without the user knowing. Simply put, there is a tradeoff between ease of use and security. Increasing needs for security demand more checks and restrictions, which translates into less friendliness and fewer features. It may very well be that there is an inherent and permanent contradiction between the ease of use of a system and its security.

Triojan Horses One important tool in gaining unauthorized access is a **Trojan horse.** Trojans are remote access management consoles (sometimes called **rootkits**) that enable users to access a computer and manage it from afar. If you see free software that will enable you to control your computer from anywhere, be careful; the software may also

TECHNICAL FOCUS 11.5 OPEN SOURCE VERSUS CLOSED SOURCE SOFTWARE

*"**A** cryptographic system should still be secure if everything is known about it except its key. You should not base the security of your system upon its obscurity."—Auguste Kerckhoffs (1883).*

Auguste Kerckhoffs was a Flemish cryptographer and linguist who studied military communications during the Franco-Prussian War. He observed that neither side could depend upon hiding their telegraph lines and equipment from the other side because the enemy would find the hidden telegraph lines and tap into the communications. One could not rely upon their system being obscure. In 1948, Claude Shannon of Bell Labs extended Kerckhoffs' Law when he said, "Always assume that the enemy knows your system." Cryptographers and military colleges teach Kerckhoffs' and Shannon's laws as fundamental rules in information security.

How does this apply to computer security? There are a few basics that we should understand first: programmers write their code in human-readable source code, which is then compiled to produce binary object code (i.e., zeros and ones); very few people can read binary code. For-profit developers do *not* release their source code when they sell software; they only release the binary object code. This **closed source** code is their proprietary "crown jewels," to be jealously guarded. In contrast, **open source** software is not-for-profit software in which the source code is provided along with the binary object code so that other developers can read the code and write new features or find and fix bugs.

So, does this mean that closed source is safer than open source because no one can see any bugs or security holes that might be hidden in the source code? No. With closed source, there is the temptation to use "security via obscurity." The history of security holes is that they become well known. Why? First, because there may be literally hundreds of people with access to the source code. Some of those people come and go. Some take the code with them. And some talk to others, who post it on the Internet.

And then there are the decompilers. A decompiler converts binary object code back into source code. Decompilers do not produce exact copies of the original source code, but they are getting better and better. With their use, attackers can better guess where the security holes are.

There is also a tendency within the closed source community to rely upon the source code being hidden as a line of defense. In effect, they drop their guard, falsely thinking that they are safe behind the obscurity of hidden code. The open source community has far more people able to examine the code than any closed source system. One of the tenets of the open source community is "No bug is too obscure or difficult for a million eyes."

Also, the motives of the developers are different. Open source coders generally do not write for profit. Closed source developers are inevitably writing for profit. With the profit motive comes more pressure to release software quickly to "beat the market." Rushing code to market is one of the surest ways of releasing flawed code. This pressure does not exist in the open source world since no one is going to make much money on it anyway.

Can there be secure closed source software? Yes. But the developers must be committed to security from the very beginning of development. By most reasonable measures, open source software has been and continues to be more secure than closed source software. This is what Auguste Kerckhoffs would have predicted.

permit an attacker to control your computer from anywhere! Trojans are more often concealed in other software that unsuspecting users download over the Internet (their name alludes to the original Trojan horse). Music and video files shared on Internet music sites are common carriers of Trojans. When the user downloads and plays a music file, it plays normally and the attached Trojan software silently installs a small program that enables the attacker to take complete control of the user's computer, so the user is unaware that anything bad has happened. The attacker then simply connects to the user's computer and has the same access and controls as the user. Many Trojans are completely undetectable by the very best antivirus software.

One of the first major Trojans was Back Orifice, which aggressively attacked Windows servers. Back Orifice gave the attacker the same functions as the administrator of the infected server, and then some: complete file and network control, device and registry access, with packet and application redirection. It was every administrator's worst nightmare, and every attacker's dream.

More recently, Trojans have morphed into tools such as MoSucker and Optix Pro. These attack consoles now have one-button clicks to disable firewalls, antivirus software, and any other defensive process that might be running on the victim's computer. The attacker can choose what port the Trojan runs on, what it is named, and when it runs. They can listen in to a computer's microphone or look through an attached camera—even if the device appears to be off. Figure 11.13 shows a menu from one Trojan that illustrates some of the "fun stuff" that an attacker can do, such as opening and closing the CD tray, beeping the speaker, or reversing the mouse buttons so that clicking on the left button actually sends a right click.

Not only have these tools become powerful, but they are also very easy to use—much easier to use than the necessary defensive countermeasures to protect oneself from them. And what does the near future hold for Trojans? We can easily envision Trojans that schedule themselves to run at, say 2:00 AM, choosing a random port, emailing the attacker that the machine is now "open for business" at port # NNNNN. The attackers can then step in, do whatever they want to do, run a script to erase most of

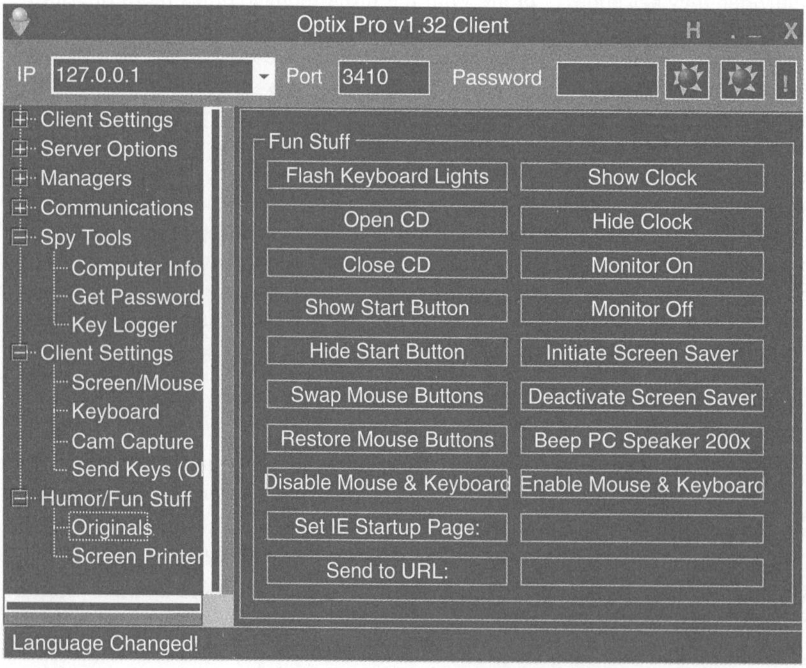

FIGURE 11.13 One menu on the control console for the Optix Pro Trojan

MANAGEMENT FOCUS 11.7 SONY'S SPYWARE

Sony BMG Entertainment, the music giant, included a spyware rootkit on audio CDs sold in the fall of 2005, including CDs by such artists as Celine Dion, Frank Sinatra, and Ricky Martin. The rootkit was automatically installed on any PC that played the infected CD. The rootkit was designed to track the behavior of users who might be illegally copying and distributing the music on the CD, with the goal of preventing illegal copies from being widely distributed.

Sony made two big mistakes. First, it failed to inform customers who purchased its CDs about the rootkit, so users unknowingly installed it. The rootkit used standard spyware techniques to conceal its existence to prevent users from discovering it. Second, Sony used a widely available rootkit, which meant that any knowledgeable user on the Internet could use the rootkit to take control of the infected computer. Several viruses have been written that exploit the rootkit and are now circulating on the Internet. The irony is that rootkit infringes on copyrights held by several open source projects, which means Sony was engaged in the very act it was trying to prevent: piracy.

When the rootkit was discovered, Sony was slow to apologize, slow to stop selling rootkit-infected CDs, and slow to help customers remove the rootkit. Several lawsuits have been filed in the United States and abroad seeking damages.

SOURCE: J.A. Halderman and E.W. Felton, "Lessons from the Sony CD DRM Episode," working paper, Princeton University, 2006; and "Sony Anti-Customer Technology Roundup and Time-Line, "*www.boingboing.net,* February 15, 2006.

their tracks, and then sign out and shut off the Trojan. Once the job is done, the Trojan could even erase itself from storage. Scary? Yes. And the future does not look better.

Spyware, adware, and DDoS agents are three types of Trojans. DDoS agents were discussed in the previous section. As the name suggests, spyware monitors what happens on the target computer. Spyware can record keystrokes that appear to be userids and passwords so the intruder can gain access to the user's account (e.g., bank accounts). Adware monitors user's actions and displays pop-up advertisements on the user's screen. For example, suppose you clicked on the Web site for an online retailer. Adware might pop-up a window for a competitor, or, worse still, redirect your browser to the competitor's Web site. Many anti-virus software packages now routinely search for and remove spyware, adware, and other Trojans and special purpose antispyware software is available (e.g., Spybot). Some firewall vendors are now adding anti-Trojan logic to their devices to block any transmissions from infected computers from entering or leaving their networks.

Encryption

One of the best ways to prevent intrusion is **encryption,** which is a means of disguising information by the use of mathematical rules known as *algorithms.*[10] Actually, *cryptography* is the more general and proper term. *Encryption* is the process of disguising information whereas **decryption** is the process of restoring it to readable form. When

[10]For more information on cryptography, see the FAQ at www.rsa.com.

information is in readable form, it is called **plaintext;** when in encrypted form, it is called **ciphertext.** Encryption can be used to encrypt files stored on a computer or to encrypt data in transit between computers.[11]

There are two fundamentally different types of encryption: symmetric and asymmetric. With **symmetric encryption,** the key used to encrypt a message is the *same* as the one used to decrypt it. With **asymmetric encryption,** the key used to decrypt a message is *different* from the key used to encrypt it.

Single Key Encryption Symmetric encryption (also called single-key encryption) has two parts: the **algorithm** and the **key,** which personalizes the algorithm by making the transformation of data unique. Two pieces of identical information encrypted with the same algorithm but with different keys produce completely different ciphertexts. With symmetric encryption, the communicating parties must share the one key. If the algorithm

MANAGEMENT FOCUS 11.8 **TROJANS AT HOME**

It started with a routine phone call to technical support—one of our users had a software package that kept crashing. The network technician was sent to fix the problem but couldn't, so thoughts turned to a virus or Trojan. After an investigation, the security team found a remote FTP Trojan installed on the computer that was storing several gigabytes of cartoons and making them available across the Internet. The reason for crash was that the FTP server was an old version that was not compatible with the computer's operating system. The Trojan was removed and life went on.

Three months later the same problem occurred on a different computer. Because the previous Trojan had been logged, the network support staff quickly recognized it as a Trojan. The same hacker had returned, storing the same cartoons on a different computer. This triggered a complete investigation. All computers on our Business School network were scanned and we found 15 computers that contained the Trojan. We gathered forensic evidence to help identify the attacker (e.g., log files, registry entries) and filed an incident report with the University incident response team advising them to scan all computers on the university network immediately.

The next day, we found more computers containing the same FTP Trojan and the same cartoons. The attacker had come back overnight and taken control of more computers. This immediately escalated the problem. We cleaned some of the machines but left some available for use by the hacker to encourage him not to attack other computers. The network security manager replicated the software and used it to investigate how the Trojan worked. We determined that the software used a brute force attack to break the administrative password file on the standard image that we used in our computer labs. We changed the password and installed a security patch to our lab computer's standard configuration. We then upgraded all the lab computers and only then cleaned the remaining machines controlled by the attacker.

The attacker had also taken over many other computers on campus for the same purpose. With the forensic evidence that we and the university security incident response team had gathered, the case is now in court.

[11] If you use Windows, you can encrypt files on your hard disk: Just use the Help facility and search on encryption to learn how.

is adequate and the key is kept secret, acquisition of the ciphertext by unauthorized personnel is of no consequence to the communicating parties.

Good encryption systems do not depend on keeping the algorithm secret. Only the keys need to be kept secret. The key is a relatively small numeric value (in terms of the number of bits). The larger the key, the more secure the encryption because large "key space" protects the ciphertext against those who try to break it by **brute-force attacks**—which simply means trying every possible key.

There should be a large enough number of possible keys that an exhaustive brute-force attack would take inordinately long or would cost more than the value of the encrypted information.

Because the same key is used to encrypt and decrypt, symmetric encryption can cause problems with **key management;** keys must be shared among the senders and receivers very carefully. Before two computers in a network can communicate using encryption, both must have the same key. This means that both computers can then send and read any messages that use that key. Companies often do not want one company to be able to read messages they send to another company, so this means that there must be a separate key used for communication with each company. These keys must be recorded but kept secure so that they cannot be stolen. Because the algorithm is known publicly, the disclosure of the key means the total compromise of encrypted messages. Managing this system of keys can be challenging.

One commonly used symmetric encryption technique is the **Data Encryption Standard (DES),** which was developed in the mid-1970s by the U.S. government in conjunction with IBM. DES is standardized by the National Institute of Standards and Technology (NIST). The most common form of DES uses a 56-bit key, which experts can break in less than a day (i.e., experts with the right tools can figure out what a message encrypted using DES says without knowing the key in less than 24 hours). DES is no longer recommended for data needing high security although some companies continue to use it for less important data.

Triple DES (3DES) is a newer standard that is harder to break. As the name suggests, it involves using DES three times, usually with three different keys to produce the encrypted text, which produces a stronger level of security because it has a total of 168 bits as the key (i.e., 3 times 56 bits).[12]

The NIST's new standard, called **Advanced Encryption Standard (AES),** has replaced DES. AES has key sizes of 128, 192, and 256 bits. NIST estimates that, using the most advanced computers and techniques available today, it will require about 150 trillion years to crack AES by brute force. As computers and techniques improve, the time requirement will drop, but AES seems secure for the foreseeable future; the original DES lasted 20 years, so AES may have a similar life span.

Another commonly used symmetric encryption algorithm is **RC4,** developed by Ron Rivest of RSA Data Security, Inc. RC4 can use a key up to 256 bits long but most

[12]There are several versions of 3DES. One version (called 3DES-EEE) simply encrypts the message three times with different keys as one would expect. Another version (3DES-EDE) encrypts with one key, decrypts with a second key (i.e., reverse encrypts), and then encrypts with a third key. There are other variants, as you can imagine.

commonly uses a 40-bit key. It is faster to use than DES but suffers from the same problems from brute-force attacks: its 40-bit key can be broken by a determined attacker in a day or two.

Today, the United States government considers encryption to be a weapon and regulates its export in the same way it regulates the export of machine guns or bombs. Present rules prohibit the export of encryption techniques with keys longer than 64 bits without permission, although exports to Canada and the European Union are permitted, and American banks and Fortune 100 companies are now permitted to use more powerful encryption techniques in their foreign offices. This policy made sense when only American companies had the expertise to develop powerful encryption software. Today, however, many non-American companies are developing encryption software that is more powerful than American software that is limited only by these rules. Therefore, the American software industry is lobbying the government to change the rules so that they can successfully compete overseas.[13]

Public Key Encryption The most popular form of asymmetric encryption (also called **public key encryption**) is **RSA,** which was invented at MIT in 1977 by Rivest, Shamir, and Adleman, who founded RSA Data Security in 1982.[14] The patent expired in 2000, so many new companies have entered the market and public key software has dropped in price. The RSA technique forms the basis for today's **public key infrastructure (PKI).**

Public key encryption is inherently different from symmetric single-key systems like DES. Because public key encryption is asymmetric, there are two keys. One key (called the **public key**) is used to encrypt the message and a second, very different **private key** is used to decrypt the message. Keys are often 512 bits or 1,024 bits in length.

Public key systems are based on one-way functions. Even though you originally know both the contents of your message and the public encryption key, once it is encrypted by the one-way function, the message cannot be decrypted without the private key. One-way functions, which are relatively easy to calculate in one direction, are impossible to "uncalculate" in the reverse direction. Public key encryption is one of the most secure encryption techniques available, excluding special encryption techniques developed by national security agencies.

Public key encryption greatly reduces the key management problem. Each user has its public key that is used to encrypt messages sent to it. These public keys are widely publicized (e.g., listed in a telephone book-style directory)—that's why they're called "public" keys. In addition, each user has a private key that decrypts only the messages that were encrypted by its public key. This private key is kept secret (that's why it's called the "private" key). The net result is that if two parties wish to communicate with one another, there is no need to exchange keys beforehand. Each knows the other's public key from the listing in a public directory and can communicate encrypted information

[13]The rules have been changed several times in recent years, so for more recent information, see www.bis.doc.gov.

[14]Rivest, Shamir, and Adleman have traditionally been given credit as the original developers of public key encryption (based on theoretical work by Whitfield Diffie and Martin Hellman), but recently declassified material has revealed that public key encryption was actually first developed years earlier by Clifford Cocks based on theoretical work by James Ellis, both of whom were employees of a British spy agency.

immediately. The key management problem is reduced to the on-site protection of the private key.

Figure 11.14 illustrates how this process works. All public keys are published in a directory. When Organization A wants to send an encrypted message to Organization B, it looks through the directory to find its public key. It then encrypts the message using B's public key. This encrypted message is then sent through the network to Organization B, which decrypts the message using its private key.

Authentication Public key encryption also permits the use of *digital signatures* through a process of **authentication.** When one user sends a message to another, it is difficult to legally prove who actually sent the message. Legal proof is important in many communications, such as bank transfers and buy/sell orders in currency and stock

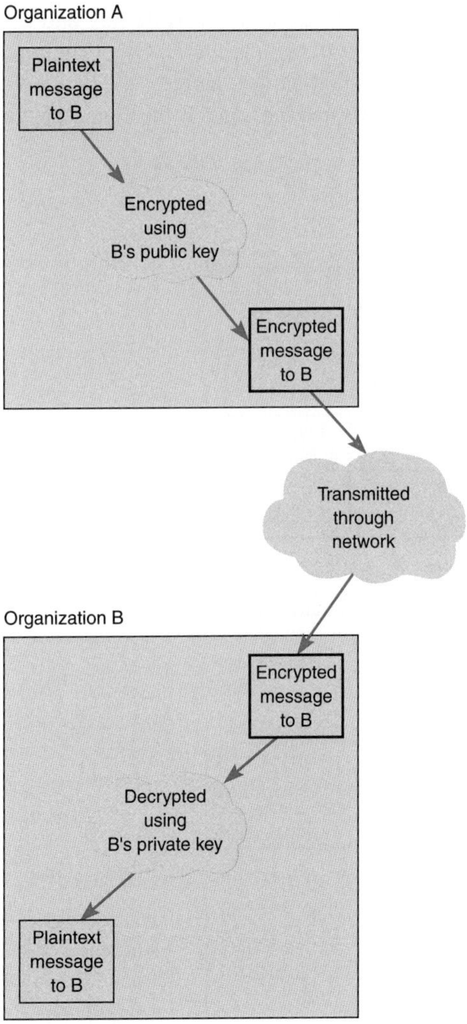

FIGURE 11.14 Secure transmission with public key encryption

trading, which normally require legal signatures. Public key encryption algorithms are *invertable,* meaning that text encrypted with either key can be decrypted by the other. Normally, we encrypt with the public key and decrypt with the private key. However, it is possible to do the inverse: encrypt with the private key and decrypt with the public key. Since the private key is secret, only the real user could use it to encrypt a message. Thus, a digital signature or authentication sequence is used as a legal signature on many financial transactions. This signature is usually the name of the signing party plus other *key-contents* such as unique information from the message (e.g., date, time, or dollar amount). This signature and the other key-contents are encrypted by the sender using the private key. The receiver uses the sender's public key to decrypt the signature block and compares the result to the name and other key contents in the rest of the message to ensure a match.

Figure 11.15 illustrates how authentication can be combined with public encryption to provide a secure and authenticated transmission with a digital signature. The plaintext message is first encrypted using Organization A's private key and then encrypted using Organization's B public key. It is then transmitted to B. Organization B first decrypts the message using its private key. It sees that part of the message (the key-contents) is still in cyphertext, indicating it is an authenticated message. B then decrypts the key-contents part

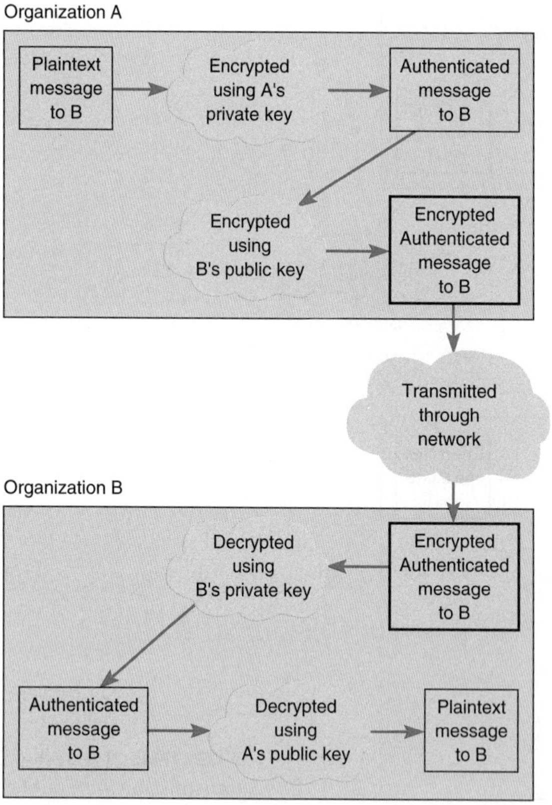

FIGURE 11.15
Authenticated and secure transmission with public key encryption

of the message using A's public key to produce the plaintext message. Since only A has the private key that matches A's public key, B can safely assume that A sent the message.

The only problem with this approach lies in ensuring that the person or organization who sent the document with the correct private key is actually the person or organization they claim to be. Anyone can post a public key on the Internet, so there is no way of knowing for sure who they actually are. For example, it would be possible for someone to create a Web site and claim to be "Organization A" when in fact they are really someone else.

This is where the Internet's public key infrastructure (PKI) becomes important.[15] The PKI is a set of hardware, software, organizations, and polices designed to make public key encryption work on the Internet. PKI begins with a **certificate authority (CA),** which is a trusted organization that can vouch for the authenticity of the person or organization using authentication (e.g., VeriSign). A person wanting to use a CA registers with the CA and must provide some proof of identity. There are several levels of certification, ranging from a simple confirmation from a valid e-mail address to a complete police-style background check with an in-person interview. The CA issues a digital *certificate* that is the requestor's public key encrypted using the CA's private key as proof of identity. This certificate is then attached to the user's e-mail or Web transactions, in addition to the authentication information. The receiver then verifies the certificate by decrypting it with the CA's public key—and must also contact the CA to ensure that the user's certificate has not been revoked by the CA.

For higher security certifications, the CA requires that a unique "fingerprint" be issued by the CA for each message sent by the user. The user submits the message to the CA, who creates the unique fingerprint by combining the CA's private key with the message's authentication key contents. Because the user must obtain a unique fingerprint for each message, this ensures that the CA has not revoked the certificate between the time it was issued and the time the message was sent by the user.

Encryption Software **Pretty Good Privacy (PGP)** is a freeware public key encryption package developed by Philip Zimmermann that is often used to encrypt e-mail. Users post their public key on Web pages, for example, and anyone wishing to send them an encrypted message simply cuts and pastes the key off the Web page into the PGP software, which encrypts and sends the message.[16]

Secure Sockets Layer (SSL) is an encryption protocol widely used on the Web. SSL operates between the application layer software and the transport layer (in what the OSI model calls the presentation layer). SSL encrypts outbound packets coming out of the application layer before they reach the transport layer and decrypts inbound packets coming out of the transport layer before they reach the application layer. With SSL, the client and the server start with a handshake for PKI authentication and for the server to provide its public key and preferred encryption technique to the client (usually RC4, DES, 3DES, or AES). The client then generates a key for this encryption technique, which is

[15]For more on the PKI, go to www.ietf.org and search on PKI.

[16]For example, Cisco posts the public keys it uses for security incident reporting on its Web site; go to www.cisco.com and search on "security incident response." For more information on PGP, see www.pgpi.org and www.pgp.com.

sent to the server encrypted with the server's public key. The rest of the communication then uses this encryption technique and key.

IP Security Protocol (IPSec) is another widely used encryption protocol. IPSec differs from SSL in that SSL is focused on Web applications, while IPSec can be used with a much wider variety of application layer protocols. IPSec sits between IP at the network layer and TCP/UDP at the transport layer. IPSec can use a wide variety of encryption techniques so the first step is for the sender and receiver to establish the technique and key to be used. This is done using **Internet Key Exchange (IKE).** Both parties generate a random key and send it to the other using an encrypted authenticated PKI process, and then put these two numbers together to produce the key.[17] The encryption technique is also negotiated between the two, often being 3DES. Once the keys and technique have been established, IPSec can begin transmitting data.

IPSec can operate in either transport mode or tunnel mode for VPNs. In **transport mode,** IPSec encrypts just the IP payload, leaving the IP packet header unchanged so it can be easily routed through the Internet. In this case, IPSec adds an additional packet (either an Authentication Header [AH] or an Encapsulating Security Payload [ESP]) at the start of the IP packet that provides encryption information for the receiver.

In **tunnel mode,** IPSec encrypts the entire IP packet, and must therefore add an entirely new IP packet that contains the encrypted packet, as well as the IPSec AH or ESP packets. In tunnel mode, the newly added IP packet just identifies the IPSec encryption agent at the next destination, not the final destination; once the IPSec packet arrives at the encryption agent, the excrypted packet is VPN decrypted and sent on its way. In tunnel mode, attackers can only learn the endpoints of the VPN tunnel, not the ultimate source and destination of the packets.

User Authentication

Once the network perimeter and the network interior have been secured, the next step is to develop a way to ensure that only authorized users are permitted into the network and into specific resources in the interior of the network. This is called **user authentication.**

The basis of user authentication is the **user profile** for each user's **account** that is assigned by the network manager. Each user's profile specifies what data and network resources he or she can access, and the type of access (read only, write, create, delete).

User profiles can limit the allowable log-in days, time of day, physical locations, and the allowable number of incorrect log-in attempts. Some will also automatically log a user out if that person has not performed any network activity for a certain length of time (e.g., the user has gone to lunch and has forgotten to log off the network). Regular security checks throughout the day when the user is logged in can determine whether a user is still permitted access to the network. For example, the network manager might have disabled the user's profile while the user is logged in, or the user's account may have run out of funds.

Creating accounts and profiles is simple. When a new staff member joins an organization, that person is assigned a user account and profile. One security problem is

[17]This is done using the Diffie-Hellman process; see the FAQ at www.rsa.com.

TECHNICAL FOCUS 11.6 CRACKING A PASSWORD

To crack Windows passwords, you just need to get a copy of the security account manager (SAM) file in the WINNT directory, which contains all the Windows passwords in an encrypted format. If you have physical access to the computer, that's sufficient. If not, you might be able to hack in over the network. Then, you just need to use a Windows-based cracking tool such as LophtCrack. Depending upon the difficulty of the password, the time needed to crack the password via brute force could take minutes or up to a day.

Or that's the way it used to be. Recently the *Cryptography and Security Lab* in Switzerland developed a new password-cracking tool that relies upon very large amounts of RAM. It then does indexed searches of possible passwords that are already in memory. This tool can cut cracking times to less than 1/10 of the time of previous tools. Keep adding RAM and mHertz and you could reduce the crack times to 1/100 that of the older cracking tools. This means that if you can get your hands on the Windows-encrypted password file, then the game *is over.* It can literally crack complex passwords in Windows in seconds.

It's different for Linux, Unix, or Apple computers. These systems insert a 12-bit random "salt" to the password, which means that cracking their passwords will take 4,096 (2^12) times longer to do. That margin is probably sufficient for now, until the next generation of cracking tools comes along. Maybe.

So what can we say from all of this? That you are 4,096 times safer with Linux? Well, not necessarily. But what we may be able to say is that strong password protection, by itself, is an oxymoron. We must combine it with other methods of security to have reasonable confidence in the system.

the removal of user accounts when someone leaves an organization. Often, network managers are not informed of the departure and accounts remain in the system. For example, an examination of the user accounts at the University of Georgia found 30 percent belonged to staff members no longer employed by the university. If the staff member's departure was not friendly, there is a risk that he or she may attempt to access data and resources and use them for personal gain, or destroy them to "get back at" the organization. Many systems permit the network manager to assign expiration dates to user accounts to ensure that unused profiles are automatically deleted or deactivated, but these actions do not replace the need to notify network managers about an employee's departure as part of the standard Human Resources procedures.

Gaining access to an account can be based on **something you know, something you have,** or **something you are.**

Passwords The most common approach is **something you know,** usually a **password.** Before users can login, they need to enter a password. Unfortunately, passwords are often poorly chosen, enabling intruders to guess them and gain access. Some organizations are now requiring that users choose passwords that meet certain security requirements, such as a minimum length or including numbers and/or special characters (e.g., $, #, !). Some have moved to **passphrases** which, as the name suggests, is a series of words separated by spaces. Using complex passwords and passphrases has also been called one of the top five least effective security controls because it can frustrate users and lead them to record their passwords in places from which they can be stolen.

Access cards Requiring passwords provides at best mid-level security (much like locking your doors when you leave the house); it won't stop the professional intruder, but it will slow amateurs. Nonetheless, most organizations today use only passwords. About a third of organizations go beyond this and are requiring users to enter a password in conjunction with *something they have,* an **access card.** A **smart card** is a card about the size of a credit card that contains a small computer chip. This card can be read by a device and in order to gain access to the network, the user must present both the card and the password. Intruders must have access to both before they can break in. The best example of this is the automated teller machine (ATM) network operated by your bank. Before you can gain access to your account, you must have both your ATM card and the access number.

Another approach is to use **one-time passwords.** The user connects into the network as usual, and after the user's password is accepted, the system generates a one-time password. The user must enter this password to gain access, otherwise the connection is terminated. The user can receive this one-time password in a number of ways (e.g., via a pager). Other systems provide the user with a unique number that must be entered into a separate handheld device (called a **token**), which in turn displays the password for the user to enter. Other systems use **time-based tokens** in which the one-time password is changed every 60 seconds. The user has a small card (often attached to a key chain) that is synchronized with the server and displays the one-time password. With any of these

MANAGEMENT FOCUS 11.9 SELECTING PASSWORDS

The key to users' accounts are passwords; each account has a unique password chosen by the user. The problem is that passwords are often chosen poorly and not changed regularly. Many network managers require users to change passwords periodically (e.g., every 90 days), but this does not ensure that users choose "good" passwords.

A good password is one that the user finds easy to remember, but is difficult for potential intruders to guess. Several studies have found that about three-quarters of passwords fall into one of four categories:

- Names of family members or pets
- Important numbers in the user's life (e.g., SSN or birthday)
- Words in a dictionary, whether an English or other language dictionary (e.g., cat, hunter, supercilious, gracias, ici)
- Keyboard patterns (e.g., QWERTY, ASDF)

The best advice is to avoid these categories because such passwords can be easily guessed.

Better choices are passwords that:

- Are meaningful to the user but no one else
- Are at least seven characters long
- Are made of two or more words that have several letters omitted (e.g., PPLEPI [apple pie]) or are the first letters of the words in phase that is not in common usage (e.g., no song lyrics) such as hapwicac (hot apple pie with ice cream and cheese)
- Include characters such as numbers or punctuation marks in the middle of the password (e.g., 1hapwic,&c for one hot apple pie with ice cream, and cheese)
- Include some uppercase and lowercase letters (e.g., 1HAPwic,&c)
- Substitute numbers for certain letters that are similar, such as using a 0 instead of an O, a 1 instead of an I, a 2 instead of a Z, a 3 instead of an E, and so on (e.g., 1HAPw1c,&c)

For more information, see www.securitystats.com/tools/password.asp.

systems, an attacker must know the user's account name, password, and have access to the user's password device before he or she can login.

Biometrics In high-security applications, a user may be required to present *something they are,* such as a finger, hand, or the retina of their eye for scanning by the system. These **biometric systems** scan the user to ensure that the user is the sole individual authorized to access the network account. About 15 percent of organizations now use biometrics. While most biometric systems are developed for high-security users, several low-cost biometric systems are now on the market. The most popular biometric system is the fingerprint scanner. Several vendors sell devices the size of a mouse that can scan a user's fingerprint for less than $100. Some laptops now come with built-in fingerprint scanners that replace traditional Windows logins. While some banks have begun using fingerprint devices for customer access to their accounts over the Internet, use of such devices has not become widespread, which we find a bit puzzling. The fingerprint is unobtrusive and means users no longer have to remember arcane passwords.

Central Authentication One long-standing problem has been that users are often assigned user profiles and passwords on several different computers. Each time a user wants to access a new server, he or she must supply his or her password. This is cumbersome for the users, and even worse for the network manager who must manage all the separate accounts for all the users.

More and more organizations are adopting **central authentication** (also called network authentication, single sign-on, or directory services), in which a login server is used to authenticate the user. Instead of logging into a file server or application server, the user logs into the **authentication server.** This server checks the userid and password against its database and if the user is an authorized user, issues a **certificate** (also called credentials). Whenever the user attempts to access a restricted service or resource that requires a userid and password, the user is challenged and his or her software presents the certificate to the authentication server (which is revalidated by the authentication server at the time). If the authentication server validates the certificate, then the service or resource lets the user in. In this way, the user no longer needs to enter his or her password to be authenticated to each new resource or service he or she uses. This also ensures that the user does not accidentally give out his or her password to an unauthorized service—it provides mutual authentication of both the user and the service or resource. The most commonly used authentication protocol is **Kerberos,** developed at MIT (see web.mit.edu/kerberos/www).

While many systems use only one authentication server, it is possible to establish a series of authentication servers for different parts of the organization. Each server authenticates clients in its domain but can also pass authentication credentials to authentication servers in other domains.

Preventing Social Engineering

One of the most common ways for attackers to break into a system, even master hackers, is through **social engineering,** which refers to breaking security simply by asking. For example, attackers routinely phone unsuspecting users and, imitating someone such as a

TECHNICAL FOCUS 11.7 INSIDE KERBEROS

Kerberos, the most commonly used central authentication protocol, uses symmetric encryption (usually DES). Kerberos is used by a variety of central authentication services, including Windows active directory services. When you login to a Kerberos-based system, you provide your userid and password to the Kerberos software on your computer. This software sends a request containing the userid but *not* the password to the Kerberos authentication server (called the Key Distribution Center [KDC]).

The KDC checks its database for the userid and if it finds it, then it accepts the login and does two things. First, it generates a service ticket (ST) for the KDC which contains information about the KDC, a time stamp, and, most importantly, a unique session key (SK1), which will be used to encrypt all further communication between the client computer and the KDC until the user logs off. SK1 is generated separately for each user and is different every time the user logs in. Now, here's the clever part: the ST is encrypted using a key based on the password that matches the userid. The client computer can only decrypt the ST if it knows the password that matches the userid used to login. If the user enters an incorrect password, the Kerberos software on the client can't decrypt the ST and asks the user to enter a new password. This way, the password is never sent over the network.

Second, the KDC creates a Ticket-Granting Ticket (TGT). The TGT includes information about the client computer and a time stamp that is encrypted using a secret key known only to the KDC and other validated servers. The KDC sends the TGT to the client computer encrypted with SK1, because all communications between the client and the server are encrypted with SK1 (so no one else can read the TGT). The client decrypts the transmission to receive the TGT, but because the client does not know the KDC's secret key, it cannot decrypt the contents of the TGT. From now until the user logs off, the user does not need to provide his or her password again; the Kerberos client software will use the TGT to gain access to all servers that require a password.

The first time a user attempts to use a server that requires a password, that server directs the user's Kerberos software to obtain a service ticket (ST) for it from the KDC. The user's Kerberos software sends the TGT to the KDC along with information about which server the user wants to access (remember that all communications between the client and the KDC are encrypted with SK1). The KDC checks to make sure that the user has not logged off and if the TGT is validated, the KDC sends the client an ST for the desired server and a new session key (SK2) that the client will use to communicate with that server, both of which have been encrypted using SK1. The ST contains authentication information and SK2, both of which have been encrypted using the secret key known only to the KDC and the server.

The client presents a login request (that specifies the userid, a time and date stamp and other information) which has been encrypted with SK2 and the ST to the server. The server decrypts the ST using the KDC's secret key to find the authentication information and SK2. It uses the SK2 to decrypt the login request. If the login request is valid after decrypting with SK2, the server accepts the login and sends the client a packet that contains information about the server that has been encrypted with SK2. This process authenticates the client to the server, and also authenticates the server to the client. Both now communicate using SK2. Notice that the server never learns the user's password.

technician or senior manager, ask for a password. Unfortunately, too many users want to be helpful and simply provide the requested information. At first, it seems ridiculous to believe that someone would give their password to a complete stranger, but a skilled social engineer is like a good con artist: he—and most social engineers are men—can manipulate people.[18]

Most security experts no longer test for social engineering attacks; they know from experience that social engineering will eventually succeed in any organization and

[18]For more information about social engineering and many good examples, see *The Art of Deception* by Kevin Mitnick and William Simon.

therefore assume that attackers can gain access at will to normal user accounts. Training end users not to divulge passwords may not eliminate social engineering attacks, but it may reduce their effectiveness so that hackers give up and move on to easier targets. Acting out social engineering skits in front of users often works very well; when employees see how they can be manipulated into giving out private information, it becomes more memorable and they tend to become much more careful.

Phishing is a very common type of social engineering. The attacker simply sends an e-mail to millions of users telling them that their bank account has been shut down due to an unauthorized access attempt and that they need to reactivate it by logging in. The e-mail contains a link that directs the user to a fake Web site that appears to be the bank's Web site. After the user logs into the fake site, the attacker has the user's userid and password and can break into his or her account at will. Clever variants on this include an e-mail informing you that a new user has been added to your paypal account, stating that the IRS has issued you a refund and you need to verify your social security number, or offering a mortgage at very low rate for which you need to provide your social security number and credit number.

Intrusion Prevention Systems

Intrusion prevention systems (IPS) are designed to detect an intrusion and take action to stop it. There are two general types of IPSs, and many network managers choose to install both. The first type is a **network-based IPS.** With a network-based IPS, an **IPS sensor** is placed on key network circuits. An IPS sensor is simply a device running a special operating system that monitors all network packets on that circuit and reports intrusions to an **IPS management console.** The second type of IPS is the **host-based IPS,** which, as the name suggests, is a software package installed on a host or server. The host-based IPS monitors activity on the server and reports intrusions to the IPS management console.

There are two fundamental techniques that these types of IPSs can use to determine that an intrusion is in progress; most IPSs use both techniques. The first technique is **misuse detection,** which compares monitored activities with signatures of known attacks. Whenever an attack signature is recognized, the IPS issues an alert and discards the suspicious packets. The problem, of course, is keeping the database of attack signatures up to date as new attacks are invented.

The second fundamental technique is **anomaly detection,** which works well in stable networks by comparing monitored activities with the "normal" set of activities. When a major deviation is detected (e.g., a sudden flood of ICMP ping packets, an unusual number of failed logins to the network manager's account), the IPS issues an alert and discards the suspicious packets. The problem, of course, is false alarms when situations occur that produce valid network traffic that is different from normal (e.g., on a heavy trading day on Wall Street, E-trade receives a larger than normal volume of messages).

IPSs are often used in conjunction with other security tools such as firewalls (Figure 11.16). In fact, some firewalls are now including IPS functions. One problem is that the IPS and its sensors and management console are a prime target for attackers. Whatever IPS is used, it must be very secure against attack. Some organizations deploy redundant IPSs from different vendors (e.g., a network-based IPS from one vendor and a host-based IPS from another) in order to decrease the chance that the IPS can be hacked.

MANAGEMENT FOCUS 11.10 SOCIAL ENGINEERING WINS AGAIN

Danny had collected all the information he needed to steal the plans for the new product. He knew the project manager's name (Bob Billings), phone number, department name, office number, computer user id, and employee number, as well as the project manager's boss's name. These had come from the company Web site and a series of innocuous phone calls to helpful receptionists. He had also tricked the project manager into giving him his password, but that hadn't worked because the company used one-time passwords using a time-based token system called Secure ID. So, after getting the phone number of the computer operations room from another helpful receptionist, all he needed was a snowstorm.

Late one Friday night, a huge storm hit and covered the roads with ice. The next morning, Danny called the computer operations room:

Danny: "Hi, this is Bob Billings in the Communications Group. I left my Secure ID in my desk and I need it to do some work this weekend. There's no way I can get into the office this morning. Could you go down to my office and get it for me? And then read my code to me so I can login?"

Operations: "Sorry, I can't leave the Operations Center."

Danny: "Do you have a Secure ID yourself?"

Operations: "There's one here we keep for emergencies."

Danny: "Listen. Can you do me a big favor? Could you let me borrow your Secure ID? Just until it's safe to drive in?"

Operations: "Who are you again?"

Danny: "Bob Billings. I work for Ed Trenton."

Operations: "Yeah, I know him."

Danny: "My office is on the second floor (2202B). Next to Roy Tucker. It'd be easier if you could just get my Secure ID out of my desk. I think it's in the upper left drawer." (Danny knew the guy wouldn't want to walk to a distant part of the building and search someone else's office.)

Operations: "I'll have to talk to my boss."

After a pause, the operations technician came back on and asked Danny to call his manager on his cell phone. After talking with the manager and providing some basic information to "prove" he was Bob Billings, Danny kept asking about having the Operations technician go to "his" office.

Finally, the manager decided to let Danny use the Secure ID in the Operations Center. The manager called the technician and gave permission for him to tell "Bob" the one-time password displayed on their Secure ID any time he called that weekend. Danny was in.

SOURCE: Kevin Mitnick and William Simon, *The Art of Deception,* John Wiley and Sons, 2002.

While IPS monitoring is important, it has little value unless there is a clear plan for responding to a security breach in progress. Every organization should have a clear response planned if a break-in is discovered. Many large organizations have emergency response "SWAT" teams ready to be called into action if a problem is discovered. The best example is CERT, which is the Internet's emergency response team. CERT has helped many organizations establish such teams.

Responding to an intrusion can be more complicated than it at first seems. For example, suppose the IPS detects a DoS attack from a certain IP address. The immediate reaction could be to discard all packets from that IP address; however, in the age of IP spoofing, the attacker could fake the address of your best customer and trick you into discarding packets from it.

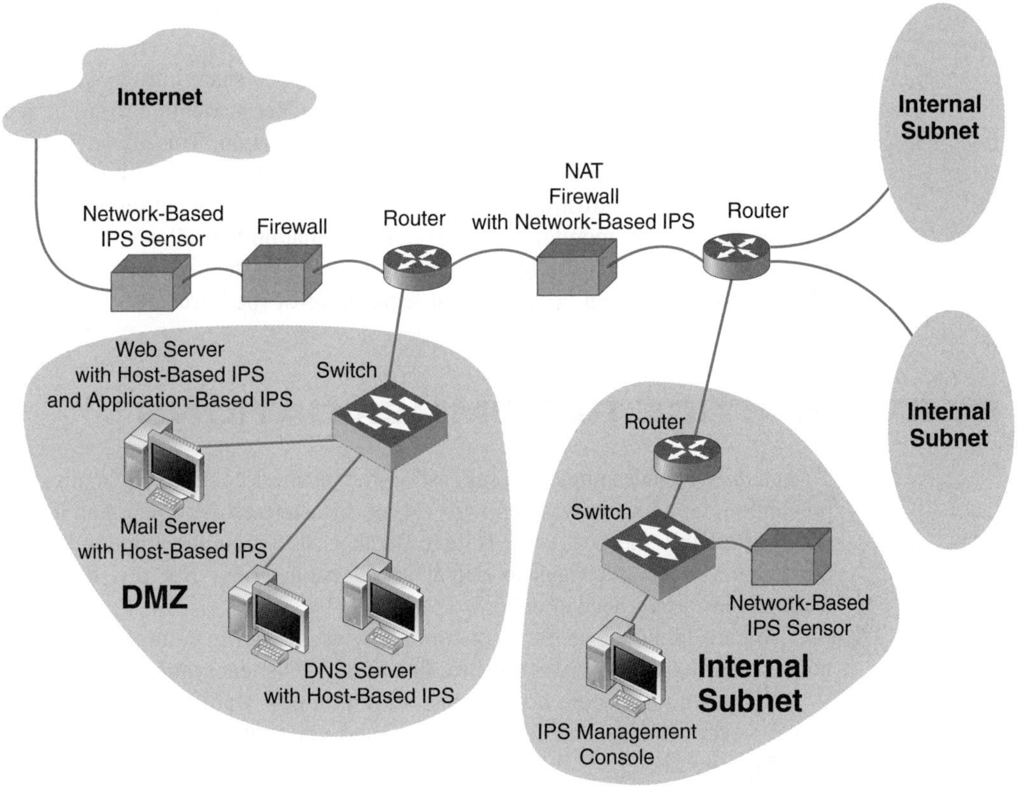

FIGURE 11.16 Intrusion prevention system (IPS). DMZ = demilitarized zone; DNS = Domain Name Service; NAT = network address translation

Intrusion Recovery

Once an intrusion has been detected, the first step is to identify how the intruder gained unauthorized access and prevent others from breaking in the same way. Some organizations will simply choose to close the door on the attacker and fix the security problem. About 30 percent of organizations take a more aggressive response by logging the intruder's activities and working with police to catch the individuals involved. Once identified, the attacker will be charged with criminal activities and/or sued in civil court. Several states and provinces have introduced laws requiring organizations to report intrusions and theft of customer data, so the percent of intrusions reported and prosecuted will increase.

A whole new area called **computer forensics** has recently opened up. Computer forensics is the use of computer analysis techniques to gather evidence for criminal and/or civil trials. The basic steps of computer forensics are similar to those of traditional forensics, but the techniques are different. First, identify potential evidence. Second, preserve evidence by making backup copies and use those copies for all analysis. Third, analyze the evidence. Finally, prepare a detailed legal report for use in prosecutions. While companies are sometimes tempted to launch counterattacks (or counterhacks) against intruders, this is illegal.

Some organizations have taken their own steps to snare intruders by using **entrapment** techniques. The objective is to divert the attacker's attention from the real network to an attractive server that contains only fake information. This server is often called a **honey pot.** The honey pot server contains highly interesting, fake information available only through illegal intrusion to "bait" the intruder. The honey pot server has sophisticated tracking software to monitor access to this information that allows the organization and law enforcement officials to trace and legally document the intruder's actions. Possession of this information then becomes final legal proof of the intrusion.

BEST PRACTICE RECOMMENDATIONS

This chapter provides numerous suggestions on business continuity planning and intrusion prevention. Good security starts with a clear disaster recovery plan and a solid security policy. Probably the best security investment is user training: training individual users on data recovery and ways to defeat social engineering. But this doesn't mean that technologies aren't needed either.

Figure 11.17 shows the most commonly used security controls. Most organizations now routinely use antivirus software, firewalls, VPNs, encryption, and IPS.

Even so, rarely does a week pass without a new warning of a major vulnerability. Leave a server unattended for two weeks, and you may find that you have five critical patches to install.

People are now asking, "Will it end?" Is (in)security just a permanent part of the information systems landscape? In a way, yes. The growth of information systems, along with the new and dangerous ability to reach into them from around the world, has created new opportunities for criminals. Mix the possibilities of stealing valuable, marketable information with the low possibilities for getting caught and punished, and we would expect increasing numbers of attacks.

Perhaps the question should be: Does it have to be this bad? Unquestionably, we could be protecting ourselves better. We could better enforce security policies and restrict

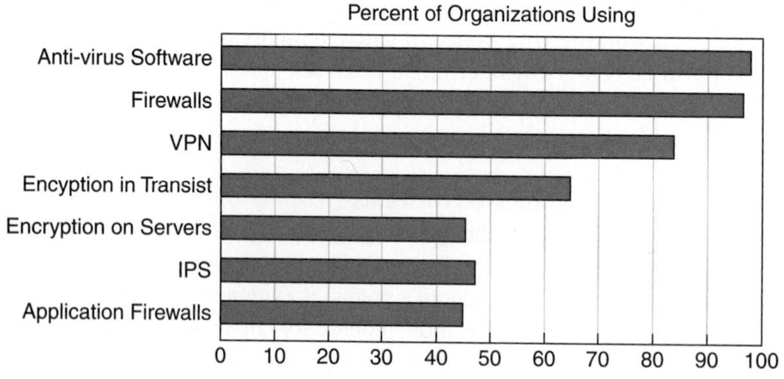

FIGURE 11.17 What security controls are used

access. But all of this has a cost. Attackers are writing and distributing a new generation of attack tools right before us—tools that are very powerful, more difficult to detect, and very easy to use. Usually such tools are much easier to use than their defensive countermeasures.

The attackers have another advantage, too. Whereas the defenders have to protect *all* vulnerable points *all the time* in order to be safe, the attacker just has to break into *one place one time* to be successful.

So what may we expect in the future in "secure" organizational environments? We would expect to see strong **desktop management,** including the use of thin clients (perhaps even network PCs that lack hard disks). Centralized desktop management, in which individual users are not permitted to change the settings on their computers, may become common, along with regular reimaging of computers to prevent Trojans and viruses and to install the most recent security patches. All external software downloads will likely be prohibited.

Continuous content filtering, in which all incoming packets (e.g., Web, e-mail) are scanned, may become common, thus significantly slowing down the network. All server files and communications with client computers would be encrypted, further slowing down transmissions.

Finally, all written security policies would be rigorously enforced. Violations of security policies might even become a "capital offense" (i.e., meaning one violation and you are fired).

We may look forlornly back to the early days of the Internet when we could "do anything" as its Golden Days.

IMPLICATIONS FOR MANAGEMENT

Network security was once an esoteric field of interest to only a few dedicated professionals. Today, it is the fastest-growing area in networking. The cost of network security will continue to increase as the tools available to network attackers become more sophisticated, as organizations rely more and more on networks for critical business operations, and as information warfare perpetrated by nations or terrorists becomes more common. As the cost of networking technology decreases, the cost of staff and networking technologies providing security will become an increasingly larger proportion of an organization's networking budget. As organizations and governments see this, there will be a call for tougher laws and better investigation and prosecution of network attackers.

Security tools available to organizations will continue to increase in sophistication and the use of encryption will become widespread in most organizations. There will be an ongoing "arms race" between security officers in organizations and attackers. Software security will become an important factor in selecting operating systems, networking software, and application software. Those companies that provide more secure software will see a steady increase in market share while those that don't will gradually lose ground.

A Day in the Life: Network Security Manager

"Managing security is a combination of detective work and prognostication about the future."

A network security manager spends much of his or her time doing three major things. First, much time is spent looking outside the organization by reading and researching potential security holes and new attacks because the technology and attack opportunities change so fast. It is important to understand new attack threats, new scripting tools used to create viruses, remote access Trojans and other harmful software, and the general direction in which the hacking community is moving. Much important information is contained at Web sites such as those maintained by CERT (www.cert.org) and SANS (www.sans.org). This information is used to create new versions of standard computer images that are more robust in defeating attacks, and to develop recommendations for the installation of application security patches. It also means that he or she must update the organization's written security policies and inform users of any changes.

Second, the network security manager looks inward toward the networks he or she is responsible for. He or she must check the vulnerability of those networks by thinking like a hacker to understand how the networks may be susceptible to attack, which often means scanning for open ports and unguarded parts of the networks and looking for computers that have not been updated with the latest security patches. It also means looking for symptoms of compromised machines such as new patterns of network activity or unknown services that have been recently opened on a computer.

Third, the network security manager must respond to security incidents. This usually means "firefighting"—quickly responding to any security breach, identifying the cause, collecting forensic evidence for use in court, and fixing the computer or software application that has been compromised.

With thanks to Kenn Crook

SUMMARY

Types of Security Threats In general, network security threats can be classified into one of two categories: (1) business continuity and (2) intrusions. Business continuity can be interrupted by disruptions that are minor and temporary, but some may also result in the destruction of data. Natural (or man-made) disasters may occur that destroy host computers or large sections of the network. Intrusion refers to intruders (external attackers or organizational employees) gaining unauthorized access to files. The intruder may gain knowledge, change files to commit fraud or theft, or destroy information to injure the organization.

Risk Assessment Developing a secure network means developing controls that reduce or eliminate threats to the network. Controls prevent, detect, and correct whatever might happen to the organization when its computer-based systems are threatened. The first step in developing a secure network is to conduct a risk assessment. This is done by identifying the key assets and threats and comparing the nature of the threats to the controls designed to protect the assets. A control spreadsheet lists the assets, threats, and controls that a network manager uses to assess the level of risk.

Business Continuity The major threats to business continuity are viruses, theft, denial of service attacks, device failure, and disasters. Installing and regularly updating antivirus software is one of the most important and commonly used security controls. Protecting against denial of service attacks is challenging and often requires special hardware. Theft is one of the most often overlooked threats and can be prevented by good physical security, especially the physical security of laptop computers. Devices fail, so the best way to prevent network outages is to ensure that the network has redundant circuits and devices (e.g., switches and routers) on mission critical network segments (e.g., the Internet connection and core backbone). Avoiding disasters can take a few commonsense steps, but no disaster can be completely avoided; most organizations focus on ensuring important data are backed up off-site and having a good, tested, disaster recovery plan.

Intrusion Prevention Intruders can be organization employees or external hackers who steal data (e.g., customer credit card numbers) or destroy important records. A security policy defines the key stakeholders and their roles, including what users can and cannot do. Firewalls often stop intruders at the network perimeter by permitting only authorized packets into the network, by examining application layer packets for known attacks, and/or by hiding the organization's private IP addresses from the public Internet. Physical and dial-up security are also useful perimeter security controls. Patching security holes—known bugs in an operating system or application software package—is important to prevent intruders from using these to break in. Single key or public key encryption can protect data in transit or data stored on servers. User authentication ensures only authorized users can enter the network and can be based on something you know (passwords), something you have (access cards), or something you are (biometrics). Preventing social engineering, where hackers trick users into revealing their passwords, is very difficult. Intrusion prevention systems are tools that detect known attacks and unusual activity and enable network managers to stop an intrusion in progress. Intrusion recovery involves correcting any damaged data, reporting the intrusion to the authorities, and taking steps to prevent the other intruders from gaining access the same way.

KEY TERMS

access card
access control list (ACL)
account
Advanced Encryption Standard (AES)
adware
algorithm
anomaly detection
antivirus software
application-level firewall
asset
asymmetric encryption
authentication
authentication server
automatic number identification (ANI)
availability
biometric system
brute-force attack
business continuity
central authentication
certificate
certificate authority (CA)
ciphertext
closed source
Computer Emergency Response Team (CERT)
computer forensics
confidentiality
continuous data protection (CDP)
control spreadsheet
controls
corrective control
cracker
Data Encryption Standard (DES)
DDoS agent
DDoS handler
decryption
Delphi team
denial-of-service (DoS) attack
desktop management
detective control
disaster recovery drill
disaster recovery firm
disaster recovery plan
disk mirroring
distributed denial-of-service (DDoS) attack
eavesdropping
encryption
entrapment
fault-tolerant server
firewall
hacker
honey pot
host-based IPS
information warfare
integrity
Internet Key Exchange (IKE)
intrusion prevention system (IPS)
IP Security Protocol (IPSec)
IP spoofing
IPS management console
IPS sensor
IPSec transport mode
IPSec tunnel mode
Kerberos
key
key management
mission-critical application
misuse detection
NAT firewall
network address translation (NAT)
network-based IPS
one-time password
online backup
open source
packet-level firewall
passphrase

password
patch
phishing
physical security
plaintext
Pretty Good Privacy (PGP)
preventive control
private key
public key
public key encryption
public key infrastructure (PKI)
RC4
recovery controls
redundancy
redundant array of independent disks (RAID)
risk assessment
rootkit
RSA
script kiddies
secure sockets layer (SSL)
secure switch
security hole
security policy
smart card
sniffer program
social engineering
something you are
something you have
something you know
spyware
symmetric encryption
threat
time-based token
token
traffic analysis
traffic anomaly analyzer
traffic anomaly detector
traffic filtering
traffic limiting
triple DES (3DES)
Trojan horse
uninterruptible power supply (UPS)
user profile
user authentication
virus
worm
zero day attack

QUESTIONS

1. What factors have brought increased emphasis on network security?
2. Briefly outline the steps required to complete a risk assessment.
3. Name at least six assets that should have controls in a data communication network.
4. What are some of the criteria that can be used to rank security risks?
5. What are the most common security threats? What are the most critical? Why?
6. Explain the primary principle of device failure protection.
7. What is the purpose of a disaster recovery plan? What are five major elements of a typical disaster recovery plan?
8. What is a computer virus? What is a worm?
9. How can one reduce the impact of a disaster?
10. Explain how a denial-of-service attack works.
11. How does a denial-of-service attack differ from a distributed denial-of-service attack?
12. What is a disaster recovery firm? When and why would you establish a contract with them?
13. What is online backup?
14. People who attempt intrusion can be classified into four different categories. Describe them.
15. There are many components in a typical security policy. Describe three important components.
16. What are three major aspects of intrusion prevention (not counting the security policy)?
17. How do you secure the network perimeter?
18. What is physical security and why is it important?
19. What is eavesdropping in a computer security sense?
20. What is a sniffer?
21. How do you secure dial-in access?
22. Describe how an ANI modem works.
23. What is a firewall?
24. How do the different types of firewalls work?
25. What is IP spoofing?
26. What is a NAT firewall and how does it work?
27. What is a security hole and how do you fix it?
28. Explain how a Trojan horse works.
29. Compare and contrast symmetric and asymmetric encryption.
30. Describe how symmetric encryption and decryption work.
31. Describe how asymmetric encryption and decryption work.
32. What is key management?
33. How does DES differ from 3DES? From RC4? From AES?
34. Compare and contrast DES and public key encryption.

35. Explain how authentication works.
36. What is PKI and why is it important?
37. What is a certificate authority?
38. How does PGP differ from SSL?
39. How does SSL differ from IPSec?
40. Compare and contrast IPSec tunnel mode and IPSec transfer mode.
41. What are the three major ways of authenticating users? What are the pros and cons of each approach?
42. What are the different types of one-time passwords and how do they work?
43. Explain how a biometric system can improve security. What are the problems with it?
44. Why is the management of user profiles an important aspect of a security policy?
45. How does network authentication work and why is it useful?
46. What is social engineering? Why does it work so well?
47. What techniques can be used to reduce the chance that social engineering will be successful?
48. What is an intrusion prevention system?
49. Compare and contrast a network-based IPS, and a host-based IPS.
50. How does IPS anomaly detection differ from misuse detection?
51. What is computer forensics?
52. What is a honey pot?
53. What is desktop management?
54. A few security consultants have said that broadband and wireless technologies are their best friends. Explain.
55. Most hackers start their careers breaking into computer systems as teenagers. What can we as a community of computer professionals do to reduce the temptation to become a hacker?
56. Some experts argue that CERT's posting of security holes on its Web site causes more security break-ins than it prevents and should be stopped. What are the pros and cons on both sides of this argument? Do you think CERT should continue to post security holes?
57. What is one of the major risks of downloading unauthorized copies of music files from the Internet (aside from the risk of jail, fines, and lawsuits)?
58. Suppose you started working as a network manager at a medium-sized firm with an Internet presence, and discovered that the previous network manager had done a terrible job of network security. Which *four* security controls would be your *first* priority? Why?
59. How can we reduce the number of viruses that are created every month?
60. While it is important to protect all servers, some servers are more important than others. What server(s) are the most important to protect and why?

EXERCISES

11-1. Conduct a risk assessment of your organization's networks. Some information may be confidential, so report what you can.

11-2. Investigate and report on the activities of CERT (the Computer Emergency Response Team).

11-3. Investigate the capabilities and costs of a disaster recovery service.

11-4. Investigate the capabilities and costs of a firewall.

11-5. Investigate the capabilities and costs of an intrusion prevention system.

11-6. Investigate the capabilities and costs of an encryption package.

11-7. Investigate the capabilities and costs of an online backup service.

MINI-CASES

I. Belmont State Bank

Belmont State Bank is a large bank with hundreds of branches that are connected to a central computer system. Some branches are connected over dedicated circuits and others use the dial-up telephone network. Each branch has a variety of client computers and ATMs connected to a server. The server stores the branch's daily transaction data and transmits it several times during the day to the central computer system. Tellers at each branch use a four-digit numeric password, and each teller's computer is transaction-coded to accept only its authorized transactions. Perform a risk assessment.

II. Western Bank

Western Bank is a small, family-owned bank with six branches spread over the county. It has decided to move onto the Internet with a Web site that permits customers to access their accounts and pay bills. Design the key security hardware and software the bank should use.

III. Classic Catalog Company, Part 1

Classic Catalog Company runs a small but rapidly growing catalog sales business. It outsourced its Web operations to a local ISP for several years but as sales over the Web have become a larger portion of its business, it has decided to move its Web site onto its own internal computer systems. It has also decided to undertake a major upgrade of its own internal networks. The company has two buildings, an office complex, and a warehouse. The two-story office building has 60 computers. The first floor has 40 computers, 30 of which are devoted to telephone sales. The warehouse, located 400 feet across the company's parking lot from the office building, has about 100,000 square feet, all on one floor. The warehouse has 15 computers in the shipping department located at one end of the warehouse. The company is about to experiment with using wireless handheld computers to help employees more quickly locate and pick products for customer orders. Based on traffic projections for the coming year, the company plans to use a T1 connection from its office to its ISP. It has three servers: the main Web server, an e-mail server, and an internal application server for its application systems (e.g., orders, payroll). Perform a risk assessment.

IV. Classic Catalog Company, Part 2

Read Minicase III above. Outline a brief business continuity plan including controls to reduce the risks in advance as well as a disaster recovery plan.

V. Classic Catalog Company, Part 3

Read Minicase III above. Outline a brief security policy and the controls you would implement to control unauthorized access.

VI. Classic Catalog Company, Part 4

Read Minicase III above. Reread Management Focus box 11.6. What patching policy would you recommend for Classic Catalog?

VII. Personal Security

Conduct a risk assessment and develop a business continuity plan and security policy for the computer(s) you own.

CASE STUDY

NEXT-DAY AIR SERVICE

See the Web site.

HANDS-ON ACTIVITY

Securing Your Computer

This chapter has focused on security, including risk analysis, business continuity, and intrusion prevention. At first glance, you may think security applies to corporate networks, not your network. However, if you have a LAN at your house or apartment, or even if you just own a desktop or laptop computer, security should be one of your concerns. There are so many potential threats to your business continuity—which might be your education—and to intrusion into your computer(s) that you need to take action.

You should perform your own risk analysis, but this section provides a brief summary of some simple actions you should take that will greatly increase your security. Do this this week; don't procrastinate. Our focus is on Windows security, because most readers of this book use Windows computers, but the same advice (but different commands) applies to Apple computers.

Business Continuity

If you run your own business, then ensuring business continuity should be a major focus of your efforts. But even if you are "just" an employee or a student, business continuity is important. What would happen if your hard disk failed just before the due date for a major report?

1. The first and most important security action you can take is to configure Windows to perform automatic updates. This will ensure you have the latest patches and updates installed.
2. The second most important action is to buy and install antivirus software such as that from Symantec. Be sure to configure it for regular updates too. If you perform just these two actions, you will be relatively secure from viruses, but you should scan your system for viruses on a regular basis, such as the first of every month when you pay your rent or mortgage.
3. Spyware is another threat. You should buy and install antispyware software that provides the same protection that anti-virus software does for viruses. Spybot is a good package. Be sure to configure this software for regular updates and scan your system on a regular basis.
4. One of the largest sources of viruses, spyware, and adware is free software and music/video files downloaded from the Internet. Simply put, don't download any file unless it is from a trusted vendor or distributor of software and files.
5. Develop a disaster recovery plan. You should plan today for what you would do if your computer was destroyed. What files would you need? If there are any important files that you wouldn't want to lose (e.g., reports you're working on, key data, or precious photos), you should develop a backup and recovery plan for them. The simplest is to copy the files to a shared directory on another computer on your LAN. But this won't enable you to recover the files if your apartment or house was destroyed by fire, for example (see Management Focus 11.5). A better plan is to suscribe to a free online backup service such as mozy.com (think CDP on the cheap). If you don't use such a site, buy a large USB drive, copy your files to it, and store it off-site in your office or at a friend's house. A plan is only good if it is followed, so your data should be regularly backed up, such as doing so the first of every month.

Intrusion Prevention

With the increase of Internet-based attacks, everyone's computer is at greater risk for intrusion, not just the computers of prominent organizations. There are a few common-sense steps you can take to prevent intrusion.

1. Think good physical security. Always turn off your computer when you are finished using it. A computer that is off cannot be attacked, either over the Internet or from someone walking by your desk.
2. Windows has the ability to have multiple user accounts. The default accounts are Administrator and Guest. You should disable the Guest account and to change the name of the administrator account so that any intruders attacking the computer will have to guess the user names as well as the passwords. It's also a good idea to create an account other than the administrator account that you can use on a day-to-day basis. The administrator account should only be used when you are installing software or changing configurations that require administrator privileges on your computer. You can manage these user accounts from the Control Panel, User Accounts. Be sure to add passwords that are secure, but easy to remember for all the accounts that you use.
3. Turn on the Windows Firewall. Use Control Panel, Security Center to examine your security settings, including the "firewall" built into Windows. The firewall is software that prevents other computers from accessing your computer. You can turn it on and examine the settings. The default settings are usually adequate, but you may want to make changes. Click on Internet Options. This will enable you to configure the firewall for four different types of site: the Internet, your local intranet (i.e., LAN), trusted sites (that have a valid PKI certificate), and restricted sites (that are sites of known hackers). Figure 11.18 shows some of the different security settings.

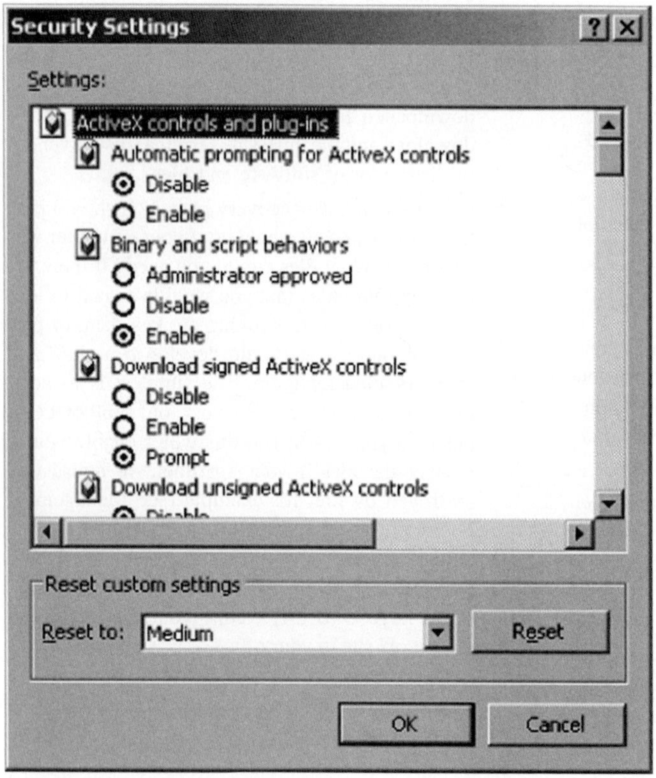

FIGURE 11.18 Security controls in Windows

4. Disable unneeded services. Windows was designed to support as many applications as the developers could think of. Many of these services are not needed by most users, and unfortunately, some have become targets of intruders. For example, Windows is a Telnet server (see Chapter 2) so that anyone with a Telnet client can connect to your computer and issue operating system commands. The Telnet server is usually turned off by the person who installed Windows on your computer, but it is safer to make sure.
   a. Right click on My Computer and select Manage
   b. Click on Services and Applications and then click on Services
   c. You should see a screen like that in Figure 11.19. Make sure the Telnet service says "Disabled." If it doesn't, right click on it, Select Properties, and change the Startup Type to Disabled.
   d. Three other services that should be set to disabled are Messenger (don't worry, this is *not* any type of Instant Messenger), Remote Registry, and Routing and Remote Access.
5. If you have a LAN in your apartment or house, be sure the router connecting you to the Internet is a NAT firewall. This will prevent many intruders from attacking your computers. The Disable WAN connections option on my router permits me to deny any TCP request from the Internet side of the router—that is, my client computer can establish outgoing TCP connections, but no one on the Internet can establish a TCP connection to a computer in my LAN.
6. In Chapter 6, we described how to share files on your LAN. If you don't need to share files right now, this capability should be turned off. See Chapter 6 for more details.
7. Avoid phishing attacks. A recent analysis of e-mail found that 80 percent of all e-mail was spam and phishing attacks. That's right, "real" e-mail is outnumbered more than two-to-one by fake e-mail. Do not *ever* click on a link in an e-mail. No exceptions. *Never* click an e-mail link. Even if you are a valued customer, have been offered a chance to participate in a survey, or receive a low cost mortgage. Even if the e-mail appears to be from a well-known firm. Let us say that again: *Never* click an e-mail link. If you want to visit a Web site mentioned in an e-mail, open a new browser window and manually type the correct address. Figure 11.20 shows a phishing attack I received. Looks real, doesn't it? I particularly enjoyed the parts that talk about spotting and avoiding fraudulent e-mails. If I had clicked on the link, it would have taken me to a Web site owned by a Singaporean company.

HANDS-ON ACTIVITY

Testing Your Computer's Intrusion Prevention

There are many ways an intruder could attack your computer. Many attacks use well-known weaknesses in Windows and Mac operating systems that can easily be used by novice hackers. There are several Web sites that will test your computer's vulnerability to these commonly used attacks. Our favorite is Shields-Up by Gibson Research Corporation.

1. Go to the Gibson Research home page at www.grc.com and click on the link to Shields-Up.
2. The first screen will provide some background information on the tests to be conducted and then will provide the application layer name of your computer (if it has one). After you read the details, click the Proceed Button.
3. Figure 11.21 displays the main menu page. Shields Up can conduct four different security tests: file sharing, port scanning, messenger spam, and browser information.
4. The file sharing test will see if your computer is set up to enable other users to read files on your computer. Windows was originally designed to be very simple to operate in a LAN environment in a peer-to-peer sharing mode using NetBIOS and NetBEUI. Unfortunately, most users don't want

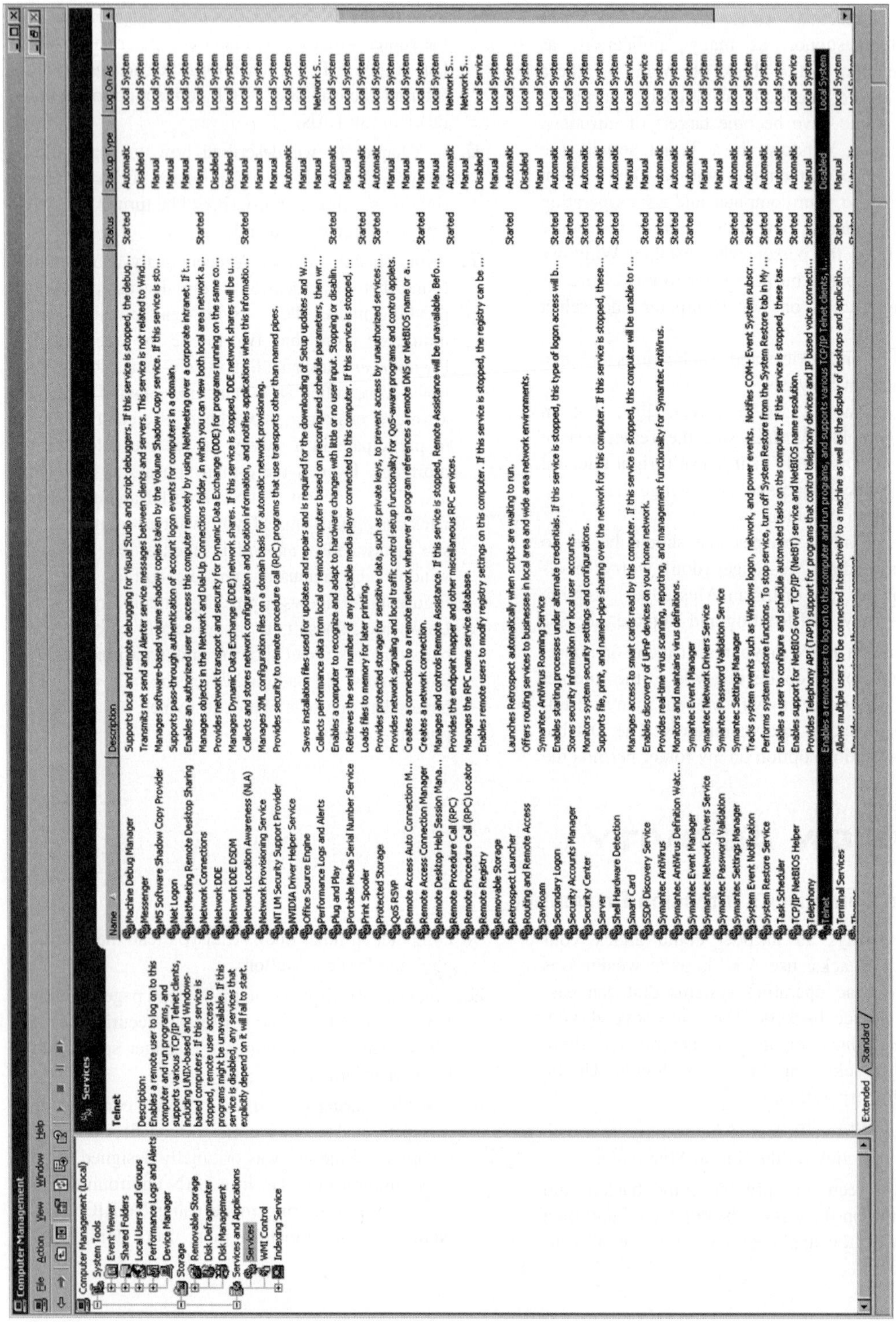

FIGURE 11.19 Windows services management

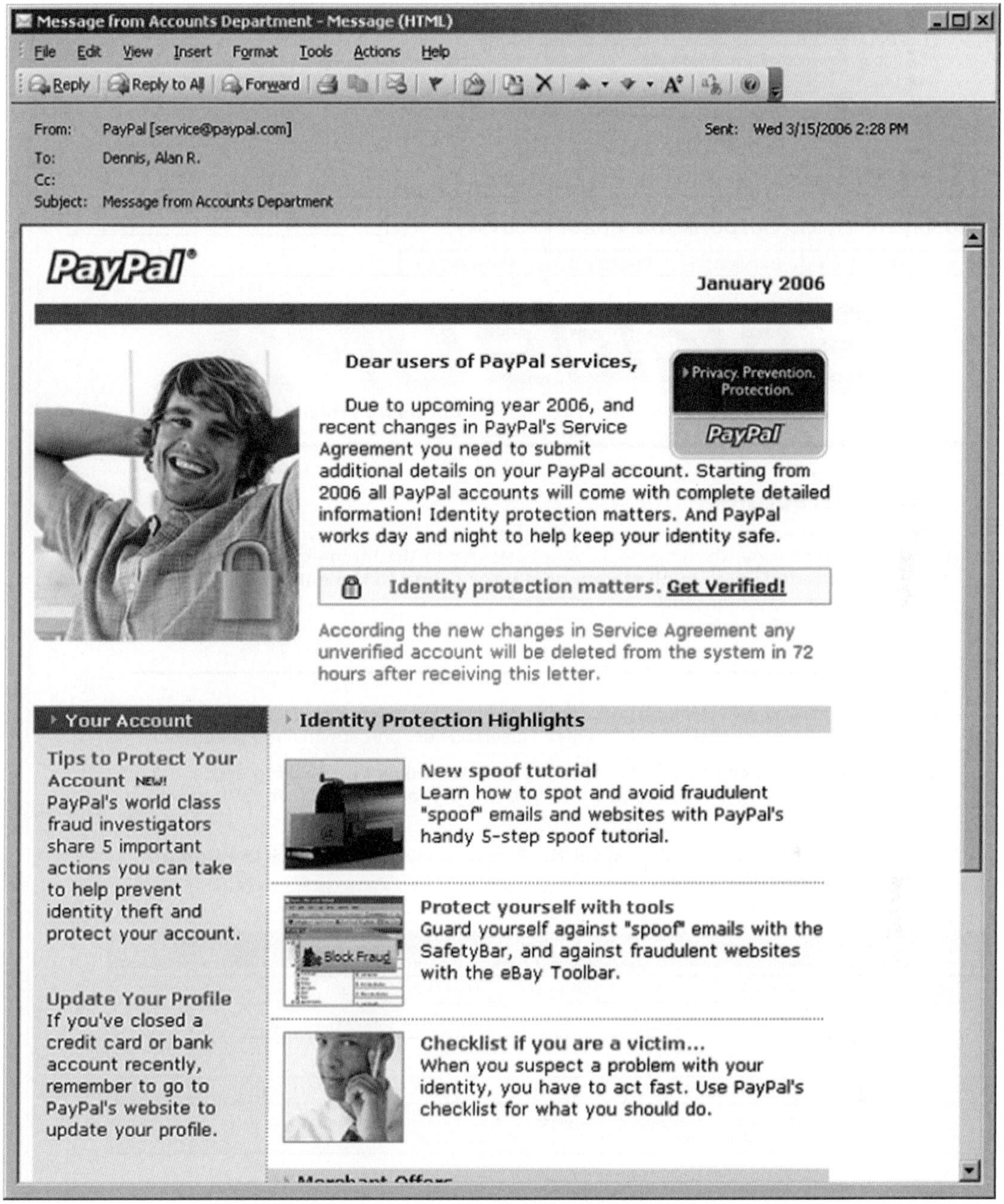

FIGURE 11.20 Phishing attack

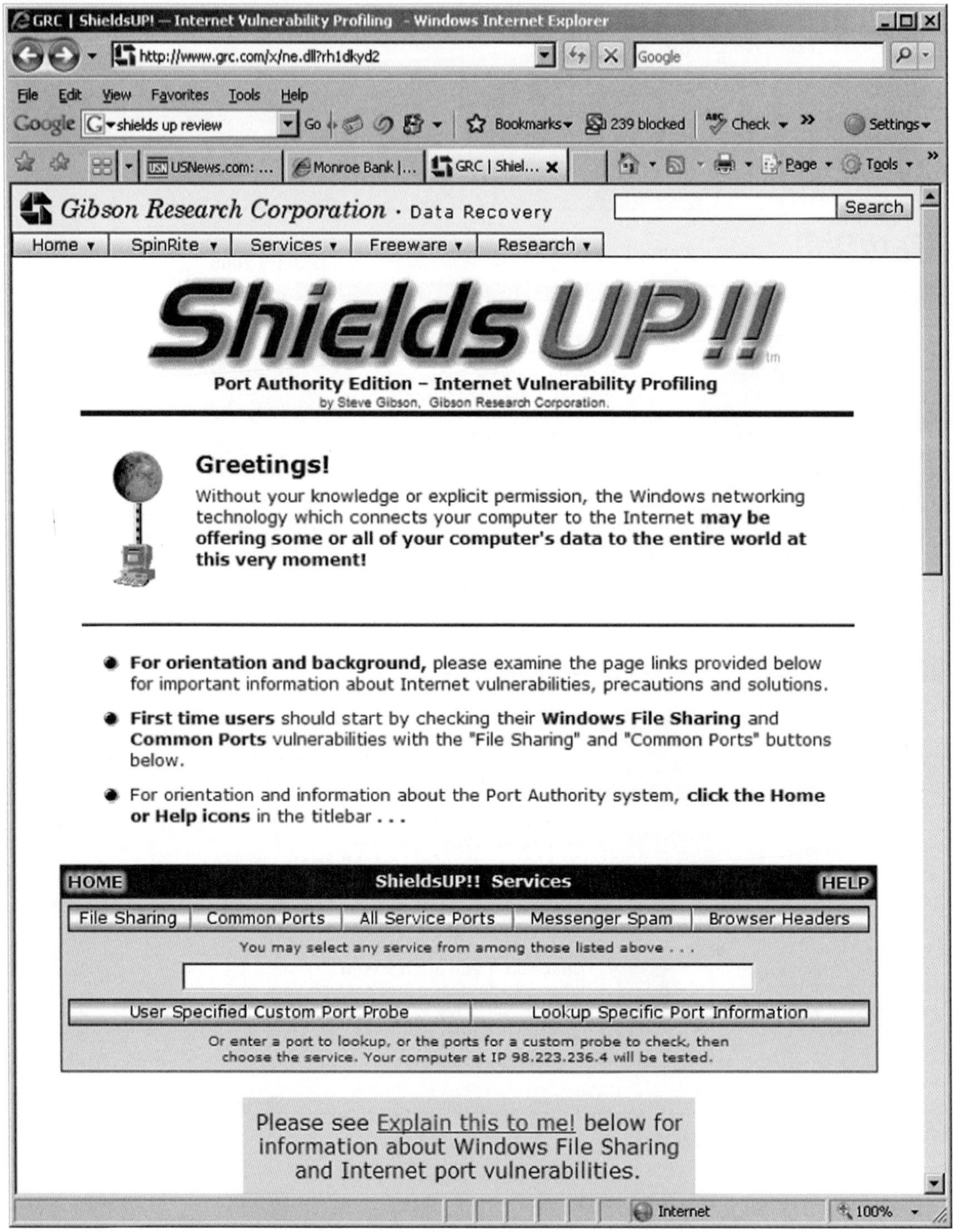

FIGURE 11.21 Shields Up main menu page

their computer to share their personal files with anyone on the Internet who knows how to issue these requests. Click the File Sharing button to run the test.

5. Figure 11.22 shows the test results for my computer. My computer has this function disabled so it is secure from this type of attack. If your computer fails this test, Shields Up will explain what you need to do.
6. Scroll this screen and near the bottom of the page, you will see the main menu again. Let's run the port scanning test. As we explained in Chapter 5, TCP ports are used to connect the network to the application software. There are about two dozen commonly used ports for standard Internet applications such as Web servers (80), SMTP e-mail (25), Telnet (23), and so on. It is not unusual for Windows computers to have some of these ports operational; for example, Windows has a built-in Web server that operates on port 80. Hackers who know this and have the right software can send HTTP messages to your computer's Web server and use it to break into your computer and read your files.
7. Figure 11.23 shows the results of the port scan on common ports for my computer. I have disabled all of the standard ports on my computer because I do not want anyone to use these ports to talk to software on my computer. If your computer fails this test, Shields Up will explain what you need to do.
8. Scroll this screen and near the bottom of the page, you will see the main menu again. You can also scan all service ports, which literally scans every port number that is possible to define on your computer, not just the commonly used port (this takes a long time). This is useful in detecting Trojan horses that have installed themselves and are using a noncommon port to send and receive messages.
9. The next test is the messenger spam test. In addition to Instant Messenger (IM), AOL IM, MSN Messenger, and all those applications, Windows also provides Messenger. Messenger is a separate application that was designed to be used by network administrators to send short messages to users. This means that anyone with the right tools (e.g., a spammer) can send your computer a message that will pop up on your screen. Scroll to the bottom of this screen to see the main menu again. Click the Messenger Spam button.
10. This will show a page that enables you to type a message and send it to your computer via Messenger. If you receive the spam message, you can read the prior Hands-On activity for information on how to turn off Messenger.
11. Scroll to the bottom of this screen and use the main menu to do the Browser test. This will show you the information your Web browser is sending as part of the HTTP request header.

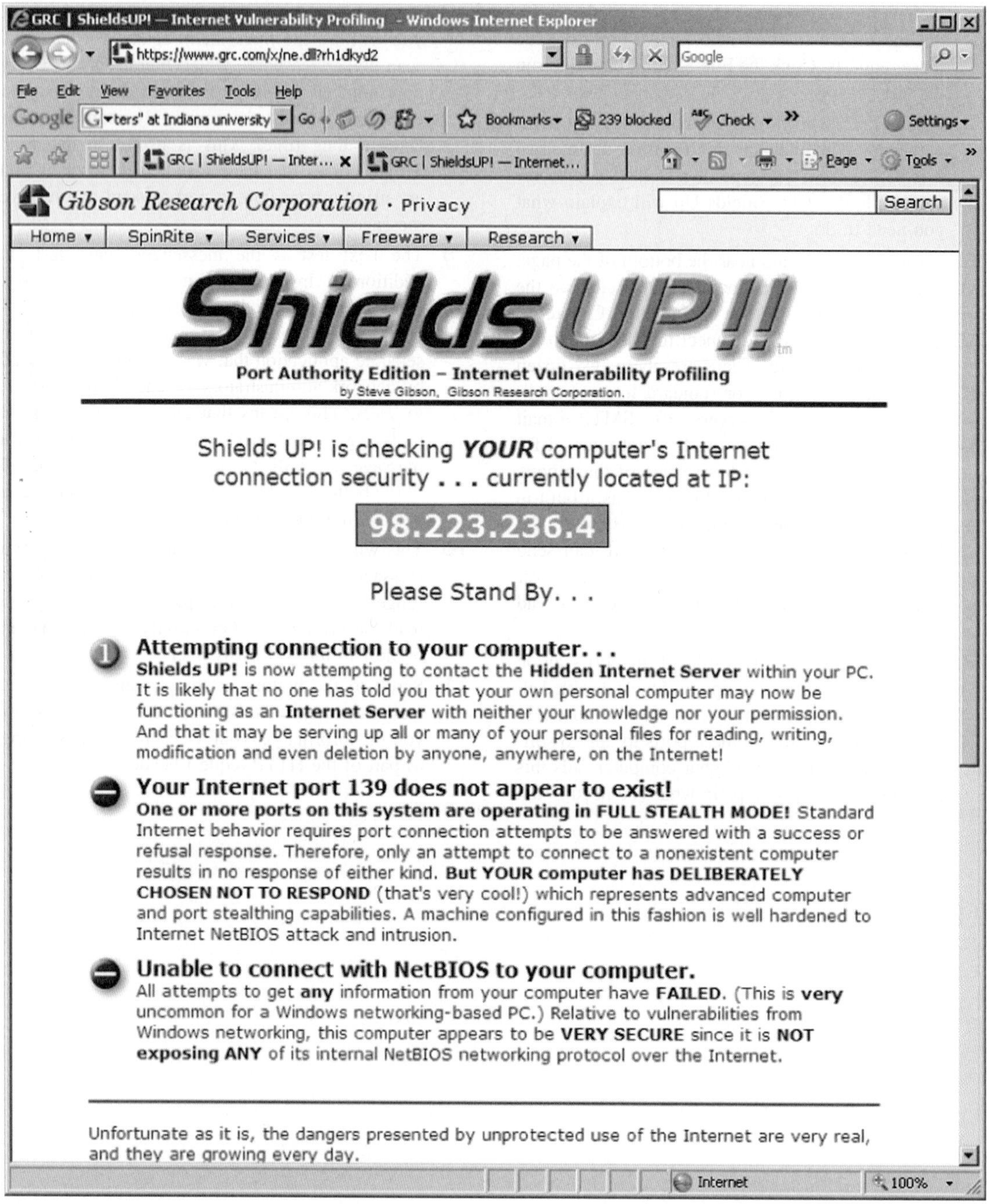

FIGURE 11.22 Shields Up scanning test

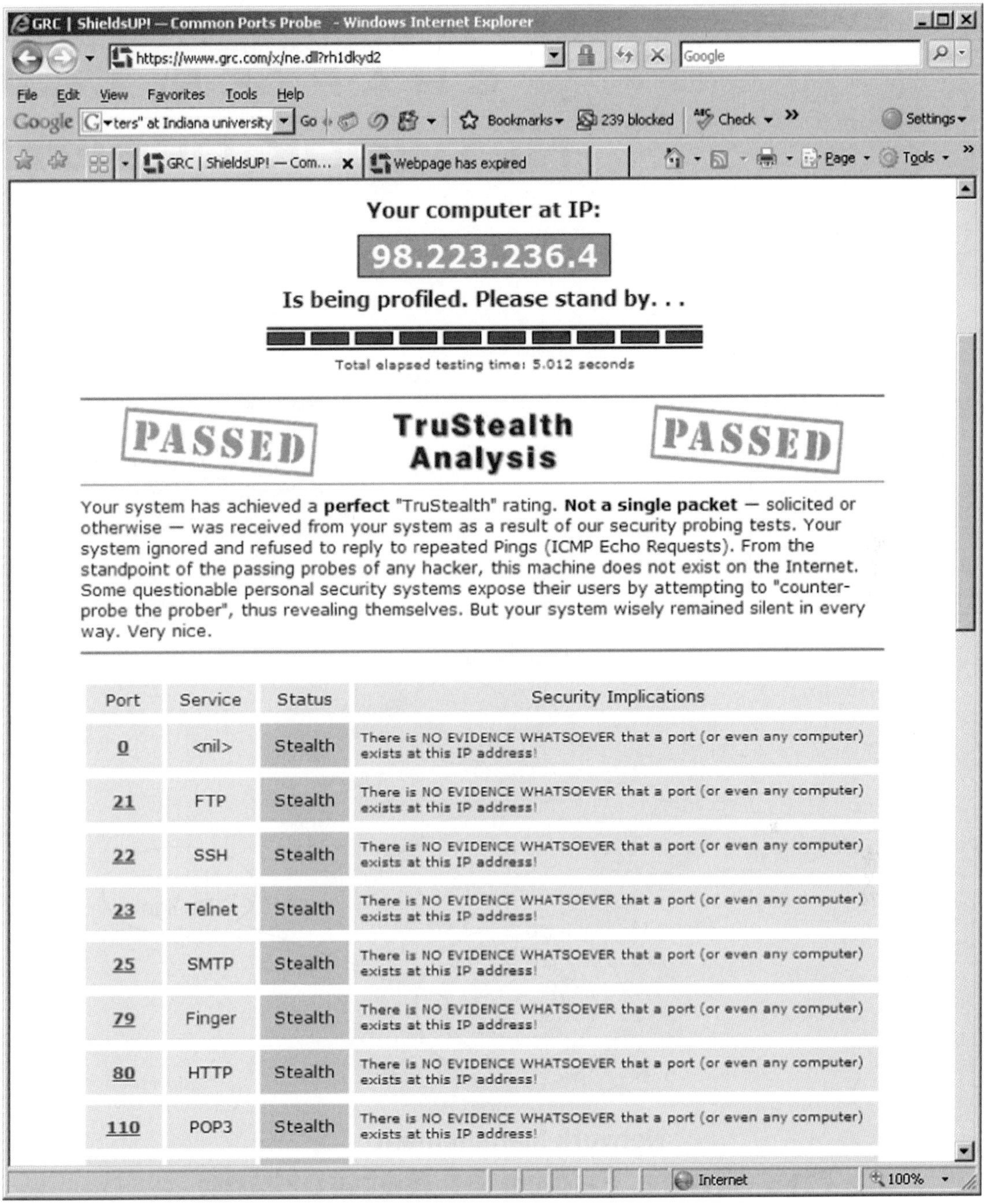

FIGURE 11.23 Shields Up port Scanning test

CHAPTER 12
NETWORK DESIGN

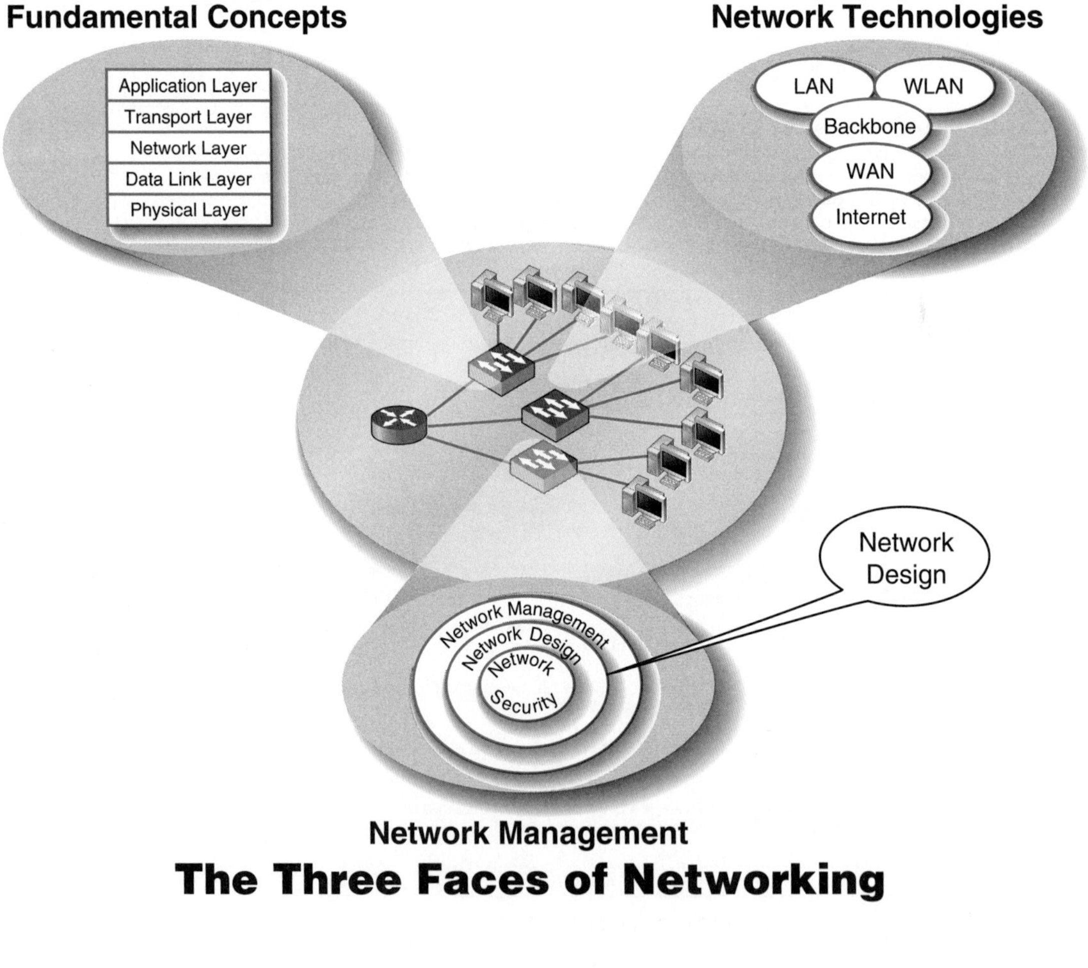

The Three Faces of Networking

NETWORK MANAGERS perform two key tasks: (1) designing new networks and network upgrades and (2) managing the day-to-day operation of existing networks. This chapter examines network design. Network design is an interative process in which the designer examines users' needs, develops an initial set of technology designs, assesses their cost, and then revisits the needs analysis until the final network design emerges.

OBJECTIVES ▼

- Be familiar with the overall process of designing and implementing a network
- Be familiar with techniques for developing a logical network design
- Be familiar with techniques for developing a physical network design
- Be familiar with network design principles
- Understand the role and functions of network management software
- Be familiar with several network management tools

CHAPTER OUTLINE ▼

INTRODUCTION

All but the smallest organizations have networks, which means that most network design projects are the design of upgrades or extensions to existing networks, rather than the construction of entirely new networks. Even the network for an entirely new building is likely to be integrated with the organization's existing backbone or WAN, so even new projects can be seen as extensions of existing networks. Nonetheless, network design is very challenging.

The Traditional Network Design Process

The **traditional network design process** follows a very structured systems analysis and design process similar to that used to build application systems. First, the network analyst meets with users to identify user needs and the application systems planned for the network. Second, the analyst develops a precise estimate of the amount of data that each user will send and receive and uses this to estimate the total amount of traffic on each part of the network. Third, the circuits needed to support this traffic plus a modest increase in traffic are designed and cost estimates are obtained from vendors. Finally, 1 or 2 years later, the network is built and implemented.

This traditional process, although expensive and time consuming, works well for static or slowly evolving networks. Unfortunately, networking today is significantly different from what it was when the traditional process was developed. Three forces are making the traditional design process less appropriate for many of today's networks.

First, the underlying technology of the client and server computers, networking devices, and the circuits themselves is changing very rapidly. In the early 1990s, mainframes dominated networks, the typical client computer was an 8-MHz 386 with 1 megabyte (MB) of random access memory (RAM) and 40 MB of hard disk space, and a typical circuit was a 9,600-bps mainframe connection or a 1-Mbps LAN. Today, client computers and servers are significantly more powerful, and circuit speeds of 100 Mbps and 1 Gbps are common. We now have more processing capability and network capacity than ever before; both are no longer scarce commodities that we need to manage carefully.

Second, the growth in network traffic is immense. The challenge is not in estimating today's user demand but in estimating its rate of growth. In the early 1990s, e-mail and the Web were novelties primarily used by university professors and scientists. In the past, network demand essentially was driven by predictable business systems such as order processing. Today, much network demand is driven by less predictable user behavior, such as e-mail and the Web. Many experts expect the rapid increase in network demand to continue, especially as video, voice, and multimedia applications become commonplace on networks. At a 10 percent growth rate, user demand on a given network will increase by one-third in three years. At 20 percent, it will increase by about 75 percent in three years. At 30 percent, it will double in less than three years. A minor mistake in estimating the growth rate can lead to major problems. With such rapid growth, it is no longer possible to accurately predict network needs for most networks. In the past, it was not

MANAGEMENT FOCUS 12.1 AVERAGE LIFE SPANS

A recent survey of network managers found that most expect their network hardware to last three to five years—not because the equipment wears out, but because rapid changes in capabilities make otherwise good equipment obsolete. As Joel Snyder, a senior partner at OpusOne (a network consulting firm), puts it: "You might go buy a firewall for a T-1 at a remote office and then two weeks later have your cable provider offer you 7 Mbps."

Life expectancy for selected network equipment:

Rack mounted switch	4.5 years	Wi-Fi access point	3 years
Chassis switch	4.5 years	Desktop PC	3.5 years
Backbone router	5 years	Laptop PC	2.5 years
Branch office router	4 years	Mainframe	8.5 years

SOURCE: "When to Upgrade," *Network World*, November 28, 2005, pp. 49–50.

uncommon for networks to be designed to last for five to ten years. Today, most network designers use a three- to five-year planning horizon.

Finally, the balance of costs have changed dramatically over the past ten years. In the early 1990s, the most expensive item in any network was the hardware (circuits, devices, and servers). Today, the most expensive part of the network is the staff members who design, operate, and maintain it. As the costs have shifted, the emphasis in network design is no longer on minimizing hardware cost (although it is important); the emphasis today is on designing networks to reduce the staff time needed to operate them.

The traditional process minimizes the equipment cost by tailoring the equipment to a careful assessment of needs but often results in a mishmash of different devices with different capabilities. Two resulting problems are that staff members need to learn to operate and maintain many different devices and that it often takes longer to perform network management activities because each device may use slightly different software.

Today, the cost of staff time is far more expensive than the cost of equipment. Thus, the traditional process can lead to a false economy—save money now in equipment costs but pay much more over the long term in staff costs.

The Building-Block Network Design Process

Some organizations still use the traditional process to network design, particularly for those applications for which hardware or network circuits are unusually expensive (e.g., WANs that cover long distances through many different countries). However, many other organizations now use a simpler approach to network design that we call the **building-block process.** The key concept in the building-block process is that networks that use a few standard components throughout the network are cheaper in the long run than networks that use a variety of different components on different parts of the network.

Rather than attempting to accurately predict user traffic on the network and build networks to meet those demands, the building-block process instead starts with a few standard components and uses them over and over again, even if they provide more capacity than is needed. The goal is simplicity of design. This strategy is sometimes called "narrow and deep" because a very narrow range of technologies and devices is used over and over again (very deeply throughout the organization). The result are a simpler design process and a more easily managed network built with a smaller range of components.

In this chapter, we focus on the building-block process to network design. The basic design process involves three steps that are performed repeatedly: needs analysis, technology design, and cost assessment (Figure 12.1). This process begins with **needs analysis,** during which the designer attempts to understand the fundamental current and future network needs of the various users, departments, and applications. This is likely to be an educated guess at best. Users and applications are classified as typical or high volume. Specific technology needs are identified (e.g., the ability to dial in with current modem technologies).

The next step, **technology design,** examines the available technologies and assesses which options will meet users' needs. The designer makes some estimates about the network needs of each category of user and circuit in terms of current technology (e.g., 100Base-T, 1000Base-T) and matches needs to technologies. Because the basic network design is general, it can easily be changed as needs and technologies change. The difficulty, of course, lies in predicting user demand so one can define the technologies needed. Most organizations solve this by building more capacity than they expect to need and by designing networks that can easily grow and then closely monitoring growth so they expand the network ahead of the growth pattern.

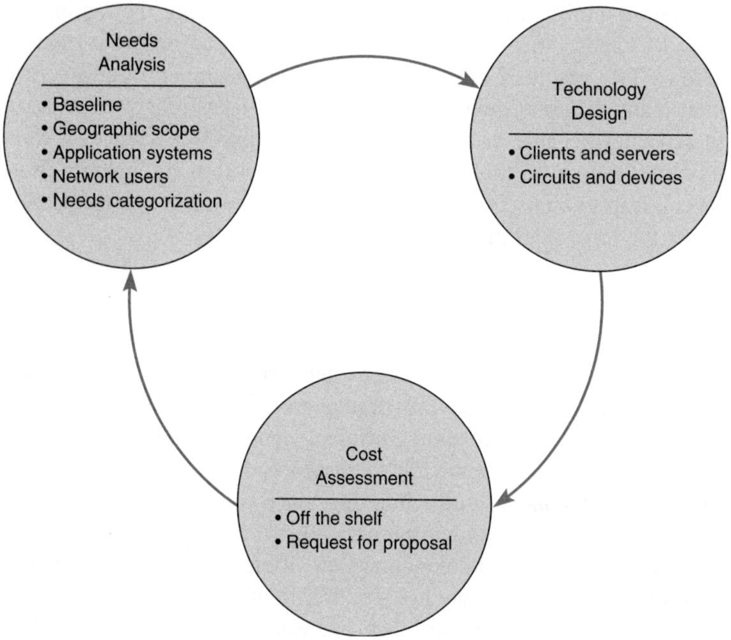

FIGURE 12.1 Network design

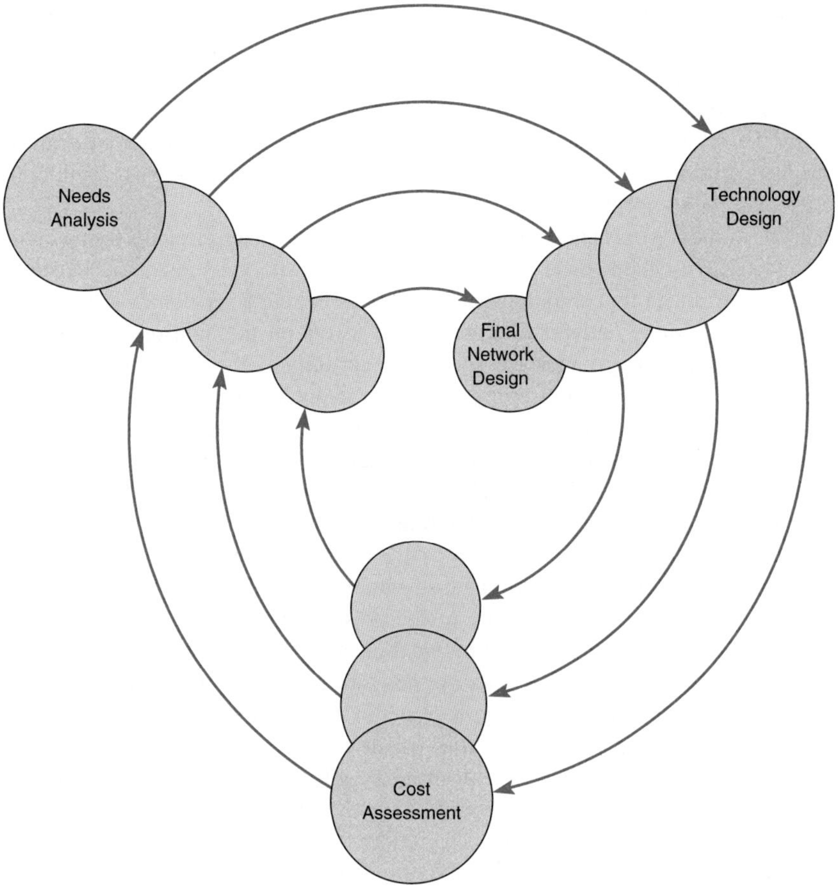

FIGURE 12.2 The cyclical nature of network design

In the third step, **cost assessment,** the relative costs of the technologies are considered. The process then cycles back to the needs analysis, which is refined using the technology and cost information to produce a new assessment of users' needs. This in turn triggers changes in the technology design and cost assessment and so on. By cycling through these three processes, the final network design is settled (Figure 12.2).

NEEDS ANALYSIS

The goal of needs analysis is to understand why the network is being built and what users and applications it will support. In many cases, the network is being designed to improve poor performance or enable new applications to be used. In other cases, the network is upgraded to replace unreliable or aging equipment or to standardize equipment so that only one type of equipment, one protocol (e.g., TCP/IP, Ethernet), or one vendor's equipment is used everywhere in the network.

Often, the goals in network design are slightly different between LANs and backbones (BNs) on the one hand and MANs and WANs on the other. In the LAN and BN environment, the organization owns and operates the equipment and the circuits. Once they are paid for, there are no additional charges for usage. However, if major changes must be made, the organization will need to spend additional funds. In this case, most network designers tend to err on the side of building too big a network—that is, building more capacity than they expect to need.

In contrast, in most MANs and WANs, the organization leases circuits from a common carrier and pays for them on a monthly or per-use basis. Understanding capacity becomes more important in this situation because additional capacity comes at a noticeable cost. In this case, most network designers tend to err on the side of building too small a network, because they can lease additional capacity if they need it—but it is much more difficult to cancel a long-term contract for capacity they are not using.

Much of the needs analysis may already have been done because most network design projects today are network upgrades rather than the design of entirely new networks. In this case, there is already a fairly good understanding of the existing traffic in the network and, most important, of the rate of growth of network traffic. It is important to gain an understanding of the current operations (application systems and messages). This step provides a **baseline** against which future design requirements can be gauged. It should provide a clear picture of the present sequence of operations, processing times, work volumes, current communication network (if one exists), existing costs, and user/management needs. Whether the network is a new network or a network upgrade, the primary objective of this stage is to define (1) the **geographic scope** of the network and (2) the users and applications that will use it.

The goal of the needs analysis step is to produce a **logical network design,** which is a statement of the network elements needed to meet the needs of the organization. The logical design does not specify technologies or products to be used (although any specific requirements are noted). Instead, it focuses on the fundamental functionality needed, such as a high-speed access network, which in the technology design stage will be translated into specific technologies (e.g., switched 100Base-T).

Geographic Scope

The first step in needs analysis is to break the network into three conceptual parts on the basis of their geographic and logical scope: the access layer, the distribution layer, and the core layer, as first discussed in Chapter 8.[1] The **access layer** is the technology that is closest to the user—the user's first contact with the network—and is often a LAN or a broadband Internet connection. The **distribution layer** is the next part of the network that connects the access layer to the rest of the network, such as the BN(s) in a specific building. The **core layer** is the innermost part of the network that connects the different distribution-layer networks to each other, such as the primary BN on a campus or a set of MAN or WAN circuits connecting different offices together. As the name suggests,

[1]It is important to understand that these three layers refer to geographic parts of the network, not the five conceptal layers in the network model, such as the application layer, transport layer, and so on.

the core layer is usually the busiest, most important part of the network. Not all layers are present in all networks; small networks, for example, may not have a distribution layer because their core may be the BN that directly connects the parts of the access layer together.

Within each of these parts of the network, the network designer must then identify some basic technical constraints. For example, if the access layer is a MAN, in that the users need to connect to the network over a broadband connection, this provides some constraints on the technologies to be used; one could not use 100Base-T Ethernet, for example. Likewise, if the access layer is a LAN, it would be silly to consider using T1 circuits.

Sometimes, the current network infrastructure also imposes constraints. For example, if we are adding a new building to an existing office complex that used 100Base-T in the access-layer LANs, then we will probably choose to use 100Base-T for the access layer in the new building. All such constraints are noted.

It is easiest to start with the highest level, so most designers begin by drawing a network diagram for any WANs with international or countrywide locations that must be connected. A diagram that shows the logical network going between the locations is sufficient. Details such as the type of circuit and other considerations will be added later. Next, the individual locations connected to the WAN are drawn, usually in a series of separate diagrams, but for a simple network, one diagram may be sufficient.

At this point, the designers gather general information and characteristics of the environment in which the network must operate. For example, they determine whether there are any legal requirements, such as local, state/provincial, federal, or international laws, regulations, or building codes, that might affect the network.

Figure 12.3 shows the initial drawing of a network design for an organization with offices in four areas connected to the core network, which is a WAN. The Toronto location, for example, has a distribution layer (a BN) connecting three distinct access-layer LANs, which could be three distinct LANs in the same office building. Chicago has a similar structure, with the addition of a fourth access part that connects to the Internet; that is, the organization has only one Internet connection, so all Internet traffic must be routed through the core network to the Chicago location. The Atlantic Canada network section has two distinct access layer parts; one is a LAN and one access layer is a MAN (e.g., dial-up). The New York network section is more complex, having its own core network component (a BN connected into the core WAN), which in turn supports three distribution-layer BNs. Each of these support several access-layer LANs.

Application Systems

Once the basic geographic scope is identified, the designers must review the list of applications that will use the network and identify the location of each. This information should be added to the emerging network diagrams. This process is called baselining. Next, those applications that are expected to use the network in the future are added.

In many cases, the applications will be relatively well defined. Specific internal applications (e.g., payroll) and external applications (e.g., Web servers) may already be part of the "old" network. However, it is important to review the organization's long-range and short-range plans concerning changes in company goals, strategic plans,

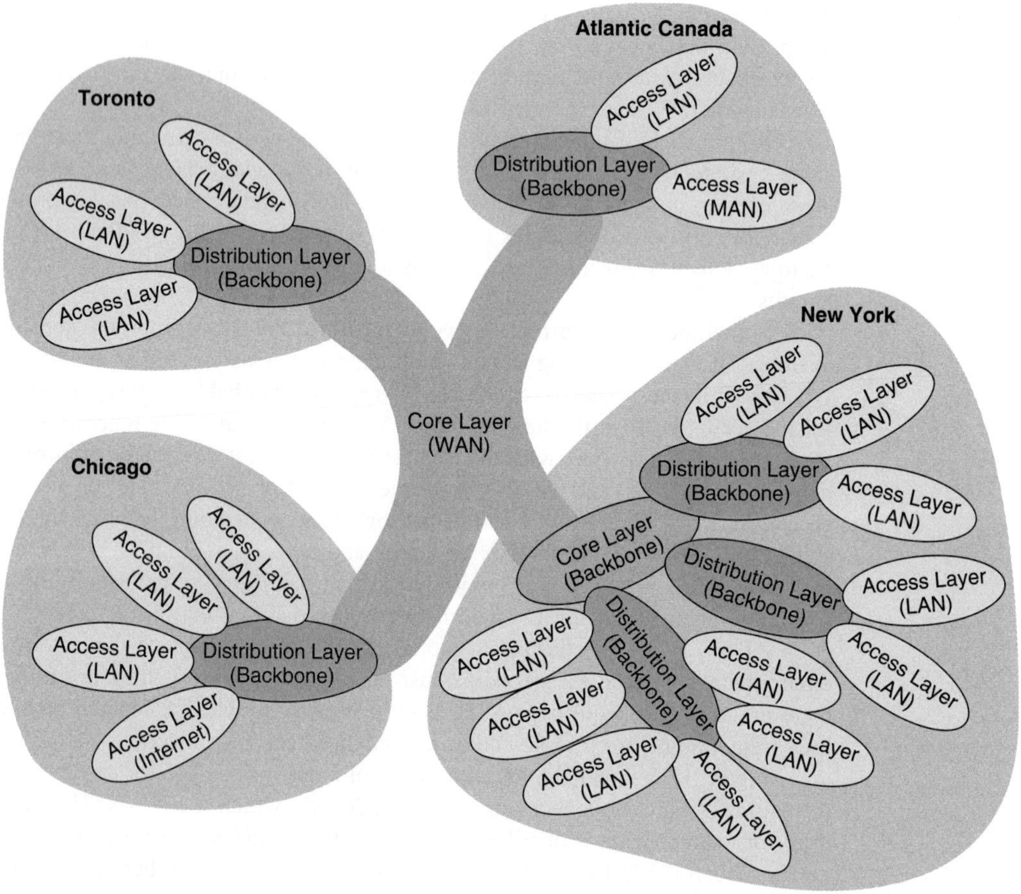

FIGURE 12.3 Geographic scope. LAN = local area network; MAN = metropolitan area network; WAN = wide area network

development plans for new products or services, projections of sales, research and development projects, major capital expenditures, possible changes in product mix, new offices that must be served by the communications network, security issues, and future commitments to technology. For example, a major expansion in the number of offices or a major electronic commerce initiative will have a significant impact on network requirements.

It also is helpful to identify the hardware and software requirements of each application that will use the network and, if possible, the protocol each application uses (e.g., HTTP over TCP/IP, Windows file access). This knowledge helps now and will be particularly useful later when designers develop technological solutions.

Network Users

In the past, application systems accounted for the majority of network traffic. Today, much network traffic is produced by the discretionary use of the Internet. Applications such as e-mail and the Web are generating significant traffic, so the network manager is no longer in total control of the network traffic generated on his or her networks. This is likely to continue in the future as network-hungry applications such as desktop videoconferencing become more common. Therefore, in addition to understanding the applications, you must also assess the number and type of users that will generate and receive network traffic and identify their location on the emerging network diagram.

Categorizing Network Needs

At this point, the network has been designed in terms of geographic scope, application systems, and users. The next step is to assess the relative amount of traffic generated in each part of the network. With the traditional design approach, this involves considerable detailed analysis. With the building-block approach, the goal is to provide some rough assessment of the relative magnitude of network needs. Each application system is assessed in general terms to determine the amount of network traffic it can be expected to generate today and in the future, compared with other applications. Likewise, each user is categorized as either a typical user or a high-traffic user. These assessments will be refined in the next stage of the design process.

This assessment can be problematic, but the goal is some relative understanding of the network needs. Some simple rules of thumb can help. For example, applications that require large amounts of multimedia data or those that load executables over the network are likely to be high-traffic applications. Applications that are time sensitive or need constant updates (e.g., financial information systems, order processing) are likely to be high-traffic applications.

Once the network requirements have been identified, they also should be organized into **mandatory requirements, desirable requirements,** and **wish-list requirements.** This information enables the development of a minimum level of mandatory requirements and a negotiable list of desirable requirements that are dependent on cost and availability. For example, desktop videoconferencing may be a wish-list item, but it will be omitted if it increases the cost of the network beyond what is desired.

At this point, the local facility network diagrams are prepared. For a really large network, there may be several levels. For example, the designer of the network in Figure 12.3 might choose to draw another set of diagrams, one each for Toronto, Chicago, Atlantic Canada, and New York. Conversely, the designer might just add more detail to Figure 12.3 and develop separate, more detailed diagrams for New York. The choice is up to the designer, provided the diagrams and supporting text clearly explain the network's needs.

Deliverables

The key deliverable for the needs assessments stage is a set of logical network diagrams, showing the applications, circuits, clients, and servers in the proposed network, each categorized as either typical or high traffic. The logical diagram is the conceptual plan for the network and does not consider the specific physical elements (e.g., routers, switches, circuits) that will be used to implement the network.

Figure 12.4 shows the results of a needs assessment for one of the New York parts of the network from Figure 12.3. This figure shows the distribution and access parts in

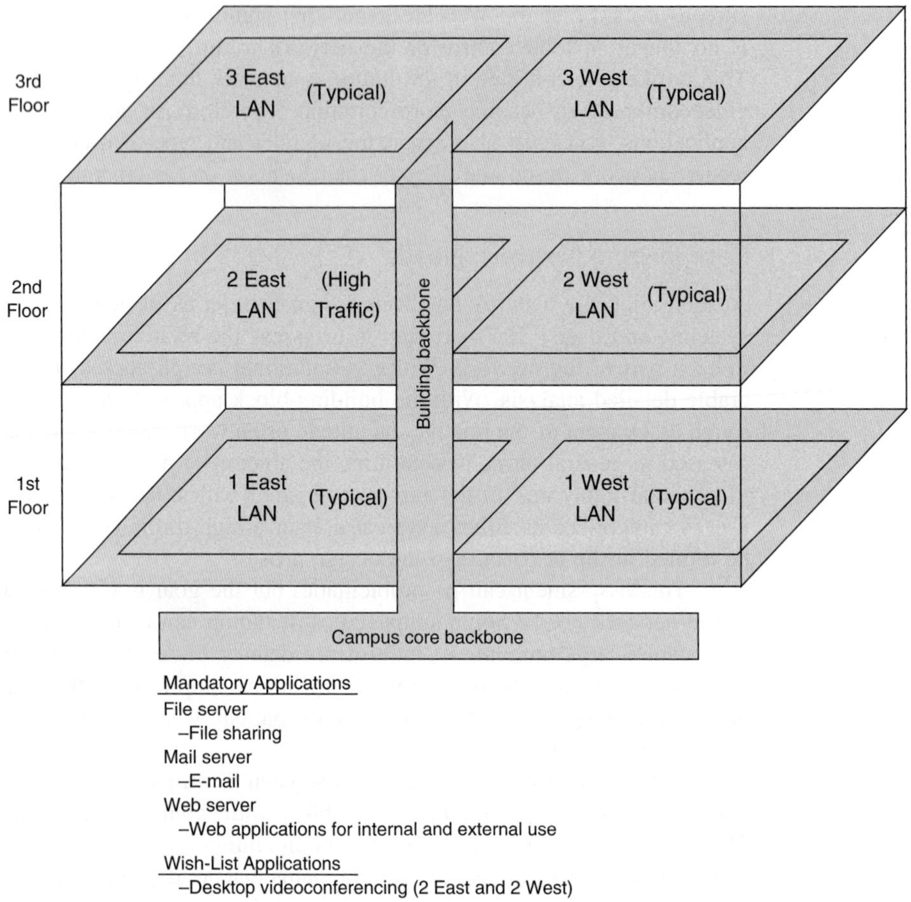

FIGURE 12.4 Sample needs assessment. LAN = local area network

the building with the series of six access LANs connected by one distribution BN, which is in turn connected to a campus-area core BN. One of the six LANs is highlighted as a high-traffic LAN whereas the others are typical. Three mandatory applications are identified that will be used by all network users: e-mail, Web, and file sharing. One wish-list requirement (desktop videoconferencing) is also identified for a portion of the network.

TECHNOLOGY DESIGN

Once the needs have been defined in the logical network design, the next step is to develop a **physical network design** (or set of possible designs). The physical network design starts with the client and server computers needed to support the users and applications. If the network is a new network, new computers will need to be purchased. If the network is an existing network, the servers may need to be upgraded to the newest technology. Once these are designed, then the circuits and devices connecting them are designed.

Designing Clients and Servers

The idea behind the building-block approach is to specify needs in terms of some standard units. Typical users are allocated the base-level client computers, as are servers supporting typical applications. Users and servers for applications needing more powerful computers are assigned some advanced computer. As the specifications for computers rapidly improve and costs drop (usually every six months), today's typical user may receive the type of computer originally intended for the advanced user when the network is actually implemented, and the advanced users may end up with a computer not available when the network was designed.

Designing Circuits and Devices

The same is true for network circuits and devices (e.g., hubs, routers, switches). There are two interrelated decisions in designing network circuits and devices: the fundamental technology and protocols (e.g., Ethernet, T1, TCP/IP) and the capacity of each circuit (e.g., 100 Mbps, 1,000 Mbps). These are interrelated, because each technology offers different circuit capacities.

Designing the circuit capacity means **capacity planning,** estimating the size and type of the standard and advanced network circuits for each type of network (LAN, BN, WAN). For example, should the standard LAN circuit be shared or switched 100Base-T? Likewise, should the standard BN circuit be 100Base-T or 1GbE?

This requires some assessment of the current and future **circuit loading** (the amount of data transmitted on a circuit). This analysis can focus on either the *average* circuit traffic or the *peak* circuit traffic. For example, in an online banking network, traffic volume peaks usually are in the midmorning (bank opening) and just prior to closing. Airline and rental car reservations network designers look for peak volumes before and during holidays or other vacation periods whereas telephone companies normally have their highest peak volumes on Mother's Day. Designing for peak circuit traffic is the ideal.

The designer usually starts with the total characters transmitted per day on each circuit or, if possible, the maximum number of characters transmitted per two-second interval if peaks must be met. You can calculate message volumes by counting messages in a current network and applying some estimated growth rate. If an existing network is in place, network monitors/analyzers (see Chapter 13) may be able to provide an actual circuit character count of the volume transmitted per minute or per day.

A good rule of thumb is that 80 percent of this circuit loading information is easy to gather. The last 20 percent needed for very precise estimates is extremely difficult and expensive to find. However, precision usually is not a major concern because of the stairstep nature of communication circuits and the need to project future needs. For example, the difference between 100Base-T and 1GbE is quite large, and assessing which level is needed for typical traffic does not require a lot of precision. Forecasts are inherently less precise than understanding current network traffic. The **turnpike effect** is an expression that means that traffic increases much faster than originally forecast. It comes from the traffic forecasting that was done for the construction of the early interstate highways. When a new, faster highway (or network) is built, people are more likely to use it than the old slow one because it is available, is very efficient, and provides new capabilities. The annual growth factor for network use may vary from 5 to 50 percent and, in some cases, may exceed 100 percent for high-growth organizations.

Although no organization wants to overbuild its network and pay for more capacity than it needs, in most cases, upgrading a network costs 50 to 80 percent more than building it right the first time. Few organizations complain about having too much network capacity, but being under capacity can cause significant problems. Given the rapid growth in network demand and the difficulty in accurately predicting it, most organizations intentionally overbuild (build more capacity into their network than they plan to use), and most end up using this supposedly unneeded capacity within 3 years.

Network Design Tools

Network modeling and design tools can perform a number of functions to help in the technology design process. With most tools, the first step is to enter a diagram or model of the existing network or proposed network design. Some modeling tools require the user to create the network diagram from scratch. That is, the user must enter all of the network components by hand, placing each server, client computer, and circuit on the diagram and defining what each is (e.g., 10Base-T, frame relay circuit with a 1-Mbps committed information rate).

Other tools can "discover" the existing network; that is, once installed on the network, they will explore the network to draw a network diagram. In this case, the user provides some starting point, and the modeling software explores the network and automatically draws the diagram itself. Once the diagram is complete, the user can then change it to reflect the new network design. Obviously, a tool that can perform network discovery by itself is most helpful when the network being designed is an upgrade to an existing network and when the network is very complex.

Once the diagram is complete, the next step is to add information about the expected network traffic and see if the network can support the level of traffic that is expected. **Simulation,** a mathematical technique in which the network comes to life and behaves as it would under real conditions, is used to model the behavior of the communication network. Applications and users generate and respond to messages while the simulator tracks the number of packets in the network and the delays encountered at each point in the network.

Simulation models may be tailored to the users' needs by entering parameter values specific to the network at hand (e.g., this computer will generate an average of three 100-byte packets per minute). Alternatively, the user may prefer to rely primarily on the set of average values provided by the network.

Once the simulation is complete, the user can examine the results to see the estimated response times throughout. It is important to note that these network design tools provide only estimates, which may vary from the actual results. At this point, the user can change the network design in an attempt to eliminate bottlenecks and rerun the simulation. Good modeling tools not only produce simulation results but also highlight potential trouble spots (e.g., servers, circuits, or devices that experienced long response times). The very best tools offer suggestions on how to overcome the problems that the simulation identified (e.g., network segmentation, increasing from T1 to T3).

Deliverables

The key deliverable is a set of one or more physical network designs. Most designers like to prepare several physical designs so they can trade off technical benefits (e.g., performance) against cost. In most cases, the critical part is the design of the network circuits and devices. In the case of a new network designed from scratch, it is also important to define the client computers with care because these will form a large portion of the total cost of the network. Usually, however, the network will replace an existing network and only a few of the client computers in the existing network will be upgraded.

Figure 12.5 shows a physical network design for the simple network in Figure 12.4. In this case, a 1GbE collapsed backbone is used in the distribution layer, and switched 100Base-T Ethernet has been chosen as the standard network for typical users in the access layer. High-traffic users (2 East) will use 1GbE. The building backbone will be connected directly into the campus backbone using a router and will use fiber-optic cable to enable the possible future addition of desktop videoconferencing.

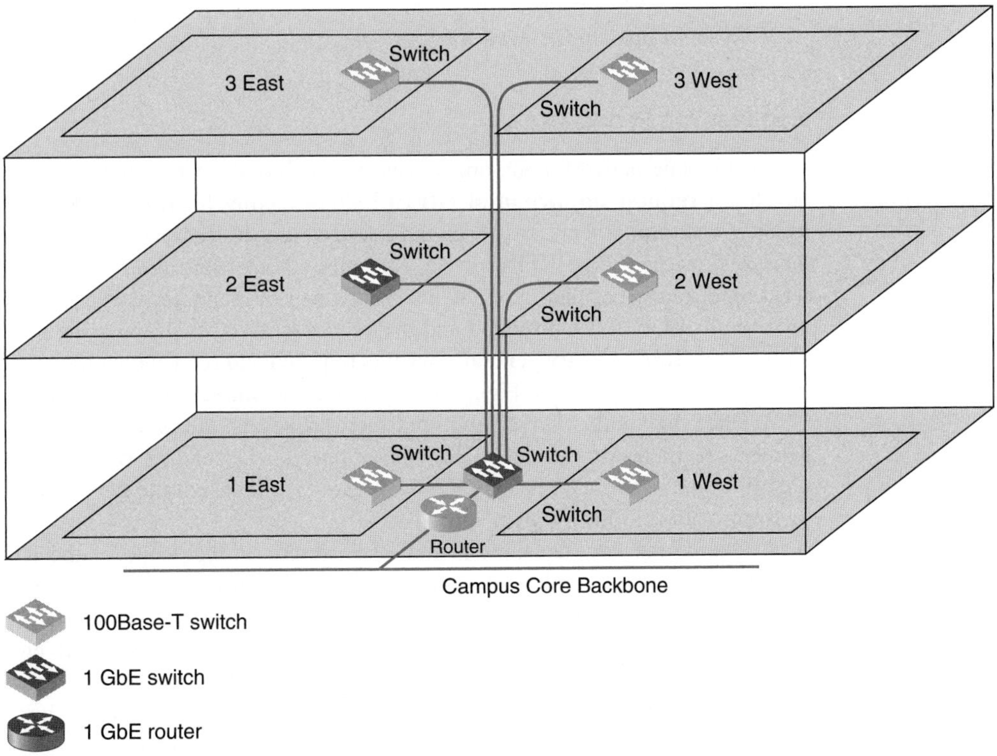

FIGURE 12.5 Physical network design

COST ASSESSMENT

The purpose of this step is to assess the costs of various physical network design alternatives produced in the previous step. The main items are the costs of software, hardware, and circuits. These three factors are all interconnected and must be considered along with the performance and reliability required. All factors are interrelated with regard to cost.

Estimating the cost of a network is quite complex because many factors are not immediately obvious. Some of the costs that must be considered are

- Circuit costs, including costs of circuits provided by common carriers or the cost of purchasing and installing your own cable
- Internetworking devices such as switches and routers
- Hardware costs, including server computers, NICs, hubs, memory, printers, uninterruptible power supplies, and backup tape drives
- Software costs for network operating system, application software, and middleware
- Network management costs, including special hardware, software, and training needed to develop a network management system for ongoing redesign, monitoring, and diagnosing of problems
- Test and maintenance costs for special monitoring equipment and software, plus the cost of onsite spare parts
- Costs to operate the network

Request for Proposal

Although some network components can be purchased off the shelf, most organizations develop a **request for proposal (RFP)** before making large network purchases. RFPs specify what equipment, software, and services are desired and ask vendors to provide their best prices. Some RFPs are very specific about what items are to be provided in what time frame. In other cases, items are defined as mandatory, important, or desirable, or several scenarios are provided and the vendor is asked to propose the best solution. In a few cases, RFPs specify generally what is required and the vendors are asked to propose their own network designs. Figure 12.6 provides a summary of the key parts of an RFP.

Once the vendors have submitted their proposals, the organization evaluates them against specified criteria and selects the winner(s). Depending on the scope and complexity of the network, it is sometimes necessary to redesign the network on the basis of the information in the vendors' proposals.

One of the key decisions in the RFP process is the scope of the RFP. Will you use one vendor or several vendors for all hardware, software, and services? Multivendor environments tend to provide better performance because it is unlikely that one vendor makes the best hardware, software, and services in all categories. Multivendor networks also tend to be less expensive because it is unlikely that one vendor will always have the cheapest hardware, software, and services in all product categories.

Multivendor environments can be more difficult to manage, however. If equipment is not working properly and it is provided by two different vendors, each can

Information in a Typical Request for Proposal

- Background information
  - Organizational profile
  - Overview of current network
  - Overview of new network
  - Goals of new network
- Network requirements
  - Choice sets of possible network designs (hardware, software, circuits)
  - Mandatory, desirable, and wish-list items
  - Security and control requirements
  - Response-time requirements
  - Guidelines for proposing new network designs
- Service requirements
  - Implementation time plan
  - Training courses and materials
  - Support services (e.g., spare parts on site)
  - Reliability and performance guarantees
- Bidding process
  - Time schedule for the bidding process
  - Ground rules
  - Bid evaluation criteria
  - Availability of additional information
- Information required from vendor
  - Vendor corporate profile
  - Experience with similar networks
  - Hardware and software benchmarks
  - Reference list

FIGURE 12.6 Request for proposal

blame the other for the problem. In contrast, a single vendor is solely responsible for everything.

Selling the Proposal to Management

One of the main problems in network design is obtaining the support of senior management. To management, the network is simply a cost center, something on which the organization is spending a lot of money with little apparent change. The network keeps on running just as it did the year before.

The key to gaining the acceptance of senior management lies in speaking management's language. It is pointless to talk about upgrades from 100 Mbps to 1GbE on the backbone because this terminology is meaningless from a business perspective. A more compelling argument is to discuss the growth in network use. For example, a simple graph that shows network usage growing at 25 percent per year, compared with network budget growing at 10 percent per year, presents a powerful illustration that the network costs are well managed, not out of control.

Likewise, a focus on network reliability is an easily understandable issue. For example, if the network supports a mission-critical system such as order processing or moving point-of-sale data from retail stores to corporate offices, it is clear from a business perspective that the network must be available and performing properly, or the organization will lose revenue.

Deliverables

There are three key deliverables for this step. The first is an RFP that goes to potential vendors. The second deliverable, after the vendor has been selected, is the revised physical network diagram (e.g., Figure 12.5) with the technology design complete. Exact products and costs are specified at this point (e.g., a 16-port 100Base-T switch). The third deliverable is the business case that provides support for the network design, expressed in business objectives.

DESIGNING FOR NETWORK PERFORMANCE

At the end of the previous chapters we have discussed the best practice design for LANs, backbones, MANs, WANs, and WLANs and examined how different technologies and services offered different effective data rates at different costs. In the backbone and MAN/WAN chapters we also examined different topologies and contrasted the advantages and disadvantages of each. So at this point, you should have a good understanding of the best choices for technologies and services and how to put them together into a good network design. In this section, we examine several higher-level concepts used to design the network for the best performance.

Managed Networks

The single most important element that contributes to the performance of a network is a **managed network** that uses **managed devices.** Managed devices are standard devices, such as switches and routers, that have small onboard computers to monitor traffic flows through the device as well as the status of the device and other devices connected to it. Managed devices perform their functions (e.g., routing, switching) and also record data on the messages they process. These data can be sent to the network manager's computer when the device receives a special control message requesting the data, or the device can send an **alarm** message to the network manager's computer if it detects a critical situation such as a failing device or a huge increase in traffic.

In this way, network problems can be detected and reported by the devices themselves before problems become serious. In the case of the failing network card, a managed device could record the increased number of retransmissions required to successfully transmit messages and inform the network management software of the problem. A managed hub or switch might even be able to detect the faulty transmissions from a failing network card, disable the incoming circuit so that the card could not send any more messages, and issue an alarm to the network manager. In either case, finding and fixing problems is much simpler, requiring minutes not hours.

Network Management Software A managed network requires both hardware and software: hardware to monitor, collect, and transmit traffic reports and problem alerts, and network management software to store, organize, and analyze these reports and alerts. There are three fundamentally different types of network management software.

Device management software (sometimes called point management software) is designed to provide information about the specific devices on a network. It enables the network-manager to monitor important devices such as servers, routers, and gateways, and typically report configuration information, traffic volumes, and error conditions for each device. Figure 12.7 shows some sample displays from a device management package running at Indiana University. This figure shows the amount of traffic in terms of inbound traffic (light gray area) and outbound traffic (dark gray line) over several network segments. The monthly graph shows, for example, that inbound traffic maxed out the resnet T3 circuit in week 18. This tool is available on the Web at netstats.indiana.edu, so you can investigate the network structure and performance.

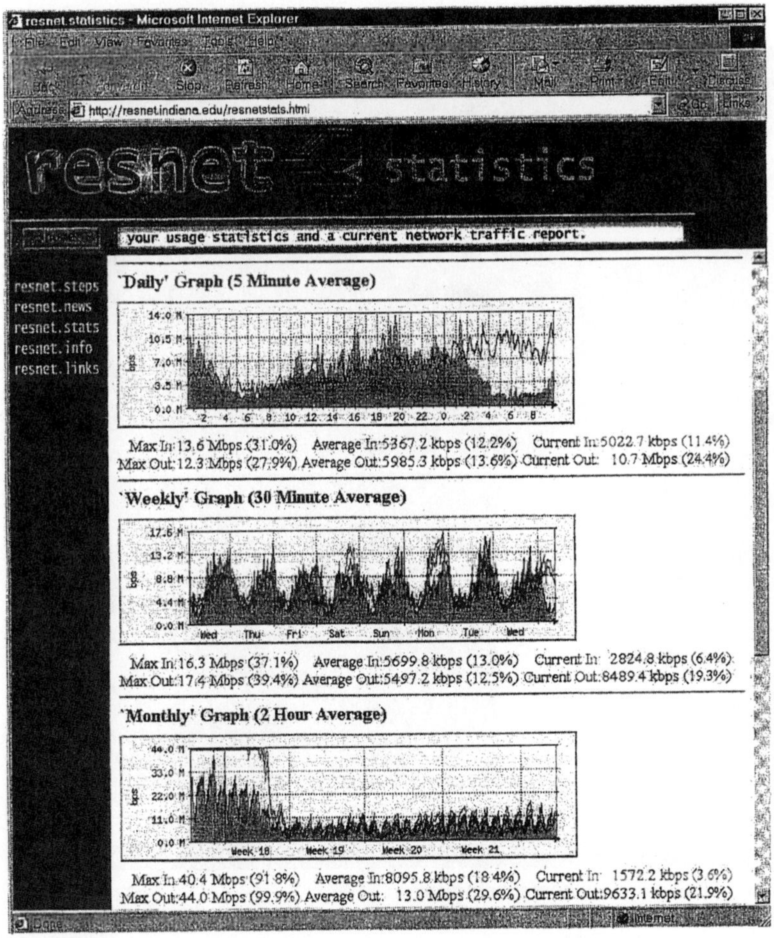

FIGURE 12.7 Device management software

System management software (sometimes called enterprise management software or a network management framework) provides the same configuration, traffic, and error information as device management systems, but can analyze the device information to diagnose patterns, not just display individual device problems. This is important when a critical device fails (e.g., a router into a high-traffic building). With device management software, all of the devices that depend on the failed device will attempt to send warning messages to the network administrator. One failure often generates several dozen problem reports, called an **alarm storm,** making it difficult to pinpoint the true source of the problem quickly. The dozens of error messages are symptoms that mask the root cause. System management software tools correlate the individual error messages into a pattern to find the true cause, which is called **root cause analysis,** and then report the pattern to the network manager. Rather than first seeing pages and pages of error messages, the network manager instead is informed of the root cause of the problem. Figure 12.8 shows a sample from HP OpenView. This is available on the Web at www.openview.hp.com.

Application management software also builds on the device management software, but instead of monitoring systems, it monitors applications. In many organizations,

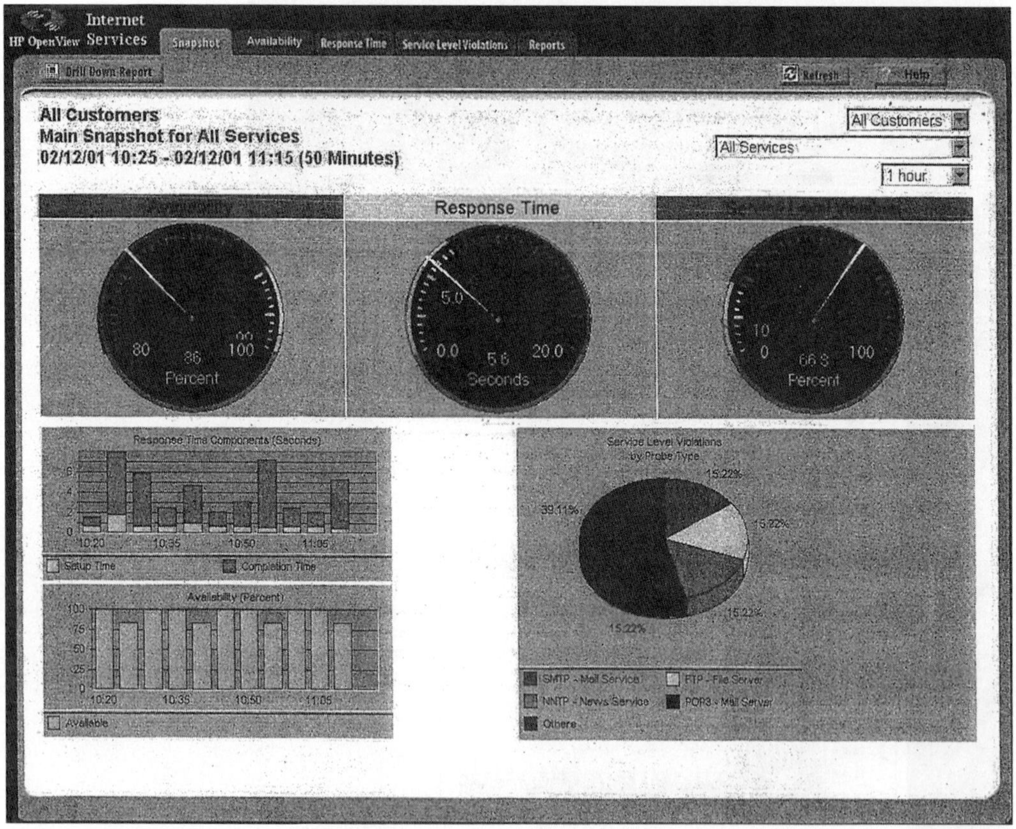

FIGURE 12.8 Network management software
Source: HP OpenView

there are mission-critical applications that should get priority over other network traffic. For example, real-time order-entry systems used by telephone operators need priority over e-mail. Application management systems track delays and problems with application layer packets and inform the network manager if problems occur.

Network Management Standards

One important problem is ensuring that hardware devices from different vendors can understand and respond to the messages sent by the network management software of other vendors. By this point in this book, the solution should be obvious: standards. A number of formal and de facto standards have been developed for network management. These standards are application layer protocols that define the type of information collected by network devices and the format of control messages that the devices understand.

The two most commonly used network management protocols are **Simple Network Management Protocol (SNMP)** and **Common Management Interface Protocol (CMIP).** Both perform the same basic functions but are incompatible. SNMP is the Internet network management standard while CMIP is a newer protocol for OSI-type networks developed by the ISO. SNMP is the most commonly used today although most of the major network management software tools understand both SNMP and CMIP and can operate with hardware that uses either standard.

SNMP was developed originally to control and monitor the status of network devices on TCP/IP networks, but it is now available for other network protocols (e.g., IPX/SPX). Each SNMP device (e.g., router, gateway, server) has an **agent** that collects information about itself and the messages it processes and stores that information in a central database called the **management information base (MIB).** The network manager's management station that runs the **network management software** has access to the MIB. Using this software, the network manager can send control messages to individual devices or groups of devices asking them to report the information stored in their MIB.

Most SNMP devices have the ability for **remote monitoring (RMON).** Most first-generation SNMP tools reported all network monitoring information to one central network management database. Each device would transmit updates to its MIB on the server every few minutes, greatly increasing network traffic. RMON SNMP software enables MIB information to be stored on the device itself or on distributed **RMON probes** that store MIB information closer to the devices that generate it. The data are not transmitted to the central server until the network manager requests, thus reducing network traffic (Figure 12.9).

Network information is recorded based on the data link layer protocols, network layer protocols, and application layer protocols, so that network managers can get a very clear picture of the exact types of network traffic. Statistics are also collected based on network addresses so the network manager can see how much network traffic any particular computer is sending and receiving. A wide variety of alarms can be defined, such as instructing a device to send a warning message if certain items in the MIB exceed certain values (e.g., if circuit utilization exceeds 50 percent).

As the name suggests, SNMP is a simple protocol with a limited number of functions. One problem with SNMP is that many vendors have defined their own extensions to it. So the network devices sold by a vendor may be SNMP compliant, but the MIBs

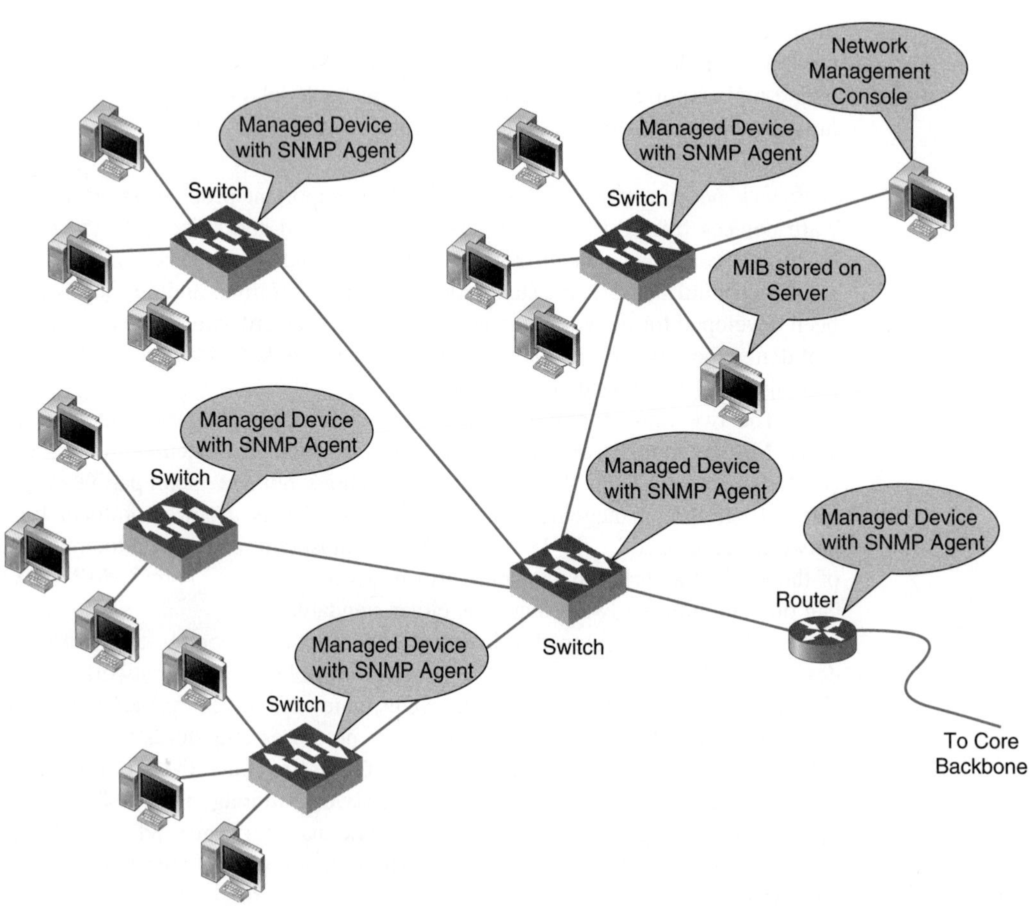

FIGURE 12.9 Network Management with Simple Network Management Protocol (SNMP). MIB = management information base

they produce contain additional information that can be used only by network management software produced by the same vendor. Therefore, while SNMP was designed to make it easier to manage devices from different vendors, in practice this is not always the case.

Policy-Based Management With **policy-based management,** the network manager uses special software to set priority policies for network traffic that take effect when the network becomes busy. For example, the network manager might say that order processing and videoconferencing get the highest priority (order processing because it is the lifeblood of the company and videoconferencing because poor response time will have the greatest impact on it). The policy management software would then configure the network devices using the quality of service (QoS) capabilities in TCP/IP and/or ATM and/or its VLANs to give these applications the highest priority when the devices become busy.

MANAGEMENT FOCUS 12.2 NETWORK MANAGEMENT TOOLKITS VERSUS NETWORK MANAGEMENT FRAMEWORKS

There is a running debate about the value of network management toolkits (also called device management software) and network management frameworks (also called system management software). Toolkits are cheaper, quicker to install, but provide fewer features than the industrial-strength frameworks.

The U.S. Department of Agriculture (USDA) Food Safety and Inspection Service has a network of 23 sites throughout the United States, including its headquarters in Washington, D.C. Before they implemented a managed network, they relied on users to inform them of problems: when a WAN link went down, irate users would begin calling the help desk and that would trigger the network management team to act. The USDA wanted a fast implementation of a network management solution that would enable them to monitor their network and detect problems quickly. They chose WebNM (www.sonix.com), an inexpensive network management toolkit. It was installed in 3 days in the Washington, D.C., office at a cost of $30,000, and then rolled out to the other 22 sites. WebNM provides alarms as well as routine usage statistics that can help the USDA in capacity planning.

In contrast, the U.S. Internal Revenue Service (IRS) operates a network with 11 major data centers, dozens of regional offices, and more than 400,000 attached computers and devices. They chose to implement the Tivoli (www.tivoli.com) network management framework, along with the CiscoWorks software (www.cisco.com). They added two large servers to manage the MIB and RMON data, as well as installing dozens of RMON probes throughout the network. The implementation was extensively planned and completed in less than a year. The system produces over 9,000 scheduled reports per year including alarms, network utilization, network response time by device, circuit and network segment, device reliability, persistent problem detection, event correlation analyses, root cause analyses, automated correction, and a network weather map.

Although the two agencies took very different approaches to network management, both are pleased with their results.

SOURCE: "Toolkits vs. Frameworks for Network Management," *ServerWorld,* August 2001, and IRS Network Management Center, Concord User Group (www.echug.com), October 2003.

Network Circuits

In designing a network for maximum performance, it is obvious that the network circuits play a critical role, whether they are under the direct control of the organization itself (in the case of LANs, backbones, and WLANs) or leased as services from common carriers (in the case of MANs and WANs). Sizing the circuits and placing them to match traffic patterns is important. We discussed circuit loading and capacity planning in the earlier sections. In this section we also consider traffic analysis and service level agreements, which are primarily important for MANs and WANs, because circuits are most important in these networks in which you pay for network capacity.

Traffic Analysis In managing a network and planning for network upgrades, it is important to know the amount of traffic on each network circuit to find which circuits are approaching capacity. These circuits then can be upgraded to provide more capacity

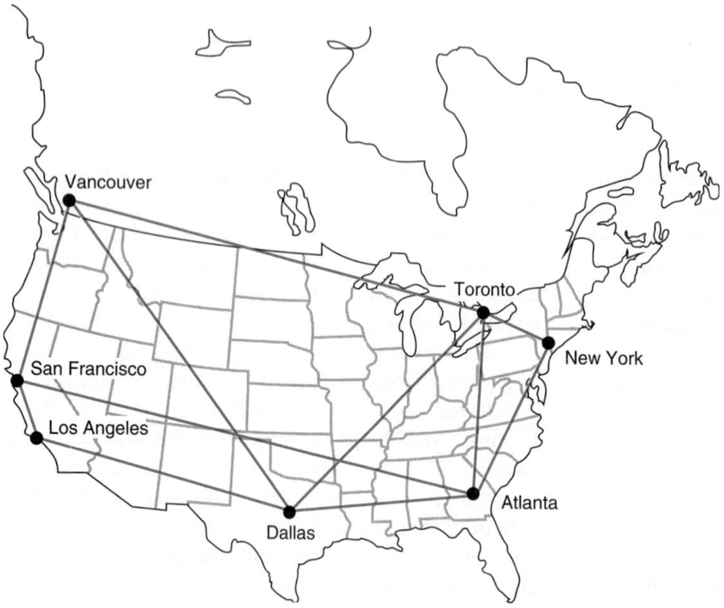

FIGURE 12.10 Sample wide area network

and less-used circuits can be downgraded to save costs. A more sophisticated approach involves a **traffic analysis** to pinpoint *why* some circuits are heavily used.

For example, Figure 12.10 shows the same partial mesh WAN we showed in Chapter 9. Suppose we discover that the circuit from Toronto to Dallas is heavily used. The immediate reaction might be to upgrade this circuit from a T1 to a T3. However, much traffic on this circuit may not originate in Toronto or be destined for Dallas. It may, for example, be going from New York to Los Angeles, in which case the best solution is a new circuit that directly connects them, rather than upgrading an existing circuit. The only way to be sure is to perform a traffic analysis to see the source and destination of the traffic.

Service Level Agreements Most organizations establish a **service level agreement (SLA)** with their common carrier and Internet service provider. An SLA specifies the exact type of performance that the common carrier will provide and the penalties if this performance is not provided. For example, the SLA might state that circuits must be available 99 percent or 99.9 percent of the time. A 99 percent availability means, for example, that the circuit can be down 3.65 days per year with no penalty, while 99.9 percent means 8.76 hours per year. In many cases, SLA includes maximum allowable response times. Some organizations are also starting to use an SLA internally to clearly define relationships between the networking group and its organizational "customers."

Network Devices

In previous chapters, we have treated the devices used to build the network as commodities. We have talked about 100Base-T switches and routers as though all were the same. This not true; in the same way that computers from different manufacturers provide different capabilities, so too do network devices. Some devices are simply faster or more reliable than similar devices from other manufacturers. In this section we examine four factors important in network performance: device latency, device memory, load balancing, and capacity management.

Device Latency

Latency is the delay imposed by the device in processing messages. A high-latency device is one that takes a long time to process a message, while a low-latency device is fast. The type of computer processor installed in the device affects latency. The fastest devices run at **wire speed,** which means they operate as fast as the circuits they connect and add virtually no delays.

For networks with heavy traffic, latency is a critical issue because any delay affects all packets that move through the device. If the device does not operate at wire speed, then packets arrive faster than the device can process them and transmit them on the outgoing circuits. If the incoming circuit is operating at close to capacity, then this will result in long traffic backups in the same way that long lines of traffic form at tollbooths on major highways during rush hour.

Latency is less important in low-traffic networks because packets arrive less frequently and long lines seldom build up even if the device cannot process all packets that the circuits can deliver. The actual delay itself—usually a few microseconds—is not noticeable by users.

Device Memory

Memory and latency go hand-in-hand. If network devices do not operate at wire speed, this means that packets can arrive faster than they can be processed. In this case, the device must have sufficient memory to store the packets. If there is not enough memory, then packets are simply lost and must be retransmitted—thus increasing traffic even more. The amount of memory needed is directly proportional to the latency (slower devices with higher latencies need more memory).

Memory is also important for servers whether they are Web servers or file servers. Memory is many times faster than hard disks so Web servers and file servers usually store the most frequently requested files in memory to decrease the time they require to process a request. The larger the memory that a server has, the more files it can store in memory and the more likely it is to be able to process a request quickly. In general, it is always worthwhile to have the greatest amount of memory practical in Web and file servers.

Load Balancing

In all large-scale networks today, servers are placed together in **server farms** or **clusters,** which sometimes have hundreds of servers that perform the same task. Yahoo.com, for example, has hundreds of Web servers that do nothing but respond to Web search requests. In this case, it is important to ensure that when a request arrives at the server farm, it is immediately forwarded to a server that is not busy—or is the least busy.

A special device called a **load balancing switch** or **virtual server** acts as a router at the front of the server farm (Figure 12.11). All requests are directed to the load balancer at its IP address. When a request hits the load balancer it forwards it to one specific server using its IP address. Sometimes a simple round-robin formula is used (requests go to each

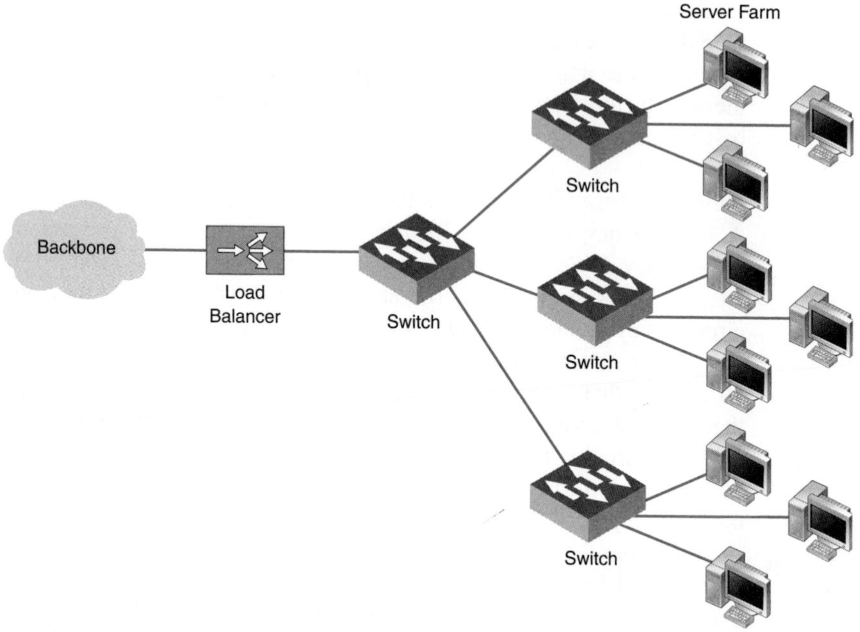

FIGURE 12.11 Network with load balancer

server one after the other in turn), while in other cases, more complex formulas track how busy each server actually is. If a server crashes, the load balancer stops sending requests to it and the network continues to operate without the failed server. Load balancing makes it simple to add servers (or remove servers) without affecting users. You simply add or remove the server(s) and change the software configuration in the load balancing switch; no one is aware of the change.

Capacity Management Most network traffic today is hard to predict. Users choose to download large software or audio files or have instant messenger voice chats. In many networks, there is greater capacity within a LAN than there is leading out of the LAN into the backbone or to the Internet. In Figure 12.5, for example, the building backbone has a capacity of 1 Gbps, which is also the capacity of just one LAN connected to it (2 East). If one user in this LAN generates traffic at the full capacity of this LAN, then the entire backbone will become congested, affecting users in all other LANs.

Capacity management devices, sometimes called **bandwidth limiters** or **bandwidth shapers,** monitor traffic and can act to slow down traffic from users who consume too much capacity. These devices are installed at key points in the network, such as between a switch serving a LAN and the backbone it connects into, and are configured to allocate capacity based on the IP address of the source (or its data link address) as well as the application in use. The device could, for example, permit a given user to generate a high amount of traffic for an approved use, but limit capacity for an unofficial use such as MP3 files. Figure 12.12 shows the control panel for one device made by *NetEqualizer.*

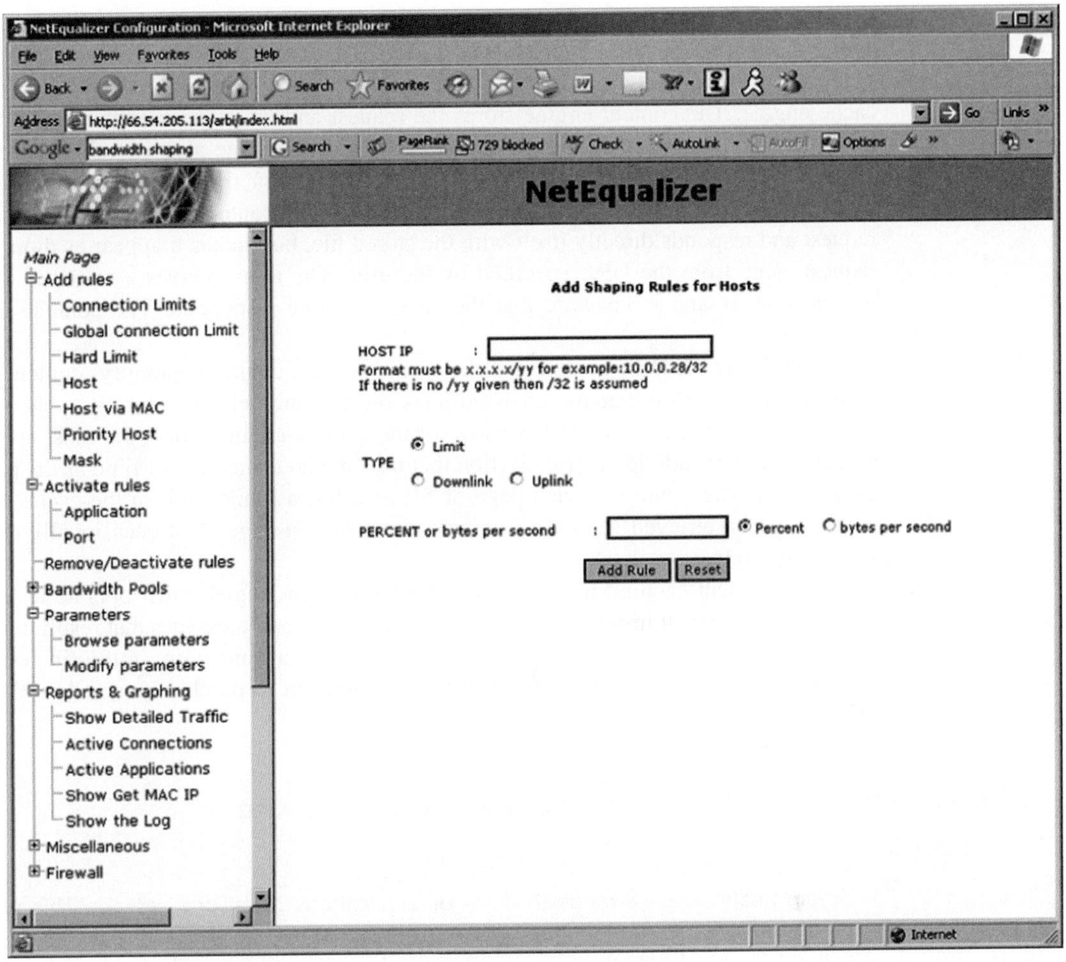

FIGURE 12.12 Capacity management software

Minimizing Network Traffic

Most approaches to improving network performance attempt to maximize the speed at which the network can move the traffic it receives. The opposite—and equally effective approach—is to minimize the amount of traffic the network receives. This may seem quite difficult at first glance—after all, how can we reduce the number of Web pages people request? We can't reduce all types of network traffic, but if we move the most commonly used data closer to the users who need it, we can reduce traffic enough to have an impact. We do this by providing servers with duplicate copies of commonly used information at points closer to the users than the original source of the data. Two approaches are emerging: content caching and content delivery.

Content Caching

The basic idea behind **content caching** is to store other people's Web data closer to your users. With content caching, you install a **content engine** (also called a *cache engine*) close to your Internet connection and install special content management software on the router (Figure 12.13). The router or routing switch directs all outgoing Web requests and the files that come back in response to those requests to the cache engine. The content engine stores the request and the static files that are returned in response (e.g., graphics files, banners). The content engine also examines each outgoing Web request to see if it is requesting static content that the content engine has already stored. If the request is for content already in the content engine, it intercepts the request and responds directly itself with the stored file, but makes it appear as though the request came from the URL specified by the user. The user receives a response almost instantaneously and is unaware that the content engine responded. The content engine is *transparent.*

While not all Web content will be in the content engine's memory, content from many of the most commonly accessed sites on the Internet will be (e.g., yahoo.com, google.com, Amazon.com). The contents of the content engine reflect the most common requests for each individual organization that uses it, and changes over time as the pattern of pages and files changes. Each page or file also has a limited life in the cache before a new copy is retrieved from the original source so that pages that occasionally change will be accurate.

For content caching to work properly, the content engine must operate at almost wire speeds, or else it imposes additional delays on outgoing messages that result in worse performance, not better. By reducing outgoing traffic (and incoming traffic in response to requests), the content engine enables the organization to purchase a smaller WAN or

MANAGEMENT FOCUS 12.3 LOAD BALANCING AT BRYAM HEALTHCARE

Bryam Healthcare is a medical supply company serving more than 300,000 customers from 17 operating centers. When its sales representatives began complaining about the slow response times for e-mail, Web, and other key applications, Anthony Acquanita, Byram's network manager, realized that the network architecture had reached its limits.

The old architecture was a set of four servers each running specific applications (e.g., one e-mail server, one Web server). At different points in the week, a different server would become overloaded and provide slow response times for a specific application—the e-mail server first thing Monday morning as people checked their e-mail after the weekend, for example.

The solution was to install a load balancing switch in front of the servers and install all the major applications on all the servers. This way when the demand for one application peaks, there are four servers available rather than one. Because the demand for different applications peaks at different times, the result has been dramatically improved performance, without the need to buy new servers. The side benefit is that it is now simple to remove one server from operations at nonpeak times for maintenance or software upgrades without the users noticing (whereas in the past, server maintenance meant disabling an application (e.g., e-mail) for a few hours while the server was worked on).

SOURCE: "Load Balancing Boosts Network," *Communications News,* November 2005, pp. 40–42.

MANAGEMENT FOCUS 12.4

CONTENT CACHING AT THE SALT LAKE CITY OLYMPIC GAMES

The 2002 Olympic Winter Games in Salt Lake City needed a network infrastructure that would deliver real-time results, athlete biographies, transportation information, competition schedules, medal counts, competition results, and more to thousands of users (media, Olympic athletes, and staff) at sporting venues, Olympic villages, administrative offices, media centers, and external Web sites. The network had to guarantee maximum reliability 24 hours a day, seven days a week.

The Salt Lake City Olympic Committee established a primary data center with two high-performance load balancing switches in a standby/failover configuration supporting a server farm (see Figure 12.14) so that if one switch failed, the standby switch would detect the failure and automatically take over. The load balancing capability of the switches ensured that incoming traffic was routed to the least busy server, thereby ensuring maximum performance.

The primary data center was connected via a pair of routers (again in a standby/failover configuration) through T-3 lines to a secondary data center with a similar structure that would be used in the event of problems with the primary data center. The primary data center was connected via a pair of T-1 lines to the Media Center, to the Athletes Village, and to each of the 10 Competition Venues.

The network at the Media Center, the Athletes Village, and Competition Venues had a similar standby paired router/paired switch configuration, with the addition of a content engine to reduce traffic over the T-1 lines to the primary data center.

The resulting network design ensured maximum reliability due to the paired circuits/routers/switches to all locations. The content engines also provided increased reliability and significantly reduced network traffic to the primary data center, thus reducing the capacity needed by the circuits and servers.

SOURCE: "IKANO Deploys Cisco Content Networking Solutions," www.cisco.com, 2004.

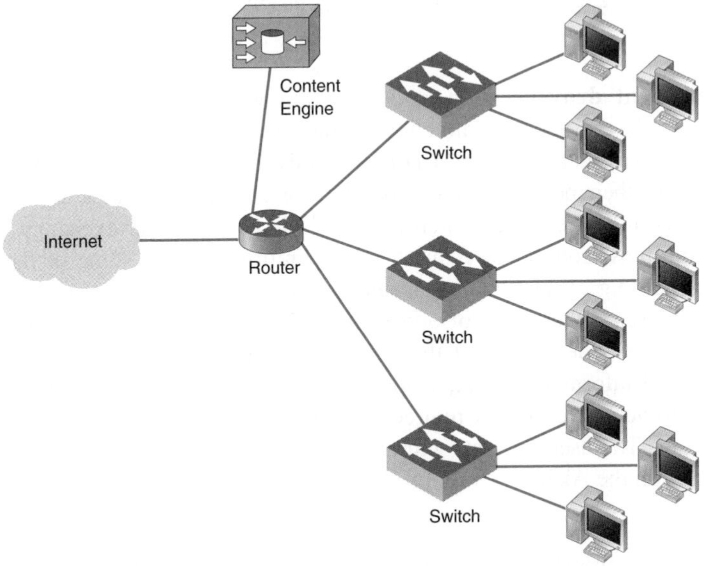

FIGURE 12.13 Network with content engine

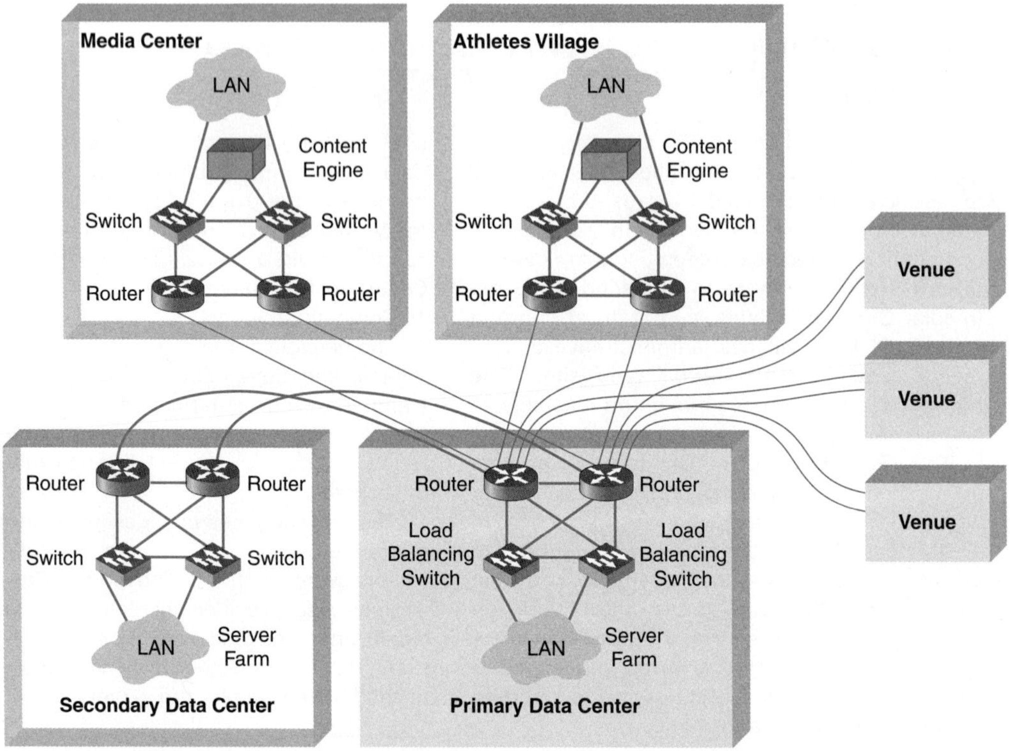

FIGURE 12.14 Olympic network. LAN = local area network

MAN circuit into the Internet. So not only does content caching improve performance, but it can also reduce network costs if the organization produces a large volume of network requests.

Content Delivery **Content delivery,** pioneered by **Akamai,**[2] is a special type of Internet service that works in the opposite direction. Rather than storing other people's Web files closer to their own internal users, a **content delivery provider** stores Web files for its clients closer to their potential users. Akamai, for example, operates almost 10,000 Web servers located near the busiest Internet NAPs, MAPs, and other exchanges. These servers contain the most commonly requested Web information for some of the busiest sites on the Internet (e.g., yahoo.com, monster.com, ticketmaster.com).

When someone accesses a Web page of one of Akamai's customers, special software on the client's Web server determines if there is an Akamai server containing any static parts of the requested information (e.g., graphics, advertisements, banners) closer to the user. If so, the customer's Web server redirects portions of the request to the Akamai server nearest the user. The user interacts with the customer's Web site for dynamic content or HTML pages with the Akamai server providing static content. In Figure 12.15,

[2]Akamai (pronounced *AH-kuh-my*) is Hawaiian for intelligent, clever, and "cool." See www.akamai.com.

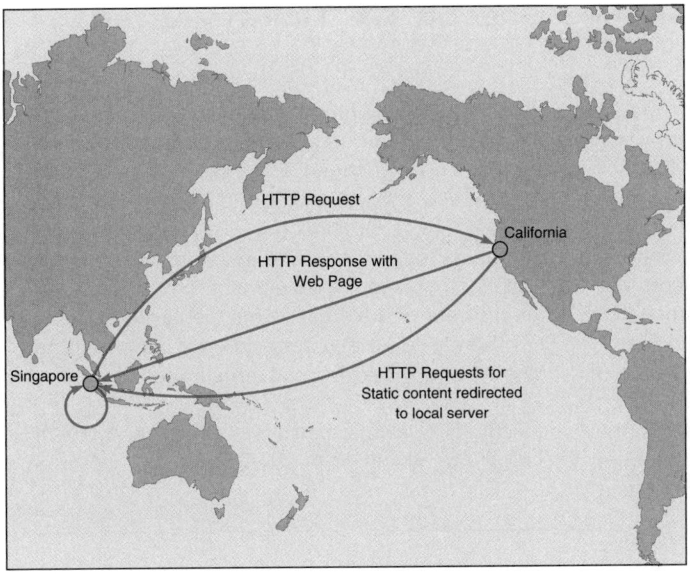

FIGURE 12.15 Network with content delivery

for example, when a user in Singapore requests a Web page from yahoo.com, the main yahoo.com server farm responds with the dynamic HTML page. This page contains several static graphic files. Rather than provide an address on the yahoo.com site, the Web page is dynamically changed by the Akamai software on the yahoo.com site to pull the static content from the Akamai server in Singapore. If you watch the bottom action bar closely on your Web browser while some of your favorite sites are loading, you'll see references to Akamai's servers.

Akamai servers benefit both the users and the organizations that are Akamai's clients, as well as many ISPs and all Internet users not directly involved with the Web request. Because more Web content is now processed by the Akamai server and not the client organization's more distant Web server, the user benefits from a much faster response time; in Figure 12.15, for example, more requests never have to leave Singapore. The client organization benefits because it serves its users with less traffic reaching its Web server; Yahoo! for example, need not spend as much on its server farm or the Internet connection into its server farm. In our example, the ISPs providing the circuits across the Pacific benefit because now less traffic flows through their network—traffic that is not paid for because of Internet peering agreements. Likewise, all other Internet users in Singapore (as well as users in the United States accessing Web sites in Singapore) benefit because there is now less traffic across the Pacific and response times are faster.

IMPLICATIONS FOR MANAGEMENT

Network design was at one time focused on providing the most efficient networks custom tailored to specific needs. Today, however, network design uses a building-block approach. Well-designed networks use a few common, standardized, network

MANAGEMENT FOCUS 12.5 AKAMAI SPEEDS UP TICKETMASTER

Ticketmaster is one of the largest online sellers of tickets in the world and one of the busiest sites on the Internet when tickets for certain events go on sale. On peak days, Ticketmaster serves 10 million page views, with most of that occurring within a 45-minute period. Ticketmaster's Online-Citysearch is a related portal that provides in-depth content for more than 30 metropolitan areas around the United States. San Francisco, for example, has 40,000 pages of information.

Both parts of Ticketmaster use the Akamai content delivery service. Since implementing the service, Ticketmaster has seen a 50-percent reduction in download times and a 40-percent reduction in the load on Ticketmaster's own servers and switches. Ticketmaster was able to prevent a $1 million addition to its own Web site.

Users have noticed the difference too. The number of page views and average duration of a visit has increased by 70 percent. This means that the number of advertisements displayed to users has increased 70 percent as well, thus providing a noticeable increase in advertising revenue.

SOURCE: "Ticketmaster Online-Citysearch: A Tale of Two Sites," Akamai.com, 2004.

technologies over and over again throughout the network even though they might provide more capacity than needed. Under ideal circumstances, the organization will develop deep relationships with a very small set of vendors.

As the cost to operate and maintain networks gradually becomes more expensive than the cost to purchase network technologies in the first place, good network design commonly results in the purchase of more expensive equipment in order to save significantly more money in reduced network management costs over the life of the network. While there is a temptation to go with the lowest bidder and buy inexpensive equipment, in many cases this can significantly increase the lifecycle cost of a network. The use of sophisticated network design tools and network management tools has become a key part of almost all new networks installed today.

SUMMARY

Traditional Network Design The traditional network design approach follows a very structured systems analysis and design process similar to that used to build application systems. It attempts to develop precise estimates of network traffic for each network user and network segment. Although this is expensive and time consuming, it works well for static or slowly evolving networks. Unfortunately, computer and networking technology is changing very rapidly, the growth in network traffic is immense, and hardware and circuit costs are relatively less expensive than they used to be. Therefore, use of the traditional network design approach is decreasing.

Building-Block Approach to Network Design The building-block approach attempts to build the network using a series of simple predefined building components, resulting in a simpler design process and a more easily managed network built with a smaller range of components. The basic process involves three steps that are performed repeatedly. Needs analysis involves developing a logical network design that includes the geographic scope of the network and a categorization of current and future network needs of the various network segments, users, and applications as either typical or high traffic. The next step, technology design, results in a set of one or more physical network designs. Network design and simulation tools can play an important role in selecting the technology that typical and high-volume users, applications, and network segments will use. The final step, cost assessment, gathers cost information for the network, usually through an RFP that specifies what equipment, software, and services are desired and asks vendors to provide their best prices. One of the keys to gaining acceptance by senior management of the network design lies in speaking management's language (cost, network growth, and reliability), not the language of the technology (Ethernet, ATM, and DSL).

Designing for Performance Network management software is critical to the design of reliable, high-performance networks. Device management software provides statistics about device utilizations and issues alerts when problems occur. System management software provides the same information, but also provides analysis and diagnosis to help the network manager make better decisions. Small networks often use device management software, while larger, more complex networks often use system management software. SNMP and CMIP are a common standard for network management software and the managed devices that support it. Load balancing devices shift network traffic among servers in a server farm to ensure that no one server is overloaded with traffic. Content caching and content delivery are commonly used to reduce network traffic.

KEY TERMS

access layer
Akamai
agent
alarm
alarm storm
application management software
bandwidth limiter
bandwidth shaper
baseline
building-block process
capacity management
capacity planning
circuit loading
cluster
Common Management Interface Protocol (CMIP)
content caching
content delivery
content delivery provider
content engine
core layer
cost assessment
desirable requirements
device management software
distribution layer
geographic scope
latency
load balancing switch
logical network design
managed device
managed network
management information base (MIB)
mandatory requirements
needs analysis
needs categorization
network management software
physical network design
policy-based management
remote monitoring (RMON)
request for proposal (RFP)
RMON probe
root cause analysis
server farm
service level agreement (SLA)
Simple Network Management Protocol (SNMP)
simulation
system management software
technology design
traditional network design process
traffic analysis
turnpike effect
virtual server
wire speed
wish-list requirements

QUESTIONS

1. What are the keys to designing a successful data communications network?
2. How does the traditional approach to network design differ from the building-block approach?
3. Describe the three major steps in current network design.
4. What is the most important principle in designing networks?

5. Why is it important to analyze needs in terms of both application systems and users?
6. Describe the key parts of the technology design step.
7. How can a network design tool help in network design?
8. On what should the design plan be based?
9. What is an RFP and why do companies use them?
10. What are the key parts of an RFP?
11. What are some major problems that can cause network designs to fail?
12. What is a network baseline and when is it established?
13. What issues are important to consider in explaining a network design to senior management?
14. What is the turnpike effect and why is it important in network design?
15. How can you design networks to improve performance?
16. How does a managed network differ from an unmanaged network?
17. Compare and contrast device management software, system management software, and application management software.
18. What are SNMP and RMON?
19. What is a traffic analysis and when is it useful?
20. What is a service level agreement?
21. How do device latency and memory affect performance?
22. How does a load balancing switch work?
23. How does content caching differ from content delivery?
24. Why do you think some organizations were slow to adopt a building-block approach to network design?
25. For what types of networks are network design tools most important? Why?

EXERCISES

12-1. What factors might cause peak loads in a network? How can a network designer determine if they are important, and how are they taken into account when designing a data communications network?

12-2. Collect information about two network design tools and compare and contrast what they can and cannot do.

12-3. Investigate the latest versions of SNMP and RMON and describe the functions that have been added in the latest version of the standard.

12-4. Investigate and report on the purpose, relative advantages, and relative disadvantages of two network management software tools (e.g., OpenView, Tivoli).

12-5. Explore the network management software demo from Tivoli (www-306.IBM.com/software/tivoli/library/demos/twa-demo.html).

MINI-CASES

I. Computer Dynamics

Computer Dynamics is a microcomputer software development company that has a 300-computer network. The company is located in three adjacent five-story buildings in an office park, with about 100 computers in each building. The current network is a poorly designed mix of Ethernet and token ring (Ethernet in two buildings and token ring in the other). The networks in all three buildings are heavily overloaded, and the company anticipates significant growth in network traffic. There is currently no network connection among the buildings, but this is one objective in building the new network. Describe the network you would recommend and how it would be configured with the goal of building a new network that will support the company's needs for the next 3 years with few additional investments. Be sure to include the devices and type of network circuits you would use. You will need to make some assumptions, so be sure to document your assumptions and explain why you have designed the network in this way.

II. Drop and Forge

Drop and Forge is a small manufacturing firm with a 60-computer network. The company has one very large manufacturing plant with an adjacent office building. The office building houses 50 computers, with an additional 10 computers in the plant. The current network is an old 1-Mbps Ethernet that will need to be completely replaced. Describe the network you would recommend and how it would be configured. The goal is to build a new network that will support the company's needs for the next 3 years with few additional investments. Be sure to include the devices and type of network circuits you would use. You will need to make some assumptions, so be sure to document your assumptions and explain why you have designed the network in this way.

III. Mary's Manufacturing

Mary's Manufacturing is a small manufacturing company that has a network with eight LANs (each with about 20 computers on them using switched 10Base-T) connected via 100Base-F over fiber-optic cable into a core switch (i.e., a collapsed BN). The switch is connected to the company's ISP over a fractional T1 circuit. Most computers are used for order processing and standard office applications, but some are used to control the manufacturing equipment in the plant. The current network is working fine and there have been no major problems, but Mary is wondering whether she should invest in network management software. It will cost about $5,000 to replace the current hardware with SNMP capable hardware. Mary can buy SNMP device management software for $2,000 or spend $7,000 to buy SNMP system management software. Should Mary install SNMP, and if so, which software should she buy? Why?

IV. AdviceNet

AdviceNet is a consulting firm with offices in Toronto, New York, Los Angeles, Dallas, and Atlanta. The firm currently uses the Internet to transmit data, but its needs are growing and it is concerned over the security of the Internet. The firm wants to establish its own private WAN. Consultants in all offices are frustrated at the current 56-Kbps modems they use for Internet access, so the firm believes that it needs faster data transmission capabilities. The firm has no records of data transmission, but it believes that the New York and Toronto offices send and receive the most data. The firm is growing by 20 percent per year and expects to open offices in Vancouver and Chicago within the next 1 or 2 years. Describe two alternatives for the network and explain what choice you would make under what assumptions.

V. Toolkits versus Frameworks

Reread Management Focus 12.2. Compare and contrast the decisions made by the USDA and the IRS. Do you think they made the right decisions? Why or why not?

VI. Salt Lake City Olympics

Reread Management Focus 12.4. Do you think the Salt Lake City Olympic network was a good design? How might you have improved it? How might you have reduced costs?

CASE STUDY

NEXT-DAY AIR SERVICE

See the Web site

HANDS-ON ACTIVITY

Network Design Software

There are many different network design software tools. Some are simple drawing tools, while others offer powerful network simulation modeling capabilities. One powerful tool that provides a free demo version that can be downloaded is SmartDraw.

The first step is to download and install the SmartDraw software. The software is available at www.smartdraw.com.

SmartDraw comes with a variety of network icons and templates that can be used to quickly build network diagrams. Figure 12.16 shows the main drawing screen in SmartDraw and a network diagram.

HANDS-ON ACTIVITY

Monitoring AT&T's WAN

AT&T permits you to monitor their Global IP network. Go to ipnetwork.bgtmo.ip.att.net and click on Look at your world wide network.

You'll see a screen like that in Figure 12.17 which shows the average delay ("latency") of all the circuits at each of the major PoPs in their global IP network. You can select a city and see the round-trip delay (from the city to the other city and back again). Figure 12.17 shows the delays to and from Indianapolis. All are highlighted in green, which means the delays are below the desired maximum. They range from a low of 13 ms to St. Louis to a high of 60 ms to San Diego.

This also displays the percent of packets that have been lost in transit (either due to errors or overloading of circuits). All circuits are below the target maximum of 0.1 percent.

The tabs across the top of the screen (e.g., Network Delay, Network Loss, Averages) show summary data across the entire network.

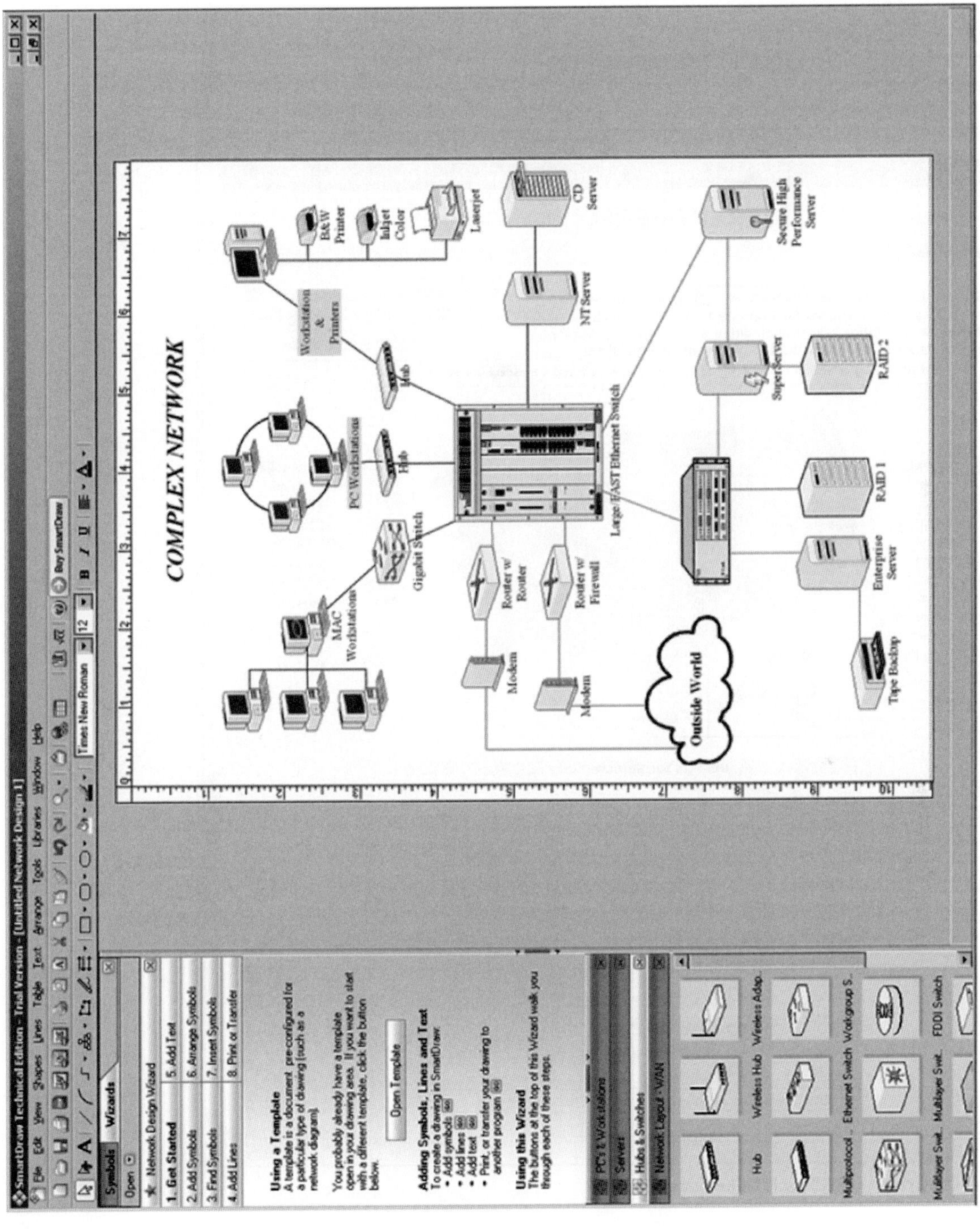

FIGURE 12.16 SmartDraw software

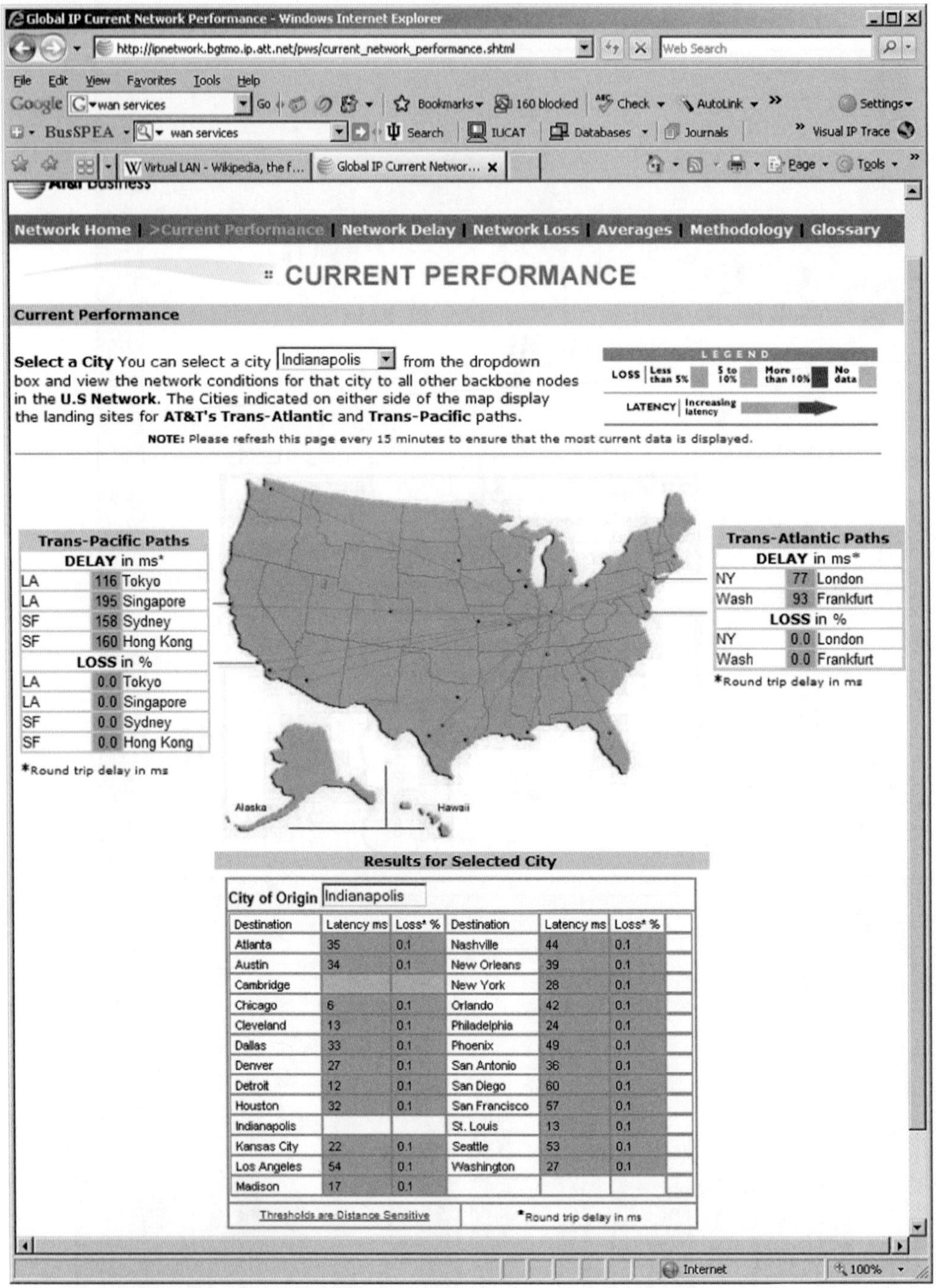

FIGURE 12.17 AT&T's global/IP network

CHAPTER 13

NETWORK MANAGEMENT

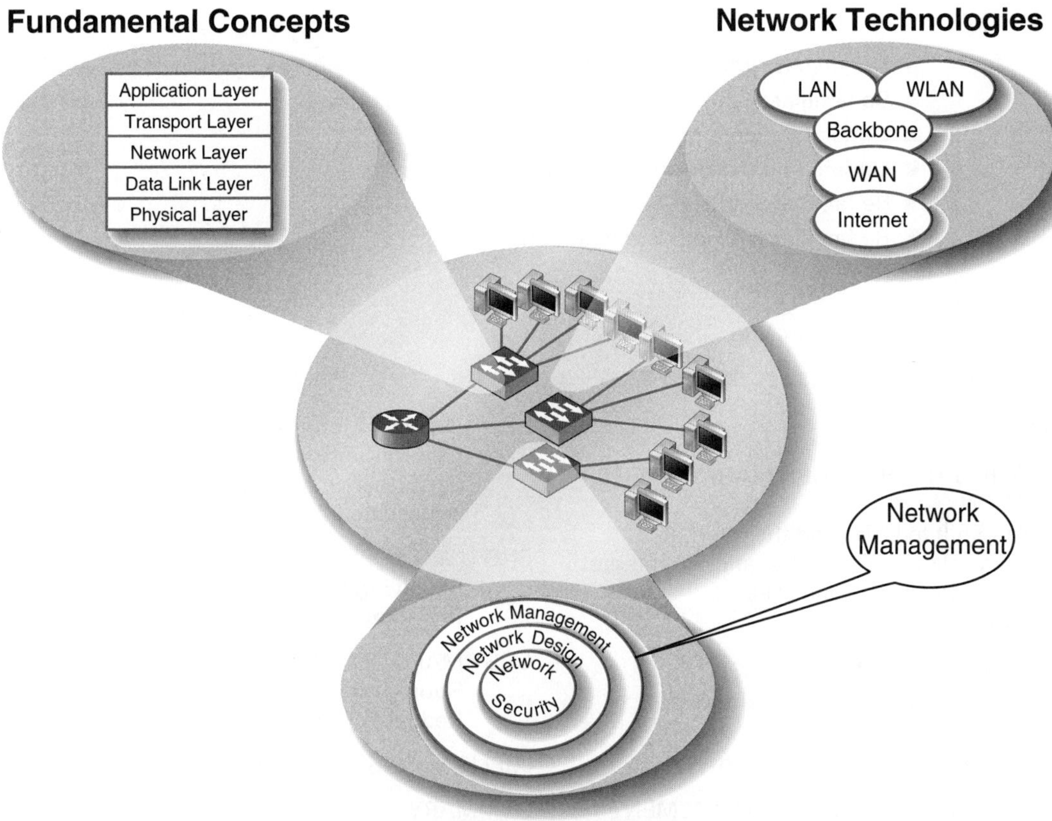

Network Management

The Three Faces of Networking

NETWORK MANAGERS perform two key tasks: (1) designing new networks and network upgrades and (2) managing the day-to-day operation of existing networks. This chapter examines day-to-day network management, discussing the things that must be done to ensure that the network functions properly. We discuss the network management organization and the basic functions that a network manager must perform to operate a successful network.

OBJECTIVES ▼

- Understand what is required to manage the day-to-day operation of networks
- Be familiar with the network management organization
- Understand configuration management
- Understand performance and fault management
- Be familiar with end user support
- Be familiar with cost management

CHAPTER OUTLINE ▼

INTRODUCTION

Network management is the process of operating, monitoring, and controlling the network to ensure it works as intended and provides value to its users. The primary objective of the data communications function is to move application-layer data from one location to another in a timely fashion and to provide the resources that allow this transfer to occur. This transfer of information may take place within a single department, between departments in an organization, or with entities outside the organization across private networks or the Internet.

Without a well-planned, well-designed network and without a well-organized network management staff, operating the network becomes extremely difficult. Unfortunately, many network managers spend most of their time **firefighting**—dealing with breakdowns and immediate problems. If managers do not spend enough time on planning and organizing the network and networking staff, which are needed to predict and prevent problems, they are destined to be reactive rather than proactive in solving problems.

In this chapter, we examine the network management function. We begin by examining the job of the network manager and how the network management function can be organized within companies. We then break down the activities that network managers perform into four basic functions: configuration management (knowing what hardware and software are where), performance and fault management (making sure the network operates as desired), end user support (assisting end users), and cost management (minimizing the cost of providing network services). In practice, it is difficult to separate the network manager's job into these four neat categories, but these are useful ways to help understand what a network manager does.

ORGANIZING THE NETWORK MANAGEMENT FUNCTION

Communication and networking functions present special organizational problems because they are both centralized and decentralized. The developers, gatherers, and users of data are typically decentralized. The need for communications and networking affects every business function, so the management of voice and data communications has traditionally been highly centralized. Networks and mainframe servers were "owned" and operated by centralized IT departments that were used to controlling every aspect of the IT and communication environment.

The Shift to LANs and the Internet

Since the late 1980s, this picture has changed dramatically. There has been an explosion in the use of microcomputer-based networks. In fact, more than 90 percent of most organizations' total computer processing power (measured in millions of instructions per seconds) now resides on microcomputer-based LANs. Since the early 1990s, the number of computers attached to LANs has grown dramatically. Today, the host mainframe computer provides less than 10 percent of the organization's total computing power whereas the number of Internet-based servers (e.g., Web servers, mail servers) has grown dramatically.

Although the management of host-based mainframe networks will always be important, the future of network management lies in the successful management of multiple clients and servers communicating over LANs, BNs, and the Internet. Many LANs and Web servers were initially designed and implemented by individual departments as separate networks and applications, whose goals were to best meet the needs of their individual owners, not to integrate with other networks and applications.

Because each LAN was developed by a different department within the organization, not all LANs used the same architecture (e.g., shared 100Base-T versus switched 10Base-T, routed backbone versus switched backbone). The more types of network technology used, the more complex network management becomes.

Integrating LANs, WANs, and the Internet

The key to integrating LANs, WANs, and the Internet into one overall organization network is for both LAN/Web and WAN managers to recognize that they no longer have the power they once had. No longer can network managers make independent decisions without considering their impacts on other parts of the organization's network. There must be a single overall communications and networking goal that best meets the needs of the entire organization. This will require some network managers to compromise on policies that are not in the best interests of their own departments or networks.

The central data communication network organization should have a written charter that defines its purpose, operational philosophy, and long-range goals. These goals must conform both to the parent organization's information-processing goals and to its own departmental goals. Along with its long-term policies, the organization must develop

MANAGEMENT FOCUS 13.1 WHAT DO NETWORK MANAGERS DO?

If you were to become a network manager, some of your responsibilities and tasks would be to

- Manage the day-to-day operations of the network
- Provide support to network users
- Ensure the network is operating reliably
- Evaluate and acquire network hardware, software, and services
- Manage the network technical staff
- Manage the network budget, with emphasis on controlling costs
- Develop a strategic (long-term) networking and voice communications plan to meet the organization's policies and goals
- Keep abreast of the latest technological developments in computers, data communications devices, network software, and the Internet
- Keep abreast of the latest technological developments in telephone technologies and metropolitan area and local area network services
- Assist senior management in understanding the business implications of network decisions and the role of the network in business operations

MANAGEMENT FOCUS 13.2 FIVE KEY MANAGEMENT TASKS

Planning activities require

- Forecasting
- Establishing objectives
- Scheduling
- Budgeting
- Allocating resources
- Developing policies

Organizing activities require

- Developing organizational structure
- Delegating
- Establishing relationships
- Establishing procedures
- Integrating the smaller organization with the larger organization

Directing activities require

- Initiating activities
- Decision making
- Communicating
- Motivating

Controlling activities require

- Establishing performance standards
- Measuring performance
- Evaluating performance
- Correcting performance

Staffing activities require

- Interviewing people
- Selecting people
- Developing People

individual procedures with which to implement the policies. Individual departments and LAN/Web managers must be free to implement their own policies and procedures that guide the day-to-day tasks of network staff.

Integrating Voice and Data Communications

Another major organizational challenge is the integration of the voice communication function with the data communication function. Traditionally, voice communications were handled by a manager in the facilities department who supervised the telephone switchboard systems and also coordinated the installation and maintenance of the organization's voice telephone networks. By contrast, data communications traditionally were handled by the IT department because the staff installed their own communication circuits as the need arose, rather than coordinating with the voice communications staff.

This separation of voice and data worked well over the years, but today changing communication technologies are causing enormous pressures to combine these functions. These pressures are magnified by the high cost of maintaining separate facilities, the low efficiency and productivity of the organization's employees because there are two separate network functions, and the potential political problems within an organization when neither manager wants to relinquish his or her functional duties or job position. A key factor in voice/data integration might turn out to be the elimination of one key management position and the merging of two staffs.

MANAGEMENT FOCUS 13.3 NETWORK MANAGER JOB REQUIREMENTS

Being a network manager is not easy. We reviewed dozens of job posting for the key responsibilities, skills, and education desired by employers. Those responsibilities listed below were commonly mentioned.

Responsibilities:

- Determine network needs and architect solutions to address business requirements.
- Procure and manage vendor relations with providers of equipment and services.
- Deploy new network components and related network systems and services, including the creation of test plans and procedures, documentation of the operation, maintenance and administration of any new systems or services, and training.
- Develop, document, and enforce standards, procedures, and processes for the operation and maintenance of the network and related systems.
- Manage the efficiency of operations of the current network infrastructure, including analyzing network performance and making configuration adjustments as necessary.
- Administer the network servers and the network-printing environment.
- Ensure network security including the development of applicable security, server and desktop standards, and monitoring processes to ensure that mission critical processes are operational.
- Manage direct reports and contractors. This includes task assignments, performance monitoring, and regular feedback. Hire, train, evaluate, and terminate staff and contractors under the direction of company policies and processes.
- Assist business in the definition of new product/service offerings and the capabilities and features of the systems in order to deliver those products and services to our customers.

Skills required:

- Strong, up-to-date technology skills in a variety of technologies
- LAN/WAN networking experience working with routers and switches
- Experience with Internet access solutions, including firewalls and VPN
- Network architecture design and implementation experience
- Information security experience
- Personnel management experience
- Project management experience
- Experience working in a team environment
- Ability to work well in an unstructured environment
- Excellent problem-solving and analytical skills
- Effective written and oral communication skills

Education:

- Bachelor's degree in an information technology field
- Security Certification
- Microsoft MCSE Certification preferred
- Cisco CCNA Certification preferred

There is no perfect solution to this problem because it must be handled in a way unique to each organization. Depending on the business environment and specific communication needs, some organizations may want to combine these functions whereas others may find it better to keep them separate. We can state unequivocally that an organization that avoids studying this situation might be promoting inefficient communication systems, lower employee productivity, and increased operating costs for its separate voice and data networks.

In communications, we are moving from an era in which the computer system is the dominant IT function to one in which communications networks are the dominant IT function. In some organizations, the total cost of both voice and data communications will equal or exceed the total cost of the computer systems.

CONFIGURATION MANAGEMENT

Configuration management means managing the network's hardware and software configuration, and documenting it, and ensuring it is updated as the configuration changes.

Configuring the Network and Client Computers

One of the most common configuration activities is adding and deleting user accounts. When new users are added to the network, they are usually categorized as being a member of some group of users (e.g., faculty, students, accounting department, personnel department). Each user group has its own access privileges, which define what file servers, directories, and files they can access and provide a standard log-in script. The log-in script specifies what commands are to be run when the user first logs in (e.g., setting default directories, connecting to public disks, running menu programs).

Another common activity is updating the software on the client computers attached to the network. Every time a new application system is developed or updated (or, for that matter, when a new version is released), each client computer in the organization must be updated. Traditionally, this has meant that someone from the networking staff has had to go to each client computer and manually install the software, either from diskettes/CDs or by downloading over the network. For a small organization, this is time consuming but not a major problem. For a large organization with hundreds or thousands of client computers (possibly with a mixture of Windows and Apples), this can be a nightmare.

Electronic software distribution (ESD), sometimes called **desktop management** or automated software delivery, is one solution to the configuration problem. ESD enables network managers to install software on client computers over the network without physically touching each client computer. Most ESD packages provide application-layer software for the network server and all client computers. The server software communicates directly with the ESD application software on the clients and can be instructed to download and install certain application packages on each client at some predefined time (e.g., at midnight on a Saturday or as requested by the user. Microsoft and many antivirus software vendors use ESD to deliver updates and patches to their software).

ESD software greatly reduces the cost of configuration management over the long term because it eliminates the need to update each and every client computer manually. It also automatically produces and maintains accurate documentation of all software installed on each client computer and enables network managers to produce a variety of useful reports. However, ESD increases costs in the short term because it costs money (typically $50 per client computer) and requires network staff to install it manually on each client computer. Desktop Management Interface (DMI) is the emerging standard in ESD software.

Documenting the Configuration

Configuration documentation includes information about network hardware, network software, user and application profiles, and **network documentation.** The most basic information about network hardware is a set of network configuration diagrams that document the number, type, and placement of network circuits (whether organization owned or leased from a common carrier), network servers, network devices (e.g., hubs, routers), and client computers. For most organizations, this is a large set of diagrams: one for each LAN, BN, MAN, and WAN. Figure 13.1 shows a diagram of network devices in one office location.

These diagrams must be supplemented by documentation on each individual network component (e.g., circuit, hub, server). Documentation should include the type of

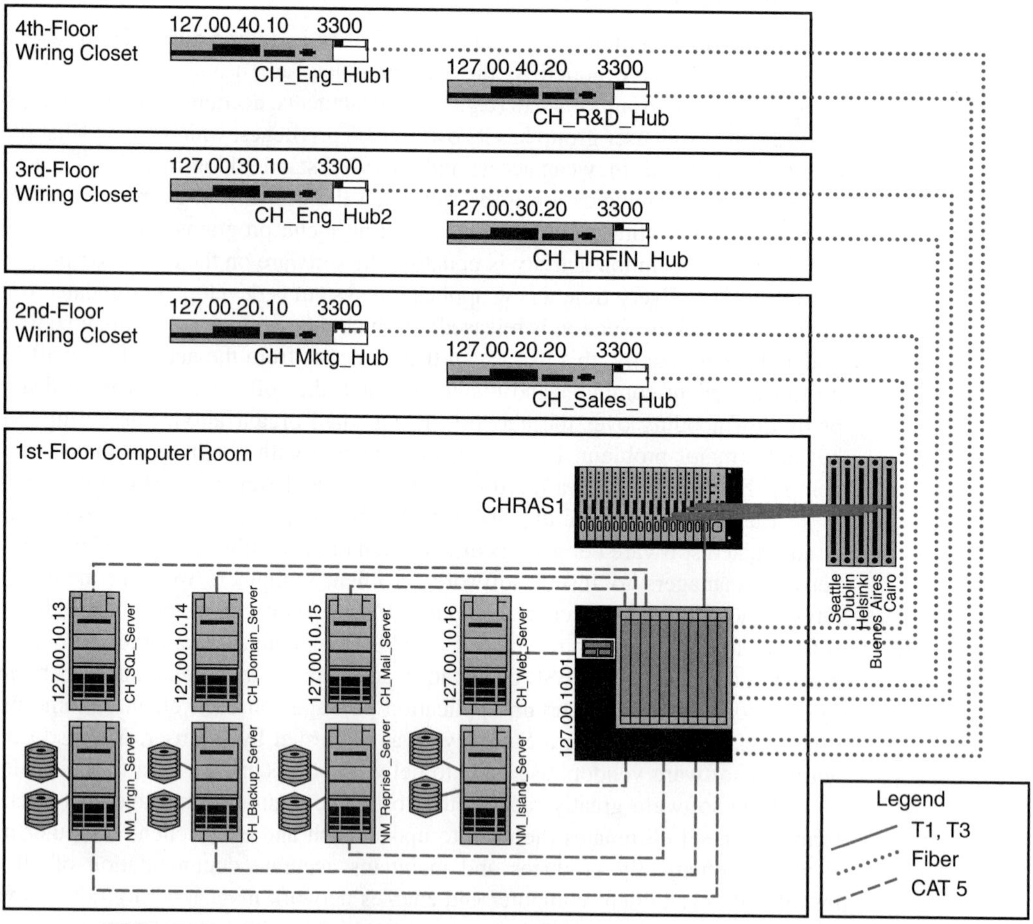

FIGURE 13.1 Network configuration diagram
Source: netViz

device, serial number, vendor, date of purchase, warranty information, repair history, telephone number for repairs, and any additional information or comments the network manager wishes to add. For example, it would be useful to include contact names and telephone numbers for the individual network managers responsible for each separate LAN within the network, and common carrier telephone contact information. (Whenever possible, establish a national account with the common carrier rather than dealing with individual common carriers in separate states and areas.)

A similar approach can be used for network software. This includes the network operating system and any special-purpose network software. For example, it is important to record which network operating system with which version or release date is installed on each network server. The same is true of application software. As discussed in Chapter 6 on LANs, sharing software on networks can greatly reduce costs although it is important to ensure that the organization is not violating any software license rules.

Software documentation can also help in negotiating site licenses for software. Many users buy software on a copy-by-copy basis, paying the retail price for each copy. It may be cheaper to negotiate the payment of one large fee for an unlimited use license for widely used software packages instead of paying on a per-copy basis.

The third type of documentation is the user and application profiles, which should be automatically provided by the network operating system or additional vendor or third-party software agreements. These should enable the network manager to easily identify the files and directories to which each user has access and each user's access rights (e.g., read-only, edit, delete). Equally important is the ability to access this information in the "opposite" direction; that is, to be able to select a file or directory and obtain a list of all authorized users and their access rights.

In addition, other documentation must be routinely developed and updated pertaining to the network. This includes network hardware and software manuals, application software manuals, standards manuals, operations manuals for network staff, vendor contracts and agreements, and licenses for software. The documentation should include details about performance and fault management (e.g., preventive maintenance guidelines and schedules, disaster recovery plan, and diagnostic techniques), end user support (e.g., applications software manuals, vendor support telephone numbers), and cost management (e.g., annual budgets, repair costs for each device). The documentation should also include any legal requirements to comply with local or federal laws, control, or regulatory bodies.

Maintaining documentation is usually a major issue for most organizations. Have you written programs? How well did you document them? Many technicians hate documentation because it is not "fun" and doesn't provide immediate value the same way that solving problems does. Therefore, it is often overlooked so when someone leaves the organization, the knowledge of the network leaves with them.

PERFORMANCE AND FAULT MANAGEMENT

Performance management means ensuring the network is operating as efficiently as possible whereas **fault management** means preventing, detecting, and correcting faults in the network circuits, hardware, and software (e.g., a broken device or improperly

A Day in the Life: Network Policy Manager

All large organizations have formal policies for the use of their networks (e.g., wireless LAN access, password, server space). Most large organizations have a special policy group devoted to the creation of network policies, many of which are devoted to network security. The job of the policy officer is to steer the policy through the policy making process and ensure that all policies are in the best interests of the organization as a whole. Although policies are focused inside the organization, policies are influenced by events both inside and outside the organization. The policy manager spends a significant amount of time working with outside organizations such as the U.S. Department of Homeland Security, CIO and security officer groups, and industry security consortiums. The goal is to make sure all policies (especially security policies) are up-to-date and provide a good balance between costs and benefits.

A typical policy begins with networking staff writing a summary containing the key points of the proposed policy. The policy manager takes the summary and uses it to develop a policy that fits the structure required for organizational policies (e.g., date, rationale, scope, responsible individuals, and procedures). This policy manager works with the originating staff to produce an initial draft of the proposed policy. Once everyone in the originating department and the policy office are satisfied with the policy, it is provided to an advisory committee of network users and network managers for discussion. Their suggestions are then incorporated in the policy or an explanation is provided is to why the suggestions will not be incorporated in the policy.

After several iterations, a policy becomes a draft policy and is posted for comment from all users within the organization. Comments are solicited from interested individuals and the policy may be revised. Once the draft is finalized, the policy is then presented to senior management for approval. Once approved, the policy is formally published, and the organization charged with implementing the policy begins to use it to guide their operations.

With thanks to Mark Bruhn

installed software). Fault management and performance management are closely related because any faults in the network reduce performance. Both require **network monitoring,** which means keeping track of the operation of network circuits and devices to ensure they are functioning properly and to determine how heavily they are used.

Network Monitoring

Most large organizations and many smaller ones use *network management software* to **monitor** and control their networks. One function provided by these systems is to collect operational statistics from the network devices. For small networks, network monitoring is often done by one person, aided by a few simple tools (discussed later in this chapter). These tools collect information and send messages to the network manager's computer.

In large networks, network monitoring becomes more important. Large networks that support organizations operating 24 hours a day are often mission critical, which means a network problem can have serious business consequences. For example, consider the impact of a network failure for a common carrier such as AT&T or for the air traffic control system. These networks often have a dedicated **network operations center (NOC)** that is responsible for monitoring and fixing problems. Such centers are staffed by a set of skilled network technicians that use sophisticated network management software. When a problem occurs, the software immediately detects the problems and sends an

MANAGEMENT FOCUS 13.4 NETWORK MANAGEMENT SALARIES

Network management is not easy, but it doesn't pay too badly. Here are some typical jobs and their respective salaries.

Network Vice President	$150,000
Network Manager	90,000
Telecom Manager	77,000
LAN Administrator	70,000
WAN Administrator	75,000
Network Designer	80,000
Network Technician	60,000
Technical Support Staff	50,000
Trainer	50,000

alarm to the NOC. Staff members in the NOC diagnose the problem and can sometimes fix it from the NOC (e.g., restarting a failed device). Other times, when a device or circuit fails, they must change routing tables to route traffic away from the device and inform the common carrier or dispatch a technician to fix or replace it.

Figure 13.2 shows the NOC at Indiana University. The NOC is staffed 24 hours a day, 7 days a week to monitor the networks at Indiana University. The NOC also has responsibility for managing portions of several very high-speed networks including the Abilene Network of Internet2 (see Management Focus Box 13.5).

The parameters monitored by a network management system fall into two distinct categories: physical network statistics and logical network information. Gathering statistics on the **physical network parameters** includes monitoring the operation of the network's modems, multiplexers, circuits linking the various hardware devices, and any other network devices. Monitoring the physical network consists of keeping track of circuits that may be down and tracing malfunctioning devices. **Logical network parameters** include performance measurement systems that keep track of user response times, the volume of traffic on a specific circuit, the destination of data routed across various networks, and any other indicators showing the level of service provided by the network.

Some types of management software operate passively, collecting the information and reporting it back to the central NOC. Others are active, in that they routinely send test messages to the servers or application being monitored (e.g., an HTTP Web page request) and record the response times. One common type of monitoring approach is the **network weather map,** which displays the usage of all major circuits in the network in real time.[1]

[1]One example of network weather maps for the Internet that provides a simple overview is www.InternetTrafficReport.com.

FIGURE 13.2 The Global Research Network Operations Center at Indiana University
Source: John Herrin, Indiana University Information Technology Services

Performance tracking is important because it enables the network manager to be proactive and respond to performance problems before users begin to complain. Poor network reporting leads to an organization that is overburdened with current problems and lacks time to address future needs. Management requires adequate reports if it is to address future needs.

Failure Control Function

Failure control requires developing a central control philosophy for problem reporting, whether the problems are first identified by the NOC or by users calling in to the NOC or a help desk. Whether problem reporting is done by the NOC or the **help desk,** the organization should maintain a central telephone number for network users to call when any problem occurs in the network. As a central troubleshooting function, only this group or its designee should have the authority to call hardware or software vendors or common carriers.

Many years ago, before the importance (and cost) of network management was widely recognized, most networks ignored the importance of fault management. Network devices were "dumb" in that they did only what they were designed to do (e.g., routing packets) but did not provide any network management information.

For example, suppose a network interface card fails and begins to transmit garbage messages randomly. Network performance immediately begins to deteriorate because these random messages destroy the messages transmitted by other computers, which need to be retransmitted. Users notice a delay in response time and complain to the network

MANAGEMENT FOCUS 13.5 INTERNET2 WEATHER MAP

The Abilene network is an Internet2 high-performance backbone that connects regional gigapops to provide high-speed network services to over 220 Internet2 university, corporate, and affiliate member institutions in all 50 states, the District of Columbia, and Puerto Rico. The current network is primarily an OC-192c (10 Gbps) backbone employing optical transport technology and advanced high-performance routers.

The network is monitored 24 hours a day, seven days a week from the network operations center (NOC) located on the campus of Indiana University in Indianapolis. The NOC oversees problem, configuration, and change management; network security; performance and policy monitoring; reporting; quality assurance; scheduling; and documentation. The NOC provides a structured environment that effectively coordinates operational activities with all participants and vendors related to the function of the network.

The NOC uses multiple network management software running across several platforms. Figure 13.3 shows one of the tools used by the NOC that is available to the general public: the Internet2 Weather Map. Each of the major circuits connecting the major Abilene gigapops is shown on the map. Each link has two parts, showing the utilization of the circuits to and from each pair of gigapops. The links are color-coded to quickly show the utilization of the link. Figure 13.3 is not in color so it is difficult to read, but if you visit the Abilene Web site (the URL is listed below), you can see that circuits with very low utilization are different shades of blue, which turn to green and then yellow and orange as utilization increases to 10 percent of capacity. Once utilization climbs above 30 percent, the link is shown in deeper shades of red and then purple. If you look back at the photo in Figure 13.2 you'll see the weather map displayed on the large screen in the NOC.

The link from the Chicago gigapop to the New York City gigapop, for example, indicates that over the last few minutes, an average of 546 Mbps has been transmitted, giving a 10 percent utilization. The link from New York City to Chicago shows that over the last few minutes, an average of 6.2 Gbps has been transmitted, giving a 70 percent utilization.

If you look carefully at the utilization rates and percentages, you will see that not all circuits in the Abilene network were 10 Gbps when this weather map was done. All circuits will shortly be upgraded.

SOURCE: abilene.internet2.edu.

support group, which begins to search for the cause. Even if the network support group suspects a failing network card (which is unlikely unless such an event has occurred before), locating the faulty card is very difficult and time consuming.

Most network managers today are installing *managed devices* that perform their functions (e.g., routing, switching) and also record data on the messages they process (see Chapter 12). These data can be sent to the network manager's computer when the device receives a special control message requesting the data, or it can send an *alarm* message to the network manager's computer if the device detects a critical situation. In this way, network faults and performance problems can be detected and reported by the devices themselves before they become serious. In the case of the failing network card, a managed device could record the increased number of retransmissions required to successfully transmit messages and inform the network management software of the problem. A managed hub or switch might even be able to detect the faulty transmissions from the failing network card, disable the incoming circuit so that the card could not

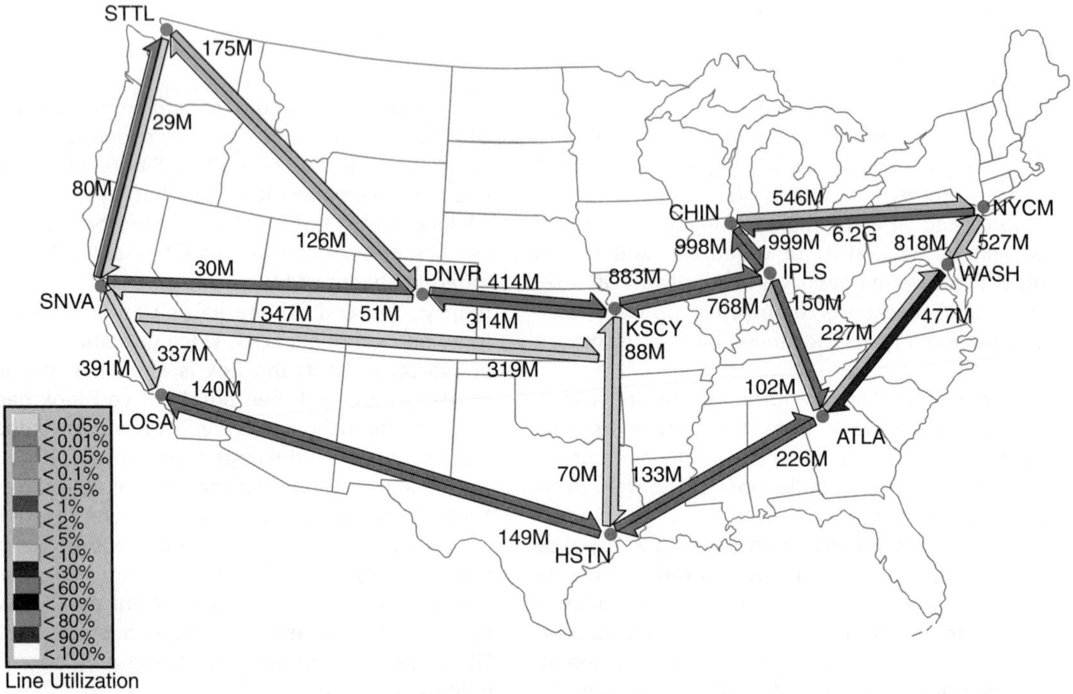

FIGURE 13.3 Internet2 Weather Map

send any more messages, and issue an alarm to the network manager. In either case, finding and fixing the fault is much simpler, requiring minutes, not hours.

Numerous software packages are available for recording fault information. The reports they produce are known as **trouble tickets.** The software packages assist the help desk personnel so they can type the trouble report immediately into a computerized failure analysis program. They also automatically produce various statistical reports to track how many failures have occurred for each piece of hardware, circuit, or software package. Automated trouble tickets are better than paper because they allow management personnel to gather problem and vendor statistics. There are four main reasons for trouble tickets: problem tracking, problem statistics, problem-solving methodology, and management reports.

Problem tracking allows the network manager to determine who is responsible for correcting any outstanding problems. This is important because some problems often are forgotten in the rush of a very hectic day. In addition, anyone might request information on the status of a problem. The network manager can determine whether the problem-solving mechanism is meeting predetermined schedules. Finally, the manager can be assured that all problems are being addressed. Problem tracking also can assist in problem resolution. Are problems being resolved in a timely manner? Are overdue problems being flagged? Are all resources and information available for problem solving?

Problem statistics are important because they are a control device for the network managers as well as for vendors. With this information, a manager can see how well the network is meeting the needs of end users. These statistics also can be used to determine

TECHNICAL FOCUS 13.1 TECHNICAL REPORTS

Technical reports that are helpful to network managers are those that provide summary information, as well as details that enable the managers to improve the network. Technical details include:

- Circuit use
- Usage rate of critical hardware such as host computers, front-end processors, and servers
- File activity rates for database systems
- Usage by various categories of client computers
- Response time analysis per circuit or per computer
- Voice versus data usage per circuit
- Queue-length descriptions, whether in the host computer, in the front-end processor, or at remote sites
- Distribution of traffic by time of day, location, and type of application software
- Failure rates for circuits, hardware, and software
- Details of any network faults

whether vendors are meeting their contractual maintenance commitments. Finally, they help to determine whether problem-solving objectives are being met.

Problem prioritizing helps ensure that critical problems get priority over less important ones. For example, a network support staff member should not work on a problem on one client computer if an entire circuit with dozens of computers is waiting for help. Moreover, a manager must know whether problem-resolution objectives are being met. For example, how long is it taking to resolve critical problems?

Management reports are required to determine network availability, product and vendor reliability (mean time between failures), and vendor responsiveness. Without them, a manager has nothing more than a "best guess" estimate for the effectiveness of either the network's technicians or the vendor's technicians. Regardless of whether this information is typed immediately into an automated trouble ticket package or recorded manually in a bound notebook-style trouble log, the objectives are the same.

The purposes of the trouble log are to record problems that must be corrected and to keep track of statistics associated with these problems. For example, the log might reveal that there were 37 calls for software problems (3 for one package, 4 for another package, and 30 for a third software package), 26 calls for cable modem problems evenly distributed among two vendors, 49 calls for client computers, and 2 calls to the common carrier that provides the network circuits. These data are valuable when the design and analysis group begins redesigning the network to meet future requirements.

Performance and Failure Statistics

There are many different types of failure and recovery statistics that can be collected. The most obvious performance statistics are those discussed above: how many packets are being moved on what circuits and what the response time is. Failure statistics also tell an important story.

One important failure statistic is **availability,** the percentage of time the network is available to users. It is calculated as the number of hours per month the network

TECHNICAL FOCUS 13.2 ELEMENTS OF A TROUBLE REPORT

When a problem is reported, the trouble log staff members should record the following:

- Time and date of the report
- Name and telephone number of the person who reported the problem
- The time and date of the problem (and the time and date of the call)
- Location of the problem
- The nature of the problem
- When the problem was identified
- Why and how the problem happened

is available divided by the total number of hours per month (i.e., 24 hours per day $\times$ 30 days per month $=$ 720 hours). The **downtime** includes times when the network is unavailable because of faults and routine maintenance and network upgrades. Most network managers strive for 99 to 99.5 percent availability, with downtime scheduled after normal working hours.

The **mean time between failures (MTBF)** is the number of hours or days of continuous operation before a component fails. Obviously, devices with higher MTBF are more reliable.

When faults occur, and devices or circuits go down, the **mean time to repair (MTTR)** is the average number of minutes or hours until the failed device or circuit is operational again. The MTTR is composed of these separate elements:

$$MTTRepair = MTTDiagnose + MTTRespond + MTTFix$$

The **mean time to diagnose (MTTD)** is the average number of minutes until the root cause of the failure is correctly diagnosed. This is an indicator of the efficiency of problem management personnel in the NOC or help desk who receive the problem report.

The **mean time to respond (MTTR)** is the average number of minutes or hours until service personnel arrive at the problem location to begin work on the problem. This is a valuable statistic because it indicates how quickly vendors and internal groups respond to emergencies. Compilation of these figures over time can lead to a change of vendors or internal management policies or, at the minimum, can exert pressure on vendors who do not respond to problems promptly.

Finally, after the vendor or internal support group arrives on the premises, the last statistic is the **mean time to fix (MTTF).** This figure tells how quickly the staff is able to correct the problem after they arrive. A very long time to fix in comparison with the time of other vendors may indicate faulty equipment design, inadequately trained customer service technicians, or even the fact that inexperienced personnel are repeatedly sent to fix problems.

For example, suppose your Internet connection at home stops working. You call your ISP, and they fix it over the phone in 15 minutes. In this case, the MTTRepair is 15 minutes, and it is hard to separate the different parts (MTTD, MTTR, and MTTF). Suppose you call your ISP and spend 60 minutes on the phone with them, and they can't

TECHNICAL FOCUS 13.3 MANAGEMENT REPORTS

Management-oriented reports that are helpful to network managers and their supervisors provide summary information for overall evaluation and for network planning and design. Details include:

- Graphs of daily/weekly/monthly usage, number of errors, or whatever is appropriate to the network
- Network availability (**uptime**) for yesterday, the last 5 days, the last month, or any other specific period
- Percentage of hours per week the network is unavailable because of network maintenance and repair
- Fault diagnosis
- Whether most response times are less than or equal to 3 seconds for online real-time traffic
- Whether management reports are timely and contain the most up-to-date statistics
- Peak volume statistics as well as average volume statistics per circuit
- Comparison of activity between today and a similar previous period

fix it over the phone; instead, the technician arrives the next day (18 hours later) and spends one hour fixing the problem. In this case MTTR = 1 hour + 18 hours + 1 hour = 20 hours.

The MTBF can be influenced by the original selection of vendor-supplied equipment. The MTTD relates directly to the ability of network personnel to isolate and diagnose failures and can often be improved by training. The MTTR (respond) can be influenced by showing vendors or internal groups how good or bad their response times have been in the past. The MTTF can be affected by the technical expertise of internal or vendor staff and the availability of spare parts onsite.

Another set of statistics that should be gathered are those collected daily by the network operations group, which uses network management software. These statistics record the normal operation of the network, such as the number of errors (retransmissions) per communication circuit. Statistics also should be collected on the daily volume of transmissions (characters per hour) for each communication circuit, each computer, or whatever is appropriate for the network. It is important to closely monitor usage rates, the percentage of the theoretical capacity that is being used. These data can identify computers/devices or communication circuits that have higher-than-average error or usage rates, and they may be used for predicting future growth patterns and failures. A device or circuit that is approaching maximum usage obviously needs to be upgraded.

Such predictions can be accomplished by establishing simple **quality control charts** similar to those used in manufacturing. Programs use an upper control limit and a lower control limit with regard to the number of blocks in error per day or per week. Notice how Figure 13.4 identifies when the common carrier moved a circuit from one microwave channel to another (circuit B), how a deteriorating circuit can be located and fixed before it goes through the upper control limit (circuit A) and causes problems for the users, or how a temporary high rate of errors (circuit C) can be encountered when installing new hardware and software.

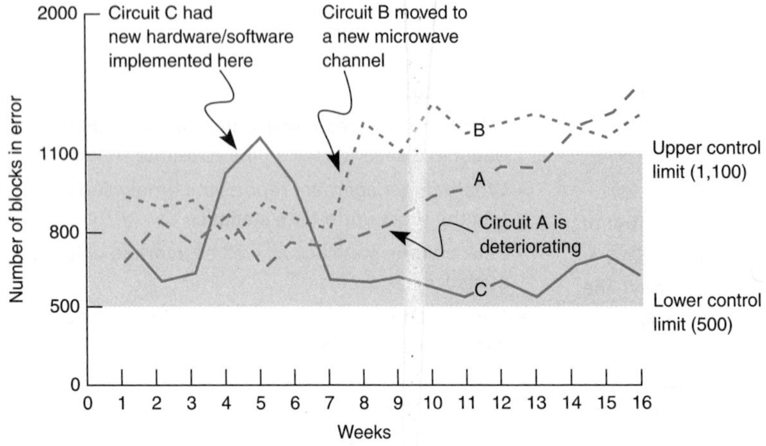

FIGURE 13.4 Quality control chart for circuits

Improving Performance

The chapters on LANs, BNs, MANs, and WANs discussed several specific actions that could be taken to improve network performance for each of those types of networks. There are also several general activities to improve performance that cut across the different types of networks.

Policy-Based Management A new approach to managing performance is policy-based management. With *policy-based management,* the network manager uses special software to set priority policies for network traffic that take effect when the network becomes busy. For example, the network manager might say that order processing and videoconferencing get the highest priority (order processing because it is the lifeblood of the company and videoconferencing because poor response time will have the greatest impact on it). The policy management software would then configure the network devices using the QoS capabilities in TCP/IP and/or ATM to give these applications the highest priority when the devices become busy.

Server Load Balancing *Load balancing,* as the name suggests, means to allocate incoming requests for network services (e.g., Web requests) across a set of equivalent servers so that the work is spread fairly evenly across all devices. With load balancing, a separate load-balancing server (sometimes called a virtual server), or a router or switch with special load-balancing software, allocates the requests among a set of identical servers using a simple round-robin formula (requests go to each server one after the other in turn) or more complex formulas that track how busy each server actually is. If a server crashes, the load balancer stops sending requests to it and the network continues to operate without the failed server.

Service-Level Agreements More organizations establish **service-level agreements (SLAs)** with their common carriers and Internet service providers. An SLA specifies the exact type of performance and fault conditions that the organization will accept. For

TECHNICAL FOCUS 13.4 INSIDE A SERVICE-LEVEL AGREEMENT

There are many elements to a solid service-level agreement (SLA) with a common carrier. Some of the important ones include

- Network availability, measured over a month as the percentage of time the network is available (e.g., [total hours – hours unavailable]/total hours) should be at least 99.5 percent
- Average round-trip permanent virtual circuit (PVC) delay, measured over a month as the number of seconds it takes a message to travel over the PVC from sender to receiver, should be less than 110 milliseconds, although some carriers will offer discounted services for SLA guarantees of 300 milliseconds or less
- PVC throughput, measured over a month as the number of outbound packets sent over a PVC divided by the inbound packets received at the destination (not counting packets over the committed information rate, which are discard eligible), should be above 99 percent—ideally, 99.99 percent
- Mean time to respond, measured as a monthly average of the time from inception of trouble ticket until repair personnel are on site, should be 4 hours or less
- Mean time to fix, measured as a monthly average of the time from the arrival of repair personnel on-site until the problem is repaired, should be 4 hours or less

SOURCE: "Carrier Service-Level Agreements," International Engineering Consortium Tutorial, www.iec.org, February 2001.

example, the SLA might state that network availability must be 99 percent or higher and that the MTBF for T1 circuits must be 120 days or more. In many cases, SLA includes maximum allowable response times. The SLA also states what compensation the service provider must provide if it fails to meet the SLA. Some organizations are also starting to use an SLA internally to define relationships between the networking group and its organizational "customers."

END USER SUPPORT

Providing **end user support** means solving whatever problems users encounter while using the network. There are three main functions within end user support: resolving network faults, resolving user problems, and training. We have already discussed how to resolve network faults, and now we focus on resolution of user problems and end user training.

Resolving Problems

Problems with user equipment (as distinct from network equipment) usually stem from three major sources. The first is a failed hardware device. These are usually the easiest to fix. A network technician simply fixes the device or installs a new part.

The second type of problem is a lack of user knowledge. These problems can usually be solved by discussing the situation with the user and taking that person through the process step by step. This is the next easiest type of problem to solve and can often be done by e-mail or over the telephone, although not all users are easy to work with. Problematic users are sometimes called ID ten-T errors, written ID10T.

The third type of problem is one with the software, software settings, or an incompatibility between the software and network software and hardware. In this case, there may be a bug in the software or the software may not function properly on a certain combination of hardware and software. Solving these problems may be difficult because they require expertise with the specific software package in use and sometimes require software upgrades from the vendor.

Resolving either type of software problem begins with a request for assistance from the help desk. Requests for assistance are usually handled in the same manner as network faults. A trouble log is maintained to document all incoming requests and the manner in which they are resolved. The staff member receiving the request attempts to resolve the problem in the best manner possible. Staff members should be provided with a set of standard procedures or scripts for soliciting information from the user about problems. In large organizations, this process may be supported by special software.

There are often several levels to the problem-resolution process. The first level is the most basic. All staff members working at the help desk should be able to resolve most of these. Most organizations strive to resolve between 75 and 85 percent of requests at this first level in less than an hour. If the request cannot be resolved, it is escalated to the second level of problem resolution. Escalation is a normal part of the process and not something that is "bad." Staff members who handle second-level support have specialized skills in certain problem areas or with certain types of software and hardware. In most cases, problems are resolved at this level. Some large organizations also have a third level of resolution in which specialists spend many hours developing and testing various solutions to the problem, often in conjunction with staff members from the vendors of network software and hardware.

Providing End User Training

End user training is an ongoing responsibility of the network manager. Training is a key part in the implementation of new networks or network components. It is also important to have an ongoing training program because employees may change job functions and new employees require training to use the organization's networks.

Training usually is conducted through in-class, one-on-one instruction, and online self-paced courses. In-class training should focus on the 20 percent of the network functions that the user will use 80 percent of the time instead of attempting to cover all network functions. By getting in-depth instruction on the fundamentals, users become confident about what they need to do. The training should also explain how to locate additional information from online support, documentation, or the help desk.

COST MANAGEMENT

One of the most challenging areas of network management over the past few years has been **cost management.** Data traffic has been growing much more rapidly than has the

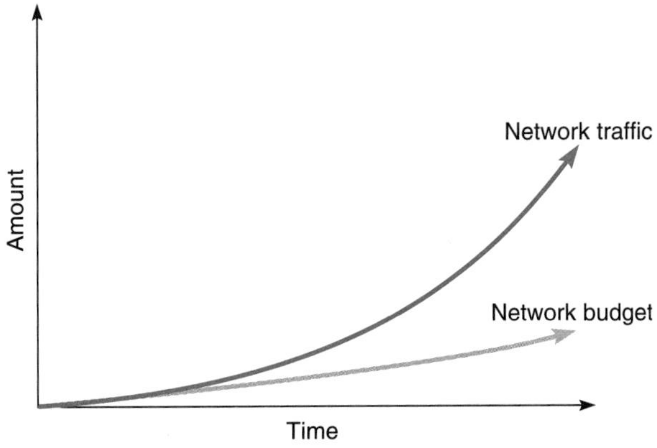

FIGURE 13.5 Network traffic versus network management budgets

network management budget, which has forced network managers to provide greater network capacity at an ever lower cost per megabyte (Figure 13.5). In this section, we examine the major sources of costs and discuss several ways to reduce them.

Sources of Costs

The cost of operating a network in a large organization can be very expensive. Figure 13.6 shows a recent cost analysis to operate the network for one year at Indiana University, a large Big Ten research university serving 36,000 students and 4,000 faculty and staff. This analysis includes the costs of operating the network infrastructure and standard applications such as e-mail and the Web, but does not include the costs of other applications such as course management software, registration, student services, accounting, and so on. Indiana University has a federal IT governance structure, which means that the different colleges and schools on campus also have budgets to hire staff and buy equipment for their faculty and staff. The budget in this figure omits these amounts, so the real costs are probably 50 percent higher than those shown. Nonetheless, this presents a snapshot of the costs of running a large network.

The largest area of costs in network operations is the $7.4 million spent on WAN circuits. Indiana University operates many high speed networks (including Internet2) so these costs are higher than might be expected. This figure also shows the large costs of e-mail, Web services, data storage, and security. The cost of end user support is the next largest cost item. This includes training as well as answering users' questions and fixing their problems. The remaining costs are purchasing new and replacement hardware and software. But, once again, remember that this does not include the hardware and software purchased by individual colleges and schools for their faculty and staff which does not come from the central IT budget.

The **total cost of ownership (TCO)** is a measure of how much it costs per year to keep one computer operating. TCO includes the actual direct cost of repair parts, software upgrades, and support staff members to maintain the network, install software, administer the network (e.g., create user IDs, back up user data), provide training and technical support, and upgrade hardware and software. It also includes the indirect cost

Network Operations		$14,871,000
Account Administration	275,000	
Authentication Services	257,000	
Directory Services Infrastructure (incl DHCP, DNS)	746,000	
E-mail and Messaging	1,434,000	
Mainframe and Cluster Operations	633,000	
Mass Data Storage	1,424,000	
Policy Management	75,000	
Printing	201,000	
Security Administration	1,270,000	
WAN Operations	7,410,000	
Web Services	1,146,000	
End User Support		$6,544,000
Departmental Technology Support	553,000	
Instructional Technology Support	856,000	
Student Residence Halls Support	279,000	
Student Technology Centers Support	1,288,000	
Support Center (Help Desk)	2,741,000	
Training and Education	827,000	
Client Hardware		$3,901,000
Classroom Technology Equipment and Supplies	844,000	
Student Residence Halls Equipment and Supplies	601,000	
Student Technology Centers Equipment and Supplies	2,456,000	
Application Software		$3,729,000
Software Site Licenses	2,540,000	
Student Residence Halls Software	146,000	
Student Technology Centers Software	1,043,000	
Total		$29,045,000

FIGURE 13.6 Annual networking costs at Indiana University

of time "wasted" by the user when problems occur, when the network is down, or when the user is attempting to learn new software.

Several studies over the past few years by Gartner Group, Inc, a leading industry research firm, suggest that the TCO of a computer is astoundingly high. Most studies suggest that the TCO for typical Windows computers on a network is about $7,000 *per computer per year.* In other words, it costs almost five times as much *each year* to operate a computer than it does to purchase it in the first place. Other studies by firms such as IBM and *Information Week,* an industry magazine, have produced TCO estimates of between $5,000 and $10,000 per year, suggesting that the Gartner Group's estimates are reasonable.

Although TCO has been accepted by many organizations, other firms argue against the practice of including indirect in the calculation. For example, using a technique that includes indirect, the TCO of a coffee machine is more than $50,000 per year—not counting the cost of the coffee or supplies. The assumption that getting coffee "wastes"

12 minutes per day times 5 days per week yields 1 hour per week, or about 50 hours per year, of wasted time. If you assume the coffeepot serves 20 employees who have an average cost of $50 per hour (not an unusually high number), you have a loss of $50,000 per year.

Some organizations, therefore, prefer to focus on costing methods that examine only the direct costs of operating the computers, omitting softer indirect costs such as “wasted” time. Such measures, often called **network cost of ownership (NCO)** or real TCO, have found that NCO ranges between $1,500 and $3,500 *per computer per year.* The typical network management group for a 100-user network would therefore have an annual budget of about $150,000 to $350,000. The most expensive item is personnel (network managers and technicians), which typically accounts for 50 to 70 percent of total costs. The second most expensive cost item is WAN circuits, followed by hardware upgrades and replacement parts.

Calculating TCO for univerisites can be difficult. Do we calculate TCO for the number of computers or the number of users. Figure 13.6 shows an annual cost of $29 million. If we use the number of users, the TCO is about $725 ($29 million divided by 40,000 users). If we use the number of computers, TCO is $4,800 ($29 million divided by about 6,000 computers owned by the university).

There is one very important message from this pattern of costs. Because the largest cost item is personnel time, the primary focus of cost management lies in designing networks and developing policies to reduce personnel time, not to reduce hardware cost. Over the long term, it makes more sense to buy more expensive equipment if it can reduce the cost of network management.

Figure 13.7 shows the average breakdown of personnel costs by function. The largest time cost (where staff members spend most of their time) is systems management, which includes configuration, fault, and performance management tasks that focus on the network as a whole. The second largest item is end user support.

Network managers often find it difficult to manage their budgets because networks grow so rapidly. They often find themselves having to defend ever-increasing requests

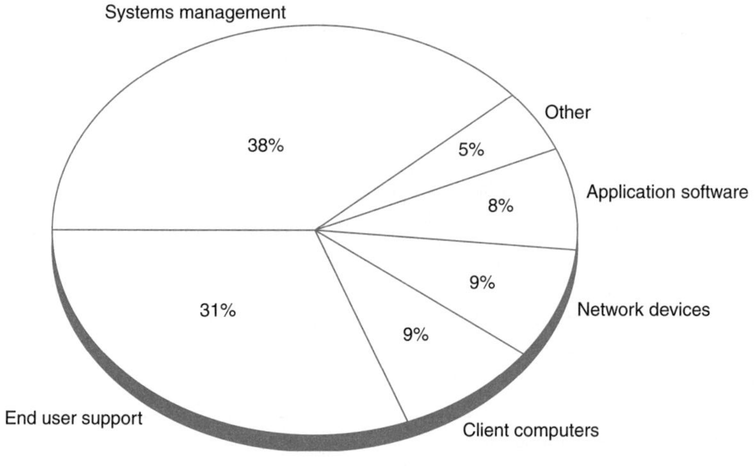

FIGURE 13.7 Network management personnel costs

for more equipment and staff. To counter these escalating costs, many large organizations have adopted **charge-back policies** for users of WANs and mainframe-based networks. (A charge-back policy attempts to allocate the costs associated with the network to specific users.) These users must "pay" for their network usage by transferring part of their budget allocations to the network group. Such policies are seldom used in LANs, making one more potential cultural difference between network management styles.

Reducing Costs

Given the huge amounts in TCO or even the substantial amounts spent in NCO, there is considerable pressure on network managers to reduce costs. Figure 13.8 summarizes five steps to reduce network costs.

The first and most important step is to develop standards for client computers, servers, and network devices (i.e., switches, routers). These standards define one configuration (or a small set of configurations) that are permitted for all computers and devices. Standardizing hardware and software makes it easier to diagnose and fix problems. Also, there are fewer software packages for the network support staff members to learn. The downside, of course, is that rigid adherence to standards reduces innovation.

The second most important step is automate as much of the network management process as possible. ESD can significantly reduce the cost to upgrade when new software is released. It also enables faster installation of new computers and faster recovery when software needs to be reinstalled and helps enforce the standards policies. Dynamic address assignment (e.g., DHCP; see Chapter 5) can reduce time spent on managing TCP/IP addresses. The use of network management software to identify and diagnose problems can significantly reduce time spent in performance and fault management. Likewise, help desk software can cut the cost of the end support function.

A third step is to do everything possible to reduce the time spent installing new hardware and software. The cost of a network technician's spending half a day to install and configure new computers is often $300 to $500. ESD is an important step to reducing costs, but careful purchasing can also go a long way. The installation of standard hardware and software (e.g., Microsoft Office) by the hardware vendor can significantly reduce costs. Likewise, careful monitoring of hardware failures can quickly identify vendors of less reliable equipment who should be avoided in the next purchasing cycle.

Traditionally, help desks have been decentralized into user departments. The result is a proliferation of help desks and support staff members, many of whom tend to

Five Steps to Reduce Network Costs

- Develop standard hardware and software configurations for client computers and servers.
- Automate as much of the network management function as possible by deploying a solid set of network management tools.
- Reduce the costs of installing new hardware and software by working with vendors.
- Centralize help desks.
- Move to thin-client architectures.

FIGURE 13.8 Reducing network costs

MANAGEMENT FOCUS 13.6 TOTAL COST OF OWNERSHIP IN MINNESOTA

Total Cost of Ownership (TCO) has come to the classroom. As part of a national TCO initiative, several school districts, including one in Minnesota, recently conducted a TCO analysis. The school district was a system of eight schools (one high school, one middle school, and six elementary schools) serving 4,100 students in kindergarten through grade 12. All schools are connected via a frame relay WAN to the district head office.

Costs were assessed in two major groups: direct costs and indirect costs. The direct costs included the costs of hardware (replacement client computers, servers, networks, and printers and supplies), software, internal network staff, and external consultants. The indirect costs included staff training and development. "Wasted time" was not included in the TCO analysis.

The district examined its most recent annual budget and allocated its spending into these categories. The district calculated that it spent about $1.2 million per year to support its 1,200 client computers, providing a TCO of about $1,004 per client computer per year. Figure 13.9 provides a summary of the costs by category.

A TCO of $1,004 is below average, indicating a well-managed network. The district had implemented several network management best practices, such as using a standardized set of software, using new standardized hardware, and providing professional development to teachers to reduce support costs. One other major contributing factor was the extremely low salaries paid to the IT technical staff (less than $25,000 per year) because of the district's rural location. Had the district been located in a more urban area, IT staff costs would double, bringing TCO closer to the lower end of the national average.

SOURCE: "Minnesota District Case Study," Taking TCO to the Classroom, k12tco.gartner.com, 2004.

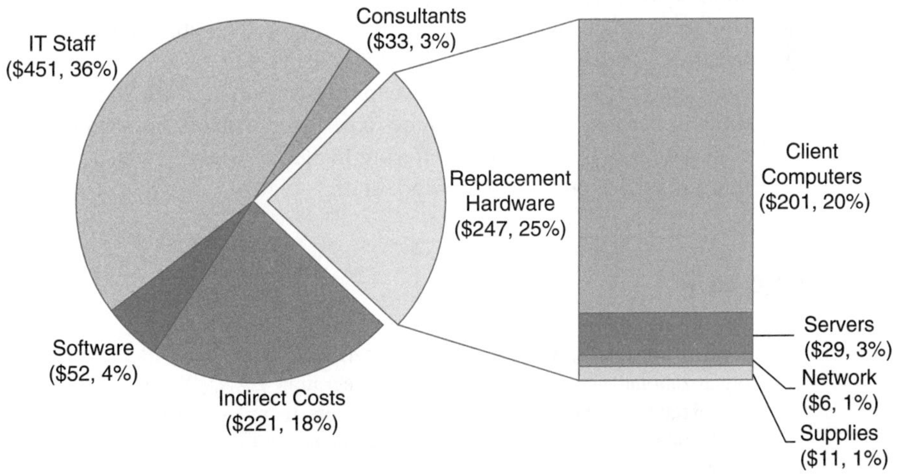

FIGURE 13.9 Total Cost of Ownership (per client computer per year) for a Minnesota school district

be generalists rather than specialists in one area. Many organizations have found that centralizing help desks enables them to reduce the number of generalists and provide more specialists in key technology areas. This results in faster resolution of difficult problems. Centralization also makes it easier to identify common problems occurring in different parts of the organization and take actions to reduce them.

Finally, many network experts argue that moving to thin-client architectures, just Web browsers on the client (see Chapter 2), can significantly reduce costs. Although this can reduce the cost to buy software, the real saving lies in the support costs. Because they are restricted to a narrow set of functions and generally do not need software installations, thin-client architectures become much easier to manage. TCO and NCO drop by 20 to 40 percent. Most organizations anticipate using thin-client architectures selectively, in areas where applications are well defined and can easily be restricted.

IMPLICATIONS FOR MANAGEMENT

Network management is one of the more challenging functions because it requires a good understanding of networking technologies, an ability to work with end users and management, and an understanding of the key elements driving networking costs. Normally no one notices it until something goes wrong.

As demand for network capacity increases, the costs associated with network management have typically increased in most organizations. Justifying these increased costs to senior management can be challenging because senior management often do not see greatly increasing amounts of network traffic—all they see are increasing costs. The ability to explain the business value of networks in terms understandable to senior management is an important skill.

As networks become larger and more complex, network management will increase in complexity. New technologies for managing networks will be developed, as vendors attempt to increase the intelligence of networks and their ability to "self-heal." These new technologies will provide significantly more reliable networks, but will also be more expensive and will require new skills on the part of network designers, network managers, and network technicians. Keeping a trained network staff will become increasingly difficult because once staff acquire experience with the new management tools, they will be lured away by other firms offering higher salaries ... which, we suppose, is not a bad thing if you're one of the network staff.

SUMMARY

Integrating LANs, WANs, and the Internet Today, the critical issue is the integration of all organizational networks. The keys to integrating LANs, WANs, and the Web into one overall organization network are for WAN managers to recognize that LAN/Web managers can make independent decisions and for LAN/Web managers to realize that they need to work within organizational standards.

Integrating Voice and Data Communications Another major challenge is combining voice communications with data and image communications. This separation of voice and data worked well for years, but changing communication technologies are generating enormous pressures to combine them. A key factor in voice/data integration might turn out to be the elimination of one key management position and the merging of two staffs into one.

Configuration Management Configuration management means managing the network's hardware and software configuration, documenting it, and ensuring the documentation is updated as the configuration changes. The most common configuration management activity is adding and deleting user accounts. The most basic documentation about network hardware is a set of network configuration diagrams, supplemented by documentation on each individual network component. A similar approach can be used for network software. ESD plays a key role in simplifying configuration management by automating and documenting the network configurations. User and application profiles should be automatically provided by the network and ESD software. There are a variety of other documentation that must be routinely developed and updated, including users' manuals and organizational policies.

Performance and Fault Management Performance management means ensuring the network is operating as efficiently as possible. Fault management means preventing, detecting, and correcting any faults in the network circuits, hardware, and software. The two are closely related because any faults in the network reduce performance and because both require network monitoring. Today, most networks use a combination of smart devices to monitor the network and issue alarms and a help desk to respond to user problems. Problem tracking allows the network manager to determine problem ownership or who is responsible for correcting any outstanding problems. Problem statistics are important because they are a control device for the network operators as well as for vendors.

Providing End User Support Providing end user support means solving whatever network problems users encounter. Support consists of resolving network faults, resolving software problems, and training. Software problems often stem from lack of user knowledge, fundamental problems with the software, or an incompatibility between the software and the network's software and hardware. There are often several levels to problem resolution. End user training is an ongoing responsibility of the network manager. Training usually has two parts: in-class instruction and the documentation and training manuals that the user keeps for reference.

Cost Management As the demand for network services grows, so does its cost. The TCO for typical networked computers is about $10,000 per year per computer, far more than the initial purchase price. The network management cost (omitting "wasted" time) is between $1,500 and $3,500 per year per computer. The largest single cost item is staff salaries. The best way to control rapidly increasing network costs is to reduce the amount of time taken to perform management functions, often by automating as many routine ones as possible.

KEY TERMS

availability
charge-back policy
configuration management
cost management
desktop management
downtime
electronic software distribution (ESD)
end user support
fault management
firefighting
help desk
logical network parameters
mean time between failures (MTBF)
mean time to diagnose (MTTD)
mean time to fix (MTTF)
mean time to repair (MTTR)
mean time to respond (MTTR)
monitor
network cost of ownership (NCO)
network documentation
network management
network monitoring
network operations center (NOC)
network weather map
performance management
physical network parameters
problem statistics
problem tracking
quality control chart
service-level agreement (SLA)
total cost of ownership (TCO)
trouble ticket
uptime

QUESTIONS

1. What are some differences between LAN and WAN management?
2. What is firefighting?
3. Why is combining voice and data a major organizational challenge?
4. Describe what configuration management encompasses.
5. People tend to think of software when documentation is mentioned. What is documentation in a network situation?
6. What is electronic software delivery and why is it important?
7. What is performance and fault management?
8. What does a help desk do?
9. What do trouble tickets report?
10. Several important statistics related to network uptime and downtime are discussed in this chapter. What are they and why are they important?
11. What is an SLA?
12. How is network availability calculated?
13. What is problem escalation?
14. What are the primary functions of end user support?
15. What is TCO?
16. Why is the TCO so high?
17. How can network costs be reduced?
18. What do network management software systems do and why are they important?
19. How does network cost of ownership differ from total cost of ownership? Which is the most useful measure of network costs from the point of view of the network manager? Why?
20. Many organizations do not have a formal trouble reporting system. Why do you think this is the case?
21. Early in the chapter, there is a box entitled Key Network Management Skills. Compare and contrast the skills labeled "very important" with those labeled "moderately important" and "less important." What patterns do you notice? Why do you think there are such patterns?

EXERCISES

13-1. What factors might cause peak loads in a network? How can a network manager determine if they are important and how are they taken into account when designing a data communications network?

13-2. Today's network managers face a number of demanding problems. Investigate and discuss three major issues.

13-3. Research the networking budget in your organization and discuss the major cost areas. Discuss several ways of reducing costs over the long term.

13-4. Explore the Internet2 weather map at abilene .internet2.edu.

13-5. Do the puzzle on the next page.

Across

5. A measure of cost effectiveness that includes direct and indirect costs
9. The first step in network design is to examine user ______
11. A device that sends requests to different servers in a cluster
15. A measure of cost effectiveness that focuses only on direct costs
16. This form of encryption has two keys
17. One of the most common security threats
18. This fixes a security hole
19. A device that prevents power loss
21. The document asking vendors to bid on a proposal
24. A non-technical way to get someone's password
25. Storing your content on other people's servers

Down

1. The average time it takes to fix a broken device
2. Documenting the network is part of ______ management
3. A system to prevent intrusion
4. A contract with a common carrier always has this
6. A strong encryption standard
7. This device limits the amount of network capacity available to a user
8. Denial of service
10. Storing other people's Web content on your network
12. Obsolete encryption standard
13. The highest level of security is to check something you ____
14. Staff working in this organization monitor the network
18. Using e-mail to trick users into revealing their password
20. This form of encryption has one key
22. The largest single part of a networking budget is the cost of _____
23. A network management standard

MINI-CASES

I. City School District, Part 1

City School District is a large, urban school district that operates 27 schools serving 22,000 students from kindergarten through grade 12. All schools are networked into a regional WAN that connects the schools to the district central office and each other. The district has a total of 5,300 client computers. The table below shows the annual costs. Calculate the real TCO (without wasted time).

Budget Item	Annual Cost
IT Staff Salaries	$7,038,400
Consultants	1,340,900
Software	657,200
Staff training	545,900
Client computers	2,236,600
Servers	355,100
Network	63,600
Supplies and parts	2,114,700

II. City School District, Part 2

Read and complete Mini-case I above. Examine the TCO by category. Do you think that this TCO indicates a well-run network? What suggestions would you have?

III. Central Textiles

Central Textiles is a clothing manufacturer that operates 16 plants throughout the southern United States and in Latin America. The Information Systems Department, which reports to the vice president of Finance, operates the central mainframe and LAN at the headquarters building in Spartanburg, South Carolina, and the WAN that connects all the plants. The LANs in each plant are managed by a separate IT group at each plant that reports to the plant manager (the plant managers report to the vice president of Manufacturing). The telephone communications system and long-distance agreements are managed by a telecommunications department in the headquarters that reports to the vice president of Finance. The CEO of Central Textiles has come to you asking about whether this is the best arrangement, or whether it would make more sense to integrate the three functions under one new department. Outline the pros and cons of both alternatives.

IV. Internet2

Reread Management Focus 13.5. If the weather map shown in Figure 13.3 is a typical traffic pattern for Internet2, how would you suggest that they improve performance?

CASE STUDY

NEXT-DAY AIR SERVICE

See the Web site.

HANDS-ON ACTIVITY

Network Monitoring

One of the key tasks of network management is monitoring the network to make sure everything is running well. There are many effective network monitoring tools available and several have demonstrations you can view on the Web. One of my favorites is solarwinds.net. They have a live demonstration of their network management software available at npm.solarwinds.net.

Once you arrive at their page you can select which part of their network to examine. Figure 13.10 shows the U.S. portion of the network. It shows a map of the network with circuits and locations color coded to show their status (green for good, yellow for some problems, and red for major problems), although the colors are hard to see in the figure. You can click on a circuit, a city, or a link on the bottom of the page to obtain more information about that part of the network.

The Tulsa Office shows green on the map, with a small red box next to it in the more detailed listing below the map. This indicates that the network is operating well, but that there is minor trouble with some part of the network that is not having a major impact.

Figure 13.11 shows what happened when I clicked on the Tulsa Office. We now see the details of the network in Tulsa. It has a set of switches and routers, all of which are green, except the Amsterdam Lab Router (GWC198) which is shown in bright red (although it's hard to see the real colors from this figure). The table below the network map also says that the router is down, again in bright red letters, in addition to a red bullet in front of the line.

You can click on any device in the picture or in the table to obtain more information about it. Figure 13.12 shows the status of the Gateway Router which connects the Tulsa Office to the 12vBNS network at the top of the display. At first glance, you can see the four "dashboard gauges" that show that response time is good at below 150 milliseconds, that there is no noticeable packet loss, that the CPU load is good at less than 30 percent, and that memory usage is hitting the high level at almost 75 percent. Memory usage is not yet a problem, but it's probably time to plan for a memory upgrade before the device begins to have problems from running out of memory.

The two graphs in this figure show data over the past 12 hours for comparison. The first graph shows a few spikes in response time in the morning (a Monday morning) as people returning from the weekend begin reading e-mail, but nothing that would be a problem. Likewise, between 2 A.M. and 5 A.M., something happened to cause some packet loss but it was not substantial (major thunderstorms swept through Tulsa overnight, so they may have been to blame). The second graph shows that the CPU load was fairly constant over the last 12 hours, always below 30 percent.

The rest of the display shows additional information about the device, such as what it is (a Cisco 1601 router), what version of the operating system it is running (12.0(8)), its IP address (65.113.77.57), and when it was last booted (2:33 A.M., March 2, 2006).

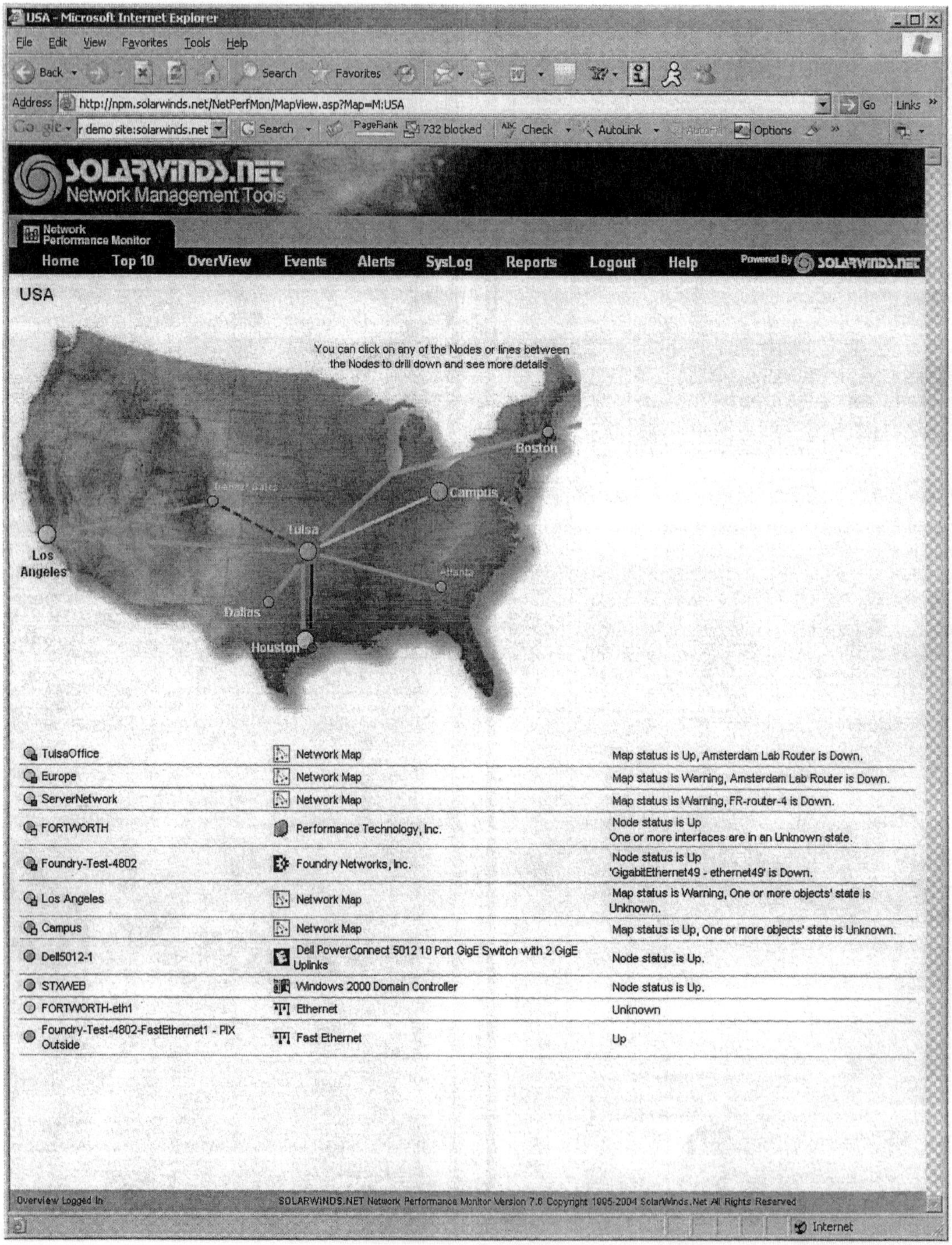

FIGURE 13.10 Solarwinds.net network monitoring software

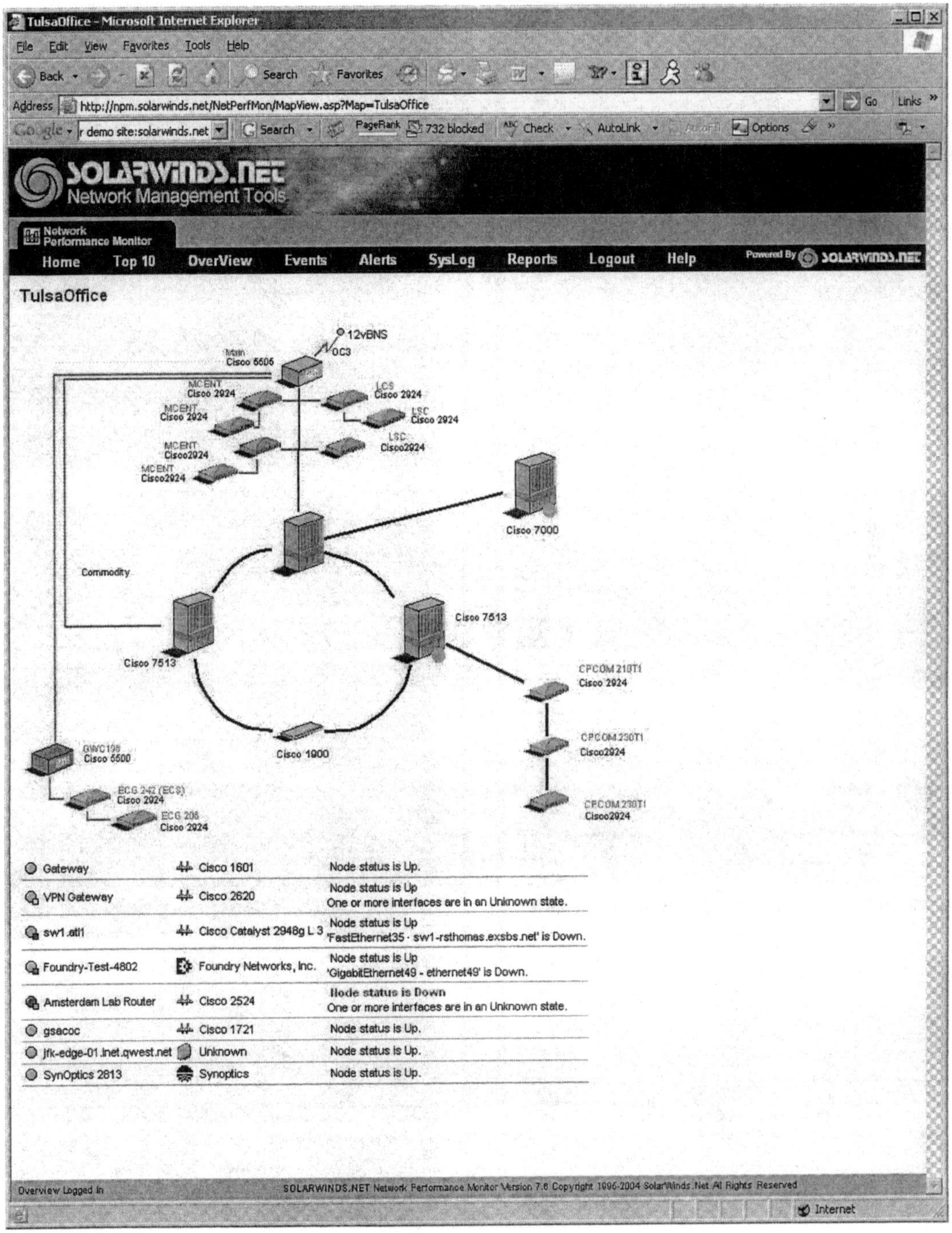

FIGURE 13.11 Status of the Tulsa office

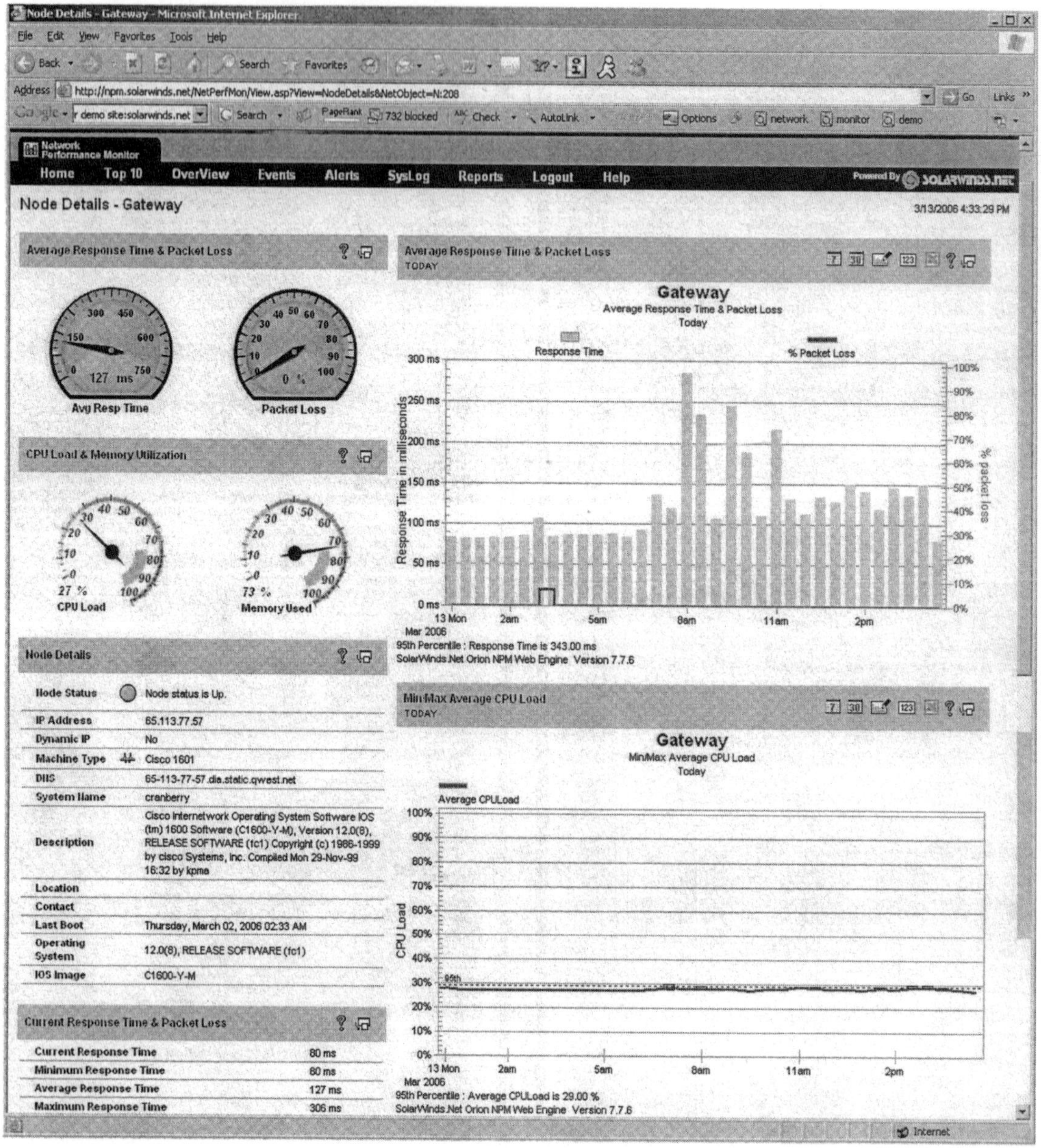

FIGURE 13.12 Information about the Gateway router

PART FIVE

APPENDICES

APPENDIX A
CONNECTOR CABLES

When a message leaves the microcomputer or terminal and begins to move onto the network, the first component it encounters is the *connector cable* between the microcomputer (or terminal) and the circuit. When people discuss connector cables, the focus is on the standards (such as RS232 or RS449).

RS232 (DB-25)/RS449 (DB-9)

When people talk about connector cables, they frequently refer to them as a *RS232, DB-25, RS449,* or *DB-9.* This is because each connector cable is based on a specified standard. Calling the connector by its standard designation allows everyone to know precisely which connector is being discussed.

The RS232 standard is the most frequently mentioned. It was first issued in 1962, and its third revision, RS232C, was issued in 1969. The RS232D standard was issued in 1987 to expand on RS232C. The RS232D standard is also known as the EIA-232-D.

The RS232 connector cable is the standard interface for connecting *data terminal equipment (DTE)* to *data circuit terminating equipment (DCE).* The newer RS232D is specified as having 25 wires and using the DB-25 connector plug like the one used on microcomputers. If this connector cable is attached to a microcomputer, people may refer to it simply as DB-25; if it is not attached to a microcomputer, they may refer to it as the RS232 interface.

DTE comprises the data source, the data sink, or both. In reality, it is any piece of equipment at which a data communications path begins or ends, such as a terminal. DCE provides all the functions required to establish, maintain, and terminate a connection. This includes signal conversion and coding between the DTE and the common carrier's circuit, including the modem. A modem is DCE.

Figure A.1 shows a picture of the RS232D interface plug and describes each of its 25 protruding pins. It is the standard connector cable (25 wires/pins) that passes control signals and data between the terminal (DTE) and the modem (DCE). This standard has been supplied by the Electronic Industries Association (EIA). Outside the United States, this RS232D connector cable is known as the V.24 and V.28. The V.24 and V.28 standards have been accepted by the international standards group known as the ITU-T. These standards provide a common description of what the signal coming out of and going into the serial port of a computer or terminal looks like electrically. Specifically, RS232 provides for a signal changing from a nominal +12 volts to a nominal–12 volts. The standard also defines the cables and connectors used to link data communications devices. This is the cable that connects an external modem to your microcomputer.

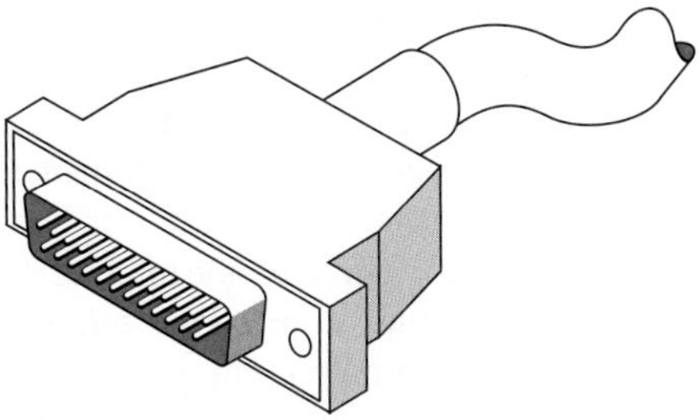

Pin	Circuit Name
1	Shield
2	Transmitted data
3	Received data
4	Request to send
5	Clear to send
6	DCE ready
7	Signal ground
8	Received line signal detector
9	(Reserved for testing)
10	(Reserved for testing)
11	(Unassigned)
12	Secondary received line signal detector/data signal rate select (DCE source)
13	Secondary clear to send
14	Secondary transmitted data
15	Transmitter signal element timing (DCE source)
16	Secondary received data
17	Receiver signal element timing (DCE source)
18	Local loopback
19	Secondary request to send
20	DTE ready
21	Remote loopbacks/signal quality detector
22	Ring indicator
23	Data signal rate select (DTE/DCE source)
24	Transmitter signal element timing (DTE source)
25	Text mode

FIGURE A.1 RS232 cable specifications. DCE = data circuit terminating equipment; DTE = data terminal equipment

The RS232 has a maximum 50-foot cable length, but it can be increased to 100 feet or more by means of a special low-capacitance, extended-distance cable. This is not advised, however, because some vendors may not honor maintenance agreements if the cable is lengthened beyond the 50-foot standard.

In illustration, we present the cable distances for Texas Instruments' products. The cable length of the RS232 varies according to the speed at which you transmit. For Texas

Instruments, the connector cable length can be up to 914 meters (1 meter = 1.1 yards) when transmitting at 1,200 bps, 549 meters when transmitting at 2,400 bps, 244 meters when transmitting at 4,800 bps, and 122 meters when transmitting at 9,600 bps. When end users operate equipment at maximum distances, it is important to remember that they must meet the restrictions on all types of equipment used, including the electrical environment, cable construction, and cable wiring. This means that when you want to operate at a maximum cable distance, you must contact the terminal and/or modem vendors to obtain their maximum cable distance before you proceed.

The RS449 standard has been adopted as U.S. Federal Standard 1031. The RS449 is shown in Figure A.2. A 4,000-foot cable length can be used, there are 37 pins instead of 25 (useful for digital transmission), and various other circuit functions have been added, such as diagnostic circuits and digital circuits. In addition, secondary channel circuits (reverse channel) have been put into a separate 9-pin connector known as a DB-9. The serial port on your microcomputer may be either a DB-9 or a DB-25.

For some of the new features, look at pin 32 (Select standby). With this pin, the terminal can instruct the modem to use an alternate standby network such as changing from a private leased line to a public packet network, either for backup or simply to access another database not normally used. In other words, a terminal can be connected to two different networks, and the operator can enter a keyboard command to switch the connection from one network to another. With regard to loopback pins 10 and 14, the terminal can allow basic tests without special test equipment or the manual exchanging of equipment or cables.

With microcomputers, the RS232 and RS449 also are referred to as D-type connectors. As stated above, the RS232 may be called a DB-25, and the 9-pin RS449 may be called a DB-9. Look at Figure A.3 to see the microcomputer pin configurations for these two connectors.

There are also X.20 and X.21 interface cables. The *X.20* interface is for asynchronous communications, and the *X.21* is for synchronous communications. Each is based on only 15 pins (wires) connecting the DTE and the DCE; the presence of fewer pins requires an increased intelligence in both the DTE and the DCE. X.20 and X.21 are international standards intended to provide an interface with the X.25 packet switching networks discussed elsewhere in this book.

Another option that may become available in the near future is a fiber-optic cable in place of the standard RS232 electrical cables. Currently, by using fiber-optic cable, we can locate a terminal 1,000 meters (3,280 feet) from a host mainframe computer. With a 1,000-meter fiber-optic cable, these products can communicate at speeds ranging from 19,200 bps to twice that speed. Therefore, you get not only greater distance (1,000 meters) but also greater speed. This may be another example in which fiber optics eventually will replace electronics.

The *high-speed serial interface (HSSI)* is beginning to appear in new products. HSSI defines the physical and electrical interface between the DTE and the DCE equipment. It was developed by Cisco Systems of Menlo Park, California, and T3plus of Santa Clara, California. They have submitted it to the American National Standards Institute, which also formalized the EIA-232 and V.35 standards. HSSI allows data transfers over the connector cable at 52 million bps, whereas RS-449 cannot handle more than 10 million bps. HSSI is a 50-pin connector using shielded twisted-pair cabling.

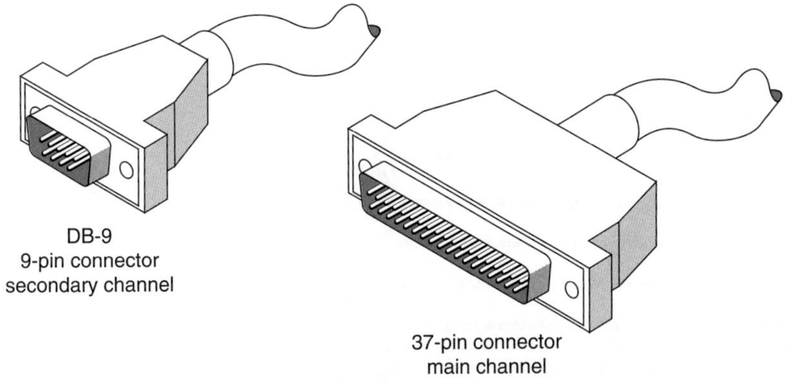

37-Pin Connector				9-Pin Connector	
Pin	First Segment Assignment Function	Pin	Second Segment Assignment Function	Pin	Function
1	Shield	20	Receive common	1	Shield
2	Signaling rate indicator	21	(Unassigned)	2	Secondary receiver
3	(Unassigned)	22	Send data ready	3	Secondary send data
4	Send data	23	Send timing	4	Secondary receive data
5	Send timing	24	Receive data	5	Signal ground
6	Receive data	25	Request to send	6	Receive common
7	Request to send	26	Receive timing	7	Secondary request to send
8	Receive timing	27	Clear to send	8	Secondary clear to send
9	Clear to send	28	Terminal in service	9	Send common
10	Local loopback	29	Data mode		
11	Data mode	30	Terminal ready		
12	Terminal ready	31	Receiver ready		
13	Receiver ready	32	Select standby		
14	Remote loopback	33	Signal quality		
15	Incoming call	34	New signal		
16	Select frequency/signaling rate selector	35	Terminal timing		
		36	Standby indicator		
17	Terminal timing	37	Send common		
18	Test mode				
19	Signal ground				

FIGURE A.2 RS449 cable specifications

NULL MODEM CABLE CONNECTIONS

Null modem cables allow transmission between two microcomputers that are next to each other (6 to 8 feet apart) without using a modem. If you discover that the diskette from your microcomputer will not fit into another one, that transmitting over telephone lines is impossible, or that you cannot transmit data easily from one microcomputer to another for any reason, then it is time to get a null modem cable.

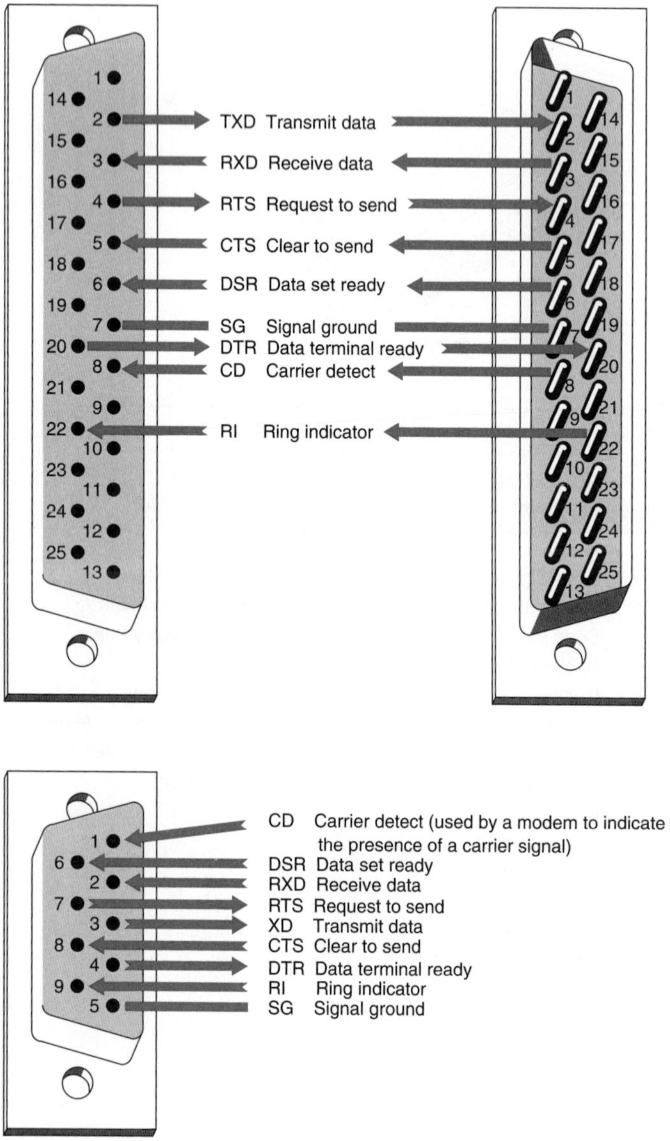

FIGURE A.3 Pin configurations

First, bring the two microcomputers close together. Next, obtain a null modem cable (more on the pin connections shortly). The cable runs from the serial communication port on the first microcomputer to the serial communication port on the second one. The cable is called a *null* modem cable because it eliminates the need for a modem. You can either build a null modem cable or buy one from any microcomputer store. Null modem connector blocks are available to connect between two cables you already own.

To transfer data between two microcomputers, just hook the null modem cable between them and call up one of the computers by using the communication software you normally use. To do so, put one microcomputer in answer mode and use the other one to call it, but skip the step of dialing the telephone number. After the receiving computer has answered that it is ready, the data can be sent, just as you would on a normal long-distance dial-up connection. Basically, a null modem cable switches pins 2 and 3 (Transmit and Receive) of the RS232 connector plug.

DATA SIGNALING/SYNCHRONIZATION

Let us look at *data signaling* or *synchronization* as it occurs on a RS232 connector cable. Figure A.4 shows the 13 most frequently used pins of the 25-pin RS232 connector cable. A microcomputer is on the left side of the figure and a modem is on the right.

Do you ever wonder what happens when you press the "send" key to transmit synchronous data? When a synchronous block of data is sent, the microcomputer and the modem raise and lower electrical signals (plus and minus polarity) between themselves over the RS232 connector. This is usually a nominal +12 or −12 volts. For example, a modem with a RS232 interface might indicate that it is on and ready to operate by raising the signal on pin 6, *Data set ready.* (*Data set* is an older term for a modem.) When a call comes in, the modem shows the microcomputer that the telephone line is ringing by raising a signal on pin 22, the *Ring indicator.* Raising a signal means putting +12 volts

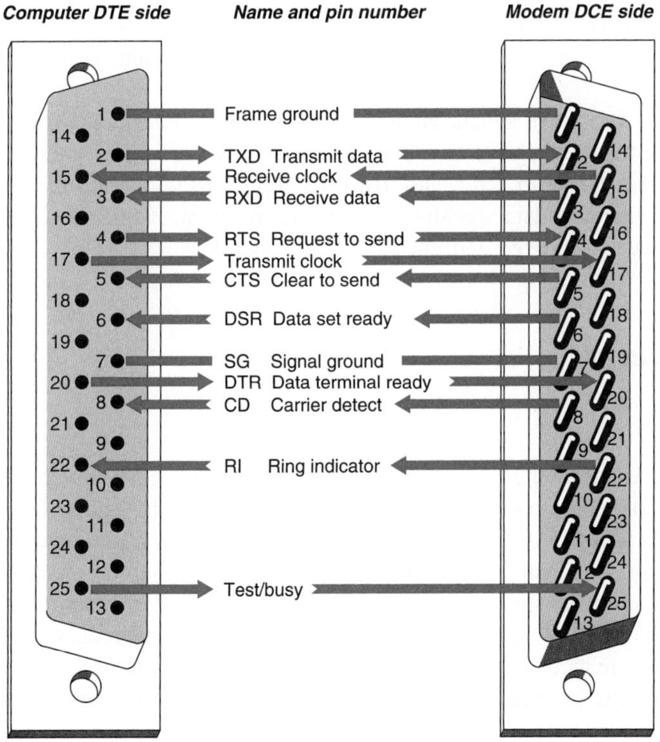

FIGURE A.4 Data signaling with RS232 cables. DCE 1-1-data circuit terminating equipment: DTE 1-1-data terminal equipment

on the wire or pin. The microcomputer may then tell the modem to answer the call by raising a signal on pin 20, *Data terminal ready.* After the modems connect, the modem may indicate the connection status to the microcomputer by raising a signal on pin 8, *Carrier detect.* At the end of the session, the microcomputer may tell the modem to drop the telephone call (release the circuit) by lowering the signal on pin 20, *Data terminal ready.* The *Request to send* and *Clear to send* signals go over pins 4 and 5, respectively, which are used in half-duplex modems to manage control of the communication channel. Incidentally, some of these basic procedures may vary slightly from one manufacturer to another.

Follow the pins and signal direction arrows in Figure A.4 as we discuss an example that handles the flow of a block of synchronous data. When the microcomputer operator presses the "send" key to transmit a block of data, pin 4, *Request to send,* transmits the signal from the microcomputer to the modem. This informs the modem that a block of data is ready to be sent. The modem then sends a *Clear to send* signal back to the microcomputer by using pin 5, thus telling the microcomputer that it can send a synchronous block of data.

The microcomputer now outpulses a serial stream of bits that contain two 8-bit SYN characters in front of the message block. A SYN character is 0110100 (decimal 22 in ASCII code). This bit stream passes over the connector cable to the modem using pin 2, *Transmit data.* The modem then modulates this data block to convert it from the digital signal (plus and minus polarity) to an analog signal (discussed in the next section). From the modem, the data go out onto the local loop circuit between your business premises and the telephone company central office. From there, it goes to the long-distance IXC and the receiving end's telephone company central office. Then it moves to the local loop, into the modem, across the connector cable, and into the host mainframe computer at the other end of the circuit.

This process is repeated for each synchronous message block in half-duplex transmission. The data signaling that takes place between the microcomputer and the modem involves the *Request to send, Clear to send,* and *Transmit data* pins. Accurate timing between blocks of data is critical in data signaling and synchronization. If this timing is lost, the entire block of data is destroyed and must be retransmitted.

ETHERNET AND RJ-45

10Base-T

Today, Ethernet 10Base-T is most often wired with cat 5 cable, which has four pairs of wire in each cable, but only two pairs are used so that cat 3 cable can still be used if desired. One pair of two wires is used to transmit from the computer to the hub (or switch), while the other pair of two wires is used to receive data from the hub (or switch). Both wires in each pair transmit the same signal but with opposite polarity; the transmit + wire uses positive charges while the transmit—uses negative charges. This redundancy helps reduce errors and also reduces interference between the wires in the pair. Thus, 10Base-T is capable of full-duplex transmission at the hardware level, but it usually is only implemented as half-duplex.

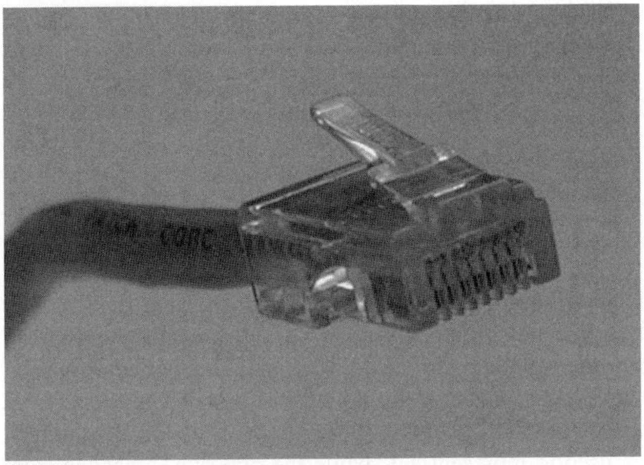

Pin number	Color (EIA/TIA 568B standard)	Name
1	White with orange stripe	Transmit +
2	Orange with white stripe or solid orange	Transmit –
3	White with green stripe	Receive +
4	Blue with white stripe or solid blue	Not used
5	White with blue stripe	Not used
6	Green with white stripe or solid green	Receive –
7	White with brown stripe or solid brown	Not used
8	Brown with white stripe or solid brown	Not used

FIGURE A.5 Pins used by 10Base-T and 100Base-T at the computer end

Figure A.5 shows the way in which cat 5 cables are wired. The cable is wired into an RJ–45 connector,[1] which is an 8-pin connector used to plug into NICs, hubs, and switches. Pins 1 and 2 are the wires used to transmit from the computer's NIC while pins 3 and 6 are used to receive transmissions at the computer's NIC. The pins on the hub or switch are reversed; that is, pins 1 and 2 deliver the computer's NIC's transmissions, so they are the receive pins at the hub or switch, while 3 and 6 are the receive pins at the hub or switch. Any time you want to directly connect two computer NICs or two hubs/switches, you must use a crossover cable, which connects pins 1 and 2 at one end to pins 3 and 6 at the other (and vice versa).

[1]To be very precise, it is not an RJ-45 connector, but rather a version of the RJ-45 designed for network use. The RJ-45 is designed for telephone use, which tolerates higher interference. Just about everyone calls it an RJ-45 connector, but if you ever buy a "real" RJ-45 connector designed for telephone use and try to build a LAN cable yourself to save a few dollars, it won't work.

In order to successfully send and receive messages, both the sender and receiver have to agree how bits will be transmitted over the specific wires in the cable. They must understand both how fast the data will be sent and what electrical voltages will be used to represent a binary 1 and a binary 0. 10Base-T transmits at a rate of 10 Mbps, or 10 million bits per second. This means that the computers divide each second into 10 million time periods in which they can send data. Each time period (100 *nanoseconds* [i.e., 100 billionths of a second]) contains one bit, either binary 1 or a binary 0. Thus each wire in the cat 3 or cat 5 cable must be capable of carrying a signal that changes 10 million times per second; we call this a *signaling rate* of 10 million Hertz, or 10 MHz.

One of the challenges in transmitting this fast is making sure that the clock at the receiver is synchronized with the clock at the sender so they can both understand when one of these 100-nanosecond time periods starts and stops. This is done by using *Manchester encoding,* a special type of signaling in which the signal is changed from high voltage (2 volts) to low voltage (0 volts) or vice versa in the middle of the signal. A change from low to high is used to represent a 1, while the opposite (a change from high to low) is used to represent a 0. Thus, in the exact middle of each time period, the signal voltage changes. This "heartbeat" synchronizes the clocks.

100Base-T

Ethernet 100Base-T also transmits data over cat 5 cables. It uses exactly the same wiring and connector pin configurations as 10Base-T so that the wiring for the two types of LANs is identical.

100Base-T does not use Manchester encoding. 100Base-T uses *4B5B coding,* in which the data are sent in groups of 5 bits, the first 4 of which are data and the last one is used for clock synchronizing purposes and to minimize interference. The fifth bit is chosen to ensure than no more than 4 out of the 5 bits have the same value. Because of the high speed at which the data is being transmitted, a long series of all ones or all zeros would result in a long transmission of positive or negative voltage, which has a greater chance of causing interference to other wires than an alternating positive and negative pattern of voltages. Also, without regular changes in signal as is done in Manchester encoding, it becomes increasingly difficult to ensure that the clocks on the sender and receiver are synchronized. Adding this extra fifth bit every 4 bits of data ensures no long single-level transmissions are sent and ensures a transition for clock synchronizing.

In order to achieve a data rate of 100 Mbps when using 4B5B, the sender and receiver have to operate at 125 MHz, because only 4 out of every 5 bits transmitted contain data. 100Base-T uses a technique called *Multi-Level Transmission–3 Level* (MLT-3) to transmit the 4B5B codes through the cable. With MLT-3, three levels of voltage are defined, +1 volts, 0 volts, and −1 volts. MLT-3 is based on changes in voltages like Manchester encoding, but in a different way. To send a binary zero, MLT-3 simply maintains the same voltage as used in the previous time slot. To transmit a binary 0, the voltage is changed to an adjacent level (e.g., from −1 to 0 or 0 to +1).

1 GbE

The version of 1 GbE that runs over twisted-pair cables is called 1000Base-T and runs over one cat 5 cable by using parallel transmission. That is, it uses each of the four pairs of wires in the cat 5 cable as a separate half-duplex circuit with a transmit and receive wire pair. We now have four parallel circuits running through one cable, so in each clock tick we can send four signals at a time through the cable. 100Base-T Ethernet uses a 4B5B coding scheme in which the set of 5 bits (4 data, one overhead) were transmitted at 125 MHz (i.e., 125 million times per second), giving a speed of 100 Mbps. 125 MHz is the fastest data rate at which the wires in cat 5 can reliably transmit for any reasonable distance. However, 125 MHz times 4 bits per signal equals only 500 Mbps. In order to get 1000 Mbps, we have to do something more creative.

Until now, we talked about transmitting one bit in each time interval by using a higher voltage and a lower voltage (e.g., see Manchester encoding). Gigabit Ethernet uses the same 125 MHz clock speed as 100Base-T Ethernet, but sends 2 bits in each time interval using *Pulse Amplitude Modulation–5* (PAM-5). With PAM-5, five different voltage levels are defined, ranging from +1 volts to −1 volts. Four of these voltage levels are used to send data. One voltage is defined to be the 2-bit pattern 00, another is defined to be 01, another 10, and another 11. The fifth voltage level is used for the fifth control bit. So, in each time period, the sender sends one electrical pulse at one of the five defined voltages, which represents a certain pattern of 2 bits, rather than just 1 bit as with Manchester encoding. Two bits per time interval times 125 time intervals per second times four separate circuit pairs in each cat 5 cable equals 1000 Mbps.

Because we are now sending 2 bits per signal using five different voltage levels rather than just two voltage levels as with Manchester encoding or 4B5B, the signal is more susceptible to noise or interference. This is because it is more difficult for the NIC to distinguish among differences in five voltage levels rather than two voltage levels because the differences between levels are smaller. It takes a much smaller amount of noise to trick the NIC into thinking a signal sent at one voltage level is actually a different level. For this reason, most organizations use cat 5e cable for 100Base-T; cat 5e is a version of cat 5 cable specially modified to reduce errors when used in 1000Base-T installations. Cat 6 cable has also been proposed, which has a capacity of 250 MHz. The maximum length of cat 5/5e/6 cable for 1000Base-T is 100 meters from the computer to the hub or switch.

UNIVERSAL SERIAL BUS

Universal Serial Bus (USB) is another commonly used data transfer standard. Older USB devices will support serial data transfer at either 1.5 Mbps or 12 Mbps. Devices that conform to the USB 2.0 standard will support both these older speeds, plus 480 Mbps, which is sometimes called *Hi-Speed USB*.

USB cables have a host end and a device end, each of which have different styles of connectors (Figure A.6). Inside the cable, there are four wires. One is a ground wire and one (VBUS) is used to send a +5 volt power signal to the USB device. The two D wires are used to transmit the data in two separate serial data streams using a nonreturn to zero technique. The D+ wire sends the data with a positive charge while the D- wire sends the identical data with an offsetting negative charge to reduce interference and error.

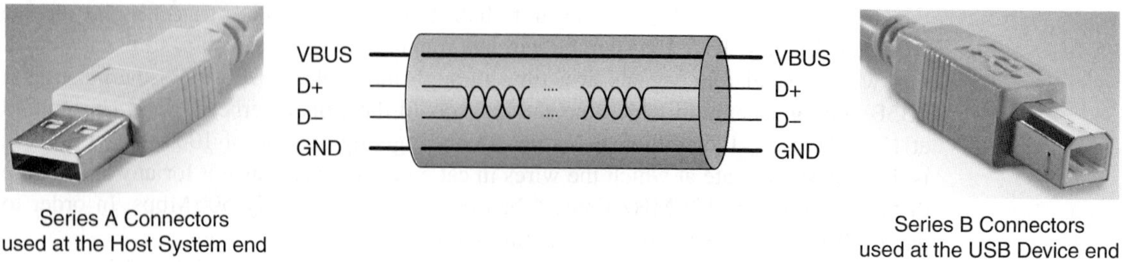

FIGURE A.6 USB cables

FIREWIRE

Firewire, a competitor to USB, was originally developed by Apple computer in thc early 1990s and was standardized as IEEE 1394a-2000. Like USB, it is a serial bus connector. Firewire is also called i.Link.

Modern 1394a-2000 Firewire devices will support serial data transfer at 400 Mbps. Firewire cables have either a 4-pin or 6-pin configuration with a variety of different types of connectors. Inside the cable there are six wires (Figure A.7). Two are used to send 8–40 volts of power to the Firewire device. The other wires are two pairs of two wires used to transmit the data in two separate serial data streams using a nonreturn to zero technique. Within each pair, the D+ wire sends the data with a positive charge while the D- wire sends the identical data with an offsetting negative charge to reduce interference and error.

Because there are two pairs of wires, Firewire could be configured to transmit in parallel, but it is not. Instead, one pair of wires is used to send data and the other pair is used to continuously send clocking signals to minimize the chance of error.

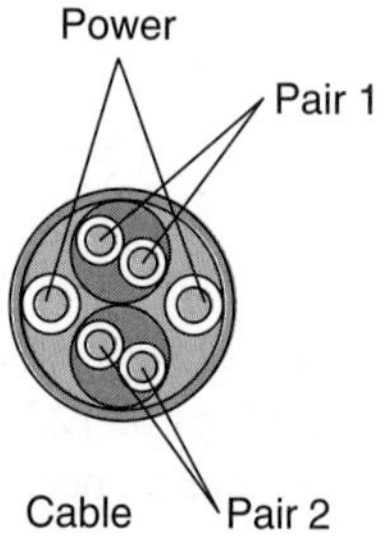

FIGURE A.7 Firewire cables

APPENDIX B
SPANNING TREE PROTOCOL

Redundancy is an important element of good network design (see Chapter 12). Redundant circuits and devices mean that the network can continue to operate even if one circuit or device fails. For example, if a device has a 99.99 percent reliability, there is a .01 percent chance of failing. This means on average that the device will fail for about one hour per year. With two devices, the reliability increases to 99.9999 percent, or less than one minute of expected downtime per year.

Figure B.1 shows a common redundant network design. Two LAN segments (LAN 1 and LAN 2) are connected to two separate switches (A and B), that are in turn connected to two separate routers (X and Y) connected to the corporate WAN. Each switch has 4 ports; port 1 on switch A connects to LAN 1, port 2 connects to LAN 2, port 3 connects to router X, and port 4 connects to router Y. In this way, both LAN 1 and LAN 2 can continue to operate and send messages to and from each other and the WAN if any one circuit or device fails. For example, if switch A fails, all traffic into LAN 1 can still flow

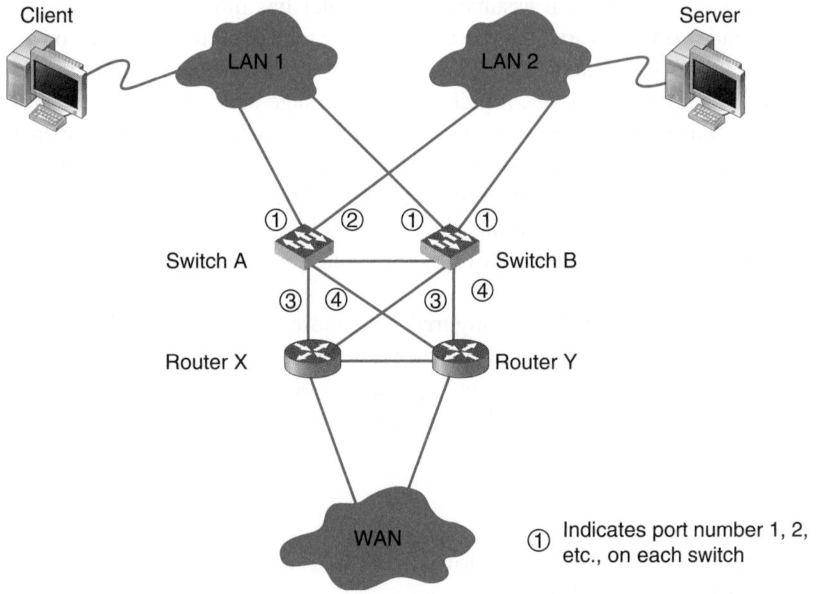

FIGURE B.1 Network design with redundant circuits and devices. LAN = local area network; WAN = wide area network

through switch B. Likewise, if router X fails, if the circuit from switch A to router X fails, or if port 3 on switch A fails, then traffic can flow through switch A to router Y and then into the WAN.

The challenge with redundant designs is to prevent broadcast storms. Remember that when switches are first turned on, they act like bridges, sending all messages in all directions, until they learn which device can be reached through which port (see Chapter 6). This means, for example, when the network in Figure B.1 is first turned on, neither switch A nor switch B will know where any device is. Assume that the client computer wants to send a message to the server. The message will enter LAN 1 from the client computer and be sent to switch A via the circuit connected to switch A's port 1. Switch A will learn that the client is on port 1. It won't know where the server is, so it will forward the packet on all remaining ports (2, 3, and 4). Router X on port 3 and router Y on port 4 will read the Ethernet address and ignore the message because it is not addressed to them. Eventually, the message will reach the server on LAN 2 via the message sent on port 2. The server will receive the message and send a response message to the client. The response message will hit switch A on port 2 (switch A will learn that the server is on port 2) and it will forward the response message to the client via port 1.

So far, so good. Now the problems start. Switch B is also on LAN 1, so it too will receive the very first message sent by the client, and will do exactly the same thing as switch A: it will learn that the client is on its port 1, and forward the message on its ports 2, 3, and 4. Once again, routers X and Y will ignore the message because it is not addressed to them (although the duplicate message has used up some of their processing capacity needlessly). When the message is sent to LAN 2 via port 2, the server sees it and starts to process it; we now have a duplicate message being processed twice.

But it gets worse. Switch A is also on LAN 2, so it receives all messages sent on LAN 2. When switch B sends the message from the client to the server into LAN 2, switch A also receives it, this time on its port 2. It now learns that the client is on port 2 (not port 1 as it originally thought; it assumes the computer has moved and updates its forwarding table), and promptly forwards the message a second time to the server on all remaining ports (1, 3, and 4). Routers X and Y see the message a third time and ignore it, but because switch B is also on LAN 1, it picks up the message again, thinks it is a new message, and again transmits the message on all other ports, which, of course, means that switch A gets the message again and forwards it again, and therefore switch B gets it again and forwards it, and so on, in a never-ending cycle. The same thing happens with the response message from the server to the client, and in fact, with all messages. They circulate forever through the circular loops in the redundant network, until the network collapses under the storm.[1]

The solution is to have switches configured with these redundant *physical* loops, but to create a way for the switches to recognize these physical loops and block them so that we create a different *logical* topology that does not have a loop. The method used to create this logical topology is called the *spanning tree protocol* and has been standardized as IEEE 802.1D.

[1]You may recall that an IP packet has a maximum hop count (also called time to live) to prevent this endless looping (see Chapter 5). Switches operate at the data link layer and therefore do not read the IP packet; the maximum hop count won't prevent looping at this layer.

With the spanning tree protocol, one switch is designated the *root node* or *root switch.* The cost to reach every computer, switch, or other device on the network from the root switch is calculated based on the "cost" of the intervening circuits (a 10 GbE circuit costs 2, 1 GbE costs 4, 100Base-T costs 19, and 10Base-T costs 100). The switches calculate the cost from the root switch to every device by sending information on the circuits they have to the switches around them using a special control message called a *Bridge Protocol Data Unit (BPDU).*[2] Switches send BPDUs every 2 seconds so that the network can quickly learn the logical topology and adjust to changes (e.g., if a circuit fails).

Once the switches determine the cost to reach other devices, they select one port as the *designated port* for each device and block all the other ports so that all messages to any one device use only the designated port. For example, in Figure B.1, switch A can reach the client via port 1 through one circuit. If all the circuits in the figure are 100Base-T, then the cost from switch A to the client via port 1 is 19. Switch A can also reach the client via port 2 through three circuits at a cost of 57 (to LAN 2, to switch B, to LAN 1). Ports 3 and 4 do not reach the client. Port 1 has the lowest cost, so it becomes the designated port for the client, and ports 2, 3, and 4 are marked as blocked for all traffic to the client (a blocked port is also called a *discarding port*). Likewise, switch A's port 2 is the designated port for traffic to the server (and ports 1, 3, and 4 are blocked for traffic to the server).

A bridge only listens, learns, and forwards packets it receives on a designated port. In some cases, the network will change or a circuit may go down, meaning that the switch needs to be able to move from blocking a port to marking it as the designated port. If a circuit or device goes down, a switch can recognize it from the changes in the BPDUs it receives from the other switches in the network (or from the failure to receive BPDUs on that port). When a switch realizes that a designated port no longer reaches the target destination (or the cost has suddenly increased), then it recalculates the costs and designates a new port.

One challenge is to determine how fast a switch should alter its designated port. If the time is set too short, then loops may develop and the network becomes unstable. If time is too long, then the network takes too long to respond to problems and users experience delays. In the original version of the spanning tree standard (IEEE 802.1D), switches were set to take 50 seconds to change designated ports. Because networks are more reliable today and they are less likely to lose BPDUs unless a circuit goes down, the newer version of spanning tree standard (IEEE 802.1 w) waits only 15 seconds.

When a switch first starts up, it does not know the cost to any devices, to what devices it is connected, which ports should be designated and blocked, or which switch is the root switch. It must learn all of these. The switch starts by presuming that it is the root switch and sending out BPDUs on all ports. These BPDUs identify the switch and start by assuming a cost of 32,768 to reach other devices (i.e., that the distance is very far). If there are no other switches, then it remains the root switch (although because there are no other switches, there is no redundancy and spanning tree is not needed).

[2]The spanning tree protocol was originally developed to be used by bridges and other layer-2 devices. Today, bridges are almost obsolete, so you are more likely to see spanning tree in a switched environment, but the terminology still reflects the origin with bridges.

If there are other switches in the network, then the switch starts receiving BPDUs from the switches around it and starts updating its cost table. Gradually the artificially high costs are replaced by actual ones and the switch is able to build an accurate forwarding table and determine whether or not it is the root node.

APPENDIX C

IP TELEPHONY

IP Telephony refers to the use of Internet protocols to provide voice, video, and data in one integrated service over LANs, BNs, MANs, and WANs. When most people talk about IP Telephony, they mean *Voice over IP* (*VoIP*). *Voice over ATM* (*VoATM*) and *Voice over Frame Relay* (*VoFR*) are also fairly common, and, as the names suggests, are close cousins to VoIP.

VoIP provides three key benefits compared to traditional voice telephone services. First, it minimizes the need for extra wiring in new buildings (there is one cable for both voice and data, not two). Second, it provides easy movement of telephones and the ability of phone numbers to move with the individual (the number is installed in the telephone, much like an IP address, so anywhere the phone is connected or the phone number programmed, the phone will connect, even if it is halfway around the world). Finally, VoIP is generally cheaper to operate because it requires less network capacity to transmit the same voice telephone call over an increasingly digital telephone network.

VoIP requires a VoIP *Private Branch Exchange* (*PBX*), which connects the organization's internal telephone network into the *public switched telephone network* (*PSTN*). The PBX can also be connected into the organization's WAN and be configured to route calls through the WAN to other organization locations (or even over the Internet), thereby bypassing any long-distance charges in the PSTN (although the call does use up network capacity on the organization's WAN or Internet connection).

The VoIP PBX can be considered a gateway that connects the internal IP telephones to the PSTN.[1] When the IP telephone user lifts the receiver off the hook to place a call, the IP telephone sends a message to the PBX, which responds by sending a dial tone. Once the number has been dialed, the IP telephone then sends a message to the PBX with the telephone number, and the PBX connects the telephone into the PSTN or over the organization's WAN to the VoIP PBX at the other location.

VoIP often uses H.323 at the application layer (see Chapter 2), although *Session Initiation Protocol* (*SIP*) is also common. *Media Gateway Control Protocol* (*MGCP*) and *Skinny Call Control Protocol* (*SCCP*) are other competing application layer protocols although they offer fewer features than H.323 and SIP. All four protocols (H.323, SIP, MCGP, and SCCP) operate at the application layer and contain all the functions needed to start and end telephone calls, as well as to transmit the call data. MCGP and SCCP

[1]Another type of VoIP PBX uses regular telephones and regular analog circuits inside the organization, and the PBX does all the conversion between the analog telephone and the digital network. This is an older, temporary approach that is quickly disappearing.

require the PBX to act as a server and communicate with other MCGP and SCCP devices only through the PBX server; H.323 and SIP can both communicate with other H.323 and SIP clients without needing to go through the PBX (except for telephone number resolution, which is a process much like using a DNS to resolve an application layer name into an IP address [see Chapter 5]). SIP is a newer and more efficient protocol than H.323, and was developed using HTTP as its core, which means that it is simpler to debug and can be easily integrated into Web-based applications and SMTP e-mail applications.

In order to use VoIP, a device such as an IP telephone must support H.323, SIP, MCGP, or SCCP, and also contain a *CODEC* to convert the incoming analog voice signal into a digital bit stream (see Chapter 3). The CODEC is also used at the receiving end to convert the digital data back into the analog voice data. The most commonly used digital voice protocols are 64 Kbps *PCM,* 32 Kbps *ADPCM* (see Chapter 3), and more recent variants on them, such as 8 Kbps G.729 (also called CELP) or 6.3 Kbps G.723 (also called MPMLQ). As might be expected from their lower bandwidth requirements, sound quality can become an issue.

A technique called *Mean Opinion Score (MOS)* has been developed by ITU-T to subjectively rate the voice quality of different CODEC standards. A MOS of 5 is the theoretical maximum (meaning excellent) while a 1 is the lowest score (very poor quality). A 4 is generally regarded as an acceptable level of quality, with barely perceptible levels of quantizing error. PCM has a MOS of 4.1; ADPCM, 3.85; G.729, 3.92; and G.723 (at 6.3 Kbps), 3.9.

Once the CODEC has produced the digital data, the data is surrounded by an application layer packet. H.323 often uses *RTP* (see Chapter 5) for transmission through an IP-based network. The RTP packet in turn is surrounded by UDP, IP, and data link layer packets (e.g., Ethernet, frame relay) for transmission through the network. Voice data packets tend to be very small, and thus the packets added at layers 5, 4, 3, and 2 can add considerable overhead to the transmission. A new version of RTP called *Compressed Real Time Protocol* (CRTP) has been developed that enables the set of RTP, UDP, and IP packets to be compressed to 2 bytes, thus significantly reducing the overhead.

Voice Activity Detection (*VAD*) is another way of reducing the network capacity required to send VoIP calls. With VAD, the end VoIP device monitors the analog voice signal and if the signal drops below a certain amplitude, then the device assumes that no one is speaking and stops sending packets. Since most conversations are silent at least half the time, this can significantly reduce the bandwidth required. VAD must be done carefully to avoiding clipping the speech (cutting off the beginning and end).

The other problem with VAD is that because no data packets are transmitted, the line is completely silent. We are so used to experiencing background noise from interference on traditional analog telephone calls that silence is usually interpreted as meaning the call has been disconnected. Therefore, several vendors have begun to add in background *comfort noise* (sometimes call pink noise) when no data packets are flowing. The VAD device at the sender's location initially sends some ambient background noise packets, which are recognized by the receiving device. After a few seconds, the VAD sending device begins operating normally and no longer sends background noise packets when speech ends. When the receiver detects the slowdown in packets, it repeatedly reproduces the ambient background noise packets to fill the "dead air" so that the receiver does not think the call has been disconnected.

As a result of VAD, the network capacity requirements for VoIP on Ethernet networks ranges from about 8 Kbps using G.729 and CRTP to 45 Kbps using PCM with RTP. On ATM networks, it ranges from about 6 Kbps using G.723 and CRTP to 53 Kbps using PCM.

One of the key issues in VoIP is ensuring that the network has sufficient capacity to send the VoIP packets. While users will accept a few second delays in Web traffic or e-mail, most people cannot tolerate delays in voice conversations over about 250 milliseconds (a quarter of a second). Therefore, VoIP is only practical in networks that enable *Quality of Service* (*QoS*) routing at the IP layer (see Chapter 5) and ideally matching QoS at the data link layer. Most organizations that deploy VoIP, therefore, use IP with QoS and also have policy-based VLANs at the data link layer (see Chapter 8).

APPENDIX D
CELLULAR TECHNOLOGIES

Cellular technology is becoming increasingly popular. Its most common use is to provide *cellular telephone* services, but the cellular network is also being used more and more often by data communication devices such as pagers, personal digital assistants (PDAs), and handheld computers.

Cellular technology is a form of high frequency radio in which antennas are spaced strategically throughout a service area. The service area is divided into many cells, each with its own antenna. This arrangement generally provides subscribers with reliable mobile telephone service of a quality almost that of a hardwired telephone system. Users (voice or data transmission) dial or login to the system, and their voices or data are transmitted directly from their telephone to one of these antennas. In this way, the cellular system replaces the hardwired local loop. Each phone service provider uses a different part of the radio frequency spectrum, which is why cell phones designed for one provider's network often won't work on another provider's network.

This network of cell antennas is an intelligent system. For example, as you drive your car through the service area, you move away from one antenna and closer to another. As the signal weakens at the first antenna, the system automatically begins picking up your signal at the second antenna. Transmission is switched automatically to the closest antenna without communication being lost.

The current technology used for cell phones is digital (not analog; see Chapter 3), and is sometimes called *2G wireless* because it is the second-generation mobile phone service (old analog cell phones were the first generation). A 2G phone has a built-in CODEC that converts the analog voice data into digital signals for transmission. These phones enable limited data transfer, often only 19.2 Kbps, because the cell phone network was designed primarily for phone calls, not data transmission.

There are three incompatible standards for cell phone technology that are commonly used around the world. *Code Division Multiple Access (CDMA)* is a spread spectrum technology that works by digitizing multiple conversations, attaching a code known only to the sender and receiver and then dicing the signals into bits for transmission and reassembling them at the receiving device. *Time Division Multiple Access (TDMA)* allows multiple users to share the same voice channel by having each conversation transmitted alternately over short lengths of time (statistically time division multiplexing). *Global System for Mobile Communication (GSM)* is a TDMA-like digital system that transmits digital voice data in bursts during brief time slots allocated to multiple subscribers sharing a radio channel. GSM is the standard in most of the world, except for the United States and Canada, which still use a mix of CDMA, TDMA, and GSM.

One of the newest forms of mobile wireless is *3G wireless,* so called because it is the third generation of public wireless networks. 3G wireless is still under development with no clear winners at this point. Several industry groups are racing to provide high-speed digital telephone and wireless Internet services. Most "high-speed" cell technologies currently deployed are called 2.5G because they serve as a stepping stone to 3G.

Two sets of technologies are leading in the 3G race. The first is *Enhanced Data GSM Environment (EDGE),* a 2.5G step along the path to *Wideband Code Division Multiple Access (WCDMA)* as the 3G standard. As the name suggests, EDGE is an enhancement of the current GSM and provides a data rate of 384 Kbps (it is sometimes called GSM384). WCDMA provides 2.3 Mbps. For more information, see www.umts-forum.org.

The second technology group sponsors *CDMA2000* (2.5G) and *CDMA2000 1X* (3G). As the names suggest, CDMA2000 and CDMA2000 1x are extensions to CDMA that provide 153 Kbps and 2.4 Mbps, respectively. For more information, see www.cdg.org.

Meanwhile, other vendors are beginning to talk about *4G wireless* services—that is, the next generation after 3G—because 2–3 Mbps data rates are not as powerful as current wireless LAN technologies such as 802.11 (see Chapter 7). Some vendors have begun to call for universal public 802.11 access as a 4G option, with 802.11 hot spots being deployed in major urban areas. In other words, your cell phone would have both the 2.5G or 3G antenna, plus an 802.11 antenna to enable faster data transfer in areas covered by 802.11. While the standard version of 802.11 has a very short range, new emerging versions of 802.11 designed for outdoor use have ranges of 20 miles or more.

Stay tuned because this battle is just starting.

APPENDIX E

TCP/IP GAME

INTRODUCTION

The purpose of this game is to help you better understand how messages are transmitted in TCP/IP-based computer networks. Players are organized into five-person teams that represent different computers in the network. Each person in the team assumes the role of one layer of software or hardware on that computer (e.g., data link layer) and works with the others to send messages through the network.

General Rules

1. This is a team game. The class will be broken into a set of five-member teams, with each team being one computer in the communications network. Each person in the team will role-play one layer in the computer, either the application layer, the transport layer, the network layer, the data link layer, or the physical layer.
2. Messages will be created by the application layer and passed to the transport layer. The transport layer will break the message into several smaller messages if necessary and pass them to the network layer. The network layer will address and route the message and pass the message to the data link layer. The data link layer will format the message and perform error control (which will involve sending ACKs and NAKs) and pass the message to the physical layer for transmission. The physical layer will transmit the message to the physical layer of the destination computer. Messages are sent using the forms in Figure E.1. Be sure to make lots of copies of the forms before the game starts.
3. Each layer will have a set of instructions to follow to ensure the messages are sent and received properly. Follow them carefully. These instructions explain what you are to write on the message forms. Never write anything on the message form in an area used by another layer.
4. At some point, someone will make a mistake. If you receive a message that contains an error, hand it back to the person who gave it to you and explain the error to that person.
5. And remember, the game is meant to be fun, too!

SMTP	From	To	Message	

TCP	Sequence Number	User Data
	of	

IP	Final Destination	Next Node	User Data

Ethernet	Source	Destination	Control	Message #	Error	User Data

FIGURE E.1 Forms for the TCP/IP game

APPLICATION LAYER

Activities

1. Send messages to other computers
2. Respond to messages from other computers

Tools Needed

- Several blank SMTP forms
- List of messages
- Network map (Figure E.2 shows an example; the instructor will draw one for your class)
- A blank piece of paper

Sending Outgoing Messages

To send a message, you must:

1. Find a blank SMTP packet.
2. Write the *IP address* of your computer in the **From** box.
3. Use the network map to select a computer as the destination for this message. Write the *IP address* of the destination computer in the **To** box. Don't send all your messages to one computer; we want to even out the messages. Try to send a few messages to computers close to you and a few to computers far away.
4. Write the message you wish to send in the **Message** box. To make the message simple to understand, please use a hyphen (-) to indicate spaces between words.

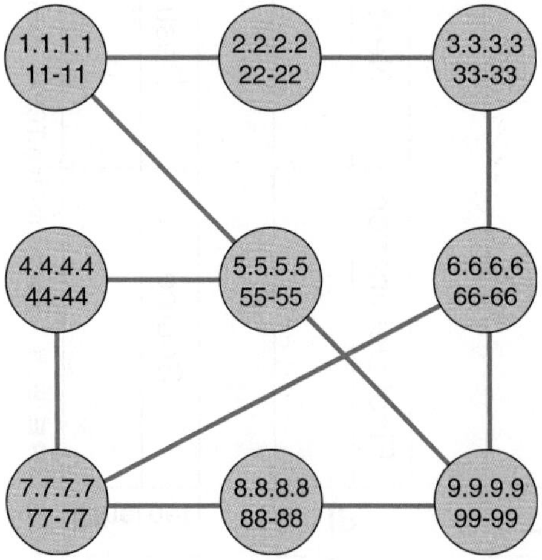

FIGURE E.2 Sample network map

Select a message from the list of messages (see below). Try to have at least one hyphen in the message (this is to help the data link layer do error control) or add one at the end or at the start if you must.

5. Write the message and the name of the computer to which you send the message on the blank piece of paper. This will help you understand the responses you get to your messages.
6. Pass the message to the transport layer.

Responding to Incoming Messages

Eventually, you will receive an incoming message from the transport layer that was sent to you by some other computer asking you a question. To respond to the message, you will send a message that answers the question. Follow the same steps above to send a message, but in step 4, write your answer in the **Message** box. For example, if the message you received asked what your favorite color was, you might write *red* or *blue* in the **Message** box.

List of Messages

Here are a list of messages you can send. Remember to use a hyphen instead of a space to separate the words. Rather than writing the entire message, you can omit the words *What is your.*

- What is your favorite color?
- What is your birthday?
- What is your phone number?
- What are your favorite holidays?
- What is your favorite car?

TRANSPORT LAYER

Activities

1. Accept outgoing SMTP messages from the application layer, packetize them, and pass them to the network layer.
2. Accept incoming messages from the network layer and, if they are made up of several packets, assemble the entire SMTP message before passing it to the application layer.

Tools Needed

- TCP forms
- Tape

Accepting Outgoing Messages from the Application Layer

Every few minutes, the application layer will hand you an outgoing message to transmit. To transmit them, you must:

1. Break the SMTP message into smaller packets. Tear the SMTP packet into two parts at the dotted line. If there is writing on both parts, then you must send each part as a separate message. If the second half of the SMTP packet has no writing on it, throw it away and ignore it.
2. Find one or two blank TCP packets.
3. Fill in the **Sequence Number** box. If there is only one part of the SMTP packet, write "1 of 1" in the **Sequence Number** box. If there are two parts of the SMTP packet, write "1 of 2" on the first TCP packet and "2 of 2" on the second TCP packet.
4. Tape the SMTP packet(s) to the TCP packet(s) over the **User Data** space. (The packet(s) will be too big to fit, but don't worry about it.)
5. Pass the TCP + SMTP packet(s) to the network layer.

Accepting Incoming Messages from the Network Layer

Every few minutes, the network layer will hand you an incoming message. To process it, you must:

- **If the message is complete (that is, if the** Sequence Number **box says "1 of 1"):**
  1. Take the TCP packet off of the SMTP packet and throw away the TCP packet.
  2. Pass the SMTP packet to the application layer.
- **If the message is not complete (that is, if the** Sequence Number **box says "1 of 2"):**
  1. Wait for the second part of the message to arrive.
  2. Take the TCP packets off of both SMTP packets and throw away the TCP packets.
  3. Tape the two parts of the SMTP packet back together.
  4. Pass the SMTP packet to the application layer.

NETWORK LAYER

Activities

1. Accept messages from the transport layer, route them, and pass them to the data link layer.
2. Accept messages from the data link layer and, if they are addressed to you, pass them to the transport layer; if they are not addressed to you, route them and pass them back to the data link layer.

Tools Needed

- IP forms
- Tape
- Network map

Accepting Outgoing Messages from the Transport Layer

Every few minutes, the transport layer will hand you an outgoing message to transmit. To transmit them, you must:

1. Find a blank IP packet.
2. Address the message by copying the IP address from the **To** box of the SMTP packet into the **Final Destination** box of the IP packet.
3. Route the message by finding the next computer in the network map to which the message should be sent and writing its Ethernet address in the **Next Node** box. If your computer is directly connected to the final destination computer, the next node is the same as the final destination. If your computer is not directly connected to the destination, you must select the best route that the message should follow and specify one of the computers to which you are connected.
4. Tape the TCP + SMTP packet to the IP packet over the **User Data** space. (It will be too big to fit, but don't worry about it.)
5. Pass the IP + TCP + SMTP packet to the data link layer.

Accepting Incoming Messages from the Data Link Layer

Every few minutes, the data link layer will hand you a message to process. You must:

- **If the message is addressed to you (that is, if the** Final Destination **box in the IP packet lists your IP address):**
  1. Remove the IP packet from the SMTP + TCP packet and throw the IP packet away.
  2. Pass the SMTP + TCP packet to the transport layer.
- **If the message is not addressed to you (that is, if the** Final Destination **box in the IP packet lists someone else's IP address):**
  1. Scratch out or erase the address in the **Next Node** box.
  2. Route the message by finding the next computer in the network map to which the message should be sent and writing its data link layer address in the **Next Node** box. If your computer is directly connected to the destination computer, the next node is the same as the final destination. If your computer is not directly connected to the destination, you must select the best route that the message should follow and specify one of the computers to which you are connected.
  3. Pass the message to the data link layer.

DATA LINK LAYER

Activities

1. Accept outgoing messages from the network layer, format them, add error-control information, and pass them to the physical layer.
2. Accept incoming messages from the physical layer. If they are data messages and contain no errors, send an ACK and pass them to the network layer. If they are data messages with an error, send an NAK. If they are an ACK, destroy the message they acknowledge. If they are an NAK, retransmit the original message.

Tools Needed

- Ethernet forms
- Tape
- Network map
- Some blank pieces of paper. You will discover that you are receiving and storing many different types of messages. To help you organize those messages, we suggest that before you begin, you use three blank pieces of paper to create three message storage piles:
  - Label one pile **Messages from the Network Layer.**
  - Label the second pile **Messages from the Physical Layer.**
  - Label the third pile **Messages Transmitted.**

Accepting Outgoing Messages from the Network Layer

Every few minutes, the network layer will hand you a message to transmit. If you receive more messages from the network layer than you can process right away, put them in the **Messages from the Network Layer** pile until you can process them. For each message, you must:

1. Find a blank Ethernet packet.
2. Format the message for the physical layer by writing your Ethernet address in the **Source** box. Copy the Ethernet address from the **Next Node** box in the IP packet into the **Destination** box. Write an asterisk (*) in the **Control** box.
3. Number the message. Write a two-digit number in the **Message Number** box. This should be *01* for the first message you send, *02* for the second, and so on. Use the blank piece of paper to help you remember what numbers you have used.
4. Add error-control information. Most error control is very sophisticated, but in this game, we'll use something very simple. Count the number of hyphens in the user data (the SMTP packet, the TCP packet, and the IP packet [but not the Ethernet packet]) and write this number in the **Error** box on the Ethernet packet.

5. Tape the SMTP + TCP + IP packet to the Ethernet packet over the **User Data** space. (It will be too big to fit, but don't worry about it.)
6. Pass the message to the physical layer. In a few moments, the physical layer will return the packet to you. *Save it* in the **Messages Transmitted** pile!

Accepting Incoming Messages from the Physical Layer

Every few minutes, the physical layer will hand you a message to process. If you receive more messages than you can process right away, put them in the **Messages from the Physical Layer** pile. These messages will either be data messages, ACKs, or NAKs. Each is processed differently.

- **If the** Control **box contains an asterisk (*), this is a data message. Do the following:**
  1. Perform error checking. Count the number of hyphens in the user data (the SMTP packet, the TCP packet, and the IP packet [but not the Ethernet packet]). If this number is the same as the number in the **Error** box, no errors have occurred. If they are different, an error has occurred.
  2. If no errors have occurred, you must send an ACK to the sender and send the incoming message to the next layer:
     a. Find a blank Ethernet packet.
     b. Write your Ethernet address in the **Source** box. Write the Ethernet address contained in the **Source** box of the incoming message in the **Destination** box of your message. (This ACK message is going to the sender of the original message.) Write *ACK* in the **Control** box. Write the two-digit number contained in the **Message Number** box of the incoming message in the **Message Number** box.
     c. Pass the outgoing ACK message to the physical layer.
     d. Remove the Ethernet packet from the incoming message and throw the Ethernet packet away.
     e. Pass the incoming SMTP + TCP + IP packet to the network layer.
  3. If an error has occurred, you must send an NAK to the sender and discard the incoming message:
     a. Find a blank Ethernet packet.
     b. Write your Ethernet address in the **Source** box. Write the Ethernet address contained in the **Source** box of the incoming message in the **Destination** box of your message. (This NAK message is going to the sender of the original message.) Write *NAK* in the **Control** box. Write the two-digit number contained in the **Message Number** box of the incoming message in the **Message Number** box.
     c. Pass the outgoing NAK message to the physical layer.
     d. Throw away the incoming message containing the error.
- **If the** Control **box contains an ACK, this is an ACK message. Do the following:**
  1. Find the original message you sent, in the **Messages Transmitted** pile, that has the same message number as the ACK.
  2. Destroy the original message and the ACK.

- **If the** Control **box contains an NAK, this is an NAK message. Do the following:**
  1. Find the original message you sent, in the **Messages Transmitted** pile, that has the same message number as the NAK.
  2. Give the original message to the physical layer to transmit again. In a few moments, the physical layer will return the packet to you. *Save it* in the **Messages Transmitted** pile.
  3. Destroy the NAK.

PHYSICAL LAYER

Activities

1. Accept messages from the data link layer and pass them to the physical layer of the computer to which they are to go, possibly introducing a transmission error.
2. Accept messages from the physical layer of other computers and pass them to the data link layer.

Tools Needed

- Ethernet forms
- IP forms
- TCP forms
- SMTP forms
- Network map
- Transmission forms
- Two coins

Accepting Messages from the Data Link Layer

Every few minutes, the data link layer will hand you a message to transmit. These messages will either be data messages or control messages (ACKs or NAKs). Each is processed differently.

- **If the** Control box **contains an asterisk (*), this is a data message. Do the following:**
  1. Determine if there will be an error in transmission by tossing two coins; if they are both heads, you will introduce an error.
  2. Copy the entire contents of the message packet onto new forms; that is, copy the SMTP packet to a new SMTP packet, the TCP packet to a new TCP packet, the IP packet to a new IP packet, and the Ethernet packet to a new Ethernet packet. If you are to introduce an error, omit all the data in the **SMTP Message** box. Be sure to tape the packets together in the right order.

3. Pass the copied SMTP + TCP + IP + Ethernet packet to the physical layer of the computer whose address is listed in the **Destination** box.
4. Pass the original SMTP + TCP + IP + Ethernet packet back to the data link layer and make sure that that person understands that you are giving back the message that he/she just gave you to transmit.

- **If the** Control box **contains an ACK or an NAK, this is a control message. Do the following:**
  1. Simply pass the Ethernet packet to the physical layer of the computer whose address is listed in the **Destination** box. Things are complicated enough without ACKs and NAKs getting destroyed.

Accepting Messages from the Physical Layer of Another Computer

Every few minutes, the physical layer of another computer will hand you a message. Simply hand the message to the data link layer.

NOTE TO INSTRUCTORS

Background

This game helps students *really* understand what the various layers actually do and how they must work together to send a message. Reading about it is one thing; having to perform a simple version of the function is something else altogether. Experiential learning can be an extremely powerful tool. I have noticed a distinct improvement in students' understanding of this material since I have begun using the game.

The game is an extremely simplified version of what happens in a real TCP/IP network. Nonetheless, it can be complicated. Students have to work together and sometimes make mistakes. Ideally, students will recognize mistakes themselves and will help one another learn. Participation is key to the learning objectives. It's also key to making a somewhat dry conceptual set of issues more real—and more fun.

When I teach the course, I usually use this game after I complete Chapter 5, **The Network and Transport Layers.** At this point students will have learned everything they need to know to run the game, and it will reinforce the material.

PREPARING TO TEACH THE GAME

This game contains all the materials you will need to run the game, except a set of coins and paper (which you can rely on students to have), enough tape for each group (bring several rolls), and a network map (which you draw on the board just before the game starts). You will also have to make copies of the four types of packets. It takes an average of three SMTP, TCP, and IP forms and four Ethernet forms for each message, so you will need a lot of them. I usually plan on the class sending about 10–15 messages per team; for a 40-person class, this means you will need 250–350 SMTP, TCP, and IP forms and 350–500 Ethernet forms.

I have found from experience that it takes the students a little while to catch on to the game. Be sure to tell the students to read the game before they come to class.

TEACHING THE GAME

It usually takes 20 minutes before the game gets going. The first step is to organize the class into five-person teams. Each team represents one computer in the network. If there are more than five people in a team, have two people play the data link layer; if there are less than five, then combine the application, transport, and/or network layers.

Draw the network map on the board. The map will have a circle to represent each team (i.e., computer). Try to draw the circles to represent the actual physical placement of the teams within the classroom. Inside each circle, write:

- The IP address (e.g., 1.1.1.1). Arbitrarily choose a number for each team but keep it short and easy to remember.
- The Ethernet address (e.g., 11-11). Arbitrarily choose a number for each team but keep it short and easy to remember. It helps if it matches the IP address in some way. Be sure to have at least one hyphen in the address to help reinforce the error-control concepts.

Next, connect the computers (i.e., teams) by drawing lines (i.e., circuits) between the circles. Don't draw in all possible circuits, because you want some teams to have to route messages through other teams to reach their final destination. Likewise, don't put too few circuits, or else all messages will take a long time to send.

Do a simple example. Walk through the sending of one message on the board and have the students follow by replicating each step you do for one of their own messages. Once the message has reached the physical layer on the next computer, I turn the students loose and let them play. I usually walk around the classroom answering questions and listening in on discussions as the game progresses.

Because each layer performs a unique function, it is useful to have each student play each layer if time permits. I try to have students rotate layers after 15 minutes. I keep the game going so that the students playing one layer need to explain to the person taking over their layer what is going on and how to play. The easiest way to rotate is downward; that is, the person playing the application layer moves to the transport layer, and so on.

Discussion Questions

After each person has had the opportunity to play several layers, it is useful to ask what the students have learned. This gives you the opportunity to reinforce the concepts the game was designed to teach. Some possible discussion questions are:

1. Why are standards important?
2. How could you improve network performance by changing the topology?
3. What layer is the busiest? How could you improve network performance by changing the protocol at this layer?

APPENDIX F
WINDOWS SERVER

Windows server is one of the most popular operating systems for servers. The server operating system enables you to share resources such as files, applications, and printers with other computers. In this section, we will explain how to set up Windows Server to share files.

MANAGING USER ACCOUNTS

Every user who wants to use the server must have an account that specifies what they can and cannot access. There are two types of accounts. A *local account* is an account that is managed on just one computer. A *domain account* is an account that is managed by *Active Directory* and can provide access rights to many different computers through a single login. For this activity, we will assume you are working with local accounts, although the processes for managing domain accounts is almost identical to the process for managing local accounts.

The administrator account is the account that controls the server. The administrator has the rights to add users, change their rights, and control who can do what on the server. In order to manage user accounts, you must login as the administrator. We will assume that you have already logged in as the administrator for the rest of this activity.

Each user account belongs to a *group*. For example, we might create groups by function with one group for sales, one group for accounting, one for production, and so on. We might also create groups by region so that we have one group for Los Angeles, one group for Toronto, one group for New York, and so on. Groups can be organized in a hierarchy so that we can start by defining groups by region, and then add the functional groups below the region so that we have Los Angeles staff, Los Angeles sales staff, Los Angeles accounting staff, and so on.

We can set individual access rights user by user. We can also set access rights by group so that all members of the same group receive the rights for the group. Groups make it simpler to manage user accounts because we do not need to enter information for every user, just every group.

Creating Users

To create a local user, click Start, Administrative Tools, Computer Management. This will show you the list of objects on the server, including folders, users, and groups. Figure F.1

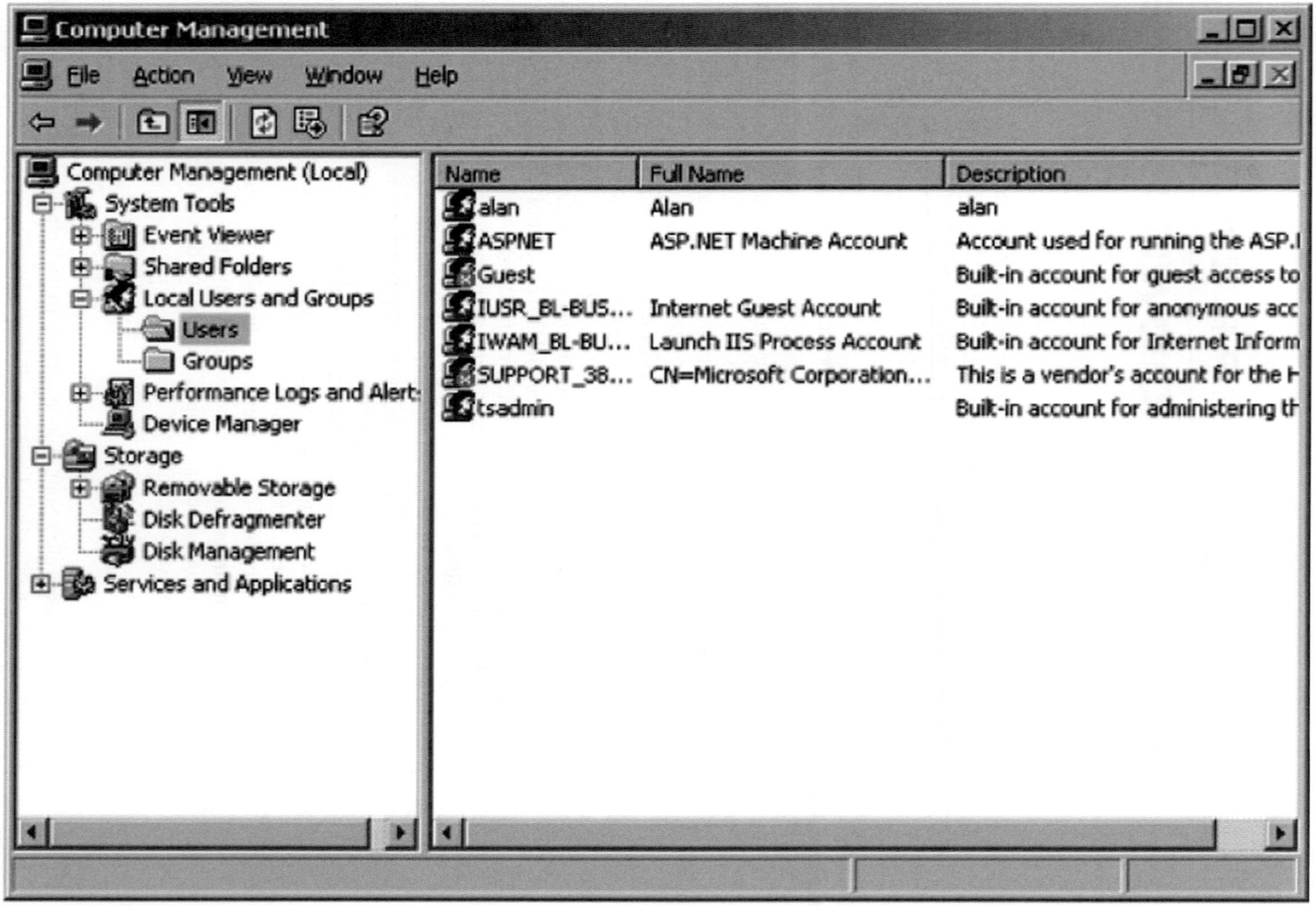

FIGURE F.1 List of users

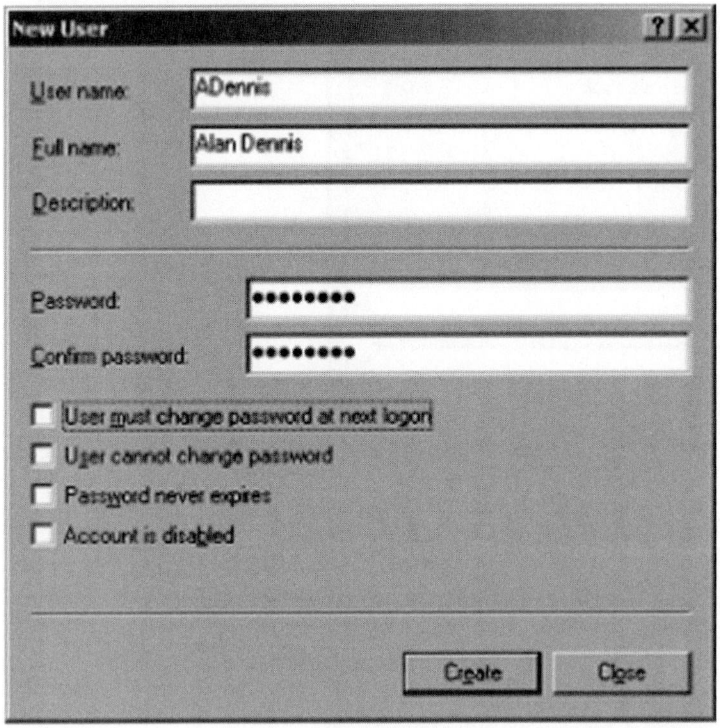

FIGURE F.2 Creating a user

shows the display after clicking on Local Users and Groups and then Users. This shows all currently defined users, which are those that were created automatically by Windows.[1]

To create a user, right click on the Users and then choose New User. You can then enter the information about the user such as the user name (i.e., userid) he or she will use to login as well as his or her full name and description (see Figure F.2). You also enter the password associated with the account, as well as the policies associated with the password. You can, for example, require the user to change the password when he or she next logs in, or prevent the user from changing the password. Click Create to add the user.

Setting User Properties

There are dozens of properties you can set for each user. After you have created the user, the user name will appear in the list shown in Figure F.1. Right click on the user name and then click Properties. You can record additional information about the user, define what groups the user belongs to (more on that in a moment), and even restrict what hours the account can be used (See Figure F.3).

[1]To create a domain account using Active Directory, click Start, Administrative Tools, Active Directory Users, and Computers. The screen in Figure F.1 would display the domains rather than users, which you could then click on to see the users and groups.

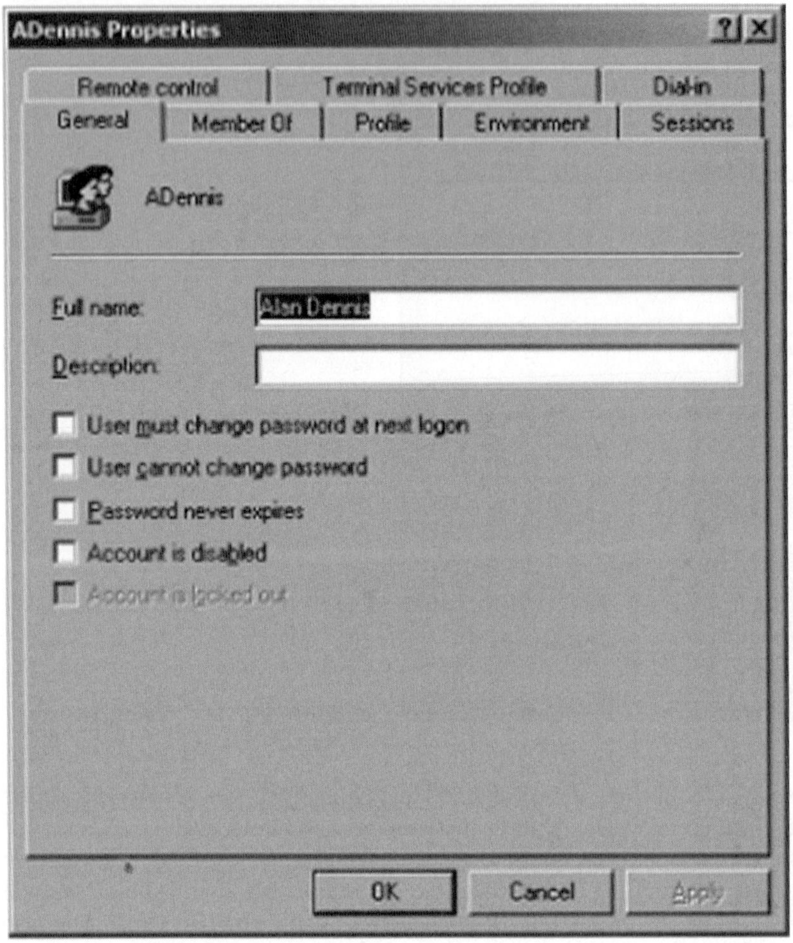

FIGURE F.3 Managing user properties

Creating Groups

Before you create groups, you should have a plan. Prepare a list of groups you would like to create and determine the hierarchy of the groups you want to implement.

To create a group, click Start, Administrative Tools, Computer Management, and then click on Groups. This will show you the list of currently defined groups which are those automatically defined by Windows (see Figure F.4).

Right click on Groups and then choose New Group. You can then enter the information about the group, including its name. This is very similar to creating a new user.

Adding Users to Groups

To add users to a group, click Start, Administrative Tools, Computer Management, and click on Users. This will show you the list of currently defined users as in Figure F.1.

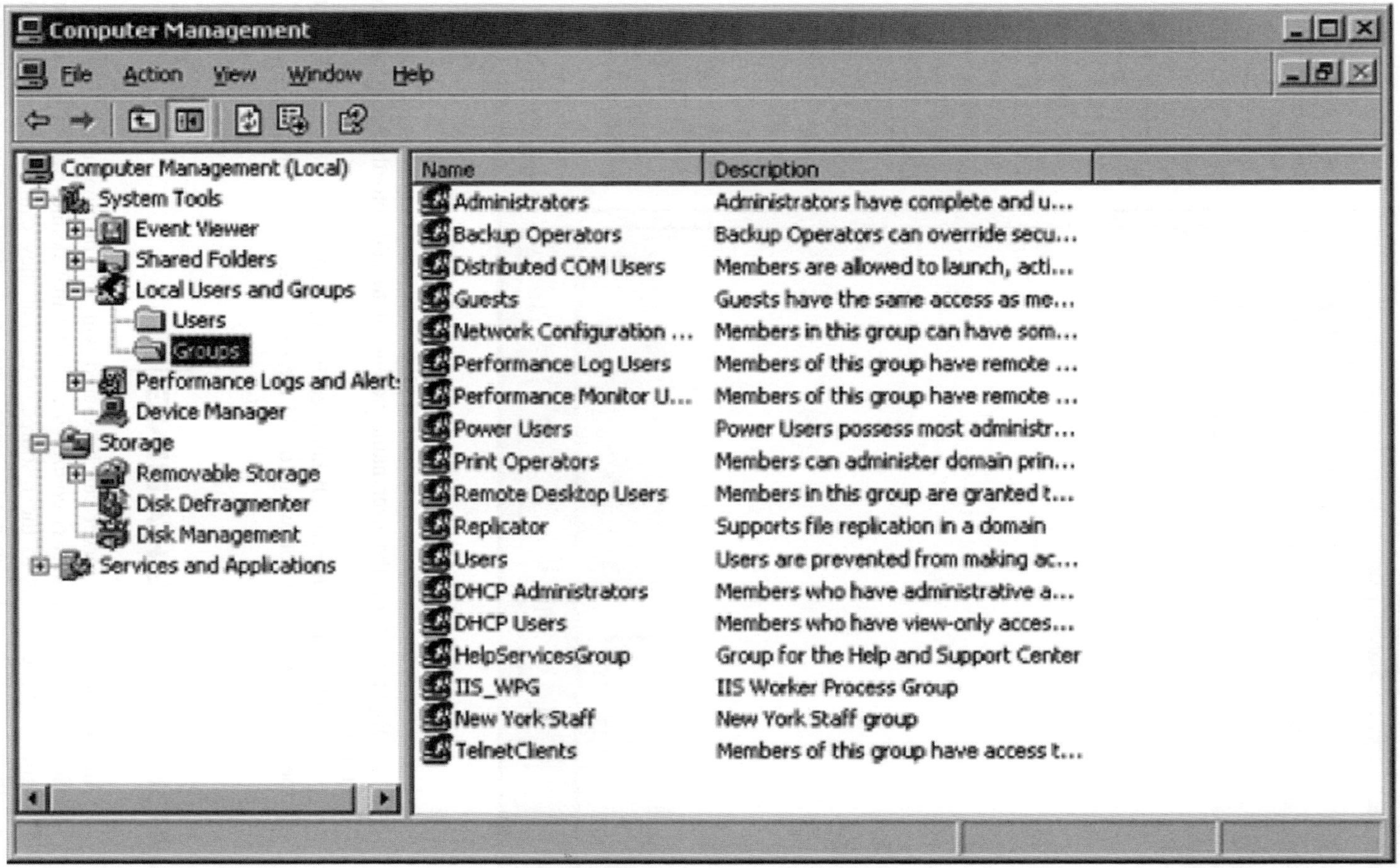

FIGURE F.4 User groups

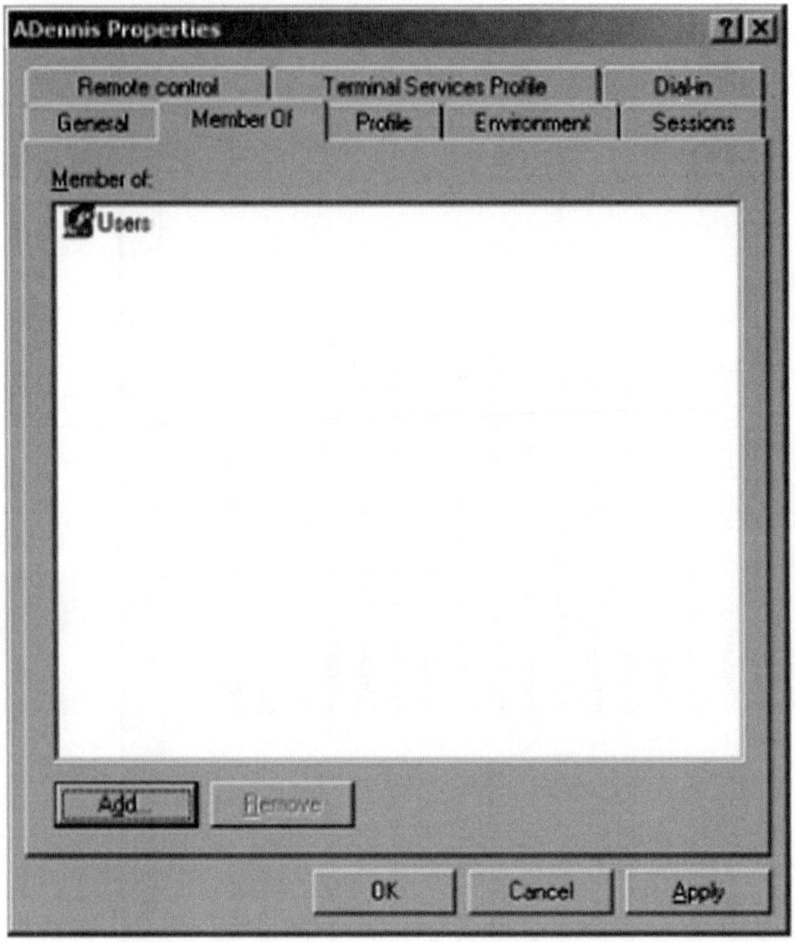

FIGURE F.5 Adding users to groups

Right click on the user name you want to add into the group. Then select the Properties.

Click on the Member Of tab (See Figure F.5). Click Add and select the name of the group into which you want to add the user. Then click OK.

MANAGING FILE SHARING

Any resource on the server can be shared with one or more users. Each resource (e.g., file, printer) has an *access control list* (ACL) that defines which user(s) and/or which group(s) have access to the resource and what they can do with it—in other words, their *permissions*. For example, some users might have permission only to read files in

Permission	When Applied to a File	When Applied to a Folder
List Folder Contents	This applies only to folders.	Permits the user to view the folder contents, but to do nothing else.
Read	Permits the user to read the file.	Permits the user to view the folder contents and to read every file in the folder.
Read and Execute	Permits the user to read a file and execute it, if it is a program.	Permits the user to view the folder contents and read or execute any file it contains.
Write	Permits the user to change the contents of a file or its attributes.	Permits the user to add new files and subfolders to the folder, but not to change any existing files in the folder.
Modify	Permits the user to change the contents of a file.	Permits the user to add new files and subfolders to the folder, and to change or delete any existing files and their attributes in the folder.
Full Control	Permits the user to do anything to the file.	Permits the user to do anything to the folder.

FIGURE F.6 File and folder permissions

a shared directory, others might have permission only to add new files to the directory, while others might have permission to change or delete existing files. Figure F.6 lists the basic permissions you can set. There are also more advanced *special permissions* that can be set as well.

Permissions can be assigned to folders or to files. If you assign a permission to a folder, all the files and subfolders it contains receive the same permissions unless you specifically change the permissions of the files and subfolders. Likewise, if you grant a permission to a group, all users in the group and all subgroups receive the same permissions.

Creating a Shared Folder

To create a shared folder, you must first create the folder exactly as you would in Windows on your desktop computer. Open Windows Explorer (click Start, Programs, Accessories, Windows Explorer). Click on the folder in which to place the shared folder and click File, New, Folder. Then type the name of the folder.

There are two steps in permitting users to access the shared folder. First, you must enable sharing for the folder and then define the security ACL. This is rather cumbersome, but this is how Windows requires you to do it.

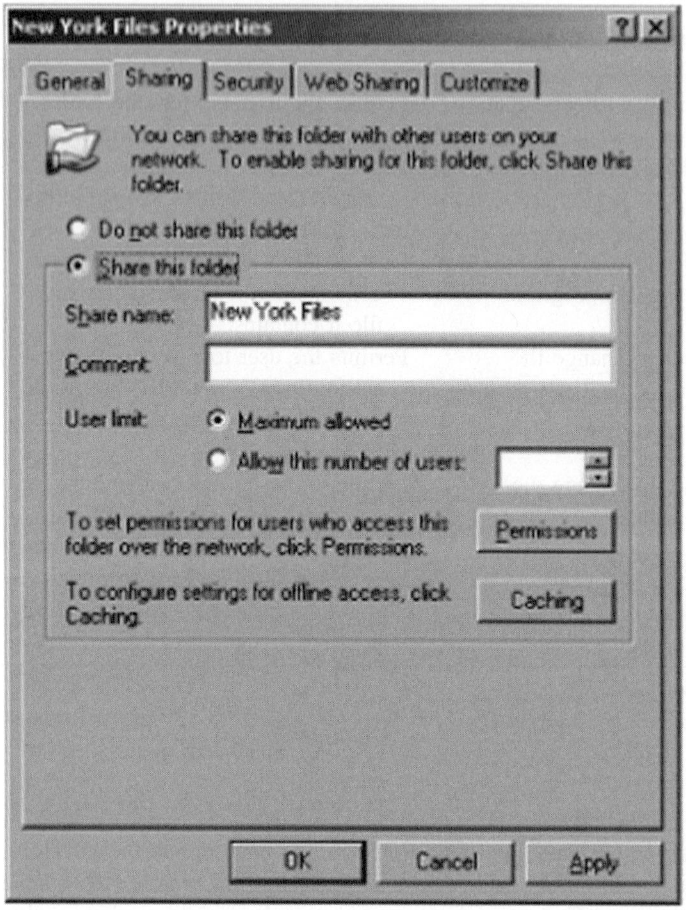

FIGURE F.7 Enabling sharing

Enabling Sharing

In Windows Explorer right click on the folder and Select Properties. The click the Sharing tab (see Figure F.7). Click the radio button to Share this folder. Then type the name that the folder will be known as to users.

Next, click Permissions. This will show you the list of users who can access this folder (see Figure F.8). By default, Windows permits the group named Everyone to access all shared folders. The Everyone group is exactly what it sounds like—every user name on the server. Typically, network managers start by removing the Everyone group and adding in only those users or groups who should have access to the folder. Click the Remove button to remove the Everyone group.

Click Add to grant permission to access this folder to a user (see Figure F.9). In the window, type the name of the group or user with whom you want to share the folder and click Check Names. Then click OK.

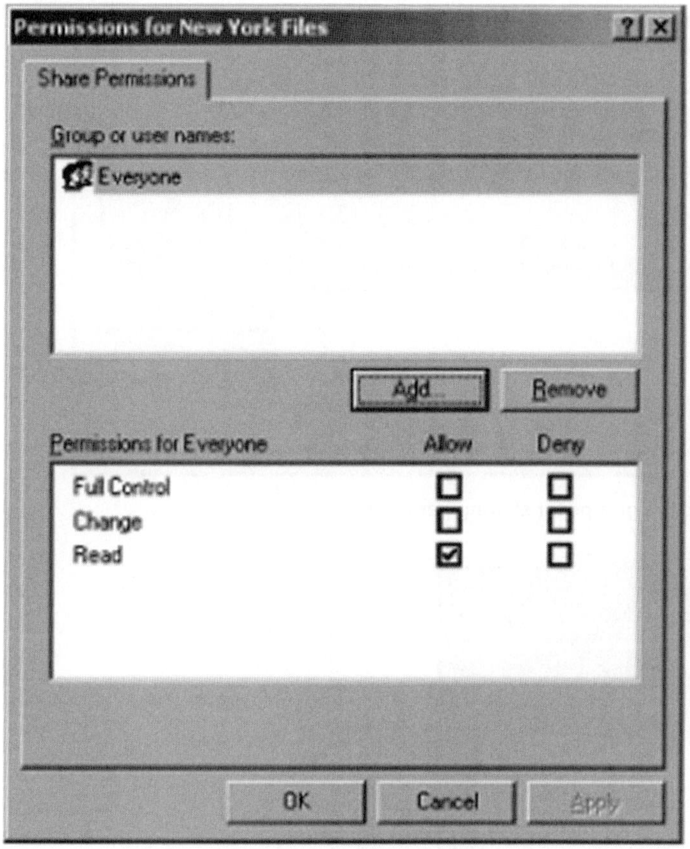

FIGURE F.8 Viewing sharing permissions

Once the user name is found, you can then define the type of access to permit (see Figure F.10). In this figure, you can see that we've granted access to the group called New York Staff. The types of access are fewer than those shown in Figure F.6, but there will be more options shortly. Then click OK.

At this point, the folder is now available to be shared to those users or groups to whom you have granted permission. However, they still cannot access the folder. You must define the security access list first.

Defining Security

In Windows Explorer, right click on the folder and Select Properties and then click the Security tab (see Figure F.11). This will display all users and groups who have security access to the folder. You will see that New York Staff does not appear in this list. Even though they were granted sharing permission, this does not grant security permission. Click Add and enter the New York Staff group as a permitted group.

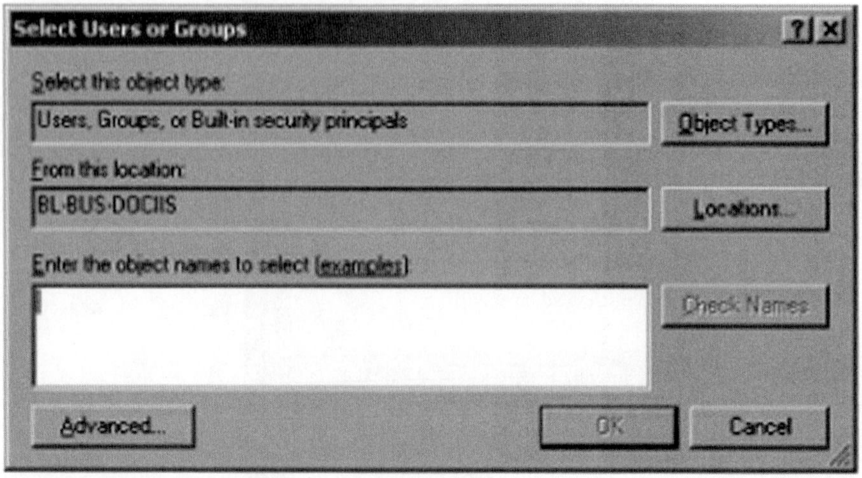

FIGURE F.9 Selecting groups for sharing permissions

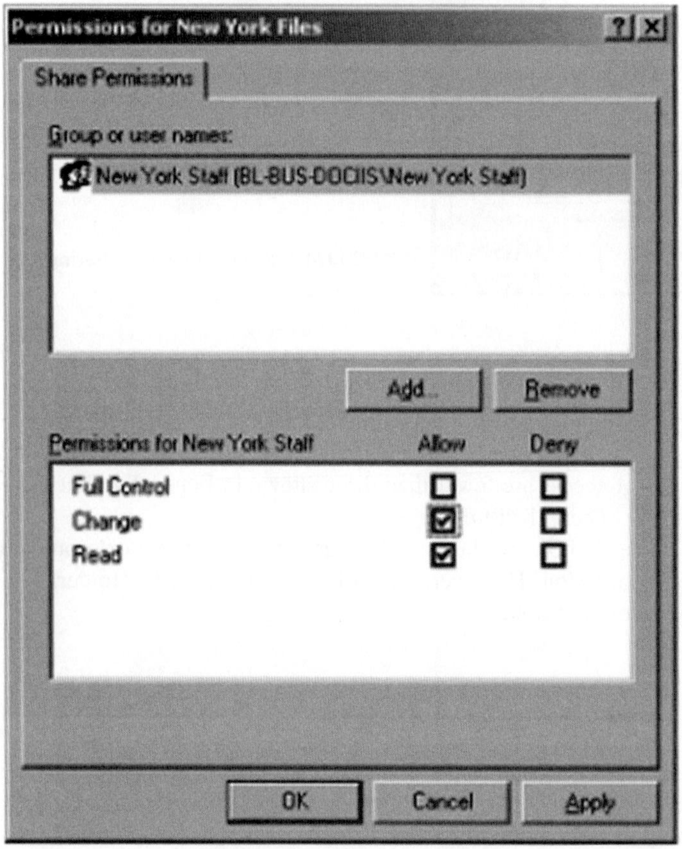

FIGURE F.10 Setting sharing permissions

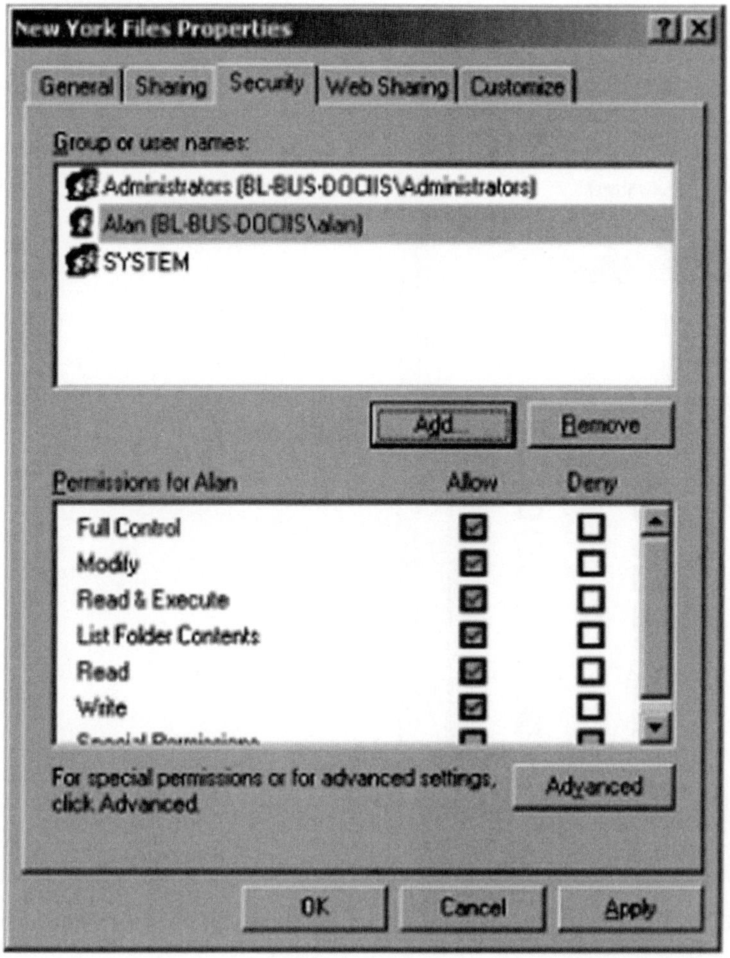

FIGURE F.11 Viewing security permissions

You can then grant the types of permissions this group has (see Figure F.12). This is the same list of options as described in Figure F.6.

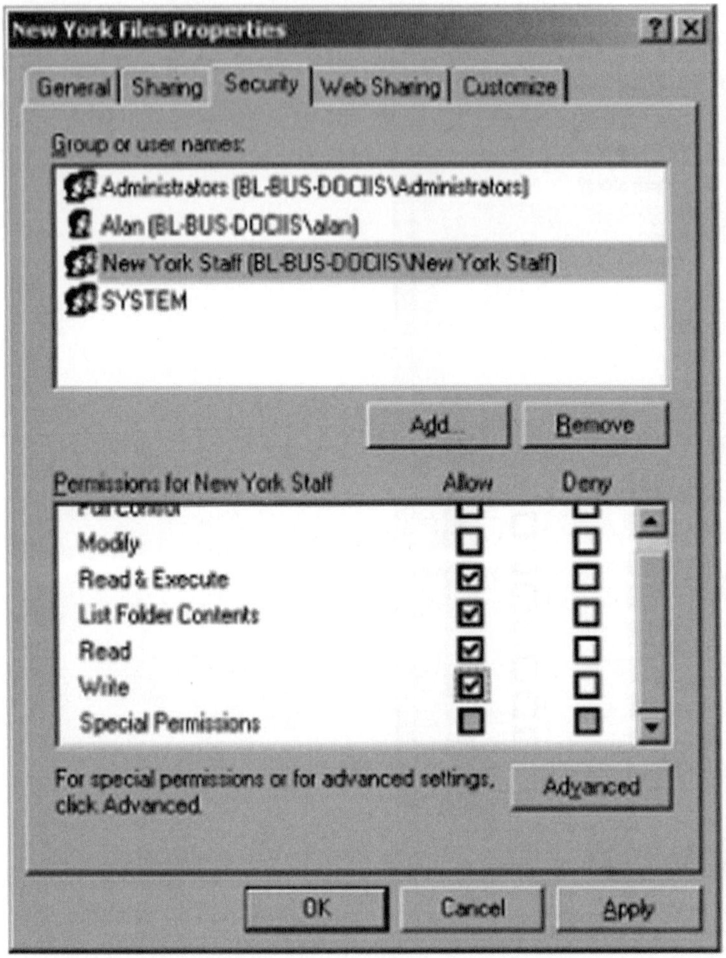

FIGURE F.12 Granting security permissions

GLOSSARY

A

Abilene network: The Abilene network is the part of Internet2 that is run by Indiana University.

access layer: The access layer is the part of a network that connects clients or servers to the rest of the network. It is often a LAN.

access point (AP): The part of the wireless LAN that connects the LAN to other networks.

ACK: *See* **acknowledgment (ACK)**.

acknowledgment (ACK): A character indicating a positive acknowledgment that a message has been received correctly.

ACM: Association for Computing Machinery. The ACM is an association of computer professionals.

acronym: A word formed from the initial letters or groups of letters of words in a phrase. An example is the word *laser*, which means *l*ight *a*mplification by *s*timulated *e*mission of *r*adiation.

address: A coded representation of the destination of data or of its originating source. For example, multiple computers on one communication circuit must each have a unique data link layer address.

address resolution: The process of determining the lower-layer address from a higher-layer address. For example, IP address resolution means determining the IP address from the application-layer address, whereas data link layer address resolution means determining the data link layer address from an IP address.

Address Resolution Protocol (ARP): The network-layer protocol standard for data link layer address resolution requests.

ADSL: *See* **asymmetric DSL (ADSL)**.

Advanced Encryption Standard (AES): A new single-key encryption standard authorized by NIST that replaces DES. It uses the Rijndael (pronounced "rain doll") algorithm and has key sizes of 128, 192, and 256 bits. NIST estimates that using the most advanced computers and techniques available today, it will require about 150 trillion years to crack AES by brute force.

Advanced Research and Development Network Operations Center (ARDNOC): The agency funded by the Canadian government to develop new Internet2 technologies and protocols.

AES: *See* **Advanced Encryption Standard (AES).**

American National Standards Institute (ANSI): The principal standards-setting body in the United States. ANSI is a nonprofit, nongovernmental organization supported by more than 1,000 trade organizations, professional societies, and companies. It belongs to the ITU-T CCITT and the ISO.

American Standard Code for Information Interchange: *See* **ASCII**.

amplifier: A device used to boost the strength of a signal. Amplifiers are spaced at intervals throughout the length of a communication circuit to increase the distance a signal can travel. *See also* **repeater**.

amplitude modulation: *See* **modulation, amplitude**.

analog: Pertaining to representation by means of continuously variable quantity, such as varying frequencies. Physical quantities such as temperature are continuous variable, and therefore are "analog."

analog signal: A signal in the form of a continuously varying quantity such as amplitude, which reflects variations in the loudness of the human voice.

analog transmission: Transmission of a continuously variable signal as opposed to a discrete on/off signal. The traditional way of transmitting a telephone or voice signal is analog.

ANI: *See* **automatic number identification (ANI).**

anonymous FTP: *See* **File Transfer Protocol (FTP).**

ANSI: *See* **American National Standards Institute (ANSI).**

AP: *See* **access point (AP).**

API: Application Program Interface. API is the way IBM links incompatible equipment for microcomputer-to-mainframe links. API allows applications on microcomputers and mainframes to speak directly to each other at the application software level, even though the equipment is from different vendors.

Apple Talk: A set of communication protocols that defines networking for Apple computers. Rarely used today.

application service provider (ASP): An application service develops an application system (e.g., an airline reservation system, a payroll system) and companies purchase the service, without ever installing the software on their own computers. They simply use the service the same way you might use a Web hosting service to publish your own Web pages rather than attempting to purchase and operate your own Web server.

ARCnet: Attached Resource Computing network. A proprietary token-bus LAN developed by the Datapoint Corporation.

ARDNOC: *See* **Advanced Research and Development Network Operations Center (ARDNOC).**

ARP: *See* **Address Resolution Protocol (ARP).**

ARPANET: One of the early packet-switching networks. ARPANET was developed by the U.S. Department of Defense Advanced Research Projects Agency. It was the predecessor of the Internet.

ARQ: Automatic Repeat reQuest. A system employing an error-detecting code so conceived that any error initiates a repetition of the transmission of the incorrectly received message.

ASCII: American Standard Code for Information Interchange. Pronounced "ask-e." An eight-level code for data transfer adopted by the ANSI to achieve compatibility among data devices.

asymmetric DSL (ADSL): A data link layer technology that provides high-speed ("broadband") communication over traditional telephone lines. A DSL modem is used to provide three channels: a traditional voice channel, an upstream channel for communicating from the client to the ISP (often at speeds of 64 to 640 Kbps), and a downstream channel for communicating from the ISP to the client (often at speeds of 640 Kbps to 6 Mbps).

asynchronous transfer mode (ATM): A communication switch that handles interface speeds ranging from 25 million to 622 million bps. It multiplexes data streams onto the same BN by using cell relay techniques. ATM switches can handle multimedia traffic, such as data, graphics, voice, and video.

asynchronous transmission: Transmission in which each information character is individually synchronized, usually by start and stop bits. The gap between each character is not a fixed length. *Compare with* **synchronous transmission**.

ATM: *See* **asynchronous transfer mode (ATM)**. In banking, an **automated teller machine**.

attenuation: As a signal travels through a circuit, it gradually attenuates, or loses power. Expressed in decibels, attenuation is the difference between the transmitted and received power caused by loss of signal strength through the equipment, communication circuits, or other devices.

authentication: A security method of guaranteeing that a message is genuine, that it has arrived unaltered, and that it comes from the source indicated.

automatic number identification (ANI): The process whereby a long-distance common carrier provides its customers with a visual display of an incoming caller's telephone number.

Automatic Repeat reQuest: *See* **ARQ.**

B

backbone network (BN): A large network to which many networks within an organization are connected. It usually is a network that interconnects all networks on a single site, but it can be larger if it connects all the organization's terminals, microcomputers, mainframes, LANs, and other communication equipment.

BALUN: balanced/unbalanced. An impedance-matching device to connect balanced twisted-pair cabling with unbalanced coaxial cable.

bandwidth: The difference between the highest and lowest frequencies in a band. For example, a voice-grade circuit has a 4,000-Hz bandwidth. In common usage, *bandwidth* refers to circuit capacity; when people say they need more bandwidth, they need a higher transmission speed.

basic rate interface (BRI): In ISDN, two 64,000-bps B circuits for data transmission and one 16,000-bps D circuit for signaling (2 B+D). Also called basic rate access. *See also* **primary rate interface (PRI)**.

baud: Unit of signaling speed. Now obsolete and replaced by the term *symbol rate*. The speed in baud is the number of signal elements per second. If each signal represents only 1 bit, *baud* is the same as *bits per second (bps)*. When each signal contains more than 1 bit, *baud* does not equal *bps*.

BCC: *See* **block check character (BCC)**.

BER: bit-error rate. The number of bits received in error divided by the total number of bits received. An indicator of circuit quality.

BERT: bit-error rate testing. Testing a data line with a pattern of bits that are compared before and after the transmission to detect errors.

BGP: *See* **Border Gateway Protocol (BGP).**

binary: A number system using only the two symbols 0 and 1 that is especially well adapted to computer usage because 0 and 1 can be represented as "on" and "off," respectively, or as negative charges and positive charges, respectively. The binary digits appear in strings of 0's and 1's.

bipolar transmission: A method of digital transmission in which binary 0 is sent as a negative pulse and binary 1 is sent as a positive pulse.

bit: 1. An abbreviation of the term *binary digit*. 2. A single pulse in a group of pulses. 3. A unit of information capacity.

bit-error rate (BER): *See* **BER.**

bit-error rate testing (BERT): *See* **BERT.**

bit rate: The rate at which bits are transmitted over a communication path, normally expressed in bits per second (bps). The bit rate should not be confused with the data signaling rate (*baud*), which measures the rate of signal changes being transmitted. *See also* **bps.**

bit stream: A continuous series of bits being transmitted on a transmission line.

bits per second (bps): *See* **bps.**

BKER: Block-error rate. The number of blocks received in error divided by the total number of blocks received.

BKERT: Block-error rate testing. Testing a data link with groups of information arranged into transmission blocks for error checking.

block: Sets of contiguous bits or bytes that make up a message, frame, or packet.

block check character (BCC): The character(s) at the end of a binary synchronous communications (BSC) message used to check for errors.

block-error rate (BKER): *See* **BKER.**

block-error rate testing (BKERT): *See* **BKERT.**

Bluetooth: A standard for short-distance wireless communication.

BN: *See* **backbone network (BN)**.

BOC: *See* **RBOC.**

BONDING: BONDING (Bandwidth on Demand Interoperatibility Networking Group) is an inverse multiplexing proposal for combining several 56-Kbps or 64-Kbps circuits into one higher-speed circuit.

Border Gateway Protocol (BGP): A network-layer standard protocol used to exchange route information between routers using dynamic decentralized routing. Used only between different TCP/IP autonomous systems (i.e., major sections of the Internet).

bps: Bits per second. The basic unit of data communication rate measurement. Usually refers to rate of information bits transmitted. *Contrast with* **baud** and **bit rate.**

BRI: *See* **basic rate interface (BRI)**

bridge: A device that connects two similar networks using the same data link and network protocols. *Compare with* **gateway, router**, and **brouter**.

broadband circuit: An analog communication circuit.

broadband communications: Originally, the term referred to analog communications, but it has become corrupted in common usage so that it now usually means high-speed communications networks, typically Internet access technologies with access speeds of 1 Mbps or higher.

broadband Ethernet: The 10Broad36 version of Ethernet IEEE 802.3, meaning that it transmits at 10 millions bps in broadband with a maximum distance of 3,600 meters.

broadcast routing: *See* **decentralized routing**.

brouter: A piece of hardware that combines the functions of a bridge and a router. *See also* **bridge** and **router**.

brute-force attack: A way of breaking an encrypted message by trying all possible values of the key.

buffer: A device used for the temporary storage of data, primarily to compensate for differences in data flow rates (for example, between a terminal and its transmission circuit) but also as a security measure to allow retransmission of data if an error is detected during transmission.

burst error: A series of consecutive errors in data transmission. Refers to the phenomenon on communication circuits in which errors are highly prone to occurring in groups or clusters.

bus: A transmission path or circuit. Typically an electrical connection with one or more conductors in which all attached devices receive all transmissions at the same time.

byte: A small group of data bits that is handled as a unit. In most cases, it is an 8-bit byte and it is known as a *character*.

C

call-back modem: When a user calls a host computer, the modem disconnects the call after receiving the password and calls back to the caller's predefined telephone number to establish a connection.

CA*net: CA*net is the Canadian network that forms part of Internet2.

carrier: An analog signal at some fixed amplitude and frequency that then is combined with an information-bearing signal to produce an intelligent output signal suitable for transmission of meaningful information. *Also called carrier wave* or **carrier frequency**.

carrier frequency: The basic frequency or pulse repetition rate of a signal bearing no intelligence until it is modulated by another signal that does impart intelligence.

Carrier Sense Multiple Access: *See* **CSMA/CA** and **CSMA/CD.**

CCITT: *See* **Consultative Committee on International Telegraph and Telephone (CCITT).** Now obsolete and renamed **International Telecommunications Union—Telecommunications (ITU-T).**

CD: 1. Collision detection in the CSMA (Carrier Sense Multiple Access) protocol for LANs. 2. Carrier detect occurs when a modem detects a carrier signal to be received.

central office: The switching and control facility set up by the local telephone company (common carrier) where the subscriber's local loop terminates. Central offices handle calls within a specified geographic area, which is identified by the first three digits of the telephone number. *Also called* an **end office** or **exchange office.**

Central processing unit (CPU): *See* **CPU.**

CENTREX: A widespread telephone company switching service that uses dedicated central office switching equipment. CENTREX CPE is where the user site also has customer premises equipment (CPE).

CERT: *See* **Computer Emergency Response Team (CERT).**

certificate authority (CA): A CA is a trusted organization that can vouch for the authenticity of the person or organization using authentication (e.g., VeriSign). A person wanting to use a CA registers with the CA and must provide some proof of identify. CA issues a digital certificate that is the requestor's public key encrypted using the CA's private key as proof of identity that can be attached to the user's e-mail or Web transactions.

channel: 1. A path for transmission of electromagnetic signals. *Synonym for* **line** or **link**. *Compare with* **circuit**. 2. A data communications path. Circuits may be divided into subcircuits.

character: A member of a set of elements used for the organization, control, or representation of data. Characters may be letters, digits, punctuation marks, or other symbols. *Also called* a **byte**.

cheapnet: *See* **thin Ethernet**.

checking, echo: A method of checking the accuracy of transmitted data in which the received data are returned to the sending end for comparison with the original data.

checking, parity: *See* **parity check**.

checking, polynomial: *See* **polynomial checking**.

circuit: The path over which the voice, data, or image transmission travels. Circuits can be twisted-wire pairs, coaxial cables, fiber-optic cables, microwave transmissions, and so forth. *Compare with* **channel, line**, and **link**.

circuit switching: A method of communications whereby an electrical connection between calling and called stations is established on demand for exclusive use of the circuit until the connection is terminated.

cladding: A layer of material (usually glass) that surrounds the glass core of an optical fiber. Prevents loss of signal by reflecting light back into the core.

client: The input–output hardware device at the user's end of a communication circuit. There are three major categories of clients: microcomputers, terminals, and special-purpose terminals.

cluster controller: A device that controls the input–output operations of the cluster of devices (microcomputers, terminals, printers, and so forth) attached to it. Also called a *terminal controller*. For example, the 3274 Control Unit is a cluster controller that directs all communications between the host computer and remote devices attached to it.

CMIP: *See* **Common Management Interface Protocol (CMIP)**.

coaxial cable: An insulated wire that runs through the middle of a cable. A second braided wire surrounds the insulation of the inner wire like a sheath. Used on LANs for transmitting messages between devices.

code: A transformation or representation of information in a different form according to some set of preestablished conventions. *See also* **ASCII** and **EBCDIC**.

codec: A codec translates analog voice data into digital data for transmission over computer networks. Two codecs are needed—one at the sender's end and one at the receiver's end.

code conversion: A hardware box or software that converts from one code to another, such as from ASCII to EBCDIC.

collapsed backbone network: In a collapsed BN, the set of routers in a typical BN is replaced by one switch and a set of circuits to each LAN. The collapsed backbone has more cable but fewer devices. There is no backbone cable. The "backbone" exists only in the switch.

collision: When two computers or devices transmit at the same time on a shared multipoint circuit, their signals collide and destroy each other.

common carrier: An organization in the business of providing regulated telephone, telegraph, telex, and data communications services, such as AT&T, MCI, Bell-South, and NYNEX. This term is applied most often to U.S. and Canadian commercial organizations, but sometimes it is used to refer to telecommunication entities, such as government-operated suppliers of communication services in other countries. *See also* **PTT**.

Common Management Interface Protocol (CMIP): CMIP is a network management system that monitors and tracks network usage and other parameters for user workstations and other nodes. It is similar to SNMP, but it is more complete and is better in many ways.

communication services: A group of transmission facilities that is available for lease or purchase.

comparison risk ranking: The process by which the members of a Delphi team reach a consensus on which network threats have the highest risk. It produces a ranked list from high risk to low risk.

component: One of the specific pieces of a network, system, or application. When these components are assembled, they become the network, system, or application. Components are the individual parts of the network that we want to safeguard or restrict by using controls.

compression: *See* **data compression.**

Computer Emergency Response Team (CERT): The job of CERT, located at Carnegie Mellon University, is to respond to computer security problems on the Internet, raise awareness of computer security issues, and prevent security breaches. It was established by the U.S. Department of Defense in 1988 after a virus shut down almost 10 percent of the computers on the Internet. Many organizations are starting their own computer emergency response teams, so the term is beginning to refer to any response team, not just the one at Carnegie Mellon University.

concentrator: A device that multiplexes several low-speed communication circuits onto a single high-speed trunk. A remote data concentrator (RDC) is similar in function to a multiplexer but differs because the host computer software usually must be rewritten to accommodate the RDC. RDCs differ from statistical multiplexes because the total capacity of the high-speed outgoing circuit, in characters per second, is equal to the total capacity of the incoming low-speed circuits. On the other hand, output capacity of a statistical multiplexer (stat mux) is less than the total capacity of the incoming circuits.

conditioning: A technique of applying electronic filtering elements to a communication line to improve the capability of that line so it can support higher data transmission rates. *See also* **equalization.**

configuration: The actual or practical layout of a network that takes into account its software, hardware, and cabling. Configurations may be multidrop, point-to-point, LANs, and the like. By contrast, a topology is the geometric layout (ring, bus, star) of the configuration. Topologies are the building blocks of configurations. *Compare with* **topology.**

connectionless routing: Connectionless routing means each packet is treated separately and makes its own way through the network. It is possible that different packets will take different routes through the network depending on the type of routing used and the amount of traffic.

connection-oriented routing: Connection-oriented routing sets up a virtual circuit (one that appears to use point-to-point circuit switching) between the sender and receiver. The network layer makes one routing decision when the connection is established, and all packets follow the same route. All packets in the same message arrive at the destination in the same order in which they were sent.

Consultative Committee on International Telegraph and Telephone (CCITT): An international organization that sets worldwide communication standards. Its new name is **International Telecommunications Union—Telecommunications (ITU-T).**

content caching: Storing content from other Web sites on your network to reduce traffic on your Internet connection. A content engine regularly stores incoming static content such as banners and graphics files so that future requests for those items can be processed internally.

content delivery: Storing content for your Web sites on the content delivery provider's servers spread around the Internet to reduce traffic on your Internet connection. The content delivery provider's servers contain the static content on your pages such as banners and graphics files. Software on your Web server locates the nearest content delivery server to the user (based on his or her IP address) and changes the references on your Web pages to draw the static content from that server. Content delivery was pioneered by Akamai, which is one of the leading content delivery services on the Internet.

contention: A method by which devices on the same shared multipoint circuit compete for time on the circuit.

control: A mechanism to ensure that the threats to a network are mitigated. There are two levels of controls: system-level controls and application-level controls.

control character: A character whose occurrence in a particular context specifies some network operation or function.

control spreadsheet: A two-dimensional matrix showing the relationship between the controls in a network, the threats that are being mitigated, and the components that are being protected. The controls listed in each cell represent the specific control enacted to reduce or eliminate the exposure.

core layer: The core layer is the central part of a network that provides access to the distribution layer. It is often a very fast BN that runs through the center of a campus or office complex.

COS: Corporation for Open Systems. An organization of computer and communications equipment vendors and users formed to accelerate the introduction of products based on the seven-layer OSI model. Its primary interest is the application layer (layer 7) of the OSI model and the X.400 e-mail standard.

CPE: *See* **customer premises equipment (CPE).**

CPU: central processing unit.

CRC: Cyclical redundancy check. An error-checking control technique using a specific binary prime divisor that results in a unique remainder. It usually is a 16- to 32-bit character.

CSMA/CA: Carrier Sense Multiple Access (CSMA) with Collision Avoidance (CA). This protocol is similar to the Carrier Sense Multiple Access (CSMA) with Collision Detection (CD) protocol. Whereas CSMA/CD sends a data packet and then reports back if it collides with another packet, CSMA/CA sends a small preliminary packet to determine whether the network is busy. If there is a collision, it is with the small packet rather than with the entire message. CA is thought to be more efficient because it reduces the time required to recover from collisions.

CSMA/CD: Carrier Sense Multiple Access (CSMA) with Collision Detection (CD). A system used in contention networks. The network interface unit listens for the presence of a carrier before attempting to send and detects the presence of a collision by monitoring for a distorted pulse.

customer premises equipment (CPE): Equipment that provides the interface between the customer's CENTREX system and the telephone network. It physically resides at the customer's site rather than the telephone company's end office. *CPE* generally refers to voice telephone equipment instead of data transmission equipment.

cut through switching: A type of switching in which messages are forwarded as they arrive, almost on a bit-by-bit basis.

cyclical redundancy check (CRC): *See* **CRC.**

D

data: 1. Specific individual facts or a list of such items. 2. Facts from which conclusions can be drawn.

data circuit terminating equipment (DCE): *See* **DCE.**

data compression: The technique that provides for the transmission of fewer data bits without the loss of information. The receiving location expands the received data bits into the original bit sequence.

Data Encryption Standard (DES): *See* **DES.**

Data over Cable System Interface Specification (DOCSIS): A de facto data link layer standard for transmitting data via a cable modem using Ethernet-like protocols.

Data-over-Voice (DOV): When data and voice share the same transmission medium. Data transmissions are superimposed over the voice transmission.

data terminal equipment (DTE): *See* **DTE.**

datagram: A datagram is a connectionless service in packet-switched networks. Each packet has a destination and sequence number and may follow a different route through the network. Different routes may deliver packets at different speeds, so data packets often arrive out of sequence. The sequence number tells the network how to reassemble the packets into a continuous message.

dB: *See* **decibel (dB).**

DCE: Data circuit terminating equipment. The equipment (usually the modem) installed at the user's site that provides all the functions required to establish, maintain, and terminate a connection, including the signal conversion and coding between the data terminal equipment (DTE) and the common carrier's line.

DDoS attack: *See* **distributed denial-of-service (DDoS) attack**.

decentralized routing: With decentralized routing, all computers in the network make their own routing decisions. There are three major types of decentralized routing. With static routing, the routing table is developed by the network manager and remains unchanged until the network manager updates it. With dynamic routing, the goal is to improve network performance by routing messages over the fastest possible route; an initial routing table is developed by the network manager but is continuously updated to reflect changing network conditions, such as message traffic. With broadcast routing, the message is sent to all computers, but it is processed only by the computer to which it is addressed.

decibel (dB): A tenth of a bel. A unit for measuring relative strength of a signal parameter such as power and voltage. The number of decibels is ten times the logarithm (base 10) of the ratio of the power of two signals, or ratio of the power of one signal to a reference level. The reference level always must be indicated, such as 1 milliwatt for power ratio.

dedicated circuit: A leased communication circuit that goes from your site to some other location. It is a clear, unbroken communication path that is yours to use 24 hours per day, 7 days per week. Also called a *private circuit* or **leased circuit**.

delay distortion: A distortion on communication lines that is caused because some frequencies travel more slowly than others in a given transmission medium and therefore arrive at the destination at slightly different times. Delay distortion is measured in microseconds of delay relative to the delay at 1,700 Hz. This type of distortion does not affect voice, but it can have a serious effect on data transmissions.

delay equalizer: A corrective device for making the phase delay or envelope delay of a circuit substantially constant over a desired frequency range. *See also* **equalizer**.

Delphi group: A small group of experts (three to nine people) who meet to develop a consensus when it may be impossible or too expensive to collect more accurate data. For example, a Delphi group of communication experts might assemble to reach a consensus on the various threats to a communication network, the potential dollar losses for each occurrence of each threat, and the estimated frequency of occurrence for each threat.

denial of service (DoS) attack: A DoS attempts to disrupt the network by flooding the network with messages so that the network cannot process messages from normal users.

DES: Data Encryption Standard. Developed by IBM and the U.S. National Institute of Standards, this widely used single-key encryption algorithm uses a 64-bit key.

desktop videoconferencing: With desktop videoconferencing, small cameras are installed on top of each user's computer so that participants can hold meetings from their offices.

DHCP: *See* **Dynamic Host Control Protocol (DHCP).**

digital signal: A discrete or discontinuous signal whose various states are discrete intervals apart, such as +15 volts and -15 volts.

digital subscriber line (DSL): A data link layer technology that provides high-speed ("broadband") communication over traditional telephone lines. A DSL modem is used to provide three channels: a traditional voice channel, an upstream channel for communicating from the client to the ISP (often at speeds of 64 to 640 Kbps), and a downstream channel for communicating from the ISP to the client (often at speeds of 640 Kbps to 6 Mbps).

distortion: The unwanted modification or change of signals from their true form by some characteristic of the communication line or equipment being used for transmission—for example, delay distortion and amplitude distortion.

distortion types: 1. *Bias:* A type of distortion resulting when the intervals of modulation do not all have exactly their normal durations. 2. *Characteristic:* Distortion caused by transient disturbances that are present in the transmission circuit because of modulation. 3. *Delay:* Distortion occurring when the envelope delay of a circuit is not consistent over the frequency range required for transmission. 4. *End:* Distortion of start–stop signals. The shifting of the end of all marking pulses from their proper positions in relation to the beginning of the start pulse. 5. *Jitter:* A type of distortion that results in the intermittent shortening or lengthening of the signals. This distortion is entirely random in nature and can be caused by hits on the line. 6. *Harmonic:* The resultant process of harmonic frequencies (due to nonlinear characteristics of a transmission circuit) in the response when a sinusoidal stimulus is applied.

distributed denial of service (DDoS) attack: With a DDoS attack, a hacker breaks into and takes control of many computers on the Internet (often several hundred to several thousand) and uses them to launch the DoS attack from thousands of computers at the same time.

distribution layer: The distribution layer is the part of a network that connects the access layer to other access layers and to the core layer. It is often a BN in a building.

DNS: *See* **Domain Name Service (DNS)**.

DOCSIS: *See* **Data over Cable System Interface Specification (DOCSIS)**.

Domain Name Service (DNS): A server that provides a directory used to supply IP addresses for application-layer addresses—that is, a server that performs IP address resolution.

DoS attack: *See* **denial of service (DoS) attack**.

download: The process of loading software and data into the nodes of a network from the central node. Downloading usually refers to the movement of data from a host mainframe computer to a remote terminal or microcomputer.

DPSK: Differential phase shift keying. *See* **modulation, phase**.

DSL: *See* **digital subscriber line (DSL)**.

DTE: Data terminal equipment. Any piece of equipment at which a communication path begins or ends, such as a terminal.

duplexing: An alternative to the process of mirroring, which occurs when a database server mirrors or backs up the database with each transaction. In mirroring, the server writes on two different hard disks through two different disk controllers. Duplexing is more redundant and therefore even safer than mirroring, because the database is written to two different hard disks on two different disk circuits. *Compare with* **mirroring**.

Dynamic Host Control Protocol (DHCP): A network-layer protocol standard used to supply TCP/IP address information using dynamic address assignment.

dynamic routing: *See* **decentralized routing**.

E

e-mail: *See* **electronic mail (e-mail)**.

EBCDIC: Extended Binary Coded Decimal Interchange Code. A standard code consisting of a set of 8-bit characters used for information representation and interchange among data processing and communication systems. Very common in IBM equipment.

echo cancellation: Used in higher-speed modems to isolate and filter out (cancel) echoes when half-duplex transmissions use stop and wait ARQ (Automatic Repeat reQuest) protocols. Needed especially for satellite links.

echo checking: *See* **checking, echo**.

echo suppressor: A device for use in a two-way telephone circuit (especially circuits over 900 miles long) to attenuate echo currents in one direction caused by telephone currents in the other direction. This is done by sending an appropriate disabling tone to the circuit.

ECMA: *See* **European Computer Manufacturers Association (ECMA)**.

EDI: *See* **Electronic Data Interchange (EDI)**.

EIA: *See* **Electronic Industries Association (EIA)**.

Electronic Data Interchange (EDI): Electronic Data Interchange for Administration, Commerce, and Transport. Standardizes the electronic interchange of business documents for both ASCII and graphics. Endorsed by the ISO. Defines major components of the ANSI X.12 EDI standard.

Electronic Industries Association (EIA): Composed of electronic manufacturers in the United States. Recommends standards for electrical and functional characteristics of interface equipment. Belongs to ANSI. Known for the RS232 interface connector cable standard.

electronic mail (e-mail): A networking application that allows users to send and receive mail electronically.

electronic software distribution (ESD): ESD enables network managers to install software on client computers over the network without physically touching each client computer. ESD client software is installed on each client and enables an ESD server to download and install certain application packages on each client at some predefined time (e.g., at midnight on a Saturday).

emulate: Computer vendors provide software and hardware emulators that accept hardware and software from other vendors and enable them to run on their hardware or software.

encapsulation: A technique in which a frame from one network is placed within the data field of the frame in another network for transmission on the second network. For example, it enables a message initiated on a coaxial cable-based Ethernet LAN to be transmitted over an ATM fiber-optic–based network and then placed onto another Ethernet LAN at the other end.

encryption: The technique of modifying a known bit stream on a transmission circuit so that to an unauthorized observer, it appears to be a random sequence of bits.

end office: The telephone company switching office for the interconnection of calls. *See also* **central office**.

envelope delay distortion: A derivative of the circuit phase shift with respect to the frequency. This distortion affects the time it takes for different frequencies to propagate the length of a communication circuit so that two signals arrive at different times.

equalization: The process of reducing frequency and phase distortion of a circuit by introducing time differences to compensate for the difference in attenuation or time delay at the various frequencies in the transmission band.

equalizer: Any combination (usually adjustable) of coils, capacitors, or resistors inserted in the transmission circuit or amplifier to improve its frequency response.

error control: An arrangement that detects the presence of errors. In some networks, refinements are added that correct the detected errors, either by operations on the received data or by retransmission from the source.

ESD: *See* **electronic software distribution (ESD)**.

Ethernet: A LAN developed by the Xerox Corporation. It uses coaxial cable or twisted-pair wires to connect the stations. It was standardized as IEEE 802.3.

European Computer Manufacturers Association (ECMA): Recommends standards for computer components manufactured or used in Europe. Belongs to the International Organization for Standardization (ISO).

exchange office: *See* **central office**.

exposure: The calculated or estimated loss resulting from the occurrence of a threat, as in "The exposure from theft could be $42,000 this year." It can be either tangible and therefore measurable in dollars or intangible and therefore not directly measurable in dollars. *See also* **comparison risk ranking**.

Extended Binary Coded Decimal Interchange Code (EBCDIC): *See* **EBCDIC**.

extranet: Using the Internet to provide access to information intended for a selected set of users, not the public at large. Usually done by requiring a password to access a selected set of Web sites.

F

FCC: *See* **Federal Communications Commission (FCC)**.

FCS: *See* **frame check sequence (FCS)**.

FDDI: *See* **fiber distributed data interface (FDDI)**.

FDM: Frequency division multiplexing. *See* **multiplexer**.

feasibility study: A study undertaken to determine the possibility or probability of improving the existing system within a reasonable cost. Determines what the problem is and what its causes are and makes recommendations for solving the problem.

FEC: *See* **forward error correction (FEC)**.

Federal Communications Commission (FCC): A board of seven commissioners appointed by the U.S. president under the Communication Act of 1934, having the power to regulate all interstate and foreign electrical communication systems originating in the United States.

FEP: *See* **front-end processor (FEP)**.

fiber distributed data interface (FDDI): A token ring–like LAN technology that permits transmission speeds of 100 million bps using fiber-optic cables (ANSI standard X3T9.5).

fiber-optic cable: A transmission medium that uses glass or plastic cable instead of copper wires.

fiber optics: A transmission technology in which modulated visible lightwave signals containing information are sent down hair-thin plastic or glass fibers and demodulated back into electrical signals at the other end by a special light-sensitive receiver.

File Transfer Protocol (FTP): FTP enables users to send and receive files over the Internet. There are two types of FTP sites: closed (which require users to have an account and a password) and anonymous (which permit anyone to use them).

firewall: A firewall is a router, gateway, or special-purpose computer that filters packets flowing into and out of a network. No access to the organization's networks is permitted except through the firewall. Two commonly used types of firewalls are packet level and application level.

firmware: A set of software instructions set permanently or semipermanently into read-only memory (ROM).

flow control: The capability of the network nodes to manage buffering schemes that allow devices of different data transmission speeds to communicate with each other.

forward error correction (FEC): A technique that identifies errors at the received station and automatically corrects those errors without retransmitting the message.

fractional T1 (FT1): A portion of a T1 circuit. A full T1 allows transmission at 1,544,000 bps. A fractional T1 circuit allows transmission at lower speeds of 384,000, 512,000, or 768,000 bps. *See also* **T carrier**.

fragment free switching: A type of switching that is a cross between store and cut through. Messages are stored until the header has been checked for errors and then the message is forwarded without checking for errors in the rest.

frame: Generally, a group of data bits having bits at each end to indicate the beginning and end of the frame. Frames also contain source addresses, destination addresses, frame type identifiers, and a data message.

frame check sequence (FCS): Used for error checking. FCS uses a 16-bit field with cyclical redundancy checking for error detection with retransmission.

frame relay: Frame relay is a type of packet-switching technology that transmits data faster than the X.25 standard. The key difference is that unlike X.25 networks, frame relay does not perform error correction at each computer in the network. Instead, it simply discards any messages with errors. It is up to the application software at the source and destination to perform error correction and to control for lost messages.

frequency: The rate at which a current alternates, measured in Hertz, kilohertz, megahertz, and so forth. Other units of measure are cycles, kilocycles, or megacycles; *hertz* and *cycles per second* are synonymous.

frequency division multiplexing (FDM): *See* **multiplexer**.

frequency modulation: *See* **modulation, frequency**.

frequency shift keying (FSK): *See* **FSK**.

front-end processor (FEP): An auxiliary processor that is placed between a computer's CPU and the transmission facilities. This device normally handles housekeeping functions like circuit management and code translation, which otherwise would interfere with efficient operation of the CPU.

FSK: Frequency shift keying. A modulation technique whereby 0 and 1 are represented by a different frequency and the amplitude does not vary.

FTP: *See* **File Transfer Protocol (FTP)**.

full duplex: The capability of transmission in both directions at one time. *Contrast with* **half-duplex** and **simplex**.

G

gateway: A device that connects two dissimilar networks. Allows networks of different vendors to communicate by translating one vendor's protocol into another. *See also* **bridge, router**, and **brouter**.

Gaussian noise: *See* **noise, Gaussian**.

Gbps: Gigabit per second; 1 Gbps is equal to 1 billion bps.

GHz: Gigahertz; 1 GHz is equal to 1 billion cycles per second in a frequency.

gigabyte: One billion bytes.

G.Lite: One de facto standard form of ADSL.

guardband: A small bandwidth of frequency that separates two voice-grade circuits. Also, the frequencies between subcircuits in FDM systems that guard against subcircuit interference.

H

hacker: A person who sleuths for passwords to gain illegal access to important computer files. Hackers may rummage through corporate trash cans looking for carelessly discarded printouts.

half-duplex: A circuit that permits transmission of a signal in two directions but not at the same time. *Contrast with* **full duplex** and **simplex**.

Hamming code: A forward error correction (FEC) technique named for its inventor.

handshaking: Exchange of predetermined signals when a connection is established between two data set devices. This is used to establish the circuit and message path.

HDLC: *See* **high-level data link control (HDLC)**.

Hertz (Hz): Same as cycles per second; for example, 3,000 Hz is 3,000 cycles per second.

high-level data link control (HDLC): A bit-oriented protocol in which control of data links is specified by series of bits rather than by control characters (bytes).

home page: A home page is the main starting point or page for a World Wide Web entry.

host computer: The computer that lies at the center of the network. It generally performs the basic centralized data processing functions for which the network was designed. The host used to be where the network communication control functions took place, but today these functions tend to take place in the front-end processor or further out in the network. *Also called* a *central computer*.

hotline: A service that provides direct connection between customers in various cities using a dedicated circuit.

HTML: Web text files or pages use a structural language called HTML (Hypertext Markup Language) to store their information. HTML enables the author to define different type styles and sizes for the text, titles, and headings, and a variety of other formatting information. HTML also permits the author to define links to other pages that may be stored on the same Web server or on any Web server anywhere on the Internet.

hub: Network hubs act as junction boxes, permitting new computers to be connected to the network as easily as plugging a power cord into an electrical socket, and provide an easy way to connect network cables. Hubs also act as repeaters or amplifiers. Hubs are sometimes also called concentrators, multistation access units, or transceivers.

Hypertext Markup Language (HTML): *See* **HTML**.

Hz: *See* **Hertz (Hz)**.

I

IAB: *See* **Internet Architecture Board (IAB)**.

IANA: *See* **Internet Assigned Numbers Authority (IANA)**.

ICMP: *See* **Internet Control Message Protocol (ICMP)**.

idle character: A transmitted character indicating "no information" that does not manifest itself as part of a message at the destination point.

IDS: *See* **intrusion detection system (IDS)**.

IEEE: *See* **Institute of Electrical and Electronics Engineers (IEEE)**.

IESG: Internet Engineering Steering Group.

IETF: Internet Engineering Task Force.

IMAP: *See* **Internet Mail Access Protocol (IMAP)**.

impulse noise: *See* **noise, impulse**.

in-band signaling: The transmission signaling information at some frequency or frequencies that lie within a carrier circuit normally used for information transmission.

Institute of Electrical and Electronics Engineers (IEEE): A professional organization for engineers in the United States. Issues standards and belongs to the ANSI and the ISO. IEEE has defined numerous standards for networks; see Chapters 6–10.

integrated services digital network (ISDN): *See* **ISDN**.

interexchange circuit (IXC): A circuit or circuit between end offices (central offices).

interLATA: Circuits that cross from one LATA (local access and transport area) into another.

intermodulation distortion: An analog line impairment whereby two frequencies create a third erroneous frequency, which in turn distorts the data signal representation.

International Organization for Standardization (ISO): *See* **ISO**.

International Telecommunications Union—Telecommunications (ITU-T): An international organization that sets worldwide communication standards. Its old name was **Consultative Committee on International Telegraph and Telephone (CCITT)**.

Internet: The information superhighway. The network of networks that spans the world, linking more than 20 million users.

Internet Architecture Board (IAB): IAB provides strategic architectural oversight (e.g., top-level domain names, use of international character sets) that can be passed on as guidance to the IESG or turned into published statements or simply passed directly to the relevant IETF working group. The IAB does not produce polished technical proposals but rather tries to stimulate action by the IESG or the IETF that will lead to proposals that meet general consensus. The IAB appoints the IETF chair and all IESG members.

Internet Assigned Numbers Authority (IANA): IANA governs the assignment of IP numbers.

Internet Control Message Protocol (ICMP): A simple network layer protocol standard intended to exchange limited routing information between routers. Most commonly known as a ping, after the DOS and UNIX command.

Internet Engineering Steering Group (IESG): The IESG is responsible for technical management of IETF activities and the Internet standards process. It administers the process according to the rules and procedures and is directly responsible for the actions associated with entry into and movement along the Internet "standards track," including final approval of specifications as Internet standards. Each IETF working group is chaired by a member of the IESG.

Internet Engineering Task Force (IETF): IETF is a large, open international community of network designers, operators, vendors, and researchers concerned with the evolution of the Internet architecture and the smooth operation of the Internet. IETF operates through a series of working groups, which are organized by topic (e.g., routing, transport, security). The requests for comment (RFCs) that form the basis for Internet standards are developed by the IETF and its working groups.

Internet Mail Access Protocol (IMAP): An application-layer protocol standard that covers communication between an e-mail client and an e-mail server.

Internet Research Task Force (IRTF): IRTF operates much like the IETF, through small research groups focused on specific issues. Although IETF working groups focus on current issues, IRTF research groups work on long-term issues related to Internet protocols, applications, architecture, and technology. The IRTF chair is appointed by the IAB.

Internet service provider (ISP): ISPs offer connections to the Internet. Some access providers charge a flat monthly fee for unlimited access (much like the telephone company), whereas others charge per hour of use (much like a long-distance telephone call).

Internet Society (ISOC): ISOC is the closest the Internet has to an owner. ISOC is an open-membership professional society with more than 175 organizational and 8,000 individual members in over 100 countries and includes corporations, government agencies, and foundations that have created the Internet and its technologies.

internetworking: Connecting several networks together so workstations can address messages to the workstations on each of the other networks.

Internet2: There are many different organizations currently working on the next generation of the Internet, including the Abilene network, vBNS, and CA*net. Although each is working in a slightly different fashion, they join together with each other and parts of the regular Internet at gigapops (gigabit points of presence).

interoperability: The interconnection of dissimilar networks in a manner that allows them to operate as though they were similar.

IntraLATA: Circuits that are totally within one LATA (local access transport area).

intranet: Using Internet protocols on a network internal to an organization so that information is accessible using a browser, for example, but only by employees, not the public at large. Usually done by requiring a password to access a selected set of Web sites and protecting the site by a firewall so no outsiders can access it.

intrusion detection system (IDS): An IDS monitors a network segment, a server, or an application on the server for signs of unauthorized access and issues an alarm when an intrusion is detected. A misuse detection IDS compares monitored activities with signatures of known attacks, whereas an anomaly detection IDS compares monitored activities with the "normal" set of activities.

inverse multiplexer: Hardware that takes one high-speed transmission and divides it among several transmission circuits.

IPX/SPX: Internetwork packet exchange/ sequenced packet exchange (IPX/SPX), based on a routing protocol developed by Xerox in the 1970s, is the primary network protocol used by Novell NetWare. About 40 percent of all installed LANs use it.

IRTF: *See* **Internet Research Task Force (IRTF)**.

ISDN: Integrated services digital network. A hierarchy of digital switching and transmission systems. The ISDN provides voice, data, and image in a unified manner. It is synchronized so all digital elements speak the same "language" at the same speed. *See also* **basic rate interface (BRI)** and **primary rate interface (PRI)**.

ISO: International Organization for Standardization, in Geneva, Switzerland. The initials *ISO* stand for its French name. This international standards-making body is best known in data communications for developing the internationally recognized seven-layer network model called the Open Systems Interconnection (OSI) Reference model. *See also* **OSI model**.

ISOC: *See* **Internet Society (ISOC)**.

ISP: *See* **Internet Service Provider (ISP)**.

ITU-T: *See* **International Telecommunications Union—Telecommunications (ITU-T)**.

IXC: *See* **interexchange circuit (IXC)**.

J

jack: The physical connecting device at the interface that mates with a compatible receptacle—a plug.

jitter: Type of analog communication line distortion caused by the variation of a signal from its reference timing positions, which can cause data transmission errors, particularly at high speeds. This variation can be in amplitude, time, frequency, or phase.

jumper: 1. A small connector that fits over a set of pins on a microcomputer circuit card. 2. A patch cable or wire used to establish a circuit for testing or diagnostics.

K

K: A standard quantity measurement of computer storage. A K is defined loosely as 1,000 bytes. In fact, it is 1,024 bytes, which is the equivalent of 2^{10}.

Kbps: Kilobits per second. A data rate equal to 10^3 bps (1,000 bps).

Kermit: Kermit is a very popular asynchronous file transfer protocol named after Kermit the Frog. The Kermit protocol was developed by Columbia University, which released it as a free software communications package. Various versions of Kermit can be found on public bulletin board systems for downloading to a microcomputer.

key management: The process of controlling the secret keys used in encryption.

KHz: Kilohertz; 1 KHz is equal to 1,000 cycles per second in a frequency.

kilobits per second (Kbps): *See* **Kbps**.

kilometer: A metric measurement equal to 0.621 mile or 3,280.8 feet.

L

LAN: *See* **local area network (LAN)**.

laser: *L*ight *a*mplification by *s*timulated *e*mission of *r*adiation. A device that transmits an extremely narrow and coherent beam of electromagnetic energy in the visible light spectrum. (*Coherent* means that the separate waves are in phase with one another rather than jumbled as in normal light.)

LATA: Local access transport area. One of approximately 200 local telephone service areas in the United States roughly paralleling major metropolitan areas. The LATA subdivisions were established as a result of the AT&T/Bell divestiture to distinguish local from long-distance service. Circuits with both end points within the LATA (intraLATAs) generally are the sole responsibility of the local telephone company. Circuits that cross outside the LATA (interLATAs) are passed on to an interexchange carrier like AT&T, MCI, or US Sprint.

latency: The delay between when the first bits of a message arrive at a device and when it begins transmitting them.

leased circuit: A leased communication circuit that goes from your site to some other location. It is a clear, unbroken communication path that is yours to use 24 hours per day, 7 days per week. *Also called private circuit* or **dedicated circuit**.

line: A circuit, channel, or link. It carries the data communication signals. An early telephone technology term that may imply a physical connection, such as with a copper wire. *Compare with* **channel, circuit**, and **link**.

link: An unbroken circuit path between two points. *Sometimes called* a **line, channel**, or **circuit**.

Listserv: A listserver (or Listserv) is a mailing list. One part, the Listserv processor, processes commands such as requests to subscribe, unsubscribe, or to provide more information about the Listserv. The second part is the Listserv mailer. Any message sent to the Listserv mailer is resent to everyone on the mailing list.

LLC: The logical link control, or LLC, sublayer is just an interface between the MAC sublayer and software in layer 3 (the network layer) that enables the software and hardware in the MAC sublayer to be separated from the logical functions in the LLC sublayer. By separating the LLC sublayer from the MAC sublayer, it is simpler to change the MAC hardware and software without affecting the software in layer 3. The most commonly used LLC protocol is IEEE 802.2.

local access transport area (LATA): *See* **LATA**.

local area network (LAN): A network that is located in a small geographic area, such as an office, a building, a complex of buildings, or a campus, and whose communication technology provides a high-bandwidth, low-cost medium to which many nodes can be connected. These networks typically do not use common carrier circuits, and their circuits do not cross public thoroughfares or property owned by others. LANs are not regulated by the FCC or state public utilities commissions.

local exchange carrier: The local telephone company, such as one of the seven regional Bell operating companies (RBOCs).

local loop: The part of a communication circuit between the subscriber's equipment and the equipment in the local central office.

log: 1. A record of everything pertinent to a system function. 2. A collection of messages that provides a history of message traffic.

logical link control (LLC): *See* **LLC**.

longitudinal redundancy check (LRC): A system of error control based on the formation of a block check following preset rules. The check formation rule is applied in the same manner to each character. In a simple case, the LRC is created by forming a parity check on each bit position of all characters in the block. (That is, the first bit of the LRC character creates odd parity among the 1-bit positions of the characters in the block.)

LRC: *See* **longitudinal redundancy check (LRC).**

M

M: Mega. The designation for 1 million, as in 3 megabits per second (3 Mbit/s).

MAC: *See* **media access control (MAC).**

MAN: *See* **metropolitan area network (MAN).**

management information base (MIB): The extent of information that can be retrieved from a user microcomputer when using the Simple Network Management Protocol (SNMP) for network management. MIBs are sets of attributes and definitions that pertain to specific network devices.

Manchester encoding: The digital transmission technique used in the physical layer of Ethernet LANs. See Chapter 3.

Mbps: A data rate equal to 10^6 bps. Sometimes called megabits per second (1,000,000 bps).

mean times: *See* **MTBF, MTTD, MTTF**, and **MTTR**.

media access control (MAC): A data link layer protocol that defines how packets are transmitted on a local area network. *See also* **CSMA/CD, token bus**, and **token ring**.

medium: The matter or substance that carries the voice or data transmission. For example, the medium can be copper (wires), glass (fiber-optic cables), or air (microwave or satellite).

megabit: One million bits.

megabyte: One million bytes.

mesh network: A network topology in which there are direct point-to-point connections among the computers.

message: A communication of information from a source to one or more destinations. A message usually is composed of three parts: (1) a heading, containing a suitable indicator of the beginning of the message together with some of the following information: source, destination, date, time, routing; (2) a body containing the information to be communicated; (3) an ending containing a suitable indicator of the end of the message.

message switching: An operation in which the entire message being transmitted is switched to the other location without regard to whether the circuits actually are interconnected at the time of your call. This usually involves a message store and forward facility.

meter: A metric measurement equal to 39.37 inches.

metropolitan area network (MAN): A network that usually covers a citywide area. Because MANs use LAN and fiber-optic technologies, transmission speeds can vary between 2 million and 100 million bps.

MHz: megahertz; 1 MHz is equal to 1 million cycles per second in a frequency.

MIB: *See* **management information base (MIB).**

MIME: *See* **Multipurpose Internet Mail Extension (MIME).**

MIPS: One million instructions per second. Used to describe a computer's processing power.

mirroring: A process in which the database server automatically backs up the disk during each database transaction. During this process, the computer writes on two different hard disks on the same disk circuit every time the hard disk is updated. This creates two mirror images of the database data. Disk mirroring can be accomplished only when the database server contains two physical disk drives, because the records or data structures are written to both disks simultaneously. Should a problem develop with one disk, the second disk is available instantly with identical information on it. *Compare with* **duplexing**.

mnemonic: A group of characters used to assist the human memory. A mnemonic frequently is an acronym.

modem: A contraction of the words ***mo***dulator-**dem**odulator. A modem is a device for performing necessary signal transformation between terminal devices and communication circuits. Modems are used in pairs, one at either end of the communication circuit.

modulation, amplitude: The form of modulation in which the amplitude of the carrier is varied in accordance with the instantaneous value of the modulating signal.

modulation, frequency: A form of modulation in which the frequency of the carrier is varied in accordance with the instantaneous value of the modulating signal.

modulation, phase: A form of modulation in which the phase of the carrier is varied in accordance with the instantaneous value of the modulating signal. Phase modulation has two related techniques. Phase shift keying (PSK) uses a 180° change in phase to indicate a change in the binary value (0 or 1), Differential phase shift keying (DPSK) uses a 180° change in phase every time a bit is transmitted; otherwise, the phase remains the same.

modulation, pulse code: *See* **pulse code modulation (PCM)**.

MTBF: mean time between failures. The statistic developed by vendors to show the reliability of their equipment. It can be an actual calculated figure that generally is more accurate, or it can be a practical (theoretical) figure.

MTTD: Mean time to diagnose. The time it takes the network testing and problem management staff to diagnose a network problem.

MTTF: Mean time to fix. The time it takes vendors to remedy a network problem once they arrive on the premises.

MTTR: 1. Mean time to repair—the combination of mean time to diagnose, mean time to respond, and mean time to fix, indicating the entire length of time it takes to fix a fault in equipment. 2. Mean time to respond—the time it takes the vendor to respond when a network problem is reported.

multidrop (multipoint): A line or circuit interconnecting several stations/nodes in a sequential fashion.

multiplexer: A device that combines data traffic from several low-speed communication circuits onto a single high-speed circuit. The two popular types of multiplexing are FDM (frequency division multiplexing) and TDM (time division multiplexing). In FDM, the voice-grade link is divided into subcircuits, each covering a different frequency range in such a manner that each subcircuit can be employed as though it were an individual circuit. In TDM, separate time segments are assigned to each terminal. During these time segments, data may be sent without conflicting with data sent from another terminal.

multiplexing (MUX): The subdivision of a transmission circuit into two or more separate circuits. This can be achieved by splitting the frequency range of the circuit into narrow frequency bands (frequency division multiplexing) or by assigning a given circuit successively to several different users at different times (time division multiplexing).

Multipurpose Internet Mail Extension (MIME): An application-layer standard protocol that enables SMTP mail messages to transfer nontext characters such as graphics and software. The sending e-mail client translates the nontext characters into something that resembles text using MIME codes and attaches it to the message. The receiving e-mail client translates the MIME codes back into the original graphic or software file.

MUX: *See* **multiplexing (MUX)**.

N

NAK: *See* **negative acknowledgment (NAK)**.

nanosecond: One billionth ($^{1}/1{,}000{,}000{,}000$) of a second or 10^{-9}.

NAP: *See* **network access point (NAP)**.

NAT: *See* **network address translation (NAT)**.

National Institute of Standards and Technology (NIST): Formerly the National Bureau of Standards. The agency of the U.S. government responsible for developing information processing standards for the federal government.

NCO: *See* **network cost of ownership (NCO)**.

negative acknowledgment (NAK): The return signal that reports an error in the message received. The opposite of **acknowledgment (ACK)**.

network: 1. A series of points connected by communication circuits. 2. The switched telephone network is the network of telephone lines normally used for dialed telephone calls. 3. A private network is a network of communication circuits confined to the use of one customer.

network access point (NAP): An "intersection" on the Internet where many national and regional ISPs connect to exchange data.

network address translation (NAT): NAT is the process of translating between one set of private IP addresses inside a network and a set of public IP addresses outside the network for use on the Internet. NAT is transparent in that no computer notices that it is being done.

network cost of ownership (NCO): NCO is a measure of how much it costs per year to keep one computer operating. NCO includes the cost of support staff to attach it to the network, install software, administer the network (e.g., create user IDs, back up user data), provide training and technical support, and upgrade hardware and software. NCO is often $1,500 to $3,500 per computer per year. *Compare with* **total cost of ownership (TCO)**.

network interface card (NIC): An NIC allows the computer to be physically connected to the network cable; the NIC provides the physical-layer connection from the computer to the network.

network operating system (NOS): The NOS is the software that controls the network. The NOS provides the data link and the network layers and must interact with the application software and the computer's own operating system. Every NOS provides two sets of software: one that runs on the network server(s) and one that runs on the network client(s).

network operations center (NOC): Any centralized network management control site.

network profile: Every LAN microcomputer has a profile that outlines what resources it has available to other microcomputers in the network and what resources it can use elsewhere in the network.

network service: An application available on a network—for example, file storage.

NIC: *See* **network interface card (NIC)**.

NIST: *See* **National Institute of Standards and Technology (NIST)**.

NOC: *See* **network operations center (NOC)**.

node: In a description of a network, the point at which the links join input–output devices. It could be a computer or a special-purpose device such as a router.

noise: The unwanted change in waveform that occurs between two points in a transmission circuit.

noise, amplitude: A sudden change in the level of power with differing effects, depending on the type of modulation used by the modem.

noise, cross-talk: Noise resulting from the interchange of signals on two adjacent circuits; manifests itself when it is possible to hear other people's telephone conversations.

noise, echo: The "hollow" or echoing characteristic that is heard on voice-grade lines with improper echo suppression.

noise, Gaussian: Noise that is characterized statistically by a Gaussian, or random, distribution.

noise, impulse: Noise caused by individual impulses on the circuit.

noise, intermodulation: Noise that occurs when signals from two independent lines intermodulate. A new signal forms and falls into a frequency band differing from those of both inputs. The new signal may fall into a frequency band reserved for another signal.

NOS: *See* **network operating system (NOS)**.

NRZ: Nonreturn to zero. A binary encoding and transmission scheme in which 1's and 0's are represented by opposite and alternating high and low voltages, and in which there is no return to a reference (zero) voltage between encoded bits.

NRZI: Nonreturn to zero inverted. A binary encoding scheme that inverts the signal on a 1 and leaves the signal unchanged for a 0, and in which a change in the voltage state signals a 1-bit value and the absence of a change denotes a 0-bit value.

null character: A control character that can be inserted into or withdrawn from a sequence of characters without altering the message.

null modem cable: A 6- to 8-foot RS232 cable that makes the two microcomputers connected at each end of the cable think they are talking through modems.

O

office, central or end: The common carrier's switching office closest to the subscriber.

100Base-T: An Ethernet LAN standard that runs at 100 million bps and uses unshielded twisted-pair wires.

1000Base-T: An Ethernet LAN standard the runs at 1 billion bps and uses unshielded twisted-pair wires.

Open Shortest Path First (OSPF): A network-layer standard protocol used to exchange route information between routers using dynamic decentralized routing.

Open Systems Interconnection (OSI) Reference model: *See* **OSI model**.

optical fibers: Hair-thin strands of very pure glass (sometimes plastic) over which light waves travel. They are used as a medium over which information is transmitted.

OSI model: The seven-layer Open Systems Interconnection (OSI) Reference model developed by the ISO subcommittee. The OSI model serves as a logical framework of protocols for computer-to-computer communications. Its purpose is to facilitate the interconnection of networks.

OSPF: *See* **Open Shortest Path First (OSPF)**.

out-of-band signaling: A method of signaling that uses a frequency that is within the passband of the transmission facility but outside of a carrier circuit normally used for data transmission.

overhead: Computer time used to keep track of or run the system, as compared with computer time used to process data.

overlay network: A network (usually a WLAN) used to supplement a primary network (usually a wired LAN).

P

packet: A group of binary digits, including data and control signals, that is switched as a composite whole. The data, control signals, and error-control information are arranged in a specific format. A packet often is a 128-character block of data.

packet assembly/disassembly (PAD): *See* **PAD**.

Packet Layer Protocol (PLP): *See* **PLP**.

packet switching: Process whereby messages are broken into finite-size packets that always are accepted by the network. The message packets are forwarded to the other party over a multitude of different circuit paths. At the other end of the circuit, the packets are reassembled into the message, which is then passed on to the receiving terminal.

packet switching network (PSN): A network designed to carry data in the form of packets. The packet and its format are internal to that network. The external interfaces may handle data in different formats, and format conversion may be done by the user's computer.

PAD: Packet assembly/disassembly. Equipment providing packet assembly and disassembly between asynchronous transmission and the packet-switching network.

PAM: *See* **pulse amplitude modulation (PAM)**.

parallel: Describes the way the internal transfer of binary data takes place within a computer. It may be transmitted as a parallel word, but it is converted to a serial or bit-by-bit data stream for transmission.

parity bit: A binary bit appended to an array of bits to make the number of 1 bits always be odd or even for an individual character. For example, odd parity may require three

1 bits and even parity may require four 1 bits.

parity check: Addition of noninformation bits to a message to detect any changes in the original bit structure from the time it leaves the sending device to the time it is received.

Pbps: Petabits per second. A data rate equal to 1 quadrillion bits per second (1,000,000,000,000,000).

PBX: private branch exchange. Telephone switch located at a customer's site that primarily establishes voice communications over tie lines or circuits as well as between individual users and the switched telephone network. Typically also provides switching within a customer site and usually offers numerous other enhanced features, such as least-cost routing and call detail recording.

PCM: *See* **pulse code modulation (PCM)**.

PDN: *See* **public data network (PDN)**.

PDU: Protocol Data Unit.

peer: A dictionary definition of *peer* is "a person who is equal to another in abilities." A peer-to-peer network, therefore, is one in which each microcomputer node has equal abilities. In communications, a peer is a node or station that is on the same protocol layer as another.

peer-to-peer communications: 1. Communication between two or more processes or programs by which both ends of the session exchange data with equal privilege. 2. Communication between two or more network nodes in which either side can initiate sessions because no primary–secondary relationship exists.

peer-to-peer LAN: A network in which a microcomputer can serve as both a server and a user. Every microcomputer has access to all the network's resources on an equal basis.

permanent virtual circuit (PVC): A virtual circuit that resembles a leased line because it can be dedicated to a single user. Its connections are controlled by software.

phase modulation: *See* **modulation, phase.**

pirate: A person who obtains the latest software programs without paying for them. A skilled software pirate is able to break the protection scheme that is designed to prevent copying.

PKI: *See* **public key infrastructure (PKI)**.

plain old telephone network (POTS): The nickname for the public switched telephone network. Often used when referring to dial-up Internet access using a modem.

PLP: Packet Layer Protocol (PLP) is the routing protocol that performs the network layer functions (e.g., routing and addressing) in X.25 networks.

point of presence (POP): The physical access location of an ISP or voice or data communications carrier.

point-to-point: Denoting a circuit or line that has only two terminals. A link. An example is a single microcomputer connected to a mainframe.

polling: Any procedure that sequentially queries several terminals in a network.

polling, hub: A type of sequential polling in which the polling device contacts a terminal, that terminal contacts the next terminal, and so on, until all the terminals have been contacted.

polling, roll call: Polling accomplished from a prespecified list in a fixed sequence, with polling restarted when the list is completed.

polynomial checking: A checking method using polynomial functions to test for errors in data in transmission. Also called **cyclical redundancy check (CRC)**.

POP: 1. *See* **Post Office Protocol (POP)** and **point-of-presence (POP)**.

port: One of the circuit connection points on a front-end processor or local intelligent controller.

Post Office Protocol (POP): An application-layer standard used to communicate between the client and the e-mail server.

POTS: *See* **plain old telephone network (POTS)**.

PPP: PPP (multilink Point-to-Point Protocol) is an inverse multiplexing protocol for combining circuits of different speeds (e.g., a 64,000-bps circuit with a 14,400-bps circuit), with data allocated to each circuit is based on speed and need. PPP enables the user to change the circuits allocated to the PPP multiplexed circuit in mid-transmission so that the PPP circuit can increase or decrease the capacity. PPP is the successor to SLIP.

primary rate interface (PRI): In ISDN, twenty-three 64,000 bits per second D circuits for data and one 64,000 bits per second B circuit for signaling (23 B+D). See also **basic rate interface (BRI)**.

private branch exchange (PBX): *See* **PBX**.

propagation delay: The time necessary for a signal to travel from one point on the circuit to another, such as from a satellite dish up to a satellite or from Los Angeles to New York.

protocol: A formal set of conventions governing the format and control of inputs and outputs between two communicating devices. This includes the rules by which these two devices communicate as well as handshaking and line discipline.

protocol stack: The set of software required to process a set of protocols.

PSK: Phase shift keying; *see* **modulation, phase**.

PSN: *See* **packet switching network (PSN)**.

PTT: Postal, telephone, and telegraph. These are the common carriers owned by governments; the government is the sole or monopoly supplier of communication facilities.

public data network (PDN): A network established and operated for the specific purpose of providing data transmission services to the public. It can be a public packet-switched network or a circuit-switched network. Public data networks normally offer value-added services for resource sharing at reduced costs and with high reliability. These time-sharing networks are available to anyone with a modem.

public key encryption: Public key encryption uses two keys. The public key is used to encrypt the message and a second, very different private key is used to decrypt the message. Even though the sender knows both the contents of the outgoing message and the public encryption key, once it is encrypted, the message cannot be decrypted without the private key. Public key encryption is one of the most secure encryption techniques available.

public key infrastructure (PKI): The PKI is the process of using public key encryption on the Internet. PKI begins with a certificate authority (CA), which is a trusted organization that can vouch for the authenticity of the person or organization using authentication (e.g., VeriSign). The CA issues a digital certificate that is the requestor's public key encrypted using the CA's private key as proof of identity. This certificate is then attached to the user's e-mail or Web transactions. The receiver then verifies the certificate by decrypting it with the CA's public key—and must also contact the CA to ensure that the user's certificate has not been revoked by the CA.

pulse amplitude modulation (PAM): Amplitude modulation of a pulse carrier. PAM is used to translate analog voice data into a series of binary digits before they are transmitted.

pulse code modulation (PCM): Representation of a speech signal by sampling at a regular rate and converting each sample to a binary number. In PCM, the information signals are sampled at regular intervals and a series of pulses in coded form are transmitted, representing the amplitude of the information signal at that time.

Q

QAM: Quadrature amplitude modulation. A sophisticated modulation technique that uses variations in signal amplitude, which allows data-encoded symbols to be represented as any of 16 states to send 4 bits on each signal.

Quality of Service (QoS): The ability of devices to give different priorities to different types of messages so that some messages (e.g., voice telephone data) are transmitted faster than other messages (e.g., e-mail).

quantizing error: The difference between the PAM signal and the original voice signal. The original signal has a smooth flow, but the PAM signal has jagged "steps."

R

RBOC: Regional Bell operating company. One of the seven companies created after divestiture of the old Bell system to provide local communications. Includes Ameritech, Bell Atlantic, BellSouth, NYNEX, Pacific Telesis, Southwestern Bell, and US West.

reclocking time: *See* **turnaround time.**

redundancy: The portion of the total information contained in a message that can be eliminated without loss of essential information.

regional Bell operating company (RBOC): *See* **RBOC**.

reliability: A characteristic of the equipment, software, or network that relates to the integrity of the system against failure. Reliability usually is measured in terms of mean time between failures (MTBF), the statistical measure of the interval between successive failures of the hardware or software under consideration.

repeater: A device used to boost the strength of a signal. Repeaters are spaced at intervals throughout the length of a communication circuit.

request for comment (RFC): A proposed standard for the Internet on which anyone in the world is invited to comment.

request for proposal (RFP): A request for proposal is used to solicit bids from vendors for new network hardware, software, and services. RFPs specify what equipment, software, and services are desired and ask vendors to provide their best prices.

response time: The time the system takes to react to a given input; the time interval from when the user presses the last key to the terminal's typing the first letter of the reply. Response time includes (1) transmission time to the computer; (2) processing time at the computer, including access time to obtain any file records needed to answer the inquiry; and (3) transmission time back to the terminal.

retrain time: *See* **turnaround time**.

RFC: *See* **request for comment (RFC)**.

RFP: *See* **request for proposal (RFP)**.

ring: 1. The hot wire in a telephone circuit. 2. An audible sound used for signaling the recipient of an incoming telephone call. 3. A LAN topology having a logical geometric arrangement in the shape of a ring.

RIP: *See* **Routing Information Protocol (RIP)**.

risk: The level or amount of exposure to an item when compared with other items. It is a hazard or chance of loss. Risk is the degree of difference, as in, "What level of risk does one threat have when compared to the other threats?"

risk assessment: The process by which one identifies threats, uses a methodology to determine the tangible or intangible exposures, and develops a sequenced list of the threats from the one having the highest risk to the one having the lowest risk. The list may be in a sequence based on tangible dollar losses or on intangible criteria such as public embarrassment, likelihood of occurrence, most dangerous, most critical to the organization, and greatest delay. *Also called risk ranking* or *risk analysis*.

RMON: Remote monitoring. The definitions of what is stored and therefore retrievable from a remote user microcomputer when using the Simple Network Management Protocol (SNMP). It is referred to as the RMON MIB (management information base). *See also* **management information base (MIB)** and **Simple Network Management Protocol (SNMP)**.

router: A device that connects two similar networks having the same network protocol. It also chooses the best route between two networks when there are multiple paths between them. *Compare with* **bridge, brouter**, and **gateway**.

Routing Information Protocol (RIP): A network-layer standard protocol used to exchange route information between routers using dynamic decentralized routing.

RS232: A technical specification published by the Electronic Industries Association that specifies the mechanical and electrical characteristics of the interface for connecting data terminal equipment (DTE) and data circuit terminating equipment (DCE). It defines interface circuit functions and their corresponding connector pin assignments.

RS449: An Electronic Industries Association standard for data terminal equipment (DTE) and data circuit terminating equipment (DCE) connection that specifies interface requirements for expanded transmission speeds (up to 2 million bps), longer cable lengths, and 10 additional functions.

S

SDLC: *See* **synchronous data link control (SDLC)**.

serial: 1. Transmitting bits one at a time and in sequence. 2. The sequential or consecutive occurrence of two or more related activities in a single device or circuit.

server: A computer that provides a particular service to the client computers on the network. In larger LANs, the server is dedicated to being a server. In a peer-to-peer LANs, the server may be both a server and a client computer. There may be file, database, network, access, modem, facsimile, printer, and gateway servers.

server farm: A LAN segment containing many servers.

service-level agreement (SLA): An SLA specifies the exact type of performance and fault conditions that the organization will accept and what compensation the service provider must provide if it fails to meet the SLA. For example, the SLA might state that network availability must be 99 percent or higher and that the MTBF for T1 circuits must be 120 days or more.

Service Set Identifier (SSId): A simple, easily broken approach to WLAN security.

session: A logical connection between two terminals. This is the part of the message transmission when the two parties are exchanging messages. It takes place after the communication circuit has been set up and is functioning.

signal: A signal is something that is sent over a communication circuit. It might be a control signal used by the network to control itself.

signal-to-noise ratio: The ratio, expressed in dB, of the usable signal to the noise signal present.

Simple Mail Transfer Protocol (SMTP): An application-layer protocol standard used to transfer e-mail messages across the Internet.

simplex: A circuit capable of transmission in one direction only. *Contrast with* **full duplex** and **half-duplex**.

Simple Network Management Protocol (SNMP): An application-layer protocol standard used in network management for monitoring and configuring network devices. *See also* **management information base (MIB)** and **RMON**.

single cable: A one-cable system in broadband LANs in which a portion of the bandwidth is allocated for "send" signals and a portion for "receive" signals, with a guardband in between to provide isolation from interference.

SLIP: Serial Line Internet Protocol (SLIP) is a proposed standard for inverse multiplexing. It has been surpassed by PPP.

SMTP: *See* **Simple Mail Transfer Protocol (SMTP)**.

SNA: *See* **systems network architecture (SNA)**.

SNMP: *See* **Simple Network Management Protocol (SNMP)**.

SONET: *See* **synchronous optical network (SONET)**.

spanning tree protocol: A data link layer protocol used to prevent broadcast storm in networks that have redundant links providing multiple paths between LAN segments.

spike: A sudden increase of electrical power on a communication circuit. *Spike* is a term used in the communication industry. *Contrast with* **surge**.

spread spectrum: The U.S. military developed spread spectrum through-the-air radio transmission technology primarily to overcome the problem of intentional interference by hostile jamming and secondarily for security. A spread spectrum signal is created by modulating the original transmitted radio frequency (RF) signal with a spreading code that causes "hopping" of the frequency from one frequency to another. By contrast, conventional AM and FM radio uses only one frequency to transmit its signal.

start bit: A bit that precedes the group of bits representing a character. Used to signal the arrival of the character in asynchronous transmission.

static routing: *See* **decentralized routing**.

statistical multiplexer: Stat mux or STDM. A time division multiplexer (TDM) that dynamically allocates communication circuit time to each of the various attached terminals, according to whether a terminal is active or inactive at a particular moment. Buffering and queuing functions also are included. *See also* **concentrator**.

stop bit: A bit that follows the group of bits representing a character. Used to signal the end of a character in asynchronous transmission.

store and forward switching: A switching technique that accepts messages, stores them, and then forwards them to the next location after ensuring they contain no errors as addressed in the message header.

STX: A control character used in ASCII and EBCDIC data communications to mean start of text.

surge: A sudden increase in voltage on a 120-volt electrical power line. A term used in the electric utilities industry. *Contrast with* **spike**.

switch: Switches connect more than two LAN segments that use the same data link and network protocol. They may connect the same or different types of cable. Switches typically provide ports for 4, 8, 16, or 32 separate LAN segments, and most enable all ports to be in use simultaneously, so they are faster than bridges.

switched circuit: A dial-up circuit in which the communication path is established by dialing. If the entire circuit path is unavailable, there is a busy signal, which prevents completion of the circuit connection.

Switched Multimegabit Data Service (SMDS): *See* **SMDS**.

switched network: Any network that has switches used for directing messages from the sender to the ultimate recipient.

switched network, circuit switched: A switched network in which switching is accomplished by disconnecting and reconnecting lines in different configurations to set up a continuous pathway between the sender and the recipient. *See also* **circuit switching**.

switched network, store and forward: A switched network in which the store-and-forward principle is used to handle transmission between senders and recipients. *See also* **store-and-forward-switching**.

switching: Identifying and connecting independent transmission links to form a continuous path from one location to another.

symbol rate: The speed in baud is the number of symbols per second. If each signal represents only one bit, *symbol rate* is the same as *bits per second*. When each signal contains more than one bit, *symbol rate* does not equal *bits per second*.

Synchronization character (SYN): An 8-bit control character that is sent at the beginning of a message block to establish synchronization (timing) between the sender and the receiver. Term used for the characters preceding an Ethernet packet. Term used for a TCP open connection request.

synchronous data link control (SDLC): A protocol for managing synchronous, code-transparent, serial bit-by-bit information transfer over a link connection. Transmission exchanges may be full-duplex or half-duplex and over switched or nonswitched links. The configurations of the link connection may be point-to-point, multipoint, or loop. SDLC is the protocol used in IBM's systems network architecture.

synchronous optical network (SONET): The National Exchange Carriers Association standard for optical transmission at gigabits-per-second speeds. For example, digital signals transmit on T1 circuits at 1,544,000 bps and on T3 circuits at 44,376,000 bps. The slowest SONET OC-1 optical transmission rate of 51,840,000 bps is slightly faster than the T3 rate.

synchronous transmission: Form of transmission in which data is sent as a fixed-length block or frame. *Compare with* **asynchonous transmission**.

systems network architecture (SNA): The name of IBM's conceptual framework that defines the data communication interaction between computer systems or terminals.

T

T carrier: A hierarchy of digital circuits designed to carry speech and other signals in digital form. Designated T1 (1.544 Mbps), T2 (6.313 Mbps), T3 (44.736 Mbps), and T4 (274.176 Mbps).

tariff: The formal schedule of rates and regulations pertaining to the communication services, equipment, and facilities that constitute the contract between the user and the common carrier. Tariffs are filed with the appropriate regulatory agency (FCC or state public utilities commission) for approval and published when approved.

TASI: Time assisted speech interpolation. The process of interleaving two or more voice calls on the same telephone circuit simultaneously.

Tbps: Terabits per second. A data rate equal to 1 trillion bits per second (1,000,000,000,000).

TCM: Trellis-coded modulation (TCM) is a modulation technique related to QAM that combines phase modulation and amplitude modulation. There are several different forms of TCM that transmit 5, 6, 7, or 8 bits per signal, respectively.

TCP/IP: Transmission Control Protocol/Internet Protocol is probably the oldest networking standard, developed for ARPANET, and now used on the Internet. One of the most commonly used network protocols.

TDM: *See* **multiplexer**.

telecommunications: A term encompassing voice, data, and image transmissions that are sent over some medium in the form of coded signals.

telecommuting: Telecommuting employees perform some or all of their work at home instead of going to the office each day.

teleconferencing: With teleconferencing, people from diverse geographic locations can "attend" a business meeting in both voice and picture format. In fact, even documents can be shown and copied at any of the remote locations.

telephony: A generic term to describe voice communications. Pronounced "tel-ef-on-e," not "tel-e-fon-e."

Telnet: Telnet enables users on one computer to log in to other computers on the Internet.

10Base-T: An Ethernet LAN standard (IEEE 802.3) that runs at 10 million bps and uses unshielded twisted-pair wires.

10Base2: An Ethernet LAN standard that runs at 10 million bps, uses baseband transmission techniques, and allows 200 meters maximum cable length.

10Base5: An Ethernet LAN standard that runs at 10 million bps, uses baseband transmission techniques, and allows 500 meters maximum cable length.

10Broad36: An Ethernet LAN standard that runs at 10 million bps, uses broadband transmission techniques, and allows 3,600 meters maximum cable length.

thick Ethernet: Refers to the original Ethernet specification that uses thick coaxial cable that is both grounded and shielded. The many layers of shielding are of polyvinyl and aluminum, which make the cable wider in diameter than other Ethernet cables. The heavy shielding also makes the cable more expensive and less flexible; therefore, it is impractical for many installations.

thin Ethernet: Refers to the 10Base2 baseband Ethernet, meaning the version that transmits at 10 million bps in baseband at 200 meters maximum. It uses thin coaxial cable. *Also called* **cheapnet.**

threat: A potentially adverse occurrence or unwanted event that could be injurious to the network, the computing environment, the organization, or a business application. Threats are acts or events the organization wants to prevent from taking place, such as lost data, theft, disasters, virus infections, errors, illegal access, and unauthorized disclosure. In other words, threats are events no one wants to occur.

3DES: *See* **triple DES (3DES).**

throughput: The total amount of useful information that is processed or communicated during a specific time period.

Time assisted speech interpolation (TASI): *See* **TASI.**

Time division multiplexing (TDM): *See* **multiplexer.**

token: The special sequence of characters used to gain access to a token ring or token-bus network to transmit a packet.

token bus: A LAN with a bus topology that uses a token-passing approach to network access. In a token-bus LAN, the next logical node or station is not necessarily the next physical node because it uses preassigned priority algorithms. Message requests are not handled in consecutive order by stations. *Contrast with* **token ring.**

token passing: A method of allocating network access wherein a terminal can send a message only after it has acquired the network's electronic token.

token ring: A LAN with a ring topology that uses a token-passing approach to network access. In a token ring LAN, the next logical station also is the next physical station because the token passes from node to node. *Contrast with* **token bus.**

topology: The basic physical or geometric arrangement of the network—for example, a ring, star, or bus layout. The topology is the network's logical arrangement, but it is influenced by the physical connections of its links and nodes. This is in contrast to its configuration, which is the actual or practical layout, including software and hardware constraints. Topologies are the building blocks of a network configuration. *Compare with* **configuration.**

total cost of ownership (TCO): TCO is a measure of how much it costs per year to keep one computer operating. TCO includes the cost of support staff to attach it to the network, install software, administer the network (e.g., create user IDs, back up user data), provide training and technical support, and upgrade hardware and software, along with the cost of "wasted time" when the network is down. TCO is often $10,000 per computer per year. *Compare to* **network cost of ownership (NCO).**

transceiver: A device that transmits and/or receives data to or from computers on an Ethernet LAN. Also a hub.

transmission rate of information bits (TRIB): *See* **TRIB.**

tree: A network arrangement in which the stations hang off a common "branch," or data bus, like leaves on the branch of a tree.

TRIB: Transmission rate of information bits. A TRIB is the network's throughput. It is the effective rate of data transfer over a communication circuit per unit of time. Usually expressed in bits per second.

triple DES (3DES): 3DES is a symmetric encryption technique that involves using DES three times, usually with three different keys, to produce the encrypted text, which produces a stronger level of security than DES, because it has a total of 168 bits as the key (i.e., 3×56 bits).

trunk: A voice communication circuit between switching devices or end offices.

turnaround time: The time required to reverse the direction of transmission from send to receive or vice versa on a half-duplex circuit.

twisted pair: A pair of wires used in standard telephone wiring. They are twisted to reduce interference caused by the other twisted pairs in the same cable bundle.

Twisted-pair wires go from homes and offices to the telephone company end office.

U

UDP: *See* **User Datagram Protocol (UDP).**

uniform resource locator (URL): *See* **URL.**

uninterruptible power supply (UPS): Provides backup electrical power if the normal electrical power fails or if the voltage drops to unacceptably low levels.

unipolar transmission: A form of digital transmission in which the voltage changes between 0 volts to represent a binary 0 and some positive value (e.g., +15 volts) to represent a binary 1. *See also* **bipolar transmission.**

unshielded twisted-pair (UTP) wires: The type of wiring used in 10Base-T Ethernet networks. Same as **twisted pair.**

upload: The process of loading software and data from the nodes of a network (terminals or microcomputers), over the network media, and to the host mainframe computer.

UPS: *See* **uninterruptible power supply (UPS).**

URL: To use a browser to access a Web server, you must enter the server's addresses or URL (uniform resource locator). All Web addresses begin with seven characters: http://.

USASCII: *See* **ASCII.**

User Datagram Protocol (UDP): A connectionless transport layer protocol standard used by TCP to send short messages such as DNS requests.

user profile: The user profile specifies what data and network resources a user can access, and the type of access (read-only, write, create, delete, etc.).

UTP: *See* **unshielded twisted-pair (UTP) wires.**

V

V.*nn*: The V.*nn* series of ITU-T standards relating to the connection of digital equipment to the analog telephone network. Primarily concerned with the modem interface. See Chapter 3 for definitions.

value-added network (VAN): A corporation that sells services of a value-added network. Such a network is built using the communication offerings of traditional common carriers, connected to computers that permit new types of telecommunication tariffs to be offered. The network may be a packet switching or message switching network.

VBNS: *See* **very-high-performance backbone network service (vBNS).**

VDSL: *See* **very-high-data-rate digital subscriber line (VDSL).**

VDT: Video display terminal.

vertical redundancy check (VRC): *See* **parity check.**

very-high-data-rate digital subscriber line (VDSL): A form of DSL that provides very high speed transmission (e.g., up to 51 Mbps) over traditional telephone lines for very short distances.

very-high-performance backbone network service (vBNS): One part of Internet2 run by MCI World-Com.

video teleconferencing: Video teleconferencing provides real-time transmission of video and audio signals to enable people in two or more locations to have a meeting.

virtual: Conceptual or appearing to be, rather than actually being.

virtual circuit: A temporary transmission circuit in which sequential data packets are routed between two points. It is created by the software in such a way that users think they have a dedicated point-to-point leased circuit.

virtual private network (VPN): A hybrid network that includes both public and private facilities. The user leases a bundle of circuits and configures the VPN on an as-needed basis so that some traffic travels on the private leased network and some travels on the common carrier's public network.

virus: Viruses are executable programs that copy themselves onto other computers.

Most viruses attach themselves to other programs or to special parts on disks, and as those files execute or are accessed, the virus spreads. Viruses cause unwanted events—some are harmless (such as nuisance messages) and others are serious (such as the destruction of data). Some viruses change their appearances as they spread, making detection more difficult.

voice-grade circuit: A term that applies to circuits suitable for transmission of speech, digital or analog data, or facsimile, generally with a frequency range of about 300 to 3,300 Hz contained within a 4,000-Hz circuit.

VPN: *See* **virtual private network (VPN).**

VRC: Vertical redundancy check. Same as **parity check.**

W

WAN: *See* **wide area network (WAN).**

WAP: *See* **Wireless Application Protocol (WAP).**

warchalk: marking (usually using chalk on pavement) the location and information for unsecured WLANs.

wardriving: The act of finding unsecured WLAN access points (usually by driving around).

weather map: A network map showing real-time utilization on each circuit.

Web: *See* **World Wide Web.**

Web browser: A software package on the client computer that enables a user to access a Web server.

Web crawler: A Web crawler searches through all the Web servers it knows to find information about a particular topic.

Web server: A Web server stores information in a series of text files called pages. These text files or pages use a structured language called HTML (Hypertext Markup Language) to store their information.

Wide Area Network (WAN): A network spanning a large geographical area. Its nodes can span city, state, or national boundaries. WANs typically use circuits provided by common carriers. *Contrast with* **backbone network (BN), local area network (LAN)**, and **metropolitan area network (MAN)**.

Wi-Fi: The trademarked name for 802.11b.

Wi-Fi Protected Access (WPA): A technique for providing security in WLANs.

Wired Equivalent Privacy (WEP): A technique for providing security in WLANs that is not very effective.

Wireless Application Protocol (WAP): A de facto standard set of protocols for connecting wireless devices to the Web. WAP provides a variety of protocols at the application, transport, and network layers to enable devices with a very small display screen to display standard Web information.

wire speed: Operating at the same speed as the incoming circuit; having extremely low latency.

wiring closet: A central point at which all the circuits in a system begin or end, to allow cross-connection.

World Wide Web: The Web provides a graphical user interface and enables the display of rich graphical images, pictures, full-motion video, and sound clips.

X

X.*nn*: The X.*nn* series of ITU-T standards relating to transmission over public data networks.

X.400: An OSI standard that defines how messages are to be encoded for the transmission of e-mail and graphics between dissimilar computers and terminals. X.400 defines what is in an electronic address and what the electronic envelope should look like. Approved by the CCITT.

X.500: An OSI standard that defines where to find the address to put on the electronic envelope of a X.400 transmission. X.500 is the directory of names and addresses similar to the yellow pages of a telephone directory.

Xmodem: Xmodem is an asynchronous file transmission protocol that takes the data being transmitted and divides it into blocks. Each block has a start of header (SOH) character, a 1-byte block number, 128 bytes of data, and a 1-byte checksum for error checking.

Y

Ymodem: Ymodem is an asynchronous file transmission protocol. The primary benefit of the Ymodem protocol is CRC-16 error checking.

Z

Zmodem: Zmodem is a newer asynchronous file transmission protocol written to overcome some of the problems in older protocols. It uses CRC-32 with continuous ARQ and dynamically adjusts its packet size according to communication circuit conditions to increase efficiency. It usually is the preferred protocol of most bulletin board systems.

INDEX

D

E

X

Y

Z